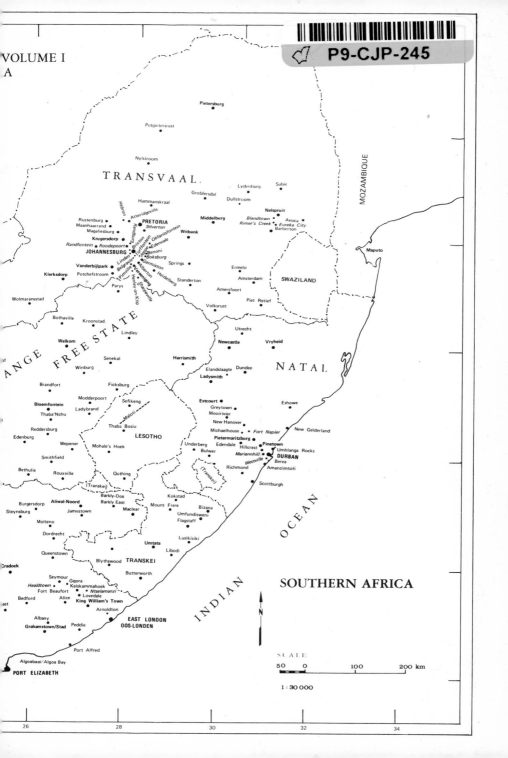

SOUTH AFRICAN MUSIC ENCYCLOPEDIA

General Editor
DR JACQUES P. MALAN

VOLUME I
A-D

A publication of the
Human Sciences Research Council
Pretoria

1979
OXFORD UNIVERSITY PRESS
CAPE TOWN

Oxford University Press
OXFORD   LONDON   GLASGOW
NEW YORK   TORONTO   MELBOURNE   WELLINGTON
NAIROBI   DAR ES SALAAM   CAPE TOWN
KUALA LUMPUR   SINGAPORE   JAKARTA   HONG KONG   TOKYO
DELHI   BOMBAY   CALCUTTA   MADRAS   KARACHI

INSTITUTE FOR LANGUAGES, LITERATURE AND ARTS
Director: *Dr K.P. Prinsloo*
Head, Research Centre for South African Music: *Prof. Dr J.P. Malan*

Typography: Martin von Kloëg
Set in 9/10pt. Garamond by Sonja Walsh
Institute for Information and Special Services, HSRC, Pretoria

Logo by Elizabeth Couzyn

ISBN 0 86965 586 8
Hierdie publikasie is ook beskikbaar in Afrikaans (ISBN 0 86965 579 5)

Published for the Human Sciences Research Council by
Oxford University Press, Harrington House,
Barrack Street, Cape Town 8001, South Africa
Printed and bound by Citadel Press, Lansdowne, Cape

PREFACE

The South African Music Encyclopedia (SAME) is a project that was initially launched under the auspices of the National Bureau for Educational and Social Research and has since 1969 become the responsibility of the Human Sciences Research Council (HSRC). In all, 17 years' work has gone into this project and the appearance of Volume I represents an important milestone in the documentation of South African music.

However, the Encyclopedia is not the HSRC's only undertaking in the field of music. The National Documentation Centre for Music of the HSRC, which has to some extent been active in the same field as that covered by the SAME, was established in 1973. The logical step was to merge these two undertakings so that one centre for music research in South Africa could come into being. This merger duly occurred in 1979 and the new centre will in future be able to handle enquiries, at the national level as well as in the broader international context, on the music life of South Africa.

Music in South Africa has reached the stage where it is desirable that the development of its various components (European, Coloured, Indian, African and indigenous) be traced in detail so that this development can be seen in overall perspective. The compilers of the SAME have undertaken this task and hope that the Encyclopedia will lead to further research and documentary work in this field.

It is envisaged that all four volumes of the Encyclopedia will have been published by 1982.

A. L. Kotzee

PRESIDENT

Editorial team:

Full-time: Elizabeth Couzyn (secretary: 1969-1974), Mrs E.H. Snyman (1965-1968), Dr Lily Wolpowitz (1966-1969), Dr C.G. Henning (1970-1973), Mrs A.M. Wepener (from 1976)

Part-time: Mrs Eva Malan (1962-1964), Mrs M. Thomas (from 1977)

Typists (part-time): Mrs R. Eyssell, Mrs B. Auret, Mrs D.R. Bower

Supplementary information since 1974: Dr C.G. Henning on behalf of the Music Documentation Centre, HSRC.

Translators (Afrikaans/English):
Prof. L.H. Hugo
Dr G.S. Jackson
Prof. J.P. Malan

Language Editors:
Prof. A.C. Partridge
Mr Thys Uys
Prof. J.P. Malan

Advisory committee (1962-1974):
Dr A.C. Hartman *(Chairman),* Prof. P.R. Kirby, Dr F.C.L. Bosman, Mr D.I.C. de Villiers, Dr Yvonne Huskisson, Prof. J.J.A. van der Walt, Dr A.J. van Rooy *(Vice-president of the HSRC),* Dr P.G. du Plessis *(Director of the Institute for Languages, Literature and Arts),* Prof. Dr Jacques P. Malan *(General Editor).*

INTRODUCTION

The South African Music Encyclopedia is the result of a project which was commenced on a part-time basis under the Bureau of Social and Educational Research in 1962, and reached publication stage under the Human Sciences Research Council in 1974. At no time did the General Editor have more than two full-time assistants for the work: there were two consecutive editorial clerks who served between 1965 and 1974, and two consecutive research officers in the period 1966 to the end of 1973. I recall the zeal and the spirit of adventure that marked the work of this tiny editorial team, with gratitude. The Encyclopedia would have been delayed even longer, had it not been for their diligence and capacity for hard work.

When Dr F.C.L. Bosman, chairman of the South African Music Council, advanced the idea of a reference work on music in South Africa to the Bureau (as it was then called), an Advisory Committee was appointed, with Dr Anton Hartman as chairman. The official blessing of the University of Pretoria, enabled the General Editor to be freed from university duties one day a week, and to devote a segment of his time to the compilation of this encyclopedic work on South African music.

Editorial policy was initially formulated along the following lines:

(a) It was decided to limit the contents to South African music history between 1652 and the last year of the Union of South Africa (1960).

(b) In addition to European music, the musics and musical instruments of the South African Blacks and Coloureds were to receive extensive coverage.

(c) Ballet and artists of that profession were to be included.

(d) Besides biographical articles, accounts of music in cities and towns, church music, theatres and concert halls, music education, musical instruments, Afrikaans folk music, visiting artists from overseas, the early years of the gramophone industry and musical societies which had functions other than that of a collective impresario, were all marked for treatment.

(e) In the selection of names for inclusion, the guiding principles were that a musician had to be of intrinsic or at least temporary significance to a community; that his personality or musical work had to have a quality which justified his inclusion; or that his career cast some light on the musical progress of the community(ies) where he worked.

In 1975 the HSRC decided, however, that the whole Encyclopedia should be revised, with a view to supplementing especially the biographies. The fifteen years between 1960 and 1975, regarded from a purely biographical point of view, are quite a considerable stretch of time in which much may have happened. But in the meantime the cause of South African musicology had gained ground at the South African universities, the HSRC had created a centre for music documentation and an appreciable amount of new facts and bibliographical details had come to light. These also called for revision. As a consequence the limit set at 1960 often had to be advanced and can no longer be regarded as absolute. On the other hand, it proved to be impossible, at the existing level of music ethnological research, to give a complete account of the music systems of the non-white races in South Africa. Despite this relative incompleteness, about one eighth of the entire Encyclopedia has been devoted

i

to this facet of musical life in South Africa.

It soon became apparent that the combined results of all South African research on the country's music were insufficient for the demands of an encyclopedic work of this stature. The obvious solution was to compile the majority of articles from primary sources, such as newspapers, periodicals, library material, archives, letters and personal notes or documents. Unfortunately, contributors with the training and background to maintain a scientific standard of work were initially few. Eventually 155 authors were made responsible for the complete contents of the Encyclopedia; excluding the editorial team, thirteen persons each contributed a series of articles. In grateful recognition, their names are: Dr George Jackson, Dr Jan Bouws, Dr Lily Wolpowitz, Prof. P.R. Kirby, Hermien Dommisse, Marina Grut, Rev. A. Pierce-Jones, Dr G.G. Cillié, Mr Walter Swanson, Mr Frits Stegmann, Dr H.H. Maske, Dr Jan Ploeger and Dr C.G. Henning.

To accomplish complete coverage of South African music history in this way proved to be extremely difficult, on the part-time basis to which the acquisition of material was committed. The ideal of completeness had to be shelved when the Advisory Committee decided in December 1968 that all attempts at increasing the store of available information should cease by the end of 1970, so that the material on hand could be edited for publication. As a consequence there are gaps, notably in the series devoted to cities and towns. Important centres, especially in the Western Province, are missing, or are only partially represented, although individual accounts have been devoted to the musical leaders and organisations of each of these communities. In the final product, however, the Encyclopedia has achieved a broad purview of South Africa's musical life between 1652 and 1960 and could serve as a cornerstone for South African musicologists to build on in the years to come.

Apart from the problems caused by the retarded condition of South African music research, the Editor had to cope with insufficient co-operation: repeated requests leading to no or scant results; incomplete information, ascribed to the bashful way in which some musicians consider their dates of birth, or to a natural reluctance to publish details of their careers. There were fortunately only a few cases in which there was no co-operation at all, the persons refusing to appear in this publication. All articles had to be checked, revised, sometimes partially or wholly recast and details had to be reconciled with new information; most articles had to be rewritten on an average two to three times. Editorial responsibility not only included research and coordination of material, it also resembled the functions of a mill and of a harvesting combine.

The South African Music Encyclopedia is equipped with an extensive system of cross-indexing, which ought to improve its usefulness. Bold type has been used for entries; for all persons or matters to which an article refers, and which have received detailed treatment under their own headings, an * has been inserted. The asterisk is confined to the first mention of a person or matter in any specific article. Furthermore, named subjects on which there was a paucity of material, have been given their own entries, followed by references to the article(s) in which they are mentioned. The titles of works have been printed in italics throughout, with the exception of work lists where normal type is used. To avoid repetition, a title has been quoted in English if the performance was obviously in English *(Messiah, Magic flute)* the Afrikaans

ii

title has been quoted if an Afrikaans translation was used in performance *(Messias Die towerfluit)*. Doubtful or unknown cases have been cited in English or in the original language.

The work lists of composers have been compiled as accurately as our present knowledge allows. In the case of vocal music, the author of the text (if available) has been named in brackets after the title. The vexatious question of the form in which details of works were to be presented, was established experimentally by the Editor, after consulting various works of reference. The often meagre bibliographies at the conclusion of articles reflect, as nothing else can, the relatively neglected condition of South African music in South African musicology.

The HSRC's long-suffering patience and vigilant interest in the growth of this project is recorded with gratitude. The confidence with which Dr P.M. Robbertse and Dr A.L. Kotzee (consecutive Presidents of the HSRC), Dr P.G. du Plessis and Dr K.P. Prinsloo (consecutive Directors of the Institute for Languages, Literature and Arts), and members of the Administrative personnel have abided by the completion of the work, contributed immeasurably to the creation of an atmosphere favourable to its growth.

South African libraries have, in the compilation of this Encyclopedia, maintained their excellent reputation for service, and are thanked most sincerely. The Archives of the Cape Colony, Transvaal, Free State and Natal, the Film Board, the Department for Coloured Affairs and the former Department for Bantu Administration and Development, as well as a number of town clerks were especially willing to assist in this project.

In conclusion, the Editor thanks those university departments that have embraced the cause of South African musicology and for much basic research conducted cheerfully.

DR JACQUES P. MALAN

Pretoria
1979

CONTRIBUTORS IN THE ALPHABETICAL ORDER OF THEIR INITIALS

ACH	Anton C. Hartman
AdK	A. de Klerk
AEBS	A.E. Barry Smith
AEH	A.E. Honey
AJJT	A.J.J. Troskie
AL	Arnold Lorie
ALMB	Alice L.M. Bilmark
AMR	A.M. Richards
AP	Andrew Porter
AP-J	Rev. A. Pierce-Jones
AST	A.S. Thomas
AXS	A.X. Smith
BG	Bruce Gardiner
BJO	B.J. Odendaal
BK	B. Krüger
BM	Beatrice Marx
BMH	Bertha M. Hamman
BMO	B.M. Offenberg
BR	B. Rees
BS	Barend Smulian
BT	Basil Taylor
CAA	C.A. Angermann
CC	Cyril Chambers
CG	Con Groenewald
CGH	C.G. Henning
CGSdV	C.G.S. de Villiers
CH	Chris Heyns
CHN	Charles H. Norburn
CHJS	C.H.J. Schutte
CJP	C.J. Prinsloo
CK	Charles Kreitzer
CLV	Chris L. Venter
CMF	C.M. Fisher
CO	Charles Oxtoby
CvW	C. van Wyk
CW	Cyril Wright
DdV	Dirkie de Villiers
DH	Deirdre Hansen
DI	Donald Inskip

DK	Dirk Koenderman
DKR	David K. Rycroft
DR	Daphne Rees
EC	Elizabeth Couzyn
Ed.	Denotes articles compiled by the editorial staff from information supplied by the person in question and/or from various sources.
ED	E. Druker
EH	E. Hildyard
EHS	E. Heila Snyman
EM	Ella Malan
EV	Ellen Vlok
EVe	E. Vermeulen
FDC	F.D. Croney
FE	Fanny Emdon
FJ	F. Jacobs
FS	Frits Stegmann
GDR	G.D. Roos
GF	Gideon Fagan
GGC	G.G. Cillié
GMW	G.M. Wareham
GSJ	George S. Jackson
HA	Hans Adler
HB	Hans Bodenstein
HD	Hermien Dommisse
HdP	Hubert du Plessis
HG	Harold Greenwood
HGA	H.G. Ashworth
HHM	H.H. Maske
HHvdS	H.H. van der Spuy
HJM	H.J. Moolman
HM	H. Müller
HMOT	H.M.O. Turnbull
HN	H. Nevill
HS	Helena Strauss
HT	H. Temmingh
HTH	Hugh T. Hewartson
HW	Herbert Woodhouse

JARB	J.A.R. Blacking
JB	Jan Bouws
JCvH	J.C. van Hille
JD	John Dunn
JdV	Jean de Villiers
JdW	Jack de Wet
JGJ vd G	J.G.J. van de Geest
JHP	J.H. Potgieter
JJA vd W	J.J.A. van der Walt
JJKK	J.J.K. Kloppers
JLKH	J.L.K. Human
JM	Joubero Malherbe
JMe	Jack Metz
JP	Jan Ploeger
JPdL	J.P. de Lange
JPe	Judith Pellissier
JPM	Jacques P. Malan
JSM	Joseph S. Manca
JU	Johanna Uys
JW vd M	Josias W. van der Merwe
KA	Kathleen Alister
KAb	Keith Abendroth
KFH	K.F. Heimes
KRT	Kenneth R. Thomas
LF	Lourens Faul
LJM	Louisa J. Muller
LM	Lily Morison
LW	Lily Wolpowitz
M	Sister Magdalen
MB	Maude Barlow
MG (MK)	Marina Grut (Marina Keet)
MGl	Mauryn Glenton
MH	Mary Hamblin
MJ	Molly Joubert
MK (MG)	Marina Keet (Grut)
MKl	Marion Klewansky
ML	Merle Loveless
MVH	Mildred V. Harris
MWC	M.W. Carter
NB	Nancy Berthauer

OB	Ockert Botha
OW	O. Wagner
PdP	Piet du Plessis
PGB	P.G. Bray
PGMS	P.G.M. Scholtz
PHJ	P.H. Jackson
PHL	P.H. Langenhoven
PJAdB	P.J.A. de Bruine
PJvE	P.J. van Eck
PlR	Pietie le Roux
PMP	Philippa M. Podlashuc
PNB	P.N. Basson
PRK	Percival R. Kirby
PW	Phyllis Wille
REO	Reino E. Otterman
REP	Rykie E. Pienaar
RFMI	R.F.M. Immelman
RL	Ruth Ladley
RRWN	R.R.W. Nixon
RS	Rupert Stoutt
RWB	R.W. Ballantine
SA	Solly Aronowsky
SHE	Stephen H. Eyssen
SK	S. Kilian
TB-D	Thomas Barrow-Dowling
TB-V	T. Brüning-Voigt
TC	Tjaart Coetzee
TJ	Thomas Johnston
VC	Victor Couzyn
VSTF	Vernon S.T. Fincken
WAS	W.A. Stevens
WD	Walter Dedekind
WDS	Walter D. Swanson
WFL	W.F. Loots
WFL	W.F. Loots
WHlR	W.H. le Roux

WM	Willem Mathlener
WSJG	W.S.J. Grobler
WT	William Tozer
W vd N	W. van der Nest
WvW	Willem van Warmelo
YH	Yvonne Huskisson

ALPHABETICAL LIST OF CONTRIBUTORS

Abendroth, Keith	KAb
Adler, Hans	HA
Alister, Kathleen	KA
Angermann, C.A.	CAA
Aronowsky, Solly	SA
Ashworth, H.G.	HGA
Ballantine, R.W.	RWB
Barlow, Maude	MB
Barrow-Dowling, Thomas	TB-D
Basson, P.N.	PNB
Berthauer, Nancy	NB
Bilmark, Alice L.M.	ALMB
Blacking, J.A.R.	JARB
Bodenstein, Hans	HB
Botha, Ockert	OB
Bouws, Jan	JB
Bray, P.G.	PGB
Brüning-Voigt, T	TB-V
Carter, M.W.	MWC
Chambers, Cyril	CC
Cillié, G.G.	GGC
Coetzee, Tjaart	TC
Couzyn, Elizabeth	EC
Couzyn, Victor	VC
Croney, F.D.	FDC
De Bruine, P.J.A.	PJAdB
Dedekind, Walter	WD
De Klerk, A.	AdK
De Lange, J.P.	JPdL

De Villiers, C.G.S.	CGSdV
De Villiers, Dirkie	DdV
De Villiers, Jean	JdV
De Wet, Jack	JdW
Du Plessis, Hubert	HdP
Du Plessis, Piet	PdP
Dommisse, Hermien	HD
Druker, E.	ED
Dunn, John	JD
Ed.	Denotes articles compiled by the editorial staff from information supplied by the person in question and/or from various sources
Emdon, Fanny	FE
Eyssen, Stephen H.	SHE
Fagan, Gideon	GF
Faul, Lourens	LF
Fincken, Vernon S.T.	VSTF
Fisher, C.M.	CMF
Gardiner, Bruce	BG
Glenton, Mauryn	MGl
Greenwood, Harold	HG
Grobler, S.W.J.	SWJG
Groenewald, Con	CG
Grut (Keet), Marina	MG(MK)
Hamblin, Mary	MH
Hamman, Bertha M.	BMH
Hansen, Deirdre	DH
Harris, Mildred V.	MVH
Hartman, Anton C.	ACH
Heimes, K.F.	KFH
Henning, C.G.	CGH
Hewartson, Hugh T.	HTH
Heyns, Chris	CH
Hildyard, E.	EH
Honey, Arthur E.	AEH
Human, J.L.K.	JLKH
Huskisson, Yvonne	YH

Immelman, R.F.M.	RFMI
Inskip, Donald	DI
Jackson, George S.	GSJ
Jackson, P.H.	PHJ
Jacobs, F.	FJ
Johnston, Thomas	TJ
Joubert, Molly	MJ
Keet, Marina (Grut)	MK (MG)
Kilian, S.	SK
Kirby, Percival R.	PRK
Klewansky, Marion	MKl
Kloppers, J.J.K.	JJKK
Koenderman, Dirk	DK
Kreitzer, Charles	CK
Krüger, B.	BK
Ladley, Ruth	RL
Langenhoven, P.H.	PHL
Le Roux, Pietie	PlR
Le Roux, W.H.	WHlR
Loots, W.F.	WFL
Lorie, Arnold	AL
Loveless, Merle	Ml
Magdalen, Sister	M
Malan, Ella	EM
Malan, Jacques P.	JPM
Malherbe, Joubero	JM
Manca, Joseph S.	JSM
Marx, Beatrice	BM
Maske, H.H.	HHM
Mathlener, Willem	WM
Metz, Jack	JMe
Moolman, H.J.	HJM
Morison, Lily	LM
Muller, Louisa J.	LJM
Müller, Hans	HM
Nevill, H.	HN
Nixon, R.R.W.	RRWN
Norburn, Charles H.	CHN
Odendaal, B.J.	BJO

Offenberg, B.M.	BMO
Ottermann, Reino E.	REO
Oxtoby, Charles	CO
Pellissier, Judith	JPe
Pienaar, Rykie E.	REP
Pierce-Jones, Rev. A.	AP-J
Ploeger, Jan	JP
Podlaschuc, Philippa M.	PMP
Porter, Andrew	AP
Potgieter, J.H.	JHP
Prinsloo, C.J.	CJP
Rees, B.	BR
Rees, Daphne	DR
Richards, A.M.	AMR
Roos, Gideon D.	GDR
Rycroft, David K.	DKR
Scholtz, P.G.M.	PGMS
Schutte, C.H.J.	CHJS
Smith, A.E. Barry	AEBS
Smith, A.X.	AXS
Smulian, Barend	BS
Snyman, E. Heila	EHS
Stegmann, Frits	FS
Stevens, W.A.	WAS
Stoutt, Rupert	RS
Strauss, Helena	HS
Swanson, Walter D.	WDS
Taylor, Basil	BT
Temmingh, H.	HT
Thomas, A.S.	AST
Thomas, Kenneth R.	KRT
Tozer, William	WT
Troskie, A.J.J.	AJJT
Turnbull, H.M.O.	HMOT
Uys, Johanna	JU
Van de Geest, J.G.J.	JGJ vd G
Van der Merwe, Josias W.	JW vd M
Van der Nest, W.	W vd N

Van der Spuy, H.H.	HH vd S
Van der Walt, J.J.A.	JJA vd W
Van Eck, P.J.	PJ v E
Van Hille, J.C.	JC v H
Van Warmelo, Willem	WvW
Van Wyk, C.	CvW
Venter, Chris L.	CLV
Vermeulen, E.	EVe˙
Vlok, Ellen	EV
Wagner, O.	OW
Wareham, G.M.	GMW
Wille, Phyllis	PW
Wolpowitz, Lily	LW
Woodhouse, Herbert	HW
Wright, Cyril	CW

ABBREVIATIONS USED IN THIS ENCYCLOPEDIA

ACT	African Consolidated Theatres
ARAM	Associate, Royal Academy of Music
ARCM	Associate, Royal College of Music
ARCO	Associate, Royal College of Organists
Arr	Arranged
ASB	Afrikaanse Studentebond
ATCL	Associate, Trinity College, London
CAPAB	Cape Performing Arts Board
CHE	Christian Higher Education
CJV	Christelike Jeugvereniging
CNE	Christian National Education
Comp.	Composed
CT	Cape Town
DRC	Dutch Reformed Church
ed	editorial
EL	East London
FRCO	Fellow, Royal College of Organists
FTCL	Fellow, Trinity College, London
GR	Graaff Reinet
HAUM	Hollands-Afrikaanse Uitgewers Maatskappy

IALY	International Arts League of Youth
IOGT	International Order of Good Templars
ISCM	International Society for Contemporary Music
KAMADS	King William's Town Amateur Music and Dramatic Society
KHS	Kaffrarian High School
KWT	King William's Town
LRAM	Licentiate, Royal Academy of Music
LRSM	Licentiate, Royal Schools of Music
LTCL	Licentiate, Trinity College, London
NAPAC	Natal Performing Arts Council
NP	Nasionale Pers
NU	Natal University
OB	Ossewa-Brandwag
ODMS	Onderwys Diploma in Musiek, Stellenbosch
PACOFS	Performing Arts Council, Orange Free State
PACT	Performing Arts Council, Transvaal
PE	Port Elizabeth
Publ	published
PU(C) for CHE	Potchefstroom University (College) for Christian Higher Education
RAM	Royal Academy of Music
RCM	Royal College of Music
RU	Rhodes University
SABC	South African Broadcasting Corporation
SACM	South African College of Music
SAMT	South African Music Teacher
SASMT	South African Society of Music Teachers
SWA	South West Africa
SWAPAC	South West African Performing Arts Council
UALM	University Accompanists' Licentiate in Music
UCT	University of Cape Town
UNISA	University of South Africa
UOFS	University of the Orange Free State
UP	University of Pretoria
UPE	University of Port Elizabeth

UPLM	University Performers' Licentiate in Music
US	University of Stellenbosch
UTLM	University Teachers' Licentiate in Music
UW	University of the Witwatersrand
VVOOZA	Vereeniging van Onderwijzers en Onderwijzeressen in Zuid Afrika. (Oldest known teachers' association, precursor to the Transvaal Teachers' Association)
YMMIS	Young Men's Mutual Improvement Society
ZAR	Zuid Afrikaansche Republiek
*	indicates date of birth
o	indicates date of death
* (in the course of an article)	indicates that a separate article has been devoted to the person or matter thus marked.

ABC SYMPHONY ORCHESTRA Johannesburg 3(i)

ABENDROTH, GUSTAV ERNST, *20 May 1844 in Pirna, Saxony; °27 March 1928 in Harrismith, OFS. Music teacher and organist.

A member of a well-known German musical family, Abendroth was trained at the Dresden Conservatorium of Music. After graduating, he went to Constance, where he taught music and was organist of the Roman Catholic Cathedral. He was acquainted with celebrities of the day such as Joseph Joachim, Clara Schumann, Anton Rubinstein and Meyerbeer. On account of ill-health, he came to South Africa from Lausanne in 1888, settling in Harrismith, where he set up a music teaching practice and was the local representative of the London College of Music. During his stay of forty years in Harrismith, more than 1 100 pupils passed through his hands, among them Isaac Bloch, the violinist. In 1890 he founded the Harrismith Brass Band, which he conducted until it ceased to exist in 1893. He was also the conductor of the Harrismith Philharmonic Society between 1890 and 1897, and of a string orchestra, which was known during the different stages of its existence as Prof. Abendroth's String Band, Prof. Abendroth's Orchestral Society and Prof. Abendroth's Orchestra. This orchestra performed in Harrismith until 1927 and at one time comprised 30-40 players. When Harrismith's Town Hall was inaugurated in September 1908, Abendroth conducted a choir and orchestra of 100 performers in a performance of Gaul's *The Holy City*. He was appointed organist of the Dutch Reformed Church in Harrismith in January 1895 and after more than thirty years' service, retired in August 1927. Of his descendants, two became well-known as musicians: Otto Hooper, a grandson of his second marriage, as violinist; and William Abendroth (°3 March 1963), an only son by his third marriage, as pianist, organist and violinist in Pretoria. The family possesses, amongst other things, a Steiner violin which was used by Gustav Ernst. Abendroth is known to have composed music which was performed both in Germany and in South Africa, but only three works performed in 1891 by the Harrismith Brass Band are known today.

WORKS
German medley. My darling, galop. Pell mell.

BIBLIOGRAPHY
FEINSTEIN, DAVID. The late Gustav Ernst Abendroth — An appreciation and some reminiscences. *The Harrismith Chronicle*, 1928. A book of newspaper cuttings, which had belonged to Prof. Abendroth, in the Johannesburg Public Library.

—K.Ab.

ABENDROTH, WILLIAM G.E. Abendroth

ACADEMY OF MUSIC, CAPE TOWN E.K. Green

ADAMS COLLEGE Bantu Composers of South Africa, R.T. Caluza, K. Mngoma

ADAMS, REV. H. Barberton III/3

ADAMS, H.L. King William's Town 10

AD ARTEM QUARTET Durban, Chamber Music Groups

ADÈ, J.C. Piano Music, South African II/2

ADELER, EDGAR, *7 December 1895 in Birmingham; in Durban in 1976. Dance band leader, pianist and composer of light music.

Adeler emigrated to South Africa in 1912 and was articled to a firm of quantity surveyors. On his return from active service after the First World War, he became a dance band pianist and on 11 November 1918 entered into a partnership with Jimmy Clark, an entertainment artist. The partnership flourished and at one time controlled 10 dance bands and one military band. They played at receptions and other social events for four consecutive Governors General, but in 1922 Clark received an advantageous offer from England and left South Africa. Adeler followed him in 1924 for a visit which was planned to last 6 months and in the event continued for 10 years. During this time he visited the Far East, returning via Holland to England. He lived in Germany for eight years with visits to Finland, Denmark and Hungary, but returned to England in 1933. The next year he signed a contract with the Blue Cosmo Night Club in Johannesburg and then became a partner in the Cosmo Night Club in Durban. During the Second World War he served in the Entertainment Unit and travelled widely in Ethiopia, Iraq and Northern Africa. After a few years spent in commerce, Adeler has returned to music and composed the music for *The King of Diamonds*. Some of his well-known melodies are Here's to South Africa (Sari Award in 1962), Soweto sweat (1965), Voortrekker valse (1965), OK baby (1968), C'mon the mealie boys (1968), A new life begins (1968), Daddy's coming home (1970), Answer to God (1970), Harry op (1972), Guido (1972), Taki talisman (1973), Roadhouse on the roadway (1974). The following melodies were all written in the early years: Karroo (publ. by B. Feldman & Co., London, 1922), In a day or two (publ. by Transvaal Music Supply, Johannesburg, n.d.), In the Valley of a Thousand Hills (publ. by Knox Printing and Publishing Co., n.d.), Karroo and the cactus (publ. by Gallo of Johannesburg, 1945). Adeler is well known in Durban for the Sing Along trend he started in 1970 and for his pianoforte entertainment in prominent hotels and restaurants. He acted as musical director for Brian Brook when the latter toured South Africa and Rhodesia with *The boy friend* and again for Adam Leslie when he put on the revue *Don't stop the carnival,* for which Adeler had written the music.

—Ed.

ADLER, BOBBY   Max Adler

ADLER COLLECTION. Hans Adler* possesses probably the largest private collection of printed music, books on music and historical keyboard instruments in the Republic of South Africa. His collection of printed music comprises mainly chamber music, piano scores, piano duets and works for 2 pianos, amongst them many first editions and collectors pieces; there are also sets of the complete works of composers such as Bach, Brahms and Mozart. The book section includes a comprehensive selection of reference books in many languages. The collection of keyboard instruments includes fine examples of early clavichords, harpsichords and rare specimens of an old Italian virginal and French glasscord. The principal items are: a 17th century upright Italian clavicytherium; an early 17th century two-manual Italian harpsichord; a single-keyboard harpsichord, made by Ferdinandus Weber, 1750; a virginal made by Joannis Andreae Menegoni Veneti, 1689; an early 18th century clavichord; an 18th century fortepiano made by Georg Winkler; a glass harmonica made by Beyer, 1786. —H.A.

ADLER, HANS G. *25 February 1904 in Frankfurt-am-Main, son of L. Adler, Chief Magistrate at Frankfurt and of Johanna née Nathan, a Lieder and oratorio singer; at present in Johannesburg. Connoisseur and organiser of music, who specialises in the collection of musical antiques and rarities.

Adler studied Law and Musicology at the Frankfurt and Berlin Universities and practical music (pianoforte and harpsichord) at the Hoch Conservatoire under Prof. Jung and also worked temporarily in the publishing houses of Breitkopf und Haertel and of Steingraeber. He settled in South Africa towards the end of 1933, and in Johannesburg in 1936. He is married to Gertrud Adler, M.D. Besides being Director of Companies of numerous trading concerns, he has devoted much of his interest to the furtherance of music and art generally. In 1952 he became Vice Chairman and in 1955 Chairman of the Johannesburg Musical Society,* which has become one of the strongest musical organisations in the Republic. Since 1974 he has been the Hon. President of this Society. Adler is the owner of a large and extremely rare collection of music, books on music and historical keyboard instruments. He has broadcast and lectured on the latter subject.

—Ed.

ADLER, MAX, *23 October 1917 in Johannesburg; now in Cape Town. Accordion player. This article also refers to his wife, Bobby Adler.

Between 1923 and 1927, Adler had lessons from G. Barclay Donn* in Johannesburg, passed pianoforte examinations and had many successes at eisteddfodau. The family moved to Bloemfontein in 1928 where Max was taught pianoforte by Mrs Victor Pohl until the middle of 1930. Then followed a partially successful attempt to earn money for further tuition with a concert tour (1930-1931) and a subsequent move to Johannesburg where he started playing accordion in 1935 and created the Max Adler Accordion School in 1936. During the War he served in the Entertainment Unit (after 1942) and afterwards he resumed his career in Johannesburg as accordion soloist, leader of a dance band, director of musical shows, and as conductor of a salon group which made frequent broadcasts. In 1953 he opened a branch of the South African College of Accordionists in Cape Town and has remained its principal ever since. As a result of his efforts, the South African College of Music* instituted accordion as a principal practical subject for B.Mus. and Adler became the first lecturer on this instrument. He is chairman of the SA Accordion and Harmonica Society and of the Accordion Club in Cape Town.   In 1943 he married Bobby Adler, a teacher at the SA College of Accordionists. She had been trained as a pianist and for a while she was a member of a cabaret act which included piano playing and dancing. Mrs Adler accompanied her husband on his tour of Rhodesia and was a member of a light entertainment group which visited Rhodesia and the (former) Belgian Congo.

SOURCE

Who's who of Southern Africa, 1959-1960. Wootton and Gibson, Johannesburg 1961.   —Ed.

ADULT EDUCATION MOVEMENT,   After a study tour of Denmark where he visited the well-known Adult Education Schools and studied their constructive influence on the spiritual life of the Danish people, Dr S.H. Pellissier* began, in 1936, to adapt the principles of this movement to conditions in South Africa. He organised a spring school (lenteskool) attended by almost 200 people in Bethlehem during the winter vacation of 1936 followed by annual, sometimes biannual schools at Free State centres until he moved to Pretoria in 1951. With similar enthusiasm he introduced the idea of these schools in the Transvaal and by 1958 the movement was introduced in the Cape Province as well. In addition to lectures on religious, historical, literary, social, scientific and racial matters, the movement from its early stages emphasized folk singing and folk dancing and obtained the co-operation of competent leaders in these fields. Folk dancing had been popular in Smithfield from as early as 1937 – three years before the first course in folk dancing was held in Bloemfontein in October 1940. Throughout, the aim of these courses was to make Afrikaners aware of their history, to recall important historical events in their own particular environment and to educate them in cultural matters. Constant, practical participation in folk singing and dancing undoubtedly contributed to an awareness of the Afrikaans heritage. This movement was never given financial support by the State. Throughout its existence it has remained financially self-reliant.

—Ed.

AEOLIAN ORCHESTRA OF GILBERT HARRIS   Johannesburg 3a

AEOLIAN PLAYERS   Durban, Chamber Music Groups

AFRICANA COLLECTION OF THE JOHANNESBURG CITY LIBRARY   Discography, Higher Educational Institutions I/4, P.R. Kirby, C.M. Kruger, J.M.C. Schonegevel

AFRICAN BROADCASTING COMPANY (ABC)   C. Berman, Cape Town Studio Orchestra, R. Caprara, Discography, J. Idelson, Johannesburg 2, 3(i), Pretoria 3, Pretoria Male Voice Choir, G.D. Roos, E. Schneider, J. Schulman, W. Swanson, V. Tailleur, G. Tobias, J.H. van Loggerenberg, T. Wendt.

AFRICAN CONSOLIDATED SOUND INDUSTRIES   Pietermaritzburg, Durban 2, 3, Polliack

AFRICAN CONSOLIDATED THEATRES (ACT, AFRICAN THEATRES, AFRICAN THEATRES TRUST)   Ballet I/1, 6, 9, 10, Maude Barlow, Cape Town Ballet Club, A. Cherniavsky, I. Conmée, H. Coulthard, Faith de Villiers, I.M. de Villiers, M. Doré, Durban 7, K. Espen, G. Fagan C. Fiore, Signor Foli, Francis Foster, P. Frames, H.T. Hewartson, J. Idelson, Johannesburg 3(i), N. Kofsky, R. Kofsky, Ø. Liltved, H. Lyell-Tayler, L. Pearce, Port Elizabeth II/2(ii), Pretoria 3, A. Rainier, Madame Ravodna, J.H. Stodel, V. Tailleur, Theatres and Concert Halls II/2, 3, IV/2, 3, T. Wendt

AFRICAN MUSIC AND BOOK CO   Boosey and Hawkes

AFRICAN MUSIC AND DRAMA ASSOCIATION (AMDA)   Bantu Music Corporations of Johannesburg, A. Feldman, S. Glasser, J. Schneider

AFRICAN MUSIC, INTERNATIONAL LIBRARY OF   Indigenous Musics of South Africa (bibliographies), H.T. Tracey

AFRICAN MUSIC SOCIETY   Indigenous Musics of South Africa (bibliographies), Potchefstroom University for CHE Institute for South African Music, H.T. Tracey

AFRIKAANS CHURCH AND MISSION MUSIC
  I.   The Psalms in the musical history of South Africa
  II.   Sacred song in South Africa
  III.   The origin and development of the choir in Afrikaans churches
  IV.   The song-books of the Afrikaans mission churches

  I.   THE PSALMS IN THE MUSICAL HISTORY OF SOUTH AFRICA
  1.   Experimentation: first phase (1852-1895)
  2.   Experimentation: second phase (1895-1932)
  3.   Consolidation (1933-1937)
  4.   The old melodies
  5.   The new melodies

4

6. Revision of the Psalm-tunes (1952-1967)

7. Afrikaans Psalm-tunes of 1937

When Van Riebeeck arrived in South Africa in 1652, he had in his possession the Dutch State Bible (authorised version), the Articles of Faith of the Reformed Church and the Dathenus Psalter, the official psalm-book of the Church. The tunes in this were exactly the same as those in the first complete Genevan Psalter of 1562, which followed in the wake of Calvinism as it spread through European and colonial lands. Thus, when the French Huguenots arrived in South Africa in 1688, they heard their own familiar tunes sung by their future compatriots – a significant factor in the welding of the two national groups at the Cape. —The eighteenth century in South Africa witnessed the progress of white civilisation eastwards and its firm entrenchment at the Cape and its environs. For the Trek-boers the psalms were the most important musical component of the daily round. Written and oral tradition relate the practice among the early settlers of assembling in the early morning before sunrise to praise and offer thanksgiving to God by singing psalms; at the end of the day, after supper, family and servants would assemble for religious devotions, an indispensable feature again being the singing of a psalm.—An ordinance of 1714 made provision for the instruction of children in the singing of psalms; it would seem that this aspect of their education had some priority. Singing ability was expected of all teachers so that justice could be done to the instruction in psalm singing. The psalms were also continually prominent in the education of slave children and in missionary work. —The Dutch rhymed metrical versions of the psalms of 1773 also found their way to South Africa. Until 1814 only these psalms and certain hymns *(Eenige Gezangen)* were sung in South African churches, to the old tunes of 1562. But in 1814 the collection known as *Evangelische Gezangen,* first used in the Dutch Reformed Church in 1805, was accepted for use in Afrikaans churches. In the farm homesteads other sacred songs, notably those of Groenewegen and Sluyters, were also sung, but these were never elevated to the status of liturgical music. — Over the centuries the Genevan psalm-tunes saw remarkably few alterations to the notation appearing in the various psalm-books. A few sharps were inserted, mainly where notes had always been sung to a higher pitch in spite of an anomalous notation. The rhythm remained unaltered in the notation, although isometric singing gradually became universal. Apart from such modifications, there is no evidence in South Africa, before the year 1852, of moves on the part of the Church to replace the old tunes with new ones.

1. Experimentation: first phase (1852-1895)

In 1852 a request that the Synod should consider replacing a few of the old tunes with newer ones came from Paarl. This took the form of a definite proposal: "To introduce new tunes in place of those psalm-tunes that are almost unsingable" *(Acta, Algemene Sinode van die Gereformeerde Kerk van Z.A.,* p.7). On a majority vote it was decided to comply with the request. A committee consisting of four ministers and one elder was entrusted with the task of putting this resolution into effect. It is illuminating to discover that those who opposed the idea and asked that their objections be recorded, came from the remoter areas, such as Burgersdorp, Colesberg and Smithfield where congregations were inclined to be more conservative. — Apparently this committee achieved very little, and in 1876 the Church Council of Swellendam put before the Synod precisely the same request. Again it was resolved – this time unanimously – that a committee should undertake the finding and selecting of more suitable psalm-

5

tunes. The efforts of this committee resulted in the first specimen copy in which some psalms were set to new tunes. A volume appeared in 1883 which was recommended to "the sympathetic consideration of the Church" by the Synod. It was entitled *Halleluja! Psalmen en Gezangen der Ned. Geref. Kerk van Zuid-Afrika* and compiled by J.S. de Villiers,* a well-known organist of Paarl. The book contained new melodies for Psalms 5, 8, 9, 23, 24, 27, 31, 48, 51, 65, 91, 92 and 130, the ones with "almost unsingable" tunes. —Though there was no opposition within the Synod to this new experiment, some people did make their objections known to the Synod of 1883, in the form of a petition entitled: *Memorie tegen nieuwigheden*. They were church members who took exception to the meddling with the original tunes, but four years later the Synod of 1886 thought it advisable to give the *Halleluja!* a chance to prove itself. The petition was shelved, and the committee asked to continue its appointed task. — Unfortunately the committee's report to the 1890 Synod is not available, but we can gather the gist of it from the following resolution: "The Synod decides to issue an edition of our psalms and hymns in a four-part setting in two note values, and to appoint a committee for this purpose. The Synod also suggests that the completely unsingable tunes, wherever they may occur, should either be adapted or replaced" *(Acta, Algemene Sinode van de Nederduitsch Gereformeerde Kerk in Zuid-Afrika, 1890, p.61).* — This resolution came to fruition in 1895, with the appearance of a volume containing the new musical settings for some of the psalms and hymns. In spite of the prevailing sentiment that, where new tunes were necessary, they should be taken from those available in the *Halleluja!* of J.S. de Villiers, all the new tunes in the proof-copy were provided by S. de Lange of Stuttgart. Forty-two psalms were provided with new tunes as alternatives to the originals, but only twenty-nine different melodies were used as indicated: 2, 5, 8, 9, 12, 13, 15, 17, 18, 20, 22, 23, 24, 26, 30, 31, 33, 46, 51, 62(=24), 63(=17), 64(=5), 67(=33), 69(=51), 70(=17), 71(=31), 76(=30), 82(=46), 87, 91, 92, 94, 95(=24), 103, 111(=24), 113, 115, 130, 139(=30), 144(=18), 146, 147. In connection with the innovations, De Lange let slip the following comment: "The reproach of having presumed to improve on some of the very beautiful melodies (e.g. in Psalms 24, 51, 130; Hymns 17, 36) in the original can hardly be directed at me. I have complied with instructions ..." (Preface to proof-copy, p. vi). Apart from the composition of new tunes which were in accordance with "the spirit of the time" (De Lange), he had tried to simplify the rhythmical shape of the Genevan melodies by removing irregularities of rhythm. He also gave thought to raising the pitch of individual notes, in order to preserve the implied cadences. But by eliminating all other accidentals that had been introduced over the years he succeeded in restoring, to some extent, the modal character of the originals.

2. Experimentation: second phase (1895-1932)

During the period 1895 to 1915 little was achieved to realize the ideal of a new church psalter. The 1906 solfa edition of the psalms and hymns commissioned by the 1903 Synod of the "Nederduitsch Gereformeerde Kerk in Zuid-Afrika" must have suffered an early eclipse as nothing further was heard about it. The De Lange volume also met with a poor response, as appears from what P.G.J.M. (Rev. P.G.J. Meiring) wrote in *De Kerkbode* of 28 September 1911. An extract from this article gives a clear indication of the way people thought: "Regarding the tunes, no one could say that our psalter has been a success. The music may be all very fine for the connoisseur, but I have made a few notes on the psalms used in public worship, and I find that of the 150 only 25 are sung by the congregation. If at a service any of the remaining 125 are chosen, a few people may participate, but the congregation as a whole remains silent. Whether it is that people don't know the tunes, or that these tunes are virtually unsingable, I don't know. The question is: did our fathers sing them with any enthusiasm? In 1894 a committee appointed by the Synod was responsible for an edition of our hymn-book, suitably enriched with a number of new tunes in place of the unsingable psalms and hymns. The composition of these melodies was entrusted to one man - a certain de Lange, a musician of high reputation. But it is too much to expect that any one man, however competent he may be, should have to compose sacred tunes by the dozen. Inevitably the result has been disappointing; and so far as I am aware, not one of his tunes has become popular. Most of the hymn-books printed at the expense of the Synod remain unsold in the office of the church administrator who, as I imagine, would like to dispose of them at a greatly reduced price. Before I leave this topic, let me say something in praise of the 25 singable psalm-tunes: visitors from other parts of the world have often remarked that nowhere have they heard anything more beautiful, or more impressive". — A reply to this article came from J.H.M. (J.H. Malan) of Oudtshoorn, and appeared in *Die Brandwag* of 1 November 1911. The writer, a staunch supporter of the old Genevan tunes, blamed the Church ministers for the congregation's ignorance of the tunes, and pointed out that theological students at the Seminary should, as part of their studies, be trained to sing. Acquaintance with the tunes of the psalms and hymns might ensure that the artistic creations of Calvin and Beza were not "ruined by novices and tinkerers of the art". He put the matter thus: "Because 125 psalms are unfamiliar to the congregation, should they be consigned to ignonimious oblivion and replaced by others? And what are the other tunes? Church Praise – Edinburgh hymns!" He added that nobody had ever insisted that the tunes of the psalms and hymns should be taught at boarding school or at day school; instead, children for many years had been inoculated with the music of *Church Praise* which had become "singable". Malan maintained that in the church at De Rust (in the district of Oudtshoorn), any so-called "unsingable" tune could be announced at the service and the visitor would be surprised at the result as regards time, rhythm and tasteful rendering. Nobody would ever think of changing a note where change is so unnecessary. The writer of this article believed that a later generation might assume responsibility for replacing the musical work of the reformers - though any twenty of the old melodies contained more genuine church music than the whole content of *Church Praise*, Edinburgh choruses included. "In the meantime, while we live, let intending reformers direct attention to some of the symptoms that, with a few exceptions, are assuredly causing actual concern in the bosom of the Church". — Articles like these were possibly responsible for the action taken by the 1915 Synod, when attention was again focussed on the "unsingable" tunes. Once more a committee was appointed to consider new tunes from South African and overseas composers, and to use existing collections such as the *Halleluja!* of J.S. de Villiers, the De Lange compositions, and the work of F.W. Jannasch,* all of whom had given practical consideration to the problem of replacing the original tunes with new creations. —The hymn-tune committee of the 1915 Synod obtained the co-operation of similar committees appointed by the federated Dutch Reformed Churches (OFS, Natal, CP), and compiled a list of 92 psalms for which new tunes were needed. The Synods of 1919, 1922 and 1928 approved the new tunes, which had appeared in the years 1919, 1922 and 1926. The following table gives a synopsis of details arising from the work by the federal committee:

NEW TUNES

Psalms requiring new tunes	Approved in 1919, composed by	Approved in 1922, composed by	Approved in 1928, composed by
2	J.H.D.		
4	A.C. v. V		
5		P.K. de V§ and M.L. de V	
6	P.K. de V.		
7			
8	S. de L.§		
9	F.W.J.		
10			
11	J. de H.§		
12	P.K. de V.§		
13	F.W.J.§		
14	J.H.D.		
15	M.L. de V.		
16	F.W.J. and A.C. v.V.§		
17	J.H.D.		
18	P.K. de V.§		
20		M.L. de V.	
22			M.L. de V.
23	F.W.J.§		
26	P.K. de V.		
28	F.W.J.		
30	S. de L.§		
31	J.S. de V.§		
33	A.C. v.V.§		
34	A.C. v.V.§		
35	M.L. de V.		
37	J.H.D.		
39			P.K. de V.
40			
41			M.L. de V.
44	J. de H.§		
46	F.W.J.		
48	J.S. de V.§		
50			M.L. de V.
51	P.K. de V.		
53	P.K. de V.		
54			Retained old tune
56		J. de H.	
57			
59			
61			

Psalms requiring new tunes	Approved in 1919, composed by	Approved in 1922, composed by	Approved in 1928, composed by
62		S. de L.	
63	J.H.D.	J. de H.	
64			
69	P.K. de V.		
70	J.H.D.		
71			
76	S. de L.§		
78	F.W.J.		
80	Tune of Ps. 105		
82			
83			
85			
87			A.C. v.V.
88			
90	F.W.J.§		
91	F.W.J.§		
92	J.H.D.		
94			
96	F.W.J.		
100	Tune of Ps. 134		P.K. de V.
102	J. de H.		
104			
106		A.C. v.V.	
107	J. de H.§		
109			
110	P.K. de V.		Retained old tune
112		P.K. de V§	
114		J. de H.	
115		S. de L.	
120			
123			
125		F.G.B.	
126			
128		M.L. de V.	
129			
130	F.W.J.	Voortrekker tune	
131			
132			
137		F.G.B.	
139		S. de L.	
141			P.K. de V.
142	J.A. Malherbe		
143		J. de H.	
144		S. de L.	
145			P.K. de V.

Psalms requiring new tunes	Approved in 1919, composed by	Approved in 1922, composed by	Approved in 1928, composed by
146	Folksong-tune		
147		P.K. de V.§	
148	J. de H.		
149		P.K. de V.	

Code:

J.H.D.	= J.H. Deelman
A.C. v. V.	= A.C. van Velden*
P.K. de V.	= P.K. de Villiers*
S. de L.	= S. de Lange (1895)
F.W.J.	= F.W. Jannasch
J. de H.	= J. de Heer
M.L. de V.	= M.L. de Villiers*
J.S. de V.	= J.S. de Villiers
F.G.B.	= F.G. Beversluis

The tunes that were ultimately included in the Afrikaans Psalter are indicated by an § after the initials of the composer. In 1919 a subcommittee consisting of F.W. Jannasch, P.K. de Villiers and A.C. van Velden was appointed to scrutinise the tunes submitted. This was the first time that musicians had been included as members of any committee concerned with the setting of the psalms. These members were also composers of new tunes. The question of "short and long notes" remained an open one; on the subject of rhythm, composers were allowed complete freedom. In the first psalters to be tested both isometric and "rhythmic" tunes were offered. In the subcommittee's report the secular tune of Ps. 146 was described as "the one now in use". The tune referred to is probably the one ultimately used for Ps. 146 in the Afrikaans psalter of 1937. The tune for Ps. 112 in the proof-copy of 1922 was finally accepted with considerable modification. Since P.K. de Villiers served on the selection committee of the 1922 collection, it is confidently assumed that he was himself responsible for the modifications. These provide reasonable clarity regarding the methods of melody-building applied by this composer of psalm-tunes. The tune for Ps. 112 in the Afrikaans Psalter was derived from that used in the edition of 1922 along the following lines:

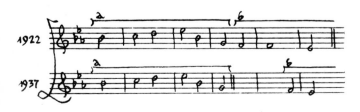

By 1926 the versification of the psalms in Afrikaans became of absorbing interest in church circles throughout the country. The work undertaken by the hymn committee of the Federated Dutch Reformed Churches, was temporarily retarded, since the Afrikaans versification might employ a metrical foot differing from the original, which would involve a further revision of the melodies. The poet was requested to maintain the metre of the Dutch psalms, but it was not long before he had to insist on a relaxation of this restriction. A close scrutiny of its reports delivers convincing proof that the committee was not thoroughly acquainted with the psalm-tunes that were to be replaced. There are curious procedures such as the recommendation of two different tunes for Psalms 14 and 53, both of which are rhymed identically. Again, the tune for Psalm 33 was to be replaced, while the other one for Psalm 67 (precisely the same tune) was to remain. Other similar inconsistencies may be found. It is important to bear in mind the two principles that were followed in the preparation of this psalter: (i) More than one melody for a single psalm is permissible; this has been applied to six of the psalms, e.g. Ps. 5 (P.K. de Villiers and M.L. de Villiers in 1922) and Ps. 16 (F.W. Jannasch and A.C. van Velden in 1922). This was the first time in the history of any Dutch Psalter that more than one tune per psalm was prescribed. (ii) As far as possible recently composed tunes were to be sought as replacements for those that were rejected. In two instances only, old tunes were offered as replacements: Ps. 80 (to the tune of Ps. 105) and Ps. 100 (to the tune of Ps. 134).

3. Consolidation (1933-1937)

The Nederduitse Hervormde Kerk (NHK) of Africa made the first move towards the acquisition of a communal psalter by enlisting the co-operation of all three Afrikaans churches; and in 1933 an *ad hoc* committee representing all three churches met for the first time. Progress up to that time was as follows: (i) There were metrical arrangements of 110 of the psalms in Afrikaans, some of which deviated from the metrical patterns used in the Dutch (Nederlands) versions. (ii) The Federated

11

Dutch Reformed Churches had obtained new tunes for 74 of the 92 psalms chosen for replacement by the 1919 Synod. (iii) The Gereformeerde Kerk (Reformed Church) of South Africa felt that new tunes were needed for 29 of the psalms, and actually had available a number of appropriate suggestions. The modified Afrikaans versions of 15 of the 29 necessitated new tunes and it must be assumed that the other 14 were in this case also encumbered with "unsingable" tunes. A further recommendation of this Church was that there should be a "rhythmic edition" of the psalter. —It should be evident that, in the choosing of suitable tunes, there was a marked divergence of opinion among the members of the Joint Committee. On the one hand, the Reformed Church was in favour of preserving as many of the original melodies as possible; and on the other, the Dutch Reformed Church had already gone far towards eliminating most of them. —Another cause of disagreement arose from the controversial question of an edition in which the old melodies were to retain their original rhythmic patterns. Though it had been decided to publish an edition of the psalter "with tunes set in the manner of a chorale", the 1937 edition used note values of varying duration (so-called "short and long notes"). As the Rev. J.V. Coetzee had the task of editing the tunes, he may be regarded as responsible for their ultimate appearance in "rhythmic" form. It appears that at the outset his intention was to have the tunes printed without bar-lines; but in this he was opposed by P.K. de Villiers and A.C. van Velden, the members of the committee who acted as musical advisers. The Rev. E.G. Malherbe reports that the Rev. Coetzee also submitted unapproved melodies to the SA Bible Society for publication. Some had actually been rejected. In certain instances he interchanged first and second choices recommended by the Committee. Nothing could be done at that stage, however, as the psalter was well on the way towards final publication.—Three factors helped to resolve these difficulties: a common agreement regarding alternative tunes for a psalm, a more or less uniform taste on the subject of new melodies, and the ideal solution that there should be one psalter for all three Afrikaans churches. Consequent upon the attitude of the Reformed Church, and especially of the Rev. J.V. Coetzee, the Afrikaans psalter of 1937 retained a fair number of old tunes, though frequently as alternatives to the other tunes. The sacrifice of so many of the old melodies was necessary, if only to ensure that the ideal referred to should not miscarry. —Towards the end of 1935 the task of the Joint Music Committee had, in the main, been accomplished, and the year 1936 was taken up with preparations for the publication of the completed psalter. In 1937, with great joy and thanksgiving, the new psalter was brought into use by the Reformed Church, and a few years later (after the music of the hymns had been edited) by the other two Afrikaans churches.

4. The old melodies

In contrast with the Genevan Psalter of 1562, in which three or four composers were responsible for 123 different tunes, the Afrikaans Psalter represents the work of almost thirty different composers; and although there are 140 different tunes in the book only 128 of the psalms have individual tunes. This is because alternative tunes are offered; the rest of the psalms, as in the French Psalter, borrow tunes from each other. One hundred and fifty versifications are by Dr. J.D. du Toit (Totius), one by Dr G.B.A. Gerdener (Psalm 23), and another by the Rev. J.J. Kühn (Ps. 130). It is generally acknowledged that the metrical versions of the psalms by Totius are among the best in Dutch literature. —Seventy of the Genevan melodies have been retained in the Afrikaans Psalter (cf. the table at the conclusion of this article). This high total may be partly ascribed to the existence for several psalms of two melodies - an old and a new tune. In some instances, where a new tune had been deemed necessary, the original tune was transferred from that psalm to another, as in the case of Psalms 83 and 115. —Though it is possible to illustrate stylistic differences between groups of Genevan melodies, they have many features in common. This is because they belong to the same period of musical history. In addition, Calvin himself had clearly defined prerequisites for a psalm-tune, and must have exerted an overall influence that shaped the melodies homogeneously. (For a discussion of the musical and aesthetic qualities of the Genevan melodies the reader is referred to the author's *Die Afrikaanse Psalmmelodieë,* Potchefstroom, 1962). —For several reasons the Genevan melodies were not taken over unaltered for use in the Afrikaans Psalter. On the one hand the committee was faced with the same problem as De Lange in editing the same tunes; and on the other, many of the tunes had to be adapted to a versification that deviated from the metre of the original. The modifications made to rhythmic patterns may be considered in four groups: (i) The results of eliminating syncopation. Except in 6a, all syncopation was removed by reconstructing the rhythmic pattern of the relevant line. (ii) In many instances the rhythmic pattern of individual lines had to be altered, to suit the Afrikaans text, e.g. in 33g and 84a. (iii) Where the original melody admitted trochaic feet in the versification, the rhythm in the Afrikaans version was often either modified to two (or multiples of two) short notes between the long notes (29c); or dotted minims were employed (42a). (iv) For many lines it was not possible to find a satisfactory reason for modifying the rhythmic pattern of the original, e.g. 32c, 33a, 121f, 130 a b c d e f g h, etc. —The practice of introducing leading notes in the Dutch Psalter, was also adopted in preparing the Afrikaans version. Here and there sharps were inserted to make the melody sound a little more "modern", e.g. in 5c. Tunes with a rising movement at the end of a line were provided with leading-notes, unless a Phrygian cadence was obviously intended, e.g. Ps. 17a, 51g, etc. The tunes of Ps. 10, 60, 79, 97, 101 and 140 were drastically altered to make them suit the Afrikaans words. —The Rev. J.V. Coetzee was responsible for the final editing of the melodies, so that there is no doubt who introduced the various modifications. In the task entrusted to him there were evidently two vital considerations: preservation of the maximum number of Genevan melodies; and reduction to a minimum of what might be regarded as "unsingable" melodies. The first entailed the adaption of old tunes to a new versification and the transference of an original tune from one psalm to another; the second made it necessary to raise the pitch of certain notes by introducing accidentals and to eliminate syncopated rhythms. The editor was not equal to such a specialised task, as is evident from the ragged aspect of many of the melodies published. But it was due especially to his efforts that these tunes were retained; and the revision of the existing tunes is now a far less arduous task than trying (after 25 years) to get the old tunes re-accepted into the psalter.

5. The new melodies

As a result of their altered versification, the following 35 psalms had to be supplied with different tunes: 2, 7, 11, 12, 14, 18, 20, 28, 37, 45, 46, 50, 53, 63, 64, 69, 70, 78, 82, 83, 88, 96, 102, 104, 109, 112, 114, 115, 119, 120, 125, 137, 145, 147 and 149. For Psalms 83 and 115 other Genevan melodies were introduced; while the melodies chosen for Psalms 28, 46 and 63 were the same as those used for Psalms 37, 82 and 70 respectively, leaving only 30 entirely new tunes to be provided.—For the following 31 psalms new melodies were also published, although the old ones could have been retained: 4, 8, 9, 13, 16, 23, 26, 31, 40, 41, 44, 48, 57, 61, 71, 76, 80, 90, 91, 92, 94, 100, 107, 110, 126, 128, 129, 142, 144, 146 and 148. As the melodies for Psalms 31 and 71 were identical, only 30 new tunes were actually used. For 5 psalms in the two groups (8, 12, 64, 109 and 125) and for 7 of the old tunes (5, 6, 33, 34, 51, 130, 131) alternative tunes were provided. Hence the total number of new psalm-tunes is 72. Four of the tunes (to Psalms 12 (no. 2), 28(=37), 46(=82) and 104) date from the sixteenth century; another (Ps. 128) is from the seventeenth century; and three (Psalms 53, 78, 88) are from the eighteenth century. The rest are from the nineteenth and twentieth centuries. —Twenty two tunes were selected from the various proof-copies of the Dutch Reformed Church (1919, 1922 and 1926); fourteen melodies came from hymn books used at this period, viz. *Church Praise, Evangelic Hymns* and *Elberfeld* and thirty-six were selected from melodies that had been submitted during the period 1933-1937. The new melodies represent the work of many different composers, yet there is remarkable uniformity of style. One significant reason is that the tunes, in greater or lesser degree, were modelled on specimens in the English Hymnody. This influence was strongly manifested in the music of P.K. de Villiers and A.C. van Velden; but it becomes less evident in F.W. Jannasch (Ps. 13), in a few tunes by W. de Vries (Ps. 145) and P. van den Burg* (Psalms 41, 45). The declining impact of the English hymn coincided with the growing influence of the old melodies, more especially as regards their rhythmic devices; but this was never as strong a force as the English hymn. —Apart from isolated instances of chromaticism, the newer melodies are diatonic. All diatonic intervals, up to and including the octave, are freely used in both ascending and descending passages, except for the interval of the seventh, of which there is only one example (125 d). Conjunct movement accounts for 60 to 70 percent of all melodic progressions. The two limits between which these percentages fluctuate are 85 percent (Ps. 11) and 55 percent (Ps. 23). The high percentage of leaps can be explained by the employment of broken chords, and certain harmonic uses. The extensive reliance on leaps and melodic triads is largely responsible for the "porous" texture of so many of these tunes. In a few of the melodies (P.K. de Villiers) the monotone is used, usually by repeating the note three times; but there are instances of four-fold repetition (2c, 2d, 119e, 130e), and one where the note is repeated five times (110a). Melodic sequences are used freely. The range of the melodies fluctuates between a sixth and a twelfth (octave + fourth). There are four times as many tunes with a range exceeding the octave as there are tunes composed within the octave. —In contrast with the Genevan tunes conceived as purely melodic lines, the new melodies are actually four-part compositions requiring analyses of harmonic progression for their definition. The harmonic resources are essentially those of the early romantic period: major and minor triads; dominant 7ths, 9ths, 11ths and 13ths (also used as secondary dominants); secondary 7ths, 9ths (mainly on the supertonic); chords of the augmented 6th (German 6th etc.). The frequent use of higher dissonant chords is especially characteristic of P.K. de Villiers, A.C. van Velden and J.S. de Villiers. These chords invariably occur in stereotyped combinations. The inner voices are for the most part stationary, and there is seldom any suggestion of polyphonic part-writing. —The melodic patterns of the new tunes are, in general, a direct outcome of an harmonic way of thinking. Conjunct thirds and fourth constructions are in evidence, but there is an overall preponderance of melodic triads. — Three groups of rhythmic structures can be distinguished: (i) Rhythms based on the same principles as those used for the Genevan melodies, e.g. 11, 13, 23, 40, 110 etc.; (ii) Rhythms in which the dotted minim was introduced as a new metrical element, e.g. 2, 4, 6, 8, 57, 69, 144 etc.; (iii) The isorhythmic melodies, e.g. 5, 7, 28, 48, 114, 148 etc. — The rhythms of the melodies in the second group exhibit the influence of the English hymn. In eleven of the nineteen melodies in this group all the lines in each melody have the same or almost identical rhythmic patterns (2, 6 18, 50, 51, 69, 102, 120, 142, 144, 147). An innovation in some melodies is the use of triple time (4, 59, 69). — Although isometric melodies represent a style of singing formerly usual in the Protestant churches, the appropriate notation was first used in this country in the Afrikaans Psalter. Of the 68 melodies under consideration, six are in the minor key and the rest in the major. Evidently the choice of the minor key was dictated by certain textual associations. — In quite a number of tunes repetition of lines occurs in much the same way as in the old melodies, giving rise to shapes of a similar nature, e.g. in 16, 41, 92, 102, etc. A new feature, however, is the melody with two identical parts (e.g. in 2, 4, 18, 51 and 144). This is in fact a division of each psalm verse into two verses. — Since the publication of the Afrikaans Psalter in 1937, there has been some sharp criticism of its music, especially from Hollanders. D.W.L. Milo described the musical part of the Totius Psalter as a "nasty conglomeration of conventional, unorthodox and frivolous tunes", and refers to the mutilation of old melodies. — He criticised the new melodies very severely: "Another example is Psalm 130. Here is a tune suitable for a camp-fire or happy wanderer's song, which has to do duty 'De profundis' to Psalm 130. We sing the choice words of Totius 'Uit Dieptes, gans verlore'. ...('Out of the depths ...') and establish that this psalm has with its profane tune now become both unsingable and unmusical" ("Het Afrikaanse Psalter" in *Organist en Eeredienst* XIII/142, Nov. 1947). The tune for Psalm 2 he regards as a "vulgar march", and the isometric melodies as belonging to the category of "dragging, dreary isorhythmic concoctions". With pained surprise, he sees how far the "peculiar character of the sacred song" in South Africa has strayed from the old Reformed style (preface by the Music Committee to the Afrikaans Psalter, 1937). — The comments of the Rev. H. Hasper *(Wat nu?,* The Hague, 1937) and Dr G. van der Leeuw *(Beknopte Geschiedenis van het Kerklied,* Groningen, 1948) sound more moderate. The former writes "... the beautiful versification of the psalms by Professor J.D. du Toit has not, alas! been set to sublime melodies that will enrapture the heart. The ultimate achievement of the 'Joint Musical Committee of the Hollands-Afrikaans Churches' is unfortunately weighed down with all the disadvantages arising from compromises reached by co-operating committees ...Hitherto Africa has had the best edition of the psalm-tunes that exists in modern notation ... but the best has now ceased to exist. That the adapted tune used for Psalm 79 could ever have found supporters must be ascribed to considerations that we in Holland are not in a position to comprehend". Van der Leeuw regrets the disappearance of many traditional melodies: "Our Afrikaans brothers have replaced many beautiful psalm-tunes with so-called 'new tunes'; not all of them are bad, but without exception they are far below the standard of the originals." — Criticisms of the new psalter have also been strongly expressed in South Africa. Initially, persons closely associated with the preparation of the psalter expressed, defended or attacked different points of view. (See Ds. J.V. Coetzee: "Ons Psalms en Gesange - hoe die musiek daarvan gekies is", *Die Huisgenoot,* 22 June 1945; P.K. de Villiers: "Ons Psalms en Gesangwysies", *Die Huisgenoot,* 19 October 1945). In these articles there was no thorough musical assessment. But gradually it became possible to consider the book more objectively.

Almost without exception the opinions expressed by later writers are based on stylistic analyses, and more or less coincide with the criticisms of the Dutch authors. The gist is appreciation for the retention of the old Genevan melodies (though in a modified form), and confirmation of the regrettably low standard of church music, represented by the new melodies. These betray the influence of Methodist hymn tunes (see articles such as: J.P. Malan's* Die Afrikaner en sy Kerkmusiek in *Standpunte*, New Series XIV/3, 4, 5 and XV/2, 3). — The Afrikaans Psalter of 1937 is an exceedingly complex document which reflects cultural and ecclesiastical aspects of Afrikaner life during its formative years. Totius's versification of the psalms is a triumph of Afrikaans which embodies purely Calvinistic convictions. The deterioration of sacred melodies during four centuries, from the artistically impeccable Genevan melodies (which owe their form to words), to sensuously popular songs, parallels the increasing emphasis placed on a subjective approach to Christian religion. There was a descent from the heights of an authentic "soli Deo gloria" reached by the Calvinistic reformation in the sixteenth century to the humanized, emotive religion of the nineteenth century. — Resorting to inferior music (for new melodies in the Afrikaans Psalter) reveals the consequences of the outcry for singable tunes. Not only has the musical standard of the psalter been seriously impaired, but we are also faced with an entirely new concept of church song, opposed to the Calvinistic tradition embodied in the old tunes. In the new tunes there flourishes a concept of church song that was prevalent in South Africa during the second half of the nine-teenth century, nourished by the over-zealous singing and dissemination of songs bearing the indelible stamp of both Wesleys and of Moody and Sankey as in *Kinder-harp, Sionsharp, Halleluja!*, etc. The "unsingability" of many Genevan melodies was proclaimed, and in the effort to provide "singable" music, hardly any thought was given to the requirements of an artistic standard of composition, to a decorous alliance between words and music. There was a shift to emotional appeal, sensuous joy in singing and pleasurable ease of execution. — Charles Wesley wrote about his songs, that any poem could be sung to any tune in the book; in similar vein J.S. de Villiers, writing in the preface to his *Halleluja!*, admits that he strove to compose singable tunes, and therefore paid less attention to artistic qualities. The comments of P.G.J.M. in the *Kerkbode* of 28 September 1911, suggest that the worth of the melody was considered to be of secondary importance: "Music may be all very fine for connoisseurs of that art but ..." Evidently singability and music of a high standard were thought to be irreconcilable. These two conditions are, however, compatible. We have evidence of this in the Dutch Psalter. J.H. Malan in his article *(Die Brandwag,* 1 November 1911) places the emphasis where it belongs: *Church Praise* has become singable through constant use in the schools and elsewhere; the Genevan melodies could have been made just as singable, if approached with understanding, and exercised as systematically. The critic's reference to the congregation of De Rust gives substantial support to his contention.

6. Revision of the Psalm-tunes (1952-1967)

Since the early 1950 s there has been agitation for the revision of the psalm-tunes. In the Reformed Church (Gereformeerde Kerk) the psalter of 1937 is still regarded as a proof-copy. It is therefore not surprising that at the 1952 Synod of this church one of the matters discussed was the need to revise the music of the psalter. The point of view was that "There has been enough time in which to review these tunes, and to make alterations and improvements to both melodies and rhythms in the light of criticisms that have been published" (Church Council of Potchefstroom). The Synod appointed delegates for the revision and instructed them to seek the co-operation of the two other Afrikaans churches. — From the report submitted by this delegation to the 1955 Synod, it appears that the revision was launched at a meeting of representatives of the Gereformeerde Kerk, Dutch Reformed Church of the OFS and Cape, and the Hervormde Kerk. This meeting was held at Bloemfontein on 3 and 4 July 1953. The most significant aspect of the report was a marked inclination to retain as many of the old Genevan tunes as possible in their original rhythmic forms, and to reduce the number of alternative melodies. — A second interchurch meeting could not be held before October 1960. On this occasion all the melodies were discussed, and practically all the new ones of 1937 were rejected; but the difficulty of finding replacements for the latter tunes could not be resolved. — This action of the churches was accompanied by simultaneous moves that created an advantageous atmosphere. First, there were the nation-wide performances by the Stellenbosse Kweekskoolkoor,* under their conductor Dr G.G. Cillié*, in which the old melodies figured prominently. Then there were articles and a series of radio talks (given by Dr J.P. Malan, Rosa Nepgen,* Dr G.G. Cillié, the Rev. W.E.H. Söhnge*), which stressed the aesthetic, historical and liturgical values of the Genevan tunes. There were also regular broadcasts of many of the old melodies, and courses on church music were held at the Theological College in Stellenbosch and the Theological College of the Reformed Church at Potchefstroom, again with the emphasis on the Genevan melodies. The commemoration of the four-hundredth anniversary of the Genevan Psalter in 1962 was the occasion for festivals throughout the country. Well-known and lesser-known psalm-tunes, often in sixteenth century arrangements, were sung by massed choirs. Through lectures given at different centres it was possible to gauge the extent to which the Genevan tunes were cherished in Afrikaans church music and a plea was made for the restoration of a rich heritage. — Since 1966 the interchurch revision committee has assembled twice yearly, to conduct their work to a satisfactory conclusion.

7. Afrikaans Psalm-tunes of 1937

Composers/sources, and date of origin of the melodies in the Afrikaans Psalter of 1937:

Ps.		Ps.	
1	ST 39	12	P.K. de Villiers, 1937
2	P.K. de Villiers, 1937	12	Day's Psalter, 1563
3	GE 51	13	F.W. Jannasch, 1919
4	P.K. de Villiers, 1937	14	P.K. de Villiers, 1937
5	P.K. de Villiers, 1937	15	ST 39
5	GE 42	16	A.C. van Velden, 1919
6	P.K. de Villiers, 1937	17	GE 51
6	GE 42	18	P.K. de Villiers, 1937
7	P.K. de Villiers, 1937	19	GE 42
8	S.J. de Villiers	20	Evangelische Gezangen, 1804
8	S. de Lange, 1895	21	GE 51
9	J. de Heer, 1937	22	GE 42
10	GE 51	23	F.W. Jannasch, 1919
11	Rosenburg, 1937	24	GE 42

25	GE 51
26	J.S. de Villiers
27	GE 51
28	Notker
29	GE 51
30	GE 51
31	J.S. de Villiers, 1882
32	Bg 47a
33	A.C. van Velden, 1919
33	ST 45
34	A.C. van Velden, 1919
34	GE 51
35	GE 51
36	ST 39
37	= 28
38	GE 42
39	GE 51
40	J.H. Groothengel, 1937
41	P. van den Burg, 1937
42	GE 51
43	MO 46
44	J. de Heer, 1919
45	P. van den Burg, 1937
46	M. Luther
47	GE 51
48	J.S. de Villiers, 1882
49	GE 62
50	J. Stainer nineteenth century
51	P.K. de Villiers, 1937
51	GE 51
52	GE 62
53	J.F. Lampe, eighteenth century
54	GE 62
55	GE 62
56	GE 62
57	P.K. de Villiers, 1937
58	GE 62
59	A.C. van Velden, 1937
60	GE 62
61	J.A. Malherbe, 1937
62	= 24
63	J. de Heer, 1922
64	P.K. de Villiers, 1937
64	W. de Vries, 1937
65	= 72
66	= 118

67	= 33(2)
68	= 36
69	P.K. de Villiers, 1937
70	= 63
71	= 31
72	ST 45
73	GE 51
74	GE 62
75	GE 62
76	S. de Lange, 1895
77	= 86
78	J. Wainwright, eighteenth century
79	ST 45
80	F. Molenaar, 1937
81	GE 62
82	= 46
83	= 3
84	GE 62
85	GE 62
86	ST 45
87	GE 62
88	S. Howard, eighteenth century
89	GE 62
90	F.W. Jannasch, 1919
91	F.W. Jannasch, 1919
92	P. van den Burg, 1937
93	GE 62
94	= 105
95	= 24
96	= 21
97	GE 62
98	= 118
99	'GE 62
100	P.K. de Villiers, 1926
101	GE 51
102	P.K. de Villiers, 1937
103	ST 39
104	M. Luther
105	GE 62
106	GE 62
107	J. de Heer, 1919
108	= 60
109	P.K. de Villiers, 1937
109	W. de Vries, 1937
110	P.K. de Villiers, 1919
111	= 24

Ps.		Ps.	
112	P.K. de Villiers, 1922	131	GE 51
113	GE 51	131	M.L. de Villiers, 1937
114	P.K. de Villiers, 1937	132	GE 51
115	= 135	133	GE 51
116	= 74	134	GE 51
117	= 127	135	GE 62
118	ST 45	136	GE 62
119	P.K. de Villiers, 1937	137	?
120	P.K. de Villiers, 1937	138	Bg 47a
121	GE 51	139	= 30
122	GE 51	140	= T.G.
123	GE 51	141	GE 62
124	GE 51	142	P.K. de Villiers, 1937
125	P.K. de Villiers, 1937	143	ST 39
125	J. Barnby, nineteenth century	144	P.K. de Villiers, 1919
126	J.A. Malherbe, 1937	145	W. de Vries, 1937
127	GE 51	146	F.G. Bäsler, 1804
128	M. Teschner, seventeenth century	147	P.K. de Villiers, 1922
129	J.A. Malherbe, 1937	148	J. de Heer, 1919
130	P.K. de Villiers, 1937	149	Crasselius
130	ST 39	150	GE 62

Commentary:

a. Where the tune has been borrowed from another psalm, the reference refers in each case to the psalm in which text and tune were originally used together. For new tunes it was not always possible to establish their original association with a text. b. 1882, 1895, 1919, 1922, 1926 refer to specimen copies that were published in these years.

BIBLIOGRAPHY:

BON, G: Die musiekkuns van die Afrikaner. *Kultuurgeskiedenis van die Afrikaner* III. Cape Town, 1950. DEKKER, G: *Die Afrikaanse Psalmberyming*. Pretoria, 1938. HANEKOM, T.N: *Die liberale rigting in Suid-Afrika*. Stellenbosch, 1951. HASPER, H: *Wat nu? Verweerschrift tegen aanvallen op het Boek der Psalmen*. The Hague, 1937. PIENAAR, E.C: *Die ontstaan van ons Afrikaanse Psalm- en Gesangboeke*. Cape Town, 1944. STEYN, J.L: *Totius as Psalmberymer*. Potchefstroom, 1951. VAN DER MERWE, P.C: *Die verhaal van ons geestelike liedere*. Cape Town, 1948. VAN DER WALT, J.J.A: *Die Afrikaanse Psalmmelodieë*. Potchefstroom, 1962.

SOURCES:

Acta Synodi, Gereformeerde Kerk van Suid-Afrika, 1862-1936. Acta Synodi, Nederduits Gereformeerde Kerk Kaapland, 1824-1936. Acta Synodi, Nederduitse Gereformeerde Kerk, 1915-1936. Almanak van die Gereformeerde Kerk van Suid-Afrika, 1938. APEL, W: The partial signatures in the sources up to 1450. *Acta Musicologica* X/1-2, 1938. Aulcuns Pseaulmes et Cantiques mys en chant. Strassburg, 1539 (facsimile). BOUWS, J: Die Kaapse musieklewe in die Hollandse tyd. *Tydskrif vir Volkskunde en Volkstaal* III/3, Feb. 1947. BOUWS, J: Die musieklewe van Kaapstad in die beginjare van die negentiende eeu en sy verhouding tot die Europese musieklewe. *Tydskrif vir Wetenskap en Kuns*, Nuwe Reeks XII/tweede aflewering, 1952. BOUWS, J: Die musieklewe in Suid-Afrika buite die Kaapkolonie in die tweede helfte van die neëntiende eeu. *Tydskrif vir Wetenskap en Kuns*,

Nuwe Reeks VIII/tweede aflewering, 1948. BOUWS, J: Drie eeue Afrikaanse musieklewe. *Jaarboek van die Afrikaanse Skrywerskring* XI, 1946. De Psalmen der Hollandsche Gereformeerde Kerk. Cape Town, 1895. COETZEE, J.V: Ons Psalms en Gesange — hoe die musiek daarvan gekies is. *Die Huisgenoot,* 22 June 1945. DE VILLIERS, P.K: Ons Psalm- en Gesangwysies. *Die Huisgenoot,* 19 October 1945. DE VILLIERS, J.S: *Hallelujah! Psalmen en Gezangen der Ned. Geref. Kerk van Zuid-Afrika,* 1882. DU TOIT, J.D. and JANNASCH, F.W.: 36 *Psalme in Afrikaans.* Cape Town, 1923. MALAN, J.H. (J.H.M.): Nieuwe wysies, ons Psalm- en Gezangboek. *Die Brandwag* II/11, 1 Nov. 1911. MALAN, J.P.: Die Afrikaner en sy kerkmusiek. *Standpunte,* Nuwe Reeks XIV/3, 4, 5 and XV/2, 3. MEIRING, P.G.J: Hiervan en daarvan. *De Kerkbode* II/38, 28 Sept. 1911. MILO, D.W.L: Het Afrikaanse Psalter. *Organist en eeredienst* XIII/142. *Nieuwe melodieën voor eenige der psalmen.* Cape Town, 1919, 1922, 1926. VAN DER WALT, J.J.A: Twee teëgestelde kerkliedbegrippe. *Koers* XXX/5 and 6, Nov./Dec. 1962.

—J.J.A. v.d. W.

II. SACRED SONG IN SOUTH AFRICA
1. Sluyter and Groenewegen
2. Old hymn-books in manuscript
3. Printed editions of sacred songs
4. The influence of "Slaven Gezangen" ("Slave tunes") on the Afrikaans heritage of sacred songs
5. "Liederwysies" and their origin

1. Sluyter and Groenewegen
From the earliest days in South Africa a feature of the family prayers was the singing of sacred songs, in addition to the psalms and hymns from the authorized song-books of the church. This practice may be assumed from the possession in many homes today of collections by Willem Sluyter (*1627) and the brothers Johannes and Jacob Groenewegen. In the Sluyter books no music is provided with the words; but at the beginning of each lyric there is a reference to a suitable tune from the psalter, and/or to an alternative that might be used. For example, one of the songs has the title: "Gebed tot Christus, om naar zijn voorbeeld geduldig te lijden" ("Prayer to Christ that we may with patience follow His example in our suffering") and suggestions for a tune run thus:
Tune: Psalm 146 or: Rosemond die lag gedoken.
Similarly, in the Groenewegen collection only the words are printed; but here only a single choice is given — either a psalm or another tune. No doubt the purpose of these early collections was that the lyrics should be sung: in fact, as we may read in Groenewegen's Preface, even before publication they were sung with great effect from manuscript copies at prayer and testimony meetings on Sunday evenings. — It has not been easy to ascertain the extent to which the songs of Sluyter and Groenewegen were sung in South Africa. In his research into the origins of so-called "liederwysies" (tunes adapted for church use) Willem van Warmelo came across isolated examples of lyrics from both of these collections, where the musical notation had been added to the text; other tunes were sung to him. We can therefore be fairly certain that in the early days some of these sacred songs were sung in this country. Possibly the suggested psalm-tune was used in some cases; but for most, other suitable tunes were chosen. There is no recorded instance of an association between the sung melody and the tune referred to above the text. Sometimes the reference is to a secular song of the sixteenth

century, but we may be fairly sure that the eighteenth century singers would no longer have been acquainted with it. Perhaps only a few lyrics from Sluyter and Groenewegen were actually sung; others were probably read aloud for the sake of spiritual edification.

2.   Old hymn-books in manuscript

Van Warmelo recounts the story of a missionary-explorer, John Campbell, who made a journey through the Caledon district. On one occasion he spent the night at the house of a certain Mr Roos. His host "produced a small manuscript book of hymns, which the family seemed to prize as more precious than gold. They formed a circle and sang three or four hymns without intermission". As a number of these manuscript hymn-books have been preserved, it seems likely that they were in fairly common use. Van Warmelo came across a valuable copy of such a book in the possession of Mrs A.J. du Plooy of Retreat, in the Cape. It had belonged to her father, S.G. du Plooy, and contained various forms of most of the better-known sacred tunes. An exceptional feature of the Du Plooy Manuscript is that Mr Du Plooy had been able to write down both the words and the tunes. In 1950 Mrs Egbert Olivier of Steynsrust in the Free State presented the present writer with another old manuscript hymn-book, containing both words and music. She said that the original had belonged to the Burger family of Piquetberg. This manuscript is now in the Church Archives of the Cape, and contains a number of psalms with neat musical notation, as well as a number of sacred songs. For most of the latter there are references to the tunes which could be used; for the rest, only the text is given. Those with musical notation are Christmas carols; among the others is an occasional song described thus: "Song composed to mark the occasion of the arrival of Rev. Mr M.C. Vos as Minister to the Congregation of War(v)eren. To the tune of 'Geeft een Aalmoes Voor de Blinde' ('Give Alms for the Blind') 1794". Dr Jan Bouws,* with the assistance of Dr Marie Veldhuyzen of Amsterdam, has been successful in tracing the tune of this song. — Prof. J.P. Malan of the University of Pretoria has in his possession a precious document of a similar kind, though of later date. It is a small manuscript book containing the following: 17 Psalms (38, 42, 77, 86, 88, 100, 102, 103, 118, 128, 130, 134, 136, 138, 139, 142, 146); A morning hymn; 5 poems by Sluyter, together with the tunes to which they were sung and 2 ABC's with two different tunes.   — Throughout, the melodies are in the chorale (plainsong) notation of the Nederlandse Psalmboek (Dutch Psalter), and quite obviously they were jotted down by ear, or from memory. The evidence for this is   (a) that with few exceptions all have been written in the key of C;   (b) that they are written with quite exceptional signs, not unlike the old neumes, representing the "scoops" and "turns" of the old Boer style of sacred singing;   (c) for the ABC's at the end of the book, chorale notation has also been used, but without indicating the rhythm of the melodies;   (d) the persistent recurrence of certain spelling errors.   — This collection was written on ruled school exercise-book paper, the pages being secured by means of a needle and thread in the cover of the periodical *Veritas Vincet*, issued by the College Department of the Theological Seminary of the Reformed Church in Potchefstroom. The cover is of later date than the manuscript, which can be dated as late nineteenth century.   — There is also in existence a small hymn-book dated "8 Januarius Anno 1799". This belonged to Susanne Magritha Liebenberg, and contains nine sacred songs, the tunes referred to being Psalms 38 and 128; also a number of sacred songs and folk songs, among which are the names of melodies found in the Sluyter and Groenewegen collections. — Many of the texts found in the old song-books were taken from printed books, such as the Psalmboek (Psalter) and the collections by Sluyter and Groenewegen. There are also occasional songs such as Christmas carols, and the M.C. Vos song mentioned above. It is impossible to say definitely that any of these lyrics was original, but the likelihood is that some original poems were included, especially if one bears in mind an episode concerning Helena Haubtfleisch (née Leroux), a folk poetess of the last century of whom I have knowledge. On the occasion of the 16th birthday of her youngest daughter, Petronella, she presented her with a copy of Groenewegen. Bound into the beginning of the book are three transcribed poems. The first, in 10 stanzas, "Op mijn geboortendag Den 1 September" ("On my birthday, 1 September") was intended to be sung to the tune of Psalm 8. Then follows a long poem of 97 stanzas "Een lied tot gedagtenis geschreven bij het geven van Dit boek" ("A song of remembrance written on the occasion of the presentation of this book"), to the tune of Psalm 130. The first stanza begins thus:

> Ik mag die dag beleven
> zolang door mij begeerd,
> dit boekje u te geven .....

> (I may live to see,
> the day for which I've longed,
> to give this book to thee ...)

On the 36th page at the end of the 97th stanza is the word "einde" ("end"). Then follows:

> Ontvang die bladeren van mijn,
> tot uwen nut geschreven
> en laat het tot gedagt'nis zijn,
> als ek niet meer zal leven,
> Helena Haubtfleisch, gebore Leroux.

> (Receive these pages of me,
> for thy dear use inscribed,
> and let them for remembrance be
> when I shall live no more,
> Helena Haubtfleisch, née Leroux).

The third poem fills two pages and ends thus:

> Ontvang die boek wilt biddend zingen,
> leer hier den toon der hemelingen,
> opdat als gij van hier eens ga,
> voor eeuwig zing haleluya.

> (Receive this book and sing your prayers,
> and learn the songs of heavenly choirs,
> and when thou shalt depart from here,
> thou'lt ever sing 'haleluya').

From accounts of the existence, contents and use of old manuscript books of sacred song, there would seem to be adequate evidence for concluding that, even before 1800, sacred songs, apart from psalms, were sung in South Africa – usually within the family circle.

3. Printed editions of sacred songs

"See, for example, what a difference there is between Dutch and German church music on the one hand, and English on the other. While the two former are dignified and strong in character, the latter is lively, sometimes even frivolous. We soon tire of the latter, while the former remains forever fresh and beautiful". This was written by an anonymous author (perhaps Dr S.H. Hofmeyr) in the periodical *Elpis* published in Cape Town in 1857. He went on to say that while even the humblest in the congregation would sing heartily any of the Dutch and German tunes, a large section of the congregation never dared to join in singing the English ones. Though we need not take exception to the writer's musical assessment of the old Dutch psalm- and hymn-tunes, as compared with English tunes, history after 1860 reveals that he was incorrect in his pronouncement on the relative popularity of the two kinds of sacred melodies.   Ever since 1876, when the Rev. C. Murray* of Graaff Reinet issued his first edition of *De Kinderharp*, a collection of sacred songs (with four-part setting) for "Home and School", the melodies of English songs have become increasingly popular among Afrikaans-speaking people. The songs in this book were, in the main, translations of English sacred songs into Dutch – many of them of the "revivalist" type. In contrast with the long, often tortuous and "rugged" melodies of the old psalms and hymns, these simple, often sentimental, tunes soon came into favour. With the issue of a second edition in 1880, the original *Kinderharp* became appreciably larger, and gained an important place in the home and in Sunday Schools. — Meanwhile there appeared, under the authorship of the Rev. A.M. McGregor, a similar collection, *Zionsliederen*, also intended for use in the family circle, in the Sunday School and at prayer meetings. In the 7th edition of this collection (1896), music was first added to the text, the latter consisting of translations from English sacred songs, some of inferior quality. — In 1903 appeared the first edition of a long line of Halleluja books. The full title of the original was: "Halleluja Liederen voor Zondagscholen, Strevers – en Jongelings – Vereenigingen, Conferenties, en Bijzondere Diensten. Bijeengebracht door C. Murray" ("Halleluja Songs for Sunday Schools, Christian Endeavour Societies, Young People's Associations, Conferences and Special Services. Compiled by C. Murray."). The publishers were the Z.A. Bijbel Vereeniging (S.A. Bible Society), Cape Town. In the preparation of this book the Rev. Murray borrowed much of his material from the *Kinderharp,* and supplemented it with other songs. This Halleluja book, printed in Dutch, remained unaltered through a number of editions. Towards the end of the 1920's it became apparent that the Halleluja, like the psalms and hymns, would have to be translated into Afrikaans. This task was entrusted to Dr (later Professor) G.B.A. Gerdener, who not only translated, but supplemented the new edition with a number of psalms and hymns in Afrikaans. He also believed that the Afrikaans Halleluja would ultimately be accepted by the Federation of Dutch Reformed Churches, as an official hymn-book containing all the psalms and hymns and, in addition, "a sufficient number of sacred songs to fill in the gaps in those collections already in use". The first edition of the *Nuwe Halleluja* appeared in 1931. — In 1945 the Cape Synod issued instructions that the *Nuwe Halleluja* be thoroughly revised, with special reference to its "musical, literary and doctrinal contents". This revision was undertaken in difficult circumstances. Strong opposition came from many church members who had, over the years, come to cherish an affection for the songs in the *Nuwe Halleluja* and its predecessors. So strong was this feeling against drastic change that less than 100 of the tunes were displaced from the old edition: they were replaced by tunes by South African composers, mainly those of P.K. de Villiers. But under pressure from the church authorities, several of the rejected tunes were re-instated in the second edition. Besides songs that had become well-known over the years, an appreciable number of psalms and hymns were added in the 1951 edition, and the contents were enlarged still further by the inclusion of Christmas carols and choral songs. — In the past hundred years the *Halleluja* and its predecessors have had a far-reaching influence on the taste for sacred music among a large section of the Afrikaner people. The ministers responsible for the pioneer work were A.C. Murray, C. Murray and A. McGregor. Descended from Scottish families, all three strove to give the Afrikaner people the songs for which they had a strong affection. From a cultural point of view, this was an unfortunate endeavour – the priceless heritage of sixteenth century France, Germany and the Netherlands was often exchanged for a less worthy heritage that came out of England and America. "As ek die kruishout gadeslaan", "As Hy weerkom", "Blye versekering, Jesus is myn", "Daar's 'n dierb're ou Kruis" and "Ek sien 'n poort wyd ope staan" – to mention only a few from the *Halleluja* – are today much closer to the hearts of the people than "Ontferm, o God, ontferm U tog oor my" (Ps. 51), "Ek hef my oë bergwaarts heen" (Ps. 121) and "O Hoof, bedek met wonde" (Hymn 121). Up to the present, efforts to make members of the church realize that they have rejected a heritage of inestimable value, for something inferior, have not been entirely successful.

4. **The influence of "Slaven Gezangen" ("Slave tunes") on the heritage of sacred songs.**

In her youthful reminiscences written in 1909, Maria Neethling, wife of the Rev. Neethling of Stellenbosch, and one of the daughters of the Rev. Andrew Murray of Graaff Reinet, relates how the family would travel once in five years by horse-cart from Graaff Reinet to Cape Town to attend Synod. On their 10-day journey it was a customary and pleasant diversion for all of them to sing during the first hour of the morning and the last hour in the evening, as they rode along. "Those were the days", she writes, "long before Sankey or Church Praise or even Bateman existed; but what a rich store we had, both in Dutch and English! The Dutch psalms and hymns so sacred, so familiar, so tender to us Cape people! We had the Scotch Paraphrases too, and the Cottage Hymns and Olney Hymns; and, best of all, a little stock in our memories of what we called "Slaven Gezangen", compiled for the use of native congregations; so simple and so sweet, they were loved most of all. The favourites were: "Liefste Heiland Uw genade", "Mijn Heiland! ek verloren kind", "Hij die den Heiland nog niet heeft", and "Ik ben een worm, gansch arm en klein". — The "Slaven Gezangen", to which Maria Neethling refers with so much affection, were collected for use in the churches of the "natives" – as she puts it. Judging by examples she gives, they were borrowed from the hymn-books of the Rhenish and Berlin Missionary Societies in South Africa. Collections of these songs were published during the 1850 s. It is certain that the non-white servants of the Murray family learned these songs in the mission church, and that they sang them to the children of that family; and this, possibly, is how whites in many families learnt the songs of the mission churches; and this is probably how songs of German origin became known to the Afrikaner people. — The hymn-books used in South Africa by non-white Christians included the following: the *Rhenish Hymn Book* (2nd Edition 1856), the *Paarl Hymn Book*

(1869), and the *Berlin Hymn Book*. These books contained mainly translations of German sacred songs into Dutch. In 1949 there appeared an Afrikaans volume, *Sionsgesange,* for use in the Dutch Reformed Mission Church in South Africa, largely the work of the Rev. E. Hartwig.* The sacred songs of the non-whites also had their influence on the sacred songs of the whites in South Africa. There is, for instance, a melody for the old Dutch Hymn 17: "Wie maar den goeden God laat zorgen", which is well-known throughout this country. It is, in fact, the tune of the German song "Mir ist Erbarmung widerfahren", which does not appear in any of the abovementioned song collections used by whites, but certainly in every book used by coloured persons. This is clearly an instance of whites having taken over a tune to be found in collections normally used by non-whites.

5. "Liederwysies" and their origin

In October 1950, a small group, including some of the older residents of Maanhaarrand, Magaliesburg, sang a number of old traditional songs, which I noted down.   (i) "The Magaliesburg Evensong" (FAK, No. 308);   (ii) a tune for Psalm 65;   (iii) "Prepare your lamps" (a song on the parable of the ten virgins); (iv) two tunes for Psalm 100, one of them identical with the tune of the song "Die rivier is vol en die trane rol";   (v) the well-known tune for Psalm 38 (FAK, No. 299);   (vi) Psalm 126, verse 3, sung to a tune generally used with the words of Hymn 17, and originally the German tune for the chorale "Mir ist Erbarmung widerfahren" (FAK, No. 300). I was able to trace the tune for Psalm 65 in the collection of psalms and hymns in the *Halleluja,* published in 1883 by Juta of Cape Town; in all probability it is the work of Jan S. de Villiers (Jan Orrelis). — Although it cannot be said with certainty where these and other sacred tunes originated, a few sources can be indicated: (i) Tunes that originated as authorized Psalm melodies.   Van Warmelo has pointed out that portions of the sacred tunes he noted down for Psalms 42, 138, 84 and 77 can be traced to the Genevan melodies used for these psalms. But as there is no instance of any resemblance between the opening of the tune and the Genevan melody, it is hardly self-evident that one tune was derived from the other. Usually the words and music of the opening line remain longest in memory.   (ii) Tunes borrowed from folksongs. As already mentioned, one instance is Ps. 100, sung to the tune of "Die rivier is vol en die trane rol". The four lines of the stanza are not sung consecutively in accordance with the lines of the melody. The first line of the text is sung three times (in the same way as the tune is sung to the secular words), then follows the second line of the text, sung to the fourth line of the melody. Then the whole procedure is repeated with the third and fourth lines of the text. — Sung in this way, the four verses of the rhymed version of Psalm 100 become virtually eight, and the words of every odd line are repeated three times, a practice that extends the short Psalm 100 to twice its original length. Van Warmelo cites also Hymn 28, sung to the tune of *Clementine*. This hymn has six lines, and *Clementine* only four. In order to match the tune to the words of the hymn, the second and third lines of the melody are repeated for lines four and five of the text. — An instance where a secular original of the sacred tune is not so evident is to be found in the Morning Hymn (Hymn 179, FAK No. 305), certainly derived from the student song *Gaudeamus igitur.* Van Warmelo maintains that the well-known Voortrekker melody of Psalm 130 evolved in various stages from the drinking-song *Io vivat.*   (iii) Sacred tunes derived from printed collections. It is difficult to provide

25

a definition that conveys satisfactorily the idea of what a "sacred tune" is. It is assumed that, where such a tune differs from the authorised melody of the psalm or hymn, it has not simply been taken from a hymn-book currently in use. One would hardly describe the tune of "Bly by my, Heer" as the "liederwysie" of Psalm 93, although the latter is normally sung to this melody. If, however, the tune for a psalm or hymn has been taken from an old collection, of which few have heard, it might in the course of time, qualify as a "sacred tune". —Thus the Bäsler tune for Psalm 146 ("Prys die Heer") and the Viner tune for Hymn 12 ("O goedheid Gods") could both be described as "sacred tunes". Both are so widely accepted that they are printed as the official tunes of the relevant psalm and hymn in the Afrikaans Hymn Book. However, the fitting solemnity of the tune for Psalm 146 makes one reluctant to call it a "sacred tune"; but the Viner tune for Hymn 12, with its secular, sprightly character, may be aptly described in this way. —Van Warmelo gives an example of a "sacred tune" that hardly qualifies: the tune for Psalm 130, which he wrote down in Paarl, and which is apparently known in Calvinia! It is a melody by F.W. Jannasch of Stellenbosch, composed for Psalm 130, and it appears in a specimen volume of psalm-tunes printed in 1919. What is more, it has been printed as an alternative choice for Hymn 7. The melody composed by Jan S. de Villiers for Psalm 65, first published in 1883, might qualify as a "sacred tune". The small volume in which it appeared is not now in general use. —With the passage of time, the origins of many more of the "sacred tunes" in printed collections may be determined. At present, the origins of the great majority still remain obscure.

BIBLIOGRAPHY

VAN WARMELO, W.: *Afrikaanse liederwysies.* Cape Town, 1948.   VAN WARMELO, W.: *Liederwysies van vanslewe.* Amsterdam, Cape Town, 1958.

SOURCES

BOUWS, J.: *Die Burger,* Cape Town, 15 December, 1966.   CILLIÉ, G.G.: *Handhaaf,* Johannesburg, August 1964.   *Geestelijke Gezangen ten gebruike van Evangelische Gemeenten in Zuid-Afrika.* Published by the Berlin Missionary Society, Berlin, 1853.   *Geestelijke Gezangen ten gebruike van Evangelische Gemeenten uit de Heidenen in Zuid-Afrika.* Published by the Rhenish Missionary Society, 2nd Edition, Cape Town, 1856.   *Gezangboek der Vereenigde Evangelische Broedergemeente.* Amsterdam, 1773, with Appendix, Genadendal, 1855.   GERDENER, G.B.A.: *Die Nuwe Halleluja, Psalms, Gesange en ander liedere vir Huis, Dag- en Sondagskool en Jongeliedeverenigings.* Die SA Bybelvereniging, Cape Town, 1931. GREYLING, P.F. AND OTHERS: *Die Halleluja, Psalms, Gesange en ander liedere vir Huis, Dag- en Sondagskool en Jeugverenigings.* Die Ned. Geref. Kerk-Uitgewers van Suid-Afrika, Cape Town, 1951.   *Halleluja! Eene Bloemlezing uit de Psalmen en Gezangen der Ned. Geref. Kerk van Zuid-Afrika ten dienste van School en Huisgezin.* J.C. Juta, Cape Town, 1883.   HARTWIG, E: *Sionsgesange vir gebruik in die Ned. Geref. Sendingkerk in SA.* Cape Town, 1948.   McGREGOR, A.: *Zionsliederen.* 7th edition, Amsterdam, Cape Town, 1896.   MURRAY, C.: *De Kinderharp.* 2nd edition, Cape Town, Port Elizabeth, Johannesburg, 1894.   MURRAY C: *Halleluja, Liederen voor Zondagscholen, Strevers- en Jongelings-Vereningen, Conferenties, en Bijzondere Diensten.* Z.A. Bijbel Vereeniging. Cape Town, 1903.   NEETHLING, MARIA: *Unto Children's Children.* Private circulation, printed by T.H. Hopkins and Son, London, 1909.

—G.G.C.

III. THE ORIGIN AND DEVELOPMENT OF THE CHOIR IN AFRIKAANS CHURCHES

The form of worship laid down by Calvin made no provision for independent choral singing, that is for songs sung by a choir on behalf of the congregation. He expected all members of the congregation to raise their voices in praise of God. In Geneva he did make use of a children's choir to lead the singing, especially in the rendering of psalms that were not well known to the congregation; but he went no further. In some churches of the Calvinist confession the use of the organ was at first forbidden; but since the early years the organ has steadily improved its position and has acquired the function of a valuable adjunct to the services of the Reformed Churches. —The choir, however, in these churches has right up to the present time no recognised status in the order of service; its position is still very insecure. How has it come about that in the Dutch Reformed Church of South Africa, in many respects steeped in the traditions of Calvinism, such an "un-Reformed" institution as a choir has become so general? — It should be remembered that the Dutch Reformed Church grew out of the Nederlandse Hervormde Kerk (NHK) of which, until early in the last century, it formed an integral part. Even at the present time the NHK does not use the choir as an independent entity in the service. Clearly the origin of the choir in the Dutch Reformed Church arises from special local circumstances, most notably English influence. Choirs appeared in Cape Town during the first half of the nineteenth century, on special occasions such as festival days (one of great importance being Reformation Day), or at inaugural ceremonies or the laying of foundation stones. These choirs were not church choirs, however, but secular choirs, for instance, that of the music society "Harmonie en Eendragt" ("Harmony and Unity"), or of the "Liefhebbery Zangkoor" ("Music Lovers' Choral Union) which was under the direction of Ludwig Beil* and F. Logier.* — The historian of the Groote Kerk in Cape Town, Rev. H.C. Hopkins, found positive evidence in tracing the origin of the choir of this church to the English services that were held there. He pointed out that in 1866 the Honorary Secretary of the DR Church Psalmody Class or Zang Koor Gezelschap (Choral Society) sought the permission of the church council to devote half of the weekly practice hour (normally taken up with rehearsing the hymns for the following Sunday) to the singing of anthems. According to Hopkins, choirs from 1868 became an indispensable part of the service on Reformation Day. On this day in 1872 there was a large attendance in the Groote Kerk, and a meagre one at the Nieuwe Kerk, "because people knew that there would be no choir in the latter". — The next move towards establishing a church choir in the Groote Kerk, for the services in Hollands, was made in 1887 when two gentlemen of the congregation, J.C. Hofmeyr and Daniël Haupt, offered the sum of R50 each as an annual donation to provide remuneration for a regular director of the choir, and for prizes awarded to its most loyal members. The choir was expected to perform at the two Sunday services in Hollands, and on the usual feast days. The underlying idea was that attendances at these services would be greatly improved, owing to "the charm of the music and a permanent choir". — In his book, *Die Kerk van Stellenbosch,* Dr A.M. Hugo comments on the activities of the choir before the year 1880. In 1847 the council of the Church of Stellenbosch appointed Pieter Hugo (1811-1861) as organist, upon two specified conditions: that he was to give (free of charge) practical instruction in church music, and that he should take immediate steps to form a choral society. At the dedication of the new organ in Stellenbosch in 1858, a children's choir made its appearance under the direction of Hugo; and in 1859, on the occasion of the festive opening of the Seminary a "fairly numerous choir" sang (among other items) a *Sanctus* by Mozart in the church, again under his direction. Attie Hofmeyr, a son of

Professor N.J. Hofmeyr, was organist at Stellenbosch from the year 1877, and he continued the choral tradition started by Hugo. The previous year (1876) he had presented a concert of sacred songs with a choir of 120 boys and girls and in 1877 he founded the Gewijde Zangvereniging (Sacred Harmonic Society) of Stellenbosch. — With Denholm Walker* in Cape Town and F.W. Jannasch in Stellenbosch, an important stage was reached in the development of Afrikaans church choirs. The former, with an English background, took up his appointment in the Groote Kerk; Jannasch had been brought up in the German tradition. During Denholm Walker's term of office as organist (1898-1914) the choir made great strides. According to Frits Stegmann,* Walker succeeded in attracting, as members of his church choir, practically all the important male and female singers of Cape Town. Through performances in and outside the church, and early gramophone records of sacred songs, the choir became widely known. The choral numbers Walker selected for church services were mainly English anthems, the words of which had been translated into Dutch, a practice continued for many years after his retirement. — More thoughtful, and of greater influence than the choral work of Walker with his English background were the ideals that the German F.W. Jannasch set out to realize in the Mother Church at Stellenbosh. Until his death at the age of 78, in 1930, after more than 40 years as organist and choirmaster at Stellenbosch, he contributed much to the improvement of Afrikaans church music. He was a pioneer of a new church tradition of worthy church music. According to manuscripts that have been preserved, Jannasch regarded the church choir as an important instrument which could support the organ in leading the singing of the congregation. He believed that in the service there is room for independent singing by the choir; as he wrote, this is a noble art "dedicated to the service of the Lord". But he did emphasise that choir-singing should not be practised as art for art's sake. The words sung must grip the attention, music and beautiful rendering serving only to underline their meaning. To prevent the choir's singing becoming an item in the liturgy, the need for close co-operation between the pulpit in the body of the church, and the choir in the gallery was emphasized; thus the singing of the choir would be in keeping with the spiritual message of the occasion. — Jannasch applied these principles for many years, and was able in Stellenbosch every year to mould hundreds of students who came from all parts of the country, and among them most of the future ministers of the Dutch Reformed Church. This achievement justifies the reputation of Jannasch as the most significant single influence in the establishment and promotion of choirs in the Dutch Reformed Church. — But the introduction of choral singing was not achieved without some opposition. J.C. Pauw writes in the Memorial Volume of the Paarl congregation that while Rocco de Villiers, his son and son-in-law, successively held the post of organist, choirs appeared only on special occasions in the historic Strooidakkerk ("Thatched-roof Church"). When A.C. van Velden was appointed organist in 1913, he asked whether he might establish a permanent church choir. The church council granted permission only on condition that he introduced choral items "tactfully" into the evening services. Some of the older church members walked out while the choir was singing. The same happened in the Mother Church at Stellenbosch before 1920, when individual members showed their displeasure at the singing of a choir (directed by Professor Jannasch), by getting up and walking out. Such demonstrative protests against choral singing may be partly attributed to the lack of provision for it in the order of service; and this is still the case. For many this was a strange new departure in church, and possibly they felt that choral singing as a part of divine service might easily lead to undesirable practices. — Higher authorities of the Dutch Reformed Church in South Africa have not yet come to a decision on the function of church choirs; nor have they found a suitable niche for choral singing in the service. In 1966 the General Synod of the Dutch Reformed Church had before it a report of the Committee for Church Music and Liturgy. This requested the Synod to endorse the view that the choir is an integral part of the service, but that "its function should be subservient to the promotion of congregational singing". In the opinion of the committee the choir should not be "an independent entity"; therefore the suggestion was made that the choir should sing during the offertory; or antiphonally with the congregation, or during the preparation of the Communion Table. The report, with its recommendations, was merely noted by the Synod. — Today (1976), in nearly every congregation of the Dutch Reformed Church, there is a more or less permanent choir; and in the majority of congregations the organist is also the choirmaster. Most church councils stipulate as one condition of the appointment of a new organist, that he should be responsible for training the choir. By implication, church councils thus allow choral singing during divine worship; indeed, most demand that there shall be choral singing. In the past, if the choir sang only one independent piece during the service it was customary for the item to be placed either after the reading from the Scriptures and before the congregational prayer from the pulpit, or just before, during or after the offertory. The first requires that the choir shall deliver a song of praise or a prayer of supplication, as the item comes near the beginning of the service. When the choir sings during the offertory, towards the end of the service, it is expected that the choice should be in keeping with the spirit of thanksgiving or dedication. — Church choirs usually have a dozen to fifty members, mainly adult members of the congregation. In many choirs there is a shortage of male voices, the singing being dominated by a disproportionate number of sopranos. In the larger congregations, especially if the choirmaster is an enthusiast, the choir sings every Sunday; but in smaller congregations, the choir does not "perform" with the same regularity. There is little evidence that the ideals of Jannasch have been taken to heart, for the ability of the choir to lead congregational singing is not often regarded as its main function. — Deficient knowledge of the art of singing, and the lack of good Afrikaans choral pieces, hamper the choral work in many congregations. Too often choirmasters take refuge in easy four-part songs from the *Halleluja,* or similar collections. Too rarely does one hear choral pieces of Bach, Handel, and other celebrated composers of the past; they are not often available in the choir books with Afrikaans texts. With few exceptions indigenous composers have not, up to the present, produced works of significance. Choral singing is consequently poor in singleness of purpose and musical quality. South Africa has the singers, but lacks skilful choirmasters and suitable choral music.

List of the most important choral collections, with Dutch and Afrikaans texts, in use by choirs of the Dutch Reformed Churches during the past 30 years.

DUTCH

1. *Koorzangen: Een versameling van doelmatige en gemakkelike Koorzangen voor gebruik in de kerk en C.J. Verenigingen in Tonic Solfa en Stafnotatie* bewerkt door W. Fouché, deel I. Bayley & Ferguson, London. 2. *Koorzangen uit het Engelsch* toegepast en verzameld door H.A. Marais, deel II (geheel nieuwe uitgawe). J.C. Juta,

Cape Town, 1902. 3. *Koorboek* zamengesteld door F.W. Jannasch. R. Müller, Cape Town, n.d. 4. *Koorzangen en enige Psalmen en Gezangen* zamengesteld door F.W. Jannasch. Nasionale Pers Ltd, Cape Town, n.d. 5. *Koorboek,* verzameling van vierstemmige liederen, verzameld, bewerkt of getoonzet door W. van Oosten. R. Müller, Cape Town, 1933.

AFRIKAANS

6. R. Müller's Kerk-koorboek, 'n reeks van uitgesoekte koorstukke vir alle geleenthede van die jaar, deel I. R. Müller (Pty) Ltd, Cape Town, n.d. 7. R. Müller's Jubilate, Tweede Kerk-koorboek bevattende 'n reeks van uitgesoekte koorstukke vir alle geleenthede van die jaar, deel 2. R. Müller (Pty) Ltd, Cape Town, n.d. 8. Afrikaanse Kerkkoor, dertig uitgesoekte kerk-, fees- en geleentheidsliedere. HAUM, Cape Town; J.H. de Bussy, Pretoria, 1929. 9. Afrikaanse Kerkkoor, twintig uitgesoekte kerk-, fees- en geleentheidsliedere, derde vermeerderde uitgawe byeengebring deur ds. D. Rossouw, eerste bundel. HAUM, Cape Town; J.H. de Bussy, Pretoria, 1942. 10. Afrikaanse Kerkkoor, twintig uitgesoekte kerk-, fees- en geleentheidsliedere, derde vermeerderde uitgawe byeengebring deur ds. D. Rossouw, tweede bundel. HAUM; J.H. de Bussy, Pretoria, 1944. 11. Lofgesang, Kerk-koorboek deur S. le Roux Marais.* Boosey and Hawkes, Cape Town, 1957. 12. FAK-Kerkkoorboek I. Federasie van Afrikaanse Kultuurvereniginge, Johannesburg, 1956. 13. Hosanna, Kerk-koorboek. Boosey and Hawkes, Cape Town, n.d. 14. Koorboek vir ons Afrikaanse Kerke saamgestel deur dr. G. Cillié en ander, deel een. NG Kerk-uitgewers, Cape Town, Pretoria, 1962. 15. Koorboek vir ons Afrikaanse Kerke, deel twee, saamgestel deur dr. G. Cillié. NG Kerk-uitgewers, Cape Town, Pretoria, 1964. 16. Die Nuwe Lied, koorsange deur W.E.H. Söhnge, 1965.

Many church choirs make use of four-part songs from the following collections: 17. Die Halleluja. NG Kerk-uitgewers, Cape Town, Pretoria (various editions). 18. Evangelie-liedere. Christelike Uitgewers-Maatskappy, Johannesburg, n.d. 19. Nuwe FAK-Sangbundel. Nasionale Boekhandel Ltd, Cape Town, Bloemfontein, Johannesburg, 1961. 20. Met Hart en Mond, 'n vierstemmige verwerking vir koorgebruik van al 150 psalms volgens die beryming van Totius, deur Rosa Nepgen.* NG Kerk-uitgewers, Cape Town, Pretoria, 1966.

BIBLIOGRAPHY

BOUWS, JAN: *Die musieklewe van Kaapstad, 1800-1850.* Cape Town, 1966. HOPKINS, H.C.: *Die moeder van ons almal.* Cape Town, 1965. HUGO, A.M. and VAN DER BIJL, J.: *Die kerk van Stellenbosch.* Cape Town, 1963. VAN DER LEEUW, G.: *Beknopte geschiedenis van het kerklied.* Groningen, 1948. *Kwartmillennium Gedenkboek van die NG Gemeente, Paarl (1691-1941).* Paarlse Drukpers Mpy, 1941.

SOURCES

CILLIÉ, G.G.: Kerkorrel waarvan dele onder die see was. *Die Burger,* Cape Town, 1946. JANNASCH, F.W.: *Het kerkelike koorgezang* (in manuscript). *Proceedings, Second General Synod of the DR Church.* Bloemfontein, 1966. STEGMANN, FRITS: Articles on Die Groote Kerkkoor in *Die Burger* (Cape Town) and *Eikestadnuus* (Stellenbosch) during 1965 and 1966.

—G.G.C.

IV. SONG-BOOKS OF THE AFRIKAANS MISSION CHURCHES

1. Sionsgesange (Hymns of Zion)
2. Dumisani
3. Incwadi Yamaculo
4. Incwadi Yemiculo
5. Kopelo
6. Nyimbo za Mulungu
7. Nziyo dze Kereke
8. Hymnal of the DR Church in Africa.

1. Sionsgesange

The Dutch Reformed Mission Church of South Africa was founded on 5 October 1881, in Wellington. With 192 congregations scattered throughout the Republic, it was by 1966 serving 112 000 church members and 342 000 people, that is 23 percent of the total coloured population. Today it has its own statute book, catechism book and periodical, *Die Ligdraer,* with 21 000 subscribers (1967). It has a synod hall, church office, school for the deaf, school for epileptics, three schools for committed persons and orphans, two training colleges for teachers and, with the aid of the Mother Church, an institution for the training of social workers and a Theological College where students can be trained as future ministers of the church. — In its early days, the Mission Church used the hymn-book and sacred song-book of the Mother Church. In time many coloured people from other denominations joined the Mission Church and, naturally, they were much attached to the hymn- and sacred song-books they had used before. Thus when the Rhenish Missionary Society was taken over, some 25 000 new members joined the DR Mission Church; consequently there were, at one time, as many as six different hymn-books in use. This lack of uniformity resulted in a certain amount of confusion. — As early as 1908 the Synod of the DR Mission Church had discussed the need for having its own hymn-book; but it was not until 1942 that the Synod, acting on representations made by the Presbytery of Kimberley, appointed a permanent hymn-book committee to consider the matter. The committee consisted of the Rev. W.F. Loots, representing De Doorns at the time, the Rev. (now Professor) E.H. Holzapfel, then still in Ceres; and Mr Jack Viljoen, school principal and elder of the church in Caledon. — There were several matters for this committee to consider: the problem of catering for a diversity of needs and abilities in a community comprising educated and working classes; the need for the book to serve as a combined song book, hymn book and choral book; respect for the rooted traditions of song books which usage had hallowed for different sections of the community. — The hymn-book committee soon found that the Rev. E. Hartwig, a missionary of the Rhenish Church in Carnarvon, had been working on a similar enterprise for the past twenty years. The committee thoroughly examined the volume he had prepared, and presented to the synod of 1946 a report which, with certain provisions and instructions, was accepted. The book was to be purchased, pending an investigation by a team of experts as to its suitability. The committee was therefore enlarged by the appointment of new members: the Rev. W.R.J. Burger, successor to the Rev. E. Hartwig at Carnarvon, and the Rev. M.C. Dippenaar, at that time minister of Sandveld. Doctrinal and linguistic assessment was undertaken by Professor Dr Jac. J. Muller of Stellenbosch, and C.H. Weich* ("EMOL") and the composer Stefans Grové* were responsible for the musical aspects. — When the 1946 synod was in session, a

31

temporary committee prepared a report on the completed manuscript, which included the following: "Your committee cannot refrain from commenting on the high standard of this manuscript, a veritable work of art, a credit to our church". The members of the committee recommended "that a letter be sent to Pastor E. Hartwig expressing the warmest thanks and appreciation of the Dutch Reformed Mission Church for this great work of a lifetime, the fruits of his God-given talents, the product of his devoted labours and dedication". — On completion of the editorial work, the first edition of 29 000 copies (words only) was issued by the SABV, later to be merged with the publishing house known as the NG Kerk-uitgewers. The official adoption of the hymn-book of the Dutch Reformed Mission Church of South Africa, the *Sionsgesange* (Hymns of Zion) was arranged throughout the country for Sunday 10 April 1949. The highlight of the occasion was a radio service held in the Sionskerk in Paarl. Many congregations arranged festival programmes to be presented in their churches on Sunday, 17 April, of the same year. — The publication of the *Sionsgesange* with musical notation, printed by Messrs Marshall, Morgan and Scott in London, entailed a great deal of work and raised many problems, mainly owing to war-time conditions. It was not until 20 December 1951, that the first consignment of this edition arrived in Table Bay. Because the Mission Church had as yet no bookshop, the Rev. E. Holzapfel was obliged to undertake the distribution of the new hymn-book himself. This he did with the assistance of Mr T.F. Holzapfel (at that time a teacher at Riversdale), and the writer of this article. The arrangement continued until a permanent bookshop was opened in the building near the Synod Hall in Worcester. Since the first appearance of *Sionsgesange* in 1949 it has become very popular: about 10 000 copies are sold every year. — The "Sionsgesange" were all adapted from the originals to Afrikaans by the compiler himself. The book naturally has much in common with the Afrikaanse Psalm- en Gesangboek, but as is to be expected, there are considerable disparities in the versification. Consequently, at the time of its publication, the committee tried to obtain the Mother Church's permission to use its versions of the psalms and hymns. This might have proved particularly useful e.g. on occasions when there were combined services. Unfortunately, the Mother Church did not agree; but the versification of the mission psalms and hymns is in no way inferior to what is found in the official book used by the Mother Church. — For example, the wording of Psalm 100 in the book used by the Mother Church is as follows:

"Juig al wat leef, juig voor die Heer!
Dien God met blydskap, gee Hom eer;
kom nader voor sy aangesig,
en prys Hom met 'n lofgedig".

The wording of Hymn 112 (Psalm 100) in *Sionsgesange* runs thus:

"Juig aarde! Juig voor God die Heer;
dien Hom met blydskap, gee Hom eer;
kom met 'n vrolik lofgedig
en jubel voor Sy aangesig".

—W.F.L.

2.. Dumisani (Zulu — You must Praise)

Zulu-speaking people strongly felt the need for a hymn-book in their own language. The Advisory Council of Mission Churches and the Joint Committee of Church Offices (bodies of representatives of the Dutch Reformed Mission Churches in the OFS, Transvaal, Natal and Cape) were prevailed upon to issue a hymn-book provisionally, pending the publication of a complete common hymnal. Acting promptly, the Natal Mission Church instructed the Rev. (now Dr) A.M. Dekker and Mr J. Xulu to select and translate 100 to 150 sacred songs. — On 19 November 1957, the Joint Committee of Church Offices arranged for the printing of 2 000 copies of this volume, with a four-part setting in tonic-solfa; and another 5 000 copies were to contain the words only. To meet the great demand, it was decided at a subsequent meeting to print another 10 000 of the latter; reprints appeared in 1959, 1962 and 1964. Today the book consists of 137 songs, compiled from *Incwadi Yemiculo* by the Rev. L.H.M. Jandrell, from *Incwadi Yamaculo* of the Dutch Reformed Bantu Church, and from psalms and hymns and other collections used in Protestant churches. Also included are a number of Bantu-tunes and songs of which the words were written by the Bantu themselves. Three of the melodies were composed by the late Rev. E.B. Cadle, four by the Rev. D.P. Myburgh,* three are Bantu tunes, and one is by the evangelist Z.B. Nkosi.

3. Incwadi Yamaculo (Xhosa song-book)

This book, compiled and translated by the Rev. J.C. Oosthuysen sen., of Stellenbosch, was issued by the Dutch Reformed Bantu Church in the Cape Province. First published in 1940, it was intended as a temporary expedient to meet an urgent need for a separate hymn-book, translated into Xhosa for the Dutch Reformed Church. It was to be used pending the publication of a common, joint volume of songs. Since the original issue a number of amendments have been made and to each of the eight editions new songs have been added. In 1959 an edition with tonic-solfa notation was made available and there was a separate volume containing the words only. There are at present 131 songs in this book, with translations from psalms and hymns, from the *Halleluja* and from other collections used in Protestant churches. The book also contains a number of Bantu tunes.

4. Incwadi Yemiculo (Zulu song-book)

At a Synodal Committee meeting of the Dutch Reformed Mission Church of the Transvaal, the Rev. J.H.M. Stofberg, mission secretary, expressed the view that separate hymn-books should be published in the various Bantu languages. The Rev. L.H.M. Jandrell of Standerton immediately embarked on the task of compiling in Zulu a book consisting of 115 unison songs. In June 1948 the volume appeared in print with tonic-solfa notation. — The Rev. Jandrell called it a "specimen copy", and stated in the preface that he had not used any translations of hymns from other collections, but had tried to reformulate poetically the thoughts of the better-known psalms, hymns and sacred songs. The book was published on the authority of the Synodal Committee mentioned. Unfortunately, it had only limited appeal, and was never re-printed. In its place there appeared the Zulu collection *Dumisani*. Though the Rev. Jandrell's book is not classified under specific headings, it does cover the Holy Trinity, the Christian Life and Occasional Hymns.

5. Kopelo (Tswana song-book)

This volume was compiled and issued by the Dutch Reformed Mission Church. As far as can be ascertained, all the hymns are translations from other song-books. — The first songs appeared in the period when the Rev. E. Beyer (1886-1895) of the Berlin Mission was active at the Mission Station of Mochudi. A revised edition was brought out between 1898 and 1907, when the Rev. P. Stofberg was the incumbent. The five editions that followed were edited by the Rev. A.M. Scheffler and the Rev. J.L. Reyneke. They contain unison songs, with tonic-solfa notation. — In 1907 there appeared another complete volume of songs about which no details are available, except that it consisted of 361 songs, with tonic-solfa notation for four vocal parts. On the title page is the following:

Lifela Tsa Sione
  (Songs of Zion)
  tsa (=of)
Tirelo ea Molimo
  (In the service of God)
  mo (=in)
Kereken Le Sekolen
  (the churches and schools)
Text: Ephesians 5:19 is quoted.
Printed by the Religious Tract Society for the Dutch
Reformed Church Missionary Society,
Cape Colony, South Africa, 1907.
There is no preface or further explanation.

6. Nyimbo za Mulungu (Songs of God — Zolembedwa M'Cinyanja)

A committee called the Consultative Board of Federated Missions of Nyasaland compiled this volume from song-books used by missionary churches and churches of various denominations; the sources were mainly the *Church Hymnary* and *Sacred songs and solos.* Formerly, some of the missions, for example the DRC, used their own books, which provided material for the volume used by the Federated Missions of Nyasaland, known today as The Fellowship of Christian Churches. With few exceptions, the songs are therefore translated. The DR Mission Church in Northern Rhodesia, now referred to as the Bantu Reformed Church of DR affiliation in Zambia, also uses this book. — In 1934 the Consultative Board appointed a committee to revise the book and to supplement the indigenous songs. In the preface to a revised edition of 1954 it is acknowledged that this objective has not yet been attained, although a number of songs were taken from the Tumbuka book, *Suma za Ukristo* (Tumbuka is the language spoken in the northern province). The songs in the latter book are arrangements of old Zulu war-songs, and they are among the most beautiful of the indigenous sacred songs in Africa. However, for speakers of Nyanja, on whom the impact of the Zulu language is not so evident, these songs are as "foreign" as European songs. When the book was revised in 1964 the committee made another attempt to incorporate more indigenous songs, especially from the rich treasure of local songs which church choirs and choral societies have distributed aurally throughout the country. — Versification is not at all popular among these people, or any other of the Bantu races. There are no songs taken from the psalms and hymns, except those also to be found in English collections, for example Hymns 7 and 27, Psalms 23, 100 and 134. — The first volume of *Nyimbo za Mulungu* appeared in 1916. It was revised and enlarged in 1954 and again in 1964.

7. Nziyo dze Kereke (Shona songs of the Church):

This was compiled by the DR Mission Church in Mashonaland, or, as it is now called, the Bantu Reformed Church in Southern Rhodesia (NGK). All the songs are translations and, as far as can be ascertained, this book contains no songs whose words or music were written or composed by Bantu members of the church. — When the wife of the Rev. A.A. Louw visited Mashonaland in 1894, and had learnt the Shona language sufficiently well, she began the translations of certain well-known songs, for example: *Gaan my nie verby, o Heiland; Wat 'n Vriend het ons in Jesus;* also some of the psalms and hymns, such as *Op berge en in dale.* The first volume of 198 songs was printed and published about the year 1910. Later the wives of the Rev. H.W. Murray and the Rev. (now Dr) Johan Reyneke of Pretoria revised the book and added a few more translations. The book has been through several editions, and each time new songs have been added. Today this volume of songs is the most widely used among this language group.

8. Hymnal of the DR Church in Africa

There is still no final decision on a title for this volume. — A committee appointed by the General Synod of the DRC in Africa (formerly: DR Mission Churches – Bantu) was responsible for the compilation of this book. Through the years these churches made use of hymn-books commonly used by other Protestant churches. Some of the collections described in the foregoing account have been used in the meantime, a state of affairs that does encourage a common hymn-book. — At a meeting held on 24 April 1947, the Synod of the DR Mission Church accepted the suggestion of the Rev. (now Dr) B.J. Odendaal that a separate hymn-book for mission churches of the OFS, Transvaal, Natal and the Cape should be compiled for the Bantu people in the five main Bantu languages: South and North Sotho, Zulu, Xhosa and Tswana. It had to be uniform for all the language groups, so that numbers, tunes and contents could be consistent. This matter was referred to the Advisory Council of the DR Mission Churches, representing all mission churches. — On 17 August 1953, the Joint Committee of Church Offices, another body representing the Bantu Churches in the four provinces, and responsible for the administrative work of the four churches, heard that the Rev. L.H.M. Jandrell of Standerton had compiled such a volume in Afrikaans and Zulu. The question was again referred to the Advisory Council of Mission Churches. The committee which was appointed to investigate and report on the book consisted of the Rev. (now Dr) M.L. Maile, Dr H. Gonin, the Rev. J.C. Oosthuysen sen. and the Rev. W.E.H. Söhnge, with power to co-opt (among others) Dr B.J. Odendaal. Much preliminary work was done especially regarding selection. At the OFS Missionary Synod in October 1959, a report was tabled to the effect that 300 songs had been chosen and were ready for translation. At the same Synod a further committee was entrusted with the translation of these songs into Southern Sotho. — When the four mission churches were united at the General Synod of May 1963, it was announced that considerable progress had been made with the drafting of the new hymn-book. The Southern Sotho translation was completed, and in use by the year 1966. Meanwhile rapid strides had been made with translations into the remaining four Bantu languages. The Rev. H.C.S. v.d. Merwe and his wife, of Welkom, were responsible for editing the tunes, many of Bantu origin, that had never before been recorded in notation. Many of the songs were written and composed by the Bantu themselves, while the remainder were translations of existing Protestant songs. Some were taken from the *Halleluja,* others from the psalms and hymns. In all there are 450 songs in this volume.

—B.J.O.

AFRIKAANS FOLK MUSIC J. Bouws, H. du Plessis, J. Fourie, E. Hullebroeck, National Council for Folk Singing and Folk Dancing, H. Pellissier, W. Spiethoff, J. van Niekerk

AFRIKAANS-HOLLANDSE LIEDERBUNDEL N. Mansvelt, Joan van Niekerk

AFRIKAANS LIGHT MUSIC AND BOEREMUSIEK O. Andrésen, C. Blignaut, R. da Costa, I.M. de Villiers, Discography, P.J. du Plessis, L. Fillis, F. Fischer, J.E. Fourie, G. Gibson, H. Gouws, Dan Hill, I. Hoogenhout, T. Kikillus, F.J. Muller, J.L. Pohl, Polliack, B. Raubenheimer, D. Ravenscroft, Stellenbosch Boereorkes, Tierberg Mannekwartet, J. van Loggerenberg.

AFRIKAANS MUSIC CLUB OF PRETORIA, THE This club was founded on 24 June 1941 at a meeting in the home of the South African singer Nunez Holtzhausen.* The following executive members were elected: the Rev. (later Prof.) P.F.D. Weiss (Chairman), Mrs H. Weiss, Miss N. Holtzhausen, Mrs Tina Stoffberg and Mr M. Meij (Secretary). The aim of the Music Club was to promote music in general and South African talents in particular, especially youthful talent and choral singing. Since 1952 the Club has annually presented a bursary to a promising music student. The following have been awarded bursaries: Liselotte Menge, Merena Combrinck, Ilse von Staden, Blanche Terblanche, Philip Markgraaff,* Margaret van der Post,* Louise Wessels, Susan Steenkamp and Paulette Germond. —The Music Club Choir – the Sangluskoor – until the sixties performed annually at one of the four club concerts. Highlights have been performances in the City Hall of *Die Skepping* (Haydn), *Messias* (Handel) and *Requiem* (Verdi), with Prof. David Roode* conducting. Others who have given invaluable service to the choir are Mr Stephen Eyssen,* Miss Helena Strauss,* Mrs Dr Pienaar, Mrs Hannatjie Dönges, Mrs Helena Erasmus, Prof. Gerrit Bon,* Messrs Bothma, Brandt, Le Roux, Malan, Mathlener* and Mr Ras. The Music Club has also promoted music in country towns and has given concerts in the following places: Ermelo, Brandfort, Groblersdal, Nelspruit,* Nylstroom, Sabie, Utrecht, Volksrust and Witbank. Although the Club is still in existence (1970), it has been more or less inactive since the creation of the Performing Arts Council of the Transvaal (PACT) in 1962.

—J.P.M.

AFRIKAANS MUSIC TERMINOLOGY FAK and Afrikaans Music, J.P. Malan, M.C. Roode

AFRIKAANS OPERETTAS O. Andrésen, S. Blakemore, L.B. de Kock, L. Faul, J. Pierre Malan, R. Pienaar, J.L. Pohl, A. Rudolph, M. Wessels

AFRIKAANS SONGS Afrikaans Church and Mission Music Song-books, O. Andrésen, D. Balfoort, P. Benoit, J. Bouws, Brandts-Buys family, Cape Malay Music, Centenary Treksongs, G.G. Cillíe, A.F. Clauset, D. Clement, C.G. de Jonge, L.B. de Kock, Betsy de la Porte, Dr C.G.S. de Villiers, M.L. de Villiers, P.K. de Villiers, Discography, C. Dopper, H. du Plessis, S.H. Eyssen, FAK Volksangbundel, J.E. Fourie, Dr H. Gutsche, Hollandsch Mannenkoor Pretoria, E. Hullebroeck, L. Knobel, G. Korsten, A. Lambrechts-Vos, P.J. Lemmer, S. le Roux Marais, O.A. Lewald, E. Lowenherz, Dr N. Mansvelt, H.T. Matthews, R. Mengelberg, A. Meulemans, E.W. Mulder, F.J. Muller, the Rev. D. Myburg, C. Nel, R. Nepgen, Flor Peeters, R.E. Pienaar, J.L. Pohl, S. Richfield, J. Röntgen, D.J. Roode, M.C. Roode, A. Rudolph, W. Spiethoff, A. Spoel, F.R. Statham, W. Swanson, J.H. ten Brink, A.W. Tideman-Wijers, J.F. Tierie, L. Toebosch, P. van Antwerpen, H. van der Mark, W.J. van Gorkom, J. van Niekerk, H.J.

van Oort, C.F. van Rees, A. van Wyk, C.A. van Wyk, L. Veremans, W. Versveld, H. Visscher, C. Wessels, J.P. Wierts, W. Wijdeveld, A. Zulman

AFRIKAANSE STUDENTEBOND (ASB)   FAK Volksangbundel

AFRIKAANSE TAAL EN KULTUURVERENIGING (ATKV)   Beaufort West, Centenary Treksongs

AHLERS, HENK   Higher Educational Institutions II/1

ALBANY INSTITUTE   Grahamstown 3

ALBERTYN, E.W.   Heidelberg 1, S.A. Army Band

ALBU, MARGARET,   *13 March 1907 in Johannesburg, daughter of Cecilia and Henry Albu; married in London the late John Logie Baird, the inventor of television, in 1931; living in Newlands, Cape Town. Pianist and music teacher.

Margaret Albu studied pianoforte as a child in Johannesburg under Annie Lynn and then under Sydney Rosenbloom* at Maud Harrison's Conservatoire of Music. By 1923 she had obtained the LTCL diploma and had been awarded the Trinity College Exhibition, several gold and silver medals and the University Exhibition. This was followed by the overseas scholarship of UNISA in 1924. The following year she entered the RCM, obtained the LRAM and ARCM degrees within eighteen months and returned to Johannesburg where she gave piano recitals and joint recitals with the cellist, Herman Becker* (1926). Together with Becker and Otto Menge* (violinist) she formed the Johannesburg Trio which gave concerts at the Grand National Hotel (July 1927). She was often soloist at John Connell's* Sunday evening organ recitals at the City Hall and played movements from piano concertos in Joubert Park with the festival orchestra conducted by Connell (e.g. 28 August 1927). — From 1928 until 1958 she lived in England where she played with various orchestras and gave public and radio recitals before 1939. Since her return to this country in 1958 Margaret Baird has given broadcast performances and recitals in the main centres, as well as undertaking concert tours in the Cape Province, Orange Free State and Natal. In 1965 she revisited England, gave a recital in the Wigmore Hall, and the following year performed in The Hague and Brussels. As Margaret Baird she wrote a book entitled *Television Baird, the story of the man who invented television* (HAUM, Cape Town, 1973).

—L.W.

ALHAMBRA HALL (PRESIDENT THEATRE, EMPRESS THEATRE)   Pretoria 1

ALHAMBRA THEATRE, CAPE TOWN   EOAN Group, Johannesburg 3(iii), Theatres and Concert Halls 2(iii), Tierberg Mannekwartet

ALHAMBRA THEATRE, DURBAN   Durban 10, Durban Amateur Operatic Society

ALI-BEN-SOU-ALLE   Touring Theatre Groups 3

ALISTER, KATHLEEN CAMERON,   *in Cape Town; at present in Johannesburg. Harpist. After preliminary study on the Celtic harp in Johannesburg under Francis Foster,* Kathleen Alister graduated to the the pedal harp and at the age of six years made her first public appearance as soloist at an organ recital by John Connell* in the City Hall. This was followed during the same year by further appearances at a concert of Isobel McLaren* in the City Hall and at a monthly meeting in the Jewish Guild Hall. Since then she has given over 200 broadcast-recitals, played under the batons of Beecham,

37

Sargent, Stravinsky, Horenstein, Galliera, Pierre Boulez, and has toured extensively as a recitalist. Prominent among the works she has performed with the orchestras of the SABC and the City of Durban are the *Doppio Concerto* for harp and oboe by H.W. Henze and Pizetti's *Concerto* for harp. She toured in Israel in 1961 and returned there in 1962, at the invitation of the Israeli Department of Special Events, to act as Judge of Honour at the Second International Harp Contest. She also attended the world conference of the International Association of Harpists and Friends of the Harp held in Israel at the same time, and has since then formed the Harp Society of South Africa,* which is affiliated to the International Association. In 1963 she was made an honorary member of the American Harp Society and a life member of the Scottish Clarsach Society. The Kathleen Alister Ensemble* has done much to propagate the harp and its literature. A trio has been specially composed for this Ensemble by the prize-winning composer Ami Ma'Ayani of New York and Tel Aviv. In 1973 the trio changed its name to Nederburg Trio but the members are still Alister, Lucien Grujon (flute) and Walter Mony (violin and viola). Between 1973 and 1976 the trio has toured in Europe, Great Britain, Rhodesia and South West Africa. Some of their programmes have been broadcast in both England and South Africa. A portrait of Kathleen Alister playing the harp was painted by the miniature painter K.B. Estcourt, RMS.

—Ed.

ALLEN, A.V.   Cooper, Gill & Tomkins

ALLEN, DENISE,   *in London; now in Johannesburg. Coloratura soprano.

Daughter of a professional pianist and singer and grand-daughter of an Australian singer, Denise Allen came to South Africa in 1940, returned to England in 1946 for further study at the RAM and has since appeared in coloratura parts of operettas and operas produced by the Johannesburg Operatic and Dramatic Society* and OPSA.* In collaboration with Richard Cherry,* who arranged the pianoforte accompaniments, she has also written scripts and composed. Since 1970 Denise Allen has often taken part in cabaret shows for which she sings mainly continental songs in eight languages; for radio and television she has also prepared programmes of folk songs. Since 1949 she has composed about 28 lyrics, both words and music, often in English and Afrikaans.

OTHER WORKS

In praise of South Africa, for chorus. Ms., 1949.   City of gold, a march. Ms., 1950.   Swiss interlude, an operetta. Ms., 1961.

—Ed.

ALLEN, REGINALD GEORGE,   ° 18 April 1918, in Johannesburg. Conductor and violinist.

Recognised as a fine violinist, Allen performed as soloist and as a member of a chamber group with Beatrice Stuart (Marx),* Mrs J. Vincent and Signor P. Grimaldi, at several of the meetings of the Johannesburg Musical Society.* A conductor of talent, he helped to develop the public's appreciation of good orchestral music at the beginning of the 20th century. He was largely responsible for the establishment of a symphony orchestra of professional instrumentalists, and was appointed conductor of the Johannesburg Symphony Orchestra, which gave its first concert at the Masonic Hall on 5 September 1909. A tremendous step forward was the decision of the Town Council to subsidise the orchestra for a series of three concerts. After this Allen joined forces with the Johannesburg Philharmonic Society* and conducted several successful choral-orchestral concerts during 1910. There is no further record of his Orchestra, which is remembered as another unsuccessful experiment in Johannesburg's orchestral history. Allen also played frequently at the Anglo-Austrian Cafe, where many of Johannesburg's artists gave recitals.

—L.W.

ALPER, ROSE (MRS H.L. MAGID), *In Wynberg, C.P.; at present in Durban. Soprano.

In 1922, a few days after her arrival in London from South Africa, Rose Alper, still in her early teens, won the Campbell-Clarke Scholarship which entitled her to three years' tuition at the RAM. She was regarded as an outstanding student and the scholarship was extended for an extra year. She made her first operatic appearance in London as Pamina in *The magic flute*, and was professionally engaged by the producer-manager, Sir Nigel Playfair, to understudy and perform Clarissa in *Lionel and Clarissa* (Dibden), an eighteenth century opera which was revived at the Lyric Theatre, Hammersmith in October 1925. It had a run of 171 evenings. — The tour of the Royal Carl Rosa Opera Company in South Africa (1937) marked the commencement of her association with this British institution. The director of the company H.B. Phillips, invited her to sing as a principal in the company; until the outbreak of the Second World War she was prominent in their productions in Great Britain, as leading lyric soprano. She sang the part of Oscar in a new production of *The masked ball* (Verdi), which was broadcast on transmissions of the BBC and enjoyed the honour of singing *Mary* in the first broadcast of *Hugh the drover* (Vaughan Williams), under supervision of the composer. In addition, she recorded for two companies, and appeared in concert halls and theatres in England, Scotland and Wales, invariably billed as "The South African Soprano". — In 1939, she returned to South Africa and played a prominent part in the opera seasons directed by John Connell* in South African centres. She had a repertoire of more than 30 operas, but was also an oratorio (e.g. *Messiah* in Johannesburg, 1930) and concert artist, one of the first invited by the SABC to undertake a national broadcast tour. In South Africa she was the first to sing *Four last songs* (Richard Strauss) and the *Ode to a nightingale* (Hamilton Harty). For her contribution to music in Britain and South Africa she was elected an Associate of the RAM. In Durban, she was nominated the Woman of the Year for "fostering the arts, particularly in the field of music" in 1965.

—F.S.

ALTER, LOUIS, *In Kovno, Lithuania; at present in Johannesburg. Mandoline soloist and conductor of mandoline, balalaika and Yugoslav tamburitza ensembles.

Alter studied violin, piano and theatrical subjects at the State Conservatoire of Music in Kovno, whilst teaching mandoline, balalaika, domra and other Russian national instruments, as a hobby. He emigrated to South Africa in 1927 and established a reputation as mandoline soloist on the radio and in theatres, also appearing as soloist with symphony orchestras conducted by Wm. Pickerill,* John Connell* and Jeremy Schulman.* His balalaika orchestra was formed in 1930 and since then he has also become conductor of a Yugoslav tamburitza orchestra. During the War he served in the Entertainments Unit, but has latterly gone into business.

—Ed.

ALTMANN, H.   Pretoria 2, H. Newboult

AMACITIA (SINGING SOCIETY) Pretoria 1

AMM, ROSS Johannesburg 3(iii)

AMORISON, E. D.J. Balfoort, Hollandsch Mannenkoor, Onze Taal, Rederijkerskamer, Pretoria 1, 2

ANDALUSIA INTERNMENT CAMP W. Frewer, Windhoek 2

ANDERSON, IAN BRUCE, *4 September 1905 in Southport, Lancashire, England; in Johannesburg permanently since 1947. Baritone, actor, producer and singing teacher. Bruce Anderson was educated in St Paul's School in London and studied singing on a scholarship of the RAM under Thomas Meux (1924-1927). This led to further studies in Milan where he made his operatic debut at the Teatro Duse in *Madame Butterfly* (Puccini). Back in England, he sang for various opera companies and in broadcasts, as well as in Noel Coward's *Bitter sweet* (New York). His connection with South Africa started in 1936, when he was a member of the company that toured this country with *White Horse Inn.* He returned in 1937 to join the SABC, establishing a reputation as a producer of radio opera productions and as a solo and operatic singer. After 1938 he collaborated with John Connell* in his Music Fortnights, participating mainly on the operatic side. — At the outbreak of war, Anderson joined the First South African Brigade and was transferred to the Mobile Recording Unit, becoming the first South African to be awarded the OBE in recognition of his work as a war correspondent. After the war he was on the staff of the South African Embassy in Rome (1945-1947), where he resumed his singing career. In 1947 he returned to South Africa to take over the teaching practice of Margaret Roux, and to participate in Connell's opera seasons as a singer and producer. Until 1950 he was active as a teacher of singing, and as singer-producer in a variety of works, including *Fledermaus* (J. Strauss), *Tannhäuser* and *Aïda* (1949), *Faust* and *I Pagliacci* (Leoncavallo) in 1950. Anderson also exerted himself in the creation of a National Opera Company and was one of the members of the committee of the National Opera Association* formed by Alexander Rota in 1955. In June 1958 he produced *Gianni Schicchi* (Puccini), one of the four operas staged at the Reps Theatre by the federated National Opera Association of South Africa* and Die Operavereniging van Suid-Afrika* (OPSA). — Bruce Anderson has also become well-known as an actor in a variety of theatre productions and was featured in the film *Cry the beloved country* (Alan Paton). He is married to Erica Jolley who was trained as a violinist at Trinity College, London, and played in the SABC Orchestra for many years after 1937. She made valuable contributions to Johannesburg's musical life as a member of Hermann Becker's* Johannesburg String Quartette (1942-1943) and of Jeremy Schulman's* quartette in 1943.

—L.W.

ANDERSON, K. Johannesburg 3 (iii)

ANDREWS, E. Queenstown 2

ANDREWS, JOHN Higher Educational Institutions II, Saline Koch, A.J. Louw

ANDRÉSEN, HANS OLAF WALDEMAR RUDIGER FELIX JANUARIUS (OLAF ANDRÉSEN, ANDRIES CILLIERS), *14 January 1902 in Berlin; 1974 in Johannesburg. Composer, mainly of light vocal works; author of most of the song texts, as well as printer and distributor of his own works.

Olaf Andrésen's musical talent became apparent at an early age, with the result that he was enrolled, whilst still at school, as a pupil at H. and P. Heller's Conservatoire in Berlin. Although his music studies concentrated on the violin, he also received tuition in theory and composition. At the age of 14 years he made his public debut as violinist, and in 1920 embarked on a world tour which lasted approximately 6 years. His journey took him to the then Dutch East Indies, British India, the Philippines, Hong Kong, China, Japan, Honolulu, the USA, Canada, once again Japan, Mauritius, Lourenco Marques and eventually South Africa. He earned his living as a bookkeeper (he had passed an auditing examination in California); and wherever he went he associated with groups of musicians, playing mostly dance music but sometimes chamber music as well. Another benefit of this extended tour was that he acquired a working knowledge of a good many languages. — From South Africa he returned to Germany but within a few months he had left on another tour, this time to South America, the oil fields of Colombia and Venezuela, and once again bookkeeping was his livelihood. In Venezuela he regularly played in a group of eight musicians. He left the sub-continent during the depression of the early thirties, spent a few months in Germany and then again visited South Africa. Here he trudged many miles on foot (Durban to Cape Town and Cape Town to Johannesburg and back!) and earned a living as an insurance agent. In 1938 he briefly visited his mother in Germany and returned to his fiancée in Johannesburg in April 1939. She was Marthel (Martha) Dittrich, an Afrikaans girl of Austrian descent. At the outbreak of war, he was interned in Leeukop Prison but within 8 months he had escaped and spent 11 months as a fugitive (in all the provinces except Natal). During this time he composed 22 marches for the Ossewa Brandwag, all within 3 months, several of which were broadcast by Zeesen in Germany. One of these tunes became the signature tune of their Afrikaans programme. They were published in South Africa under the pseudonym Andries Cilliers. He and Marthel crossed the border into Portuguese East Africa in 1942. He was given asylum but she was deported to South Africa and had to serve a sentence of three years in jail. After the war they were married in Lourenco Marques (1946), and upon the election victory of the Nationalist Party in 1948 they returned to Johannesburg. It was here that Andrésen became a professional composer, earning a living in earnest from his music. He established an own publishing concern, the Melotoon Musiekuitgewers, printing and distributing his compositions and even cutting and selling his own records for many years. — Andrésen composed close on 400 works, including marches, dance music, one symphony and three operettas; but the majority were songs. The marches were arranged for military band by Lt Charles Donne, and the operettas, which incorporated many of his earlier melodies, are well suited for school use and have been performed hundreds of times. His most famous song is *Heidelied* the words of which were inspired by the heath on a trip through the Western Province. Sixteen years later it was played at the inauguration of the Voortrekker Monument, whereafter it became a national favourite. It is also well known in Lüneburg (Germany) and New Jersey (USA), and is used as a march by the South African Army.

WORKS

(Note: a) Except where indicated, both words and music are by the composer; b) all numbers are those assigned by the composer himself; c) the letters in brackets following on the titles refer to translations thus: (A) Afrikaans (E) English (F) French

(G) German; d) arrangements for small, large, instrumental/vocal combinations have not been listed).

A. Vocal

Operettas

Die heidenooientjie, in 3 acts, 1957.   Die drie astertjies, in 3 acts, 1960.   Die mieliefeetjie, in 2 acts, 1961.

Songs for voice and pianoforte

Ossewa-Brandwagbundel (nom-de-plume, Andries Cilliers). Voortrekkerpers, Johannesburg, 1941:

1. Ossewa-Brandwag (song).   2. Die dag sal kom (march song).   3. Opsaal, Boere! (battle song).   4. Vry Suid-Afrika! (march song).   5. Gee pad! (battle song).   6. Eer die son verdwyn.   7. Wapenbroers (march).   8. Majuba (song).   9. Burger, jou eer! (battle song).   10. Op kommando! (cavalry march).   11. OB-Penkoppe (march song).   12. Eerste kolonne (march).   13. Los van dwingeland! (battle song).   14. Plig, diens ter ere (march song).   15. Kort galop (cavalry march).   16. Hou koers! (song of greeting).   17. Hoor, hulle kom! (battle song).   18. Die lied van die vlag (song).   19. Tot weersiens! (march song).   20. Goeienag (waltz).   21. Triomfmars (march).   22. Dogters van Suid-Afrika (song).

The following songs have appeared in separate publications between 1949 and 1973:

26. Lebewohl (E), slow foxtrot.   29. Ruiter (G) (H. van der Westhuysen).   30. Vat die geweer.   35. Hulde (H. van der Westhuysen).   41. Die lied van my tuiste (E) (G), slow foxtrot (1949).   45. Ek dink aan jou (G), slow foxtrot.   46. So alone.   47. Maratina, tango.   49. Die Heidelied (E) (F) (G), tango, composed 1932 (1949).   50. Nur bei dir ist mein Glück.   52. Long ago.   60. Beautiful eyes, slow foxtrot.   62. Sê net goeie-nag (E), slow foxtrot.   66. Net vir jou.   68. Peasant song.   69. My eie land.   70. Memories.   71. Carefree.   72. Soldier's song.   74. Met 'n glimlag en 'n grap, foxtrot.   75. Im grünen Wald.   80. Frauenherz.   81. Das deutsche Freiheitslied.   84. Gee my 'n walsie.   85. Surrender, waltz.   86. Bocamba.   89. Der Glückliche.   90. Parole (J. von Eichendorff).   91. Aandgebed (G) (H. van der Westhuysen).   92. Die kleintjie (G) (J. von Eichendorff).   93. Vyf hoendertjies (E) (G) (Victor Blüthgen).   94. Gelyk en gelyk (G) (J.W. von Goethe).   95. Die bloue lenteogies (G) (H. Heine).   96. Im wunderschönen Monat Mai (H. Heine).   97. Gekommen ist der Mai (H. Heine).   98. Herz, mein Herz (H. Heine).   99. Ich halte ihr die Augen zu (H. Heine).   100. An die lieben.   101. Das Reh (L. Uhland).   103. Die klok (E) (G).   104. Wenn ich bei meinem Liebsten bin (H. Heine).   108. Shadows of the night, waltz, song.   112. Umantombi.   116. Sambreeltjies (E).   117. Lullaby (poem ex Royal Reader, No. 1).   118. One day, slow foxtrot.   120. Sympathy.   124. Forget-me-not.   126. My lovely Irish vale.   127. A dream come true.   129. Ek het jou lief (E).   136. You couldn't be true, my dear.   137. Memento.   138. Let's walk together, slow foxtrot.   140. Moedertjie (Whispering past), slow foxtrot.   141. Ukusamasama, for voice, piano and 2 violins.   142. Ob ich das Wetter.   143. Oor die wilgers by die rivier (G) (Fritz Woike).   144. Du musst nur mit den lieben Augen sehen.   145. As die liefde sagte hande (G) (Fritz Woike).   146. Für alles danken.   147. Blumen brauchen Sonnenschein.   148. Sei still, sei still.   149. Du hast mein Leben so reich gemacht.   151. Op patrollie (E), march.   152. Silwerpyl (E), march.   153. Weiche Flocken (Fritz Woike).   155. Little locket.   157. Caressing, waltz.   159. Mein Baum?   160. Night.   161. You are my choice.   163. Where the silver stars glow, slow foxtrot.   164. Serenata.   165. Always I

shall remember. 166. Carmelite. 167. Eventide. 168. Languid moon.
169. Klaasvakiewals (E) (G). 170. Dulcinee. 171. Rio Matola, tango. 172. Blue
days. 174. There's a twinkle in your eyes. 175. Echoes. 177. Together with
you. 178. Hush-a-bye, my baby darling. 179. Klein bonkie en sy donkie. 180. Mexican
lullaby, tango (Jimmy Boonzaaier). 181. A singing violin. 182. Laurentina,
tango. 183. If you were here (J.S. Wright). 184. Twee ogies (E) (G). 185. Please take
me along. 186. Troumars (E). 187. Aan jou. 188. Awendrus (H. van der Westhuysen).
189. Ja baas, nee baas. 190. Kaggeltjie (G). 191. When the bell rings for
me. 192. African moon, slow foxtrot. 194. Rio Negro. 147. 'n Lied op wieke (E)
(G), slow foxtrot. 199. As die aandklokke lui. 200. Wenn es nur will Abend
werden. 201. Die lied van die berg. 202. Sê net vir my. 203. Jeugkamerade.
204. Eensame wilgerboom. 205. Die lied van die lente (G). 206. Stellenbosch
student. 207. Heimwee (Anita Nel). 208. Die lied in my hart (G) (Frans
Henning). 209. Was ek maar (G) (Anita Nel), waltz. 210. Die koms van die poskar (G)
(Frans Henning). 211. Kersnag (G) (Frans Henning). 213. Net 'n uurtjie. 214. As
die hele wêreld. 216. So sing ons 'n lied (Frans Henning). 217. Up on the mountain
peak. 218. Vrystaatse nooi. 219. Net vir jou. 220. Weihnachtsabend.
221. Hannelie (A) (G), waltz. 223. Ek is jaloers. 224. Die maat van 'n wals. 225. Love
is all (F) (A). 226. Nee (G). 227. Hamba kahla (A) (E) (G) (Toy
Havemann). 229. Pikke Pikkewyn (G). 230. The reddest rose, waltz. 231. The night
is ours (Flora Henderson). 232. Ou moederhande (E) (G). 233. You and I (A) (G), slow
foxtrot. 234. Die kameelperdjie (G) (Bambila). 235. Daar bo in die hemel. 236. 'n
Nuwe jaar. 237. Aandlied (G) (Adelheid Dittrich). 238. Kom na my toe (C. le Grange).
239. My hart verlang na die Boland (C. le Grange). 241. Klein woelwater. 242. In der Heide
(E) (W. Groké). 243. Mütterlein. 244. Stil en sag (C. le Grange). 245. Kom saam met my
(C. le Grange). 246. Maanlig op die ou rivier (C. le Grange). 247. Die ou plaashuisie (C. le
Grange). 248. Heideklokkies (G) (1956). 249. Oerw'ouddagbreek (E)
(R.O'Keife). 250. Golden City. 251. Storm (Dedicated to the Kemp Tank
Regiment). 252. Ek dwaal so rond in die duister (G). 253. Op 'n manier (G). 254. Ek
is verlief op jou (G), slow foxtrot. 255. Aangename kennis (G). 256. Nog 'n koppie koffie
(G). 257. Oom en tante (G). 258. Inligting asseblief (G). 259. Die môre na die aand
tevore. 260. Weet jy nog? (G), waltz. 261. Die lied van die braaivleisaand (G).
262. Dis darem lekker. 263. Leef in vrede. 268. Die tikster se lied. (Mildred
Dieperink, Piet Ackerman en O.A. 271. Rondom die huis (G). 272. Wenn der
Abend naht. 273. Dorpie van drome (G). 274. Amsterdam se Landbouhoër-
skoollied. 275. Die drie astertjies. 276. Wanneer die skaduwees val, slow foxtrot.
277. Margolet, (A), (E), (G), waltz. 278. I know she'd like (G). 279. Dis
jy (G) (M. Dieperink and O.A.). 280. As twee hartjies klop. 281. Dis darem
lekker. 282. Wil jy my hê?, waltz. 283. Ek sê vir jou. 284. 'n Nuwe dag (A).
287. Ons mielieland (G). 290. My klein kwassie (G). 291. Wikkel, wikkel, woel (G).
292. Wonderland (G). 293. Net vir moeder (G) (E). 294. De Deur primary school song.
296. Ho-a-ho (G). 297. Verre lande (G). 298. Hoekom? (G). 299. So 'n dwaas (G).
300. Ek weet (G). 301. Wys my die man (G). 302. Dankie, baie dankie (G).
303. Voorwaarts (Song of the League of Internees). 307. Blou berge (E). 314. Danie
Theron school song (G.A. Watermeyer). 317. Altyd my beste (H.J. Myburgh). 318. Wees
getrou (school song of the Dr Malan High School, Meyerton). 320. Johan Steyn
(J. Steyn) (School song of 'the Elandspoort High School). 325. Certa cito (A) (E)
(O.A.I. van Loggerenberg) (Composed for the Signal Corps). 326. Lizelle se wiegelied.

328. Certa di via sumus (Frans Neethling). 329. Ons delf diep, school song.
330. Hoor my lied (E) (registered as Hear my Song). 337. Prof. Dr Barnard's prayer.
338. Das Blümchen (Neue Post, Ausgabe No. 16). 340. Die alte Kogge (A) (E) (Neue Post,
H.J. Kletzer). 341. Zufriedenheit (A) (Neue Post, Maria Pellvụchoud). 342. Golden lacht der
Sonnenschein (Neue Post, K. Kühner). 343. Letzter Hauch des Tages (Neue Post, E. Gosdorf).
344. Weisse Sterne (Neue Post, E. Wischlinski). 345. Freude (Neue Post, Dr Francken). 346.
Der Held (Neue Post, C. Broller). 347. Geh weiter (A) (E) (Neue Post, J. Pfaff). 348. Nur ein
sonniges Lächeln (A) (Neue Post, P. Klöcker). 349. Es weht ein Hauch (Neue Post, E. Pfeiffer).
350. Frühling (Neue Post, Marge Stier). 351. Frühlingserwachen (A) (Neue Post,
F. Buszemeier). 352. Mütterlein (Neue Post, U. Gretlhörster). 353. Seelen (A)
(E. Geibel). 354. Abendstille (Neue Post, E. Knöpfli). 355. So wunderschön ist
die Natur (Neue Post, W. Ludwig). 356. Der alte Musikant (Neue Post, J. Hawner).
357. Jugendzeit (Neue Post, R. Limp). 358. Zur alten Linde (Neue Post, E. Görnsdorfer).
359. Die Wolken (Neue Post, K.H. Maurer). 360. Es liegt ein Schloss am Rhein
(K. Janssen). 361. Noch heut! (Neue Post, Kurt Janssen). 362. Vorentoe! (School song
of the primary school Vryheidsmonument, Vereeniging). 363. Wenn du Liebe willst
erleben (A.G. Klöcker). 364. Capri. 365. Minnetog. 366. Vry, maar aan jou
gebonde (School song of the Jeugland High School, Kempton Park). 367. Peinsing.
372. Southern Cross (A) (P). 373. Arbeid veredel (E) (School song of the Johan
Jürgens Commercial High School, Springs, Transvaal). 374. Die President se wag.
375. Veilchen blüh'n (Erna Jüttner-Arndt) (1974). 376. Frühlingsstimmen (Erna Jüttner-
Arndt). 378. Liefde en dood (S. Ignatius Mocke).

B. *Instrumental*
(Note: All works are for piano, unless otherwise stated)
23. Die heidelied, pastorale. 24. A little tune. 25. A little interlude, intermezzo.
27. A little waltz. 36. Serenata. 38. Staan gereed, march. 42. Erewag, slow march.
51. Drakensberge, military march. 53. Longing, waltz-fantasy. 54. Sê net vir my, vastrap.
55. Ein kleiner Traum. 56. Für Freiheit und Recht, march. 57. Wiener Schelmereien.
58. Kleine Launen, waltz. 59. Olé! 61. Twilight, tone-poem. 63. Erinnerungen,
fantasy. 64. Frechdachs, foxtrot. 67. Ojos Espanoles, concert tango. 73. With flying
colours, military march. 80. Symphony. 82. Wild spirits, foxtrot. 83. Cocktail, foxtrot.
85. Surrender, waltz for piano and 4 strings. 87. Marcia do Presidente Carmona. 102. Ins
Blaue, foxtrot, for piano and 4 instruments. 105. Waldestraüme, piano and violin.
106. Doe-doe my babatjie. 107. Espana agitada, foxtrot. 108. Sombras da noite,
piano solo (E). 109. Why? (Porque?). 110. La Castiliana, pasodobles two-step.
111. Meditation. 115. I want you near me, slow foxtrot. 119. Rainbow march.
121. Shamrock, Irish song. 122. Tepping Toots, foxtrot. 123. Esmeralda, tango.
125. Temptation, tango. 128. My wonderful rose, waltz. 130. Esperanza, tango.
131. Starlight, waltz. 132. Pensamientos, tango piano and violin. 134. La Margarita,
concert tango. 135. El gaucho, concert tango. 139. Just dreams, slow foxtrot.
150. Embers, slow foxtrot. 154. Forest call, tone-poem. 156. Sunset, waltz. 158. Erin,
Irish song. 162. Morning glory, waltz. 176. Dawn, tone-poem. 267. Peinsing, reverie
without words. 269. Lanterntjies. 270. Overture for operetta Die Heidenooientjie.
285. Overture for operetta Die Drie Astertjies. 286. Notturno. 305. Wees sterk, march
(composed for the East Rand Regiment) (1962). 306. Sambreeltjies (E) march (accepted as
march of the Paratroop Regiment, in 1962). 307. Blou berge (E), march (dedicated to the
Stellenbosch Univ. Reg., 1972). 308. Die Heidelied, march (chosen as official march of the
S.A. Army, in 1962). 316. Voorwaarts, march. 332. Storm, march (composed for the

Kemp Tank Regiment). 333. Ruiter, march. 334. Wits command, march. 335. Die Kommandant-generaal, march. 336. Generaal Willie Louw, march. 339. March, untitled. 370. Potpourri, for symphony orchestra.
Unnumbered: 1. Southern Cross clarion call, march. 2. Verolme, march (1975).
This list of works has been compiled from the composer's own list, a list made available by S.A.M.R.O. and from material in the Music Documentation Centre of the H.S.R.C.

—Ed.

ANGERMANN, CARL ALFRED, *23 October 1890 in Hamburg, Germany; ° 14 September 1966 in Cape Town. Music dealer.

Angermann served his apprenticeship in the import and export firm of Coqui and Reimers, and then, in 1908, went to South West Africa. In 1911 he joined the firm of Müllers* as Richard Müller's* secretary, but a year later, evidently wishing to go to the Far East, he left the firm and returned to Germany. He had scarcely got there, however, when letters and cables from Richard Müller began arriving - all entreating him to return. He gave in and returned to Cape Town, where he made his home until his death. He, as well as other members of the staff, was interned at Fort Napier near Pietermaritzburg during and immediately after the First World War (from August 1914 until 1920). He was released because of illness but restricted to the Cape Flats and, later on, to Stellenbosch. In Stellenbosch he assisted David Justus in the local branch of R. Müller. In 1921 he was permitted to return to Cape Town to rejoin the small staff of R. Müller in Waterkant Street. He married Mary Burnie Tyler in St George's Cathedral*, Cape Town, on 7 April 1924, became a junior partner in the firm on 1 July 1930 and managing director from 5 December 1934. He kept this position until 1953, when Phil Morkel took over the business. Angermann then assumed control of the organ section, which he developed into Müller Organ Builders (Pty) Ltd with a factory at Potchefstroom in the Transvaal. This business was taken over by Suid-Afrikaanse Orrelbouers* in 1963.

—Ed.

ANGLICAN CHURCH MUSIC   Bell ringing in South Africa, C.E. Brown, Diocesan College, R.M. O'Hogan, Organs 1 (i), (vi), 2 (iv), (v), 3, 4, 5 (i), 7, 8, 9, 12, A. Pierce-Jones, Barry Smith, St George's Cathedral, C.N. Thomas.

ANGOVE, IVY ST AUBYN, *10 October 1886 in London; living in Fish Hoek since 1943. Violinist.

She started violin lessons at the age of six, and her progress was so rapid that she was accepted by Wilhelmj as a pupil at the age of eleven. Three years later she became the youngest Licentiate of the RAM, and the holder of a scholarship to study at this institution. At the termination of her studies there, she became a pupil of Sevčik in Prague and returned to London for her debut with the London Symphony Orchestra in 1904, playing three concertos. During the next 15 years she toured extensively in England and on the continent and during the Great War, played almost daily in camps and hospitals.   — After her marriage to Kenneth Holme Barnett in 1919 she came to South Africa and settled at Stellenbosch, appearing frequently at the Thursday Symphony Concerts at the City Hall, Cape Town. She made several tours of the Republic, giving concerts in schools and colleges. There have been frequent comments on the originality and variety of her programmes. Of her first South African appearance Prof. W.H. Bell* wrote: "Though I expected a good performance, I was hardly prepared for the brilliant one that was actually given." In the year of her arrival in South Africa she was appointed to the staff of respectively the SA College of Music* in Cape Town and the Conservatoire of Music of the Stellenbosch University,* occupying these positions until 1939 and 1943 respectively. Since then she has taught privately at Fish Hoek. Her pupils include Virginia-Gene Shankel (now in America), Elize de Villiers,* Margherita Bini and Elsie Dawes.

—Ed.

Apollo male voice choir   L.R. Glenton, C.H. Norburn, Pretoria 3, Pretoria Male Choir.

Archdeacon, a.   Barberton, Touring Theatre Groups 3

Arenhold, dr a. and family   Barberton, Graaff Reinet 2, 3 (iv), 6.

Armhold, adelheid, born on the Frisian Islands of a Dutch father and a Frisian mother; now in Honolulu. Mezzo-soprano and teacher of singing.

Adelheid Armhold started as a pianist and she qualified with a diploma in pianoforte at a Hamburg Conservatoire. Her training as a singer commenced at the age of 18 under Alexander Scarneo (of La Scala, Milan) and Prof. Alexander de Rival (a Russian-born expert on the French style); it was completed at the M. Ivogün School in Germany. Thus she became thoroughly acquainted with the singing traditions of the Italian, French and German schools. A soprano, with a velvety middle register and the coloratura ability to cope with Bach's *Jauchzet in allen Ländern,* she made her debut at the age of 19. Engagements followed in Germany, Switzerland, Holland and England. Her repertoire consisted mainly of Lieder, but she had much success in oratorios. Although she never specialised in opera, she has sung in productions of *Die Zauberflöte* (Pamina), *Der Freischütz* (Agatha), and *Herakles* and *Acis and Galathea* (Handel). — Her voice gradually deepened, and it was as a mezzo-soprano that she accepted an appointment as senior lecturer in singing at the College of Music,* Cape Town, at the end of 1939. Here she established a reputation not only as the teacher of successful South African singers, such as Noreen Berry, Nellie du Toit,* Desirée Talbot,* George van der Spuy,* Xander Haagen,* Joy van Niekerk* and Louise Wessels, but also as a singer. Her singing of folk songs in a variety of European languages, to her own lute accompaniment, became a feature of her appearances in Cape Town and, in 1961, in Pretoria. In 1955 she became the first singer to present at a public concert in South Africa Schönberg's setting of Stefan George's *Buch der hangenden Gärten.* She retired from the College of Music at the end of 1965. Since the beginning of 1977 she teaches singing at a music school in Honolulu.

PUBLICATION

Singing, based on irrefragable laws, with a preface by Keith Falkner, director of the RCM. Tafelberg-Uitgewers Bpk., 1963.

—Ed.

Arnold, leslie, *15 January 1906 in London; 8 April 1963 in Cape Town. Organist, lecturer and composer.

Largely self-taught, Arnold had some instruction from Cecil Hazelhurst, W.F. Jordan and Lloyd Webber, passing the Fellowship examination of the R C O in January 1933, and gaining the coveted Lafontaine Prize. After holding sundry posts as organist, he came to Simonstown in 1945, while on active service in the Royal Navy, and fell in

46

love with Cape Town. He decided to settle here after demobilisation in 1946, and was joined a few months later by his wife, Jean Agnes Nancy Arnold, an accomplished musician and a licentiate of music of the R C M Arnold was appointed city organist of Cape Town in 1946 and at the same time became organist of the Metropolitan Methodist Church on Greenmarket Square. — Apart from weekly organ recitals and the playing of accompaniments to choral works at St George's Cathedral and elsewhere, Arnold was also organ lecturer at the South African College of Music* from August 1948 until 31 December 1962. He taught organ at St Cyprian's School, class-singing at Western Province Preparatory School and Marist Brothers, Rondebosch and visited Port Elizabeth periodically to accompany the Port Elizabeth Oratorio Choir, conducted by Robert Selley.* Cape Town enjoyed the privilege of hearing him play a wide range of organ music. His recital programmes, about one hundred and sixty in number, were not repeated till two and a half years had elapsed. Arnold is remembered for outstanding performances in connection with the bicentenary of Bach's death and the Union Festival held at Bloemfontein in 1960, as well as for recitals of the works of Cesar Franck at the Diocesan College*, and of Max Reger at St. George's Cathedral.

PUBLICATIONS

Music in Church. *Sound* I/1-5, May- September, 1956.

WORKS

Organ

Sonata No. 1 in G. Ms., 1947, revised version.   Sonata No. 2 in A major. Ms., 1974, revised version.   Mjölnir, fantasia - The Hammer of Thor. Ms., 1948.   Adantino pastorale. Ms., 1949, Kokstad.   Introduction, variations and finale on a Somersetshire folk melody. Ms., January 1957.   God be in my head, five-part Introit. Ms., n.d.   A variety of organ transcriptions of orchestral works.   Two symphonies mentioned by A.P.J., no details; probably lost.

Songs and Carols

Angels from the realms of glory, carol. Ms., first performance at Carol Concert, 1953.   Magnificat, sung at Carols by Candlelight, usually to harp accompaniment. Ms., n.d.   But the souls of the righteous, contralto solo, orchestrated. Ms., n.d.   Ah, mon beau chateau, for Union Festival Choir. Ms., 1960.   The Lord is my shepherd, quartet. Ms., n.d.   O God of love. Ms., n.d.   To Thee we bow. Ms., n.d.   Wedding song, for voice and piano (William Vaughan Jenkins). Ms., n.d.   Chorale, small improvisation on the tune *Irish*. Ms., n.d.   They wait upon the Lord. Ms., n.d.   Oh, my love's like a red, red rose, ballad. Ms., n.d.

—A.P.J. (amplified)

ARNOLD, ROSANNA LOUISA SWANN (ROSE), *23 August 1868 in East London; °16 September 1940 at Arnoldton. Composer of light music.

Louisa Arnold grew up on a farm near Arnoldton where the family settled in 1874, and had little opportunity of studying music. Although she could never read music fluently, she became a proficient pianist and provided music at country dances. Later she began to compose by playing her improvisations to a friend, Margaret Gately, who wrote them down.

WORKS

Amalinda, barn dance, for piano. Franz Moeller's Music Warehouse, East London. n.d.   Amalinda march. Franz Moeller's Music Warehouse, East London, n.d.   Cheeky, barn dance. Franz Moeller's Music Warehouse, East London, n.d.   Manzi kanya (Shining waters), waltz for piano. Printed by Röder of Leipzig for Franz Moeller's Music Warehouse, East London, n.d.; reprinted in England for B.J. Ewins & Co., East London and Queenstown, n.d.   Somlanga waltz, for piano. Printed by Röder of Leipzig for Franz Moeller's Music Warehouse, East London, n.d.; reprinted in England for B.J. Ewins, East London and Queenstown, n.d.   The golden star of the veldt, waltz. Printed by Röder of Leipzig for Franz Moeller's Music Warehouse, East London, n.d.; reprinted in England for B.J. Ewins & Co., East London and Queenstown, n.d.   The motor girl, waltz. B.J. Ewins & Co., East London and Queenstown, 1936.

BIBLIOGRAPHY

VAN DER MERWE, F.Z.: *Suid-Afrikaanse Musiekbibliografie 1787-1952.* J.L. van Schaik, Pretoria, 1958.

SOURCES

Denfield Collection, Public Library, East London.   *Daily Dispatch:* 12 December 1936; 20 September 1940; 27 September 1940.   National Documentation Centre for Music, HSRC.
                                                                              —Ed.

ARONOWITZ, a family originally of King William's Town, which holds the distinction of having produced three winners of the Overseas Scholarship of the University of South Africa.*

The first to win the scholarship was the pianist, **John** (*21 March 1913 in King William's Town; °27 February 1971, in Norwich, England), who entered the RAM in December 1929 at the age of sixteen. He had received his first music lessons from Sister Cecilia at the Convent of the Sacred Heart in King William's Town, and for two years prior to winning the scholarship had been a pupil of Horace Barton* of Johannesburg, though he was still at school in East London at the time. He studied at the RAM under Claude Pollard, obtained the LRAM and ARCM diplomas, and returned to East London to open an Academy of Music (December 1935).   — During 1937 he was appointed official accompanist to the SABC Studio Orchestra in Durban and as local supervisor of gramophone-record broadcasting. He was back in London in 1939, a week before the outbreak of hostilities, and served in the armed forces until invalided out in 1942. For some years (1942-1946) he studied under Harold Craxton, and commenced giving concerts again during 1944, undertaking tours in the United Kingdom, Canada and Holland, and broadcasting for the BBC. Until 1948 he also played with a number of prominent orchestras, including the Hallé and Bournemouth orchestras. John visited Durban during 1948, where he appeared with the Durban Orchestra* as soloist, returning to England in the early fifties.   — Ill-health prevented him from continuing his career as a concert pianist and after his marriage to a ballerina, on 5th March 1954, he concentrated on composition, receiving several commissions to write incidental music for documentary films. In 1959 he and his wife opened a ballet school in Norwich (which became one of the biggest of its kind in England); he played the pianoforte and arranged and composed music for the school. According to his wife, he composed a concerto and several minor works, but, being self-critical, he did not attempt to have them published.   — John's sister **Alice** (*27 November 1914 in King William's Town) had pianoforte and cello lessons from Sister Euphonia at the same convent as her brother. She continued pianoforte study at the Training College, Grahamstown, under Archibald Iliffe-Higgo, and won the SA Scholarship for Overseas Study (1932). Continuing her study at the RAM under Arthur Alexander (pianoforte) and John Snowdon (cello) she won

48

the Leverhulme Scholarship, and has since played concertos, performed at recitals and broadcast frequently for the BBC. After her marriage in 1939 to Louis H. Yellon, she remained in England and devoted herself to the teaching of music. — The youngest member of the family, **Cecil**, (*4 March 1916) received pianoforte and violin lessons from Sister Bernado at the Sacred Heart Convent, King William's Town (1924-1928). Subsequently he entered the Training College, Grahamstown, where his violin tuition was conducted by Sister Bridgett and Miss Alexandra (1929-1933). This was followed by violin study under Stirling Robins* in Durban during 1934-1935, when he won the SA Overseas Scholarship and elected to attend the RCM. Here he studied violin and viola under Achille Rivarde, and conducting under Adrian Boult (1936-1939), winning the Leverhulme Scholarship and obtaining an Hon. ARCM. Since 1946 Cecil has specialised in viola playing and is now professor of viola and chamber music at the RCM. He has played in ensembles with artists like Oistrakh, Rostropovich, Barenboim and others, and was co-founder of the Melos Ensemble, the Musica da Camera Ensemble, the Cremona String Quartet, and the Pro Arte Piano Quartet. As soloist, he appears with leading symphony orchestras, has also given recitals, made recordings, and formed a duo sonata team with his wife, the pianist Nicola Grünberg, whom he married in 1967.

SOURCES

Daily Dispatch: 4 October 1928; 23 November 1929; 29 November 1935; 6 January 1936; 10 September 1937.   *Rand Daily Mail:* 21 July 1969.   Archives of the University of South Africa.   Correspondence with Mrs Janet Aronowitz and with Prof. Cecil Aronowitz.

—E.C.

ARONOWSKY, SOLOMON (SOLLY), *6 October 1911, in Suvalki, Poland; at present in Johannesburg. Conductor, violinist and head of the Music Library of the SABC in Johannesburg.

Solly Aronowsky studied violin and piano at the State Conservatoire in Kovno, Lithuania, from 1927 until 1935, and played as violinist in the Radio Orchestra and as leader of the Aronowsky Trio. Having obtained the BA, LL.B. degree of the University of Vytautas, Lithuania, in 1935, he came to South Africa in 1936 as a first violinist in the SABC Orchestra, a position he occupied until 1946, when he founded the Conservatoire of Music of the Jewish Musical Institute of South Africa, which he directed for the next three years. — During the early years in Johannesburg he was leader of a new Aronowsky Trio, violin master at the Marist Brothers' College, leader of the Johannesburg Symphony Orchestra* (1943-1944) and managing director of the Solly Aronowsky Concert Bureau (Pty) Ltd (1946-1949). In 1949 he was appointed Head of the Music Library of the SABC in Johannesburg and undertook a study tour of Radio and Television Music Libraries in London, Paris, Rome, Madrid, Budapest, Tel-Aviv (1953). For his thesis, *The repertoire of the modern orchestra,* the Ph.D. degree of the University of the Witwatersrand was conferred on him in 1960. — Dr Aronowsky founded the Jewish Guild Orchestra* in 1944 and a Johannesburg Promenade Orchestra in 1951, and has been the conductor of both ever since. He was also the first Resident Conductor of the shortlived South African National Youth Orchestra (1964) and since 1937 has occasionally been guest conductor of the Municipal and Radio orchestras in Johannesburg, Cape Town, Durban, Jerusalem, Bulawayo and Lourenço Marques. He has been a committee member of both the

Johannesburg City Ballet and the Operavereniging van Suid-Afrika* (OPSA) and still is a member of the International Association of Music Librarians (UNESCO). In 1970 he became a member of Unesco's International Radio Commission and a member of the International Council of the National Music Librarians' Association. He has adjudicated the string section and chamber music at National Eisteddfodau and has produced numerous music-historical radio programmes in Afrikaans and English. In 1968 he represented South Africa on an American grant at a musicological congress, and in 1971 he was the representative of the SABC at an international conference held at St Gallen in Switzerland.

PUBLICATIONS

Performing Times of Orchestral Works. Ernest Benn, London, and John de Graff, New York, 1959.   Articles in journals and newspapers since 1938.

WORKS

Incidental music for pageants and films. Ms., 1950 and later.

—Ed.

ARSENIEVA, MASHA,   *19 May 1912 in St Petersburg (Leningrad); at present in Graaff Reinet. Ballerina, choreographer and ballet teacher.

Educated in Paris, where she first studied classical ballet, she continued her studies in 1928 at the State Ballet School in Belgrade, and in 1930 achieved the status of ballerina in the Belgrade Opera House Ballet. In Belgrade she met Boris Igneff,* whom she married in 1933. Developing an interest in expressive dancing, she continued her ballet studies, as well as studies in design, costume and decor at the school of Mary Wigman in Berlin and Dresden. — She founded, and choreographed for her own ballet group in Belgrade in 1934-1935, while also assisting as choreographer at the Belgrade University Theatre and the Opera House Ballet. Until the outbreak of war, she held the post of Instructress of Ballet and Modern Dance at the Yugoslavian Art Organisation, Zvieta Zogoritch, subsequently teaching ballet in Italy. — In 1946 she undertook a tour of South Africa, and two years later decided to open a studio in Cape Town, with branches subsequently at Worcester and Robertson. By 1953, when she was appointed instructress of Modern Dance and Ballet at the East London Technical College, she had completed three tours of the Republic and two tours of South West Africa. After a fourth tour of the country districts, she settled in Graaff Reinet in 1961 and established a ballet school with branches in the neighbouring towns of Middelburg and Aberdeen. In 1974 she suffered a severe thrombosis which compelled her to terminate all teaching activities.

—C.G.H.

ASAF CHOIR, JOHANNESBURG, THE was founded on 5 July 1920 in the home of Mr and Mrs S.J. Buys of Melville, Johannesburg. The first conductor was H.A. Delen; he was succeeded in 1921 by J.B.Z. Keet* who remained conductor until 1963. The choir became a truly national choir in the sense that it was much in demand on occasions such as Kruger Day and other Afrikaans cultural festivals held in the Johannesburg City Hall. In addition, this choir performed great works of the choral repertoire such as the *Mattheuspassie*, Verdi's *Requiem* and *Messias*. The choir also took part regularly in John Connell's* opera seasons. The collaboration with Connell as conductor of the Philharmonic Choir was particularly successful. In this way, from 1939 onwards, the combined choirs performed the *Messiah* in Afrikaans on one evening and in English on another. The Asaf Choir consisted of several separate choirs which were rehearsed individually by Keet and then combined for large-scale recitals - Turffontein (1924); Brixton (1928); Germiston (1932); Alberton (1936); and Linden (1937). The first opera to be performed in Afrikaans was a memorable occasion: it was *Carmen,* presented in Johannesburg on 23 April 1946, with the choral parts sung by the Asaf Choir. From 1934 onwards the choir collaborated regularly in SABC broadcasts and often performed with the SABC Symphony Orchestra. On 21 October 1963, on J.B.Z. Keet's 79th birthday, a special tribute was paid to him in the Johannesburg Civic Centre. Danie van den Heever,* who had joined the Asaf Choir in 1928 at the age of twelve and had remained an active member throughout, succeeded J.B.Z. Keet as chairman and conductor.

—Ed.

Ascham, margaret jane (reece, maggie), *1859 in Chester; °20 June 1897 in Port Elizabeth. Contralto and wife of Roger Ascham.*

Maggie Ascham lost her eyesight at the age of 7 and was accepted as a pupil at the Academy of Music for the Blind in Upper Norwood, England, where she studied singing and eventually became a singing teacher. Here she met Roger Ascham and was married to him in 1885. Many of his songs were sung for the first time by her. Apparently she enjoyed a firm reputation in England since she sang for Queen Victoria as well as for the Royal couple of Belgium. In 1890 she accompanied her husband to South Africa and had success as a teacher of singing at the Girls' Collegiate School in Port Elizabeth. She also established a reputation as a concert singer and was able to contribute to the musical life of Port Elizabeth before her early death. She often used her maiden name, Maggie Reece, on concert programmes.

BIBLIOGRAPHY
Troskie, a.j.j.: *The musical life of Port Elizabeth, 1875-1900.* M.Mus. dissertation, UPE, 1969.
—A.J.J.T.

Ascham (askham), roger, *28 August 1864 in London; °31 March 1934 in Port Elizabeth. Organist, pianist and composer, who dominated the musical life of Port Elizabeth for forty-four years. He was born Askham but later adopted the spelling used by a namesake, the famous sixteenth century scholar and poet.

Until he was ten years old, Roger Ascham was taught music by his mother and after that he walked five miles every week to have organ lessons from Josiah Booth of Banbury. He showed much aptitude for the organ and became organist at St Clement's Church in Bournemouth at a salary of R16 per year when he was 13 years old. Two years later (1879) he received an appointment as a reader at the Normal College for the Blind, in Norwood, receiving in exchange for his services, tuition in piano (Frits Hartvigson), organ (Dr E.J. Hopkins) and harmony (Banister). At the college he met his future wife Margaret Jane (Maggie) Reece* (whom he married in 1885) and his life-long friend, the blind organist Alfred Hollins. Financial considerations obliged him to accept the post of organist of All Saints in Wellingborough in November 1883. — South Africa offered him better prospects than England and he emigrated in 1890 to become "professor of music" at the Collegiate School for Girls in Port Elizabeth and also organist of the Holy Trinity Church in Pearson Street. Both these positions he held until his death 44 years later. At his first recital in Trinity Church he had a showy programme which included a *Sonata* by Rheinberger, the *Fanfare* by

Lemmens and Widor's *Toccata* (from 5th symphony). The organ in the Feather Market Hall was completed in June 1893 and on the 16th of September he gave his first recital on the new instrument, repeating the Rheinberger Sonata and the Widor Toccata, but adding a Bach fugue and diverse pieces by Guilmant, Moszkowski and Lemmens. The City Council appointed him Municipal Organist in 1895 and his recitals in the Feather Market Hall became a regular feature of the city's life. Ascham received R200 per annum and was entitled to a benefit concert each year. After some fluctuation the recitals settled down to the convenient time of 8.30 on Sunday evenings (following on the evening service in the various churches) and were regularly presented until 1933 when he had reached a total of 1 150 recitals. The audiences were generally large, on an average about 1 000, who were attracted by the showiness of the organ playing and the intimate atmosphere established by the organist. The programmes were always printed and contained notes to introduce the public to the works they were going to hear. Gradually he made more and more use of variety in the way of guest artists, generally singers, but sometimes there were choirs, or instrumental ensembles, the PAG Band,* his own students, or a visiting Imperial Band. He would play four or five items and the rest were presented by the evening's guests. Apart from a sprinkling of serious and semi-serious works written for the organ, he generally gave the public what they wanted in the form of organ arrangements of symphonic works, songs or popular pianoforte pieces. For his 100th recital (23 December 1900) the English composers Faulkes, Wolstenholme and Hollins wrote festival compositions and the same composers with the addition of Archer, Mayo, Hilton and Morris, commemorated his 1 000th recital by contributing specially composed works to the programme. At the end of this occasion, the large audience gave way to their enthusiasm and carried the organist around the hall on their shoulders. The City Council had marked the occasion by presenting a special "Ascham Festival Week" which included choral and orchestral concerts. Many people came from as far afield as Uitenhage to listen to his playing, and the train service between this town and the Port was even regulated to suit the concerts. He loved chatting to the people and often encouraged them to submit proposals of works they would like to hear. It would be difficult to imagine a more popular or successful musician than this organist of the City of Port Elizabeth. After 1901 his duties were extended to include the organisation of municipal concerts such as the popular Saturday Evening Concerts. During the Great War these generally took the form of concerts for War Relief. — Ascham was almost equally active as a pianist. Liszt, whom he had once met in London, was his idol, though he regarded Wagner as the greatest genius of all. Shortly after his arrival he gave his first public piano recital and included one of his own compositions (*By the Sea,* opus 2) in the programme. Concertos were often included in these programmes with the orchestral part played by little more than one violin, a viola, a portable organ and piano, and sometimes by piano alone. Between 1896 and 1898 he presented four series of six fortnightly recitals each. One series was devoted to arrangements of unfamiliar orchestral works such as *Faust symphony; Tasso* and *Mazeppa,* all by Franz Liszt. With his pupil, Miss Biden, he gave another series of five recitals for two pianos in 1901 when *Till Eulenspiegel* (Richard Strauss), *Les preludes* (Liszt) and Tchaikowsky's *Sixth symphony* were performed. In his solo recitals, Liszt, Chopin and Beethoven were quite well represented, with other, lesser composers of *pièces de resistance.* In the early years of the 20th century he also visited East London, Durban, Pretoria and Johannesburg.

The concert reviews are not always very complimentary, mentioning that he had an extraordinarily fine technique but that there was nothing "that would absolutely stun people". An article in *The Tatler* of 30 September 1903, calls him the "Paderewski of South Africa" and says that Ascham commands "a musical eclecticism of his own". —The frequent performances of concertos emphasised the need for an orchestra and in June 1906 a group presented as the Ascham Symphony Orchestra made its first public appearance in Port Elizabeth. Up to 1913 they supported Ascham in about 11 concertos with the pianist acting as conductor at the piano. A few symphonic works or extracts from symphonies were included to fill these programmes. Edward Sangster acted as their conductor during 1911-1913. Ascham delighted in large ensembles and before 1915, combined his symphony orchestra with the PAG Band and the cinema orchestra which played in the Grand Theatre. These efforts added a special lustre to his own annual Benefit Concerts. In December 1915 he conducted a choir of 140 plus a combined orchestra of 50 and in August 1916 he had 120 singers under his command at a concert in the Grand Theatre. — Ascham delighted in co-operating with his colleagues in Port Elizabeth, W.H. Howse, C.W. Smart, W.H. Lee-Davies,* and Horace Barton* in presenting large-scale choral works such as standard oratorios by Handel, Haydn and Mendelssohn. But he also had his own choirs - a "select" male voice choir which made its debut in December 1911 and a women's choir which appeared for the first time in June 1917. They were still in existence in 1927 when Ascham had a festival choir of about 70 members. —The majority of his piano compositions and songs were created before 1900. They are entirely in the Romantic idiom and influenced by Liszt, Grieg and Chopin according to Ascham's own admission. The bravura element is seldom absent and is typically contrasted with flowing expressive melodies and rich chromatic harmonies in the Wagnerian style. His songs exhibit a talent for setting words to sensitive accompaniments which capture something of the spirit of the poems. Byron, Tennyson and Edgar Allan Poe were his favourite poets, though he also set a few of Heine's poems to music. Formally, his work inclines to a through-composed song with contrasting sections dictated by the words. — It was his personality as much as his talent that endeared him to the people of Port Elizabeth. Belonging to a generation when musicians were expected to look like musicians, he never abandoned the fashions of his youth - long hair, wide slouch hat, velvet jacket and flowing cravat. Among his close friends he counted Alfred Hollins who composed pieces for his organ recitals. The pianist Albert Friedenthal also knew him well and sometimes included Ascham's piano compositions in his programmes. Ascham was well loved as a teacher and drew many music students to Port Elizabeth. They appeared quite often at his organ recitals and also had to perform concertos with him. Pre-eminent among his pupils was undoubtedly Adolph Hallis.* — After Ascham's death, his family presented his extensive collection of music scores and books to the Port Elizabeth Public Library where it is housed with a memorial plaque. Two oil paintings of him were presented at the same time. The Africana Library in Johannesburg possesses a third portrait.

WORKS

It is noteworthy that Ascham used his original name of Askham* only in the case of the first two opus numbers: the song *Der Asra* and the pianoforte piece entitled *By the sea*. The decision to use Ascham must have been taken between 1885 and 1890. Also noteworthy is the fact that

Ascham started publishing his compositions after he had settled in Port Elizabeth, though many of these had apparently been written in England before he came to South Africa. After 1900 relatively little was published, so that the bulk of his published works were printed between 1890 and 1900 and thus represent the work of a young man.

A. *Instrumental*

Der Asra, op. 1, song by Rubinstein, paraphrased for piano; n.d. By the sea, op. 2, for piano. Albert Adams, Birmingham, c 1885. Three short pieces in F, op. 5, for piano, composed 1883-1886. Enoch & Sons, London, n.d. Available: 2nd edition. I love thee, op. 6, romance for piano, composed in Durban 1891. Charles Vincent, London, n.d. Available: 3rd edition. Du bist wie eine Blume, op. 7, song transcribed for piano, composed in Port Elizabeth 1893. Charles Vincent, London, n.d. First romance in F, op. 8, for violin and piano. Composed in England 1888. Enoch & Sons, London, n.d. Slumber and rest, op. 9 no. 1, berceuse for piano and violoncello or violin. G. Schirmer Ltd., London, n.d. Slumber and rest, op. 9, no. 2, an arrangement for organ. The Vincent Music Co., London, n.d.; Enoch & Sons, London, n.d. Romanze for violin and piano, op. 11. Ries & Erler, Berlin, n.d. Zwei Klavierstücke, op. 12, Ries & Erler, Berlin, n.d.: 1. Wiegenlied. 2. Etude. Trois piéces de salon pour le piano, op. 13, Ries & Erler, Berlin, n.d.: 1. Melodie. 2. Encore. 3. Danse des sorcières. Süsse Ruh', op. 17, Schlummerlied für Pianoforte. Ries & Erler, Berlin, n.d. Deuxième grandes valses de concert pour le piano, op. 18, composed in Port Elizabeth 1894. Published (a) Charles Vincent, London, n.d. (b) Oliver Ditson Co., New York, n.d. (c) Braille edition, G. Schirmer Ltd., New York, n.d. Have you forgot? (Weisst du wohl noch?) Op. 19a, romance de concert for piano. G. Schirmer Ltd., London, n.d.; The Vincent Co., London, n.d. Am Bächlein, op. 20, Concert-Studie (sic!) für das Pianoforte, composed in Port Elizabeth 1897. Charles Vincent, London, n.d.; Oliver Ditson Co., New York, n.d. Cinq piéces de salon, op. 23, Charles Vincent, London, 1900: 1. Petite valse (1897) 2. Gavotte (1896) 3. Angelus (1893) 4. Chanson sans paroles (Canterbury, 1883) 5. Caprice humoresque on the impromptu theme "O let me stay" (1894). Valse (en tierce) for piano, op. 24, composed 1896. Charles Vincent, London, n.d.; Oliver Ditson Co, New York, n.d. Cadence pour la deuxième rhapsodie Hongroise de Liszt, pour le piano, op. 24b. Charles Vincent, London, 1890; Oliver Ditson Co., New York, 1890. Fantasia on an air by Balfé "When other lips", for piano. Ms. Transcription for organ published as op. 25, Charles Vincent, London, n.d.; Oliver Ditson Co., New York, n.d. Serenade, for piano. Ms., before 1902. Sailor's dance, for organ. Ms., February 1903. Song without words, for organ. Ms., before February 1903. Ne m'oubliez pas, esquisse for piano. Ms., before December 1906. Triomphe d'amour, rhapsody for piano. Ms., before December 1906. Tout-a toi, piéce romantique for piano. Ms., before 1910. Une pensée d'amour, op. 45 no. 2, for piano. Ms., before 1912. Cantilene pastorale, concert rondo for piano. Ms., June 1916. Do you remember? for piano. Ms., 1923. I want to kiss you, intermezzo a la gavotte for orchestra. Ms., August 1927. Chanson d'amour, for piano. Ms., n.d. Concert gavotte in F, for piano. Ms., n.d. Etude in G flat, for piano. Ms., n.d. Etude on a melody by Petterson, for piano. Ms., n.d. Gavotte de concert, for piano. Ms., n.d. L'Absence, valse triste for piano. Ms., n.d. L'Antique d'amour, for piano. Ms., n.d. Love song, for piano. Ms., n.d. Night wind in the trees, concert study for piano. Ms., n.d. Passionate fantasy, for piano. Ms., n.d. Pensez a moi, romance for piano. Ms., n.d. Schlaf, Geliebter, schlaf, for piano. Ms., n.d. Song of rhapsody, for piano. Ms., n.d. Song reverie, for piano. Ms., n.d. Two pieces without titles, for piano. Ms., n.d. Une petite coquette, caprice for piano. Ms., n.d. Valse etude in E flat. Ms., n.d. Tintagel, for orchestra. Ms., n.d. Romanze ohne

Worte, for violin and piano. Ms., n.d.   Barcarolle, for violin and piano. Ms., n.d.   Interlude
to the hymn, "Lead kindly light", for organ. Ms., n.d.

B. Vocal

Album of six songs, op. 4, all composed in England. Stanley Lucas, Weber & Co., London, n.d.;
Jackson Bros., Durban, 1892:   1. Killochan (W.T. Saward), 1884.   2. Whither? (W.T.
Saward), 1884.   3. Remind me not (Byron), 1889/1890.   4. A last request (T.A.),
1888.   5. The wave (Longfellow), 1883.   6. Annabel Lee (E.A. Poe), 1886. (Has
additional parts for organ and male voice chorus).   Drei Liebeslieder, for voice and piano, op.
10 (H. Heine), composed 1890/91, G. Schirmer, London, n.d.:   1. Du bist wie eine
Blume.   2. Wenn ich in Deine Augen seh'.   3. Ich liebe Dich (first performance June
1903).   Have you forgot? Op. 19b, for voice and piano, Charles Vincent, London,
n.d.   Three songs for soprano or tenor voice, op. 21 (Byron), composed in England 1888.
Charles Vincent, London, n.d.:   1. They were alone.   2. And now 'twas done.   3. O
love.   Twelve songs, op. 22, composed in England. Charles Vincent, London, n.d.; Oliver
Ditson Co., New York, n.d.:   1. "Love me," she said (C. Barnard-Smith), 1898.   2. What is
the end of fame? (Byron), 1886.   3. When I am dead (Christina Rosetti), 1898.   4. The
day is cold (Longfellow), 1882.   5. Autumn leaves (Moore), 1894.   6. Come not when I
am dead (Tennyson), 1887.   7. In dreamland (W.T. Saward), 1884.   8. The world is too
much with us (Wordsworth), 1889.   9. When I dream that you love me (Byron),
1898.   10. Good night (Shelley), 1898.   11. Love's dream (W.T. Saward), 1885.
12. Time the tyrant   (Mary L. Pendered), 1899.   Twelve love lyrics, op. 26,
composed before 1900. The Vincent Music Co., London, c 1906; Oliver Ditson Co., New York,
n.d.; G. Schirmer, London, n.d.; G. Schirmer, New York, n.d.:   1. Love.   2. Come.   3. Pray.
4. Goodbye.   5. The request.   6. Alone.   7. To sleep.   8. Beloved.   9. If.   10. At
midnight.   11. Longing.   12. Parted.   Jack's all right, song (W.H. Paddon). Charles
Vincent, London, 1900.   The knightly host, song (W.H. Paddon), Charles Vincent, London,
1900.   . Masonic music, the Vincent Music Co., London, 1901.   The Grey, song (W. Chubb-
Meredith), first performance October 1907. Novello & Co., London, 1906.   No fear! Song for
baritone, male voice choir and orchestra (or piano) (Mary L. Pendered), first performance 1900.
Charles Vincent, London, n.d.   Sleep little child, lullaby (Ascham), Laudy & Co., London,
n.d.   The child and the flowers, song (W.T. Saward). A. Adams, Birmingham, 1885.   The
radiant morn, sacred song. Ms., before December 1900.   Because, song. Ms., before March
1903.   Homesick (G. Mathieson). Ms., before April 1903.   The rainy day. Ms., before May
1905.   The unseen master. Ms., before May 1905.   Be mine. Ms., before December
1906.   Just once. Ms., before December 1906.   Wilt thou take me for thy slave. Ms., before
December 1906.   My beloved one. Ms., before August 1908.   If I only knew. Ms., before
June 1909.   When time was naught. Ms., before June 1909.   Where art thou, for male
voice choir. Ms., before August 1912.   Silver spring, for male voice choir. Ms., before August
1912.   O love, for male voice choir. Ms., before December 1912.   When I am dead, arr. for
male voice choir. Ms., before September 1913.   I thought you once loved me, song. Ms., before
1914.   Follow, song. Ms., before 1914.   O lovely night, for male voice choir. Ms., before
February 1915.   Songs of the Dominions, arr. for soprano, tenor, mixed choir and orchestra.
Ms., before November 1915.   Mates, song (Mrs Bridgeman). Ms., November 1919.   The
song of the knights of King Arthur, composed for the festival of the 1820 Settlers, first
performed 9 and 10 April 1921.   The garden, song. Ms., before August 1927.   Sleep little
love, arr. for ladies' choir and strings. Ms., before August 1927.   I love thee. Ms., n.d.   I
love thee so. Ms., n.d.   No other. Ms., n.d.   Shrine of my heart. Ms., n.d.   O strength

and stay, sacred song. Ms., n.d.   Sleep. Ms., n.d.   National anthems of the Allies, for choir and orchestra. Ms., February 1915.   Songs of the Empire, for choir and orchestra. Ms., n.d.

C. *Transcriptions and arrangements*

Apart from the numerous pianoforte and organ arrangements that Ascham made of his own songs, he extended this art to include works by Liszt, Richard Strauss, Tchaikowsky, Moszkowski, Raff, Petterson and other lesser lights. A number of these arrangements are also housed in the Public Library at Port Elizabeth.

BIBLIOGRAPHY

TROSKIE, A.J.J.: *The musical life of Port Elizabeth, 1875-1900.* M.Mus, dissertation, UPE, 1969.   VAN DER MERWE, F.Z.: *Suid-Afrikaanse Musiekbibliografie 1787-1952.* Pretoria, Van Schaik, 1958. Bygewerk vir die RGN tot 1972 deur J. van de Graaf. Tafelberg Uitgewers, Cape Town, 1974.

SOURCES

Eastern Province Herald: 1901-1920; 1 April 1934; 18 December 1962.   *Daily Dispatch:* 18 January 1923; 22 November 1924; 19 July 1926; 8 October 1927.   *The Outspan:* 6 May 1927; 26 August 1927 (A South African organist's Thousandth Recital, by W.A. Gingell); 15 June 1934 (Roger as I knew him, by Herbert Hilton).   *The Tatler:* 30 September 1903.   TROSKIE, A.J.J.: Roger Ascham (1964-1934) - virtuoos, pedagoog en komponis. *Ars Nova* 4:2, November 1972.   Letters, programmes, cuttings, compositions and other documents in the Public Library, Port Elizabeth.   National Documentation Centre for Music, HSRC, Pretoria.
—Ed.

ASCHAM'S SYMPHONY ORCHESTRA   Port Elizabeth Amateur Choral and Orchestral Music.

ASHWORTH, ABRAHAM HARGREAVES, *10 May 1861 in Uley, Gloucestershire; °4 June 1944 in Pietersburg. Composer, choirmaster, music teacher and organist.

After two years at Borough Road College in London (1880-1881), Ashworth became assistant, and subsequently headmaster at various schools under the Leeds School Board. Concurrently, from 1891 to 1901, he was lecturer in music at Yorkshire College (later Leeds University), obtaining the Mus. Bac. degree of the University of Durham in 1898. At that time Leeds was an enthusiastic choral centre, and this is reflected in his career. He was conductor of the Leeds Musicians' Union from 1885 to 1901, choirmaster in Leeds, Saltaire and Blenheim of many prize choirs in competition events, and did a considerable amount of adjudicating of choral competitions in the North of England in 1900 and 1901. — It was one of the major disappointments of his life that the work he wanted, and for which he had been specially trained, that of inspector of vocal music in schools, was not available when he arrived in Cape Town in April 1902. He had to choose between one of two vacancies available at that time in Calitzdorp and Kimberley, and decided to accept appointment as a classteacher at the Boys' High School in Kimberley. He taught Standard 4 throughout his service there (until 1920), also giving instruction in vocal music to all classes at this school and the Girls' High School (1915-1920). Concurrently, he was Principal of the Kimberley Evening School (1905-1914). Afterwards he assisted at the Perseverance Training School (1921-1932). Ashworth's extraordinary energy in promoting the cause of music appears even from a short summary: he founded the Boys' High School Drum and Fife Band in 1902; acted as choirmaster at St Mary's Cathedral in 1902-1903, as precentor of the Baptist Union Church from 1904 to 1918, as honorary choirmaster of the Baptist Union Church from 1922 to 1936; assisted in Church Music at St Cyprian's Cathedral, the Presbyterian and Trinity Churches, St Andrew's and the Dutch Reformed Church in Beaconsfield; succeeded Frank Proudman* as honorary conductor of the Kimberley Musical Association in 1908; organised and conducted the Kimberley Amateur Orchestra (1929-1932); became the first President of the Kimberley Philharmonic Society; formed and conducted the Kimberley Male Voice Choir (1934-1936); and acted as editor of the *SA Music Teacher* in 1934. He also organised and conducted the Kimberley Junior Choral Society, conducted the Kimberley City Council Sunday evening concerts, and was instrumental in forming the Kimberley Centre of the South African Society of Music Teachers.* — Apart from all this active music-making, he wrote notes on musical subjects for the *Diamond Fields Advertiser* under the pseudonym of *Cor Anglais,* and acted as musical editor for the short-lived *Kimberley Gazette* (1904-1905). He was adjudicator of vocal music at Johannesburg, Cape Town, Pretoria, East London, Durban and Vryheid eisteddfodau, and inspector of school music in the Eastern Cape Province for the latter half of 1925. From 1902 to 1926 he acted as examiner in theory of music and tonic solfa for the Cape Department of Education, and was elected a Fellow of the Tonic Solfa College in London in 1927. He acted as examiner for the University of South Africa in 1925 and 1926. — Ashworth lived in retirement in Kimberley until within a month of his death, when he visited a daughter in Pietersburg. His wife, Louie Ashworth (née Winder), whom he had married in 1887, was an accomplished singer, pianist and organist, and taught music privately until a year before her death in 1943.

WORKS

A. Vocal

A Morning Service, for solo, choir and organ (words from the Holy Writ.). Curwen, London, n.d.   A new carol — Christ is born (Paul Gerhardt). John Rinder, Music Publisher, Leeds, n.d.   O paradise!, anthem for soprano and tenor solos and chorus (F.W. Faber). Curwen, London, n.d.   A song of England, song (C.E. Beales). Ms., n.d.   Canadian spring song, trio for SSA (J.B. Greenhough). Curwen, London, n.d.   Fill the bumper fair, for male voices. Ms., n.d.   Hail to thee, blithe spirit, part song. Ms., n.d.   Light of the world, sacred song. Ms., n.d.   Nelly was a lady, song. Curwen, London, n.d.   O, sing to me a spring song, trio for SSA (from Little Folks). Curwen, London, n.d.   Praise other lands, song. Ms., n.d.   School song, Kimberley High School (C.C. Wiles). Curwen, London, n.d.   School songs for the following schools: Darling, Indwe High School, Beaufort West School, Cradock Training College, Perseverance Training School (Kimberley), Gore Browne Native School (Kimberley), and the Windhoek Public School. Mss., n.d.   Shout! Throw your banners, trio for SSA. Curwen, London, n.d.   The house of dreams-come-true, song. Ms., n.d.   The recessional, four-part song (Rudyard Kipling). Gestetner duplication, n.d.   The shark, duet for SA (Laura E. Richards). Curwen, London, n.d.   Love's old story, song. Leadbeater & Co., Manchester, 1882.   A song of war, glee for four male voices (John Rinder). Leeds Century Music Press, Farnley, 1889.   The blue-bottle's fate, four-part song. Novello, Ewer & Co., London, 1892.   A Canadian boat-song, trio for SSA (T. Moore). Novello, Ewer & Co., London, 1893.   A song of evening, trio for SSA (Margaret Scott Haycroft). Novello, Ewer & Co., London, 1897.   Jubilate Deo (Mus. Bac. exercise). Ms., 1898.   The song of dawn, madrigal. Ms., 1901.   The brook is rippling merrily, trio for SSA (F. Valdemar). Novello and Co., London, 1902.   A hymn of Union, anthem composed for Union Day, 1910 (L.M. Hastings).

Spark and Sons, Leeds, n.d.   Die Stem van Suid-Afrika, part song. Ms., 1910.   Beatty's squadron, song (C.C. Wiles). Ms., 1916.   Pack clouds away, four-part song. Gold medal diploma, Cape Town Eisteddfod, 1925. Ms., n.d.   Weep you no more, sad fountains, four-part song. First prize, Johannesburg Eisteddfod, 1926. Ms., n.d.   The Merchant of Tarposh, opera (libretto, C.E. Beales). Ms., n.d.

B. *Instrumental*
Twelve hymn tunes. Printed by Erith, n.d.: 1. Gleaming in the sunshine 2. Gwyn 3. Consolation 4. Gentle Shepherd 5. Rest 6. Victory 7. Thornville 8. Sunny days of childhood 9. Ev'ry morning as we rise 10. Blenheim 11. Sing Hallelujah 12. Summer flowers.   Intermezzo, for oboe and orchestra. Ms., n.d.   A medley march. Ms., n.d. Melody elegie. Ms., n.d.   Rose-Mary, chansonette for oboe and small orchestra. Ms., n.d. Banquet music, for the Sons of England Society. Ms., n.d.   Short overture on Baa Baa Black Sheep. Ms., n.d.

BIBLIOGRAPHY
VAN DER MERWE, F.Z.: *Suid-Afrikaanse musiekbibliografie, 1787-1952.* J.L. van Schaik Ltd, Pretoria, 1958.

SOURCES
Chats with Yorkshire singers. *Yorkshire Musical Record,* August, 1899 (article on Mrs Ashworth).   *Zoutpansberg Review:* Obituary notice.   *Griqualand West Who's Who. Diamond Fields Advertiser,* 28 January, 1931.   *Diamond Fields Advertiser:* Obituary notice.   Abraham Hargreaves Ashworth. *South African Music Teacher,* 16 April 1939.   Autobiographical notes compiled by the late A.H. Ashworth, in the possession of his son, H.G. Ashworth.   Manuscripts housed in the library of the South African Broadcasting Corporation.   Published compositions and manuscripts in the possession of his son, H.G. Ashworth.   Published compositions and manuscripts housed in the Public Library, Kimberley.

—H.G.A.

ASHWORTH, ALEXANDER HARGREAVES (ALEX), *24 July 1895 in Leeds, Yorkshire; °20 December 1959 in Leeds. A versatile musician who enjoyed a considerable reputation in England as music critic, composer and authority on modern choral music. He was a son of Abraham Hargreaves Ashworth.*

His father had preceded his family of seven children, who followed him to South Africa a little more than a year later, in July 1903. Alec was educated at the Boys' High School in Kimberley, where his father was a teacher. On account of his growing preoccupation with music, he failed to obtain the BA Degree at the South African College (now UCT), but eventually graduated after war service in 1916 and entered the Cape Education Department as a clerk. Prof. W.H. Bell* saw some of his compositions and used his influence to admit Ashworth in 1918 to the South African College of Music,* where he studied under Bell's guidance for one year, at the end of which he was awarded the gold medal of the Cape Town City Council both for his talent and for his activities in furthering the cause of music among his fellow students. Prof. Bell typically extended his favour to obtain Ashworth an appointment as student-assistant to lecture on harmony, counterpoint and musical history, and to assist in the administrative work of the college. On the strength of this appointment, Alec continued his studies for a further period of two years to become a licentiate of the college and the possessor of a Cape Music Teacher's Diploma. —He was then appointed master of instrumental music at the Boys' High School in Kimberley, but resigned in 1922 for further study at the RCM. He obtained the Associateship of the Royal College in 1923. The following year Alec was appointed on the staff of the *Yorkshire Post* as assistant librarian, in due course becoming a reporter and eventually the deputy to the music critic, Herbert Thompson. When the latter retired in 1936, Ashworth succeeded him as music critic and became known for his fearless appreciations of then little-known composers. He returned to the educational field in 1941, however, to become lecturer on music and painting to H.M. Forces and eventually music master at Leeds and Barnsley Grammar Schools. — During the last years of his active life, he was lecturer in Music at a Teachers' Training College in Staffordshire. On retirement, he settled in Leeds, his place of birth. — Apart from his work as a journalist, Alex Ashworth was a contributor to English musical periodicals and wrote the programme notes for the Northern Philharmonic Orchestra. His chief work is a thesis on *Modern Choral Music,* which won a Music and Letters Prize in 1940. At the time of his death he was engaged in writing a text book on school music. Because of his specialised knowledge, he was invited to write an article on modern choral music for the 5th Edition of *Grove's Dictionary of Music and Musicians* (1954). On the practical side, he was a pianist and accompanied his wife, who was a singer, but he also gave individual recitals and lecture recitals. — His compositions include several settings of Afrikaans poems. His works have a poetic quality of their own; according to *Grove's Dictionary,* they slightly exhibit the influence of Delius. Unfortunately little of his music was published, and much manuscript material has been lost. Alex Ashworth was also the author of some serious verse and satire. In the following list of works the dates reflect the year of composition and the years in which works were improved upon or recast in manuscript unless stated otherwise.

WORKS

A. Vocal

Songs

A dirge (Shelley), 1914   Mother (McQueen), 1917   Thou tender flower (Cowling), 1918 Sea weed (Hull), 1920   Songs of the East Riding (Cowling), written between 1920-1940: 1. Morning song 2. Love song 3. Spring 4. Elegy 5. Sunday 6. Thou tender flower 7. Beauty or brass 8. A toddling bairn 9. The witch 10. A nattering wife 11. When skies are blue. Clouds (Hull), 1920   In Fountain Court (Symons), 1920   The Salley Gardens (Yeats), 1920, 1947   'n Kinderlied (A.D. Keet), 1921/3 1923   Adoratio (A.D. Keet), 1921, 1937, 1950/1/2   'n Lied van die see (A.D. Keet), 1921/2, 1923, 1947/53   Sonnedaal (A.D. Keet), 1921, 1947   Dis al (Jan F.E. Celliers), 1922, 1935/40, 1950/51   Lente (J.F. Celliers), 1922, 1951/52   Klaas vakie (Trad.). Nasionale Pers, 1923   An epitaph (de la Mare), 1923, 1933   Five kiddy songs (A. Ashworth), 1929   Bunches of grapes (de la Mare), 1931, 1933   Stay, thou art (Freeman), 1932   She comes not when (French), 1932   The cloud (A. Ashworth), 1932   Old Shellover (de la Mare), 1933   Meeting at night (Browning), 1933, 1935   Just as the tide (Trad.), 1933   Kaffir lullaby (Slater), 1933   Prologue and epilogue (Yeats), 1933   My delight (Bridges), 1934/39, 1940   When death (Bridges), 1934, 1936   My spirit kisseth thine (Bridges), 1934, 1936   I love all beauteous things (Bridges), 1934, 1940   Spring snow (Bridges), 1934   A widow bird (Shelley), 1934, 1952 Five nursery songs (Trans.). Nasionale Pers, 1934   Sleep comes (A. Ashworth), 1935 A Chinese screen (H. Waddell), 1936/37   Twenty towers (Childe), 1938   Garry fairies (Mitchison), 1938   These remain (Coleridge), 1938, 1948   The wind in a frolic (Howitt),

1938   Serenade in the French style (A. Ashworth), 1938   The sea poppy (Bridges), 1940 Alice in Wonderland (Carroll), 1940   The minstrel (Watson), 1948   The ballad of Semmerwater (Watson), 1948   Cakes and ale (Anon.), 1948   Vlindertjies (A.D. Keet), 1950/51/52   Die ossewa (J.F.E. Celliers), 1950, 1952   Na Dingaansdag (C. Louis Leipoldt), 1950, 1952   Winternag (E. Marais), 1950, 1952   Bruilof (J.R.L. van Bruggen), 1950, 1952   Dit moet iets wonderbaarliks wees (German, trans. into Afrikaans)   Fairy song (Yeats)

Choral

Seven choral songs for mixed voices, 1930/35:   1. Nattering wives (Cowling) 2. The witch (Cowling) 3. Fiddle-cum-Fee (Trad.) 4. Milking time (Dixon) 5. Song of the Yorkshire dales (Moorman), also in 1939   6. The thorn bush (Cowling)   7. Sunday morning (Cowling). Songs for male voices: 1. Lente (Celliers), 1922.   2. Sea shanties (Trad.), 1944 3. Cakes and ale (Anon.), 1948 4. Nattering wives (Cowling), 1949 5. A song of Finland (Palmroth), 1949 6. Ballad of Semmerwater (Watson), 1949 7. A twisted tale (Anon.), 1949 8. I was a child (Anon.), 1949 9. Winternag (E. Marais).   Songs for female or treble voices: 1. Clouds (Hull), 1919 2. In Fountain Court (Symons), 1919 3. The discontented hen (A. Ashworth), 1932 4. The cloud (A. Ashworth), 1934, 1936 5. Four rounds (Trad.), 1938, 1956 6. The owl (Tennyson), 1938, 1956 7. Bells of London town (A. Ashworth), 1946 8. Bunches of grapes 9. The witch 10. Old Shellover 11. Nocturne (Shelley)   Three unison songs for trebles

Church music:

1. Collect for peace, 1920, 1938, 1941 2. Prayer for peace, 1941 3. Cleveland patrol, 1942 4. Te Deum laudamus, unison with organ, 1944 5. Psalm CL by Stanford, arr. for unison with descant.

B. Instrumental

Two lyric pieces, for orchestra, 1919   Sketches, for piano, 1921   Kaffiresques, for piano, 1922   Kaffiresques, for piano duet, 1922   Rhapsody on Kaffir themes, for violin and piano, 1922   Six South African airs, for piano, 1923, 1948   Kaffir suite, for piano, 1923 Movement (incomplete), for piano, 1923   Scherzo, for piano, 1924   Sonata, for viola and piano, 1930   Night music (twosome, pause, company), for orchestra, 1931   Lyric movement, for viola, 1935   Elegy, for orchestra, 1936   Intermezzo, for violin and cello, 1936 October woods, for orchestra, 1936   Four nocturnes, for orchestra, 1937   Night music (nocturne, intermezzo, finale), for piano duet, 1940, 1946   25 variations, for cello and piano, 1943   Incidental music for Dear Brutus, Macbeth and the pantomine Two St Georges and the Dragon, for orchestra, 1944   South African sketchbook (15 pieces), for piano, 1947/52 Etude in B minor, for piano, 1947, 1952   In a boat, for piano, 1947   17 pieces for young players, for piano, 1947, 1952   Nocturne (In a fountain court), for piano, 1948   Nocturne (sea dreams), for piano, 1948   Kaffir dances, for piano duet, 1948   Solemn war dance, for piano duet, 1948 In the mealie fields, for piano duet, 1948   Zulus, for piano duet, 1948   In the mealie fields, for piano duet, 1948   Little Bantu suite, for orchestra, 1948, 1950   Study (thumb tune), for piano, 1949   Bantu music (5 pieces), for piano duet, 1949   Barcarolle, for piano, 1950   Bobijaan (sic!) klim die berg (variations), for piano, 1951   One and five study for piano, 1951 - Slow foxtrot for piano, 1954   25 preludes for piano, 1954   Sonata, for flute and piano, 1954 Nine easy pieces, for piano duet, 1956, 1957   Six more advanced pieces, 1956/57   11 little studies in canon, for piano, 1958   Cosy cat, for piano, 1958   Okkerneutjies, for piano, 1958 The lonely moor, for piano, 1959   The bird guest, for piano, 1959   Monkey business (a sonatina), for piano, 1959   Four pieces of moderate difficulty, for piano duet   Four Kaffiresques, for discant recorder or flute and violin   Songs of the East Riding, for orchestra

Two light pieces (andantino and scherzo), for orchestra   Divertimento (overture, nocturne, intermezzo), for orchestra   Bantu suite, for orchestra

BIBLIOGRAPHY

BLOM, ERIC: *Grove's Dictionary of Music and Musicians.* London, 1954.
VAN DER MERWE, F.Z.: *Suid-Afrikaanse musiekbibliografie, 1787-1952.* Van Schaik, Pretoria, 1958.

SOURCES

BOUWS, JAN: *Die Burger,* 27 February 1970.   *Diamond Fields Advertiser,* 12 September 1927. Original manuscripts and records, University of Cape Town Library.

—H.G.A.

ASHWORTH, LOUIE (MRS)   Abraham H. Ashworth, L. Skirving

ATHENAEUM MUSICAL AND CHORAL SOCIETY   G.G. Dunsterville, Graaff Reinet 2, 3, Port Elizabeth I/2, Port Elizabeth Amateur Choral and Orchestral Music, P. Reece.

ATHENAEUM THEATRE, CAPE TOWN   Charles du Val.

ATHLONE CULTURAL CENTRE   EOAN Group.

ATKINSON, J.   Graaff Reinet 2, 6.

AVRICH, DOROTHY,   *in De Aar; at present in Durban. Soprano.
Her musical and dramatic talents were first discovered in Cape Town by Dr William Pickerill,* conductor of the Cape Town Municipal Orchestra.* When she and her husband moved to Durban in 1951 she began training seriously under Madame Xenia Belmas.* Her first stage appearance in Durban was in *Rio Rita.* Over the years she has appeared in a number of musicals and in two one-act operas by Menotti: *The telephone* and *The medium.* Between 1960 and 1964 she took part in the Durban and Pretoria productions of the Durban Opera Company (Olympia in *Tales of Hoffman* and Susanna in *The marriage of Figaro*). In the latter role she achieved her greatest success as an operatic soprano.   —Dorothy Avrich has sung with the orchestras of Cape Town, Johannesburg and Durban, has given song recitals and has broadcast from the SABC in Durban and Johannesburg. In recent years she has produced concerts and plays for charity and *The pirates of Penzance* (1970) and *The gondoliers* (1971) for Olive Peel's Durban Opera Company.

—G.S.J.

AYLING, JOAN (MRS QUAYLE)   Leo G. Quayle

BACHELOR GIRLS   Durban 7,   Durban Amateur Operatic Society, John Whitcutt.

BAHLSEN, PAUL   Windhoek 3

BAIER, S (BAUER, BEYER)   Organs 1 (v)

BAILEY, NORMAN STANLEY,   *23 March 1933 in Birmingham; at present in London. Baritone.
Norman Bailey's parents immigrated to South Africa when he was a child. He received his schooling at the Boksburg High School and the Prince Edward School, Salisbury. In music, he was educated at Rhodes University, where he obtained the B.Mus. degree and diplomas for teaching and performance in 1955. He taught singing at Rhodes in 1956, and a year later became music teacher at Highlands School, Salisbury. In 1958 he

resigned to study at the Vienna State Academy, where he passed courses in Voice Production, Lieder, Oratorio and Opera with distinction. —His operatic career commenced at the Linzer Landestheater, where he was engaged as Italian baritone during 1960-1963. This was followed by a year at the Wupperthal Stadttheater, Germany, which he left for an appointment at the Deutsche Oper am Rhein, Düsseldorf (1964-1967). —During the period 1964-1969 he sang in guest performances in La Scala, Covent Garden, the Bayreuther Festspiele and the state operas of Hamburg, Munich and Stuttgart. He was engaged by Saddler's Wells till 1971 and then decided to launch out on his own as an operatic and concert singer. Since then he has sung in the State Opera of Vienna, in the Metropolitan, in Paris, at the Edinburgh Festival and has studied the baritone parts in most of the Wagner music dramas for performances in Bayreuth and elsewhere. He has also sung for recordings made of *Meistersinger, Walküre* and *Fliegende Holländer*. For BBC Television he has had parts in *Falstaff, La traviata* and *The flying Dutchman*. Apart from his opera engagements Norman Bailey is also active as a Lieder singer and has taken part in oratorio performances.

—Ed.

BAIN, A.G. Grahamstown 3

BAKER, T. J. Uys

BAKER, W.H. Port Elizabeth I/2, Port Elizabeth Amateur Choral and Orchestral Music

BALDWIN-TANN, W.R. Bloemfontein, King William's Town 9

BALFOORT, DIRK. *1 January 1858 in Utrecht; °24 January 1921 in The Hague. Conductor, composer and surveyor.

Balfoort was trained as surveyor in the Utrecht surveyor's office, but he had no significant training in music at all. Nevertheless, he began composing at an early age. He married Elizabeth Joanna van't Hul (1859-1945) in Nijmegen in 1883. From this marriage three children were born of whom Dirk Jacobus* (19.7.1886, Utrecht - 11.11.1964, The Hague) became a well-known violinist, conductor and an Assistant Director of the Scheurleer Collection in The Hague. — Dirk Balfoort (sen.) came to Pretoria with his family in 1890 as bookkeeper of De Volksstem Company. Later on he also wrote reviews on music and theatrical performances for his employers. Shortly after his arrival, Balfoort became an integral part of the musical life of Pretoria. On 15 October 1892, for example, he was a soloist in Haydn's *De Seisoene,* and in the same year played a role in Pauschel's comic operetta *Der goldene Hochzeitsmorgen.* His wife, who was a singer, also took part in the operetta. As producer and later conductor of the Rederijkerskamer Onze Taal* and as conductor of the Hollandsch Mannenkoor,* Balfoort made significant contributions to the musical and theatrical life of the Afrikaans-Dutch community in Republican Pretoria by having the works of contemporary Dutch and English composers performed, and by appearing as a singer at the soirées of the Rederijkerskamer. In 1897, and again in 1898 his musical setting of W.J. van Zeggelen's poem *De Haringvisschers,* in the form of a cantata for solo voices, male choir and orchestra, was performed in the city. — Balfoort and his family left the Republic on April 16, 1899 for Belgium where he became bookkeeper to the SA Republican Legation in Brussels. On his departure from the Pretoria railway station the Hollandsch Mannenkoor sang two of his compositions, *Mijne Moedertaal* and *De Banierzang* and presented him with a memorial album. After the Peace of Vereeniging the family moved back to the Netherlands. Balfoort had his own *Het Prinzesje* performed in The Hague and acted as producer to the amateur Vereeniging Toynbee. Evidence of his later career is scant.

WORKS

Vooruit, op. 10, march, dedicated to the "Algemeene Utrechtse Ijsklub Vooruit". Appears in the publication *Weekelijksche Piano Muziek*, no. 253. Johan de Liefde, Utrecht. Onze Taal, op. 17, club song (H.J.L. Th. Roorda), G.J.G.W. Maas, Utrecht, 1893. Amajoeba-feestlied, mentioned on Amajuba Day program, Feb. 1894. De Haringvisschers, op. 27, cantata (W.J. van Zeggelen). Ms., 1897. Liever dood dan onderworpen, song "made by a Transvaal couple for the benefit of the women's camps in South Africa". H. ten Hoet, Nijmegen, 1901. Ontboezeming van oud-Nederlanders in Transvaal, song. Algemeene Transvaalsche Boekhandel, Pretoria, Sept. 1898. Heilgroet aan Haare Majesteit Koningin Wilhelmina, song. Pretoria, Sept. 1898. Blijf een. Ms., n.d. Van Hollandsch vlag. Ms., n.d. Der Goldschmied. Ms., n.d. Mooi Aafje, song from De Haringvisschers. Ms., n.d. Lentelied. Ms., n.d. Mijn land is 'n land der zee. Ms., n.d. An die Musik. Ms., n.d. Het vaderland. Hollands-Afrikaanse Liederbundel (N. Mansveldt) pp. 24-25, 1907. De poppenfee. Ms., n.d. Mijne moedertaal. Ms., n.d. Het prinzesje Cilie, operetta. Ms., n.d. Banierzang, Hollandsch Mannenkoor, 1898. Only the words have been preserved. With the exception of De Haringvisschers, Heilgroet and the last two items, all the works have been presented to the Africana Museum in Johannesburg for preservation, by D.J. Balfoort Jnr.

BIBLIOGRAPHY

Standard encyclopaedia of Southern Africa, Vol. 2. Nasau Ltd., 1970. VAN DER MERWE, F.Z.: *Suid-Afrikaanse musiekbibliografie, 1787-1952.* J.L. van Schaik, Pretoria, 1958. VERMEULEN, ELIZABETH: *Die musieklewe van Pretoria tussen 1902 en 1926.* M.Mus. dissertation, UP, 1967.

SOURCES

BOUWS, JAN: Dirk Balfoort, 'n belangrike musiekbeoefenaar uit die laaste jare van die Zuid-Afrikaansche Republiek. *Historia* II/2, September 1957, Pretoria. BOUWS, JAN: Het muziekleven in Pretoria in die jaren van Krugers Hollanders. *Mens en Melodie* XIV/9, Sept. 1959. Maerten Spies Collection, State Archives, Pretoria. PLOEGER, JAN: Die klub- of bondslied van die Pretoriase rederykerskamer, Onze Taal. *Res Musicae*, Pretoria, June 1962. PLOEGER, JAN: D. Balfoort en sy Banierzang. *Res Musica* IX/1, Dec. 1962. PLOEGER, JAN: Herinneringe aan Dirk Balfoort en sy verblyf in die Transvaalse hoofstad, 1890-1899. *Lantern*, Pretoria, Dec. 1962. PLOEGER, JAN: Die Balfoort-skenking. *Africana: Aantekeninge en Nuus*, Johannesburg, March 1963. PLOEGER, JAN: Dirk J. Balfoort en die nuwe toevoeging aan die Balfoort-versameling. *Africana: Aantekeninge en Nuus,* Johannesburg, March 1964.

—J.P.

BALFOORT, DIRK JACOBUS, *19 July 1886 in Utrecht, the Netherlands; °11 November 1964 in The Hague, the Netherlands. Violinist, conductor, curator of the history of music section of the Gemeente Museum in The Hague.

Dirk Balfoort came to Pretoria with his parents at the age of three. His father played an important role in the theatrical and musical life of the Transvaal capital and Dirk at the age of nine began taking violin instruction under E. Amorison. Later he studied under M. de Groot, music and singing teacher at the Staatsmodelschool, and had the honour of being presented with a violin by Dr W.J. Leyds before Leyds's departure for Europe (1899). In April the same year the family moved to Brussels, where Balfoort's father was appointed to the South African Republic's legation, but his musical instruction was continued in Holland only after the Anglo-Boer War. In 1906 he was awarded a diploma by the Amsterdam conservatoire. After that he was associated with the Residentie Orchestra in The Hague and various other orchestras, including The Dresden Philharmonic Orchestra in Germany. After a period in Lübeck, he returned to Holland, became leader of the National Opera Orchestra, and was appointed lecturer at the Rotterdam conservatoire. From 1927 he was assistant curator of the music collection of Dr D.F. Scheurleer. When The Hague bought the collection in 1953 after Scheurleer's death, Balfoort became curator of the Gemeentemuseum in The Hague; simultaneously he served as vice-director of municipal services with regard to the fine arts. — In 1962 he donated his father's manuscripts and published compositions to the Africana Museum in Johannesburg. The memorial album which his father had received on his departure from Pretoria in 1889 was later added to this collection.

BIBLIOGRAPHY
BALFOORT, D.J.: De múziekhistorische afdeling onder dr H.E. van Gelder. Mededelingen Gemeentemuseum van Den Haag II/1, Den Haag 1956.   CHARBON, M.H.: Daniël François Scheurleer, stichter van het Muziekmuseum Scheurleer. Mededelingen Gemeentemuseum van den Haag X/2, Den Haag, 1955.   LIEVENSE, W.: Dirk J. Balfoort en zijn Museum-Kamerorkest en Museum- Kamerkoor nemen afscheid. Den Haag, 1963.
SOURCES
BOUWS, JAN: Dirk Balfoort, 'n belangrike musiekbeoefenaar uit die laaste jare van die Zuid-Afrikaanse Republiek. Historia II/2, Pretoria, September 1957.   PLOEGER, JAN: Die Balfoort-skenking. Africana: Aantekeninge en Nuus XV/5, Johannesburg, March 1963.   PLOEGER, JAN: Dirk J. Balfoort en die nuwe toevoeging aan die Balfoortversameling. Africana: Aantekeninge en Nuus XVI/1, Johannesburg, March 1964.

—J.P.

BALL, G.H.   King William's Town 9, Queenstown 2

BALLANTINE, CHRISTOPHER JOHN, *30 August 1942 in Johannesburg; at present in Durban. Musicologist and son of Ronald White Ballantine.*

After pianoforte training under Brigitte Wild and Philip Levy,* Ballantine entered the University of the Witwatersrand in 1962, obtained the degree of B.Mus. Hons. in December 1965, and was awarded the Julius Robinson Music Scholarship. During 1966 he was music critic to The Star, but relinquished this position in October, on receiving an ad hoc post-graduate scholarship from the University of the Witwatersrand.   —Ballantine continued his studies at Cambridge University (St John's College), where he undertook research concerning the 20th century symphony, and earned an M.Litt. degree (Cantab) in 1969. He has also had some success as a choral conductor. Since 1973 he had been lecturer in the Music Department of the University of Natal and in 1974 he became professor and head of the department.

PUBLICATIONS
Music and society: the forgotten relationship. University of Natal Press, Durban, 1975. Towards a theory of the modern symphony: an historical approach. Denis Dobson Ltd., London, 1977.

CONTRIBUTIONS
Contributions to music periodicals: The symphony in the twentieth century: some aspects of its tradition and innovation. *Music Review* 32/3, August 1971.   Beethoven and the Hegelian tradition. *Music Review* 33/1, Febr. 1972.   The polyrhythmic foundation of Tswana pipe melody. *African Music* 3/4, 1965.   How musical is man? *African Music* 5/3, 1974.   Towards an aesthetic of experimental music. *Musical Quarterly* LXIII, 1977.

—Ed.

BALLANTINE, RONALD WHITE, *8 February 1909, in Keiskama Hoek; at present in Johannesburg. Chemical engineer, pharmacist, amateur orchestral musician.

Ronald Ballantine had pianoforte, violin and trombone tuition during his childhood and at the age of eighteen years joined a dance band, playing both violin and trombone (1927-1933). Whilst studying at the University of the Witwatersrand for the M.Sc.Eng. (Chem.) Degree and the Pharmaceutical Diploma, he played trombone in the University Orchestra (1933-1936) and became Chairman of the Witwatersrand University Music Society in 1935. He was also a founder member and trombonist of the Johannesburg Symphony Orchestra,* served on the Orchestra's committee between 1948 and 1955 and in 1956 became its Chairman, a position he held until 1974. He is the father of Christopher John Ballantine.*

—Ed.

BALLET (UNTIL 1963)

I. *BALLET IN THE TRANSVAAL*

II. *CAPE TOWN*

III. *GREEK DANCING IN SOUTH AFRICA*

IV. *SPANISH DANCING IN SOUTH AFRICA*

V. *SOUTH AFRICAN DANCING TIMES*

I. *BALLET IN THE TRANSVAAL*
1. Early history
2. Establishment of the AOD and Cecchetti Society
3. Establishment of the South African Dancing Teachers' Association (SADTA)
4. Performances
5. Demonstrations and presentations of ballet
6. Anna Pavlova and professional ballet
7. Institution of ballet examinations and the development of the art
8. Attempts to establish a ballet club
9. Developments during the War years
10. Ballet Theatre
11. Difficult years
12. Establishment of the Johannesburg City Ballet

1. Early history
Ballet took root in the Transvaal in the nineteen-twenties, when Edouard Espinosa introduced the ballet syllabus of the British Association of Operatic Dancing (AOD). Before this there was dancing and teaching, but no progressive, planned system of tuition. The first known dancing teacher was Lilian Baylis,* who later founded the Old Vic and Sadler's Wells Companies in London. She arrived with her parents in Johannesburg in 1891. They opened a music school, formed a women's orchestra and began to give dancing lessons that probably included more than coaching in ballroom

dancing. In the same year Charles Rodney ("Uncle Charlie") added tuition in dancing to his many other activities, although in this case it was probably social dancing. His two daughters, Eileen and Kathleen, later became well-known ballet teachers in Durban. — Miss Finch-Weedon settled in Johannesburg after the Anglo-Boer War and began to give lessons in the old Wanderers' Club. Her production of *The living bridge* (a danced game of bridge) and other works caused a sensation at the time. She and her pupils also successfully produced *The four seasons;* later, Pearl Adler danced the part of Mother Nature, and the noted singer Ethel Mann had the part of Spring. When Mrs Finch-Weedon left, "Professor" West and his wife took over her studio. At that time parents were still prejudiced against ballet, holding it to be an unbecoming exercise for young girls, especially when practised in public. They preferred lessons to be conducted in their homes, and one understands why West emphasized that his wife would be present at all lessons. Miss Walter-Williams who taught in Johannesburg from 1909, gave her lessons in the stately homes of well-off citizens, where her charges met for lessons under the personal supervision of their mothers. Ballet lessons in such circumstances easily became social events. They were so profitable, however, that more studios soon appeared. — Flora Fairbairn came to Johannesburg in 1911. She had had a reasonable training in dancing in England, and was able to exert a considerable and positive influence on ballet in Johannesburg. During the First World War she arranged patriotic street processions, tableaux and dancing performances, for charity and war funds. She and Poppins Salomon were among the first teachers to give lessons in Pretoria. In addition to Miss Fairbairn, Elsa Dieseldorff came to Johannesburg before the War, and gave lessons in Corona Lodge, Hillbrow, later to become the headquarters of the Johannesburg City Ballet.* Other personalities of the time were Violet Kirby and Madge Mann. Miss Mann had achieved a sound reputation as a dancer in England, and in Johannesburg she rapidly became a popular teacher. She made arrangements with the management of the Carlton Hotel to conduct her classes on Saturday mornings in the hotel ballroom. The children occupied the dance floor next to long rows of chairs which had to serve as barres, while their mothers sat round at tables sipping tea. Under such circumstances her classes deteriorated into lessons in "fancy dancing". —There was no real possibility of serious training, because of parental attitudes and teachers' limited resources. However, there was sufficient enthusiasm for African Consolidated Theatres to appoint a permanent ballet instructress to their staff in 1915. The choice fell on Vivien Tailleur,* who settled in Johannesburg after her marriage. She was to occupy the position for nearly 20 years. Her career had begun when she was still young; she had undertaken world tours with the Diaghileff Company, and received lessons from Maestro Cecchetti, then ballet master of the company. Her first production in her new position was *The children's hour* (music: Delibes), which was successfully performed in Johannesburg, as well as in Pretoria. She was, moreover, responsible for the choreography of ACT's pantomines, which were presented every Christmas. Initially, she danced the leading roles herself. Her contract permitted her to take private pupils, who then naturally appeared in ACT's productions. — Just before and during the First World War, Miss Brito gave lessons in Spanish dancing in both cities. It was an exciting new form of dancing for girls, but did not become generally popular at the time. In Pretoria there were fairly regular ballet performances at the Opera House.* Miss Jessie Collier presented *True love in fairyland* (story: Walter Cranch) at the Opera House in 1916, with Gladys Haupt in the lead. —The long association of

Señor Edouard Espinosa and his sister, Ray, with South African ballet began towards the end of 1917. The children of famed dancers, they had toured the world with their parents. Señor Espinosa was the author of a manual on systematic ballet-teaching, in which he had used the French terms. During his visit to South Africa his book was widely read, and came increasingly to be used by local teachers. He had been contracted by ACT to undertake a Union-wide concert tour. In Johannesburg he chose Ettie Landau, Olive Hanley and the two Salomon sisters to appear with him and his sister, Ray, in their variety programme. After the première at the Empire Theatre, they visited all the major centres, presenting what was, in effect, a kind of ballet-revue. — After the tour, Espinosa left for Australia, but Ray remained in Johannesburg, opening a ballet school, in which she gave lessons as Mme Ravodna.* Marjorie Sturman* of Pretoria joined her, and opened a branch of the school in Pretoria. She was thus the first teacher to introduce the Espinosa method to Pretoria, and consistently to use the French terminology in the Capital. — A considerable number of teachers had opened studios in Pretoria and Johannesburg by the early nineteen-twenties. In addition to those already mentioned, there were Pearl Adler, Sunbeam List, Betty Brooke, Curly Clarke, Isoline Frames, Nelly McClaren, Dulcie Bailley and Miss Moorcroft-Lamb. "Dancing Displays" were the order of the day, many of them being organised in aid of War funds or charity. Pupils of the different studios took part in performances, which always had a high percentage of youthful participants. For example, in 1919 the "Lilliputians" made their appearance. This was a group of dancers that appeared fairly regularly and successfully: the youngest was Peachy Esson, aged four, who could already execute toe dancing. The well-known Poppy Frames* made her debut in this group. A typical programme of those days contained a wide variety of items, loosely connected. For example, Tromp van Diggelen would give a demonstration of muscle power, Peachy Esson would arouse great excitement with her toe dancing, and Poppy Frames would create a deep impression with her interpretation of Pavlova's famous creation, *The dying swan.*

2. Establishment of the AOD and the Cecchetti Society

During the twenties the fame of Serge Diaghileff's Ballet Russe spread throughout the western world, and great dancers such as Nijinski, Pavlova, Karsovina and others, became household names. As elsewhere, this led to the revival of the art of ballet in England. — In London in 1920 Edouard Espinosa established the Association of Operating Dancing of Great Britain (AOD), with representatives from all the important ballet schools - such as Karsovina (Russian), Germani (Italian), Adeline Genèe (Danish), Phyllis Bedells (English) and Espinosa (French) - on the executive. In 1935 the AOD became the Royal Academy of Dancing (RAD), which was to play a decisive role in the development of ballet in England, and, because of our close connection with London, in South Africa. Marjorie Sturman set the example, and more and more teachers began to teach according to the AOD manual. In the beginning, Espinosa himself came annually to South Africa to examine the pupils. Consequently, the influence of the AOD rapidly gained ground. In a couple of years representatives had to be appointed in Johannesburg, Pretoria, Cape Town and other smaller centres. — In 1920, the year that the AOD was formed, Cyril de Beaumont established the Cecchetti Society in London. A number of the maestro's pupils, such as Margaret Craske, Molly Lake, Marie Rambert, Derra de Moroda and others, associated themselves with this society from its inception. The purpose was to systematize

Cecchetti's methods, and to make them known throughout the world. Cecchetti himself accepted the chairmanship of the society. It soon became known in England, and was to play an important part in South African ballet.

3. Establishment of the South African Dancing Teachers' Association (SADTA)

These developments in England soon created the need for a similar fusion of interests in South Africa. Miss Moorcroft-Lamb and Mrs Alice Grant-Smith returned from a visit to England inspired by the tremendous developments they had observed, and called a meeting of interested people and the press to discuss the establishment of a Dancing Teachers' Association. They then decided to call a larger, more representative meeting - a decision that received some impetus in March 1923, from the visit to Johannesburg of Helen Webb's* ballet company. At an informal welcoming party for Helen Webb, it was decided to hold a meeting on 8 March 1923, at Berkeley Rooms. At this meeting Madge Mann was elected chairman, E. Ramsey honorary secretary, Mme Ravodna treasurer, and Pearl Adler as additional member. Twenty-nine teachers attended the meeting. The aims of the association were set out as follows: a. to standardise ballet teaching;   b. to create teaching facilities and to set examinations for aspirant teachers in South Africa;   c. to associate all South African teachers under SADTA;   d. to provide information about tuition to prospective pupils;   e. to fix tuition fees;   f. to promote the interests of dancing and co-operation among teachers.   — This organisation was to become a powerful motive force in the Transvaal, which already had the greatest concentration of teachers and pupils in the country. By the end of 1924 there were 41 members, and at a meeting on 5 May of the following year Pearl Adler pleaded for the first time for something that would be frequently and repeatedly discussed: State recognition of ballet teachers.   — One of the first steps was the introduction of ballet at the Cambrian Society's annual Eisteddfod in Johannesburg. As a result of the endeavours, mainly of Flora Fairbairn, ballet appeared on the programme of the 1923 Eisteddfod. There were four divisions: point dancing, classical dancing, national dancing and character dancing; and 127 entries, mainly for national dancing, were received. Curly Clarke, who then lived in Hammanskraal, adjudicated. Because the male executive of the Cambrian Society did not feel itself qualified to manage this section of the Eisteddfod, Gwen Evans took it over. She was still carrying on the work some forty years later, having presided over a phenomenal growth. Other opportunities for ballet pupils were to come later, but the Eisteddfod was the one permanent institution, and remained the most important annual event for ballet. Competition between dancers and between teachers was keen. In the course of time bursaries for the most talented participants came to be awarded; the list of winners contains the names of several dancers who subsequently achieved fame as professionals.

4. Performances

Ballet performances in Johannesburg and Pretoria during the twenties were very important, functioning as window displays for work being done in the studios. They were usually held in aid of some charity, and were well supported by parents and prominent personalities in the community. Programmes included a great variety of dance forms, from jazz to toe dancing. Some of the performances reached a high standard, with the names of subsequently well-known artists appearing on the programmes.

5. Demonstrations and presentations of ballet

On 18 October 1924, at the Grand National Hotel in Johannesburg, there was a demonstration of the work required of pupils following the British AOD syllabus. Fifteen teachers were present. The demonstration was given by Olive Hearndley, an official of the Association, who was on a visit to South Africa. — However, the AOD was not the only body to display such positive interest in South Africa. When in the same year the Cecchetti Society combined with the Imperial Society of Teachers of Dancers, they too became interested in the country. Audrey Grose and Pearl Adler were already teaching according to Cecchetti methods. Nancy Hooper in Natal and Dulcie Howes* in Cape Town were other exponents of the method. — Meanwhile SADTA was continuing with its work. In November 1925, it arranged a large ballet evening in the Standard Theatre. Eight prominent teachers took part in a variety that ranged from jazz numbers to operatic solos and group dancing. This presentation was the first of a series to be held annually.

6. Anna Pavlova and professional ballet

There was little opportunity for professional dancing in the early years of organised ballet in South Africa. The exceptions were usually when ACT arranged professional productions for visiting artists. For example, in July 1925 auditions were held to choose eight dancers for the *corps de ballet* for Anita Bronzi and Oreste Faraboni's touring company. The season opened at the Empire Theatre with a programme that included burlesque, singing, even gymnastics, as well as ballet. Ballet alone would probably not have succeeded, but needed this kind of supporting programme. — The general public saw the art of ballet at its highest level during Anna Pavlova's sensational tour. She arrived in Cape Town on 25 December 1925, with a large company of 27 dancers, among them her partner, the celebrated Laurent Novikoff. —After a short and extremely successful season in Cape Town, the company opened at the Standard Theatre, Johannesburg, on 13 January 1926, with a programme of short ballet works such as *The fairy doll; Snow ballet; Dance of the hours* (Ponchielli); *Bacchanale* (Glazounov) and Pavlova's masterpiece, *The dying swan*. —The occasion was a revelation to all devotees. It set new standards and opened up hither-to unknown vistas. Pavlova was Cecchetti's most brilliant pupil; naturally her visit to South Africa gave a tremendous boost to Cecchetti teachers. Two members of Pavlova's company, the Misses Delamore and D'Arcy, acted as examiners for the first Cecchetti examinations to be held in Johannesburg. Another development was that a branch of the Cecchetti Society was formed in South Africa, the first outside England. — Encouraged by the enthusiasm aroused by Pavlova's visit ACT invited Mme Ravodna to present *The sleeping beauty*. The project was tackled with enthusiasm, but it came to nothing because of jealousy and quarrelling. This detrimental tendency was unfortunately a characteristic of ballet in the Transvaal from the beginning. It occasionally reached such proportions that visiting examiners and adjudicators repeatedly issued warnings about the harmful effect it would have on the development of the art in the Transvaal. ACT then contracted with two dancers. Dorothy Morrison and Poppy Frames, to give dancing performances in their cinemas. Their first appearance was at the Tivoli Theatre in Cape Town, where as "Daye" and "Dawn" they gave a sort of entr'acte between films and musical items. After a moderate success in Cape Town, they gave similar performances in Durban and Johannesburg. Although their programme was artistically limited, it exhibited great improvement on the programmes presented to date by local artists. However, it was all too clear that the time was not ripe for indigenous professional ballet, even although ballet could rely on a large public in Johannesburg. Enthusiasts preferred to attend performances by foreign artists, as was proved again when the Delysia-Stroganoff Company visited South Africa in November 1927.

7.   Institution of ballet examinations and the development of the art

The first examinations for ballet pupils were conducted in Johannesburg in 1925, during the visit of the Pavlova Company to the city. Two years later SADTA invited Edouard Espinosa, as examiner of the AOD, to test affiliated members in South Africa. There was, as yet, no qualified examiner in this country. All examinations for teachers, as well as examiners, had had to be taken in England, an expensive undertaking that few aspirants could afford. As a result there were many unqualified teachers. Espinosa had only a few candidates to examine, and could complete his tour in a fortnight. Entries were for the first three grades only.   — Shortly before this, Espinosa, who had been one of the founders of the AOD, quarrelled with the Association and left it to form his own society, the British Ballet Organization (BBO). During his examination tour he widely advertised the BBO, and formed branches. From 1927 to 1933 he paid regular visits to the country to examine the pupils of affiliated members of his organisation.   — Meanwhile Audrey Grose and Pearl Adler took their examinations at the Cecchetti Society in London and, returning to South Africa in September 1927, officiated as examiners for the Cecchetti Society in Durban.   — Towards the end of the twenties there were thus four independent organisations serving the interests of ballet in South Africa. These were the AOD, the BBO, the Cecchetti Society and SADTA. The last-named society aimed at serving the interests of all teachers, and arranged for examiners of the AOD and the Cecchetti Society to come in alternate years to examine pupils of their affiliated societies. Many teachers did not, however, belong to SADTA, and went their own way. Nevertheless, by the end of the twenties ballet in the Transvaal was organized on a fairly sound basis. Indeed, South Africa was the first member country of the British Commonwealth to institute ballet examinations so as to maintain a recognised standard of tuition. There were still no professional openings for trained dancers. They were obliged to teach, and the result was a glut of teachers, many of whom did not have the necessary qualifications; there was also intensive competition to obtain talented pupils. Parents and pupils had almost always to be requested not to cause unpleasantness.   — Further developments came during the early thirties with all four organisations showing remarkable vitality. John Connell,* the Johannesburg City organist, began to play a substantial role in the furtherance of ballet at this time. Already in 1925 he had inaugurated the annual Johannesburg Music Fortnights. At the beginning of 1927 he sought the co-operation of SADTA, who put on an oriental ballet during the city's fortieth anniversary celebrations.   —The Society arranged the dances for a production of *Hiawatha* during the Music Fortnight in 1929. From this date until 1953 ballet was a regular feature of the Fortnights, and then of the Festivals. At the same time SADTA adopted Connell's suggestion and organised its first dance festival. This took place in the Wanderers Hall, Johannesburg, in September 1929. Eight studios took part in demonstrations and performances, which were adjudicated by the visiting examiner, Margaret Craske. The function was so successful that it became a regular annual event from April 1931.   — More and more teachers were now joining SADTA, which by

1931 was able to hold its own ballet championships; the visiting examiner Judith Espinosa was the adjudicator. These championships became an annual institution, and pupils of affiliated members were even prevented from taking part in future Eisteddfodau. There were then 47 Transvaal members, and a new Memorandum and Act of Association was drawn up. During the visit of Miss Phyllis Bedells, who adjudicated at the 1932 championships, the first examinations of the "Revived Greek Association" were held. A year later the first issue of the *South African Dancing Times*, the organisation's own journal, appeared. It contained news about the activities of different branches, and reports on innumerable performances by different studios. It appears from the reports that the programmes were mainly a mixture of ballet, ballroom dancing, jazz and tap dancing which was popular in those days. By 1934 SADTA felt itself in a sufficiently strong position to approach the Minister of Labour for a charter to register and protect the interests of ballet teachers.   —In 1935 there were more than 900 entries for the dance festival, and the adjudicator, Felix Demery, had to examine an additional 400 senior pupils.   —In the same year the first meeting of the General or National Council of SADTA was held, with Florence Moorcroft-Lamb in the chair; Cape Town was represented by K. Hayward, and Durban by Ida Patlansky. Marjorie Sturman was elected National Chairman, and Mr F. McCullough as secretary. The new Memorandum of Association was signed by seven of the leading members: Marjorie Sturman, Salome Alexander, Ernest Gordon, Marjorie Dyke, Poppy Frames, Marguerite Stickells and Ivy Conmée.* The aims of the Association were set out in the Memorandum, as follows: a. to promote and standardize dancing in all its aspects   b. to train and qualify dancing teachers in all aspects of the art, in South Africa and Northern and Southern Rhodesia   c. to incorporate into the Association all trained dancing teachers, and people proposing to choose dancing as a profession   d. to provide information about the qualifications of teachers to all prospective pupils   e. to promote the interests of the art, and co-operation among teachers   f. to institute lectures and discussions on dancing and related subjects, and to create a library of books on the art.   —The possibility of State registration of all member-teachers was again discussed at this meeting.   — SADTA's exceptional growth was paralleled by that of the AOD and the Cecchetti Society. After the first Cecchetti examination in Durban in 1927 the next step (in 1928) was to get the noted Cecchetti teacher, Margaret Craske, to come to South Africa as an examiner. During her first visit, the first meeting of the recently-established overseas branch of the Imperial Society of Teachers of Dancing (Cecchetti division) took place in Johannesburg, under her chairmanship, and the executive (appointed in London) was made known: Audrey Grose (chairman); Pearl Collins (nèe Adler) (hon. secretary); Agnes Bergen (the Johannesburg representative); Nancy Hooper (the Durban representative); Dulcie Howes and Maud Lloyd* (the Cape representatives). In 1931 the headquarters moved to Cape Town, but the development in Johannesburg was so rapid that they were transferred back to that city in 1933. Aimée de Nettre became the organising secretary, and held the position until 1956, whilst the chairmanship went to such prominent personalities as Audrey Grose, Pearl Collins, Vera Lane, Madge Mann, and Vivienne Keegan*. — The Society spread to Durban, Pietermaritzburg, Port Elizabeth, Bloemfontein, East London and Salisbury, while on the Witwatersrand new Cecchetti studios were continually being opened. The famous Cecchetti exponent, Derra de Moroda, came to South Africa as examiner in 1933; before her return she gave a dance

71

recital in the Empire Theatre. In the first part of the programme she presented candidates who had been successful at recent examinations in demonstrations of the Cecchetti method. In the second part, supported by Dolphine Thompson and Aimée de Nettre, she gave a performance of national dances. By 1936 the Society had expanded to such an extent that Pearl Collins and Natalie Levy felt justified in calling their first general conference in South Africa. — It took place on 7 December, and was attended by representatives from all parts of the country. When the proceedings of the congress were concluded, a number of ballet pieces were presented at the Zoo Lake, in the open air. This was the first congress of the Cecchetti Society to be held outside England. —The AOD also grew from strength to strength, during these years. In 1928 Queen Mary granted the Association her patronage, which undoubtedly gave it additional status. In 1932 when Phyllis Bedells came to South Africa as an examiner, she had to examine 700 pupils. She was able also to arrange a demonstration lecture in His Majesty's Theatre* on her association's methods of tuition. Marjorie Sturman and Vivien Tailleur were amongst those who took part. —The BBO also grew in stature. In 1934, in Pretoria alone, Edouard Espinosa examined 450 pupils of affiliated members of this organisation. The city had a number of flourishing studios that year including those of Pat Jenner, Valerie Smith and Florence Moorcroft-Lamb, and several Johannesburg teachers regularly travelled to Pretoria to give lessons. Ballet productions in Pretoria were able to rely on the assistance of Alfred Gordon Quayle, the conductor of the Iscor Orchestra.

8. Attempts to establish a ballet club

In 1934 South African ballet was again given a stimulus when Levitoff's Russian Ballet visited the country. He was already known as one of Pavlova's partners in her tour of 1925; and now, some nine years later, having been invited by the impresario Alex Cherniavsky,* he was back in South Africa with a company of 27 dancers. — In addition to the prominent names of Vera Nemchinova, Anatole Oboukov, Natasha Bojkovich and Stanley Judson, that of the South African, Eileen Keegan,* was also included in the company. The season at His Majesty's Theatre gave balletomanes the opportunity of seeing Fokine's masterpieces of choreography, and Leon Bakst's décor. Both men had earlier collaborated with Sergé Diaghileff. —With this visit fresh in their minds, Transvaal teachers at last decided to form a ballet club that would enable dancers to appear professionally in their own country. In order to devote all her energy to this undertaking, Mrs Smith resigned as secretary of SADTA, and on 12 September 1934, the provisionally entitled "South African Ballet and Production Club" held its first meeting in the Rand Women's Club. The aim was to present professional ballet performances, and to form an orchestra. Mme Ravodna became ballet mistress, and plans were made to have a production ready by May 1935. Internal dissension and discord wrecked this promising enterprize. But increasing participation in the Eisteddfod, dancing championships and other numerous performances, indicates that the art was strong and resilient enough to overcome such setbacks. — By 1935 South Africa had become an important "ballet colony" of England, and visiting examiners praised the high standard and talent of South African dancers. An important outcome was that parent bodies in England began to grant significant concessions. For example, AOD headquarters arranged that, as a special favour for South African members, dancers who had taken elementary examinations might go to England and enjoy British membership of the Association at no cost, for six months; and they could

72

take further examinations, also without payment. — In July 1935, the Cecchetti Society introduced examinations for prospective professionals. Successful candidates would in future receive a certificate from the Imperial Society. The aims of this examination were set out as follows: a. to bring members of the performing section into contact with the living professional stage   b. to develop and maintain a high standard of contemporaneous ballet   c. to help qualified members to find professional appointments. —This development of the AOD and the Cecchetti Society meant that they would inevitably compete strongly with SADTA; and gradually it became clear that SADTA would have to give way. Whereas SADTA, in consultation with the AOD and the Cecchetti Society, had previously made all arrangements concerning visiting examiners, the Cecchetti Society now decided that it would be to its advantage to conduct its own examinations. SADTA had organisational problems of its own, which made the parting of the ways easier to effect. An important aspect of the separation was that examination fees, which were substantial, would no longer remain in South Africa, but be deposited in the coffers of the parent body in London. — Another significant aspect was that SADTA, in the midst of these collapsing partnerships, felt obliged to replace imported examiners by local ones, the result being that the AOD and the Cecchetti Society were forced also to employ some locally selected examiners. — Royal patronage of the AOD was taken a step further in August 1935, when George V signed a charter granting it the status of a "Royal Academy of Dancing" (RAD). RAD's school of ballet was to develop within a few years to become the most important in Western Europe, and the nursery of British ballet companies. — SADTA faced an uphill battle against such competition. As early as 1936 RAD sent the noted British ballet teacher, Freda Grant, to South Africa as examiner, and in March of that year teachers wishing to break away from SADTA formed a separate National Association of Teachers of Dancing, and registered themselves as NATD(SA). In emulation of RAD, they visualized the establishment of a South African Dancing Academy, in which music and drama, as related arts, would be recognized. They envisaged the erection of a large building, with studios and a hall for their productions, surrounded by a garden and lawns, where "Revived Greek Dancing" could be presented in the open air. They also decided to attempt again to get State recognition of the art of ballet, and its teaching. Hector Poole was appointed secretary, but in spite of hard work and the idealism with which the scheme had been tackled, it was brought to nothing by the outbreak of the Second World War. —The differences among the various ballet organisations were accentuated when Adeline Genée, one of the founders of AOD, and then president of RAD, donated a trophy for accomplishment in South African ballet. Judith Espinosa was invited in 1937 to be examiner in South Africa, and to adjudicate at the new South African ballet championships. Dancers from all over the country took part; and the new trophy was finally awarded to Florence Read of Pretoria. ¨—Then in 1938 RAD set up a South African Advisory Committee, consisting of Marjorie Sturman, Ivy Conmée and Poppy Frames, with Hector Poole as secretary. One of its duties was to advise the London office about local arrangements, especially in connection with annual examinations. Freda Grant again came to examine; and during her visit the Advisory Committee arranged a big demonstration of teaching methods, syllabuses and work done by RAD; this took place in the Standard Theatre on 13, 14 and 15 June. John Connell conducted the City Orchestra on this occasion. In addition to the demonstrations - in which Pearl Waal, Olive Jacobs, Vera Kirsch, Hazel Cranko,

Ivan Berold, Ruth Inglestone and Eileen Salski took part - there were dances arranged by members of the Advisory Committee. One of the outstanding events was a dance specially devised by Judith Espinosa for Marjorie Sturman, Ivy Conmée and Poppy Frames. — Apart from the shows being excellent propaganda for RAD, they once more pointed to the need for South African professional ballet. The only opportunity was still the annual ballet performance, conducted by John Connell, which formed part of his Music Fortnights. — An important influence on ballet in the years before the War was the visit of the Ballet Russe de Monte Carlo, managed by René Blum. Balletomanes were entertained by some of the greatest artists such as Nemchinova, Oboukhov, Levitoff and André Eglevsky. Two South Africans, Yvonne Blake* and Unity Grantham, were in the company. The programmes were focussed mainly on Fokine's choreography, with décor and costumes by Bakst for *Prince Igor, Carnaval, Les sylphides, Spectre de la rose, Petrouschka, Coppélia, Casse noisette* and *Swan lake*, the last presented in an abridged form. The company brought its own conductor and orchestra. —This visit, offering ballet at its best, crowned the great developments of the thirties, and left a lasting impression on ballet in the Transvaal. Compared with local productions, which consisted mainly of work by less talented teachers, the visit of the René Blum company was a revelation. New standards were set, now horizons were disclosed, public interest was stimulated afresh, and local talent yearned once again for the opportunity that professional ballet would provide. — The 1937 championships achieved a remarkably high standard - further proof of the inspiring influence of the René Blum company. In 1938 Cecily Robinson* succeeded in forming a semi-professional group in Cape Town, with the ambitious name of National Ballet. A year later the editor of the *South African Dancing Times* made a strong plea for a ballet club in Johannesburg, similar to that of Marie Rambert in the Mercury Theatre, London. But rivalries and quarrels among Transvaal teachers made such a development temporarily impossible. — There was, however, an appreciable improvement in the quality of performances by different studios; those by RAD and the Cecchetti Society improved markedly. For example, on 21 October 1938, in the Pretoria City Hall, Marjorie Sturman presented a particularly notable ballet concert and demonstration of the work of RAD. Alfred Gordon Quayle conducted his orchestra on this occasion, while the costumes and décor were provided by Mesdames D.H. Ross, G. Haupt and Miss Dulcie Wiggett of Johannesburg.

9. Developments during the War years

Because communications with England and Europe were disrupted, the War actually promoted the development of ballet in the Transvaal. In addition to innumerable performances in aid of war funds, there were further attempts to establish professional ballet. In early 1940 Vivienne Keegan and Aimée de Nettre took the lead by setting up a ballet club under the chairmanship of Prof. P.R. Kirby.* Agnes Bergen was secretary and Vivienne Tailleur ballet mistress. A branch, under the chairmanship of Ida Baggott-Smith, was formed in Pretoria. — Towards the end of 1940 the first production took place in the Johannesburg Library Theatre in which RAD and the Cecchetti Society co-operated. Unfortunately, discord brought this enterprize to an end. —Meanwhile John Connell and Poppy Frames were working towards a Johannesburg Festival Ballet. Their collaboration had begun in 1927; and it was confirmed in 1937, when Poppy Frames directed the ballet in a major production of the *Bartered Bride*. She was then permanently appointed as ballet mistress for all John Connell's operatic productions. In 1941 he got Marjorie Sturman, Ivy Conmée and Lesley Hodson each to present a short ballet divertissement during the opera season. Immediately afterwards, Connell took the lead in forming the Johannesburg Festival Ballet. This company had a very successful début at the Standard Theatre on 12 May 1941, although all parts had to be danced by females, there being no male dancers in the company. — At the same time interest in the ballet section of the Eisteddfod and the SADTA championships increased to such an extent that entries for the Eisteddfod exceeded the 2 000 mark. The same kind of resurgence occurred in Cape Town, where Dulcie Howes developed the ballet school that was connected with the College of Music* of the University of Cape Town. This, like Cecily Robinson's Ballet Club, progressed so well, that Dulcie Howes could take a company on tour to Johannesburg in 1942. Her presentation took place, on Prof. Kirby's invitation, in the Great Hall of the University of the Witwatersrand, and was an enormous success. Competition between Cape Town and Johannesburg promoted standards in both centres, and the following year the Johannesburg Festival Ballet achieved a higher level, when two male dancers took part for the first time. — In December 1943, Dulcie Howes was again in Johannesburg, with a company consisting of the University Ballet and the Ballet Club of Cape Town. She had an extremely successful season, this time at the Empire Theatre. Marjorie Sturman then formed a Pretoria Ballet Club, and discussed the possibility of forming a similar club in Johannesburg with Poppy Frames, Ivy Conmée, Lesley Hodson and John Connell. This was the origin of the Johannesburg Festival Ballet Society, and the beginning of an especially active year. In April, the combined Pretoria and Johannesburg clubs presented an outstanding programme during the music festival; in July Cecily Robinson, invited by ACT, brought her ballet club to Johannesburg and Pretoria; and the annual Eisteddfod had a record number of entries in the ballet section. Miss Robinson appealed in *The Outspan* for a South African National Ballet, which would keep South African talent in the country. Public interest was so great that the Festival Ballet Society decided to risk a second season in September, on this occasion in the Standard Theatre,* under its own name. — The highlights of the year 1945 were the two seasons presented by the Festival Ballet Society, the first during the music festival, and the second in co-operation with the Pretoria Ballet Club. The movement towards independence was helped by the co-operation of the talented composer Richard Cherry,* who was to perform invaluable services for Transvaal ballet. Local choreographers, such as Marjorie Sturman and Poppy Frames, became prominent, while Helen White and Dulcie Wiggett designed décors and costumes. Dulcie Howes's second visit, with her University group, to the Witwatersrand University Great Hall was a triumph. Her company consisted of 15 women and 6 men, with outstanding talent in such dancers as Jasmine Honoré,* Delysia Jacobs, Yvonne Blake and Lionel Luyt. They used Hans Ebenstein's designs, and the brilliance of John Cranko's* choreography aroused special comment. The artistic standard achieved by this company was easily the best that South Africa could produce at the time. When the company again came to Johannesburg in 1946, talented David Poole* was its leading dancer. — Whilst ballet in the Cape went from strength to strength, and the Cape Town Ballet Club became the South African National Ballet Club (1946), its counterpart in the Transvaal was rife with discord and rivalries, and in a perpetual state of instability. SADTA, which had contributed so much of value in the thirties, was in confusion and fell into decline. Many members resigned. It was no longer possible to get examiners from overseas, and teachers had to rely on local examiners. The Association was drastically re-organised, and its affairs were partly put in order but its influence was a thing of the past. On the positive side, the mid-forties were characterized by the growth of both RAD and the Cecchetti Society, and by the heartening development of the Johannesburg Festival Ballet Society and the Pretoria Ballet Club. — An important outcome of visits by overseas and Cape Town companies was that their choreography created a desire for work of higher standard. Marjorie Sturman went to England to supplement the repertoires of the Pretoria Ballet Club and the Johannesburg Festival Ballet, with works from the classical canon. She memorized the choreographies of five classical ballets in three months and, because orchestral parts for ballet were not available after the War, she and an assistant copied the piano parts at the British Museum. After her return, Richard Cherry re-orchestrated the music. Unfortunately, these labours could not be completed in time for the 1947 season. Nevertheless, the Society presented an ambitious programme: *Incidents at a ball* (music by Richard Cherry), *The professor's mantlepiece* (music by Granville Bantock), *Russian fair* and *Impromptu*. Marjorie Sturman wrote the choreography for Richard Cherry's new ballet, and the décor and costume designs were undertaken by Hans Ebenstein, who had settled in Johannesburg.

10. Ballet Theatre

Ballet's great popularity persuaded ACT to present a programme of professional ballet on its own account. Debroy Somers, at that time under contract to ACT, was conductor, and Frank Rogaly, also under contract, was appointed to direct the show *Ace high*. Faith de Villiers,* recently back from Europe, was appointed ballet mistress, and Joyce van Geems* and Stanley Hockman were the soloists. The production was so successful that Stanley Hockman, Joyce van Geems, Ken Geyer, Arnold Dover and Faith de Villiers came together to form a semi-professional company, which they called Ballet Theatre. Frank Rogaly was appointed manager, and ACT promised its support. — It was at first hoped that the Pretoria Ballet Club and the Festival Ballet Society would amalgamate with Ballet Theatre, but Miss Sturman was not in favour of this. She was already busy rehearsing a ballet programme that included *Coppelia* and *Casse noisette*, as well as six smaller works. It was scheduled to run from 1-6 September in the Standard Theatre, and included some of the finest talents of Pretoria and Johannesburg in the cast; for instance, Dorothy Morrison, Peggy Caroline, Aileen Farrel and five men, among them Louis Godfrey,* Desmond Gullet, Danie van den Heever* and Geoffrey Farthing. — Ballet Theatre presented its first programme in July 1948 at His Majesty's Theatre. It was offered in collaboration with Dulcie Howes's University Ballet. The latter presented *La Famille* and *Les Diversions,* with choreography by Dulcie Howes; while Ballet Theatre were responsible for *Theme and Variations* (Faith de Villiers), the *Prince Igor Dances* (Lilian Graham), and *Spanish Ballet* (Ivy Conmée). Designs were by the talented artist John Dronsfield. Pat Bosman, later a member of the British Royal Ballet, danced the male leads, and the British conductor, David Ellenburg, had the baton. The production was so successful that a second season was envisaged for November of the same year. Meanwhile, personal differences had caused a rift in Ballet Theatre, and a new management had to be elected. The November programme was again presented in conjunction with Dulcie Howes, and when the Johannesburg season was concluded, the entire production was mounted at the Alhambra Theatre in Cape Town. The programme consisted of seven ballets, of which the University Ballet contributed four and Ballet Theatre three. —In September the Festival Ballet Society and the Pretoria Ballet Club also presented a season of seven ballets. The standard of the production was so high that the press as well as the public felt that South African Ballet had at last reached maturity. —The forties ended on a high note with Anton Dolin's and Alicia Markova's visit in April 1949. Alex Cherniavsky arranged the tour for ACT. While appearing in Johannesburg, they were so impressed by Marjorie Sturman's ballet corps that they agreed to appear with them. Dolin himself directed the second act of *Giselle* for the occasion. Other works on the programme were *Les sylphides, Swan lake* (a portion) and *Aurora's wedding*. The visitors appeared in all four works. Dolin also assisted the local soloists Thalia Karras, Toby Fine* and Derek Rosenberg. Dolin was profoundly impressed by Louis Godfrey's potential, and took him back to Europe so that he could pursue his career there. —During the following years Festival Ballet and Pretoria Ballet annually presented two seasons in Johannesburg, and one in Pretoria. They also visited centres on the Witwatersrand, and performed fairly regularly in Durban. Because there was no financial backing, no one received payment for services. Dancers had to provide their own shoes, and pay for their journeys. It was an uphill effort to provide costumes, and everyone made sacrifices to keep the company going. Nevertheless, Misses Sturman and Frames managed to present new ballets, and with the assistance of Richard Cherry, they were able also to introduce new compositions to the public.

11. Difficult years

The Johannesburg Civic Orchestra was dissolved in 1953. This was a blow to the various ballet groups since the annual music festival with its ballet season, fell away. Thenceforth, dancers had to rely on orchestras specially formed for the occasion, or by agreement with the SABC Symphony Orchestra, which arose from the Civic Orchestra. However, the general rule was that they danced to piano accompaniments. When Nadia Nerina* and Alexis Rassine* came to South Africa in April 1952, they were obliged to appear at His Majesty's Theatre with only a piano accompaniment. It was only too clear that ballet productions on this basis could not be successful. The companies were forced to limit practically all their presentations to centres outside the city. This state of affairs so discouraged many dancers that they left for overseas, to pursue their careers under more favourable conditions. —The drain of talent was accelerated by a visit of the Sadler's Wells Ballet Company in 1954. It brought its own orchestra and, in addition to some classical ballets, surprised South African audiences with the work of two South African choreographers, Alfred Rodrigues* and John Cranko, who had settled in England. Moreover, there were several South African dancers in the company - Maryon Lane, Patricia Miller*, David Poole*, Dudley Davies,* Gilbert Vernon and Maurice Metliss, who had all done well in England. The depressed condition of local ballet, when measured against the successes of compatriots overseas, resulted in a further exodus of talented dancers. —The presentation by the Pretoria Ballet Club and the Festival Ballet Society of Johannesburg of *Swan Lake,* during the 1956 Johannesburg Festival, was virtually their swan song. Invited by the Johannesburg City Council, the two British dancers, Margot Fonteyn and Michael Somes, came out to dance with Miss Sturman's company; the Cape Town University Ballet co-operated in a presentation of the second act of

Coppélia, and the Durban Civic Orchestra was brought to Johannesburg for the occasion, the conductors being Frits Schuurman* and Jeremy Schulman*. The season lasted a week, from 15-19 October, and the demand for tickets was so great that an open-air performance at the Zoo Lake had to be arranged for the evening of 20 October. In spite of rainy weather, over 6 000 attended the performance. But the effort involved in producing ballet under such conditons was too great, and at the end of the season both the Johannesburg and Pretoria companies were dissolved. — After this, ballet in Pretoria was kept going by Lorna Haupt, Joyce Seaborne* and Gwynne Ashton. Lorna Haupt, who had been a tower of strength in Pretoria ballet, organised an annual show with dancers of her studio, while Joyce Seaborne formed the Ci-Bonne Company, with Dr W. Nicol as patron. She mounted a programme in the Pretoria City Hall at the beginning of 1958; dancers such as Mercedes Molina,* Arnold Dover and Phyllis Spira* took part. — The Ci-Bonne Company then became the Pretoria City Ballet, which set itself the task of creating a professional ballet company in the capital. During the inauguration festivities of the Aula of the University of Pretoria,* Gwynne Ashton, Joyce Seaborne, Lorna Haupt and Aimée de Nettre presented a combined programme. They were supported by the Iscor Orchestra, conducted by Peter Rorke.* The programme included *Les sylphides* (Gwynne Ashton), *Casse noisette,* third act (Joyce Seaborne), *The lyre* with music by Scriabin (Lorna Haupt), and the *Polovtsian dances* from *Prince Igor* (Aimée de Nettre). During the second festival season in the Aula the same dancers, without Joyce Seaborne and with the addition of Dudley Davies, presented another combined programme. After this Miss Ashton left the Pretoria City Ballet, which faded away; she formed her own group called the Ashton Ballet Company. — In Johannesburg ballet virtually ceased to exist after Miss Sturman's two groups had been dissolved; and as in earlier years, the only opportunities for dancers existed in productions by the various studios, at the Eisteddfod, and in the ballet championships. Artists aspiring to a career in ballet had to go overseas, trusting that they would be engaged by a professional company.

12.   Establishment of the Johannesburg City Ballet

Towards the end of 1958, Yvonne Mounsey, a Pretoria dancer who had acquitted herself well in George Balachine's company, returned to the Transvaal, and acted as adjudicator at the Eisteddfod. Like others before her, she was so impressed with the talent of participants that she took the lead in forming a company. Initially, Faith de Villiers and Denise Schultze were her chief helpers. During 1959 they presented various programmes outside Johannesburg; and at the end of the year the company grew with the support of Reina Berman, Aileen Farrel, Ruth Inglestone, Audrey Kind, Mercedes Molina and the administrative help of Mrs Calderwood and Mr Fred Ziegler. Auditions were held, and at the end of January 1960, a strong company appeared in the YMCA Little Theatre, also in Brakpan, Klerksdorp and Blyvooruitzicht. — Their success encouraged them to form a permanent company. A committee consisting of Messrs Mandell, Salmon, Calderwood, Brodie and Ziegler was formed to go into the matter. During a civic reception given by the Mayor of Johannesburg, the company received official recognition (2 August 1960), and the city of Johannesburg offered them the use of buildings at Trematon Place. The first general meeting of the Johannesburg City Ballet took place on 6 August, and after public auditions had been held, 23 female and 6 male dancers were accepted into the company. The idea was to advance the new society and start a ballet school. A Board of

Directors was appointed on 21 November, with Mr W. Grant-Mackenzie as chairman. When one of the members resigned in 1961, Edgar Cree was appointed in his place, as director and musical adviser. — Meanwhile the company's first production took place in December 1960, in the open air at the Zoo Lake. The establishment of a ballet school went ahead, and in April 1961, Gwynne Ashton was appointed principal, as well as the company's ballet mistress and choreographer. There were more performances in various centres in the Transvaal, in Johannesburg (the music taped), and in the Aula, Pretoria (the orchestra conducted by Edgar Cree). One of the most successful productions was Frank Staff's* *Transfigured night*. When his own "South African Ballet" collapsed because of lack of funds, Staff joined the Johannesburg City Ballet, as associate choreographer and teacher. — The City Ballet also found itself handicapped by a lack of funds. However, after discussion with the Administrator of the Transvaal, the Transvaal Education Department granted a subsidy for performances at schools in Johannesburg and Pretoria. A year later, in April 1962, this concession was extended to include a limited number of country schools. The support enabled the City Ballet to carry on. Denise Schultze succeeded Miss Ashton as principal of the ballet school at the beginning of 1962, becoming at the same time the Prima Ballerina, while Hermien Dommisse* became the director of productions. Numerous programmes were arranged and performed in centres throughout the Transvaal, for schools as well as for the general public. At the end of the year the city of Johannesburg increased its subsidy, and the City Ballet was able to appear as a professional company, when the Johannesburg Civic Theatre* was opened. It presented *Coppélia* for the occasion, with David Blair and Maryon Lane of the Royal Ballet in the main rôles. —In 1962 a new development in the history of the performing arts in South Africa was reached, which proved a turning-point for ballet, as well as opera, music and drama. In February 1962, the Government decided to establish a Council for the Performing Arts in each of the four provinces. From this time there was to be no State or Provincial subsidy for any amateur or semi-professional organisation. The City Ballet could not therefore continue its work. At a general meeting on 30 July 1962, it was decided to dissolve the company, and to request the Performing Arts Council of the Transvaal to take it over. PACT formed a professional company of three male and nineteen female dancers. With this step ballet in the Transvaal at last achieved permanent professional status.

—H.D.

II. C*APE TOWN*

1. Ballet Club
2. University of Cape Town Ballet Company
3. University of Cape Town Ballet School

1. **The Cape Town Ballet Club** was founded in 1938 by Cecily Robinson when she returned to South Africa after studying dancing in Europe. She invited members of all the dance studios in Cape Town to co-operate in presenting ballet in Cape Town. They produced *Les sylphides* at the Alhambra Theatre for one week, Melvin Simmers taking the male lead. — This venture was so successful that a meeting was called and a committee appointed, with Helen Webb as President and Prof. Donald Inskip as Chairman. The club consisted of dancing members (dancers of a certain standard only were admitted), non-dancing members and associate members (children between the ages of twelve and fourteen), who met once a month for lectures on ballet and ballet

history, choreography, décor, etc. Rehearsals were held every week-end. During the two seasons presented annually, the Club performed at the City Hall and the Alhambra or Little Theatre* in co-operation with the Cape Town Municipal Orchestra.* The club proved an excellent training ground for budding choreographers. — Dancing members were paid for the first time in 1942, and the Club's own school was established by Cecily Robinson and Yvonne Blake* three years later. In 1946 the Ballet Club became a professional company, known as the South African National Ballet, under the leadership of Cecily Robinson and Yvonne Blake. This was South Africa's first professional ballet company. — When Cecily Robinson departed for Rhodesia in 1947, Yvonne Blake carried on the work alone, until Faith de Villiers* became ballet mistress in 1948. In 1949 the company merged with the Cape Town University Ballet,* to form the corps-de-ballet for a season with Alicia Markova and Anton Dolin. When the season was over, the National Ballet ceased to exist, continuing as a school only, until this also closed down. — During the eight years of its existence as the Cape Town Ballet Club, twenty-five ballets were presented, including the work of choreographers such as Petipa and Fokine, as well as original ballets by Rodrigues,* Cranko,* Blake and others. As the South African National Ballet, the club presented seventeen ballets, including five by Frank Staff.*

BIBLIOGRAPHY

GADEM, F and MAILLARD, R.: *A Dictionary of modern ballet.* Methuen and Co, London, 1959. WILSON, G.B.: *A Dictionary of ballet.* Penguin, 1957.   WORRAL, JOHN: *Ballet in South Africa.* Howard Timmins, Cape Town, n.d.

—M.G.

2. **The University of Cape Town Ballet Company,** or the UCT Ballet, as it is generally called, is the oldest existing ballet company in South Africa. —The foundations of the company were laid in 1932, when Dulcie Howes formed the Cape Town University Ballet School. Later in the same year she co-operated in a production by the College of Music,* but it was not until 1936 that the Ballet Company produced its own programmes. No exact date can be given for the formation of the company, as it gradually grew out of the School's performances, which advanced to professional rating as the standard of dancing developed. By 1940 the company was not only performing in Cape Town, but toured the country as far afield as Rhodesia, S.W. Africa and Moçambique.   —The partnership of School and Company worked very well, for the students of the School gained invaluable experience while dancing in the Company. Likewise, for the Company the School was indispensable, for it provided a continuous flow of trained dancers with a certain uniformity of style. — In spite of its name, UCT Ballet was a self-supporting body, completely separate from the University, which merely granted it the use of premises for rehearsals. Until 1963 the members of the Company, who were mainly the students and staff of the School, were not paid, the income from performances going into the Dulcie Howes Trust Fund. This fund was used for the financing of new productions, to help dancers to go overseas for further study, and to defray the expenses of guest artists. Among the latter were Alicia Markova, Anton Dolin, David Poole,* Nadia Nerina,* Alexis Rassine,* Beryl Grey, Maryon Lane and Desmond Doyle.*   — In 1963 the company became semi-professional, when it utilised the Trust Fund to employ a nucleus of paid dancers, with David Poole* as ballet-master. The University allowed it to continue using the premises for reahearsals, and CAPAB undertook to cover any losses. The

founder, Dulcie Howes, remained Director. In 1965 it became a fully professional company, with CAPAB accepting full responsibility for its finance. Thus the University Ballet ceased to exist as an independent touring company. In Cape Town, however, it continues to dance under the name of "University of Cape Town Ballet, in collaboration with CAPAB". — The UCT Ballet have in their present repertoire important works such as *Giselle, Swan lake, Coppélia, Petrouchka, The fire bird, Prince Igor, Le carnaval, Les sylphides, Casse noisette* and *The sleeping beauty,* and also ballets by modern choreographers such as De Valois, Cranko, Ashton, Rodrigues, Staff and Poole.

BIBLIOGRAPHY
WORRAL, JOHN: *Ballet in South Africa.* Howard Timmins, Cape Town, n.d.

—M.G.

3. **The University of Cape Town Ballet School.** After Dulcie Howes had returned from Europe, she was approached by Prof. W.H. Bell* in 1932 to join the staff of the South African College of Music,* then incorporated in the University of Cape Town, at Rondebosch. This meant that the University became the first in the world to present a course in Ballet. —The UCT Ballet School grew, from children's classes given by Dulcie Howes, into a school where over 300 students and children are taught by a large staff, assisted by students. Students may enter for a three-year Ballet Certificate course, which inludes not only daily ballet classes, but classes in mime, character and national dancing, Spanish dancing, and lectures on ballet history, ballet general-knowledge and art. At the end of each year the students are examined in all the above subjects. They are also trained in the dancing styles of, and required to take the examinations set by, the Cecchetti Society and the Spanish Dance Society. — Past teachers at the school have been Yvonne Blake,* Jasmine Honoré,* Richard Glasstone,* Mary Suckling and Elisabeth Coombes. It is still under the direction of Dulcie Howes, while the principal teacher, Pamela Chrimes,* is assisted by Cecily Robinson,* Marina Keet* and June Hattersly. The school has brought forth dancers such as David Poole, John Cranko, Patricia Miller,* Alfred Rodrigues, Desmond Doyle,* Johaar Mosaval,* Dudley Davies* and others, who have made a name for themselves overseas. — The school's connection with the University of Cape Town Ballet Company is most important. The school provides dancers who have had a uniform training, giving the company unity of style and technique. The company, in turn, offers the dancers employment when they have completed their course.

BIBLIOGRAPHY
WORRAL, JOHN: *Ballet in South Africa.* Howard Timmins, Cape Town, n.d.

—M.G.

III. GREEK DANCING IN SOUTH AFRICA
The art of Ancient Greek Dancing, in its form a dedication to the gods, was forgotten for centuries, until Ruby Ginner started a school in London to revive it. — In South Africa revival and recognition were due almost entirely to two of Ruby Ginner's early pupils, Jean Strapp and Lesley Hodson. After completing their studies at the Ruby Ginner School, they joined her company and toured Greece in 1930, before returning to South Africa. — Jean Strapp started a school in Durban and Pietermaritzburg in 1931. After establishing Greek Dancing in Natal, she settled in Cape Town in 1934, with the object of introducing it there. Lesley Hodson started a similar school in

Johannesburg in 1933. As a result of her efforts, Greek Dancing was accepted as a subject for the Ballet Matriculation Examination in the Transvaal.

—G.M.

IV. SPANISH DANCING IN SOUTH AFRICA

The dances of Spain, perhaps the most varied and highly developed of all folk-dances are generally classified under four headings: classical, regional, flamenco and religious. — In Cape Town this dance form was first represented by Delis Rohr, who gave recitals in the Cape from 1932; by Jasmine Honoré,* who taught Spanish dancing at the University of Cape Town Ballet School from 1947, and produced two ballets with Spanish themes; by Elizabeth Coombes, who taught in the city from 1949 to 1956, both at the Eoan Group* and for one year at the UCT Ballet School; by Marina Keet,* who teaches at the UCT Ballet School, and has been responsible for productions and recitals since 1955; by Deanna Blacher, who taught with David Poole before starting her own company; and finally by Mavis Becker (Marina Lorca), who spent some time abroad after 1958, touring with Luisillo's Spanish Dance Theatre. All these South African dancers studied in Spain, and many also under Elsa Brunelleschi in London. — Prior to 1951, Spanish dancing in Johannesburg was taught only by ballet teachers, the first of whom was Espinosa. In that year Madame Gitanilla opened the first studio of Spanish dancing. Others who helped to establish an interest were Ivy Conmée, Reina Berman, Elizabeth Coombes, Zara Kwitz and June Hern. In 1957 Luisillo and his Spanish Dance Theatre visited South Africa for the first time. From his company returned Mersyne Mavros (Mercedes Molina*), a South African who had been touring extensively with him, and is now teaching in Johannesburg. She started South Africa's first Spanish dance company in 1958, and has performed in the Republic, Rhodesia and Moçambique. Others who have danced at various times in Luisillo's company are Geoffrey Neumann (Enrique Segovia),* Rhoda Zulman (Luisa Cortes), Bernice Lloyd, Silvia Durán* and Rafael Arroyo, all from Johannesburg. Segovia danced for six years with Antonio and Paco Ruiz, and Arroyo with Marienna. — In Durban Joy Shearer* has taught since 1953, producing several programmes of Spanish dancing. — In 1965 the Spanish Dance Society was formed to set a standard for the teaching of Spanish dancing in South Africa, by compiling a uniform examination syllabus. The secretariat of the society is in Johannesburg, with Luisillo as patron.

—M.G

V. SOUTH AFRICAN DANCING TIMES

The South African Dancing Times (August 1933 - September 1955) was distributed by the Weil Publishing Company in Johannesburg until February 1940 and printed by G.M. Horne (Pty) Ltd. During the first seven years of its existence this monthly was edited by the following people: Laurence Turner, Florence Moorcroft-Lamb, Leonora G. Williams, Vera Ross Jones and C.J. Weil. From March 1940 to June 1946, W.A. Helfer was the editor, and after him William Perl took over as editor, Jack M. Woolf became the publisher and general manager, and the Dantim Publishing Company became the printers. In June 1947 Perl changed the name of the periodical to *Night and Day,* but this was not successful. Jack Woolf took over as editor and restored its original name. Eventually Gerry Gerrard became the editor and was responsible for the last two issues. — Until 1940 *The SA Dancing Times* was the South African issue of the *Dancing Times* which was published in England. The South African issue was

82

devoted to ballet and ballroom dancing and included photographs of prominent dancers, articles and general news items on ballet and dancing. The first news item from Cape Town was published in the journal in January 1934. In order to encourage local interest in South Africa, C.J. Weil, on behalf of the periodical, presented two silver trophies which were handed over at annual national competitions held by the South African Dancing Teachers' Association (SADTA). — Representatives were appointed in London and the United States and in Paris. These measures were successful. By October 1936 the periodical had become popular in South Africa. It contained many advertisements and regularly published the results of various examinations and competitions. It was also given two covers, one with a photograph of ballet dancing and the other with a photograph of ballroom dancing, to emphasise its dual function. During the difficult war years, W.A. Helfer tried to increase its circulation by including theatre news, short stories, humorous sketches and articles on elocution and music. This was so successful that by the end of 1945 the periodical had become a fairly bulky publication of 63 pages. Until about the end of 1946 it was also the official publication of the Johannesburg Festival Ballet Club and the Pretoria Ballet Club. — But William Perl took this diversity too far when he became the editor. The result was that it lost its original character and tended to become a general magazine which contained only a few items on ballet. — This change of policy was announced in an editorial dated June 1947, in which the owners and publishers - the Dantim Publishing Company - stated that they had decided to incorporate the original *SA Dancing Times* into a general publication on a wider variety of entertainment, because they believed that there was a greater demand for this kind of magazine. — Several attempts were made to restore the periodical to its previous popularity, but by the end of 1955 the entire venture had failed.

—H.D.

BAL VAN LIER, HENRIETTA CORNELIA MINETTA (BORN VAN LIER), *1861 (1862?) in Amsterdam; °18 February 1939, in Johannesburg. Singing teacher who was prominent with choirs and operettas in the musical life of Kruger's Republic.

The production of her voice, complemented by thorough anatomical studies of the vocal organs, was managed by Collin Tobisch (a former Viennese court singer), by Mathilda Marchesi in Paris and by Stockhausen in Germany. She took part in opera in Holland and Germany, and taught school music in Amsterdam, but her early marriage to G. Ribbink gave her life a decisively new direction. Ribbink emigrated to the South African Republic, where he became a loyal supporter of Kruger and eventually Director of Posts and Telegraphs. She followed him with their two sons, Gerrit and Eduard, in 1889, and after a concert appearance with Reményi* she became a well-known soloist in Johannesburg and Pretoria. Her previous experience with children's voices in Amsterdam was put to good use, and on several occasions she led school choirs at public functions which the President attended. On 21 September 1892 the President opened a Children's Exhibition at which a children's choir of 150 voices led by Mrs Bal van Lier contributed 3 items. That same evening there was a musical competition at which one of the judges of the pianoforte items was Dirk Balfoort* (sen.). — After the death of Ribbink in 1893, his wife was forced to become a singing teacher at the State School for Girls, and to co-operate with Henri van den Berg and Henri ten Brink* at their music school. In the same year this very active woman organised two subscription concerts in her Vermeulen Street studio. Well-known musicians such as Grant Fallowes, Amorison, M. Spies, J.C. Leyds and W. Baylis co-operated in these ventures. In 1895 she married J.H.E. Bal, and Henriette Villa, as their residence in Church Street was called, became the popular meeting place of the Pretoria Dramatic and Operatic Society, and of the Sancta Cecilia Ladies' Choir. Both groups were initiated by Bal van Lier to afford her pupils the opportunity of performing as soloists and in choirs. During the Anglo-Boer War she was one of the three directresses of the Republican Red Cross, and exerted herself to gather funds for War Relief among the Boers by means of concerts and performances. After the war she gradually turned her attention to English operettas, and between 1903 and 1913 she produced works such as *Iolanthe, The mikado, Trial by jury, The gondoliers, The sylph* (A. Benson) and *La mascotte* (Audran), with the Pretoria Operatic and Dramatic Society and her own Conservatoire choir. She had started her own Conservatoire in Market Street just after the war. — An estrangement came into her second marriage, and in 1910 she opened a second studio in Johannesburg, which was gradually extended through branches over the Witwatersrand, necessitating the appointment of assistants. The evidence suggests that she went to live in Johannesburg between 1910 and 1914. Mr Bal succumbed to injuries which he sustained in a dynamite explosion in their previous residence, in 1914. — Henrietta Bal van Lier continued her widespread teaching activities until 1932, when she entrusted the Pretoria branch to two of her pupils, Jenny Liebman and Minnie van Zyl. She managed her studio in Johannesburg personally until she died in 1939, after a long illness. Among her pupils were Rose Alper,* Maud Baury (Mrs Dr Watson), Joy van Rijneveld, Emile Knoll, Victor Slater and Jenny Liebman.

BIBLIOGRAPHY

VERMEULEN, ELIZABETH: *Die musieklewe in Pretoria tussen 1902 en 1926.* M.Mus. dissertation, UP, 1967.

SOURCES

Maarten Spies collection, State Archives, Pretoria. *Die Volkstem:* 9 January 1926. *Die Vaderland:* 20 February 1939. *The South African Music Teacher:* April 1932.

—Ed.

BANDS, name of an Eastern Province family of musicians.

It is possible that R. Bands (°April 1875 in Queenstown) came to South Africa as an Imperial bandsman, and that after discharge he settled in Queenstown, where for at least 40 years the name of Bands was well-known. Bands, the town gaoler, was the first bandmaster of the Queenstown Volunteer Band from 1864 until the time of his death in April 1873, when he was accorded a military funeral. He was not only musical, but probably had qualities of leadership, since the band showed improvement under his baton. From June 1864 and thereafter, monthly (or bi-monthly) promenade concerts were given, at the famous Hexagon Hotel and in the public gardens; the members also played for church, masonic and school parades, and at important occasions, such as the visit of the Governor in March 1871. Bands was also a composer: at the Queen's Birthday Ball in March 1874 the programme of 21 items contained four from his pen. — In March 1883 a Quadrille Band consisting of W. Bands (sen.), J. Bands, and Messrs Almond and G. Trollip, provided the music for the St Andrew's Lodge Ball. From April to December 1889, Bugle-Major W. Bands acted as leader, when the Volunteer Band was without the services of a bandmaster of their own. In

April 1891 it was reported from Kokstad that the "local band has a valuable addition in Mr Bands of Queenstown". — Of the second generation, J. Bands was a vocalist. At a concert given by the Volunteers in September 1885, he sang an aria from the *Flying Dutchman* (Wagner). He sang in Queenstown during the 1890's, performing leading parts in nearly all the cantata and oratorio productions of the Philharmonic Society, as well as solo parts in the Society's first two Gilbert and Sullivan productions, *Trial by jury* (October 1895) and *HMS Pinafore* (August 1896).

WORKS BY R. BANDS
Unpublished: Jenny Jones, march, 1864.   Queenstown, polka, 1864.   Traviata, mazurka, 1874.   Fanny, mazurka, 1874.   Gem, mazurka, 1874.   Oddfellows, galop, 1874.

SOURCE
Queenstown Free Press, 1864 to 1898.

—C.G.H.

BANTU COMPOSERS OF SOUTH AFRICA, THE
Editor's Note: In the final section of his introduction to *The Music of the Bantu Races of South Africa**, Professor Kirby discussed the influence of Western music on the rise of Bantu musical composition, as an addendum to his main theme. Because of the lucidly expressed views this contains, the section has been transferred from the article, where it does not properly belong, to serve as an introduction to Dr Huskisson's historical review of Bantu composers and their music. Although occasional duplication is inevitable, this step seems justified in the challenge offered by a characteristically independent mind.
1.   Introduction.
2.   Lovedale Seminary.
3.   Healdtown.
4.   Ohlange Institute.
5.   Zulu Training School (Adams), Amanzimtoti.
6.   Mariannhill Mission.
7.   Lesotho (Morija).
8.   Valdezia (Swiss Mission).
9.   Botshabelo.
10.   Kilnerton Institute.
11.   Training School, Umfundisweni.
12.   Kimberley.
13.   Grahamstown.
14.   Urbanised Bantu Music.
15.   Radio Bantu.

1.   Introduction
Hardly twelve years after Lichtenstein visited the Eastern Province in the party of Commissioner Van der Mist, a petty Xhosa chief, named Ntsikana, was converted to Christianity (1815)[1]. As a child he had heard the preaching of Dr Van der Kemp of the London Missionary Society, who began his work in "Gaikaland" in 1799. But it was not until the year 1815, or thereabouts, when Ntsikana was a grown man, with two wives as became a typical pagan polygamist, that he listened to the teaching of Rev. James Read at Gqora in the Kat River District, and was so profoundly affected that he at once

embraced Christianity, thus becoming the first Xhosa convert. Ntsikana, however, was not content merely to listen to and to participate in the hymn-singing of the missionary and his followers, but aspired to create something of the sort himself. The result was his "composition" of several little hymns, both the music and the words in his vernacular. But since Ntsikana could neither read nor write, all that has been preserved are the pieces retained in the memories of his fellow converts and their successors. His personal influence, however, was so great that, on the death of the missionary Williams (the man who followed Read), Ntsikana carried on his missionary work with great success. The three compositions by which he is still remembered, were of course only written down long after his death , though the words of his "Great Hymn", together with an English translation, were printed in the works of several travellers. John Knox Bokwe* (1855-1922) heard the story of Ntsikana from his grandparents, prepared a sketch of the Xhosa missionary's life, and became the first to note down the tunes and harmonies of his hymns in Tonic Sol-fa notation.[2] — Bokwe's rendering of these hymns would appear to indicate that even at this early stage European ideas had begun to "contaminate" aboriginal music, particularly as regards the rhythm, and to a certain extent the mode used. Nevertheless both Ntsikana's melodies and harmonies, as set down by Bokwe, retain certain unmistakably African elements. The time-values of the notes and their relation to the general rhythm of the music shows how careful Ntsikana was to avoid as far as possible distorting the Xhosa language. His hymn "Dalibom" ("Life Creator") shows this very clearly.

He! Nan-ko-k'u Da-li-bom Wa-se s'kd-we-ni

This melody is unquestionably African, though its rhythm, being set down in European musical notation, is probably less free than it was originally intended to be. Ntsikana's "Round Hymn", on the other hand, as noted down by Bokwe, contains an harmonic progression that must have been anathema to the early missionaries, and possibly also to Bokwe himself. Nevertheless, with his innate honesty he set down the music as he remembered having heard it sung to him. Since there are several versions extant, I quote from one in Bokwe's autograph, which he wrote in staff notation.[3] —It differs slighly from the printed version in Tonic Sol-fa which appears in Bokwe's *Amaculu ase Lovedale,* but all the important points are present in both.

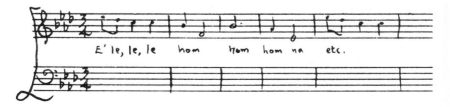

E' le, le, le hom hom hom na etc.

The second melody note in this hymn, D flat, is a passing note, and it is curious to find it present in the tune when the note D natural is so prominent in the harmony. If we analyse the scale of this tune, omitting the D flat, we find a scale that would appear to have been derived from the harmonic series, the D natural being the eleventh partial (not normally used in European art-music),

while the F may possibly have originally been the seventh partial (likewise normally unused in Europe). —The opening syllables of the text, which appear to be meaningless, sound, so Bokwe himself noticed, "pretty much like Hallelujah, Amen", which was probably the intention. —By the year 1875, when Bokwe was twenty years old, he had picked up sufficient knowledge of simple European harmony to himself set to music a number of hymns in the customary four-voice parts. His part-writing was naturally by no means perfect, for it contained minor breaches of the principles of such writing, which was undoubtedly due to his lack of systematic training. There was also little originality in either melody or harmony. Nevertheless Bokwe's vocal compositions were regularly performed, and became greatly esteemed by his Christian compatriots. They were originally written in the Tonic Sol-fa notation, but later the composer succeeded in mastering staff notation and transcribed a number of them into it. —It was in this same year, 1875, that his compilation, *Amaculu ase Lovedale* (Lovedale Music) was first published in Tonic Sol-fa notation; and it was reprinted, with additions, both in 1894 and in 1910.[4] —Bokwe's technique may be judged to some extent by one of his early compositions, *Msindisi wa boni* (Saviour of Sinners) of which a copy exists in his own handwriting, and which has also been recorded commercially.[5] On the record, however, the singers, as is so frequently the case with Black choirs, do not adhere to the notes which were written by the composer; for the parts are inverted at one point, and at another, where Bokwe introduced a flattened seventh, the vocalists sing an unaltered leading note. — By Bokwe's time the Xhosa converts had become accustomed to the perfect cadence at the ends of their hymn tunes, and also, to some extent, to the plagal cadence. It was undoubtedly these harmonic formulae that led to increasing familiarity with the heptatonic major scale. As a result, the Southern Bantu composers and singers learned to use appropriately the primary chords, though they tended to avoid minor triads (vide Ntsikana's "Round Hymn") and to alter inverted chords to root positions. In other words, they seldom sang the work of a composer as it was written, but simplified it to suit themselves, invariably "taking the line of least resistance". Incidentally, those singers who had to sing the leading note in the perfect cadence, almost always dropped to the dominant of the second chord, instead of rising to the tonic. The reason for this practice was that they disliked singing incomplete chords. —John Knox Bokwe's example was followed by many Christian converts, especially those of denominations other than Roman Catholic. Bokwe based the bulk of his compositions (with the exception of a few songs for voice with pianoforte accompaniment) on the four-part principle of the Protestant churches. In this he was followed by other Bantu composers to such an extent that it is only with difficulty that one can now hear examples of the original types of indigenous vocal music, and then as a rule only at some of the age-old ceremonies and rituals which are still practised. One example has fortunately been made readily available, and it is of such importance for a comparison of the practices of former days and those of modern times, that a description of it is here essential. The Bantu were not long in concluding that there appeared to be no reason why they themselves should not organize their own special sects. Many broke away from the orthodox practices of the Christian churches, and under the name of "Separatists" began to establish their own forms of worship. So widespread has this become, that today there are well over a thousand Native religious sects. Among these "Separatists", as most of them call themselves, the principal group known as "Nazarites" was founded in 1911 by a Zulu named Isaiah Shembe. This man endeavoured to adapt the Christian religion to Zulu custom and art. In the "Separatist" hymn *Dalela Zulu* ("Listen, ye Zulus"), Shembe made use of the tune of an old Zulu tribal song, which dates back to at least the time of the chief Mpande (reigned: 1840-1872). The original Zulu words of this song dealt with loyalty to the tyrant chief Dingane (reigned: 1828-1840); but in the new words which were fitted to it by Shembe the idea of loyalty to Christ is implied by the expressed loyalty to the tyrant, whose name is actually mentioned in the text.[6]   —There is no question but that in this hymn we can hear the authentic Zulu choral idiom, such as must have been regularly heard by the early pioneers in Natal. The main melody is pentatonic, as might be expected, and it is executed by baritone voices. Deeper voices, which would normally perform an organum, or parallel progression, at the fifth below the main melody, actually double that melody in the lower octave, in a species of Bantu magadizing, such as that of the ancient Greeks. The whole is further embroidered by the voices of women, which "embroideries", however, are of a comparatively free nature.   —In this connection it is worth while noting that the Zulu verb *vuma*, which primarily means "agree", has a secondary signification today, that of singing the bass part in a chorus. I would, however, submit that this secondary meaning is of relatively recent adoption. Father Bryant, in his Zulu Dictionary of 1905, expressed it as to "sing the low accompaniment; the second part in a song". Here he would appear to have been in error, for I have found that in Zulu the word *vuma*, and in Tshikaranga *bvumira*, which is the same word, signifies the baritone register, and that therefore the secondary meaning of the Zulu term would be better rendered as cantus firmus. This is the more interesting since it is known that in medieval times in Europe the cantus

88

firmus was performed by baritone singers, though their vocal part, which "held" or "sustained" the main melody, was known as the "tenor" (Latin: tenere). My argument would appear to be strengthened by the secondary meaning of the verb *vuma* which the old German missionary, Kropf, gave to it in his Xhosa Dictionary of 1899. In this he states that it means "To express a common sentiment in tune: one person commences, all the others fall in". — It is quite impossible here to list the numerous Bantu composers who have followed in the wake of Bokwe. I can only mention one or two who have distinguished themselves among their people by writing in a more characteristic vein than the majority of their compatriots, most of whose music consists chiefly of the repetition of well-worn formulae. — Among the more distinctive writers may be counted the Zulu Reuben Caluza* (° 1969), many of whose part-songs became very popular, especially in Natal. One of these, his Ricksha Song, contains traces of American ragtime.[7]

The text of his song describes the manner in which the typical ricksha-hauler of Durban solicits custom, and is, in a sense, a criticism of the European attitude to the African. A volume of twenty-seven of Caluza's four-part songs, in Tonic Sol-fa notation, was published in Natal, and from it one may judge the nature of his work.[8] — Enoch Sontonga* gave to the South African Bantu the part-song *Nkosi sikilel'i Africa* ("God bless Africa"), which now (with another text) has become the national anthem of the Transkei. This composition is also available on a commercial disc.[9]

The contemporary Basuto writer, J.P. Mohapeloa,* who has learned enough about European harmony to compose simple part-songs, has succeeded in retaining something of an African "flavour". Another contemporary composer is J. Foley* who, during his residence in Grahamstown, wrote many part-songs, and organised and trained a good choir to sing his works. His style is more fluent than that of most Bantu writers, and he not only succeeded in introducing a certain amount of chromaticism, but even in teaching his choralists to sing it correctly.[10] — Following the recent decision of the Pope to permit the use of vernacular in the Roman Catholic Mass, Benjamin Tyamzashe* has experimented in setting portions of the Mass in his mother tongue. He has also written trios for female voices (SSA), intended for use in Native schools.[11] This is most unusual for a Bantu composer.

A four-part song, entitled *Ama-Gora e-Mendi* (The Brave men of the Mendi), written by S.E. Mqayi and A.M. Jonas in memory of the tragic disaster to that ill-fated vessel, is remarkable for the use of harmonies that one seldom meets with in Bantu music, such as chromatic auxiliary notes, diminished sevenths, and even the "German" sixth, as well as simple modulation. Though the part-writing is generally satisfactory, it is occasionally uncertain. The whole, however, is completely European in character.[12]

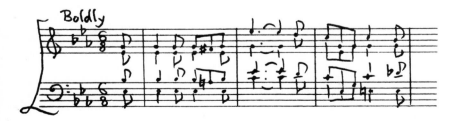

It is, of course, true that for many years Black choirs have attempted to sing, with more or less success, choruses from the oratorios of Handel and other masters, and even complete works like *Messiah*. Such performances have, however, usually been organised in the larger urban areas, and generally the trainer has been a European. With rare exceptions the instrumental accompaniments, especially when orchestral, have been rendered by Europeans. — A great many of the choral writings of Bantu composers have been printed, the principal publisher of such works being the Lovedale Press. A considerable number of these has also been recorded commercially, and these recordings have proved to be very popular among the Bantu, with whom the portable clock-work-driven gramophone is widespread. —The gramophone, however, has brought in its train vast quantities of popular American dance music, and the dissemination of this has led to the imitation of it by groups of urban Blacks, now almost completely detribalized, who have been able to acquire or to borrow the necessary musical instruments. The result of this has been the production of a regular flood of imitations of the dance music of the White man, including his simple formal structures and instrumental devices. With few exceptions these remain imitations, and often are very crude. But the fact that in such music the heptatonic scale is the basis on which the melodies are built, with occasional "altered" notes, as in the case of the "blues", has resulted in the Bantu acquiring considerable facility in singing the European major scale, and even in colouring it chromatically on occasion. Modulation, however, still remains a *terra incognita* for the majority, and the lack of genuine modulation in the European prototypes makes it unlikely that this shortcoming will be eliminated in the near future.[13] —The almost universal adoption by Bantu youths in the cities of the penny-whistle, has resulted in their becoming accustomed to the heptatonic scale, and is causing them to think in that scale and to abandon the pentatonic modes of their forefathers. The fact that this inexpensive instrument is built in perfect tune, enables the youths to use the major scale in correct intonation, and this is influencing their vocal practices to a remarkable extent. But it is in the major mode that they normally think, for, as I have already said, the average Bantu is not at home in the minor mode.   —The popular musical show, *King Kong,* is in a category of its own, for although the melodies were invented by an African, the text was devised by a European, and the harmonies and orchestration were supplied by another European. It therefore cannot legitimately be called an African work, though it was performed by an African cast. It was, however, noteworthy that the principal singer in it had assimilated European practices to such an extent that not only did he produce his voice in the European manner, but he was able to sing chromatic passages in tune with perfect ease.[14]   — In practically all the African musical compositions that have hitherto been discussed, their form is of the most rudimentary nature, consisting chiefly of orthodox musical sentences without a trace of the devices used by European composers to mitigate the "squareness" of the design or to inject vitality into the melody or character into the harmony. In other words, with very few exceptions, our African composers have made little advance in their art during the last half-century.   —The gramophone and radio may possibly change all this in time, though the fact that the majority of Africans in our country have little opportunity of hearing, let alone studying, the works of the great masters of Europe, particularly their instrumental compositions, and the fact that few have access to a piano, will undoubtedly retard their musical progress.   —There are in South Africa a number of Black brass bands, some of which are run by missions, some by the Salvation Army, and a few by Municipalities. But these are quite separate from the general musical life of our Africans, and the fact that bowed instruments are rarely studied by the Bantu, and almost exclusively only those wood-wind instruments that figure in dance bands, effectively precludes the organisation of an all-African orchestra of any size.   — As far as I am aware, only one South African Bantu composer has succeeded in writing an extended musical work, which is, *mirabile dictu,* for full modern orchestra. This is the previously mentioned Michael M. Moerane*, who spent many years in studying for the degree of Bachelor of Music of the University of South Africa, and who, after a severe struggle with almost insuperable difficulties, eventually succeeded in obtaining it. His composition exercise for the degree was his orchestral tone-poem, *Fatse la hese* (My Country), which is based on Basuto tribal songs. In writing this work Mr Moerane had the guidance of Professor F.H. Hartmann*, who at the time was head of the Music Department of Rhodes University College, now Rhodes University. Moerane's work was performed and recorded in Bedford in 1944 at a BBC concert conducted by Clifford Curzon, and later in New York and Paris at concerts conducted by the Negro Dean Dixon, who became chief conductor of a radio orchestra in West Germany. Unfortunately the recordings were not preserved. — Moerane, however, has had no successor, nor is he likely to have one until, in the fulness of time, a school of music for South African Bantu may be established. Only then will our Bantu be enabled to receive systematic training from competent instructors, and to hear appropriate works on which they may model their own; for the African has an enormous leeway to make up before he is in a position to emulate the European musician of culture. The few who are at the present time struggling seriously to master the art of music, as the European knows it, are having an uphill fight, but a fight in which they may in time be victorious. But they can never win it without the help of sympathetic and thoughtful Europeans, together with a willingness on their own part to undertake the really gruelling work that is necessary, if one desires to become a composer of any distinction. For the overdone praise and patronage extended to the Black by the uncritical and often ignorant White only serves to put the clock back on his hopes for advancement in the art.

BIBLIOGRAPHY AND NOTES

[1]BOKWE, J.K.: *Ntsikana, the story of an African convert* (second edition), Lovedale, 1914. [2]BOKWE, J.K.: *Amaculo ase Lovedale* (third edition), pp. 86-90 (in Tonic Sol-fa). [3]In a collection of Bokwe's compositions in his autograph (in staff notation) in the Cory Library, Rhodes University, Grahamstown. [4]BOKWE, J.K.: *Amaculo ase Lovedale* (third edition), Lovedale 1910, pp. 137-139; also in the Bokwe MSS in the Cory Library, Rhodes University, and recorded on Columbia, Y.E. 117, WEA. 152. [5] Vide supra. [6] Recorded on Gallotone, G.E. 996 T (A). [7]CALUZA, R.T.: Ricksha Song or Ixegwana, *Lovedale Sol-fa Leaflets* no. 2c. It was, however, originally printed in the Native Teachers Journal (Natal) in 1921. [8] CALUZA, R.T.: *Amagama Ohlange Lakwazulu.* There is no publisher's name or date on the copy presented to me by the composer, but it was subsequent to 1925, since it contains Bayete, a song written for the visit of the Prince of Wales in that year. [9] Composed in 1897 and first sung publicly in 1899, *Lovedale Sol-fa leaflets* no. 17 (n.d.). Recorded on Columbia YE 117, WEA. 189. [10]FOLEY, J.: *Umtshangase,* recorded on HMV JP 523 B. [11]Published by the Lovedale Press (n.d.). [12]*Lovedale Sol-fa Leaflets* no. 20. [13]There are scores of records of this kind issued, and their number continues to increase. The following are typical of various phases of this "imitative" music: *Ixuno zam,* HMV GU 96B (very naïve); *Myelo bebe.* Gallotone GB 1602 A (more sophisticated); *Peshaya Kweyo Ntaba,* Gallotone GE 973 A (quite remarkable). [14]WILLIAMS, P., and MATCHIKIZA, T.: King Kong and Marvellous Muscles from *King Kong* (Gallotone GB 2891, both sides).

—P.R.K.

In the various institutions where they pursued their musical studies, Bantu composers were moulded by European teachers: their earlier compositions were therefore a product of training in the Western musical idiom, especially of the missionary variety. Their own indigenous music had no marked effect on their training. Nevertheless, their rather mediocre works in the Western idiom, mostly vocal, have a distinctive quality, and this may be attributed to the advantage of their language, which is musical and highly expressive. In South Africa during the nineteenth century churches and schools adopted the Curwen system of Tonic Sol-fa notation and, very naturally, this system formed the basis of musical training in Bantu schools and colleges, where choral singing was invariably the starting point of musical education. A Zulu hymn-book in staff notation was printed in 1862 at Ifafa, but until recently it was the only one of its kind. For an adequate understanding of the achievement of the Bantu composers, one must bear in mind their training in the Curwen system, especially in view of the limitations it imposes.

2. The Lovedale Seminary

On 21 July 1841, when the Lovedale Seminary was opened at Alice with the Rev. William Goven as its first principal, there were 20 registered students. Among them was the future father of **John Knox Bokwe*** who also had his schooling there, before being trained in Scotland for the ministry. Mrs (Dr) Stewart, wife of the succeeding principal, taught Bokwe junior to play the piano and the organ. After completing his education he became, successively, bookkeeper, interpreter, private secretary to the principal, and postmaster of the college; but he also undertook the training of the choir. Arising from his interest in sacred vocal music was a little volume of 12 Xhosa songs, published in small format in 1884, under the title of *Amaculo ase Lovedale.* Subsequent editions in larger format appeared in 1894 and 1910, including some of Bokwe's own compositions, choruses in the original language (Xhosa), and translations into Xhosa of certain Scottish hymns. *Ulothixo Omkhulu,* Bokwe's arrangement of the hymn in commemoration of the conversion to Christianity of the first Xhosa, the prophet Ntsikana, is the most significant item in the second and third editions. — It was the Rev. William Chalmer who sent **Tiyo Soga** to Lovedale. After completing his education there, he went to Scotland where, in 1856, he qualified as an evangelical minister. On his return he devoted his life to the ministry among the Gcaleka of Tutura, in the vicinity of Butterworth. He was a prolific writer of songs, some of which were incorporated into *Incwadi Yama Culo Aserabe,* a hymn-book subsequently published at Lovedale. His son, **John Henderson Soga,** was trained at Lovedale. As a missionary and composer of sacred songs, he followed in his father's footsteps, but he also indulged in the composition of a few light waltzes. — **Benjamin Peter John Tyamzashe*** was at Lovedale from 1906 (when he was in Standard 6) until the completion of his training as a teacher. He taught for a short while at Lovedale, before being appointed to the Tierkloof Institution near Vryburg (1913-24), where he began composing. His first composition *S'Thandwa Sam* was published at Lovedale, and also many of his later works e.g. *Five SSC Part Songs,* for primary school choirs, which appeared in pamphlet form in 1954. The last 26 years of his teaching career were spent at Cala, where he retired in 1950; thereafter he settled in the vicinity of King William's Town. He is best known for his occasional compositions in a style conventionally Western, but he did resort to indigenous elements where he thought this appropriate to any particular song, using the hymn of Ntsikana as his main source. In fulfilment of a commission from the Roman Catholic Church at Lumko, he composed a setting of the Mass using traditional elements of the Xhosa musical heritage, in order to infuse the centuries-old liturgy with something of the spirit of the Xhosa people. He is fond of using descriptive devices: for example, the 6/8 rhythm for conveying the idea of the movement of water; and quaver and semi-quaver motifs to convey suggestions of flowing. According to Deidre Hansen*, there is little originality in his work, which is characterised by fundamental harmonies, quite simple modulations, conventional intervals, parallelism between the different voices and stereotyped forms and formulae. The melody in the top part is invariably the main point of interest in the music. — Bantu teachers trained at

Lovedale played an important part in the schools of the Transkei and Ciskei by creating a love of music among children and adults. A typical personality is **Lawrence Lusaseni,** formerly principal of Moonda School at Mount Frere (from 1934 until his death in 1969), and for many years a dynamic force in the Eisteddfodau held in the Transkei.   —When Lovedale became an institution for higher education, many of the young men who later emerged as composers went there as students. **Enoch Gwashu,** the composer of the inspired song *U-Absalom,* began his schooling at the Bantu School, Port Alfred, and completed his Standard 6 year at Lovedale. It was here that **Gibson Kente,** while studying for his matriculation, gave evidence of his musical talent by composing pieces for his fellow-students as a mere diversion. In 1959 a gramophone record company employed him as a song-writer for the singer Miriam Makeba, and later for the Manhattan Brothers. His three musical plays *Manana the Jazz prophet, Sikalo* and *Lifa* he wrote as librettist and composer, after the year 1963. — **Todd Matchikiza,** who composed the melodies for *King Kong,* was trained for the teaching profession at the Lovedale Training College and taught there for some years before moving to Johannesburg in 1947, where he continued his work as a teacher. He was successively teacher, bookseller, journalist and newspaper editor. In 1961 he went to London as a member of the King Kong company. He decided to remain in London and made a living by playing the piano, giving lectures on music, and taking part in BBC programmes, until 1965, when he was appointed announcer on the Zambian Radio. He died in Lusaka after three years, during which he played an important role in advancing Zambian cultural life.   —When St Matthew's College became an establishment for girls, **Pat Matchikiza,** nephew of Todd, continued his studies at Lovedale and obtained a teacher's diploma there in 1957. But he never actually taught, because he preferred being a professional pianist. He is now regarded as one of the outstanding Bantu jazz pianists. Another jazz pianist of high repute, "Shakes" **Mgudlwa,** completed his education at Lovedale by obtaining the junior certificate in 1952.   —Young men from other Bantu groups studied at Lovedale and a number of them benefited through the musical tradition of this institution. **Michael Moerane*** obtained the junior certificate at Lovedale, and returned there in 1927 as a part-time lecturer at the Training College. During the years 1930-1938 he was on the permanent staff of the Lovedale High School. In 1941 he obtained the B.Mus. degree through the University of South Africa, under the guidance of Professor Friedrich Hartmann. His symphonic poem, *Fatse le heso* (My land) makes use of traditional Basuto songs. In 1944 this work was performed on the BBC, and thereafter in New York and Paris by Dean Dixon.

3. Healdtown

Lovedale remained under the control of the Presbyterian Church. Fourteen miles away at Fort Beaufort, the Methodist Church offered a similar kind of education and facilities for theological study at Healdtown. One of the first ordained Methodist Xhosa ministers at Healdtown, the **Rev. Coke Miji,** and his son **Max,** wrote hymns which were incorporated in the Methodist Xhosa Hymn-book. Also the son of a Methodist minister was **Hamilton Masiza** (1894-1955). He went to school at Healdtown and was trained there as a teacher. Later, through correspondence, he obtained a licentiate diploma in Tonic Sol-fa from the Curwen Memorial College. As a teacher and school principal for more than 30 years, he was the musical mentor and conductor of the Abantu Batho Music Association in Kimberley, which became well-known for its concerts of oratorio and sacred choral music in the Cape and the

Transvaal. It was for this choir that he composed his popular song *Ngasemilanjeni Yasebabilone* (At the waters of Babylon), and his two sacred cantatas *Emnqamlezweni* (At the Cross) and *Uvuko* (The Resurrection). — **Gladson Sidyiyo** acquired his knowledge of singing at Healdtown, where he studied for the teacher's diploma. In his long career as teacher and school principal (1921-1962), mainly in Bloemfontein, he composed a series of light choral works in Xhosa and Tswana. Originally intended for his own choirs, these compositions soon became great favourites with school choirs throughout Southern Africa. Some of the works have their origins in Xhosa history, e.g. *Unongqause* (based on the story of the self-destruction of the Gaika and Gcaleka tribes); others were created from his impressions of life in the South African cities he visited: *eMuizenberg* (Cape Town), *Umzi Waserhini* (Grahamstown), *eZasebhayi* (Port Elizabeth), *Kwelase Monti* (East London). — Sidyiyo's brother, **Nathan**, wrote the junior certificate examination at Healdtown, after which he qualified as a teacher at Clarkbury Institute of Education. In 1936 he composed his first song *I-Mendi.* His training of many choirs and groups during his teaching career in the OFS, Natal and Cape, was an inducement to compose new light choral pieces for them. One of his best, *Lala Ngoxolo* (Rest in Peace) is in serious vein, as a memorial to Dr Verwoerd, deceased Prime Minister of the Republic of South Africa. —Another student of the Shawbury and Healdtown institutions was **Eric Nomvete**, whose parents were Methodist missionary workers in the Transkei. After his training as a teacher at the Adams Training College in Natal, he qualified (in 1944) at the Jan Hofmeyr School for Social Science in Johannesburg. As a welfare worker he had also acquired the reputation of a jazz musician and for a short while he directed his own Tileric Music Studio in East London. He gained some recognition from fronting leading bands on the saxophone, and was responsible for the *African revellers review,* which toured the Cape (1957-1959). With a similar show *Foundation frolics,* he had toured the whole country in 1951, and again in 1957. *Xapa goes to town* was the title of his third production in this kind. — **Benjamin Berner Myataza** was greatly influenced by his uncle, the teacher-composer **Marcus**, and like his uncle he attended the Blythswood Institute before he qualified as a teacher at Healdtown (1928-1930). His uncle's songs and books on music inspired him to embark on a musical career. At the training college his musical gift had attracted attention, and under the guidance of his uncle he began to develop his talent and original ideas. Shortly after he had commenced his teaching career, he undertook musical studies through the Trinity College of Music, and then resigned from teaching to do clerical work; but he continued with musical composition. Since 1965 he has undertaken to write new pieces for the annual National Inter-School Bantu Choir Contests. As examples of these 4 to 8-part choral works *Ingoma Phezu Kodonga Lomlambo* and *Uponi* are worthy of mention. —The principal of Healdtown, Mr J.H. Dugard, encouraged the gifted student **Richard Mfamana** to take up musical composition as a hobby. *Nge 14th May Emqwashini* was written for the Fingo festivities. *Umkosi Wemithika* was composed at the request of the Rev. J.K. Zondi and the Rev. Seth Mokotimi, for the Methodist Fraternal held at Healdtown in 1949. These compositions depict the arrival of the early missionaries in South Africa, the hardships they endured, their courage and their sacrifices.

4. Ohlange Institute

Reuben Caluza is descended from an established line of devout Methodists. His great-grandfather is regarded as the first convert of the Rev. Allison; and his grandfather, **John Mlungumnyama Caluza,** was believed to be the first choir trainer to introduce staff notation into missionary education. It was a concert given by the choirs and brass band of the Ohlange Institute at Pietermaritzburg that persuaded Reuben's father that his son should be sent to this establishment of the American mission (since 1899). By then the son could play the organ, and was accompanist to the kindergarten class. In 1910 he trained a vocal quartet and later took over the whole choir. Under his direction the choir embarked on extensive tours of the country to raise money for school funds, and it was through this that a song recently composed by **Enoch Sontonga*** entitled *Nkosi sikelel'iAfrika* became widely known. Sung to another text, this song became the national anthem of the Transkei. Caluza's compositions at Ohlange between the years 1915 and 1930 owe their origin to his duties as choir trainer, while he was still teaching. Twenty-seven of them were published by the Lovedale Press under the title of *Amagama Ohlane Lakwazulu,* and within six months 1 000 copies (at 50 cents each) were sold. In 1930, at the invitation of His Master's Voice, he went to England with ten Zulu singers to record Zulu songs. In all, 150 of these were recorded; 45 of them are by Caluza, and the rest traditional. He then went to the Hampton Insitute (Virginia, USA) to read for the BA degree in music teaching. His *Rondo for orchestra* and *Reminiscences of Africa* (for string quartet) were based on his song *Ricksha* and the Negro spiritual *Go down Moses* respectively, and submitted to Columbia University, New York, for the degree of MA. In 1937 he returned to South Africa, and for 10 years he was Head of Music at Adams College (Natal).

5. Zulu Training School (Adams), Amanzimtoti
In 1853 the medical missionary, Adams, established a school at his mission station on the Umlaas River. This became one of the most important centres of Zulu education in Natal. Today it is known as the Amanzimtoti Zulu Training School. Since 1937 it has had its own music department, of which **Reuben Caluza** was head until the year 1947. A number of composers have received their training in this department. — After teaching for three years in Lesotho, **Solomon Polile** studied music here (1941-1943), with the assistance of a scholarship awarded by the University of South Africa and the Lesotho Education Department. Some of his Sotho songs *Horolosi, Orange Express, Salang* and *Churchumankhala* can often be heard sung with great enthusiasm. — **B.S.A. Makololo** obtained a teacher's diploma at the Pax Training College near Pietersburg, after which he took a course in music at Adams (1941). **Stephen Modibedi** had his schooling in the OFS and obtained the teacher's diploma at Adams. **Todd Matchikiza** and **Eric Nomvete** matriculated at Adams. In one capacity or another all became known in the world of Bantu music. — Caluza maintained a high standard of musical training at Adams, and it was especially through his choral arrangements that he did much to arouse interest in traditional songs, particularly among fellow students and countrymen. After his retirement he started a chain of trading stores; but in 1962 he accepted the post of lecturer in music at the Zululand University College. He retired finally in 1968.

6. Mariannhill Mission (founded in 1882)
The St Francis College and printing press at Mariannhill has played an important part in Zulu education and musical training. Among the composers who derived great benefit from their training here were **Nimrod Sithole** and his nephew **Elkin,** both of whom qualified as teachers. Nimrod's songs *Bambanani, Bantwana Fundani, Nomo Kunini* and *Umcintiswano* were included in *Amaculo Ezingane Zesikole,* a song-book published by Shuter and Shooter in 1959. Elkin's song *Izimbali Zomdali* is also in this

book. For the Zululand festivities at Nongoma, Elkin was commissioned by the Natal Education Department to write a song which he called *Kithi Kwa Nongoma* (Nongoma my'home). It was performed by a massed choir of 600 voices. Apart from the privilege of receiving a first-class training in music from the sisters of the religious order at Mariannhill, Elkin was encouraged by his uncle and also by a school music inspector, who arranged that he be transferred from Indaleni to Umlazi, so that he might be closer to Durban and enjoy better facilities for the study of music. In 1965 the British Council awarded him a bursary to enable him to continue his studies at the Northern School of Music in Manchester. Later he was enrolled as a student at the Hartt College of Music of the Hartford University in Connecticut (USA), and since 1969 at the State College in Chicago. He obtained the LRAM diploma for singing in 1966. — Another product of Mariannhill is **Alexius Buthelezi,** who attended school there and subsequently obtained a teacher's diploma. In contrast to **Elkin Sithole,** he had to train himself by practising on an harmonium during the lunch hours; for this he had only a pianoforte tutor and occasional help from his fellow students. In the evenings he and his friends would listen to classical music on gramophone records they had borrowed. Gradually he mastered Tonic Sòl-fa and staff notation, and acquired a certain amount of musical background. When he was appointed to a teaching post in Newcastle, he was able to study musical theory properly under the guidance of a teacher from the local convent school, in addition to having regular lessons in piano and singing. In 1960, as a music teacher at the Amanzimtoti Zulu Training School, he obtained the LRSM teacher's diploma in singing; he also trained choirs and began composing. Among his first songs were *Unwabu* (based on a Zulu legend), and *Insimbi Yesikole* (School bells). The latter was included in the volume already referred to - *Amaculo Ezingane Zesikole.* Since his appointment as Zulu announcer for Radio Bantu in 1961, Buthelezi has written music for radio plays: *Unobhathakathi* (about witchcraft); *Nokhwezi* (a Zulu legend), *Ulindiwe* (on the tremendous part played by individuality in the life of a Zulu artist), and *Ihlahla* (a Zulu rendering of Menotti's *Amahl and the night visitors).* In this latter work he makes considerable use of traditional songs, but also of sacred and secular styles. Sixteen foreign radio stations have broadcast Buthelezi's *Nokhwezi.*

7. Lesotho (Morija)

From the year 1868 the Rev. Adolphe Mabille, of the Paris Evangelical Mission, recruited 20 young Basuto from the area round Thaba Bosiu and Morija for training as evangelists and teachers. The first school building was completed in 1870. Originally known as the Morija Normal School, it has changed its name three times: Morija Training College, Basutoland Training College (1947), Lesotho Training College (1964); however, the Bantu usually call it "Thabeng" (on the mountain). A few generations of composers have come from this College, and its printing press has provided music for both church and school; as, for example, the hymn-book *Difela tsa Sione,* which has been used in all the Sotho churches, regardless of denomination, for nearly a century. — By virtue of his clerical obligations, the Rev. Joel Mohapeloa was responsible for the supervision of all schools of the Paris Mission, throughout the whole of the Maluti area. Among other things he organised music competitions for schools. His son, **Joshua Mohapeloa*,** not only had the privilege of becoming closely acquainted, as a child, with choirmasters in various schools; but he grew up in a household where sacred and secular songs were sung regularly in the evenings by family and friends. —In the course of time the music teacher, E.F. Pester, of Morija, laid the foundations for Joshua's musical career by giving him lessons on the piano. After he had matriculated at the South African Native College, Fort Hare, he wanted to continue his studies as a medical student. Ill health prevented him from doing this, and in 1929 he was obliged to remain at home under medical supervision: so he kept himself occupied with further study through correspondence. — In this period Joshua started composing. His first song *Mutlanyana* (Song of a hare) was quickly followed by others; and in 1935 the Morija Book Depot was able to publish a collection of his compositions (32 in all), under the title *Melodi 'Le Lethallere tsa Afrika* (second edition, 1953). A second volume of 32 new songs was published by Morija in 1939 under the same title (second edition, 1945; third, 1955). In this latter collection we find *Leeba* (Dove), *Moshoashoailane* (Song of praise for Moshoeshoe, founder of the Sotho nation) and *Obe* (a creature with big ears). From these collections Sotho children were able to sing, for the first time, songs written in their own language. — On the recommendation of the Lesotho Director of Education, Mr O.B. Bull, the University of the Witwatersrand awarded Joshua a bursary, which enabled him (1938-1942) to attend lectures in musical history, harmony and counterpoint. This gave him confidence in his own ability, and a deepening insight into musical knowledge. In 1947 the Morija Press published a third volume containing 28 of his songs, under the title of *Buka ea Boraro.* — The Basutos regard Joshua Mohapeloa as their foremost composer, and up to the present he has been the most prolific, competent and versatile Bantu composer to come from their ranks. His three volumes comprise both secular and sacred compositions, and reveal a style that has had a far-reaching influence on other Bantu composers. He has a capacity for using the indigenous musical idiom of his people by adapting it to, or integrating it with, Western music, without allowing the "Africanisms" to obtrude themselves unnaturally. On the contrary, he succeeds in employing the greater and more varied resources of Western music as a means of giving an artistic shape to indigenous ideas. What is striking and easily distinguishable is, for example, the deep bass of the traditional *Mekorotlo,* as sung by Basuto men, something indispensable to any good song. — During the years 1930 and 1937 Joshua was also choirmaster at Morija. Officially known as the Morija Choristers, members of the choir called themselves "Manong". They became known throughout Lesotho, OFS and Johannesburg, as a result of their concerts. Five members of the Manong, J.C. Matsoso, L. Mtsasa, S.S. Polile, S. Ntoampe and E.E. Monese, distinguished themselves as Sotho musicians and composers. Gradually the Manong introduced Joshua's songs into the schools, and his musical influence began to spread wider. — Since 1945 Joshua has been proof-reader for the press, but still trains the Baithaopi choir. In September 1963, he was commissioned by Radio Bantu to compose the incidental music for the radio drama *Ya Ba Wa Fihla.* This symbolically expresses man's inclination to accept the Wrong in preference to the Right (messages of Hope being evaded all the time); the work has particular reference to the life of Christ. Mohapeloa's music was written for a four-part choir, which fulfils the three-fold function of narration, orchestra and chorus. After returning from the All Africa Church Music Conference (Mindolo, December 1963 - January 1964) he composed the Easter song *Mor'aMolimo Sefapanong,* which is to appear in a fourth volume containing 100 of his compositions. In many of these new works traditional music still plays an important role. — In 1937 **E.E. Monese** became the first student to gain the newly-instituted Diploma for Higher Primary Education at Morija. Subsequently he matriculated through private study. His music teacher at Morija was Mashologu. Though he was a member of the Morija Choristers, he could not afford the time to undertake the training of the choir. When, however, he became a teacher at the United Bantu Higher Primary School at Senekal, he was asked to take charge of the choir; and whenever songs were lacking, he wrote new ones himself. His *Nanabolele* and *Puleng* have both become best-sellers. — The musical **Josias Matsoso** was known to his fellow students at Morija as "Moharepa" (the harpist). Greatly influenced by the life and work of **Mohapeloa,** he too began composing. Perhaps his best work is *Sehopotso Sa Mmuso Wa Riphabik,* composed for the celebrations in connection with the Republic festival of 1965. It is a hymn of praise in memory of those who founded South Africa, and asks for the blessing of lasting peace and prosperity in our land. Since 1954 he has been a teacher at Ficksburg. — **Kekeletso Phakisi** had his schooling at Morija. While he was still in training as a teacher, he began composing English songs, among them *My native land - Basutoland.* By attending concerts he learnt new songs, and when Mohapeloa's Sotho songs appeared, this was an inspiration to follow. But Phakisi's songs were never published. He has been teaching, though not continuously, since 1923 and since 1957 has lived at Quithing. — **John Nkopane Makhetha*** of Morija was trained for the ministry at Fort Hare, and in 1942 accepted an appointment in Sefikeng in Lesotho. Sixteen years later he moved to Mohale's Hoek. Equipped with nothing but a tuning fork and his own good ear for music, he began writing songs "to make pianos and organs out of children". He does not regard himself as a composer, but says that he merely does his best: "just like the humblest of singers, he sings for his King". — After obtaining a teacher's diploma at Morija, **Mallane Maile*** was a school teacher in Lesotho and South Africa. Meanwhile he qualified himself for the ministry of the Gospel at the Stofberg Memorial School. In 1936, as a minister in the DR Mission Church, he was in Schweizer Reneke, and since 1938 has been in Bothaville. After taking a correspondence course with an American university college, he became a Doctor of Theology. He was endowed with a fine tenor voice, and while still at the theological college, wrote songs for the choir. His first composition *Teatsi la Morena* appeared in 1926, and was later included by the DRC Book Depot in the volume called *Mantloa a Kajeno.* It is significant that this song was written for a school choir, since Maile, true to his nickname Monnana-Moholwana (he who will never grow old), is very fond of young people and believes in the intrinsic value of music as a means of education. There is also a didactic quality in his songs, often presenting aspects of good and evil. His *Kodi Ya Malla* (Lamentations) are musical settings of a number of the psalms. A few of these were included in the recently published *Hosanna,* a hymn-book of the DR Mission Church. — **David Khunou** obtained the NT3 teacher's diploma at the Stofberg Memorial School in 1942, studied for the junior certificate at the Moroka Mission Institute at Thaba 'Nchu, and finally obtained the PH 1 teacher's diploma. While he was teaching at Vereeniging and Sharpeville, he studied privately for matriculation, with the intention of taking a degree by correspondence; but his father died in 1955, and this moved him to compose his first song *Aaron Khunou.* Since then the urge to write musical compositions has supplanted his earlier plans for study. His particular strength lies in sacred music, of which the song *Messia* has acquired special popularity. — While still at school **Walter Sejammutla** had a strong inclination to express his "reading and recitation" through tunes composed by himself; thus the principal of St Patrick's College in Bloemfontein (Brother Patrick True) urged him to take up music as a career. Instead,

Sejammutla went to the Modderpoort Training College, where in 1937 he completed the course for a teacher's diploma, and entered the teaching profession. From 1938 he wrote many songs, e.g. *Molaetsa* (in support of education) and *Sennanapo* (a legend). The latter is still the best song composed to a Tswana text.

8. Valdezia (Swiss mission)

The missionaries of the Swiss Reformed Church have had a profound influence on the Tsonga people of the Northern and Eastern Transvaal. In 1904 **Daniel Marivate** was taught primary school subjects by the Rev. Paul Rosset of Valdezia. Eight years later, with a view to completing a three-year teacher-training course, he registered as a student at the training institute at Elim, run by the same religious denomination. He became a teacher at the Swiss mission station, with two breaks in his teaching service (1924-1925 and 1930) when he was a student at Lovedale. At the latter institution he passed the Junior Certificate examination, and then took a further course of musical training, leading to the diploma of the Curwen School of Music, London. — In 1931 the Singer Gramophone Company invited Marivate to England to make recordings of Tsonga and Venda songs. Three years later he was in England again for a Boy Scouts' training course, and remained there until the outbreak of the Second World War. Returning to South Africa, he was attached to the field staff of the Scouts, both in South Africa and the Protectorates, until 1951. At this time the Swiss Mission was offering free study-courses in theology. Marivate enrolled, and in 1956 was ordained as a minister. Besides working as a minister of religion he continued his scouting duties until 1959, when he relinquished them to give more time to the extensive parish of the Swiss Mission at Atteridgeville, Pretoria. Marivate's songs in Tsonga were written for school, church and the Boy Scouts. Some sacred pieces were included in *Tinsimu,* a hymn-book of the Swiss Mission. He also arranged for choirs traditional songs in Tsonga. His son **Russel,** a medical doctor at Ga-Rankuwa, composes as a hobby.

9. Botshabelo

This educational institution of the Berlin Mission near Middelburg (Transvaal) acquired a name for the high level of musical training it maintained. It was here that **Nathaniel Ramokgopa,** one of the first superintendents of Bantu education in the Transvaal, learnt to play the violin, a skill used in accompanying his family when they gathered in the evening to sing. The musical taste of his son lay in the direction of light music, which he composed for groups such as the Eastern Township Charioteers, and Lo Six in Johannesburg. Not until after the death of his father in 1927 did he begin to write serious choral pieces. *Matsediso* and *Wallmansthal* (the place where he now teaches) are two songs that have been included in the repertoire of the Northern-Sotho Choir. — **Patrick Simelane** qualified as a teacher in 1945 at Botshabelo, and while he was in a teaching post embarked on further study for the BA degree and UED through the University of South Africa. In music he obtained diplomas of the Curwen Tonic Solfa College and certificates of the Royal Schools of Music. The first person to give him encouragement as a composer was W. Endemann, music teacher at Botshabelo. His earliest composition was a new song submitted in a competition. He continued creative work while carrying on his duties as teacher and school inspector. — Simelane had the habit of revising his works frequently, and considered that only about a third of the pieces started achieved a final shape. *Kunjalo,* composed to words by Emerson, and *Ujabuleleni* (Happiness), were specially written for national inter-school choir competitions. In 1952 he was asked to compose the incidental music for the Zulu radio production of *Raka* (N.P. van Wyk Louw). *Indiela Eqond'*

Ekhaya is perhaps most often sung; in this, God in Heaven is asked to protect Bantu mineworkers on the trains that bring them home, after the expiry of their service contracts. Most of his songs are settings of Zulu words, and are characterized by surging phrases, remarkable singability and well-ordered polyphony. Perhaps the quality of his melodic line is the outcome of his love of opera.

10. Kilnerton Institute

Today many Bantu teachers proudly remember the high standard of training it was their good fortune to receive at Kilnerton. **Podu Mamabolo** amused himself by making tunes, and trying to harmonize them. After he had become a teacher, he took theory lessons with **Mike Mlahleki**. Mike, who at the time was music teacher at Kilnerton, had been running his own school of music in Pretoria. Mamabolo became known as a composer with his song *Thuto* (Education), which he wrote while a teacher at Olifantsfontein (1937-1949). In this song, parents are exhorted to send their children to school; and pupils inclined to be idle or indifferent are urged to work harder.

11. Training School, Umfundisweni

Isaac Majola (1902-1959) was trained at this school near Flagstaff, and as a 20 year-old teacher started composing. In the succeeding 37 years he wrote 168 songs, most of them relating to the life and history of the Xhosa people. The progress of Xhosa development can be traced from *Unsikana* to *Ibunga* (the Parliament of the Transkei); and from *Igubu* (the drum) to *Rock-'n-Roll*. With Majola as their trainer, the Gillespie teachers' Choir won the Transkei Shield in choir competitions for three consecutive years. His son, **Hamilton**, was trained by his father in organ playing and composition, and carries on the family's musical heritage.

12. Kimberley

When A.H. Ashworth* taught music at the Perseverance training college in Kimberley, **Henry Jorha** (°1970), son of a Congregational minister, was one of his most promising pupils. Ashworth encouraged him to compose, and in 1929, under his guidance, Jorha completed the teacher's course in music and obtained the ATCL diploma in school-music teaching. Jorha could play the piano reasonably well, but like most Bantu composers, his work with school choirs interested him in choral composition. Besides such choral works as *Emakhaya,* he would also write "pop" songs such as *Ntyilo-Ntyilo*. His versatility stood him in good stead when he became senior programme compiler for the Xhosa service of Radio Bantu at King William's Town. — **Gideon Nxumalo** (°1970) learnt to play the piano at the St Boniface Mission School in Kimberley, and at the age of 9 played his first piece *Bramble Hill*. He eventually became a competent pianist and, with further training at the Roma College and University of Lesotho, a knowledgeable musician. In 1964 he was music teacher for the African Music and Drama Association (ADMA) in Johannesburg. He was partly responsible for orchestrating the music for *King Kong,* and for the incidental music to *Sponono* (text by Alan Paton). His exceptional talent and technical ability enabled him to compose for solo instruments, voices and orchestra, and for all of these in combination, both in the classical and in the jazz idiom. His music drama *At the time of Kigego* was first performed in 1967.

13. Grahamstown

Julius Mtyobo (°1967) and **Jabez Foley**, are two Bantu composers whose musical background was formed through close association with the church in Grahamstown.

Julius's father was an Anglican priest in the diocese of Grahamstown, and he himself was a choirboy under the Rev. W.Y. Stead of St Phillip's Church. After this early musical apprenticeship, he qualified as a teacher at St Matthew's College (1919) and extended his musical knowledge through private study under the guidance of James Rodgers of Cape Town and Douglas Mossop* of Johannesburg. He was further assisted by the personal interest and encouragement of Mr Farrington*, Inspector of Music Education. — At college Mtyobo had started composing, but he also undertook the training and conducting of choirs. Under his direction the Gqeberha Dramatic and Glee Society took part in a number of sacred concerts in the Feathermarket Hall in Port Elizabeth during the 1950's. After retiring in 1961, he became Assistant Director of Religious Education in the Anglican diocese of Grahamstown. He also devoted himself to training St Phillip's church choir, and to composing sacred songs for the Anglican Xhosa youth organisation of the diocese. — **Jabez Foley** succeeded his sister as organist of the Methodist Shaw Memorial Church in Grahamstown, for which his father, Moses, had composed hymns. Jabez had learnt both Tonic Sol-fa and staff notation and, as accompanist to music groups, acquired considerable musical experience. Owing to ill-health, music became his life's work. Of his many compositions the choral song *Ntshangase* has become a great favourite. He died in 1959. — **Chambers Qwesha** was trained in composition by **Julius Mtyobo,** and then by H.J.M. Masiza, Prof. Howell, and finally by Robert Selley*. After completing his first choral work, *Ndisindise O' Jehova* (1946), he wrote several others of lasting merit. — In contrast with these musically talented Bantu who received expert tuition, there were others of exceptional talent who had to struggle on their own, with occasional help from musicians who had enjoyed systematic training. One of the most prolific Xhosa composers, **Gideon Mjekula,** grew up in Peddie. Whenever he was herding the cattle, he tried to incorporate into his singing imitations of bird-song and the noise of running water. In later years he introduced imitative effects into his songs. In *Isikhova* it is the owl that calls by night and sleeps in the day-time, and in *Isinaigogo* the main character is a little bird with a black collar, pecking and crying out "Gobrogo, Gobrogo". When he was 16 years old a school principal, K.K. Mafongoz, and a teacher, H. Mpofu, encouraged him to compose and continue his musical studies. While he was working in East London, he matriculated with the help of correspondence courses. — As a little child **Alfred Assegai Kumalo** used to sing a lot, and unknown to his Christian parents also took part in traditional Zulu dancing. He would be singing all the time, while asking for food, and would keep on repeating the name of his father's wagon driver, Jiza Sikhakhane, as he walked along drumming on a bully-beef tin. He had had some musical training at school. In 1893, after passing Standard 9 at the Nuttall Training College near Edendale (Natal), he started work as a driver on transport wagons going to Johannesburg; then he became a messenger at the Jubilee Gold Mining Company, and finally an interpreter's clerk at New Hanover (Natal). In 1897 he took over the management of his father's transport business, until his trek-oxen died of rinderpest. — These difficult circumstances forced Alfred to go back to Johannesburg, where for a short time he worked for the Goldsmith Alliance. Then his career took some strange and unexpected turns. In 1900 he was a clerk in the Municipal Registration Office in Pietermaritzburg. Soon he became a volunteer in the Natal African Mounted Regiment, which fought in the Bambata Rebellion. Then he was a building contractor for corrugated-iron houses in Krugersdorp and Randfontein (1912-1916); a choirmaster and trainer of the Harmony Singers in Durban (1917-

1952); and finally telephonist at the Edenvale Hospital (1954-1961). His compositions date mostly from the Durban period; from 1961 the emphasis was on church music, most of the works being commissioned. In 1967 Shuter and Shooter published a volume of his songs, for choir, under the title *Inzingoma Zika Kumalo*. This comprises 27 songs, sacred and secular, e.g. *Woza Lapha Mfana, Woza Ngiku Tsheli Indaba, Intokozo, Menzi Wento Zonke.*

14. Urbanized Bantu music

For Bantu workers who gravitated towards the Witwatersrand, the sentimental songs of Europeans and the blaring gramophones that made them available were an attractive novelty. Trade in records and machines flourished, and as soon as Bantu singers began to record song hits, the sales increased rapidly. Then the professional Bantu singers of popular songs came to the fore, and close on their heels followed Bantu composers, writing tear-jerkers in their own language. — Since their schooldays at Pimville Government School, **Ronnie Sehume, Joseph Mogotsi, Rufus Koza** and **Dambuza Mdledle** had sung as a group; during school holidays they sang to earn a living. When they had reached their adult years they formed a "harmony group", presenting themselves as the Manhattan Brothers. At first they imitated the singing of the Mills Brothers and the Inkspots; but with experience they developed a style of their own. In 1946 they presented their Pitch Black Follies and in the following year left school to carve out a career in the world of entertainment. Gallo Africa Ltd. made their first recording in English and placed them under contract to prepare songs in Sotho, Zulu and Xhosa for the recorded music market. From then on their popularity became legendary. In 1961 they accompanied the King Kong group to London, remained there and performed as an ensemble until 1966. — There was no lack of imitators of this kind of musical expression, but most of them followed Western models, or tried to give their songs an original flavour by adapting traditional songs to the prevailing style of singing. The creators of these songs were, and still are, associated with recording companies as talent-scouts. A few deserve to be mentioned: **Rupert Bopape, Strike Vilakazi, Isaac "Zaiks" Nkosi, Cuthbert Matumba, Lebenye Matlotlo, David Thekwane, Enoch Thabethe** and **Raymond Nkue.** — With this flourishing cult of "pop" songs, there had to be a correspondingly rapid advance in instrumental playing. In the Bantu suburbs the reed-pipe flutes of children were replaced by tin whistles (kwêla flutes); when saxophones became a profitable acquisition, those who could afford it provided themselves with these instruments. At the mission schools there was a fair amount of European tuition on the piano and the organ and some of the mission societies trained the students to play wind instruments. Through singing in choirs at school and sporadic training on instruments, many pupils acquired a sufficient knowledge of musical notation and of the techniques of playing to take part in the stampede for big money, popularity and the glamour of footlights. The scope provided by the new market for light dance music justified maximum efforts, and sometimes offered highly profitable returns. Five different instrumental combinations can be distinguished: (i) the kwêla group consisting of penny (tin) whistles, guitars and sometimes home-made cellos (or double bassses). The kwêla tunes of **Lemmy "Special" (Mabaso)**, entitled *Chris special* and *See you later*, became "hits" both in South Africa and overseas; (ii) the township Bantu Jazz Orchestra consisted originally of saxophone, double bass, drums and guitars, for the so-called *Saxophone-Jive* items. From this combination there evolved a trio of fronting guitarist, rhythm-guitarist and drums, with or without a saxophone. This was obviously an imitation of the jazz style, but handicapped by the limitations of their techniques. Nevertheless the orchestras developed an individual style, and the profits were so attractive that new groups appeared like mushrooms. Their music had little constructive melody, and was limited to basic harmonies, thriving on repetition and characterized by a sameness that emphasizes the rhythm. The use of traditional musical elements ensured the success of this style among the urban Bantu. There is hardly any original work in this musical activity, and the so-called composers are no more than diligent imitators and arrangers;   (iii) the Rock-'n-Roll groups, with their guitars and drum rhythms, are also the reflected images of their European counterparts;   (iv) orchestras that play for dances follow the instrumentation and style of European dance-bands;   (v) jazz combos. Increasing numbers of Bantu are making an intensive study of the technical possibilities of their instruments (piano, cello, drums, guitar, saxophone, trombone, trumpet, vibraphone) and now speak disparagingly of "cheap, commercialized jazz". They are at home in the arts of improvisation and variation, and in the polyrhythms inherent in the traditional Bantu song and dance; and they cultivate progressive jazz, with an intuitive feeling for the use of sound in choral combination. Consequently their music sounds characteristically Bantu, a result of the traditional sonorities of untempered tuning. — During the years 1956-1960 the pioneers **Dollar Brand** (piano), **Kiepie Moeketsi** (alto-saxophone), **Jonas Gwangwa** (trombone), **Hugh Masekela** (trumpet), **Johnny Gertze** (cello) and **Mackay Ntshako** (drums) had begun to experiment with instrumental combinations. — Dollar, who was privileged to receive piano lessons at school in Cape Town, had played in a dance orchestra during his early years. He learnt a great deal from experienced orchestral players, including the art of reading musical notation with facility. With increasing experience he began to think of developing his own style. He took up pure jazz and practised from 8 to 10 hours daily in a garage furnished as a practice room. Unfortunately he discovered that this style, which he had cultivated so assiduously, did not meet with favour; so he went to Switzerland, where he played in a combo consisting of cello, drums and piano. Duke Ellington heard him and, as repertory-scout for the company Reprise, arranged to make recordings of his playing. Then followed contracts in London, the USA and a number of European countries; participation in the Newport Jazz Festival in 1965; concert appearances with Duke Ellington and the Elvin Jones Companies (1966-1967); in addition to various appearances in Village Vanguard, Village Gate, Carnegie Hall, Lincoln Centre, in radio orchestras and on television. — With enthusiastic reviews of his solo performances and recordings, Dollar acquired an international reputation in the keenly competitive world of jazz. On his return to South Africa in 1968 he toured the country, playing to capacity houses and, with his wife, the singer Bea Benjamin, is still in constant demand. With his solo piano works, in which he feels that he has reached the top level of self-expression, he by-passes progressive jazz, and in pieces like *Titinyana* he enters the new style of the electronic era. In many items there is a South African background and echoes of traditional elements of Xhosa music, as in *South Easter,* and in his suite *Portrait of a Bushman.* — Arising from the great success of *King Kong,* (text by Harry Bloom and music by **Todd Matchikiza:** Johannesburg 1960; London 1961), the Union of South African Artists (Union Artists of Dorkay House) came into being. This group was to play an important role in the promotion of light musical entertainment, and in the performance of dramatic pieces featuring professional Bantu musicians and actors. **Mackay Davashe** (° 1972) led the *King Kong* orchestra with his alto-saxophone. Since 1943 he had been a professional player in Johannesburg, had toured with the Manhattan Brothers and was leader of the jazz groups in the jazz sessions of the 1950's. *Khumbula Jane,* his first song, was composed for the Brothers. His song *Kilimanjaro* became famous through the Harmony Singers, though originally composed in another form as *Izikalo Zegoduka.* When *King Kong* was in preparation, he worked as an arranger with Stanley Glasser,* and later, on his own, composed the music for *Bobo,* a production of Union Artists (1966-1967). His song *Lakutshon'Llanga* is a Xhosa favourite.

15. Radio Bantu

By fostering the amateur and professional potentialities of the Bantu in Southern Africa, giving them guidance and encouragement through recordings and broadcasts, Radio Bantu (since its inauguration in 1960) has in many ways become a focal point of Bantu music. To composers and performing artists of all kinds it has given ample opportunity to become known. Through close liaison between school and church, serious Bantu music in all its aspects has developed a pattern, characterized, however, by strongly differentiating features of a regional nature. The knowledge that these works may now be heard on the radio in seven different language services, over the length and breadth of the country, has created conditions for comparisons, and interacting influences - needful to musical development. Radio Bantu has also brought to the fore the singer from the kraal. From a tribal background such a creative musician as **Princess Magogo Buthelezi** (daughter of the headman, Dinuzulu) has been honoured by the Zulus as a traditional singer par excellence. In songs of religious character she accompanies herself on an auto-harp, and in epic tribal songs on the Ugubu, which she herself tunes with accuracy and sensitivity. — Since 1964 lessons on Bantu composers, including examples from their works, have been broadcast on the school programmes of Radio Bantu. As a guide, the SABC published in 1969 *The Bantu composers of Southern Africa* by Yvonne Huskisson*. With this work, a book of reference has become available for schools, libraries, universities and broadcasting studios in South Africa and in foreign countries. The book contains information on 318 Bantu composers and their works, and on the development of Bantu music in Southern Africa.

BIBLIOGRAPHY

HUSKISSON, DR Y.H.: *The Bantu composers of Southern Africa.* SABC, Johannesburg, 1969.

—Y.H.

BANTU MUSICAL CORPORATIONS OF JOHANNESBURG, 1949-1976. From 1949 to 1954 a group of energetic and enthusiastic Bantu men of musical calibre tried to stimulate a love of· serious music among the Bantu of Johannesburg by getting renowned visiting artists to include in their concert schedule a concert for the Bantu, in the Bantu townships. This group called themselves the Syndicate of African Artists.

Developed concurrently, under the auspices of the Bantu Affairs Department of the Johannesburg Municipality, was an annual eisteddfod for Bantu musicians known as the *Bantu Music Festival.* It still flourishes. The Bantu Affairs Department, however, did not confine its cultural interest to this one event. They appointed a Cultural Activities Officer, attached to the Recreation and Community Services Department, who was responsible firstly, for the organisation and holding of music classes, giving individual and group instrumental and vocal tuition at various Bantu community centres; secondly, this officer's task was to promote musical appreciation in the Johannesburg township complex of Soweto. This post was held from 1957 to 1964 by Khabi Mngoma*, a Zulu tenor/pianist/conductor who had been trained as a teacher at Adams College (Natal) and then studied singing, piano and conducting privately. Initially a teacher, in 1953 he became Supervisor of the Chiawelo Community Centre in Johannesburg. —Mngoma founded the Orlando Music Society in 1948, the Moroka Township Music Appreciation Group in 1954, the Ionian Male Voice and Mixed Choirs in 1960 and shortly afterwards the first Bantu string ensemble, known as the Jubilee String Players. To launch this group he took both violin and cello lessons and the Bantu Affairs Department made a bursary available for further musical study. During the Johannesburg Festival in 1965, Soweto choirs combined under Mngoma's baton for performances of *Judas Maccabaeus* and *Samson* (Handel). As Personnel Relations Officer, Mngoma trained and conducted the Ionian Choirs, and adjudicated and lectured on choral singing. Since 1975 he has been senior lecturer in Music at the University of Zululand and head of the newly-created music department. —In 1959 the Johannesburg African Music Society came into being. Three Soweto choirs i.e. the Jabavu Choristers, Christ the King Church Choir and the St Augustine Church Choir, under their respective conductors, Ben Xatasi, Michael Rantho and Stanford Gxashe, combined to perform *Messiah* in the City Hall. The organisers were Osborn Ferdinand and J.P. Tutu, both teachers, their sponsors the Desert Lily Shell-hole of MOTHS. The JAMS have since given performances of *Messiah* and *Elijah*. In 1964 they staged a Civic Theatre presentation, *Intsholo,* a programme of Euro-Bantu choral items in S. Sotho, N. Sotho, Xhosa and Zulu, plus a few choral arrangements of indigenous traditional songs. The conductors Joseph Friedland,* Jeremy Schulman* and John Kavan and the soprano Anne Feldman* have assisted them in these efforts. — In 1960 the African Music and Drama Association (AMDA) was founded under the auspices of the Edward Joseph Memorial Trust Fund. Classes, first held at the Jubilee Social Centre, were to provide city Bantu with the opportunity to study music seriously. Several European music-teachers devoted a few hours per week each to teaching pupils free of charge and a small Bantu staff (among them Gideon Nxumalo) gave regular music instruction. AMDA is still in existence. It has always been closely affiliated to Union Artists and, since 1964, has joined forces with Union Artists and is also known as Dorkay House (the venue occupied by Union Artists since its creation in 1960). —Union Artists (Union of South African Artists) was the brain-child of Stanley Glasser*, Ian Bernhardt and Leon Gluckman, who were also responsible for the creation of AMDA. The aim of the society has been to promote the Bantu artist. It does this by staging concerts and shows in and around Johannesburg (which enable the Bantu musician and actor to make a professional living, and the new artist to become known) and by acting as an impresario for Bantu artists. Dorkay House provides practice and rehearsal-room facilities. Major productions of Union Artists have been: *Call me mister; Emperor Jones; King Kong* (a musical staged in Johannesburg, 1960, and London, 1961) and *Sponono* (a play staged in Johannesburg, 1963, and New York World Fair, 1964). — Union Artists have staged *Jazz festivals* and *Township jazz* in Johannesburg since 1961, and provided the artists for the *Batfair trade shows,* held in Bantu homelands during the years 1963 to 1965. In 1964, after the amalgamation of AMDA and Union Artists, a Music Workshop was started at Dorkay House, while under the School Theatre

Project, plays have been staged regularly at Transvaal Bantu schools. In July 1967 Khabi Mngoma became the part-time director of Dorkay House. — The Jubilee String Players, originally founded by Khabi Mngoma, then Recreation Officer of the Johannesburg Municipality in the townships, has, since 1972, become the 40 strong Soweto Symphony Orchestra directed by Shadrock Masote, under the auspices of the Johannesburg City Council Recreation Department. — The Ionian Orchestra which played under Khabi Mngoma, mainly accompanying the performances of the Ionian Choirs, are finding his dynamic leadership difficult to replace since his appointment to the Zululand University in mid 1975. — Dorkay House (Union Artists) have specialised in drama presentations, many of their professional artists having gone their separate ways. They have, however, increased the individual music teaching facilities. A Music Centre is to be erected next to the Baragwanath Hospital.

—Y.H.

BANTU SCHOOLS (1970), MUSIC IN In 1970 about 44 000 teachers were attached to more than 9 000 primary schools, 380 intermediate schools (where the courses go up to Junior Certificate) and 31 training schools for teachers. Music has been included in the syllabuses of all classes up to and including Junior Certificate, but without an examination. The training schools have an internal examination at the end of the first year to determine which practical subject (music, art, craft, needlework or gardening) is strong enough for a second year's study. To complete the course, at the end of two years, the school where the candidate does his tests is responsible for his final examination. —The department prepares the syllabuses for each class, starting with the sub-standards and going on to Junior Certificate and also prescribes the course of study for the training of future teachers in music in the two-year course. During the first school years, the children have to learn nursery rhymes and action songs in the mother tongue. One or two suitable songs in one of the official languages are prescribed for Standard 1, but such songs are strictly limited - at the end of the Higher Primary course one half of all the songs still have to be in the mother tongue. Principals and music teachers have the responsibility of selecting twelve songs in the mother tongue for the Junior Certificate course. In theory the best songs in each language group should be chosen, but in fact far too much time is devoted to competitions which prescribe songs of doubtful value. —In the first stages, songs are taught by rote, but the study courses prescribe that in Standards 2 and 3 the songs should be written in tonic solfa on a blackboard. From this stage onward the pupils are expected to acquire a knowledge of solfa and staff notation. It is by no means the exception to find that teachers, even in the secondary classes, are unable to switch over to written music and still employ singing by rote. No written theory is expected of pupils in the primary schools; in the secondary schools, this aspect of music teaching is coupled with the teaching of singing by sight. —Inspectors of the department visit the training colleges regularly twice a year and since textbooks, songbooks and blackboards with staves are readily available, the progress is generally quite satisfactory. The standard of teaching in the practical subjects was improved in 1970 by a scheme which makes it obligatory for all students in the first year to follow a course in music and three other practical subjects. Thus all are taught solfa and staff notation, selected primary school songs and teaching method. Subject to the approval of the principal, students are allowed to choose a subject in which they wish to specialise during the second year. Those who choose music have one period for each weekday during the whole year available for music and regular practical experience in teaching at the nearest available school. — Selected students at the higher or training schools of Eshowe and Hebron in Pretoria North, have been introduced to pianoforte playing since 1967. At each of these centres, three practice pianos are available for the use of students, but the progress is slow, since only one or two students have the possibility of practising during the holidays. The value of the tuition lies more in the interest that it possibly awakens, than in the practical application of pianoforte playing in class teaching.

SOURCE

REES, E.: Music in Bantu schools. *25th Newsletter,* SASMT (Pretoria Branch), October 1970.
—Ed.

Inter-school competitions are very much the order of the day. Allied to these, urban and country inter-church choir and inter-hospital choir competitions are increasing, in the case of churches to raise the standard of church music; the hospital choirs are for additional staff relaxation and social extra-mural activity. The Transkei, Ciskei, Kwazulu, Lebowa, Bophutatswana, Venda, Gazankulu and Qwaqwa governments have their own Organisers of Music/Culture operating in their own educational circuits to organise musical events, in some instances both choral and traditional, school and adult. Mr P.M. Ntloko, Cultural Organiser of the Transkei, has done Trojan work in this regard. School choirs and traditional groups competed in all 28 districts of the Transkei as part of their Independence Celebrations with the 10 top competitors performing at the Independence Stadium on the 26th October 1976. — A Music Department established at the Fort Hare (Xhosa) University near Alice in 1974, has already produced a Fort Hare University Choir which has undertaken several tours. Prof. G Gruber*, retired from Rhodes University Music Department, is at the helm, with professional instrumental tuition assistants and, since 1976 with Mr M.J.W. Sgatya, formerly Ciskei Organiser of Music, on the permanent staff. — August 1975, saw the resurrection of the Music Department of the Zululand University, with Khabi Mngoma, just returned from educational visits to the USA, UK and West Germany in 1975, appointed as senior lecturer. A Zululand University choir and orchestra are already in being. A 4-year B.Mus. degree course commences from 1977 with a core of Khabi Mngoma's own students from Johannesburg who have attained the necessary entrance qualifications. — The standard of black choirs in the Republic took a sharp downward plunge in the early 70's, but is now stabilising with a re-awareness among conductors of the finer points of choral work and the hours of practice required to achieve it. In Natal especially, thanks mainly to the untiring efforts of Patrick Buthelezi, former Training College choirmaster, appointed to the Zulu Service of the SABC to produce the music for these programmes, the past 3 years have seen a remarkable number of school choirs once again singing extremely well.
—Y.H.

BARBER, J   Durban 10, Durban Municipal Bantu Brass Band

BARBERTON, MUSIC IN (1886-1914)
    I   Introduction
    II   Music halls
    III   Societies
    IV   Operetta
    V   Variety concerts

I. INTRODUCTION

The history of Barberton and its musical life begins with the gold that a certain French Bob extracted from the Duiwels Kantoor (The Devil's Office) on a day in 1883. The Kantoor was a sweltering hot mountain basin and valley, also known as the North Kaap Valley, not far from the present town. This discovery unleashed the first of three gold rushes. At first, diggers' camps sprang up at Jamestown, Avoca, Eureka City and Blandtown - all of them ghost towns today. After the discovery of even richer alluvial deposits on thirteen farms adjoining the river in the valley - all belonging to G.P. Moodie - the second wave of fortunehunters came. From Sweden, Australia, Cornwall, Ireland, France and America, they poured in over rough paths and swollen rivers; and over the rugged mountain passes that descended abruptly, sometimes 800 metres within a few kilometres, so that wagons and their loads had, literally, to be carried by hand. They came on horseback, on foot, in scotch-carts, and wagons - adventurers such as Yankee Moore, Charley the Tinker, Californian Wilson, Rocky Mountain Thompson, Harry the Sailor, Northern Territory Jack, Canada Joe: and a few women like Cockney Liz, later to become queen of the barmaids, and Granny Klok, a widowed nurse with six children. — In 1883 the focal point of the community was Yankee Moore's shop. Beneath a gigantic bucksail, stretched over poles, he sold his merchandise, anything from mealie meal to candles and castor-oil, and any amount of gin. Here the diggers sat round on flour bags, drinking and talking. When they paid in "cash", they took out of their trouser pocket a paper bag of golddust, and carefully weighed out enough to meet the cost of their purchases. A "Diggers' Committee" not only protected the interests of the diggers, but also punished or even banished offenders. There were grievances in abundance. In 1884 Mr Moodie sent an agent to negotiate with the diggers. He was supported by a bodyguard of five tough hunters: the brothers Fred and Harry Barber (sons of an 1820 settler), their cousin and two friends. But the agent felt quite safe with the diggers, and dispensed with his bodyguard. The Barbers went hunting and prospecting in the mountains near Rimer's Creek and discovered a rich gold deposit. On 24 June the gold commissioner, David Wilson, broke a bottle of gin against the rocks and christened the place Barberton. A third wave of people eager for gold came flooding in, and within a year there were 10 000 inhabitants in Barberton. In 1885 it was publicly proclaimed as gold diggings to be governed by a resident commissioner supported by a diggers' committee. — The diggings became a mining town. Houses and shops sprang up; business people prospered; there was work everywhere; a magistrate and police were appointed. However, living conditions were hard; malaria and typhus rife, and largely responsible for the deaths in the bucksail-and-pole "hospital" (the real hospital was not built until 1886). Sanitation was primitive, and the community became isolated through lack of adequate roads and bridges during the protracted summer rains. At times not even the mule wagon bringing the post could get through. Gold was the reason for 9 000 residents leaving Barberton in 1886 for the newly-discovered reefs of Johannesburg, where many of them acquired fame: Abe Bailey, Sammy Marks, Alfred Beit, Ikey Sonnenberg, Percy Fitzpatrick (of "Jock of the Bushveld" fame), Stafford Parker; even the Barber brothers. The 1 000 people who remained at Barberton made a start with town planning, and a committee was set up to control water rights, sanitation etc. In 1887 the Republican government had refused to declare Barberton a municipality; not until 1895 did it attain the status of a town - and one that could already boast of having its own newspapers.   —Newspapers were at first printed on any bits of paper: scribbling paper, brown paper, ruled paper - even toilet paper. There were three important newspapers, of which the *Goldfields Times* (established 1886) and the *Goldfields News* (established 1886) were amalgamated in 1890, later to be merged with the *Barberton Herald*. After 1892 the only newspaper that survived was the *Goldfields News: the Barberton and Nelspruit Herald*. A.W. Bayly was editor of the *News* until his death in 1915. After that it continued until 1947, when it was incorporated with the *Lowveld Leader* (also started in 1886). Bayly, who had newly arrived from Harrismith was an enthusiastic amateur musician. He was to be until his death the king-pin of Barberton's musical life. He was a church organist; helped to found the first musical and orchestral society; often appeared in public as singer and conductor - and within a year of his arrival had opened a music shop. In 1886 there was only one piano in the town, and this belonged to a teacher, Mrs Button. Bayly borrowed it frequently for variety concerts, which, with all the singing voices and musical talent available on the diggings, were quite the order of the day.

II.   MUSIC HALLS

Until 1886 there was no hall for musical performance, and private houses, barns, business premises and hotels had to provide venues for concerts (and even church services). In that year the first church building (Roman Catholic) was started under strange circumstances. One day Father Kelly was walking back to Barberton through the rain and slush from a burial in the mountains. On the Market Square, Stafford Parker saw him approaching, tired and dirty, and exclaimed that "there is a man with neither house nor church". Within 24 hours R2 000 had been collected. This event also hastened the building of other English churches. Sometimes these churches were used for concerts of sacred music.   —Dance and music halls meant profit. Between 1886 and 1888 several of them were built, usually of corrugated iron and wood. Drinks and refreshments could be bought during the "Music Hall" items - also the practice at the later concerts of serious music. Most of these places were just beer halls. Others had high-sounding names: The Royal Albert Hall, Marble Arch, the Barberton Royal (Standard) Music Hall, The Kaap Exchange. The first municipal hall was only built in 1909.   —The Barberton Royal Music Hall, made of wood and iron, was knocked together in Pietermaritzburg in 1886, transported by wagons to Barberton, and erected on a suitable vacant stand. It covered an area of 18m x 12m and was designed by W. Thorne (the Natal stage designer) as a "music hall equipped with a stage". The owner, E. Perkins, arrived in Barberton together with his hall and a concert party and started a series of concerts (see Chapter VI). In April 1887, this hall, re-christened "The Royal Standard Music Hall", lived through yet another inaugural concert. Perkins appointed a new manager - a certain Mr Deboas - who engaged a visiting company, including "Professor" Ferreira and Messrs Goodman and Daniels, for a programme of songs, dances and variety turns. After this he advertised the hire of the hall for dances and performances as "the coolest and most comfortable hall in the town".   —The Kaap Exchange Hall, part of a building complex comprising brokers' offices and a board room, was opened on 2 February 1887, by the magistrate J.Z. de Villiers. The builder was J. Kirknis, and a certain Mr Halder was the architect. It was neatly finished off with a ceiling and had fairly good acoustics. The auditorium was 20,3m x 11,2m and the stage 4,5m x 2,4m. The *Goldfields Times* described the inaugural concert as "the first musical performance of a classical nature that had yet been given in Barberton". In spite of a torrential downpour on the iron roof, which all but drowned the voices of the singers, the audience was ecstatic in its appreciation, the favourite singer being Mrs Richards (Virginie Cheron*). But the newspaper critics intoned a refrain that recurred until 1914: "creaky-booted seat-holders" disturbed the audience by walking in and out of the hall during the items. — The Royal Albert Hall (built by a Mr Behr) was opened on 16 July 1887. With a floor space of 18,2m x 9,1m, it was a poor relation of its illustrious namesake in London. On the other hand, it could boast of genuine stained-glass windows, and it had three paintings hanging on the wall, one depicting President Kruger and the others Queen Victoria and the Prince of Wales. To the left front was a "specially decorated" platform for the orchestra. — The first municipal hall was built in 1909. In fact, it was just an old recreation hall that had been demolished and, with added improvements and facilities for artists, re-erected on a new site "to fulfil its elevated purpose until the dawn of better days". Acoustically it was poor "since, in the construction of the stage, far too much emphasis had to be given to air space". The auditorium was decorated in shades of blue, and provided with walnut seats and "artistic" lamps. The floor was reinforced for dancing, a new piano was purchased, and scenery painted for the stage. The rental was moderate. The inaugural concert on 16 February 1909, was arranged by Mrs A.E. Graham Lawrence, a well-known amateur singer. She harnessed all the local talent and rendered a few songs herself, including *Villanella* (E. dell' Agua) (sic!).

III.   S OCIETIES

1. The Smoking Club
2. Barberton Orchestral Society
3. Choral societies
4. Barberton Recreation Society

1.   The Smoking Club
In Barberton, "music" virtually meant light entertainment. The first musical society was The Smoking Club, founded in 1886 by Daniel Defries*, as a place where menfolk could enjoy pipes, cigars and "good" music (in a Victorian sense); it met once a week at an hotel. Members sang or recited for their fellows; and this was sometimes varied with "priceless imitations of the piccolo and banjo" (by a certain Mr Delmonti) or humorous sketches. The gentlemen Neale, Cohen, Fletcher, Blaine, Reinhold, Needham and others, often repeated the items at different concerts. Within a short time Defries became conductor of the Orchestral Society and a committee member of the Philharmonic Society, whose services he then commandeered for the Smoking Club. Each meeting had a different host. The programme that Clayton presented on 5 July 1887, was more or less typical:
Solo song, *Brown eyes and blue,* Blaine; solo song, *Love's labour lost,* Myers; solo song, *Once upon a time,* Clayton; recitation from *Othello,* Bennett; piano duet, Reinhold and Needham; solo song, *Sailing,* Blaine; solo song, *Three jolly sailors,* Clement; reading from Mark Twain's *Roughing it,* Dr Wolff; solo song, *The Midshi,* Myers; recitation, *The heathen Chinee,* Tallermann; piano duet; student songs; *Auld lang syne; The Transvaal Volkslied,* Reinhold and Needham.
By 7 June 1887, there were 50 members, and the fair sex could no longer be excluded.

From 17 June they were invited every month to a so-called ladies' evening. Apart from this privilege, they were not allowed membership and were not even permitted to buy tickets for the club's charity concerts. "Ladies are to be invited," said the *Goldfields News* (18 October 1887). Here the three Neale brothers made their debut as singers. Harry, the youngest, was to sing at nearly every Barberton concert. But the programmes became monotonous, and especially in August 1887, during the operetta season of the Bolder company, there was a lean period. Indeed, on 23 August there was no concert at all; according to the *Goldfields Times,* the artists had lost both their money and their enthusiasm at the horse races, and didn't turn up for the concert. — From then an effort was made to raise the standard of the programmes, with guest artists such as P. de Jongh (tenor of the Perkins company), and Professor Witte (Bolder company) with zither and zylophone solos; or with female singers, or a Minstrel evening with the Byron Amateur Minstrel Troupe (1 September). A year later the Orchestral Society provided a programme; it also played at the farewell concert for Reinhold (who left for England). Defries also intended returning to England and left in January 1889; but he got no further than Johannesburg. Enthusiasm for the club declined still further, and in 1890 it was decided that henceforth the Smokers' Evenings should be held at the Royal Albert Hall. This lasted only until February 1892, when the club again held a concert in the United South African Billiard Saloon. After that it went back to the hotels e.g. Phoenix Hotel (2 May 1892); Granville Hotel (25 October 1892) and Crown Hotel (21 March 1893). Gradually the programmes deteriorated, and on the subject of the last-mentioned concert the newspaper wrote that "songs of the *Knock'em down in the old Kent Road* type were the most prominent items". Thus the flame of the Smoking Club sometimes glowed dimly, but it never quite subsided; in 1902 the Club was still treated to lunch-hour music by the band of the Lincolnshire Regiment.

2. Barberton Orchestral Society

Early in 1887 A.W. Bayly, Daniel Defries and A.E. Graham Lawrence (cornettist and cellist and founder of the Barberton Brass Band) began discussions about an orchestral society. With the moral support of the *Goldfields News* (29 March), they called an inaugural meeting for 11 May, and Bayly was elected president; he sometimes also officiated as choirmaster and conductor. Defries was conductor and Graham Lawrence the secretary. At first the orchestra provided the usual variety concerts. On 22 March 1888, there were, for example, eight solo songs and five orchestral numbers: *Polka travestur; Iris valse;* overture to *Masaniello; The flying colours* and the *Transvaal Volkslied.* Concerts were popular, but after this concert the *Golfields Times* commented on members of the audience "who not only caused annoyance to the performers, but were being most distasteful to the audience by talking while the singers were doing their best to provide a good rendering of the music." This complaint became a recurring theme. — At first the society performed often: 19 June, 23 June, and on 24 July 1887, at one of Breakspeare Smith's concerts (see Chapter VI). On 28 August the Orchestral Society arranged a *soirée* about which the *Times* wrote: "the Society is an institution very much in evidence. The talent and services of its members, from its conductor D. Defries, that veteran wielder of the baton, down to the big drummer, are always willingly offered". The orchestra played for the Smoking Club on 24 September; and after the dance of the Orchestral Society on 26 October, a local newspaper expressed the hope that henceforth, at the big dances, piano music would be replaced by that of the orchestra! On 16 November it gave the first of a long series of concerts in the park. — Defries left in January 1889, and commended the members of the orchestra on the musical progress they had made under his direction. E.H. Cohen became conductor for six months, and when Reinhold, the accompanist left, his place was taken by A.W. Bayly, who often acted as conductor. He was complimented on the proficiency shown by the orchestra when it played under his baton. He was insistent on correct (tonal) balance and precision of attack. Especially on those occasions requiring an orchestral accompaniment, his services were greatly appreciated. He also provided musical instruments and sheet music from his shop. In July 1889, there was a complaint in the newspaper that there were too few instrumentalists. To this the secretary replied with "a concert of very up-to-date highbrow music," under the patronage of Mr Justice Esselen. For this purpose he had reorganised the society and appointed a new conductor, E.E. Vogts, who raised the standard of the programmes - a daring thing to do in Barberton! Interest was stimulated, and the Kaap Exchange was packed for the first concert in September 1889, in which the orchestral items were: *L'Espair d'Alsace,* March from *La Prophete* (Meyerbeer), Overture to *Caliph of Bagdad* (Boieldieu), *Aus dem Hochland* (Kaulich), *Souvenir de Tyrol* (Witmann) and a Strauss waltz. The programme also contained 4 instrumental duets and quartets, as well as 4 vocal solos. Immediately the public raised a storm of protest: there were too many long orchestral pieces and too few songs.   Soon afterwards (December) there was, by invitation, a concert conducted by Tallermann, but whether due to Tallermann or the programme, the dissatisfaction among the audience (see Chapter VI) rose to such a pitch that the musicians had to stop playing, and the concert ended in confusion. The newspaper, however, offered some consolation: in spite of the noise, the orchestra did succeed in giving an excellent rendering of one or two of the items. On 14 October 1890, there was a new committee, with W. Davies as chairman, while Graham Lawrence continued as secretary. The other members were W. Young, A.W. Arenhold, E.W. Knox and W.S. Riddel. Vogts was still the conductor. The programmes were planned to conform to the taste of the general public, and on 4 April A.W. Bayly conducted "a delightful programme of classical music", consisting of melodious English tunes.   —The orchestra now had 6 violins, 1 cello, 1 double bass, 2 flutes, 1 piccolo, 1 cornet, 1 French horn (J.H. Hofmeyr),   1 organ (harmonium?) and 2 pianos (played by Mrs J.H. Hofmeyr and W.S. Riddel). But many people were opposed to an orchestra, and on 20 August 1891, the *News* had to plead that "the Society must fulfil the essential but thankless role of being a true and powerful instrument for educating the public in the sphere of music". When on 15 April 1892, the orchestra played at its own dance, assisted by the Barberton Brass Band, the newspaper published a letter expressing apprehension that the Barberton Brass Band might lose its identity in the orchestra! So much opposition caused enthusiasm to wane, though the newspaper attributed the decline in the orchestra to superior performances by visiting companies and local societies, such as the Barberton Recreation Society, Amateur Dramatic Club and minstrels. A.W. Bayly deplored the lack of orchestral members; at the promenade concert of 22 January 1895, and the St Andrew's Day concert of December 1897, there were only thirteen present.   — The orchestra did not perform again in public until after the War, but on the departure of the Lincolnshire Regiment and its military band in February 1904, the newspaper expressed a yearning for the old orchestral society. Three months later A.W. Arenhold directed an "orchestra" of seven players.

However, the war had not altered the attitude of the public, and in the same year various other conductors, including J.G. Tomlinson, tried to do something about it. On 5 July Graham Lawrence, in collaboration with the conductor, W.D. McClelland, arranged a concert which included a *Cake walk* by Buccalossi. The members of the "orchestra" were A.W. Arenhold and A.W. Willis (first violins); Miss Eaton, W. Bayly and J. Roberts (second violins); A.E. Graham Lawrence (cello) and Ida Wood (piano). During the following years, the orchestra slowly emerged from the depths, until the newspaper averred in November 1909, that it was "numerically as strong as the old orchestra of the pre-war days", though not yet able to reach the same heights. —There was a chronic shortage of money. For the purchase of new instruments, music stands and sheet music, there followed on 19 November 1909, a concert under the direction of J. Thompson, with Mrs Graham Lawrence as singer. The orchestra provided eight of the twelve items. Mrs Graham Lawrence sang two operatic arias: *Ah, forse é lui (Traviata)* and the *Jewel song (Faust).* The conductor played a clarinet solo, and the string players a serenade. The orchestral numbers were light: a march, a gavotte, two selections from the operettas, a Graceful Dance from *Henry VIII* (German) and a descriptive piece, *Our branch line.* There were still a few of the original members of the orchestra: A.W. Arenhold, Graham Lawrence, W. Grubb and Mrs Wood. In addition some of their children, a few of them very young, also assisted, e.g. the two Wood boys, W. Arenhold and W. Bayly. The others were newcomers. There were 4 first and 2 second violins, 2 cellos, first and second cornet, euphonium, flute, clarinet, drum, triangle and pianoforte. — But the writing was on the wall. Trouble-makers stayed away, others sought their entertainment elsewhere, and the audience dwindled. After a concert on 18 March 1910, the following critical comment appeared in the newspaper: "Even when free concerts are offered in the municipal hall, the adults who are invited send their children instead". Two other concerts were held in 1912, but on 12 September 1913, there followed a kind of death notice in the newspaper: "During the past 12 months Barberton has been entirely without an orchestra".

3. Choral Societies

In Barberton choral music developed mainly in the English-speaking (Catholic, Anglican and Wesleyan) churches. Church leaders worked in active co-operation, in the interests of the communal musical life, and sometimes the concerts were held in the churches themselves. — An Anglican church choir was started by the Rev. H. Adams on 1 February 1887, with G.M. Cullingworth as secretary, and H.M. Martyn, H. Liddle and D.A. Ogilvie as members of the committee. A.W. Bayly was the organist of the church and conductor of the choir, consisting of 8 men, 15 women and three boys. They held weekly practices and sang at divine services, as well as at secular concerts held under the auspices of the Philharmonic Society. On 29 March 1909, the Anglican church choir, augmented by volunteer singers from the town, held a public concert in the municipal hall in aid of church funds. —The Band of Hope, an integral part of which was the Wesleyan church choir (originally six members of the Kellar family and five of the Hendry family), was founded by the Rev. Benson on 7 February 1891, and for years presented monthly programmes, geared to topics of religion and anti-alcoholism. After the founder had returned to England, the group continued to exist, and presented mainly variety concerts. On 26 March 1891, the choir sang *The temperance bells* and *Oh, if the cup you fill for me.* Four of the members sang a quartet *Wine is a wrecker.* On 2 February 1892, there were three choral items: *Oh, we are volunteers, The happy farmer* and *Oh lady stream*. The choir assisted the solo singer, Blanche Spring, with the refrain of *Carry me back to my mother's home*. Thereafter the concerts provided solo songs, recitations and instrumental playing, until 12 April 1909, when the choir once again gave its support. — The Catholic church did not use its choir for public concerts. Variety concerts for church funds were given without the choir. An exception was on 25 March 1893, when a double quartet consisting of choir members sang *Benedictus* (Weber), *God is a Spirit* (Sterndale Bennett), and a duet with "demi-chorus" composed by Rossi. This programme was received with much enthusiasm. — The Philharmonic Society, the earliest secular choral society, was founded on 12 July 1887, under the chairmanship of the Rev. H. Adams, the Anglican parson, with A.W. Bayly as conductor, R.H.F. Stranack secretary, and D. Defries, J.M. Cullingworth, W.E. Steers and P.A. Ogilvie as additional members of the committee (Bayly, Defries and Steers also belonged to the Orchestral Society; Cullingworth and Ogilvie to the Anglican church choir). At the jnaugural meeting 20 people attended, and the first choir practice was held a week later. Male members had to pay a monthly subscription of 50c , but for ladies membership was free. Sheet music was obtainable from the secretary at wholesale prices. On 22 October 1887, a concert was given with the orchestral society. The audience was satisfied and the critique favourable, especially with regard to the singing of the ladies. On the programme was Mendelssohn's *Wedding march*, a glee by the choir (described as "not very good") and solos by H. Williams *(The romany lass)* and E.H.A. Cohen *(I must forget)*. Miss Caskie, Mrs Ridette and Messrs Steers and Cullingworth sang a quartet. By request, the orchestra was obliged to repeat its second item, *Festal march*. From the start the Philharmonic Society co-operated whole-heartedly with the orchestral society, but it did not exist for very long. — Christy Minstrels appeared sporadically in various amateur forms. The Barberton Minstrels, who were the first, gave a charity concert in aid of church funds on 28 December 1886. The programme included a chorus from *The Sorcerer (Now to the banquet we press)*, and the "black" items, *All on account of Eliza,* with Kent Smith as Bones, and *It's hard to love* with L.O. Browning as Tambo. There was, in addition, the usual "variety", and Cullingworth caused emotional disturbances with *When we sleep beneath the daisies*. Yet another group, the Byron Amateur Minstrels, entertained the Smoking Club in September 1887. — In December 1893, Harry Neale, assisted by local amateurs and Christy Minstrels, gave two concerts and earned high praise for his voice, his love of music, his value to the community and his organising ability. For the benefit of the hospital, the Southern Stars Amateur Troupe of Night and Morning Minstrels presented a typical programme in October 1896:

Part I: Overture, orchestra; opening chorus, dance and song by the company; solo and chorus, *An old brass locket,* J.D. Pinnkoop and chorus; song, *Who did,* A.C. Cooper; roundelay, *Way down in Tennessee,* by the Company; comic song, *Just by luck,* W.C. Shepperd; solo and chorus, *On a cycle with the girl you love,* J. McClymont and chorus; comic song, *Fancy meeting you,* C. Dalton; song, *Avril yer aber gwine ter marry me,* H. Speed; solo and chorus, *Far away ober dere,* J.G. Rorrison and chorus; comic song, *But it is so,* W.C. Shepperd. — Part II: overture, orchestra; solo and chorus, *Darkie's love,* Mr Rorrison and orchestra; topical duet, *We shall never be happy again,* Arenhold and McClymont; morceau de fascination, *A lesson with the fan,* Miss G. Hazelhurst; comic song, *I'm waiting for you,* Mr S. King; vocal duet, *The toy duet* (from *Geisha girl*), Mrs W.A. Gregory and Mr Rorrison; trio, *The tree grows,* Dalton, McClymont and Speed; comic song, *Chin chin chinaman* (from *Geisha girl*), S. King; grand finale, *De lecture,* Mr Dalton and the Company.

The Magpie Minstrels - consisting of A. Cooper, W. Bayly, F. Crossby, C. Didcott, W. McClelland, F. Goodhead, S. King, W. Pearson, E.H. Egan, R.B. Pacy and J. McMagh - on occasion also appeared with the orchestral society. As far as is known, the American negroes led by Orpheus McAdoo, who visited Barberton twice (October 1896 and October 1897), were the only professional minstrels. —The Barberton Choral Society was founded on 21 July 1914, with W.D. McClelland (president), W. Grubb (vice-president and conductor) and C.J. Nash (secretary.)

4. Barberton Recreation Society

This society was started in 1890 by the Rev. L. Browne, a Wesleyan minister, to provide the youth of Barberton with physical, social, intellectual and cultural recreation. Although sports meetings and debates constituted a part of their activities, music was at the core. The society gave many concerts, the first of which was held in April in the Royal Albert Hall, with the co-operation of A.W. Bayly, Cullingworth, Tassart, Tallermann and Mesdames Fryer, Rush and Gilfillan. The Rev. Browne (club president) took part in this programme himself. At the next concert (12 July) seven artists provided nine songs in a programme of fifteen items. The remaining six numbers consisted of solos for the piano, violin and piccolo; an organ-and-piano duet (Mesdames Bayly and Thompson), a character piece and a humorous reading. Tallerman, Dr Wolff, Tassart and the 10-year old Grace Hazelhurst were among those who took part. A similar programme followed in September, with seven of the previous eleven artists taking part. — A.E. Graham Lawrence became secretary in October, and from 9 December all meetings were held in the Royal Albert Hall. Two months later the Rev. Browne was obliged to return to England, and the young people presented him with an illuminated address in appreciation of his work. The new president, the Rev. Fisher (Mus. Bac.), raised the musical standard of the concerts, and provided music lectures, such as the one by Father Vigneron on 7 October (supported by an illustrated programme), and another in December 1891, by Fisher himself, on the subject of the Christmas carol. He was an organist as well as a singer. On 11 November he and Miss Sheard performed a duet for piano and organ *(Mazurka);* and he joined Crossby and Shepperd in the singing of a trio *(Mijnheer Vandunck).* On 14 March 1893, Arenhold contributed a violin solo - a lachrymose rendering of *Home sweet home.* — In October 1893, there was a change in the committee. The Rev. B.G. Fitzpatrick (MA in music) became president. Concerts continued until October 1894, but ceased after Fitzpatrick became principal of the Templars' High School for boys (January 1895, see Chapter VIII); members of the society then had to join the Band of Hope or the Barberton Musical Society (founded on 27 November 1894).

IV. Operetta

This art form, and more especially the works of Gilbert and Sullivan, ranked high in Barberton. Early in 1887 Bob Bolder (in private life Robert Edney) appeared on the scene with a musical comedy group. They enticed the customers with comic pieces, zither solos *(Recollections of home,* selections from *Il Trovatore* and *Martha)* and with high-powered patriotic ballads *(True till death),* but also with scenes from Offenbach's operetta *Forty winks.* At the third concert Bolder presented a burlesque, *The great Salvation Army song,* in uniform, and with cornet, tambourine, triangle, a great, swinging umbrella and pretty girls. Besides Bolder himself (comedian), the troupe included Jane and Katie Leechman (singers and dancers), Professor A. Witte (an "expert musician" on the zither and xylophone) and one Gregg (tenor). — Engaging amateurs to help them, they commenced a season of musical comedies and operettas in July. These *(A fit of the blues, The farcical comedy, A piece of impudence* and *The goose with the golden eggs)* raked in such a rich harvest of "golden eggs" that all other entertainment, even the Smokers' Concerts, went up in smoke. In August, Bolder pushed his luck with a series of *Mikado* performances and once again his auditorium was packed. Hurrying, he brought *HMS Pinafore* on 2 September, only twelve days after the last *Mikado* performance. The newspaper criticised the slip-shod singing of the chorus and also commented: "It was a big swallow to get over the 'Little Buttercup' by Mr Myers. The words and songs were those of the Little Buttercup but the voice, ah, the voice was the voice of Myers". Despite these ominous rumblings, Bolder immediately presented *The hospital board of Bungledon,* but this was so badly bungled that the company could not continue and was disbanded. Later, shortly prior to the Anglo-Boer War, Bolder came back once more with a musical comedy, *Two sharps and a flat,* performed in Barberton on 11 August 1899. — Meanwhile the amateurs were following suit. On 24 January 1888 they presented *The sorcerer,* followed by *The pirates of Penzance* in July 1890, A.W. Bayly singing the Major General and coaching the chorus. Cohen was Frederick, L. Martyn the Pirate King, and Steers the Police Sergeant. Miss Fryer's Mabel was heartily applauded, and Riddel conducted the orchestra. After two silent years, in July 1892, Rowland presented a massive programme with a variety concert in the first half and, after the interval, a performance of *The sentinel,* all presented with amateurs. — The Barberton Dramatic Club was founded in 1893 in an attempt to co-ordinate and centralise amateur productions. This society could always raise an orchestra for its performances, even in times of orchestral paralysis. Their "orchestra" varied between seven and eleven instruments, but usually there were three violins, 1 viola, 1 cello, 1 cornet, an organ (harmonium?) and a pianoforte, with Bayly as pianist. This group also began by giving variety concerts. Their first noteworthy attempts at presenting an operetta were three performances of *HMS Pinafore* with an all-juvenile cast, aged between 11 and 17 years, under the patronage of Mr Justice Jorissen, and commencing on 19 October 1894. This proved to be the pinnacle of Barberton's musical history; new talent was discovered in the person of the young singer, Grace Hazelhurst (see Chapter VI). The children were rehearsed by Mesdames Deglon and Bowness, Miss Humphries was the singing coach and T. Powell painted the decor. The orchestral society collaborated by contributing 3 violins, 1 viola, 1 cello, double bass, two flutes, a drum, a cornet and a pianist. — Six months later the Dramatic Club presented two one-act musical comedies by A.J. Byron, *The snow drift* and *The rose bud;* and after nearly three more years they once again gave a variety concert (3 March 1897) with J. McClymont, J.G. Morrison and Mrs S.O. Holmes singing and Lazarus playing the flute. They did no more until well after the Anglo-Boer War. In the two years before the war, the professional companies of Searelle* (April 1898) and Wykeham *(The lucky feud,* March 1899) visited Barberton. — The Dramatic Club was reconstituted under the name of Operatic Company in 1904, and from 1906 it gave variety concerts, engaging the orchestra and choir of the orchestral society. After the first concert on June 4, the newspaper gratefully noted that the orchestra seemed to be alive again and hoped that it would do its bit, as it had before the war; on June 12 there was a benefit concert for Miss Nisbet in the Kaap Exchange, containing i.a. parts of the operetta *Patience,* played with decor and "stage-front scenery" (to replace the curtains which had been destroyed by fire). The hall was crammed. Encouraged by this success, the whole of the operetta *Patience* was performed on September 7, accompanied by a violin, cello and pianoforte. Although this effort was not too well received, the newspaper praised the singing of "very difficult choruses" and the accompaniment. Encouraged by this report, the operatic company devoted time and care to their next production, so that, when they presented *The Mikado* nearly a year later (3 September 1907), they could boast of costumes by Wallers of London, decor by the professional artist Chris Hallé of Durban, an orchestra of ten instruments, a ladies' chorus of ten voices, augmented by a group of schoolgirls, and a male chorus of fourteen voices. The soloists were well chosen and everyone had been thoroughly drilled. This *Mikado* created such a sensation that old Barbertonians still enthuse about it in the seventies of the present century. — Everybody hoped that music making in Barberton would blossom after this exhilirating production, but until 1914 no comparable effort could be made. Now and then an odd professional troupe visited the town, like the Wheeler-Edwardes Musical Comedy Company *(A country girl* and *The orchid* in July 1906 and *The merry widow* in October 1908) but they could not activate the Barbertonians - their musical glory had passed beyond recall.

V. *Variety concerts*

Music in Barberton was virtually synonymous with variety concerts. The public sought entertainment and diversion both from the climate and hard work, and members were sometimes outspoken in making known their displeasure, especially if a programme was too "highbrow". Neither the tireless efforts of amateur musicians such as A.W. Bayly, Mr and Mrs A.E. Graham Lawrence, and Daniel Defries, nor the English-speaking church leaders and music societies, could guide the taste of the public towards serious music. The orchestral society had to fill its programmes with variety. Even concerts in aid of church funds, by visiting artists, had to follow this pattern. As early as 1886, Bayly had organised variety concerts, often for charity, and many others followed his example, occasionally for personal gain. — The newspapers praised or disparaged the artists; but children were usually acclaimed. On 19 April 1887, the *Barberton Herald* wrote about the young daughter of S.C. Bell as follows: "the performance of a by no means easy fantasia on the violin by Irene Bell, aged 9, completely carried away the audience. This little lady seems a born violinist". Concerts were also held in the vicinity of the town; for instance, at Sheba Mine on 29 April, when there was singing and piano-playing, "Mr Nocz gave *The loves of the brave* and *Nein! Nein!* in a very good voice". There was an abundance of singing talent, and the programme of a concert on 15 September 1888 in the Central Hotel, mentions several forgotten troubadours. The singers were commended, and "the cornet solos by Mr Bawe were well appreciated, though the limited dimensions of the room were not well adapted for such a performance". Names such as Harry Neale, J. Myers, J.L. Williams, E.H.A. Cohen, Reinhold, Saunders, Tallerman and Bayly, appear frequently on the programmes, interspersed with groups of instrumentalists, or vocal quartets and duets. For instance, on 24 December Mesdames Munik (sic) and Barrett sang *List' to the convent bells,* and the daughter of De Villiers, the magistrate, made her debut as a singer. Music teacher R.B. Moorby (see Chapter VIII) often acted as accompanist up to the time of his death. Bayly appeared very frequently;

with the Rev. C. Fisher he played (for example) an *Allegro brillant* for two pianos; this was in aid of funds for the renovation of All Saint Church. Early in 1893 Frank Watkins, Barberton's junior member of the Volksraad, also held a concert, for the benefit of the widow and orphaned children of T. Cossen. — Then there were concerts by various national groups. The German community held their own concert on 12 August 1887, in the Granville Hotel; an audience of 50 Germans attended. On 24 May 1888, the local amateurs, Mesdames Krause and J.H. Wood, and Messrs Harry Neale, Myers, Williams, Cohen, Reinhold, Saunders and Tallermann, combined with the orchestral society for a concert in aid of the Jewish Benevolent Fund. Throughout St Andrew's Day, the Transvaal Scottish Clan danced and made music, and in the evening they held a concert. A newspaper advertised the concert of 1890 in these terms: "a novelty in these parts, being exclusively Scotch, and including the choicest lyric gems of Scotia:

'I will be blythe and licht,
My heart is bend upon so guid a nicht'.
Such must be the feelings pervading the hearts of all Scotia's sons and daughters on Saturday". Though the music was Scottish, those taking part - Riddell (piano), Jagger and Arenhold (1st violins), Knox and Lazarus (2nd violins), Tassart (piccolo), Moorby (euphonium) - were international. For his violin solo, *Highland wreaths,* Jagger was called "a good son of Scotland". One of the solo-singers was Mrs Bowness, who presented *Jock O'Hazeldean* and *Comin' thro' the Rye.* The following year there was an original song sung by Hugh Beacon:

Hands across the Vaal, boys,
Hands across the Vaal;
Came you from old Scotland,
From Cape Town or Natal,
Then friendship, peace and harmony, exist among us shall,
And we'll live and toil as brothers in the new Transvaal.
The 1897 concert began and ended with the playing of the bagpipes. Grace Hazelhurst (17 years old and probably home on holiday) sang with McClelland the duet *O wert thou in the 'could' blast,* a "national" band played, and McClymont sang *St Andrew's Nicht.* From Pietermaritzburg came a telegram from brother Scotsmen: "The land o' heather, hills and lakes, A' ither land surpasses Our toast the nicht's the land o' lakes". — On the international front was the Independent Order of Good Templars. On 21 October 1890, according to the *Goldfields News,* they gave the best concert ever held in Barberton; "the various items were gone through without a hitch". Of the eleven items, five were solo songs; one solo each for violin, piccolo and piano; while four members were responsible for the rest of the programme, consisting of a recitation, a reading and a (humorous) dialogue. On 25 November 1905, Brother Millan and The Templars arranged a programme of instrumental solos for the banjo, piccolo, flute, mandoline, violin, viola and piano. — From the year 1905, the gramophone also featured in programmes, especially in Coronation Park. Amateur singing - solo and choir - was mingled with gramophone records, perhaps because the orchestral society was by then virtually defunct. On 7 October 1908, in his twenty-third year as amateur musician in Barberton, A.W. Bayly was commended for his solo singing; with his beautiful baritone voice he had given an impressive rendering of *Blow, Blow.* On Christmas Eve the residents of Sheba Mine were treated to a programme consisting exclusively of recorded music. Up to the time of the First

121

World War the gramophone was used to boost amateur performances. Only in the municipal hall (from the year 1909) did the presentation of "live" music reach a higher level. The programme of 28 August 1910 (for instance), included works by Grieg, Handel, Gounod and Mendelssohn.   — The orchestral society made use of this hall, too, but its efforts did not appeal to Barberton tastes.

VI.   PROFESSIONAL ARTISTS

Rumours about the rich gold-mining town soon reached the ears of the many touring, professional concert-parties of those days, and several arrived to give performances. Two groups remained in Barberton for some time: the Perkins and the Walther companies.   — In 1886 Edgar Perkins arrived from Natal with eight musicians and a wood-and-iron hall, and even before the erection of the latter presented a programme in the Criterion Hotel, with Perkins himself as singer. The company included Miss E. Linton (dancer), Kate Roseberry (cabaret and ballad singer), Fred Linton, J. Elliot, Harry Goodman, E. Goudet and H. D'Almain (Negro comedian). Touring singers Ada Rayson, Alice Clairette and Abe Vosper also took part in a programme of musical entertainment and comic turns such as *Travelling back to Georgia, Lemuel's ghost* and the humorous sketch *Fancy*. They advertised thus: "Who cheers Ria? Roll up, boys! Special performance!"   — For Perkins these programmes were banal, and on 29 April 1887, after recruiting a chorus, his company gave a concert version of *Trial by jury* directed by E. Cohen. It was explained that the operetta was produced in London in a completely different manner - the local stage in Barberton was too small to allow a fully dramatized production. The singers were, however, made-up and the stage was adorned with a court-room set. But Perkins had been too-hurried with this production. His characters were insufficiently rehearsed and the result was disappointing. A.R. Thorn and M. Younge (RAM) used the same singers in a more successful production in the Kaap Exchange a month later (14 May). Kate Roseberry and a Mr De Jongh (tenor) took the main roles. Perkins, however, dissolved his company and henceforth used his hall for entertainment only, regardless of who provided it. In 1888-1889 he left for Johannesburg, where he collaborated in various enterprises with such people as James Henry Harper*.   — In January 1887, after a two months' tour, Carl Walther's company arrived in Barberton. He opened the new Kaap Exchange Hall, with the assistance of amateurs including Henry Leslie, V.C. Cullingworth, Messrs Williamson and Mathie (both singers) and Mr Baker (viola). The company consisted of Carl Walther (violin), H. Bomon (cello) and Mr Ramsden (a baritone who was proficient on "all" instruments). Virginie Cheron (presented as Mrs Richards), who at that time was visiting Barberton with her father, appeared in the first five concerts of the Walther company. Finally, A.W. Bayly also took part and loaned from his shop the first grand piano ever used in a Barberton concert. The standard of variety at these five concerts (three in February, one on 5 March and one on 15 April 1887) was higher than that offered by Perkins; there were string quartets by Mozart and Haydn, and works by De Beriot, Servais and Gounod. Virginie Cheron was the most popular artist. "Her popularity as a vocalist was established after she had gone through two or three bars", wrote the newspaper; and the audience threw bouquets on to the stage after she had sung as an encore *Tell me my heart* (Bishop). But even at the first concert a section of the audience became restive. After the third concert, there was criticism in the newspaper about unsatisfactory playing, and singers suffering from colds (see Chapter VII); and on 5 March the audience was very sparse. At this latter concert the programme opened with Haydn's *String quartet in*

122

G, and concluded with another string quartet. But it was impossible to play the last two movements, because of rowdy behaviour by individuals in the audience. The newspaper expressed its disapproval as follows: "It is a pity that those who call themselves human beings should have so little self-respect that they behave like this. If they want the kind of amusement where they can drink and smoke, that class of entertainment is also provided in this town". — But Walther was undaunted. He assembled an orchestra of twelve members, and six weeks later offered a concert of songs (Virginie Cheron: *Only once more, Maid of Athens, Love song*) and light orchestral music, including Mendelssohn's *Wedding march*. At this level orchestral music found favour. After this concert the company was disbanded, however; assisted by the Barberton musician Clifford Hallé, Carl Walther left on a concert tour to Pretoria, Johannesburg and Durban; Virginie Cheron returned to Natal, and the remainder made appearances in Barberton from time to time. — Other companies made brief visits to Barberton: the Charles Saunders* concert party, with Alfred Gould, Baron von Himmelstjerna* and Mrs Warden (31 January 1896); an American Negro group of eleven minstrels - Orpheus McAdoo's Jubilee Singers - with songs of "spiritual value" (October 1896); the same group as The Minstrel Vaudeville and Concert Company (October 1897); the Continental Concert Group with Jessie Walton (from London), and Mons. and Mme. Jonquier (piano and violin) from Paris (January 1897); the Company of Society Entertainers, under Signor Robertz, which included Albert Vine (piano), F. Sydney (singer) and Vera and Beryl, the young daughters of Signor Robertz (May 1903); Signor and Mme de Pasquali,* Italian tenor and soprano, with Angelique de Beer (sister of Pierre de Beer* - pianist) and C. Israel* (violin) (June 1904). —The Westminister Glee Singers, with four boy soloists of the Westminster College of Choristers, sang glees and staged *The musical village,* a humorous musical sketch (November 1904). They were very popular. The Steele-Payne Bellringers* arrived with their handbells, violin, mandoline and sleigh bells in June 1908, and visited the town again in April 1911. Mme. Bal van Lier* of Pretoria with Lettie Smook (mezzo-soprano) and Beatrice Stuart* (violin) visited the town in October 1908; on 3 November 1908, Beatrice Stuart gave a recital. She re-visited Barberton in 1909, and again on 7 July 1911, with the contralto L. Allum and the baritone Jas Pursail, with A.W. Bayly as accompanist. The Archdeacon Concert Party, directed by Tom Robinson, with Pierre de Beer (piano), Hamilton (bass from the Royal Opera, London), Beatrice McCready (contralto), John Harrison (tenor) and Emily Breare (soprano), appeared at the Kaap Exchange on 3 June 1909. — Ada Forrest*, who had lived in Barberton as a child and had had her first music lessons from the local Rabbi Woolfe, was trained in a Durban convent in preparation for her studies in London (1898). She visited the town, probably in 1909, in the company of Mme Wedlake Santanera (harp), Beatrice Stuart (violin), Gilion Evans (tenor) and J.L. Wintle (baritone). The accompanist at their concerts, L.R. Glenton*, was a humorist, and assisted as compère in presenting their programme. Maud Vernon (piano), Edith Armstrong (singer) from London, E. Philips (tenor), C.O. Brinkworth (the "George Robey of South Africa") and Adam Gordon (baritone), appeared in January 1910. The Madcaps, directed by Totten, a comedy company, visited Barberton three times: in October 1910, after that as Meyer-Caselle in November 1910, and finally as the Musical Madcaps in November 1911. — The Scarlet Troubadours (opera singers and an instrumental ensemble, directed by a Mr Edwards), and a group called the Leopold Ladies were both in Barberton in 1911; and in 1912 a small band, the Butterflies,

visited "the Flower of the Lowveld". Many individual visiting artists followed
Virginie Cheron (1887): Professor Burt (piano); Ada Rayson (singer), who repeatedly
entertained the people of Barberton with her operatic arias; Jane and Katie Leechman,
who were both singers and dancers; Chas du Val* (singer and instrumentalist), who
gave two concerts - one on 25 July 1888, under the patronage of J.Z. de Villiers, the
magistrate. They were followed by Cooper and Leonardi. Harry Cantor remained a
long time, earned good money, and then returned to England. A pianist, Herr Rainer,
gave a demonstration of tenacity rather than talent by playing non-stop for 36 hours,
and he too earned good money. The world-famous concert pianist Albert Friedenthal
sought health and sunshine on his tour to South Africa. At his own home A.W. Bayly
arranged a concert for him, at which he played the following items: *Sonata in C
sharp,* "Moonlight", Beethoven; *Funeral march,* Chopin; *Lullaby,* Grieg;
Storm scene, Wagner; *Serenade,* Liszt; *Hungarian Rhapsody No 2,* Liszt.
If it can be called "professional" to make a public appearance for personal profit, the
Barbertonians were not slow in coming forward. E. Breakspeare Smith composed a
brand-new *Grand waltz in A flat,* and staged a new "musical" called *The silver
wedding* in 1888. In December 1889, after three years as an amateur, Tallermann was
invited to conduct an orchestral concert for his own profit, but it was a failure: "We
should have to record a silly and miserable fiasco" the newspaper wrote, "a wretched
breakdown, a yelling audience and failure, and ignominy from the very rise of the
curtain" (A prophet at home?). On 24 July 1892, Rowland and local artists -
Thompson (piano) and Mrs Verey (singer) - presented a variety concert; the operetta
The sentinel was presented in the second half of the programme. Local amateurs, the
Rev. Benson, Didcott, Mc Clelland and Arenhold, assisted Mrs Wardon at her concert
in December 1896. The last-named had also visited Barberton early in 1896, with
Charles Saunders and Von Himmelstjerna. — The favourite among local talent of
Barberton in those days was Grace Hazelhurst. When she was "discovered" as a 14-
year old (see Chapter IV) she was sent to the Royal Academy for further training as a
singer. This was made possible when Bayly's newspaper started a public subscription. After her return, she sang at concerts in Johannesburg, and in October 1899,
gave a Grand Concert in Barberton, under the patronage of the Mayor and Mayoress,
and members of the Town Council. She was assisted by J.L. Wintle (baritone),
Charles Israel (violin), and Ethel Fainsinger (pianist). The programme included
works by Grieg and Dvorak, and Grace sang English ballads and "Say it once again"
from *Samson and Delilah* (Saint-Saëns). — In 1902 Miss Hazelhurst was back again
for a concert given by the Band of the Lincolnshire Regiment in the Kaap Exchange.
She lived in Johannesburg where she was married to E.J. Wood and became fairly
well-known as a singer. In April 1909, she re-visited Barberton for another Grand
Concert, in which she was assisted by Miss H. van der Hoven (soprano), and in the
same year she was once again at the Royal Academy in London, where she won a
bronze medal and, with Elsa Leviseur* as her accompanist, took part in a concert at the
home of Otto Beit, on 22 December. This was under the aegis of *African World* (edited
by Leo Weinthal), and directed by Ada Forrest for the benefit of the Rand Regiments'
Memorial Fund. The patrons included Otto Beit, Sir Abe Bailey, Dr Hans Sauer, C.
Schlesinger and Solly Joel. Other artists on the programme were Selma Sacke*
(Whitehouse), Annie Visser,* Geraldine and Frederick Dillon,* Ada Forrest and
Vera Wise. — Apart from overseas artists, few of whom were in the top flight, the
following names figure prominently in the South African musical history of this

period: Beatrice Stuart, C. Israel, Pierre de Beer, Ada Forrest, L.R. Glenton, Von Himmelstjerna, Virginie Cheron.

VII PROMENADE CONCERTS

The first so-called "promenade" concert (February 1887) was held indoors in a hall decorated with trees, ferns and flowers. The programme was too highbrow and Virginie Cheron had such a heavy cold that she was unable to sing an encore. The audience stamped from the stuffy hall with loud protests. Immediately afterwards the request was made that future promenade programmes, to be held at Coronation Park, should include only light music, ballads and selections from light opera. To begin with, the Orchestral Society was responsible for most of these concerts, with programmes such as the following (23 December 1888):

Part I: Slow march, *Honour to the brave,* Riviére; overture, *Poet and peasant,* Von Suppé; fantasia, *Alpine echoes,* Herfurth; cornet obligato by A.E. Graham Lawrence; waltz, *Luna bella,* Ougrette; selection, *Chevalier de Breton,* Herman; Galop, *Postillion,* Fourdin. Part II: overture, *Tancredi,* Rossini; gavotte, *Queen of hearts,* Le Thière; selection, *Les deux matots* (sic!), Bouillon; polka, *Carte blanche,* Hartmann; waltz, *Lac d'amour,* Hartmann; galop, *Clear the road,* Le Thière.

There were also variety concerts, and possibly because there was more freedom of movement out of doors than in halls, it rarely happened that the audience was badly behaved. The promenade concerts continued to be a recognised institution until 1914. A fair example was a concert on 22 January 1894, when the "new orchestra" performed with 3 violins, violo, cello, 2 flutes, cornet and piano. After the South African War British military bands participated. Thus on 9 February 1906, with Chinese lanterns illuminating the scene, the Manchester Military Band accompanied a 16-strong male choir, and rendered 8 items themselves. On the evening of New Year's Day 1904, there was a variety concert. On 5 May 1912, the gramophone gave support to a programme by Miss Kellar, Rev. Douthwaite and J. McClymont. A year later the Boy Scouts began Sunday concerts with their brass band, but unfortunately the outbreak of the First World War brought these to an end (see Chapter IX).

VIII EDUCATION

At first the parents of Barberton were responsible for teaching their children reading, writing and arithmetic; but soon small schools came into being, where women taught their own children along with those of their neighbours and friends. Mrs Rushby and Mrs Deglon each had such a school, while Mrs Tarpie and her daughter used a double-storeyed house in the centre of the town, near the Market Square, as a school. These schools disappeared with the advent of organised education. Mrs Button closed her school officially with a concert, which greatly impressed the *Goldfields News:* "It was without doubt one of the greatest successes and a most attractive novelty, free from ... objectionable features of the usual infant prodigy shows", wrote the reporter, and gave encouragement to this kind of education. From 1887 there were at least two music teachers in the town, Mrs Ridette and Mr R.B. Moorby. The latter had been in Pietermaritzburg (c. 1864-1882), as choirmaster of St Peter's Cathedral, and had owned a music shop (The Musical Repository). During the late 1870's he was in financial difficulties, and in 1882 he was declared insolvent. In 1883 he formed a choral society in Pretoria, and from 1887 was in Barberton, where he became a member of the Orchestral Society, for which he sometimes played the euphonium; at other times he provided piano accompaniments. He was popular as a music teacher, and when he died on 6 December 1892, his twenty music pupils were "orphaned". — On 15 April 1891, the Rev. P. Wolfers opened the Collegiate School for Girls "on a high standard basis, with preparations for Oxford and Cambridge Local Examinations". It was governed by a parents' committee and permitted the admission of small boys. An important part of the education for girls was music, which absorbed a fairly large portion of the school time-table. In January 1895, the IOGT started a high school for boys, with the Rev. Fitzpatrick acting as headmaster. Singing and music featured prominently in the syllabus. — State-aided, and under the control of a parents' committee, another school was opened on 17 April 1896. Here piano lessons could be had for a small fee. In November Dr Mansvelt* (Superintendent of Education in the Transvaal) visited the town to announce the opening of a Government school which, with 105 pupils and Mr Jansen as principal, was started in 1897. On 16 December 1902, the newspaper wrote that the annual school concert was of a high standard, and it commended the choral singing of 50 pupils from the senior classes (*Oh ye hours; The lads in navy blue* and *Chin Chin*). Three years later the "skilled tuition" and breathing exercises in the singing classes at this school became an item of news. — Many private pupils of individual music teachers were the children of artists who had taken an active part in the musical life of the town. Mrs J. Wood, for example, taught her own children Ida and Adolf, as well as Norah and Sybil Mc Clelland, Theodore White and, later, W.M. Arenhold. The first five were successful in the 1906 preparatory piano examination of the Trinity College. The presentation of 19 certificates (10 practical and 9 theory) two years later, offered an excuse for a concert, with six piano solos and two duets and, in the second half of the programme, the operetta *Snow White*. — On 9 December 1909, Mrs Wood and her pupils attempted a performance of a *Toy symphony*. The only adult musicians were Mr King (first violin) and the accompanist at the piano, Miss A. Beyerly. The first part of the programme consisted of a violin solo by Adolf Wood, a cello solo by W. Arenhold and a trio (Adolf Wood, W. Arenhold, and Ida Wood (piano)). This performance was highly praised in the local newspaper. — On 15 December 1903, assisted by a children's choir of 30 voices, B. Swords gave a concert containing songs, including *Who is Sylvia* (Schubert) and *I would that my love* (Mendelssohn); this was commended as a great achievement. "If a child learns to like fine music the educative gain is enormous", wrote the newspaper. — Miss Postma, the grand-daughter of "the well-known dopper minister of the Kruger regime", and daughter of the predikant at Middelburg, visited Barberton on 5 August 1912, and stayed two days to advertise the "Naunton method". With the aid of this, anyone would be able to play even classical pieces on the piano after eight lessons. Her visit was a social success, but was neither followed up, nor repeated. Another teacher, who for a number of years taught singing, violin and piano was E.E. Vogts. Mainly a violinist himself, he was a dedicated conductor and member of the Orchestral Society.

IX. BRASS BANDS

1. Barberton Brass Band
2. Military bands
3. Boy Scouts

1. Barberton Brass Band

From 1887, a large section of the public raised objections to what they regarded as the

126

"high classical music" provided by the Orchestral Society. They were after entertainment. There was, however, no other orchestral music, except a small German band, a private organisation with musical tastes foreign to the predominantly English community. When in 1892 the Orchestral Society began to decline in the face of this hostility, A.E. Graham Lawrence started a public subscription list; instruments were purchased, and the Barberton Brass Band (BBB) was established to provide light music in the park, and at sports meetings. On 24 March the BBB gave its first concert on the cricket ground, playing a march (Glasner); a ballroom dance; Lancers, *Favourite;* 2 waltzes, *Courtship* and *Pauline;* a fantasia, *Virginia;* and a galop, the *Maori war dance.* The programme was concluded with the "Queen". —Three weeks later the Band played with the Orchestral Society at the latter's dance, and a correspondent pointed out in the newspaper that the BBB had lost its identity. On 5 May, however, they gave another performance on the cricket ground with an entirely different programme: *Greeting to Australia* (march); *Juanita* (mazurka); *Bonaventura* (waltz); *Queen of my heart* (air); *Down among the dead men* (march); *Esmeralda* (fantasia); *Pride of the Rhine* (waltz) and *Polo* (galop). With Graham Lawrence assisting, the BBB did flirt with the Orchestral Society. When it was rumoured that the band was rehearsing for a combined concert, a contributor to the cost of the instruments asked why the BBB were holding no more concerts, and concluded that they were practising for what he presumed would be "a programme of high classical music, which most people would prefer to see relegated to the Kaap Exchange and the Orchestral Society". — Both the Orchestral Society and the BBB were discouraged, and the public had to wait until 27 June 1893 for its next concert. In June, Bayly the chairman, decided at a meeting to end this orchestral paralysis by recommending A.W. Arenhold as conductor of a BBB concert. The programme was a repetition of the items played in the first two concerts. Arenhold made it known that he was "working up some pleasing orchestral music", but when in July the band performed at a hospital bazaar (for which it was given a donation of R10), and at an athletics meeting on the 18th (its last concert), it again repeated the earlier programme. — About the year 1900 the Deutscher Verein also had a small band which, during the British occupation, staged a weekly demonstration by marching through the streets and playing German folk music.

2. Military bands

The Officer Commanding, Lt-Col Haig, who marched into Barberton with his Lincolnshire Regiment during the South African War, accommodated his troops in two large camps in Berea and Belgravia. Musical life was dominated by the military band of the Regiment's Second Battalion, which gave at least five concerts during 1902. Its repertoire included the overtures to *Fra diavolo* (Auber), *Banditenstreiche* etc. as well as selections from light opera, the *Minuet* (Paderewski) and the *Angel's serenade* (Braga). Guest soloists sang, for example, *The lost chord* (Sullivan), or played the *Polonaise in A* (Chopin). The bandmaster was A.L. Hurst. On 31 July 1902, the band accompanied Grace Hazelhurst at a concert (see Chapter VI) and its services were also made available to the Smoking Club during lunch hour, and for a presentation of Tableaux Vivants by the so-called "Barberton Loyal Women's Guild". Another busy year was 1903. Band Sergeant Dromey (cornet) and Corporals Gruber (euphonium) and Barry (saxophone) acquired reputations as soloists. Barry even became a local favourite. — On 2 February 1904, this band returned to England, leaving a void until the arrival of its replacement, the Band of the

Third Manchester Regiment, in 1906. On 9 February the new ensemble made its debut in Coronation Park in a promenade concert (see Chapter VII), and thereafter followed the pattern of its predecessor, until it was also recalled to England. The Sunday concerts in the park, which at a later date were usually given by the Boy Scouts' Band, were inspired by these two military bands.

3. Boy Scouts

One result of the Anglo-Boer War was the founding by Baden-Powell of the Boy Scout movement. Late in 1912 a Barberton laager was formed, with Colonel Spear as the Scout Master. His son Jack was allowed to join. A band of buglers and trumpeters was chosen from the members, and more instruments were purchased by means of a donation from a Mr Scott. In the December holidays the laager attended a Jamboree in Parkhurst, Johannesburg, where Spear secured the services of the retired bandmaster, James. He trained the boys so thoroughly that the band won the Gillray trophy at this camp, as the most proficient group of players. James remained their bandmaster, returned to Barberton with them, and gave them further training (assisted by his son, who played the drums). Jack Spear*, still too young to become a member of the band, was allowed to play with the band. — On 7 March 1913, in the period when there was no orchestra, this band of 40 · players gave a concert and played the marches *Debut, Viva* and *Majesty;* the waltzes *Budding flowers, Barberton troop* and *The brook;* a polka, *Massa's birthday;* and an overture, *The banquet.* Four of the members also played a quartet, *Larboard watch.* The second concert on 12 July earned money for enlarging the band; amateur artists gave their support with solo songs. Scout Munro played a solo, and for the occasion the band had learnt to play *Way down in Dixie* and *A life on the ocean wave,* much to the delight of the public. Shortly after this they were invited by the Governor-General of Moçambique to give two concerts in Lourenço Marques. — Occasionally, Dorothy Pahl was responsible for piano accompaniments and, like other girls in the town, keen on helping the boys with their concerts. She was often invited to give a solo, and would play as a cellist with the violinist Maisie Graham Lawrence. Yet another young soloist was the new scout Gregory, with his double-bass. James demanded higher standards and Barberton was enthusiastic about its children's band. The musicians were young and the training good. In April 1914, they presented the following programme at a variety concert:

March, *The new colonial,* band; song, Mr Henry; trombone solo, *In cellar cool,* scout Hauston; selection from Maritana, *Alas those chimes,* band; song, *Land of hope and glory,* Miss M. Olsen; violin solo, *Salute d'amour,* Maisie Graham Lawrence; song, *Deathless army,* Campion; Scottish selection, *The gathering of the clans:* Dorothy Pahl, scoutmaster Spear, bandmaster James and scout Lyons; selection, *All winners,* band; selection for cello, *Poet and peasant* (Suppé), Dorothy Pahl; duet for cornet and baritone, *Excelsior,* two scouts; mandoline solo, *The song that reached my heart,* Miss Lyons; march, *Don Juan,* band.

But the group did not exist very long. Most of the players were plunged into military service in the First World War. Delville Wood claimed many of the young lives. Scout Goodhead, at that time too young to join up, is still living in Barberton (1967), and he recalls the Sunday services - each week in a different church - attended by the band. He remembers also the weekly Sunday concerts in the park, and the dark days when the news of Delville Wood reached Barberton. —Since the First World War, Barberton has been living with the names and echoes of its flourishing period.

The musical life of bygone days has waned and the once active town has become, musically speaking, another dorp of the Lowveld. But in recent years there has been a revival since PACT has extended its concert tours to include Barberton.

BIBLIOGRAPHY
CURROR, W.D.: *Golden memories of Barberton.* Barberton Publicity Association, 4th edition, December 1940.   MARÉ, BLYDA: *Die musieklewe van Barberton tussen die jare 1885-1914.* B.Mus. script, UP, November 1967.
SOURCES
Correspondence with Mrs Esmé Lownds, Barberton.   Information on Moorby from Dr G.S. Jackson, Durban.

—E.C.

BARBERTON ORCHESTRAL SOCIETY   Barberton, D.N. Defries

**BARFIELD, ARTHUR, ***1827 in Dunmo, Essex; °20 June 1900 in Kimberley. Music teacher who, with his daughter Mathilda Mary, was active in the Eastern Province between 1863 and 1884.

The EP Herald of January 1863 mentions Barfield for the first time as a singer at a Glee Club concert in Port Elizabeth and on 16 October, "Mr Barfield of Uitenhage" is again mentioned in connection with a concert. With his daughter, Barfield arrived in Queenstown in January 1876 and contributed to the town's musical life with a quadrille ensemble in co-operation with Coester (violin), Harry Sawerthal* (piano), Mr Jackson (viola) and bandleader Hinds. As music teacher he organised not only entertainments in aid of a projected primary school, but also half-yearly concerts by his pupils. These are not mentioned after 1880. — Barfield played the harmonium in the Roman Catholic Church (1876-1877) and in March 1878 he became the organist of St Michael's. He also advertised his services as a tuner and was the Queenstown representative of the London Art Union. He was declared insolvent in August 1883, but in May 1884 he contributed an item to Madame Mendelssohn's* concert in King William's Town, playing with his daughter and a violinist, Griffiths. His daughter is again mentioned in connection with a concert in East London (February 1887).

SOURCES
EP Herald: 16-30 January 1863; 16 October 1863; 4 August 1864.   Register of Estates, Cape Colony: MOOC 6/9/406, DN 2516.   *Queenstown Free Press:* 3 January 1876 - 1 February 1887.

—C.G.H.

BARFIELD, MATHILDA MARY   A. Barfield

BARKER, JOYCE (MRS H.E. DYER), *6 June 1931 in Mooi River, Natal; now in Johannesburg. Soprano.

Joyce Barker's serious training started under Daisy Holmes in Durban at the age of nineteen. She won the Ernest Whitcutt Memorial Cup three years in succession and gained three different bursaries. Assisted by the overseas bursary of the RSM and a special bursary for overseas study awarded by the NSAM (Natal Society for the Advancement of Music),* she continued her training for three years in London. In 1956, at the end of this period, she became the first winner of the Kathleen Ferrier Scholarship and left for the Continent where she studied with Maria Hittorff, Paula Köhler and Reinhardt (1956-1959), eventually placing herself under the guidance of

129

Borishka Gereb and Maraio and Katerina Baziola for voice production, and Edouardo Pedrazolli for Italian opera repertoire (since 1959). During this period of preparation Joyce Barker won a variety of awards, including the Gold Medal of the International Concours de Chant (1959). —Starting with the soprano part in Mendelssohn's *Elijah* which was performed during the Canterbury Festival in 1954, she has sung with prominent conductors and appeared at Sadler's Wells and Covent Garden in *Götterdämmerung* (Wagner), *Mefistofele* (Boïto), *I Lombardi* (Verdi), *Nabucco* (Verdi) and *Walküre* (Wagner). During a season of opera in Ireland she sang in productions of *Tales of Hoffmann* (Offenbach), *Marriage of Figaro* (Mozart) and *La Bohéme* (Puccini). Other important appearances during this period include the soprano leads in Mahler's *Eighth symphony,* Nielsen's *Saul and David* and Verdi's *Aïda*. — After an absence of ten years, during which she had only one short South African tour in 1957-1958, she returned to her homeland in 1963. Since then she has established herself as a leading soprano in this country with a long run of engagements as solo recitalist with all four Regional Councils for the Performing Arts and the leading orchestras. There have been numerous broadcasts and leading soprano roles in works such as Benjamin Britten's *War Requiem,* Handel's *Messiah,* Puccini's *Turandot,* De Falla's *El Amor Brujo,* Mascagni's *Cavalleria Rusticana,* Verdi's *Aïda,* Wagner's *Der fliegende Holländer* and Cantatas by Bach.

—Ed.

BARKER, PHYLLIS ELIZABETH (MRS KENT), *27 January 1920 in Durban; at present in Westville. Composer, music teacher and organist.

Phyllis Barker received her musical training from sister Mary Gabriel* at the Maris Stella Convent in Durban (1926-1938), obtaining the UPLM and LTCL diplomas. She has taught music intermittently since 1963, mainly at the Westville Girls High School. Since 1957 she has been organist at St Elizabeth's Church in Westville. — Phyllis Barker has won several first prizes in competitions for composition. Concerts of her own works have been held at the University of Natal (1959) and in the Westville City Hall (1964).

WORKS

Eastern slave dance, pianoforte. Ms., 1931.   Gnomes and fairies, pianoforte. Ms., 1931.   March of the Empire, pianoforte. Ms., 1931.   Scherzo, pianoforte. Ms., 1933.   Abide with me, hymn. E. & H. 363, 1935.   Nero and the flea, pianoforte. Ms., 1937. Lullaby, song (anon). Ms., 1937.   Away, away, song (theme Schubert, words Evelyn Getaz). Ms., 1938.   Indian wayside sketch, song. Ms., 1938.   Musical box, pianoforte. Ms., 1939. Stellawood Government School, school song. Ms., n.d.   God's garden, song. Ms., 1951.   Jolly miller, song. Ms., n.d.   The monkeys and the crocodile, song (L. Richards). Ms., 1951.   Prelude, pianoforte. Ms., 1952.   Puck's frolics, pianoforte. Ms., 1952.   Christ was born on Christmas Day. Ms., 1952.   Coronation march, pianoforte. Ms., 1953.   Mountain fantasy, pianoforte. Ms., 1954.   Frustration, pianoforte. Ms., 1955. Sonata in F minor, for violin and pianoforte. Ms., 1956.   Christmas anthem (Una Hooper). Ms., 1956.   As Mary appeared, Christmas oratorio (Una Hooper). Ms., n.d.   O day of calm and heavenly peace (Una Hooper). Ms., n.d.   A.Y.P.A. hymn (Dorothy Anderson). Ms., n.d.   Dedication hymn. E. & H. 636, 1957.   Mother's prayer, song (Una Hooper). Ms., 1960.   Waves, song (Len Clark). Ms., 1960.   Dedication of St Elizabeth's Church, Westville, dedication anthem. Ms., 1960.   Praise the Lord of Heaven, hymn. E. & H. 534, 1961.   Little drops of water, hymn. E. & H. 600, 1961.   Durban High School, school song

130

(Charles Hoby). Ms., 1962. I saw a stranger yestreen, song (anon). Ms., n.d. Monday prayer, song. Ms., 1962. Come love ye God, carol. Oxford no. 10, 1962. Lord Jesus hath a garden, carol. Oxford 105, 1962. Hold Thou my hands, hymn. E. & H. 403, 1963. In the bleak mid-winter, hymn. E. & H. 25, n.d. Repent ye. Ms., 1963. The travellers, song (Biddy Hammond). Ms., 1964. Temptation in two minors, musical monologue (Una Hooper). Ms., 1964. Plain Jane, song (Una Hooper). Ms., n.d. There are no rules for love, song (I.F. McKinley). Ms., n.d.

—Ed.

BARLOW, MAUDE ANNE (BORN SMIT), *5 August 1883 in Bloemfontein; living in Durban in 1976. Soprano.

Maude Barlow was trained in music at the Eunice High School in Bloemfontein by the Misses Dixon and Von Steytler (1893-1899); after the South African War Florence Fraser* started training her voice (1903-1905). In August of the latter year she sang with Charles Saunders* in a performance of *Messiah* by the Combined Choirs of Bloemfontein, and the following year she was vocal soloist at two recitals given by Bosman di Ravelli.* — Mrs Barlow went with her husband to Great Britain in 1907, where she studied with Visetti at the RCM in London. There were also lessons with Darewski, who arranged an audition for her with Lyell-Tayler* in Brighton. The result was an engagement to sing Marguerite in Gounod's *Faust.* She stayed in Brighton, studying excerpts from Wagner's works with Tayler, and journeying to London once a week for lessons with Sir Henry Wood. At a commemoration concert for Richard Wagner she sang the Liebestod from *Tristan und Isolde,* and was engaged by Tayler to sing in Queen's Hall with the Brighton Orchestra, when the Barlows decided to return to South Africa on account of the War (1915). — In South Africa, Maude toured for a while for African Theatres, had a week-long engagement with the Cape Town Municipal Orchestra,* and in Bloemfontein took part in a production of *Iolanthe* by Jimmy MacQuade of *The Friend.* She then opened her own studio in Bloemfontein, and started teaching. Subsequent appearances included one in 1923, when she sang with her old mentor, Lyell-Tàyler, in the presence of the Governor-General and his wife and one in Port Elizabeth at Roger Ascham's* 932nd organ recital, in 1924. — While staying with her mother in Seymour C.P. in the early twenties, she organised local talent to produce a revue. This started her on a new career of variety shows, of which the 1932 Carnival Revue in the Feather Market Hall, Port Elizabeth, for the Mayor's emergency fund, serves as an example. The revues were invariably for charity, and continued until 1952. — During the late thirties Maude interested herself in visual art, and studied at the Technical College in Port Elizabeth, subsequently exhibiting there, and regularly in Durban and Pietermaritzburg.

—Ed.

BARNATO PARK COLLEGE OF MUSIC AND DRAMA Johannesburg 5, E. Mann

BAROEN, ARTHUR Johannesburg 2, Johannesburg Musical Society, Pretoria 2, Touring Theatre Groups 3.

BAROQUE PLAYERS Durban Chamber Music Groups

BARR, F. Organs 5(i), Port Elizabeth I/4(ii), Grahamstown 6.

131

BARRABLE, DAVID SOLOMON. *9 May 1835 in Purfleet, Essex; °22 May 1912 at "Glencoe", district Queenstown. Owner of the *Queenstown Free Press* and music dealer.

Before David Barrable arrived in Queenstown in his 23rd year, he had been an employee of the *Grahamstown Journal*. This more or less establishes the date of his arrival in South Africa between 1855 and 1857. He apparently had some capital, and started a weekly newspaper in Queenstown entitled *Queenstown Free Press*. It remained a weekly paper until April 1866, when it appeared twice a week and for three years, after 1898, it was published three times a week (until 30 September 1901). On this date it merged with the *Queenstown Daily Representative*. Barrable remained the owner and editor of the newspaper from 19 January 1859 until September 1901. In 1884 he also printed four editions of Mendelssohn's* periodical *The Cape Musical Monthly.* —With the remainder of his capital he entered the music trade and started selling sheet music. He evidently made some headway in this manner, since he was selling pianos and harmoniums in 1870 at prices which varied from R30 to R200. He stayed in the trade apparently until the end of 1889. On 9 August 1889 the last advertisement of his firm appeared, covering a full page of his newspaper. —Barrable was three times mayor of Queenstown and his children were quite active in the town's musical life.

SOURCES

Queenstown Free Press: May 1865-1898.   Registrar of Estates, Cape Province: MOOC 6/9/693, and DN 1856.

—C.G.H.

BARRATT. The names of the three Barratt brothers, Samuel, William and James, recur repeatedly in the musical history of Bloemfontein, Kimberley, East London and Bethulie, during the period 1874 to 1889. A fourth Barratt, called David, is mentioned only once in connection with a Grand Concert held in Kimberley on 2 July 1880. On this occasion *The merrie men of Sherwood Forest* (Birch) was performed under the direction of Sam Barratt, and David Barratt was one of the eight members of the "orchestra" that played the accompaniment. — There are no personal data about any of the Barratts, and the story of their activities is fragmentary, because they frequently changed their address. The available evidence indicates that they were versatile musicians, who had had a sound musical education; they appear as choral and orchestral conductors, as pianists, violinists, singers, organists and piano-tuners; some of the works they attempted were by no means easy. —J. Samuel Barratt turned up in Bloemfontein in 1874, when he became organist of St Andrew's Cathedral, as successor to G.A. White*. In the same year his brother, William S. Barratt, made an appearance as pianist in Kimberley. It thus seems that the two brothers came to South Africa in 1874. James Barratt is first mentioned in 1877. Shortly after his appointment as organist early in 1874, Samuel Barratt started the first choral society in the history of the Free State capital. The choir accompanied by an orchestra, performed five choral excerpts from *Messiah* on 16 July 1874. In addition, he became conductor of the Free State Artillery Band in 1874. After performing once in 1875, singing excerpts from *Acis and Galatea* (Handel), the Bloemfontein Choral Society was disbanded. Six months later, on 24 February 1876, Samuel's directorship of the music corps was advertised; but after that there is no mention of Samuel Barratt in Bloemfontein. It is, however, possible that he was the music master at Eunice Girls'

132

High School, mentioned in 1876. It is known that he paid a visit to Kimberley on 5 November 1874, appearing there as accompanist at a performance of *Messiah* sung by a choir of fifty, under the direction of William Barratt. William, in his turn, visited Sam on the occasion of his performance of *Acis and Galatea* in Bloemfontein. In the second half of the programme the two brothers played the complete Mozart *Quintet in A* as a piano duet. — In 1879 Sam Barratt turned up in Kimberley, where he directed the Kimberley Choral Society in a performance of *Elijah* on 13 March, and *Messiah* on 2 July. On 20 November of this active year he gave a performance of *The May Queen* (Sterndale Bennett) with the choral society, and led them again in a performance of *The merrie men of Sherwood forest* on 2 July 1880. On this occasion there was an "orchestra" of eight members, including his brother James and the unidentified David Barratt. James Barratt, who had been music teacher, piano-tuner and choir leader in Bloemfontein since 1877, left the city early in 1880 to the regret of many of its inhabitants, and joined his brother Sam in Kimberley. In 1881 the brothers gave a series of three concerts, but James must have left Kimberley again in 1884, since a press report in January 1885 mentions his return to the Free State Republic, and that he had started a practice in Bethulie, as music teacher and piano-tuner. — In the meantime, William Barratt had taken over James's practice in Bloemfontein in 1880. In August the Bloemfontein Choral Society came to life again under his direction, and in December he directed a performance of *The merrie men of Sherwood forest*, with a small orchestra. Before the society disbanded in 1884, it performed under his direction the so-called *Twelfth mass* by Mozart and *The ancient mariner* (Barnett). He was also organist and choir leader at the inauguration of the DR Church building in May 1880. Sam Barratt, in the meantime, had decided to leave Kimberley, and had arranged a large farewell concert on 15 October 1881, at which Sullivan's *The pirates of Penzance* was performed. He did not leave for New Zealand, as was reported by *The Friend* (24 November 1881), since he turned up as director of the East London Choral Society, which came into being on 22 May 1882, apparently as a result of his endeavours. He left East London after their first concert, and turned up in Bloemfontein in 1883 to rejoin William. — In this year Sam and William collaborated for the inauguration of a Broadwood grand piano and an American organ, which William had ordered for the new City Hall. It was claimed that William had given the builders of the instruments hints on how to overcome the climatic conditions of the Free State. Sam, too, in 1889, had a piano built for him by the firm Rogers and Sons in England, in which a key·rail of bronze was firmly fixed to the steel frame and the keys had ivory tops screwed down on them. In 1883 Sam and William started their own brass band, which provided music for a variety of occasions, and accompanied operettas until 1887, when it took a leading part in the Queen Victoria Jubilee festivities. The two brothers were not only collaborators in the creation of this brass band, but shared its conducting. It was at first simply called the Barratt Orchestra, and later the Orchestral Society. — On his return to Bloemfontein in 1884, Sam directed performances of *Trial by jury* (Sullivan) by the Bloemfontein Choral Society, and of *HMS Pinafore* (Sullivan), by children. *HMS Pinafore* was repeated in 1888, this time with adult singers. Sam also produced an original operetta in 1887 the title of which is unfortunately unknown. His only surviving composition is the song *Britannia's sons,* which appeared in 1887. After 1884 there is no further mention of William Barratt, and after April

1889, Sam also disappeared from the scene.

BIBLIOGRAPHY

HUMAN, J.L.K.: *Musiek in die Oranje-Vrystaat vanaf 1850 tot aan die begin van die Anglo-Boere-oorlog.* M.Mus. dissertation, UOFS, 1963.

SOURCES

The Diamond News: 1874-1878.   *The Diamond Fields Advertiser:* 1878-1881.   *The East London Dispatch:* 1882.

-J.P.M.

BARROW-DOWLING, MINNA (née GRANT), *22 December 1870 in Sibdon, Shropshire; °5 May 1962 in Salisbury, Rhodesia. Pianist, organist and journalist.

Minna Barrow-Dowling was educated at St Boniface, Isle of Wight, where she received her early training as a pianist. In 1888 she married Thomas Barrow-Dowling*, and in the same year accompanied him to Cape Town. After the birth of her second daughter in 1891, she went to London for further pianoforte study under Henry Davenport at the RAM and became a Licentiate within six months, before returning to Cape Town. In spite of her private practice as a teacher of pianoforte and singing, and her responsibilities as the mother of eventually four sons and three daughters, she found time to become proficient as an organist, an accomplishment that was to prove of great value later in her career.   — Between 1896 and 1911 Minna's name recurs constantly as accompanist in performances of the Cape Town Musical Society, under her husband's conductorship. In 1903 she accompanied Sir Charles Santley at his recital in the Dutch Reformed Church Hall. She is mentioned in his autobiography. During these years she acted as official accompanist to the combined Choral Societies and was of tremendous assistance to her husband in the production of Festival oratorios.   — 1924-1926 were to prove exacting years. During Dr Barrow-Dowling's two serious illnesses, the last of which was to prove fatal (September 1926), she stepped into the breach and carried on his work as organist and choirmistress of St George's Cathedral. She continued this work until the appointment of Alban Hamer*.   — In 1918 Mrs Barrow-Dowling had been appointed musical and dramatic critic to the *Cape Times* by the editor, Sir Maitland Park. Her wide musical knowledge and love of the theatre found fulfilment during the next fourteen years. Although an exacting critic, she was scrupulously fair in her opinions. In 1932 family affairs compelled her departure for East Africa where, in Nairobi, she joined the *East African Standard,* and for some years was organist and choirmistress of the Cathedral of the Highlands.   — She returned to South Africa in 1939.

—T.B-D.

BARROW-DOWLING ORGAN SCHOLARSHIP   T.R.W. Farrell

BARROW-DOWLING, THOMAS, *31 May 1861 in Over Wallop, Wiltshire; °5 September 1926 in Cape Town. Organist and conductor.

Barrow-Dowling was of yeoman stock and there is no record of inherited musicality in his family. Nothing is known of his early training as an organist, but his association with Salisbury Cathedral, as chorister, undoubtedly awakened his inherent love for choirs and church music, which played an important part in the shaping of his career. From January 1880 until July 1884 he studied at the RAM and was awarded a Fellowship. Between 1884 and 1885 he was organist to St Phillip's, Regent Street, London. In 1888 he married Minna Grant*, and left for Cape Town to assume the position of organist and choirmaster at St George's Cathedral*, being the successor to Neumann Thomas*. — In a lecture later published in the *Cape Times*, Dr Barrow-Dowling included the following recollection: "The Rev. John Deacon ... was Precentor when I arrived here, and there was a St George's Choral Society with Mr Deacon as conductor and Miss Bau as pianist. Mozart's *Twelfth Mass* was performed in the Cathedral shortly after I arrived. I have a keen recollection of my first hearing of the Cathedral choir that Sunday morning, 15 April 1888, which impressed me very much as regards the purity and refinement of the voices, and their rendering of a ·difficult service". — Though born with a withered leg, Thomas was a man of boundless energy and strong personality, and it was not long before he had made a considerable impact on the musical life of the city of his adoption. In the year of his arrival he became conductor of the flourishing Suburban Choral Union, when Halford Smith had to retire through ill-health, and he was also pressed to accept the post of conductor to the Cape Town Choral Society. On 27 December he performed Mackenzie's *Jason* in the Exhibition Hall with this city group; but after this there was a lapse until 1891. — The suburban group remained very active during the period 1888-1891, performing a dozen major works, including Mendelssohn's *St Paul* and *Athalie*. In 1891 the two groups joined forces, and a flourishing period of choral activity under Barrow-Dowling ensued, perhaps not equalled in Cape Town's musical history. Contemporary British composers featured prominently in the programmes, but gradually an impressive array of classical masterpieces was added to the repertoire. — In April 1895, four years after the merger of the choral unions, Barrow-Dowling accepted the conductorship of the Cape Town Musical Society, an amateur orchestral group that had regularly assisted his choral ventures in the previous years; he thus brought together the great combined choir and the only orchestra in Cape Town, under one leadership. This happy conjunction lasted until the final Festival performance of Mendelssohn's *Elijah* in 1912. The years 1895-1912 had been musically prolific: "There were hundreds of concerts given, as well as about 80 performances with the Choral Societies" *(Cape Times,* 17 July 1923). —Barrow-Dowling was fortunate in having Percy Ould* and Ellie Marx* as partners and leaders of the orchestra until 1906. The performances were generally in the Mixed Commission Room or the Mutual Hall, and after 1895 in the Good Hope Hall. With the inauguration of the City Hall on 25 July 1905, the latter became their permanent home. After that, Barrow-Dowling engaged actively in the promotion of a permanent City Orchestra, finally achieved in 1914. His efforts were, however, affected by the regrettable decline of the Musical Society, owing to the diminishing number of subscribers after 1905. During the last 7 years of its existence Barrow-Dowling's orchestra played regularly at municipal functions, and paved the way for the new City Orchestra. — Dr Barrow-Dowling's musical activities remained all-embracing. Besides the concert work, there was the responsibility of training the Cathedral Choir; he had many private pupils for singing, pianoforte and organ, and his was the educational task of choral training in a number of local schools. Faced with the imminent institution of music examinations in South Africa, on the pattern of the Associated Board in London and with examiners from Great Britain, prominent Cape Town musicians in 1893 started the Vredenburg Music School for Ladies on Overbeek Square. Barrow-Dowling was director of this school which had to prepare candidates for the examinations of the Cape University, co-operating with the Associated Board. — His keen interest in the Tonic Solfa movement and the systematic training of children in singing, led to close co-operation with Messrs Ashley, Smithers and Arthur Lee, the last being chief Music Inspector in the Education Department. The sympathetic attitude of the Superintendent of Education, Sir Thomas Muir, fostered the growth of this movement. In 1909, when Piérne's *Children's crusade* was performed with the orchestra, 600 children from the High Schools, together with the Training College and the Combined Choral Societies, participated under Barrow-Dowling's direction. The composer acknowledged this performance from Paris, in a special letter of thanks to the conductor. — After the opening of the City Hall, Barrow-Dowling was appointed joint city organist with Denholm Walker*, but later relinquished the post, when it became evident that he was dangerously overburdened. In 1910 he was responsible for the musical side of the historic Pageant in Cape Town, to celebrate the Act of Union. This was criticised, from the national point of view, by Bosman di Ravelli*. — After the establishment of the Cape Town Municipal Orchestra* in 1914, Dr Barrow-Dowling gradually withdrew from public work, owing to failing health and concentrated on Cathedral and educational work. The end came after 38 years of devoted and strenuous labour devoted to the creation of a new standard of musical activity in South Africa. This provided the tradition that enabled the first professional orchestra and the South African College of Music* to be established. — There is a tablet to his memory in St George's Cathedral, Cape Town. In January 1904, the Lambeth degree of Doctor Musicae was conferred on him by the Archbishop of Canterbury.

WORKS

Cape Town College song. Maskew Miller, n.d.   Chastelär, Gavotte de concert in E minor for the pianoforte. Hutchings and Romer, London, n.d.   The progress of prosperity, a Masque of Consummation and Consecration for the celebration of the opening of the first Union Parliament (Francis Hartman Markoë), 1910.   Fivefold Amen: Service Book of the Cape Town Diocesan Church Choirs' Association. Novello, 1910.   St. Cyprian's school song. Boosey & Co, London, 1921.

BIBLIOGRAPHY

BOUWS, JAN: *Geskiedenis van die musiekonderwys in Suid-Afrika, 1652-1902.* Nasou, Cape Town, 1972.   BROWN, JAMES, and STRATTON, STEPHEN: *British musical biography.* Birmingham, 1897.   OLIVIER, GERRIT: *Die orrel in die Stadsaal van Kaapstad.* B. Mus. script, UP, 1967. VAN DER MERWE, F.Z.: *Suid-Afrikaanse musiekbibliografie, 1787-1952.* J.L. van Schaik, Pretoria. 1958.

SOURCE

BARROW-DOWLING, T.: Music at the Cape from 1860 to 1912. *Cape Times,* 17 July 1923.

—T.B-D.

BARROWMAN, L   Pretoria 3

BARTELS, A (MRS EYSSEN)   S.H. Eyssen

BARTHELEMON, MISS   Piano Music III/2

BARTON, HORACE PERCIVAL, *20 May 1872 in Forest Gate, Essex; ° 17 September 1951 in Johannesburg. Composer, pianist and organist, who exerted considerable influence on musical life in Port Elizabeth and Johannesburg.

The Bartons were a musical family, and Horace Percival was instructed in music from his fifth year by his elder brother, William J. Barton, who was for 25 years a professor of harmony, counterpoint, orchestration and composition at the Guildhall School of

Music. Inevitably, the younger brother entered the school, where he was taught by late Victorian musicians such as J.F. Barnett, Dr J. Bridge and Dr G. Oldroyd. His curriculum included pianoforte, cello, theoretical subjects and composition, to which he eventually added organ, violin and advanced cello playing. To acquire the broadest possible basis for his future career, he also became a member of two choral societies, and gained considerable insight into choral repertoires and the art of conducting. He performed in public for the first time when he was nine years old, playing Sterndale Bennett's *Rondo a la Polonaise.* — Subsequently Barton performed at concerts in and around London. Sir George Grove, then principal of the RCM, paid a warm tribute to his pianistic ability in 1886. In due course he completed his musical education, and started his career equipped with licentiates of the Trinity College for pianoforte and composition. He was also a Fellow of Trinity College, and in later years became a member of the Royal Society of Teachers, the Incorporated Society of Musicians, the London Musicians' Club and the Performing Right Society. He had started composing in his 16th year and won a couple of awards for his works, to which, however, he attached little importance at the time. — Barton was organist of St Mary's Church, Moorfield, London, in 1897, when he was notified that he had been appointed organist of St Augustine's Roman Catholic Cathedral in Port Elizabeth, on the recommendation of Alfred Hollins. He came to South Africa in the same year, and shortly after taking up his duties, was appointed music teacher on the staff of Marist Brothers' College in Uitenhage. — He identified himself with the musical life of the city, played accompaniments for the PE Municipal Choral Society at the rate of 50c per evening, and presented two excellent concerts, playing major works by Beethoven, Schumann, Mendelssohn and Chopin. In conjunction with Ethel Biden (violin), Alice Ivimy (violin), Charles Davies (violin) and Percival Jackson (cello) he played trios by Niels Gade and Mendelssohn and other chamber music in the German Liedertafel Hall and conducted the PE Operatic Society in *Les cloches de Corneville* (Planquette) and *Dorothy* (Cellier) before February 1901. — Encouraged by successes with the Operatic Society, he revived the PE Philharmonic Society in 1905, and conducted performances of *Hiawatha* (Coleridge-Taylor), *John Gilpin* (Cowen), and Stanford's *The revenge* (May 1907). He then launched into a more ambitious repertoire with *Faust* (December 1906 and August 1910), *St Paul* (April 1906), *Elijah* (July 1907), *The creation* (July 1907), *Messiah* (August 1909), and *Judas Maccabaeus* (August 1910). — In 1907 Barton had a choir of over 200 voices, with which he inaugurated annual choral festivals, at which British soloists sang with the choir. At the opening concert in July 1907, the Philharmonic Society presented Barton with a baton in recognition of his services. At St Augustine's he played on the organ many extracts from larger works; under other conductors the choir sang extracts from classical masses and oratorios, whilst vocal and string soloists added their quota. In March 1899, he was organist at a performance of Rossini's *Stabat Mater,* conducted by C.W. Smart, the leader of the orchestra being P. Quarterman.* — In April 1911 Barton went on a five-month tour of South Africa with Ada Crossley, Gregor Cherniavsky (cello) and Stanley Newman (bass). From reports in Bloemfontein, Kimberley and Pretoria, it is concluded that he was a great success as accompanist. At the end of the tour Frank Proudman* invited him to give an organ recital in Durban, which was reputedly listened to by 5 000 people. Barton became organist at the St George's Presbyterian Church in Johannesburg in October 1911 and his career followed the same pattern as in Port Elizabeth. He established the St George's Choral

Union, which gave performances of works such as *Athalia* and *Hymn of praise* (Mendelssohn). Features of his organ recitals were his own transcriptions of symphonic works. Shortly after arrival he took over the lead of the Johannesburg Male Voice Choir, and in 1915 became musical director of the Johannesburg Philharmonic Society,* which he conducted in performances of *The creation* (Haydn), *The rose of Sharon* (Mackenzie), *The rose maiden* (Cowen) and Bach's *Christmas oratorio*. In addition, he performed as pianist, and was invited to give recitals on the newly-installed organ in the City Hall. — Maude Harrison enlisted Barton as a lecturer in theoretical subjects at her Conservatoire of Music, where he taught for six years (1911-1916). When P.R. Kirby* started the Department of Music at the University of the Witwatersrand, Barton was first choice as a lecturer in pianoforte (1923-1945) and he resigned his position as organist of St George's. Among the best-known of the students he instructed are Rosa Nepgen* (pianoforte and composition), Maisie Flink,* Jack Aronowitz* and Betty Pack.* He was also on the panel of music examiners of the University of South Africa. — With the advent of national broadcasting in South Africa during the thirties, Barton was frequently invited to give radio recitals, in which he included his own works. After 1945 failing eyesight compelled him to curtail his activities. He confined himself to teaching a few pupils, and devoted more of his time to composition. When the Society of South African Composers* was formed in 1945, Barton was one of the founder members, and served as chairman for three years. In Port Elizabeth in 1905, Barton was married to Ethel Maud Collett. One daughter, Phyllis, was born from this union.

WORKS

Orchestral

Valse fantasia, op. 17, dedicated to Signor Tardugno, bandmaster of the Prince Alfred's Guard Band. Ms., 1903.   Symphonic variations on Sarie Marais. Ms., 1932.   Four miniatures. Ms., 1938.   Valse. Ms., n.d.   Pavane. Ms., n.d.   The jovial chase. Ms., n.d.   The ghostly tale. Ms., n.d.   Nocturne. Ms., n.d.   Symphonic variations on Reveille (see vocal). Ms., n.d.   Symphonic variations on Swarte osse (see vocal). Ms., n.d.   Symphonic variations on The Scamp (see vocal). Ms., n.d.   Symphonic variations on Vegkop (see vocal). Ms., n.d.   Symphonic variations on Etude (Anton Rubinstein). Ms., n.d.

Chamber Music

Romance in A major, for violin and pianoforte, dedicated to Arthur Payne. Ms., before 1904. Trio in F minor, for violin, cello and pianoforte. Ms., 1937.   Sonata, for cello and pianoforte. Ms., 1943.   Jig, for cello and pianoforte. Ms., October 1943.   The robin, impromptu for cello and pianoforte, dedicated to Betty Pack. Ms., 31 October 1943.   Prelude and fugal fantasia, for three cellos and pianoforte. Ms., 1945.   Ballade in D minor, for cello and pianoforte. Ms., n.d.   To Proteas, for cello and pianoforte, dedicated to Betty Pack. Ms., 27 November 1945.   Sonata, for two violas and pianoforte. Ms., 1945.   Invocation, for cello and pianoforte. Ms., n.d.   Sarabande, for cello and pianoforte. Ms., n.d.   Hebrew song of supplication, for cello and pianoforte. Ms., n.d.   Minuet, for 3 flutes and triangle. Ms., n.d.

Vocal

An hour with thee (Sir Walter Scott), song. Augener & Co., London, before 1901.   The beautiful city of sleep (Edward Oxenford) song, dedicated to Mrs M. Dowar. Jackson Bros., Port Elizabeth, before 1902.   Vegkop (Totius), song. Printed by Paterson's Publications, London; publ. Nasionale Pers Beperk, Cape Town, n.d.   Daar's nog die lang rooi wapad voor my (C.L. Leipoldt), song. Printed by Paterson's Publications, London; publ. Nasionale Pers Beperk,

Cape Town, n.d.   To blossoms (Herrick), song. Paterson's Publications Ltd., London, 1935. The singer (Rosa Nepgen), song. Paterson's Publications Ltd, London, 1935.   Swarte osse (A.G. Visser), song. Paterson's Publications Ltd, London 1937.   As saans (A.D. Keet), song. Publishers and date unknown.   Reveille (E.D. van Weenen), song. Ms., 20 January 1940.   Morte d'Arthur (Tennyson), for tenor, baritone, chorus and orchestra. Ms., comp. 1947/48 under the pseudonym Excalibur.   Memory come hither (Blake), four-part song. Ms., n.d.   The scamp (E.D. van Weenen), song. Ms., n.d.   Ave Maria, song with organ accompaniment. Ms., n.d.   You can't do nothing all the time (E.D. van Weenen), song. Ms., n.d.   Serenade (Longfellow), four-part song. Ms., n.d.   Kyk hoe goed en lieflik, psalm 133, three-part song. Die Vlakte series Afrikaanse Liedere I, composed under the pseudonym Kleinjan. Nasionale Pers Beperk, n.d.

Pianoforte
Sonata in G minor. Augener & Co., London, before 1901.   Valse brillante. Augener & Co., London, before 1901.   Valse caprice. Augener Ltd, London, before 1901.   Rondo scherzando. Augener Ltd, London, before 1901.   Romance in G maj. Augener & Co., London, before 1901.   Polonaise in E min. Augener Ltd, London, before 1901.   Melody in A flat. Augener & Co, London, before 1901. Barcarolle. Augener & Co, London, before 1901. Golden hours, six easy pieces suitable for child hands. Hammond & Co, London, before 1902.   Floral emblems, six easy pieces suitable for child hands (six morceaux faciles pour piano). Printed by C.G. Röder, Leipzig; published by Jackson Bros, Port Elizabeth, before 1902.   Redowak, opus 15. Reynolds & Co, London, 1903.   Pavane, opus 16. Reynolds & Co, London, 1903.   Three cameos, opus 20. Augener Ltd, London, n.d.   Valse arabesque. Augener & Co, London, before 1904.   Waltz in B flat. Ms. under the pseudonym Templeton, n.d.

BIBLIOGRAPHY
ROUX, MARGARETHA: *Die lewe en werk van Horace Percival Barton*. B.Mus. script, UP, 1966. VAN DER MERWE, F.Z.: *Suid-Afrikaanse musiekbibliografie, 1787-1952*. J.L. van Schaik, Pretoria, 1958.   W.H.K.: *The arts in South Africa*. Knox Printing and Publishing Co, Durban, 1933.

SOURCES
IDELSON, J.: Sketches of South African composers. *Bandstand*, n.d.   National Documentation Centre for Music, HSRC, Pretoria.   *The Star:* 1911-1953.   *The Eastern Province Herald:* 1901-1911.

—P.W. (amplified)

BARTONYI, G.   G.A. Walker

BASSEL, HELGA (MRS HANNES UYS), *2 July 1908 in Berlin, of Viennese parents; °26 May 1969 in Cape Town. Pianist and piano teacher.

Helga Bassel was privileged as a young girl to receive music tuition from Jascha Horenstein and Helene Pretorius; after that she attended the Hochschule für Musik in Berlin, qualifying under Leonid Kreutzer (piano), Georg Schönemann (composition) and Bruno Kittel (choral conducting). She became known as a pianist, but a visit to her brother in Cape Town in 1937 changed the direction of her career. She was repeatedly invited by William Pickerill* to appear in concertos with the Cape Town Municipal Orchestra* and she also undertook a concert tour of South West Africa as a member of a trio in the same year. The result was that, after a brief return to Berlin, she came back to settle in South Africa in August 1939. She continued her career as a concert pianist and, in appearances with the Cape Town Orchestra, performed comparatively unknown works by the composers Liszt, Jean Françaix, Richard Strauss, Weber and Armstrong Gibbs. In addition, her playing was repeatedly broadcast. — She and

Hannes Uys* played duets on two pianos and became well-known through concert tours, appearances with the orchestras of Cape Town, Durban and Johannesburg and through radio broadcasts. They were married in 1943. In 1948 they appeared together in the first Afrikaans music film, *Kom saam vanaand*. She was a member of Charles Kreitzer's* chamber music group and was connected with the South African College of Music* and the Conservatoire of Music in Stellenbosch* (since 1952) and was a music teacher at various Cape schools for many years. — Her talented daughter, Tessa (Hannelore) Uys, is now in London, where she is preparing for a career as concert pianist. She has played in South Africa with the orchestra of the SABC.

SOURCE
National Documentation Centre for Music, HSRC, Pretoria.

—Ed.

BASSON, P.N.   Pretoria School for the Cerebral Palsied

BATCHELDER, GRACE (MRS DEANE)   W. Deane, Johannesburg 2

BAU, FRÄULEIN   T. Barrow-Dowling, Graaff Reinet 2, 3, 6

BAUMANN, ALFRED MORITZ, *28 June 1862 in Bloemfontein, son of the Bloemfontein pioneer, Isaac Baumann and Caroline Baumann (who owned the first piano in Bloemfontein); °29 July 1921 in Bloemfontein. General medical practitioner, oculist and singer.

From 1878 to 1886 Baumann received medical training in Germany, and after his return in 1887, he established himself as a general practitioner in Winburg (1888-1896), where he produced *The Mikado*. After 1896 he again left for Germany, Austria and England to qualify as an eye specialist. In Bloemfontein during the Anglo Boer War, Baumann was in command of the concentration camp and at the end of the war he remained in the capital as an eye specialist. — Beside his medical work Dr Baumann was a devoted music-lover who actively shared in Bloemfontein music until his death. In 1885, during his student years, he conducted an orchestra in a light variety programme before the State President and Mrs Brand. Later he was a vocalist who advised or even taught Bloemfontein singers. In his estate were three compositions which provide evidence that he had also studied the theoretical aspects of music, perhaps during his student years in Germany.

WORKS
Adieu, waltz for piano. Townsend and Thomson, Edinburgh, n.d.   Awake, song (Longfellow). Novello, Ewer and Co, 1896.   The night has a thousand eyes, song. Ms., n.d.

BIBLIOGRAPHY
HUMAN, J.L.K.: *Musiek in die Oranje-Vrystaat vanaf 1850 tot aan die begin van die Anglo-Boere-oorlog*. M.Mus. dissertation, UOFS, 1963.

SOURCE
The Friend: 30 July 1921.

—E.H.S.

BAUMANN FAMILY   Bloemfontein I(i), E. Leviseur

BAVIAANSPOORT   W. Frewer

BAXTER, DR WILLIAM DUNCAN, *14 June 1868 in Dundee, Scotland; °7 January 1960 in Cape Town. Benefactor of music and theatre.

Educated in Dundee, where he developed a lifelong love for reading and good music, Baxter came to Cape Town in 1886. He was active in both commerce and politics, twice President of the Cape Town Chamber of Commerce, Mayor of Cape Town in 1907-1908, and a Member of Parliament from 1908-1920. He sat on several Government Commissions in the early 1920's and served for many years on the governing body of, among others, the University of Cape Town. He was a co-founder of the South African College of Music* and a foundation member and lifelong supporter of the Cape Town Municipal Orchestra.* The University of Cape Town honoured him with an Hon. LL.D. in 1940, and in 1958 he became a Freeman of the City of Cape Town. Even at the height of his political and commercial career, he regularly attended concerts and the theatre. He constantly deplored the modern trend towards converting theatres into cinemas, without replacing them with other theatres, and expressed the hope that "the day will come when all the cities in the Union will again possess an adequate theatre and so resume what I consider indispensable to the welfare, education and enjoyment of the citizens - good plays, operas, ballets and the like". At his death in 1960, he bequeathed the bulk of his estate (some R540 000) to the University of Cape Town, stating that the money should be used to establish a theatre in Cape Town in which plays, operas, ballets and concerts could be presented.

—R.I.

BAYLIS, LILIAN MARY, *9 May 1874 in London; °25 November 1937 in Stockwell, England. Founder of the Old Vic and Sadler's Wells Companies.

Lilian's father, Newton Baylis, was a baritone and her mother, Elizabeth ("Liebe") Kons, a contralto singer and pianist. Lilian was a pupil of J.T. Carrodus, a violinist in the orchestra of Covent Garden, and appeared on the concert stage for the first time as a seven-year-old. Apart from tuition, she was indebted to Carrodus for her great love of theatre and opera.   —After she had taken part in a programme at the Aeolian Hall in London (May 1889), in which she appeared with her parents and her brother Willy, the family came to South Africa in 1890, to present variety programmes of a musico-dramatic nature in the main centres. Early in 1892 they were in Durban and, during May, in Johannesburg, where Lilian sang songs in the Wanderers' Hall, with David Foote* as her accompanist. In August the family appeared in a joint programme with the Royal Celebrated Gypsy Revellers, treating their audiences to "gypsy" music. In their advertisements, they announced themselves as the Kons-Baylis Variety Troupe. The members were Madame Kons-Baylis (contralto, pianist and guitarist), Newton Baylis (bass-baritone), Adeline Varlain (cornet), Lilian, Willy and the six-year-old "babe vocalist", Ethel. Lilian and Willy respectively played mandoline and cello, and were also announced as "the only zither players in the country".   —The family decided to settle in Johannesburg, where, during those exciting days of gold digging, they made a living by adapting their talents to the great demand for entertainment and tuition in music. They advertised lessons on the fashionable instruments of the time: guitar, banjo and mandoline; but also in violin, cello and singing. They apparently made good progress, since they ambitiously launched a Rand Academy of Music, initially in Davies Street, but later at 131 Bree Street, Doornfontein. This school of music existed until after the South African War. In 1899 dancing and gymnastics were added to the subjects taught, but by then Lilian had already been in England a year. —This emphasis on educational work may have been owing to harsh newspaper criticisms after concert appearances in 1892; at least one of the songs was condemned for its "vulgarity". However, the Baylis team remained active in the musical life of the town: Lilian was a member of von Himmelstjerna's* Ladies' Orchestra, Newton was secretary to the Johannesburg Oratorio Society, and Willy, who later became head of the Rand Academy, played cello solos during an organ recital in St Mary's Cathedral in September 1902. He also became the conductor of a theatre orchestra, and decided to settle in South Africa. —The initiative and vitality that were to make Lilian a celebrated figure in the London theatre world, led her to interesting experiments during these early years. At one time she conducted an "orchestra" consisting of the wives of Rand millionaires and other moneyed persons. The fortunes of this "orchestra" are unknown, as are those of the band of bank clerks whom she tried to forge into a banjo ensemble. Shortly before her departure she also gave dancing lessons, and it is said that, during his visit to South Africa, none less than Mark Twain was one of her pupils. He was evidently not very proficient, and could hardly manage the steps of the Lancers. — Lilian was, however, destined for greater things. Her aunt, Emma Kons, needed an assistant to manage her Royal Victoria Hall in London. Although Lilian was not inclined to leave South Africa, she accepted her aunt's offer in 1898, and during the following year appointed Charles Corri as her musical director. This was the first step in a particularly fortunate partnership that was to last more than 30 years, and improved considerably the musical aspect of her theatrical productions. When Emma Kons died in 1912, full management of the theatre passed into Lilian's hands. During the meagre theatre years of the First World War she managed to steady the financial standing of her theatre, so that prominent actors were eager to join her company. The reputation of her theatre as a home for the plays of Shakespeare became established and by 1920, when the Old Vic was one of the most important theatres in London, she had expanded her activities by the acquisition of the Sadler's Wells Theatre in Islington. She had it rebuilt during the years of financial depression, as a home for opera and ballet, and directed both theatres until her death. —Lilian Baylis retained a warm affection for South Africa. In 1924 she was here on a visit, and was acclaimed with great enthusiasm. In the same year the University of Oxford awarded her an honorary degree; in 1929 she was nominated a Companion of Honour, and in 1934 the University of Birmingham also conferred on her an honorary degree. Besides Willy, some of whose descendants still live in the vicinity of Johannesburg, Lilian's sister Ethel (Mrs Dunning) also became a citizen of South Africa.

BIBLIOGRAPHY
Dictionary of national biography. London, 1949.   The Oxford companion to the theatre. OUP.   GUTHRIE, TYRONE: A life in the theatre.   HARCOURT WILLIAMS, E.G.: Vic-Wells. The work of Lilian Baylis. London, 1938.   THORNDIKE, SYBIL and RUSSEL: Lilian Baylis. London, 1938.

SOURCES
MANDER, R.P.: The Old Vic story. Programme of the Old Vic Company in South Africa, 1952.   The Star: 1892-1902.   Diggers' News: 1892.

—E.H.S. (amplified)

BAYLY, A.W.   Barberton I, III/2, 3, 4, IV, V, VI, B.M. Marx

BEASLEY, GORDON LEONARD,*1 July 1920 in Winchester; at present in Cape Town. Pianist, accompanist.

Gordon Beasley was privately educated in music and obtained the LRSM (Performer) and LTCL (Performer) diplomas. When he was 17 years old, he became an orchestral pianist in small orchestras in the South of England and participated in piano trios. His career was interrupted by the Second World War in 1939, but in 1946 he became Musical Director for Hedley Claxton at the Playhouse, Weston-super-Mare, and after one season there, joined the Weston-super-Mare Municipal Orchestra, as pianist and accompanist. During this time he accompanied leading English singers such as Heddle Nash, Isobel Baillie, Gladys Ripley and others. — Beasley came to South Africa in September 1947, and freelanced as an accompanist and pianist. In 1960 he was appointed senior music producer at the SABC Johannesburg and since October 1968 he has been the SABC's Organiser of Music for the Western Cape Region. Since his arrival in South Africa in 1947, Beasley has become well-known as an accompanist, has toured for the Performing Arts Councils of four provinces, and taken part in many theatrical engagements, especially ballet, as accompanist to Nerina* and Rassine,* Beryl Grey, Danilova and others. He has performed in a great number of radio broadcasts, as soloist, but mainly as accompanist in sonata combinations with other instruments.
—Ed.

BEAUFORT WEST, MUSIC IN The musical history of Beaufort West did not start in a church, but with the general dealers Alport and Co., buyers of wool and hides, dealers in arms and ammunition, owners of a bottle store and a flour mill, woolwashers and building contractors, who provided for the needs of this isolated Karoo community. In November 1870 (the town was then 35 years old) members of the clerical staff in this store had the idea of also providing music for the town: one played the flute, another the cornet, two were proficient violinists and a fifth could strum a guitar - why not start a band? Their plan took shape, and by Christmas they had given an out-door performance: "their performance was very creditable" wrote the *Courier*. There must have been a Christy Minstrel group as well, because in February of the following year, when the Governor of the Cape Province, Sir Philip Wodehouse, visited the town, the "OHIO Minstrels" presented a comic show on the verandah of Alport's store. The band remained in existence, because on the occasion of Queen Victoria's Golden Jubilee Celebrations in 1887, the *Courier* reported that when, on 22 June, the express train steamed into the station, the "stoep" (platform) was packed with people and the "brass band sang (sic!) the national anthem". Between 1890 and 1899 the Alport Brass Band played at dances held at the women's club and on 31 May 1893 the management of the Lyric Hall advertised that music was provided at the roller-skating rink every night. The Alport band dominated the musical scene until the Anglo Boer War. — Soon afterwards, a new group appeared on the scene - or it could have been the same group under another name - the Beaufort West Brass Band. They too, played in the Lyric Hall which had become the venue for dances, concerts and wedding receptions (the Coronation Hall was not built until 1910; the National Theatre about 1920). In 1912, when M. van der Bent* was their leader, the band had 23 members including three young boys. Van der Bent left for Potchefstroom in 1914, after which the Rev. Whaits became the conductor. In 1915 there were three Whaits in the band, and the band had changed its name to The Earls. Their main source of income was still from playing at the roller-skating rink. A certain Joseph de Klerk also had a group, consisting of a piano, a violin, a saxophone and percussion, which provided music in the National Theatre during the projection of silent films. — The most important institution in Beaufort West's cultural life still is the Music and Drama Society. The local girls' school formerly had an Old Girls' League which disbanded in 1928. On 13 February of the following year their erstwhile members came together and founded a Beaufort West Music Club under the chairmanship of Dr J. Villett, with Mrs W.A. Jeffrey the prime mover. This society arranged musical evenings at the homes of members, presented stage performances (in 1929 it was the operetta *Floradora*) and accordingly adapted the name to Beaufort West Music, Operatic and Dramatic Club. When funds ran out, they disbanded, but there was a revival in June 1937 called the Beaufort West Dramatic and Operatic Society, which mounted a stage production every three months. The Second World War brought their initiative to a standstill and not until August 1945 did they come to life again as the Beaufort West Music and Drama Society (see above). — Before the Town Hall was built, they had no adequate hall for their meetings; the cinema was hired for an evening and the members transported pianos there and back for concerts. Usually they presented vocal items, piano and violin compositions, ballet numbers, musical sketches and stage pieces in one or two acts (the latter once a year). Sometimes after the tea interval, records were played, or lectures given on the great composers, or slides were projected by members or guests who had been overseas. Every year one concert was repeated for the staff and patients of the Nelspoort Sanatorium, 31 miles away. The society also entertained guest artists e.g. Elsie Hall* and Cecilia Wessels* (both of whom came three times), the Vienna Boys' Choir, Walter Klien, Erwin Broedrich* and others. — In 1963 they launched a ballet school, at which Judy Sillerey taught ballet and Spanish dancing to between 60 and 70 pupils. Ballet has a great following as is evidenced by the fact that the Cape Town University Ballet* have already visited the town no less than four times. —Since 1933 the ATKV has been active in organising cultural evenings with musical items, and has instituted scholarships for deserving music students. In 1938 the ATKV played a prominent role in compiling a programme for the Voortrekker festival on 8 October which included choir singing by 35 voices under the direction of J.D. Nel of the NG Kerk.

BIBLIOGRAPHY

VIVIER W.G.H. and S.: *Hooyvlakte. Die verhaal van Beaufort-Wes 1818-1968.* Nasionale Boekhandel, Cape Town, 1969.

SOURCE
Information from Mrs E.J. Truter, Beaufort West.

—J.P.M.

BEAVAN, JOHN TRYAL, *circa 1870 in England. Music teacher and choirmaster in South Africa between 1893 and 1904.

Beavan was trained at the Trinity College of Music and at the time of his leaving England in 1892, he was the holder of an ATCL diploma and a first grade certificate of the Society of Arts. He had also passed with honours in the Trinity College advanced examination in harmony and counterpoint. In Bloemfontein, where he established himself in 1893 as a teacher of piano, singing, violin, organ and theoretical subjects, Beavan was the founder of the Bloemfontein Choral Society which he directed in performances of *The rose maiden* (Cowen) and *The holy city* (Gaul). He conducted the Brandfort Choral Society at its first concert in November 1894, played the piano at concerts, gave lectures on music, and in 1895 introduced to Bloemfontein the music examinations of Trinity College. — Early in 1896, three months after his arrival in East London, he was organist and choirmaster of the Presbyterian Church, choirmaster of St John's Church and conductor of the choral section of the East London Choral and Orchestral Union which he directed in a programme of partsongs (1896). Beavan founded the Panmure Junior Singing and Instrumental Society and conducted its performance of the *Toy symphony* by Romberg and Vincent's cantata *The two cities.* As pianist he took part in four concerts and accompanied the singer Sims Reeves in East London. In 1897 he tackled larger choral works and gave performances of *The rose maiden* and the operetta *The Bohemian girl* (Balfe). But his health began to fail and after a performance of *The yeoman of the guard* (Sullivan) (September 1898) he collapsed. He had to curtail his activities considerably and only on a few occasions did he appear as conductor of the East London Choral and Orchestral Union and as a solo pianist. — In May 1900 his post at the Presbyterian Church became vacant and although the examination results of his pupils were still published in November 1900, Beavan must have left East London by then. On 23 June 1902 he married Mabel Coutts in the Presbyterian Church and with her he made a new start in the Transvaal. In 1904 he directed yet another performance of Cowen's *Rose maiden* in St Andrew's Presbyterian Church in Pretoria, but there is no further trace of him.

WORKS
Scottish folk songs arranged for choir. Ms., 1894.   Andante and rondo capriccioso, for piano. Ms., 1896.   Improvisatore, for piano. Ms., 1898.

BIBLIOGRAPHY
HUMAN J.L.K.: *Musiek in die Oranje-Vrystaat vanaf 1850 tot aan die begin van die Anglo-Boere-oorlog:* M.Mus. dissertation, UOFS, 1963. VERMEULEN, ELIZABETH: *Die musieklewe in Pretoria tussen 1902 en 1926.* M.Mus. dissertation, UP, 1967.

SOURCE
The East London Daily Dispatch: 1896-1900.

—Ed.

BECK, JOHANNES HENDRICUS MEIRING, *28 November 1855 in Worcester; ° 15 May 1919 in Cape Town. Medical doctor, politician and amateur musician.

After seeking self-expression on the cornet in Worcester, Beck had piano and violin lessons in Cape Town whilst at school there (1872-1874). He was a member of the Cape Town Music Society, at that time under the chairmanship of Professor Carl Schultz, and took part in their orchestral performances. In Edinburgh, where he began his medical studies late in 1874, Beck played for the Orchestral Society as one of the first violins (1874-1879) and acted as secretary of the university music society. There he became friendly with the musicians Sir John Hullah and Sir Herbert Oakley. Officially on the staff of the Royal Infirmary in Edinburgh, he spent his vacations in doing medical research in Vienna and Berlin. There he became acquainted with Wagner's music dramas which commanded his enthusiastic admiration. Wagner was at that time almost unknown in England. — From 1881 Beck practised medicine at first in Kimberley, then in Worcester (1883), and, after his marriage to Miss May Kuys of Stellenbosch in 1885, in Rondebosch and

Mowbray. Most of his compositions were created during these happy years - often they were improvisations, an art in which Beck excelled. Their home in Rondebosch, called "Rustenburg", was a rendezvous for many musicians of whom Reményi* was one. — It was during a visit to England in 1891 that Beck, in an interview with Sir George Grove, the first Director of the RCM, did convincing work which was to become a deciding factor in the introduction of British music examiners for examinations held in conjunction with the University of the Cape of Good Hope of whose Council he was a member. The University decided the next year to introduce music examinations, similar to those which had been instituted in England in the early seventies, and in 1893 the Vredenburg Music School for Ladies was started in Cape Town with T. Barrow-Dowling* as director, to prepare candidates for the examinations of the Cape university. Meiring Beck was one of the patrons of this music school. The agreement initiated by Meiring Beck with the Associate Board came into effect in 1894 and remained in force until 1945. — After a further visit to England in 1896, Beck entered politics in 1898, first as the elected representative for the Worcester-Tulbagh-Ceres constituency; as senator in the 1st Union Parliament; and finally in 1916 as Minister of Postal Affairs in the cabinet of General Louis Botha. In 1903 he bought and restored the dilapidated Oude Drostdy in Tulbagh as a residence for his family. It became a regular venue for home concerts of chamber and solo performances. Of his compositions one became well-known: the song of the South African College, written in 1887 for the benefit of his wife's stall at a bazaar in aid of this institution. This song became the property of the SACS and survives as an academic song of the University of Cape Town. The rest of his published work is written in a vein of rather artless sentimentality which has a certain old-world charm.

COMPOSITIONS

An deine Liebe will ich glauben, song (Egan Forst), opus 7 no. 2. A. Dixon Holloway, St Ives, Hunts., n.d. The arrowslit, song (Jean Ingelow). Published privately, Christmas, 1885. Cameraderie, a masonic march song (C. Fred Silberbauer). R. Müller, Cape Town, n.d. Chromatique valse de concert pour piano, opus 5 no. 1. Darter and Sons, n.d. Zwei Lieder. Published separately by R. Müller, Cape Town, n.d.: 1. Hoffnung (Hope), song (Schiller); 2. Gefunden (Found), song (Goethe). R. Müller, Cape Town, n.d. How strange that love should last, song. Ms., n.d. Hurrah for Table Mountain, song (C. Ray Woods). Cape Times Litho's, n.d. Lentelied, song (C.E. Viljoen). R. Müller, Cape Town, n.d. Lullaby, song (anon.). R. Müller, Cape Town, n.d. Many happy returns, birthday march. R. Müller, Cape Town, n.d. Marche triomphale. A Dixon Holloway, St Ives, Hunts, n.d. Music and moonlight their secret shall tell, song (anon.), op. 10. A Dixon Holloway, St Ives, Hunts., 1885. A national song for South Africans, song (C.E. Viljoen). 'n Volkslied vir Suid-Afrika, lied (C.E. Viljoen). Publ., n.d. Ons Vaderland. Afrikaner-Volkslied, song (Ds D.P. Faure). Published in December 1906 as supplement to "Ons Land" by Van de Sandt de Villiers Drukkers Maatschappij Bpk. Also printed in Dr. N. Mansvelt's Hollands-Afrikaanse Liederbundel (1907) and in Joan van Niekerk's Groot Afrikaans-Hollandse Liederbundel (1927). Ons land, ons land, song (Dr F.C. Kolbe). R. Müller, n.d. The SACS song (Dr F.C. Kolbe). W.A. Richards and Sons, Cape Town, 1887. Slumber, song (Eva Best). R. Müller, Cape Town, n.d. Spring, song. R. Müller, Cape Town, n.d. Summer, song. (T.E. Fuller). Enoch and Sons, London, 1890. Table Mountain echoes, waltz. opus 6 E.A. Dixon Holloway, St Ives, Hunts., n.d. Holloway printed 12 editions and two more were issued by Reynolds & Co. of London and R. Müller of Cape

Town.   The tide rises, the tide falls, song (Longfellow). Opus 7 no. 15. A. Dixon Holloway, St Ives, Hunts., n.d.   Valse minuet, for piano. R. Müller, Cape Town, n.d.   The way is clear, song. Ms., n.d.   Wonderland, song. Ms., n.d.   Suite for piano, violin and cello. Ms., n.d.

BIBLIOGRAPHY
BOUWS, JAN: *Geskiedenis van die musiekonderwys in Suid-Afrika, 1652-1902.* Nasou, Cape Town, 1972.   SCULLY, W.C.: *Sir Meiring Beck. A Memoir.* Maskew Miller, Cape Town, 1921. *South African biographical dictionary II,* 1972.   *Standard encyclopaedia of Southern Africa II,* Nasou Ltd., Cape Town, 1970.   VAN DER MERWE, F.Z.: *Suid-Afrikaanse Musiekbibliografie, 1787-1952.* J.L. van Schaik Bpk., Pretoria, 1958.

SOURCES
National Documentation Centre for Music, HSRC, Pretoria.
                                                                                    —Ed.

BECKER, HERMANN, *9 February 1888 in St Helier, the capital of Jersey Island; living in Port Elizabeth in 1969. A cellist of outstanding capability, who played a major part in South African musical life after 1914, chiefly as a performer.

Of German extraction, the Beckers produced a number of first-rate musicians, including the eminent cellist, Hugo Becker of Frankfurt, who was Hermann Becker's cousin, and two uncles prominent as cellist and organist respectively. Hermann's partiality for stringed instruments led him at the age of three to construct a crude violin out of a cigar box, and inevitably to violin lessons with a Mr McKee. At the age of five, his first public performance (*Cavalry* by Benedict) initiated a spate of concerts, in which variations on operatic airs were especially prominent. During his teens, Hermann was active in every musical organisation and event on the island, participating in performances of operas, Shakespearian productions and twice yearly in concerts of the local philharmonic society, conducted by the organist of the town church, Mr Hubert. A visit of his uncle from Frankfurt led to a new interest, the cello, on which he progressed so well that he soon became the principal cellist in the philharmonic orchestra. His father, who was a horticulturist, Fellow of the Royal Horticultural Society, and a good pianist, died in 1904, and Becker inherited his nursery. But at the age of 21 he abandoned this inheritance to leave for Guernsey, where he found employment in another nursery, and joined the local orchestra as a cellist. He also became a member of an athletic club, and distinguished himself as a marathon runner. — Becker's connection with South Africa came in 1911, when he was engaged as a cellist in the band of the *Balmoral Castle* on its maiden voyage to Cape Town. On his return to England he decided finally on a career in music, and was taken on as a cello pupil by Emily Krall, whose modern ideas on bowing and its relationship to tone production were a revelation to Becker. He held a position in the Orchestra of the Chelsea Palace Theatre, followed in succession by engagements with the Weymouth Municipal Orchestra, the South Pier Blackpool Orchestra and the Municipal Orchestra of Brighton, conducted at the time by Lyell-Tayler,* with Harold Ketelbey* as the leader. — Early in January 1914, the Cape Town Municipality advertised in London for principals in all sections of the Municipal Orchestra, then in the process of formation. Becker was appointed principal cellist and sailed for South Africa in the *Balmoral Castle,* this time as a passenger. Soon afterwards, Prof. Henry Bell* arrived to take charge of the growing College of Music* on Stalplein, and appointed Becker as lecturer in cello. In July, Theo Wendt* led his orchestra on a tour of South Africa, which culminated in

Johannesburg with a series of concerts in the Carlton Hotel Ball Room. The acquaintance with Johannesburg proved to be decisive. When the First World War ended in 1918, Becker accepted an offer as cello teacher on the staff of Miss Harrison's Conservatoire of Music, at that time the most flourishing musical institute in Johannesburg, with its own concert hall and a large staff of student lecturers and professionals, including Douglas Mossop* and Sydney Rosenbloom.* Soon after his arrival, Becker gave a cello recital for the Johannesburg Musical Society (March 1918). — Filled with an abundance of energy, optimism, enthusiasm and with encouragement from Mr Tatlow of the South African Railways Publicity Department (then Chairman of the Musical Society), Becker published a small monthly magazine called *The Student's Musical Magazine*. In this periodical Becker dealt with students' problems, local musical matters (such as the formation of a permanent civic orchestra), co-operation between teachers and artists, and the stabilization of their earnings. Although moderately successful, the magazine had to be discontinued after twelve monthly issues. Until 1923, however, he consented to act as editor of *The Music Teacher,* a quarterly journal published by the recently established Music Teachers' Society. — Becker's musical sense and personality guaranteed his success as a teacher. Among his pupils were the Pack sisters, of whom Betty Pack* became prominent, the Mason family and Betty Kendall. He formed his pupils into ensembles, with one combination in Johannesburg, one in Pretoria and one in Germiston. For special concerts, which he gave in combination with the singing pupils of Mrs Bal van Lier,* he would combine the three into one of a more equitable size. In the early days of Johannesburg, Becker found scope for his enthusiasm for chamber music, and co-operated with Lorenzo Danza* and his partner Ferramosca. — After five years, Becker emigrated with his family to the USA, and settled for a while in Chicago's Zion City, where he was a member of a religious organization and active in community life, especially its musical side. In addition to pioneering broadcasts, recitals and chamber-music performances, he wrote and published a number of short stories. He returned to Johannesburg in 1927, the proud possessor of an 1810 Lupot violoncello, which was reputed to have been made for the court of Napoleon. — Boom conditions prevailed in 1927. Becker built up his teaching practice again and entered heart and soul into the propagation of music. He gave a joint recital with Margaret Albu* at the Grand National Hotel, acted as deputy conductor for Dave Foote* at the Empire Theatre, and formed a trio with Otto Menge* and Frances Foster*, which played at the Carlton Hotel. In 1932 he announced the formation of a new asset in Johannesburg's musical life. The first combination included a brilliant young violinist, recently arrived from Amsterdam, Bram Verhoef, also Edward Foster (viola) and Mrs Bobby Evans (second violin). For special works, Lorenzo Danza* (pianoforte) and Dr Van den Bos (clarinet) were available. After weeks of daily rehearsals, Becker inaugurated a series of four concerts with his string quartette, which proved a success. The third concert formed part of John Connell's* Music Fortnight, and before the performance, Becker gave an introductory talk on *Our attitude to the music we play*. His erudite approach, judicious choice of programmes, and the sensitive team work of the ensemble, created some talk at the time. — Encouraged by this success, Becker introduced quintets with clarinet, oboe and horn, and also offered a trio repertoire. When Verhoef was engaged as leading violinist of the reorganised SABC Orchestra, Michael Doré* was enlisted, and, in company with Else Schneider* and Bobby

Evans, a series of ten monthly chamber concerts was broadcast on the SABC programmes. There were pianoforte trios and quartettes with Danza, as well as string quartettes, presented under the title: *A journey through the history of chamber music from Haydn to the present day*. The first series was followed by six more concerts in December of the same year. The response to this comprehensive series of chamber-music programmes encouraged Becker to organize a further series on the first Saturday night of each month; it was given in the Public Library Lecture Hall, which was invariably filled to capacity. The years of regular chamber music in Johannesburg continued until 1944. At the 184th and last concert on 29 March, the Quartette, then composed of Jeremy Schulman,* Erica Jolley, Lettie Vermaak* and Hermann Becker, performed the Schumann *Quartette in A minor* and the Dohnanyi *Quartette in D flat major*. — In the meantime, Becker had consented, in 1935, to form a Municipal Orchestra in Brakpan, consisting eventually of 30 players, augmented by others from the Witwatersrand, including Becker's own pupils. Guest artists such as Danza, Bruce Anderson* and Margaret Roux gave their assistance. It lasted till 1940, when the war forced the Civic Council of Brakpan to withdraw its support. Becker also conducted an amateur philharmonic orchestra in Germiston for a while and, during the War, directed the Springs Municipal Orchestra whilst its Director was on active service. — When the Johannesburg City Orchestra came into existence in 1946, Becker became principal cellist, and retained this position until the ill-fated orchestra was dissolved in 1953. He then decided to leave Johannesburg, and after one year as lecturer and head of the String Department at Rhodes University, he settled in Port Elizabeth. Here he created a new teaching practice, and soon had a Children's Orchestra, which grew to 43 performers, including 10 cellos. This group gave 20 concerts during the ten years of its existence, and managed to donate R1 000 to charity. Becker also took up chamber music again and performed in the auditorium of the new PE University in April 1968, with Sybil Whiteman* and Neil MacKay.* — Hermann was first married to Miss Marjorie Kellar, in 1921; in 1938 he married Miss Dorothy Ford of Johannesburg, a composer of songs.

WRITINGS
Editorial, *SAMT* 1, October 1931.

SOURCES
BENDER, A.: At 85 this cellist is a legend. *Opus, New Series* IV/3, March 1973.

—L.W.

BEETHOVEN COLLECTION IN WINDHOEK. This collection was built up over a long period by Marianne Steinbrink, a nurse in Otjiwarongo. After her death in 1966, it was taken over by the Windhoek branch of the Library of the South African Association of Arts. This was made possible by the donation of R540 by a businessman, Mr E. Behnsen. Marianne Steinbrink's will had stipulated that the collection should go to the Beethoven House in Bonn; but the directors turned the offer down, because of the excessive cost of transport; they wanted only a few selected items. The executor forbade this, and so the entire collection remained in Windhoek. — There are 189 books, among them biographies of Beethoven by Thayer, Schindler, Nohl, Marx, Wegeler and Ries, and studies of the composer by Frimmel and Seyfried, as well as Emily Andersen's edition of the letters and Kinsky's bibliography of the works. There is also a four-volume edition of Nottebohm's Beethoven sketches, and facsimiles of letters and some of the compositions. The collection is supplemented by printed editions of the music, gramophone records, portraits, and a copy of the famous death mask.

—H.H.M.

BEETHOVEN SCHOOL OF MUSIC   Wellington

BEHRENS, RICHARD HERMANN, *7 July 1925 in Kroondal, Rustenburg; now in Stellenbosch. Professor of Music and Director of the Conservatoire of Music, University of Stellenbosch.*

While at school in Kroondal and Rustenburg, Richard Behrens received training in pianoforte, organ and violin. Among his teachers were Lydia Wenhold and Charlotte Prinsloo. He went to Stellenbosch in 1944 and enrolled for a BA (Mus) degree, which he obtained *(cum laude)* in 1946. In 1948 he obtained a B.Mus degree under Professor Maria Fismer* and after completing his studies, became a junior lecturer at the Conservatoire of Music. The following year Richard Behrens was promoted to the post of lecturer and in 1958 to senior lecturer. In 1960 he continued his studies at the Staatliche Hochschule für Musik (Frankfurt/Main, Germany) under Helmut Walcha (organ) and Kurt Hessenberg (harmony and counterpoint). He returned in 1961 and was appointed Director of the Conservatoire of Music and promoted to the chair for Music in 1965. He has been the organist of the Lutheran congregation in Stellenbosch since 1952. — In 1958 Behrens's initiative and organising talents led to the first Stellenbosch Art Festival being held. He was also the chief organiser of subsequent festivals in 1961, 1964, 1966 (when the festival was part of the University's centenary celebrations) and in 1969. He has organised several short courses in church music, choir leadership, school music and piano teaching. Two of these courses, in 1956 and in 1959, were conducted by the German choir leader Professor Kurt Thomas. — When the Conservatoire of Music celebrated its Golden Jubilee in 1955, Richard Behrens edited a publication containing an historical survey of the Conservatoire and biographical sketches of the first four principals.

PUBLICATIONS
Die ontstaan en onwikkeling van die Konservatorium van die Universiteit van Stellenbosch. Gedenkblad, uitgegee by geleentheid van die Goue Jubileum van die Konservatorium. Stellenbosch, 1955.   75 Jaar kerkmusiekopleiding in Stellenbosch. *Die Orrel,* a periodical published by South African Organ Builders, 1959.

—Ed.

BEIL, LUDWIG HEINRICH, *December 1793 or January 1794, probably in Württemberg; °25 June 1852 at Kromboom River, Cape Flats. Organist and choirmaster.

It is not known when Beil settled in South Africa, but he was a keen amateur botanist and, together with his countryman C.F.H. Ludwig (afterwards Baron von Ludwig), he collected plants in the Swellendam district in 1826. He had been an organist in Württemberg before he came to South Africa, and was referred to as a musician when the church council asked him to inspect the new Jan Hoets organ of the Groote Kerk. At the inauguration on 11 July 1830 he also conducted the choir. — Between 1830 and 1847 Beil acted as choirmaster, in conjunction with Frederick Logier*, of the "Muzijk- en Koorzanggezelschap" during festival services. The choir held weekly practices, and appeared at many important church functions, later under the name of "Harmonie en Eendracht". Beil also maintained a children's

150

choir from 1837 to 1839, under the patronage of the Lutheran Church for which he acted as organist from 1839 to 1847. His work was, however, hampered by pecuniary difficulties and poor health. — Apparently sympathetic towards new European trends, Beil, after 1842, grasped every opportunity to apply the principles of Wilhelm, the French reformer of folk-song tuition. He used them in the singing lessons of the "Tot Nut van't Algemeen" society, and in Dr A.N.E. Changuion's school. It was at this time that Suasso da Lima referred to Beil in the weekly *De Verzamelaar* as "hervormer der Zangkunst". Recurrences of poor health and financial difficulties obliged him to retire from the music scene in 1847. He was organist and verger of the DR Church of Somerset West in the remaining years of his life. — Beil made an important contribution to the advancement of musical life in Cape Town, especially with regard to choir-singing and its tuition. His choir was the only meritorious group in the eighteen-thirties, well abreast of the latest European trends. His services were acknowledged by church and educational authorities, as well as by the press. Once he was referred to as a composer - at the laying of the foundation-stone of the DR Church at Kuipers Square in 1833 - when he conducted the singing to his own music of *Psalm 118* by the choir "Harmonie en Eendràcht".

BIBLIOGRAPHY

BOUWS, JAN: *Die musieklewe van Kaapstad, 1800 tot 1850, en sy verhouding tot die musiekkultuur van Wes-Europa.* Cape Town/Amsterdam, 1966.   BOUWS, JAN: *Nuwe strominge in die Kaapse musiekonderwys in die eerste helfte van die negentiende eeu.* Address to the South African Academy, Pretoria, 1966.   BRADLOW, FRANK R.: *Baron von Ludwig and the Ludwigsburg Garden.* Cape Town, Amsterdam, 1965.   OTTERMANN, REINO E.: *Die Kerkmusiek in die Evangeliese Lutherse Kerk in Strandstraat, Kaapstad, tussen 1780 en 1880.* M.Mus. dissertation, US, 1963.

SOURCE

BOUWS, JAN: Geskiedenis van die musiekonderwys in Suid-Afrika. *The South African Music Teacher,* nos. 72 (1967) and 74 (1968).

—J.B.

BEL CANTO SINGERS. This group of sixteen male and female voices was founded by Rupert Stoutt* in Johannesburg in 1941. The members were experienced singers, who covered wide fields in their concert and radio programmes, including choral songs, folk music, opera and musical comedy. Ability to sing in Latin, German, Italian and French, as well as the official languages, was a feature of their work.

—R.B.S.

BELL, ALFRED, *1860 in Newcastle-on-Tyne; °5 July 1935 in Johannesburg. Choral conductor and organist.

Bell was well known in the musical world of the Tyne and Derwentside from 1883 until 1891, when he came to South Africa. He established a studio in Jeppe, Johannesburg, taught at various schools, and was organist at the Methodist Church, President Street, and the Methodist Church, Jeppestown. He gave concerts with the Jeppestown Wesleyan Church Choir towards the end of 1902, and led it in a performance of the cantata, *The ten virgins* (Gaul), in 1903. — As a choral conductor, Bell was particularly successful. His mixed, ladies' and children's choirs won more than 25 gold medals at local Eisteddfodau, while his Juvenile Choir held the Mayor's Shield from 1908 to 1918 (excepting 1912). In 1920 the Sir Thomas

Price Shield for mixed choirs was presented to him, after his choir had won it every year from 1913 to 1920 (excepting 1916). They were also the winners of the Challenge Shield presented by the Pretoria Municipality in 1925.

—L.W.

BELL, DRUMMOND, *30 October 1908 in Johannesburg; living in Johannesburg. Conductor, organist and music teacher. Son of Alfred Bell.*

Drummond received his early musical education from his father, followed by lessons under Horace Barton* (pianoforte), Douglas Mossop* (singing) and John Connell* (organ). He obtained the LTCL diploma at the age of fifteen, and in 1948 passed the ARCM examination at the RCM. — Bell grew up in an environment of choirs and choir training, and at the age of sixteen he formed what was known as the Ragamuffin Choir, consisting of boys taken from street corners. This choir was placed second at the Johannesburg Eisteddfod in 1925. Since then he has upheld the tradition of his father's choir, well known to Johannesburg as regular winners of the Sir Thomas Price shield for mixed choirs. In 1934 he formed the Johannesburg Choral Society, which enjoyed a fine reputation. — Other choirs Bell trained and conducted include the choir of the Germiston Presbyterian Church (where Bell was organist and choirmaster from 1930 until 1942), the choir of the St George's Presbyterian Church, Noord Street (where he became organist in 1943), and the choirs at various schools where he taught music: King Edward School for Boys (1939-1955), Mayfair Convent (1935-1940), Yeoville Convent (1937 -   ), Parktown Convent (1937 -   ), Marist Brothers' Convent, Theck Street (1948-1965), Marist Brothers' Convent, Inanda (1949), Marist Brothers' Convent, Observatory (1951) and Pridwin School (1965). Besides teaching at schools, he also teaches privately. — Bell became the first paid conductor of the Johannesburg Philharmonic Society* in 1950. During his period as musical director of the society (1949-1952) he conducted it in performances of *Hiawatha* (Coleridge-Taylor), *Messiah* (Handel), *The gondoliers, Trial by jury* and *H.M.S. Pinafore* (Sullivan). In addition, he has been musical director of the Johannesburg Operatic and Dramatic Society* for many years (1937-1942, 1951-1960). — Besides his work as a choral conductor, Bell has given organ recitals on the Johannesburg City Hall organ* and elsewhere, and he presided at this organ for many years during the annual performances of *Messiah,* conducted by John Connell. He has also acted as adjudicator at Springs, and at several Bantu choral festivals at Alexandra Township. — He married the soprano, Mamie Dunbaron, in 1938.

WORKS

Te Deum. Ms., 1963.   Various Anthems. Mss., n.d.   A number of piano pieces. Mss., n.d.

—L.W.

BELL, HELEN (NÉE McEWEN)   W.H. Bell, G. Fagan, L. Wolpowitz.

BELL, WILLIAM HENRY, *20 August 1873 in Saracen's Head Yard, Holywell Hill, St Alban's. °13 April 1946 at Gordon's Bay. Professor of music and composer.

William Henry Bell was educated at the St Alban's Grammar School, sang as choirboy in the local cathedral and received instruction in harmony, counterpoint and pianoforte playing from Mary Toulmin. At times his father assisted him in his violin playing. Through the offices of Dr Turpin, Head of the St Alban's Music School, Bell successfully entered for the Goss Bursary Competition and became a

152

student at the RAM where the strongest influence on him was exerted by Frederick Corder who lectured on harmony, counterpoint and composition. Sir Charles B. Stanford of the Royal College also advised him in his original work. Bell's practical subjects were organ, pianoforte and violin. This period lasted until 1893 when he completed his studies at the RAM and was appointed organist of St Alban's Cathedral. At a later date he was organist at Oswestry in Shropshire. Although he composed a great deal at this time, few of his early compositions have been preserved; but on 30 April 1898, August Manns conducted Bell's *Symphonic prologue to Chaucer's Canterbury tales* at the Crystal Palace and his works achieved some recognition. Henry Wood, Thomas Beecham, Hans Richter and Arthur Nikisch all in turn conducted performances of his works. The RAM appointed him professor of harmony and counterpoint in 1903 and he became the organist of All Saints Church in London. — In January 1912 he was appointed Principal of the South African College of Music* in Cape Town and he resigned from his position at the RAM. The College was at first an independent institution in Strand Street and later in a building at Stalplein, but after it had become affiliated to the University of Cape Town, by the introduction of music as a course for the BA degree (1919), its incorporation into the University followed as a matter of course in 1923. Two years later the college moved from Stalplein to its present location on the university grounds at Strubenholm in Rosebank. The Little Theatre* was established in 1931 for drama and lesser operas, and the Ballet School* was introduced in 1934. The college was the second permanent institution for advanced music teaching in the history of South Africa and through Bell's vigour and drive it has exerted an influence felt throughout South Africa's cultural life. — Among the students at the college whilst he was principal, were J.C. Douthwaite, A. Ashworth,* Johannes Fagan,* Raie da Costa,* Cecilia Wessels,* Adelaide Newman,* Blanche Gerstman,* and Joyce Kadish. He retired in 1935 and to mark the occasion, the University of Cape Town awarded him an honorary doctorate in Law. The Bells stayed in England for a short while and then returned to South Africa and settled at Gordon's Bay. Bell was a temporary director of the college when Stewart Deas resigned (1939) and continued to teach composition. Young men who were guided by Bell's tuition until his death in 1946 were Hubert du Plessis,* John Joubert* and Stefans Grové.* — The Cape Town City Orchestra* often included Bell's works in their programmes and Betsy de la Porte* and Albina Bini* frequently appeared on the stage to sing his orchestral songs. In this way his *Five preludes* were performed on 4 June 1942, the *Songs of the last passage* (composed on the death of his son) were sung on 19 August 1943 and the *Symphonic fantasia, Aeterna Munera* was played on 11 November 1945. Usually Bell himself conducted the orchestra on these occasions. Feelings of reverence and gratitude prompted a number of his students to dedicate compositions to his memory: John Joubert's *Threnody* was performed by the City Orchestra on 8 August 1946; Stefans Grové dedicated his *String quartette in D major* to the memory of his old mentor and Hubert du Plessis' *String quartette, opus 13* (composed between 1950 and 1953) is inscribed "To the memory of William Henry Bell". — He was married to Helen McEwen, a sister of Sir John McEwen who had been principal of the RAM. She had been a student of Tobias Matthay and was an accomplished pianist.

WORKS

A. Vocal

153

1. Church music

Miserere maidens, Psalm 51, for soloist, choir, orchestra and organ. Ms., 1895. Magnificat and Nunc dimittis in G. Novello's Parish Choir Book etc., no. 194, 1895. Hearken unto me, ye holy children, anthem for baritone solo and choir. Novello's Collection of Anthems, etc., no. 773, 1903. I will magnify Thee, O Lord (Anthem for Easter) Psalm XXV, arranged for four voices and accompaniment. Novello's Collection of Anthems, etc., 760, 1903. Communion service in B flat, for voices and organ. Ms., September 1907 (9?). Maria Assumpta, dedicated to Balfour Gardiner, soprano solo, double choir, boys' choir and orchestra (based on poem: In the glorious assumption of our Blessed Lady by Richard Crashaw). Stainer & Bell, London, 1923. Missions (George Washington Doane, 1799-1859). No. 383 in The English Hymnal with Tunes, Humphrey Milford, OUP, London. A.R. Mowbray & Co. Ltd., London, 1933. Saints' Day: St John Baptist (The ven. Bede, 673-735, tr. C.S. Calverley). The English Hymnal with Tunes, no. 225, 1933. Five choral hymns. In Memoriam J.G.W. for soprano, contralto, tenor and bass unaccompanied: 1. Most glorious Lord of life (E. Spenser) 2. Lord in thine anger (Psalm 6) (J. Milton) 3. In numbers and but these few (R. Herrick) 4. Lord, how many are my foes (Psalm 3) (J. Milton) 5. O, Jehovah our Lord (Psalm 8) (J. Milton). Ms., Cape Town, 1934. Glory to God, for ladies choir (1 and 2 soprano and contralto). Ms., n.d.

2. Secular

Lasst uns erfreuen, for unaccompanied solo voice. Ms., n.d.

(i) For solo voice and pianoforte

Songs of youth and springtide - 8 songs: 1. An Interlude (for Nell's eyes only) (A. Swinburne) 2. Tarantelle (J. Russel Taylor) 3. Nay, but you who do not love her (R. Browning) 4. Summum bonum (Heine) (comp. 1892) 5. The rose and the lily (Heine) 6 & 7. Two songs from The passionate pilgrim (Shakespeare) 8. A rondel of spring (James Payne) (comp. 1896). Ms., n.d. The rose and the lily (Heine). Ms., 1892. Serenade (from a June romance) (Norman Cale). Ms., 1896. Three songs (Arthur O'Shaughnessy: 1. When the rose came (also in b flat) 2. Following a dream 3. If she but knew. Ms., 1896. Crabbed age and youth (W. Shakespeare). Ms., St Alban's, 1898. Heart of joy (E. Nesbit). Ms., St Alban's, 1898. A portrait (E. Nesbit). Ms., St Alban's, 1898. A prelude (E. Nesbut). Ms., St Alban's, 1898. Spring-song (E. Nesbut). Ms., St Alban's, 1898. Too late (E. Nesbit). Ms., 1898. Love's farewell (M. Drayton). Ms., 3 July 1902. Sing heighho (Charles Kingsley), for middle voice. Ms., 1903. A set of six love-lyrics (W.E. Henley) for contralto or baritone: 1. Gulls in an early Morrice. 2. Geraldine 3. Fill a glass with golden wine 4. The shadow of dawn 5. The nightingale and the rose 6. When you are old. Novello & Co., London, 1903. The four winds (C.H. Lüderz) for baritone. Ms., Gordon's Bay, 11 July 1905. Sappho songs (Carman Bliss). Mss., 1919-1943: 1. The Cyprus born, orchestrated 1919 and revised 1940 2. The Cretan maidens, Jan. 1941. 3. The twilight, 19 January 1941. 4. Arcturus, 1919. 5. Hesperus, n.d. 6. In the olive grove, Oct. 1942. 7. Summer, n.d. 8. Garlands, n.d. 9. In the apple-boughs, n.d. 10. The medlar tree, 1919. 11. Ecstasy, 1919. 12. Daphne and Synrix, 1941. 13. Sleep, 1943. 14. Adoration, 1941. 15. Invocation, 1941. 16. Alone, 1919. 17. Lament for Adonis, 1919. 18. Epilogue, 1919, revised 1941. Clair de lune (P. Verlaine). Ms., 5 September 1925 (rev. 30 June 1945). D'une prison (P. Verlaine). Ms., 1925? (revised 1932). Que faudre-t'il a ce coeur (J. Moreas). Ms., 1925 (June 1945). Songs: Mss., July-August 1940: 1. Summer dawn (W. Morris), 24 July 2. A calender (S. Dobell), 27 July 3. & 4. Two songs (John Skelton, 1460-1523), 20 August 5. His epitaph (S. Dawes), 6. A valentine (W.S. Blunt), 14 August. 7. To spring (W. Blake), 8. Summer (W. Blake), 9. Autumn (W.

Blake).   Six Blake songs (1st set) Mss., Gordon's Bay, August-September, 1940:   1. To spring, August   2. Summer, 29 August 3. Autumn, 8 September 4. Winter, 18 September   5. To the evening star, 19 September   6. ??   Six Blake songs (2nd set) (from Songs of Experience by Blake). Mss., September-October 1940:   1. My pretty rose tree   2. The fairy, from "Rosetti Ms."   3. In a myrtle shade, from "Rosetti Ms." 25 September 4. The birds, from "Rosetti Ms."   5. My spectre around me!   6. I heard an angel singing, 15 October. Hesperides, fifteen miniatures (1st set) (R. Herrick), for mezzo-soprano, dedicated to Albina Bini*. Mss., 1945: 1. The argument to his book, 3 June.   2. The wounded cupid, 14 May. 3. On gilly flowers begotten, 15 May.   4. To the lark, 16 May.   5. To a bed of tulips, 16 May.   6. Anacreontic,   17 May.   7. To sycamores,   20 May.   8. To Dianeme,   21 May.   9. The Valentine, 23 May.   10. Upon love, by way of question and answer, 22 May.   11. The fairies.   12. The Peter penny, 31 May. 13. Morning prayer, 29 May.   14. Upon a maid.   15. His legacy, 24 May.   Hesperides (2nd set) (R. Herrick), for mezzo soprano, dedicated to Betsy de la Porte. Mss., 1945:   1. To his muse.   2. The kiss: a dialogue, 11 June.   3. To meadows.   4. A canticle to Apollo.   5. Amaryllis, 5 June.   6. Kissing usury.   7. Love's play at pushpin, 6 June.   8. To cherry blossoms, 6 June.   9. The little spinners.   10. To violets, 20 June.   11. The hag, 23 June.   12. The bellman.   13. The scarefire.   14. The cheating cupid.   15. The mad maid's song, 11 July.   16. Meditation on his mistress, 14 July.   17. Farewell frost or welcome to spring.   Three songs: Sonnets from the Portuguese (E. Barrett Browning). Mss., probably 1945:   1. If thou must love me, 5 February.   2. I lift my heavy heart.   3. Say over again.   Two songs (N.P. van Wyk Louw): Mss., 1945:   1. My venster is 'n blanke vlak.   2. Ek het jou lief.   The parrot (J. Skelton). Ms., n.d.   Zoo teedere schade (J.W.F. Werumeus-Buning). Ms., n.d.   To Margery (J. Skelton). Ms., n.d.   The falcon (Anon. Mediaeval). Ms., n.d.   Skreeu (N.P. van Wyk Louw). Ms., n.d.   Die vlakte is so stil vannag (N.P. van Wyk Louw). Ms., n.d.   Nagrit (N.P. van Wyk Louw). Ms., n.d.   Winternag (E.N. Marais). Ms., n.d.   Le ciel est pardessus le toit (Verlaine). Ms., n.d.

(ii)   For solo voice and orchestra
The four winds, for baritone and orchestra. Ms., 11 July 1903. Orchestrated 1904; pianoforte score 1905.   Sappho (B. Carman), a song cycle dedicated to Albina Bini, for soprano and orchestra. Ms., 1920; rewritten and orchestrated, 1942.   Bhanavar the beautiful (George Meredith), for mezzo soprano and orchestra, dedicated to Betsy de la Porte. Ms., Gordon's Bay, 3 February 1943:   1. By the mountain-rill, 22 November 1942.   2. Intermezzo, 29 November 1942.   3. Bridal songs, 29 December 1942.   4. Bridal songs (2), 20 January 1943.   5. At the tomb of Ameryl.   Songs of the last passage: in memory of Oliver M. Bell (killed in action at the Wadi-Akarit, Tunisia, 7 April 1943) - Delightful to men and yet more delightful to the gods he lived not far into age. O Earth, dost thou unfold the sacred man in death, or does he still live in gladness there? (Greek mythology); Mss., Gordon's Bay, 13 July 1943: 1. Whispers of heavenly death. 2. Hushed be the camps today. 3. Song of the gray brown bird. 4. Darest thou now, o soul.   5. The last invocation.   Six songs, for solo voice and orchestra. Orchestrated 28 March 1944: 1. His epitaph (S. Dawes, °1525). 2. With margeraine gentle (J. Skelton).   3. Merry Margaret (J. Skelton).   4. The parrot (J. Skelton).   5. St Hugh's dirge (T. Dekker).   6. The month of May (T. Dekker).   Twelve Blake songs, for solo voice and orchestra. Mss., Aug.-Oct. 1940, orchestrated March 1944.   1st set: 1. Spring 2. Summer 3. Autumn 4. Winter 5. To the evening 6. To morning.   2nd set: 1. My pretty rosetree 2. The fairy.   3. In a myrtle shade.   4. The birds.   5. My spectre around us.   6. I heard an angel singing.   Seven Afrikaans songs for solo voice and orchestra. Gordon's Bay, 9 August 1944: 1. Winternag (E. Marais).   2. Die vlakte is so stil vannag (N.P. van Wyk

155

Louw). 3. Skreeu (N.P. van Wyk Louw). 4. Nagrit (N.P. van Wyk Louw). 5. My venster is 'n blanke vlak (N.P. van Wyk Louw). 6. Ek het jou lief (N.P. van Wyk Louw). 7. Zoo teedere schade (J.W.F. Werumeus-Buning). Three songs, for solo voice and orchestra. Mss., n.d.: 1. Summer dawn (W. Morris). 2. A calender (S. Dobell). 3. A valentine (W.S. Blunt). War and peace, a triptych, for solo voice and orchestra (The four Zons by W. Blake). Mss., n.d.: 1. War song of Oro. 2. Lament. 3. The tillage (unfinished). The ballad of the bird bride, baritone solo and orchestra (derives from an Eskimo legend by R. Marriot-Watson). Ms., n.d. Twelve oxen, for solo voice and orchestra. Ms., n.d. The flower of Jesse. Ms., n.d. Four songs of youth and springtime, for solo voice and orchestra. Ms., n.d.

(iii) For solo voice, choir and orchestra
The call of the sea: an ode for soprano, choir (with demi-choir) and orchestra (Frank S. Tooker). Ms., 18 Nov. 1902-1903, rewritten 1904. Song of the sinless soul, for mezzo soprano, ladies' choir and orchestra (from the poem Vala by William Blake). Ms., Gordon's Bay, 25 Feb. 1944. Threnody: Adonis, for soprano and mezzo soprano solos, ladies' choir and orchestra (The Greek of Bion, tr. E.B. Browning). Ms., May 1945. Night rises the mist, for solo voices, choir and orchestra. Ms., n.d.

(iv) Choir
Diaphenia, a part song for SATB, a capella. Ms., n.d. To music to becalm his fever, for SATB, a capella (The Hesperides, R. Herrick). Ms., n.d. A part song, a capella. Ms., n.d.

(v) Choir with pianoforte accompaniment
Sleep, sleep, mother's own pretty one, lullaby for four voices, comp. 1902. Novello's Tonic Solfa Series no. 1465; The Musical Times, no. 707. My sweet sweeting, part song for four voices (anon.), comp. 1903. The Musical Times, no. 722. Matin song, Elizabethan madrigal no. 2, song for four voices (Nathan Field), comp. 1903. Novello's Part-song Book, Second Series, no. 905. I loved a lass, part song for four voices (George Wither), comp. 1903. Novello's Part-song Book, Second Series, no. 916; Novello's Tonic Solfa Series no. 1316. Love and beauty, part song for four voices (Robert Greene), comp. 1903. Novello's Part-song Book, Second Series, no. 915; Novello's Tonic Solfa Series, no. 1386. The blind raven, part song for four male voices TTBB (Persian of Jami), comp. 1906. The Orpheus, New Series, no. 394. Der blinde Rabe, part song for four male voices TTBB (Persian of Jami, German translations E. Schreck, 1909). G.E. Schreck, Novellos Chorgesang Literatur etc., no. 13. Four mediaeval songs (1st set), for soprano I, II, contralto, dedicated to Colin Taylor.* OUP, London, 1927 (The Oxford Choral Songs, nos. 507-510): 1. Hymn to the virgin. 2. The maiden that is makeless. 3. Mater ora filium. 4. The flower of Jesse. Four mediaeval songs (2nd set): for soprano I, II, contralto, dedicated to Victor Hely-Hutchinson.* OUP, London, 1930 (The Oxford Choral Songs, nos. 525-528): 5. At Domys Day. 6. May in the greenwood. 7. Twelve oxen. 8. Hunting song. Man and woman, Elizabethan madrigal no. 6, SATB and pianoforte. Ms., n.d.

(vi) Choir and orchestra
Hawke (early work). Ms., n.d. The Baron of Brackley, a Scottish ballad (traditional). Joseph Williams, London, 1911. Prometheus unbound (Shelley). Ms., 1923/24. Dicitis philosophi, song for the University of Cape Town. (B. Farrington). Ms., n.d. Performed 26 November 1932.

(vii) Operas
Hippolytus, 3 acts (based on Euripides). Ms., 1910-1914. Isabeau, 1 act. Ms., March 1924. The mousetrap, 1 act (based on R.L. Stevenson's The Sire de Maletroits' door). Ms.,

156

1928. Doctor love, 1 act (based on L'Amour Médecin, Moliére). Ms., Cape Town, 5.1.1930. The wandering scholar, 1 act (Clifford Bax). Ms., 1934, performed Little Theatre, Cape Town, 28.10.1935. The duenna, 3 acts (Richard B. Sheridan). Ms., August 1938-June 1939. Romeo and Juliet, unfinished. Ms., "commenced August 1939".

(viii) Japanese Nō-plays

Komachi, 1 act (based on Nō-play by Kwanam, tr. A. Waley). Ms., Cape Town, Sept. 1925. Tsuneyo of the three trees (based on Nō-play by Hachi No Ki, tr. A. Waley). Ms., 8 November 1926. Hatsuyuki (Early snow), 1 act (based on Nō-play by Komparu Zembo Motoyasu (1453-1532), tr. A. Waley). Performed Little Theatre Cape Town, 19.11.1934. Publ. by The University of Cape Town, SACM, 1963 (pianoforte score). The pillow of Kantan (based on a 14th century Nō-play). Ms., Jan. 1935, perf. Little Theatre, Cape Town, 28.10.1935. Kagekiyo (based on a Nō-play by Seami (1363-1444), tr. A. Waley). Ms., London, 9.7.1936; rewritten, Jan. 1940.

(ix) Other theatre music

The vision of delight, masque (Ben Jonson). Ms., 1906, perf. Court Theatre, London. Pageant music, St Albans, Op. 18 (C.H. Ashdown). Comp. July 1907, perf. St Albans, England, 1907. Breitkopf & Härtel for C. Avison, Leipzig, n.d. Fête Champêtre, ballet. Ms., July 1935, perf. Little Theatre, Cape Town, 28 October 1935. The tumbler of Our Lady, ballet. "To Dulcie Howes* affectionately inscribed" for orchestra, 2 sop. choirs, contralto, male voice choir, priest's solo. Ms., London, 25 March 1936. La fée des sources, pantomime ballet. Ms., n.d.

B. Instrumental

1. Orchestra

A symphonic prologue to the Canterbury Tales, Op. 3. Ms., 5.2.1896. The Pardoner's Tale, symphonic tone poem. Ms., St Albans, 23.8.1898. Walt Whitman: symphony in C minor, Op. 8. Ms., 1899. A song of the morning, symphonic poem, perf. Queen's Hall orchestra. Novello & Co., London, n.d. Epithalamion, a serenade for small orchestra. Ms., 28.9.1904. Love among the ruins, orchestral tone poem based on a poem by Robert Browning. Ms., 1905-1908?; revised version, 2.12.1920. The shepherd, fantasy prelude for orchestra. Ms., 1907-1908?; rewritten 1910. Agamemnon, prelude for orchestra. Ms., 1908. Dance du tambour for orchestra. Ms., August 1909. Arcadian suite, a serenade in four movements for orchestra. Avison ed., Novello and Co., London, 1911. Prelude, based on two old English folk songs. Jenny pluck pears and Robin Hood, for orchestra. Ms., 1912, perf. Cape Town 12.4.1912. La fée des sources, symphonic tone poem for orchestra. Ms., 1912, perf. October 1914. Symphonic variations. Ms. 1915-1917; revised 1943; perf. 5.7.1915. Rosa mystica, concerto for viola and orchestra. Ms. 18.12.1916, perf. 8.11.1917. Symphony no. 2 in A minor. "To my dear friend Theo Wendt affectionately inscribed". Ms. Cape Town, 29.8.1918. Symphony no. 3 in F. maj. Ms. Cape Town, 1918-1919, perf. 25.9.1919. The portal, symphonic tone poem. Ms. Cape Town, May 1921, perf. 15.9.1921. Veldt loneliness, symphonic tone poem. Ms., n.d. A song of greeting. Ms. n.d., perf. 22.2.1922. Suite in C min. (In modo academico): prelude, allemande, courante, sarabande, gavotte, gigue, for string orchestra. Ms., Cape Town, May 1924. A South African symphony, A min. Ms. Cape Town, 27.12.1927, perf. 1 March 1928, Cape Town. An English suite: sarabande, pavane, gavotte, ?, march, march, for orchestra. Ms., n.d., perf. 25.2.1929. Symphony in F min. Ms. 6.5.1932. Aeterna munera, a symphonic fantasy. Ms., Gordon's Bay, 17.9.1941. Hamlet: five preludes for orchestra (Shakespeare). Ms. 1941-1942. Mother Carey: 1. In the night watches. 2. In the fo'c'sle, symphonic tone poem. Novello, London, n.d.

2. *Arrangements for orchestra*

Chant sans paroles (E.H. Lemare), for small orchestra. Ms., 1901.   Staines Morrice, dance. Ms., 1912, perf. Cape Town 12.4.1912.   Ständchen (Brahms), Wiegenlied (Brahms). Ms., n.d.   Die Allmacht (Schubert).   Under the greenwood tree (Arne). Ms., 1912, perf. Cape Town 12.4.1912.

3. *Incidental music*

Life's measure - morality play by Nugent Monck. Ms., 1905-1908(?)   The little corporal. Ms., 1912, perf. 18.12.1912.   The seagull, arr. for strings: Reverie, catoire, berceuse, Zoltarev-humoresque (Tchaikowsky). Ms., n.d.   Sister Beatrice (Maeterlinck). Ms., n.d.   Such men are dangerous. Ms., n.d.

4. *Chamber music*

Introduction and first movement of a quartet for pianoforte, violin, viola and cello. Ms., 23.6.1894.   String quartet in G min. Ms., Cape Town, June 1926.   String quartet in F. Ms., n.d.

5. *Pianoforte*

Arranged for piano solo: The witch's daughter (Sir A.C. Mackenzie). Ms., 1904.   Four elegiac pieces for piano. Ms., November 1940: 1. Andante grazioso 2. Allegro moderato 3. Adagio mesto 4. Andante maestro.   Chorale with variations. Ms., 5.12.1940.

6. *Organ*

Minuet and trio in C maj. Organ solos ... for recitals, no. 28 and The Organ Loft etc., book 7 no. 20. Vincent Music Co., London, 1901.   Postlude (romance, spring song), no. 300 of Original compositions for the organ. Novello and Co., London, 1902.

7. *Solo stringed instrument and piano*

Sonata for violin and piano in e. Ms., St Albans, 15.12.1897.   Cradle song, for violin and pianoforte. Novello and Co., London, 1901.   Arabesque for violin and pianoforte, comp. 1904. Breitkopf and Härtel for C. Avison, Leipzig, 1906.   Sonata in D "to Ellie Marx and Elsie Hall affectionately inscribed" for violin and pianoforte. Ms. Cape Town, 1918.   Sonata in D min, to Oliver M. Bell, for clarinet or viola and pianoforte. Ms., Claremont, Christmas 1926.   Sonata in A min, to Brian Bell, for cello and pianoforte. Ms. Cape Town, January 1927.   Sonata in F min., for violin and pianoforte. Ms., Cape Town, 27 January?

BIBLIOGRAPHY

Baker's biographical dictionary of musicians. G. Schirmer, New York.   BOUWS, JAN: *Musiek in Suid-Afrika*. Uitgeverij Voorland, Brugge, 1946.   BOUWS, JAN: *Suid-Afrikaanse komponiste van vandag en gister*. A.A. Balkema, Cape Town, 1957.   A *Dictionary of modern music and musicians*. Dutton, New York, MCMXXIV.   DU PLESSIS, HUBERT: *Letters from William Henry Bell*. Tafelberg-Uitgewers Bpk., Cape Town, 1973.   *Grove's dictionary of music and musicians*. Macmillan & Co., Ltd., London, 1954.   KIRBY, PERCIVAL R.: *Wits' End*. Howard Timmins, Cape Town, 1967.   POTGIETER, J.H.: *'n Analitiese oorsig van die Afrikaanse kunslied*. D. Mus. thesis, UP, 1967.   RACSTER, OLGA: *Curtain. up!* Juta & Co., Ltd., Cape Town, 1951.   VAN DER MERWE, F.Z.: *Suid-Afrikaanse musiekbibliografie, 1787-1952*. J.L. van Schaik Ltd., Pretoria, 1958.   VAN DER SPUY, H.H.: *W.H. Bell: Enkele aspekte van sy loopbaan en sy invloed op die Suid-Afrikaanse musieklewe*. Dissertation, UPE, 1970. W.H.K.: *The arts in South Africa*. Knox Printing and Publishing Co., Durban, 1933-1934. "Loose-leaf"-catalogue B. no. 14 of the music section of the British Museum, London. List of additional manuscripts by William Henry Bell, presented to the Cape Town University Library by Mrs Bell in 1966.   TAYLOR, L.E.: *Catalogue of the music manuscripts* of William Henry Bell, 1873-1946. University of Cape Town, 1948.

SOURCES
Die Eikestadnuus: 27 April 1962, 4 May 1962. *Die Huisgenoot:* 6 June 1914, IX/118. *Kultuur* (ed.: Filma) May 1946, 3/7; July 1946, 3/8. *Lantern:* June 1964, XIII/4. *The Musical Times:* 1 May 1920, 61/927; June 1920, 61/928; 1 July 1920, 61/929. *The Outspan:* 16 August 1946, XL/1016. *The SABC Radio Bulletin:* 7 September 1959, 5/11; 22 November 1965, 11/24. *South African Digest:* 9 January 1964. *The South African Music Teacher:* April 1935, no. 8; October 1935, no. 9; June 1946, no. 30; June 1949, no. 36. *Trek:* 3 May 1946, X/22. *The Times,* London: 15 April 1946, 50/427. University of Cape Town: Citation at conferment of the honorary degree of LL.D., December 1935.

—H.H. v.d. S. (amplified)

Bell was not only the most productive and the most important of the foreign composers who had settled in South Africa, he was also the most active of the educationists who had come to live here. The combination of composer and pedagogue is a strong one, a fact to which Bell's career in South Africa amply testifies. Under his leadership the College of Music became a conservatoire for advanced musical education with the emphasis on the practical side, an adaption to a South African University of the institutions at which he himself had been trained and which he in turn had served as teacher. Consequently, of the hundreds of students who studied at the College of Music during Bell's term as Dean of the Faculty of Music, only a handful entered for a degree in Music and slightly more were trained for a licentiate. His educational policy was simply to cater for the needs of the country, for a variety of practical musicians and not for musicologists. His own creative and hard-working example served as an inspiring model for the students at the College. Through mutual assistance in the matter of accompaniments, through public performances and the acknowledgement of their achievements by the press, they were soon welded into a homogeneous body. Bell's own weekly columns in *The Cape; The South African Nation* and *The Cape Argus,* written in an easy and fluent style of great vitality, contributed materially to the idea of the College as it existed in the mind of the Cape public. For this work of disseminating knowledge about musical matters and the importance of music in a community, he was exceptionally well equipped by his own variety of interests, first and foremost English drama and literature, but also architecture, politics and cultural interest generally (including the cinema!). The creation of the Little Theatre* owes much to his exertions on behalf of opera as a dimension of the educational work being done at the College. — With his intimate knowledge of music in all its forms (including opera and ballet) and by virtue of his logical thinking and exceptional gift for expressing himself clearly and unambiguously (often with the assistance of a considerable vocabulary of expletives), Bell was destined to be a teacher and a guide to young composers. His correspondence with Hubert du Plessis testifies to his considerable talents in this direction. The letter written to Du Plessis on the 11th of August 1942 (the year in which Du Plessis became his pupil in composition) is a fine example of his educational and powerful style: "I want you to cultivate a certain attitude towards your composition, that will keep you always cheerful, and contented, contented to wait on God's good time if and when you seem to have no ideas, or have the ideas and cannot get to grips with them ... Worry always connotes the idea of fear and the finest artist I ever knew used to say 'the greates enemy of all art is fear'. So don't worry and cultivate instead an unflagging faith, or if that sounds preachified, just call it pluck . . . . The kind of attitude towards one's art that I am trying to present to you is a certain child-like, not childish way of looking at it, the way a child looks on everything it does as a gallant adventure". How clearly he saw South African problems is exemplified by a letter written on the 11th of November 1943: "The whole issue of Afrikaner music is so confused by appallingly mediocre, if not actually *bad* music. A real Afrikaner composer could sweep everything in front of him, and establish a standard that would sweep most of what is being done at present into Limbo (a mixed metaphor I am afraid . . .)" In another letter he praises the drive of young Afrikaners (1st of July 1944,) or criticises the Afrikaner sentimentality (6th March 1944) and in a letter dated 5th of November he expresses his disappointment that South Africa had refused to consider his scheme for the advancement of young composers: "My thirty years of experience here should have taught me that so often on the verge of doing a really useful and big thing, S.A. always just stops short, and goes for a compromise . . . ." These quotes from his correspondence illustrate the fact that Bell was intensely interested in South African music and in the rise of a generation who could take the lead. — Bell's works are all in the custody of the Cape University and are still awaiting appreciation by a competent investigator who could assess them at their true worth.

—J.P.M.

BELLRINGING IN SOUTH AFRICA. To some persons bellringing means playing a tune, or chords, on bells. In South Africa much time has been devoted to producing bell music in which there is no tune, but which is composed on continually varying sequences, in each of which a bell rings once only. This is ringing "in the English style", and the reader should understand how this type of ringing is done.

At the age of 10 the writer was taught to handle a bell, by the village sexton at Stone, a small village in Worcestershire, England. To ring a bell "full circle", as the name implies, means that the bell is rung through 360 degrees; it begins and ends its swing in the mouth-upward position. By practice, a learner makes a bell do a completely-controlled series of swings, and the pause - if any - between one swing and the next is entirely at the will of the performer. This is the first stage in becoming a ringer. — In 1933, E. ("Ted") Gilbert, the conductor of the Chaddesley Corbett ringers, showed the writer how the "Grandsire" system was produced. At the Chaddesley Corbett tower he worked at both theory and practice, and after six months was sufficiently advanced to enter a tower where the ringing was more skilled - Kidderminster. By 1934 ringing had declined to some extent, but there were still a few old ringers left from whose experience one could profit. Different towers had their own practice nights, and it was possible to belong to two or more at the same time. There were times when the writer was ringing at one tower on a Sunday morning, another in the evening; during the week he would attend practices at two other places. When on holiday - usually travelling on a Sunday - he tried to be passing through a fairly large town at a time when ringing was in progress, and would join the ringers there, whenever an opportunity offered. — Coming to South Africa in 1939, the writer obtained work in Johannesburg, a city with no ring of bells, but in September 1940, he made the acquaintance of the late Canon G.H. Ridout, who had a ring of handbells. The Canon and his sister, the writer's wife and himself, met almost every week, and with the Canon and himself ringing two bells, and the others one, were able to ring the changes on six bells. Unfortunately, within six months the Canon died, and the band broke up. But later another band was formed, composed mainly of members of the Cookson family, practising Grandsire Triples single-handed on handbells. — In November 1944, the writer came to Durban, and rang at St Paul's for about two years, before joining the Greyville band, led by Densell Wittstock. When Densell went to Rhodesia, the present Captain, John Maeder, took over. Since World War II, however, recruitment at Greyville has been difficult, and in 1956 the group broke up, whereupon the writer rejoined the ringers of St Paul's. But the Vicar of Greyville, Rev. Mountford, wanted the Greyville bells to ring again, and owing largely to his enthusiasm a new band was enlisted, which by 1963 was putting in steady practice. — Bellringing in South Africa began about the year 1880, when a ring of eight bells was installed in the Cathedral at Grahamstown. Later installations were: 8 bells at St Mary's Church, Woodstock, Cape Town, 1901; 8 bells at St Paul's Church, Durban, 1921; 10 bells at St Mary's Church, Greyville, Durban, 1921. A ring is to be installed at Kimberley, and another at St George's Cathedral, Cape Town. At Grahamstown ringing will make no progress, until the bells are put in order. The installation in 1880 was made in accordance with commonly-held, but erroneous ideas about the way stresses caused by swinging bells should be borne in the tower. In spite of this handicap, students at St Paul's Theological College have made valiant efforts to ring them. — To Woodstock belongs the distinction - unique in South Africa - of having rung a peal (5 000 or more changes). This is recorded on a tablet in the tower as follows:

In this tower
on Thursday, December 15th, 1904,
in 3 hours and 7 minutes
a peal of
GRANDSIRE TRIPLES
5040 changes.
Taylor's six-part.

G.A. Davies	Treble	L. Green	5
J.F. Priest	2	J. Murray	6
H.G. Cock	3	F.P. Powell	7
E.F. Behan	4	H. Montgomery	Tenor

Conducted by F.P. Powell

This was the first peal on bells in Africa. It is said that four of the ringers were Australians, and four were Englishmen who had settled in South Africa. The Australians were returning to their country after a trip to England. A peal had been attempted at Woodstock on their way to England, but had failed. While in England they practised whenever they had opportunity, and this evidently stood them in good stead. — The only member of this band known to the writer was J.F. Priest, who rang the second. He was a retired engine-driver and came originally from Wanstead, Essex. His last peal in England before coming to South Africa was a peal of Bob Royal rung at St Mary Abbotts, High Street, Kensington, London, in 1890. He left for South Africa on 21 May 1890, and Lewis Green emigrated to South Africa about the same time. Priest died on 17 June 1954, aged 90. The conductor, F.P. Powell, was a member of the Ancient Society of College Youths in 1894, and on coming to South Africa lived at Southwold, Grahamstown. E.F. Behan was from Melbourne, Australia. He died on 15 September 1943. All that is known of J. Murray is that he died in 1946. — Woodstock may be considered the doyen of South African towers.

Its geographical position gives it an advantage over other towers, for visitors, who promote interest in good ringing. Numerous quarter peals have been rung at Woodstock, and some have been recorded on boards in the belfry. In April 1962, the writer had the pleasure of taking part in one (Grandsire Triples) conducted by R.H. Stickley. — The late Jack G. Wood probably holds the record in South Africa for unbroken ringing service in one tower. His ringing career at Woodstock covered a period of 35 years, during many of which he was captain. The present band at Woodstock is depleted, but the captain, Wm. Smith, is training a number of learners, and hopes eventually to restore the strength it once enjoyed. The "oldsters" include Ray Law, Len Hewitt, John Riley, R.H. Stickley (when in Cape Town) and J. Entzen, all of whom have rung in Durban on visits to that city. A former member of the Woodstock band, Vic Sheppard, is one whose loss to South African ringing will not easily be made good. He learnt at Woodstock, and was indefatigable in interesting new people in bellringing, in delving into, and writing about, ringing history, and in maintaining the Woodstock bells, their ropes and fittings. — At St Paul's, Durban, only call changes (an elementary system of bellringing) have, until recent years, been practised. In 1957 ringing in the English style was begun, and a quarter peal of Bob Minor was accomplished, conducted by E. Bishop. The hey-day of ringing at Greyville was in the 1920's, when Messrs Prickett, Clarkson and Simpson, all with overseas experience, were ringing there. For a time Fred May, a well-known ringer from Bristol, rang with them. These two Durban rings of bells are tuned in the modern manner, on the principles enunciated by Canon Simpson. Both rings are in steel frames, and are hung on ball-bearings. — It was largely through the influence of Canon Ridout that the two Durban rings were installed. He came of a Bourne, Lincolnshire, family, and settled in Johannesburg in 1909. He learnt to ring in his university days, and became a member of the Cambridge University Guild of Ringers. Before Johannesburg Cathedral was built, an anonymous donor had promised a ring of bells, and offered to put them up in a steel frame, round which the tower could afterwards be built. This was refused by the church authorities, who wanted the cathedral built first. By the time they were ready to have the bells installed, other buildings had sprung up in the vicinity and it was impossible to allow the installation, because of the noise. One has an inkling that the anonymous donor was none other than the Canon himself. — Canon Ridout and several members of the Cambridge University Guild learnt to ring on handbells. When the group first tried to ring tower bells, they knew what they wanted the bells to do, but could not make them respond! The Canon was a very competent handbell ringer, and especially interested in the theory and history of bells. On 6 March 1930 he rang Nos. 5 and 6 to what would have constituted a peal of Bob Minor, had the other bells been rung "double-handed" instead of "single-handed". — When living in Johannesburg, the writer met Mr Collins, a jeweller there, who told him he was one of two people who rang the tenor to the first peal in Australia. He was an old man, as a peal was rung in Australia as long ago as 1890, possibly not the first. — At Greyville, possibly on the last day of 1928, an attempt was made at a peal of Grandshire Triples, which failed after about an hour. T.A. Nash, one of those who took part, states that the band was as follows:

| F. Simpson (Senior) | Treble | F. Simpson (Junior) | 5 |
| Daisy Clarkson | 2 | T.E. Prickett | 6 |

| Fred H. May | 3 | John Prickett, conductor | 7 |
| T.A. Nash | 4 | Clarkson | Tenor |

On the occasion of a visit by Sydney Osborne of Rugby, in 1955, a quarter peal, the first since 1929, was rung at Greyville, the details being thus recorded:

Durban, South Africa
On Saturday, August 20, 1955
At the Church of St. Mary, Greyville,
A quarter peal of 1260 Grandsire Doubles

Tenor 18 cwt. 25 lb.

§William A. Gardner	Treble	§Theodore J. Maeder	4
Thomas A. Nash	2	Sydney G. Osborne	5
Cyril Chambers	3	§Rev. James Draper	Tenor

Conducted by Sydney G. Osborne

(§First quarter peal)

It often happens that the children of ringers become ringers, although no instance of this is known at Woodstock. At Greyville, sons and daughters of the families of Prickett, Clarkson and Simpson became ringers, but only one, Agnes Simpson (now Mrs Edwin Slaughter) is still an active ringer. Her brother, Frederick Louis Simpson, married Daisy Clarkson. They are both ringers, but live in Umtata, where there are no bells. Ewart Prickett, although living in Durban, gave up ringing in the 1950's. — Bellringing is undertaken by people of widely-varying ages, teenagers to octogenarians. "It is never too late to learn" - an example is the late G.E. North, who began to learn at Greyville when he was 76 years of age! Because of his keenness, a new stairway was fitted at St Paul's tower in 1961; this did away with the akward ladder-and-trap-door approach to the belfry. — For tune-playing, a considerable number of bells is required - 25 may be considered a minimum. In the towers mentioned, tune-playing is hardly possible, partly because there are not sufficient bells to produce a good musical effect. Most bells are designed to be rung - they are not capable of being chimed; for chiming a special mechanism is required, the bells themselves remaining stationary.

BIBLIOGRAPHY
MORRIS, ERNEST: *The history and art of change ringing.* Chapman & Hall Ltd, London, 1931. *The ringing world,* Official Organ of The Central Council of Church Bell Ringers, Lower Pyrford Road, Guildford, Surrey, England.

—C.C.

BELMAS, XENIA, *1891 in Kiev, Ukraine; at present in Durban. Soprano and singing teacher.

Xenia Belmas received her training at the Conservatoire in Kiev and appeared as soloist at a symphony concert when she was sixteen. After further study in Moscow she became a member of an opera company in Odessa in 1930, making her debut as Sieglinde *(Die Walküre)* and Elisabeth *(Tannhäuser).* After that she often sang in Russian operas. In 1921 she left Russia, never to return, and began a study of the Italian repertory in Milan. Four years later she had become a well-known soloist at symphony concerts in Paris and had appeared as Aïda in the Opéra. In 1928 she moved from France to Berlin where she gained a reputation as concert singer. She recorded operatic arias and Russian art songs in collaboration with her husband, the conductor Alexander Kitsching and in Wiesbaden she sang Isolde under the baton of Carl Schuricht. Following an opera tour of Australia with an Italian opera company, in which she sang roles in Wagnerian and Italian operas, she returned to Berlin and in 1931 toured Poland and the Baltic states. However, after 1933 she left Germany and returned to France where she sang at symphony concerts in Paris and Monte Carlo. — Xenia Belmas arrived in Cape Town on 25 July 1934 to give a series of twenty concerts in South African cities. After completing her commitment, she decided to settle in Durban where she became a singing teacher. Rose Alper* and Gregorio Fiasconaro* are among those who had lessons from her. It is a measure of Xenia Belmas's status that she is included in the first edition of the lexicon *Unvergängliche Stimmen*. In it her beautiful voice is described as being permeated with perfect musicality.

BIBLIOGRAPHY

KUTSCH, K.J. and RIEMENS, LEO: *Unvergängliche Stimmen: Kleines Sängerlexikon;* 1st edition, 1962 and 2nd edition, 1966.

—F.S.

BENDER, ANNA CATHERINA (MRS IAN BRINK) *6 December 1919 in Piet Retief; now in Johannesburg. Pianist and music consultant, accompanist. Since 1975 she has been a lecturer in practical subjects at the Pretoria College for Advanced Technical Education.

Until she was 7 years old, Anna was instructed in music by her mother. I.J. Haarhoff was her teacher until 1936 and taught her piano, theory and harmony. While still at school she was awarded scholarships by Trinity College and obtained several medals at Eisteddfodau. She studied for and obtained a B.A. and a Teacher's Diploma at the University of Pretoria and acted as a school teacher for a while. Concurrently she continued her musical studies under Isador Epstein* who taught her until 1946. In 1942 she became a Fellow of Trinity College. — During 1949 Anna Bender was a student of Louis Kentner in London and when she returned to South Africa the next year, she became the official accompanist to the SABC in Johannesburg. She remained in this position for 20 years and was responsible for a large number of transcription recordings with internationally famous soloists. On occasion she herself acted as soloist with several symphonic guest conductors. Her duties included playing the piano in orchestral scores and also acting as player on the harpsichord, celesta, glockenspiel and organ. During 1955/56 she was away on an extended tour of America. The collection of Afrikaans music publications is one of her interests. For the women's programmes of the SABC she often offered talks on this subject. — After leaving the SABC in 1969 Anna Bender became music consultant to the Phil Morkel Company in Johannesburg. She demonstrated electronic organs and was the editor of *Opus,* a periodical on music, published by Phil Morkel until 1974. Since 1975 she has been on the staff of the Pretoria College for Advanced Technical Education, lecturing on the Lied and also assisting the opera school as repetitor. During the last two years she has been on national tours with Gert Potgieter's* company and has accepted engagements with the Regional Councils of the Free State and Transvaal. Her connection with the SABC has been maintained by means of frequent talks and contributions to their programmes. She is a founder member of the Harp Society of South Africa*.

WRITINGS

As editor of *Opus,* regular contributions to this periodical: Volumes I/1, 2, 3, 4; II/2, 3, 4; III/1, 2, 3, 4; IV/2, 3; V/1.   Isador Epstein. *Kultuur (Filma)* III/2, October 1946.   Water in musiek. *SASMT Newsletter,* Pretoria, no. 25, 1970.

PUBLICATIONS

Vir die musiekleier. Unieboekhandel (Edms) Bpk., 1949.   24 articles for *Radio-rubriek* in *Rooi Rose,* 1954-1955.

—Ed.

BENNETT, ENA   B.M. van der Post

BENOIT, PETER,   *17 August 1834 in Harelbeke, West Flanders; °8 March 1901 in Antwerp. Belgian composer and conductor.

Benoit studied composition under F.J. Fétis (1851-1857) at the Brussels Conservatoire, concluding his studies by winning the Rome Prize. He founded the Flemish School of Music in 1867. This became the Royal Belgian Conservatoire in 1897. His children's cantata *De Wêreld in!* is still well known and has been sung in South Africa. His cantata *De Leie* was performed by Hans Endler.* His enthusiasm for the Afrikaner's struggle for freedom inspired him to write the following battle songs in 1884 and in 1901:   *In Transvaal; Transvaals krijgslied* (text of Julius de Meester).

BIBLIOGRAPHY

CORBET, A.: *Peter Benoit - leven, werk en betekenis,* 1944.   VAN DER MUEREN, FL.: *Vlaamsche muziek en componisten in de XIXde en XXste eeuw.* 's-Gravenhage, 1931.   VAN DER MUEREN, FL.: *Perspectief van de Vlaamse muziek.* Hasselt, 1961.   BOUWS, JAN: "Naar Broedren!", *Woord en Wys van die Afrikaanse Lied.* Cape Town, 1961.   SMITS, DOM. A.: *Betrekkingen tussen Vlaanderen en Zuid-Afrika.* Bruges, 1943.

—J.B.

BENZON, EUGENE   Organs 11, Pietermaritzburg, Touring Theatre Groups 3

BEREA CHORAL SOCIETY   Durban 4, 5, Durban Orchestral Society, R.H. MacDonald

BERESFORD, S.   Durban 5, 6 7

BERG, H. (PSEUDONYM OF ANN ZULMANN)   A. Zulmann

BERMAN, CHARLES,   *14 January 1912 in Johannesburg, where he still lives. Dance-band leader and composer of light music.

At eighteen Berman played the trumpet in the first South African band booked for an overseas tour. Four years later (1934) he was appointed director of a studio dance band, formed for the African Broadcasting Company. For seven years he led his own dance orchestra in Johannesburg, also playing principal trumpet in the SABC Symphony Orchestra. — In 1946 Berman spent six months in the United States of America, studying broadcasting and the manufacture of gramophone records. On his return to South Africa he started Record Industries, and at present is a director of African Radio Productions (Pty) Ltd. Since undertaking the musical direction for the first Bantu musical film, *Zonk,* he has become interested in composing background music for films and radio productions.

Melodies: Crazy zoo, foxtrot (1933); Un minuto contigo; Egoli Africa; Hibiscus waltz; Sarie; Anameno; Saddled with sunshine; Centavos and pesetas; Bright side; Good news; Happy theme.

—Ed.

BERRY, NOREEN A. Armhold, C.G. Feros, Higher Educational Institutions I/2

BERTRAND, JACQUES (FERDINAND), *probably in France; °November or December 1823 in Cape Town. Music and dancing teacher.

It is known that Bertrand contributed as ballet manager to Boniface's* and Lemming's* production of *Het beleg en het nemen van Trojen,* a ballet pantomime in three acts, in 1813. During the following 10 years he made his living as a dancing teacher, but also gave violin, guitar, zither and piano lessons, and made occasional concert appearances. But financially he struggled, and it is apparent from his frequent changes of address that he had many pecuniary problems. After his death his estate, consisting solely of "an assortment of musical instruments and music books", was auctioned.

BIBLIOGRAPHY

BOUWS, JAN: *Die musiekle we van Kaapstad, 1800 tot 1850, en sy verhouding tot die musiekkultuur van Wes-Europa.* Cape Town/Amsterdam, 1966. BOUWS, JAN: *Nuwe strominge in die Kaapse musiekonderwys in die eerste helfte van die negentiende eeu.* Address to the South African Academy, Pretoria, 1966.

SOURCES

Kaapsche Stads Courant en Afrikaansche Berigter: 1813 - 1824. *The South African Court Calendar and Directory (Geo. Ross):* 1819 - 1823.

—J.B.

BESTER FAMILY Nelspruit

BEZZIO, LUIGI, *30 September 1893 in Moncalvo, Italy; now in Pretoria. Medical doctor, composer and music teacher.

While studying to become a medical doctor, Luigi Bezzio was instructed in music by C. Tagliapietra. When he became director of a dental institute in Venice, he played the flute and later cello in the Symphony Orchestra of the Liceo Musicale and at times acted as their conductor. He also re-organised and conducted the classical plectrum orchestra, Lux Venice, established a municipal symphonic band in Padua, and was music critic of the newspaper, *Il Gazzettino.* In 1946 he settled in Pretoria where he was still teaching singing and pianoforte in 1970. For twelve years he was a member of the Executive Committee of the South African Society of Music Teachers.* In 1964 he composed an opera *The Great Trek,* on the libretto of Dr Oreste Arioli. It is the only work of its kind based on the history of the Voortrekkers.

WORKS

Opera

Il Grande Viaggio, opera in four acts (libretto, Dr Oreste Arioli). Ms., 1964.

Operetta

Pirimpaya, in three acts. Ms., n.d.

Orchestra

Adagio cantabile. Ms., n.d.

Voice and pianoforte
Jakarande in fiore, tango (L. Bezzio). Ms., 1950.   Rappelle toi (A. de Musset). Ms.,
n.d.   Barcarolle (T. Gautier). Ms., n.d.   Ottobre (Stecchetti). Ms., n.d.   O verre berge (T.
Wassenaar). Ms., n.d.   Inno del Pretoria Technical College (Brits). Ms., n.d.   Fiamme
legionarie (Bezzio). Zanibon-Padova., n.d.   Panis Angelicus. Ms., n.d.   Baccio morto (Ada
Negri). Zanibon-Padova, n.d.   Fatina d'amore (L. Bezzio). Ms., n.d.   Le jour viendra (L.
Bezzio). Ms., n.d.   Just one kiss (I. Larsen). Ms., n.d.   Il valzer della farfalla (L. Bezzio). Ms.,
n.d.   Canarino innamorato (L. Bezzio). Ms., n.d.   Voci nella notte, duet for tenor and
baritone (L. Bezzio). Ms., n.d.   Many light songs.   *Transcriptions* of operas, symphonies,
ballets, overtures, etc. for symphonic band or plectrum orchestra.

—Ed.

BIELEVELDT, J.H.   Organs 1 (v)

BIJVANCK, HENDRIK MARIE JACOBUS, *6 November 1909 at Koedoes in Java. Dutch
composer and pianist.

Bijvanck studied pianoforte (under Mrs Andrassfy) and composition (under Franz
Schmidt) in Vienna. He was repetitor of the Vienna Boys' Choir and the Vienna
National Opera, and became a concert pianist and song accompanist in Amsterdam.
Apart from a number of major works *(Bevrydingsimfonie, Requiem* for soloists,
choir and orchestra, and a piano concerto), he composed chamber music and songs
with Afrikaans texts. These were collected in the volume *Van liefde en
dood:*   1. Offerande (I.D. du Plessis)   2. Teen die helling (W.E.G.
Louw)   3. Liefde en dood (S. Ign. Mocke)   4. Wie sing?

—J.B.

BILMARK, ALICE LEONORA MARIA (NÉE HYVARD), *31 July 1901 in Copenhagen; at
present (1967) in Durban. Soprano and pianist.

Alice Bilmark started pianoforte lessons under Marius Lennó and at sixteen she
entered the Royal Danish Conservatoire in Copenhagen, where she studied piano
and singing for four years. After the first year she was chosen out of 250 students for
free tuition. Her studies completed, she was offered an engagement in the Danish
Royal Opera House, but she married Amon Bilmark,* with whom she came to South
Africa in April 1922. Six years later she continued her studies in Rome under
Alfredo Martino of the Royal Opera House. — In Durban she has given concerts
and recitals with the Durban Civic Orchestra* and for the SABC - both as pianist and
as singer.

—Ed.

BILMARK, AMON PETER JOHANNES, *2 May 1894 in Copenhagen; °2 March 1960 in
Durban. Luthier.

Amon Bilmark was a professional flautist at the age of twelve, but switched to cello
in 1913 and went to Petrograd for study under Gorski and Rubinstein after having
had private lessons in Copenhagen. In 1917 and 1918 he continued his studies under
Albrecht Loeffler in Sweden. Shortly before coming to South Africa in April 1922, he
married the Danish singer Alice Hyvard.* After six years in South Africa as
principal cellist in the Durban Civic Orchestra,* he left for Rome where he studied
cello, but also violinmaking (under Fernando Sacconi). One year later, in 1929, he
was back in Durban. — Competing with 165 instrument makers, Bilmark entered
two violins and two violas for the International Violinmaking Contest held in The

Hague in 1949 and was awarded a diploma of honour, one of the five awards made on this occasion. On 17 April 1946, a unique event was recorded at a chamber music concert in Johannesburg when all four instruments used by a quartet - Michael Doré,* J. de Almeida Gorge, Else Schneider* and Betty Pack* - were products of South African craftmanship, made by Amon Bilmark. Bilmark also made a violin entirely of South African wood; this he presented to the Africana Museum in Johannesburg as a token of his love for this country.

—A.L.M.B.

BINI, ALBINA, (MRS BERGAMASCO), *11 July 1899 in Florence; now living in Cape Town. Pianist and soprano.

Albina Bini was brought to South Africa in 1904 when her parents immigrated, and received her initial musical training at the St Mary's Convent School in Cape Town. As an 11-year-old schoolgirl, she was engaged to play piano at the Claremont Bioscope every night, for a monthly fee of three golden sovereigns (R6). At the age of 15 she began serious pianoforte study under Madame Niay Darroll,* a primary founder of the South African College of Music,* winning contests and gold medals at Eisteddfodau. She was in demand at War Relief Concerts during the First World War. — After obtaining her teachers' and performers' licentiates at the SACM, she taught pianoforte privately and made her debut as a concert pianist with the Cape Town Municipal Orchestra.* She has since become well-known both as a pianist and as a singer. Noteworthy performances range from piano recitals during the Beethoven Centenary in 1928 to her association with Albert Mallinson, the British composer, of whose songs she gave recitals between 1941 and 1945. In 1947 she sang at the Gala Concert in the Cape Town City Hall when the Municipal Orchestra was conducted by Albert Coates* in honour of the Royal family. Apart from her concert work, she has become an examiner and adjudicator of repute in South Africa and the former Rhodesias. — After the inception of the University of Cape Town's Opera School and the appointment of Giuseppe Paganelli (formerly a member of the Sistine Choir in Rome) as lecturer in singing and opera (1926), Albina Bini became his pupil and sang the role of Rosina in his first production, *The barber of Seville;* the Cape Town Municipal Orchestra was conducted by W.J. Pickerill.* This marked the beginning of an operatic career which was continued in Johannesburg, Durban, Pretoria, and in the Cape Town Opera House until the building was demolished in 1926. The erection of the Little Theatre* in 1966 gave Cape Town a new cultural centre. Further performances by the university's Opera Company were then possible and Albina was chosen to sing leading roles in *Don Pasquale, La Traviata, Rigoletto, La Bohéme The marriage of Figaro, Don Giovanni,* and a Nō Play by W.H. Bell. — Since her retirement as a pianist and a singer, she has done much adjudicating in the Cape Colony, Natal and the Transvaal. She also co-operates actively with the opera committee of Capab, of which she is a member.

—Ed.

BIRCH, THE FAMILY was prominent in Queenstown's music between 1883 and 1894. Sophie Birch and her husband, John, arrived in Queenstown in October 1883, her husband as a piano tuner to E. Mendelssohn* & Co. Sophie had studied at the Royal Academy of Music. After their arrival, Mendelssohn arranged a series of Monday Popular Promenade Concerts, with Mme Mendelssohn* and the Volunteer Band, to introduce Sophie Birch to the Queenstown public. During the next eleven years, she established a reputation as a piano teacher, and appeared at local concerts, mostly as a pianist, but on a few occasions also as a singer. — Mme Birch took part in the concerts of Gerrard and the Hilda Temple Touring Company in 1885; in December 1887, at short notice, she accompanied Reményi,* when the latter's accompanist, Charles Eberlein,* terminated his association with this violinist. She also accompanied Clifford Halle .(baritone), Carl Walther (violin), Signor Foli* (August 1889 and 1892), Mme Marie Stefani (February 1893), and Miss Nellie Ganthony (February 1894). She herself promoted a number of concerts; one in June 1886 for St Michael's Church funds, and another in August 1888, a Grand Evening Concert in the Town Hall, in aid of library funds. She also promoted children's concerts in which she co-operated with a Miss Dashwood and was associated with the violinist, George Daws.* In 1892 she became a pianist in the newly-formed Queenstown Orchestra. In May 1894, on the occasion of her departure from Queenstown, the orchestra gave her a Grand Complimentary Concert. — John Birch was a talented entertainer. In November 1883, when the Leslie Minstrel Troupe visited Queenstown, their "Tambo" fell ill, and at short notice, Birch acted as a substitute. He was subsequently a member of the "Queenstown Blackbirds". When the firm of Mendelssohn & Co. terminated their business interests in Queenstown towards the end of 1886, Birch resigned. In January 1887, he was in Natal, where he was laid up with paralysis. He recovered from this illness and he and Sophie visited England, but in August of that year they were back in Queenstown. Their daughter, Maudie Birch, was a violinist at local concerts. By 1900 the family were living in Johannesburg.

SOURCES

*Queenstown Free Press:*12 October 1883 to 8 May 1894.

—C.G.H.

BIRCH, MAUDE Birch family

BIRCHAM, W.T. Piano music IV/3

BIRKETT, C. Grahamstown 5

BIRKMANN, W. Grahamstown, Port Elizabeth, C. Pearson, C. Schulze, J. Schonegevel, Touring Theatre Groups 3

BIRKS, MOIRA Durban 8, 10

BIRT, HAROLD, REV. Diocesan College

BISHOP, ANN (NÉE ANNA RIVIÈRE), *9 January 1810 in London; °18 March 1884 in New York. English soprano born of French parents.

After initially playing pianoforte, Anna Rivière commenced her study of singing at the Royal Academy in 1824, remaining there until 1831, when she married (since 1842 Sir) Henry Rowley Bishop (1786-1855). Her reputation grew very rapidly and after an initial period devoted to oratorio and classical music, she was converted to Italian opera by Bochsa, a harpist with whom she toured in England during 1839. Shortly after their return to London during the same year, she eloped with Bochsa, deserting her husband, two daughters and a son. —From September 1839 to May 1843 she toured the musical centres of Europe and Russia with Bochsa, singing in a total of 260 concerts. They then left for Italy where in 27 months she interpreted parts in 20 operas at the San Carlo Theatre in Naples. After a short stay in England (1846), she left for America in 1847 and in 1855 she was in Australia, where Bochsa died. She returned to England via South and North America and was married in New York to her third husband, a Mr Schulz. In 1859 she was back in America, also singing in Canada and Mexico, and in February 1866 she was shipwrecked en route to China from Honolulu. After deprivations lasting 40 days, the ship's company was saved and the singer could continue her concert tour to Manila, China and India. In 1868 Ann Bishop was once more in Australia and after a visit to London, she spent the rest of her life in New York, with the exception of a period from September 1875 to November 1876, when as a last gesture, she toured South Africa, accompanied by the singer, pianist and composer, Charles Lascelles.* — Starting with her very first "Grand Concert de Salon", in the Mutual Hall in Cape Town on 22 September, she was acclaimed with unparallelled enthusiasm. She sang in a production of *Norma* and appeared in Offenbach's *Grand duchess,* but achieved her greatest successes with ballads such as *Please give me a penny.* This caused silver pennies to shower onto the stage and she had them gathered for a Robben Island Fund. From October to March she toured the Eastern Province and Natal where she produced *Grand duchess* concertante and *Il Trovatore* as an *opera di camera.* Back in Cape Town there was a measure of rivalry with the Italian Opera Company of Sign. Cagli, but after a while she co-operated with them: under the baton of Sign. Maggi she appeared in the Theatre Royal in a performance of *Norma.* In June she embarked on a second journey into the interior, up to Bloemfontein and from there to the diamond fields. In October she was back in Cape Town giving concerts and once more singing in *Norma* for her "Final Appearance and Farewell to South Africa". — With her experience, Ann Bishop knew how to excite enthusiasm in her public. Ironically, Henry Bishop's *Home sweet home* appeared regularly on her programmes, but in Cape Town she also included *Wien Neêrlandsch bloed* and in Bloemfontein, the Free State's national anthem, which she sang with excited music lovers of the town. Her voice is described as a high soprano with a brilliant quality and it is often mentioned that it was rather unsympathetic. Her farewell to South Africa was also a farewell to her career. She attempted a comeback in Islington, London, during the next year, but the impolite reaction of the public convinced her that her time had passed.

BIBLIOGRAPHY

Dictionary of national biography, II, pp. 551-552. OUP, 1970.   *Grove's Dictionary of music and musicians I.* Macmillan, 1954.   HUMAN, J.L.K.: *Musiek in die Oranje-Vrystaat vanaf 1850 tot aan die begin van die Anglo-Boereoorlog.* M.Mus. dissertation, UOFS, 1963.   JACKSON, G.S.: *Music in Durban from 1850 to 1900.* D.Phil. thesis, Wits U, 1961.

SOURCES

Het Volksblad: 1875, 1876.   *The Lantern:* 1877.

—J.B. (amplified)

BISHOP'S Diocesan College

BLACKING, JOHN ANTHONY RANDOLL,   *22 October 1928 at Guildford; at present in Belfast, Ireland. Professor of social anthropology, musicologist and composer.

As a boy he regularly sang in the choir of Salisbury Cathedral in England, often as a soloist, and studied pianoforte and composition under Reginald Moore, B.J.F. Picton and Ronald Woodham. On various occasions during his youth he appeared at concerts as a promising young pianist. Although he chose to study Social

Anthropology at Cambridge University (1950-53), he managed to develop his musical talent at the same time and organised and played at numerous public concerts which placed the emphasis on contemporary music. In 1952 he attended a course in musicology given by André Schaeffner in Paris and in 1954 he returned to Paris to continue his pianoforte studies with Suzanne Guébel. The climax to these formative years was a concert tour in South East Asia with the violinist Maurice Clare, during which his double interest in anthropology and music led him to ethnomusicological studies of Malay music. This marked a definite turning point in his career. — On completion of the eastern tour, he settled in South Africa (1954), as a musicologist to the International Library of African Music near Roodepoort and started his research into the music of the Venda of Northern Transvaal. This research was completed on a Horniman Scholarship in 1958 and cast in a definitive form for his Ph.D. thesis on "The Cultural Foundations of the Music of the Venda, with Special Reference to their Children's Songs", which was accepted by the University of the Witwatersrand in 1965. — Since the termination of his contract with the International Library, Blacking has done numerous other studies on African music. — From 1959-1965 he was lecturer, and after 1966 Professor and Head of the Department of Social Anthropology at the University of the Witwatersrand. He was also an honorary lecturer in the University's Department of Music. From 1960-1965 he conducted the University of the Witwatersrand Choir, which gave concerts on the Reef and toured Natal and the Eastern Cape. He left South Africa in 1970 and in the same year was appointed Professor at Belfast University.

PUBLICATIONS (all purely anthropological works are excluded).

Musical instruments of the Malayan aborigines. *Federation Museums Journal I and II.* Singapore, 1955. Some notes on a theory of African rhythm advanced by Erich von Hornbostel. *African Music* I/2, 1955. Eight flute tunes from Butembo. *African Music* I/2, 1955. The role of music amongst the Venda of the Northern Transvaal. *International Library of African Music,* Roodepoort, 1957. Problems of pitch, pattern and harmony in the ocarina music of the Venda. *African Music* II/2, 1959. Fieldwork co-operation in the study of Nsenga music and ritual. *Africa* XXXII/1, 1962. Patterns of Nsenga "kalimba" music. *African Music* II/4, 1961. Musical expeditions of the Venda. *African Music* III/1, 1962. The role of music in the culture of the Venda of the Northern Transvaal. *Studies in Ethnomusicology* II, New York, 1965. Studying and developing music in East Africa. East Africa's cultural heritage. *African Contemporary Monographs* No. 4, Nairobi, 1966. Culture, the arts and economic development. *East Africa Journal* III/7, 1966. The identification of different musical styles and their historical and sociological foundations, with special reference to the music of the Venda. *Music and History in Africa,* Royal Anthropological Institute, London. *Venda children's songs - a study in ethnomusicological analysis.* Witwatersrand University Press, 1967. The need for professional musicians in developing Venda church music. *African Music* IV/2, 1968. Several book reviews in *African Music, African Studies, Ethnomusicology* etc. Music from Petauke, Northern Rhodesia, Volumes 1-3. Three 12-inch long-playing records, with notes and photographs. *Ethnic Folkways Library,* New York, 1962, Fe. 4201-3. *How musical is man?* Faber & Faber, London, 1976.

WORKS

Jesu, the very thought is sweet, anthem for unaccompanied SATB. Ms., 1947. *Fair and true,* song for soprano and piano. Ms., 1951.   Incidental music for *The taming of the shrew*, for chamber ensemble. Ms., 1954.

–Ed.

·BLAKE, YVONNE (MRS BARNS), *24 November 1916 in Durban; now residing near Wellington. Ballet dancer and teacher.

Yvonne Blake received her ballet training from Helen Webb* and Dulcie Howes,* before leaving for London in 1935. She danced with the Slavinsky Russian Ballet and René Blum's Ballet Russe de Monte Carlo, while studying intermittently with Margaret Craske, Preobrajenska, Sokolova and Brunelleschi. At the request of Dulcie. Howes, she returned to South Africa in 1937 to teach ballet at the College of Music* in Cape Town. — In 1945 she joined Cecily Robinson* in forming a ballet school for the Cape Town Ballet Club,* which became the South African National Ballet in the following year. When Cecily Robinson left in 1947, Yvonne Blake continued as director of the company for a year, before also leaving Cape Town. Since then she has been teaching ballet in Wellington and Paarl. She danced in *Les sylphides, Scheherezade, Petrouchka* and other works choreographed by Fokine. Her 5 productions for the Cape Town Ballet Club included *Streetlight* (Britten) and *Légende* (Ravel).

—M.G.

BLAKEMORE, STELLA, *13 April 1906 in Lindley; now in London. Music teacher, singer and author.

Stella Blakemore's father was Captain Percy Harold Blakemore, an officer in charge of a settlement of persons who had assisted the British forces during the Anglo-Boer War. Her mother was a daughter of Theunis Krogh, one time under-secretary of Paul Kruger. The father was an optimistic gambler who left his family about 1908 to visit Canada where he hoped to "create a new home for them". They never saw him again. Her mother energetically took up the career of a teacher and came to Pretoria where she devoted herself to her daughter's future. Stella's musical education consisted of violin tuition (Hannah Selschop, Ferramosca), pianoforte tuition (Ellen Norburn,* Peter Cruse, Lorenzo Danza,* Barclay Donn,* Maud Rogers and Aileen Palmer) and eventually, singing (Paganelli of Cape Town and then Victor Booth and Frederick King of London). She passed pianoforte examinations (Licentiate, 1923) and often achieved successes in eisteddfodau in Johannesburg, Cape Town and Durban. Her mother, however, was determined to make a singer of her and after she had passed the LRAM and ARCM in London, she was sent to Dresden where she loved taking part in the opera productions of the Conservatoire. — In 1930 she returned to South Africa for a concert tour and then again left for Dresden, this time with her mother, then for Milan and eventually for London with a touring company. In these years she relished singing opera roles, but with a critical evaluation of her own accomplishments. — In June 1933 she was married in England to a civil engineer, David Owen, with whom she had become acquainted in 1927. They came to South Africa where Stella sang with the Cape Town orchestra and for the ABC before Owen, through the agency of his mother-in-law, was given a position in the department of Nature Conservation at Loskop. Stella started teaching music in Pretoria in 1935 and opened the Blakemore Studios with the co-operation of her mother in 1938. With one interruption when Stella was with her husband in Swaziland, she was a music teacher in Pretoria until 1947. During the War, while her

172

husband was on active service, her practice was extended to Johannesburg and became so successful that she had to appoint a number of assistants. Besides her teaching, she was an adjudicator at eisteddfodau, produced an abbreviated Afrikaans version of *Hansie en Grietjie* and was responsible for a theatrical presentation of *Alice in Wonderland* with ballet. There was a steady demand for her services as a singer, especially at the concerts of Gerke's Euterpe Society (from May 1926) and as a soloist in the oratorios conducted by Bon*, Gerke and Norburn* (from June 1930). — In 1947 her husband accepted a position in Ghana where he lived with Stella, his mother-in-law and two children, first in Kumasi and later in Accra. During nine years in Ghana and another two years in Nigeria, Stella continued teaching music, but sent her children to school, first in Wales and then in Ireland. In 1954 the Owens bought a country cottage in Ireland, and on visits to that country Stella acted as accompanist in Warren Point, Newry and Belfast. In Ghana and in Ireland she showed a preference for radio programmes in which she could accompany or sing, or participate as an announcer ("I like talking on radio - I am much better at it than at singing"). In 1962 the family lived in Ireland for a year, but since 1963 they have been resident in London. — Two children's operettas were written as a direct result of her music teaching - *Die goue sleutel* and *Die toweruur*. She wrote the words and the music for both of them. During 1967 and 1968 she studied composition in England, especially orchestral composition; but her creative work in music is overshadowed by the series of teenage books which she published under her maiden and married names, but also under the noms-de-plumes of Theunis Krogh, Annaliza Bierman and Dien Grimbeeck. Her literary career had started in 1931 with a volume of English poems, and a collection of travel memoirs on Ireland *(Pass no remarks)*. Stella Blakemore's books for girls about Maasdorp School, and for boys about Keurboslaan, are widely read by Afrikaans teenagers.

WORKS

Die goue sleutel, a comedy for children in one act (words and music, Stella Blakemore). It contains eight songs, published by J.L. van Schaik, Pretoria, 1931. Die toweruur, children's operetta in one act (Stella Blakemore). J.L. van Schaik, Pretoria, 1932. Folly, song (Stella Blakemore). Arthur Stockwell Ltd., London, n.d.

BIBLIOGRAPHY

VILJOEN, A.W.: *Drie Pretoriase musici: Blakemore, Yates en Gafner*. B.Mus script, UP, 1973 (contains a detailed bibliography).

—Ed.

BLIGNAUT, CHRISTIAN AUGUST (CHRIS), *27 April 1897 in Johannesburg; °21 July 1974 in Vereeniging. Singer and writer of Afrikaans light music.

It was as Harold Wise that Chris Blignaut first attracted attention. The First World War was on and overseas entertainers had practically vanished from the South African stage, so that this talented young boy of seventeen had his opportunity of singing in bioscope theatres. During the early twenties Aimee Parkerson* and then Alfred Bell,* Madame Palmer and Signor Pentuzzi worked at his voice production and in 1923 he came first in a Radio Talent Competition and started winning medal awards and diplomas at the Johannesburg Eisteddfod. During these years he once sang an Afrikaans song at a concert and was applauded so vociferously that he thought "the roof was going to come off". He had tapped the vein of Afrikaans nationalism and pride in the Afrikaans heritage, and from this time onward he concentrated on the popular song in Afrikaans. The *Star* described his art as follows: "He caught the sentiment of the words with complete fidelity in singing that gives the song a certain dignity and fervour" (29 November 1930). Add to this art a manly stature of about two metres, a sense of humour, a beautifully strong baritone voice, and the gift of accompanying himself on the ukelele or guitar and it becomes clear that Chris Blignaut was predestined to present Afrikaners with their own songs in the popular genre. Until he decided to retire from the stage in 1949, he dominated the scene as singer and entertainer. He became the first person to broadcast Afrikaans tunes, the first to play in Afrikaans films (Ou tante Koba, Een kêrel van die Paarl, Sarie Marais) and the first to achieve notable success with gramophone records. Both HMV and Columbia had him under contract to record Afrikaans songs in London. According to a statement dated 28 March 1931, Columbia had sold 54 853 records by Blignaut in three months. At two cents commission per record, this netted him about R1 165. He himself made a conservative estimate that about two million of his records were sold after 1929, giving him an estimated income of R70 000. In all, he recorded 250 tunes on 150 short-playing records and later another 120 tunes on long-playing records. During the thirties and forties he was unquestionably the most popular and most successful singer of light Afrikaans music. He also remained the most popular entertainer on the live stage, made five grand tours of South Africa and finally, in the last one, also of Rhodesia and South West Africa, usually in association with other popular entertainers such as Teddie Garratt. — In spite of his great success as singer, Chris Blignaut held an appointment as employee of an insurance company, in which he rose to become chief inspector and finally manager.

PUBLISHED MELODIES
Versameling van deuntjies in Afrikaans (with Teddie Garratt). Teddie Garratt, Johannesburg, 1931 (eight songs). Ek verlang na die Bosveld. The Singer series of Afrikaans melodies, no. 51. Gallo Africa Ltd., Johannesburg, 1945. Terug na jou. Gallo Africa Ltd., Johannesburg, 1945. Die Chris Blignaut Sangbundel. Musiekuitgewersmaatskappy van Afrika, Johannesburg, 1969(?). Populêre Sangbundel (Settings by M. Catoggio (M.L. de Villiers)). Muziekdrukkerij Dogilbert, Brussels (eight songs). Bly vir altyd by my. Intersong, Johannesburg, 1970. Daar's 'n voetpad wat kronkel. Intersong, Johannesburg, 1970. Lettie du Toit. Intersong, Johannesburg, 1970. Lulu Louw. Intersong, Johannesburg, 1970. 'n Meisie in 'n huisie in die Vrystaat. Intersong, Johannesburg, 1970 (com. 1934). My Oom Koos. Intersong, Johannesburg, 1970. My Sannie. Intersong, Johannesburg, 1970. My suikerpop. Intersong, Johannesburg, 1970. Nooietjie van my hart. Intersong, Johannesburg, 1970. Sewe jaar met 'n bevoeterde vrou. Intersong, Johannesburg, 1970. Sing vir my 'n melodietjie. Intersong, Johannesburg, 1970. Verlang na my ryperd. Intersong, Johannesburg, 1970.

BIBLIOGRAPHY
VAN DER MERWE, F.Z.: *Suid-Afrikaanse musiekbibliografie, 1787-1952.* Bygewerk deur J. van de Graaf (1953-1972). Published for the HSRC by Tafelberg-Uitgewers, Cape Town, 1974.

SOURCES
Scrapbook of newspaper cuttings and other documents in the National Documentation Centre for Music, HSRC, Pretoria.

—C.G.H.

BLOE, A.C.T. R. Müller (Pty) Ltd., Port Elizabeth I/5

Bloemfontein, music in
I. The period from 1850 to 1899
II. The period from 1900 to 1939

I. The period from 1850 to 1899

1. Orchestras
2. Opera
3. Choral societies
4. Visiting artists
5. Light music
6. State music
7. Winter evening entertainments and debating societies
8. Educational institutions and music

1. Orchestras

Orchestras in this period are usually brass bands of various sizes, some with only four and others with between 20 and 30 players. The rather primitive musical conditions at the time often made it necessary to improvise by including a pianoforte or harmonium in the "orchestra", or by adding strings to the brass when they were available. The repertoire too, was fortuitous and had to be adjusted to the available players and their varying technical facilities. The "foreigners" (uitlanders) in Bloemfontein were influenced by the traditions they had brought with them from their home countries and by the urgent desire to employ their leisure to some purpose. Entertainments were few and far between and for those who had the necessary knowledge and ability, the making of music was an obvious choice. The histories of "orchestras" and choirs reveal time and again that there were too few enthusiasts and that their public was too small to give their enterprises a reasonably permanent basis. — The first band was started by a Mr Bauer, possibly a German, in 1867. The very next year, however, his group experienced financial difficulties and despite a benefit concert organised by the Bloemfontein Amateur Dramatic Club, they disappeared from the scene. The Free State's Artillery Brigade had a small band in those years and applied for their own uniform in 1871. Sam Barratt* became the bandmaster of this group in 1874 at a salary of R400 per annum and in the same year the firm of Pallice of Strassbourg delivered eighteen instruments for their use. A commission of the Volksraad recommended in 1879 that the number of players be increased to 25. Unfortunately there are very few references to the activities of the Artillery Band, but it does appear that they played in the city and in varius country towns under the direction of August Gräder (Grader), a clarinet player who had previously played under Hans von Bülow in Hamburg and subsequently in Covent Garden. Another conductor was the teacher and musician O.T. de Villiers.* The band is mentioned for the last time in December 1890 when the railway line to Bloemfontein was inaugurated. — A year previously a second army band, that of the President Brandt Rifles, appeared on the scene. The members were volunteers who were trained and conducted by Charles Acton who previously had been a member of the Barratt Orchestra (see next paragraph). This band played at State functions such as President Reitz' wedding in 1889 and also held promenade concerts in the Government Gardens. Acton was succeeded by Edwards and then by Landgraf. The band remained active and was exceedingly popular until 1894 after which it disappeared from the scene. — This Army Band had been preceded by an amateur orchestra which was established by the Barratt Brothers* in 1883. The latter group played a leading part in Bloemfontein's musical life until 1887. Initially it was simply called the Barratt Orchestra, but later it had other names such as the Philharmonic Society or the Orchestral Band. At the time of the Queen's jubilee in 1887, the orchestra turned out for a special Cathedral service and also played at a festival concert where they accompanied a large choir of 250 members in the performance of Barratt's occasional song *Britannia's sons*. Earlier in the same year the orchestra was also engaged by Barratt in the presentation of an operetta of his own fabrication dealing with misplaced philanthropy. The available accounts do not mention the name of the operetta. After 1887 the orchestra probably dissolved. Another short-lived effort at creating an orchestra was made by A.M. Baumann* in 1885. After one single concert this band is not mentioned again. — Although the scene is one of some activity as far as bands are concerned, the players were (with rare exceptions) amateurs who had to be instructed in the use of their instruments. In the case of the artillery band, advertisements for the post of bandmaster expressly mention that the duties of the successful applicant would include instruction in the playing of the instruments. — Consequently the bands were rarely able to present an entire programme, and only contributed a few items which were supplemented by soloists, either instrumental or vocal. — With the arrival of Ivan Haarburger,* the orchestral work in Bloemfontein moved to a higher level altogether. He took the initiative in October 1893 of creating a Bloemfontein Orchestral Society which had Mr C. Fischer as chairman of the orchestral committee, Hurt as secretary and Charles Israel* as leader. The attempt was successful - by 1895 the number of players had increased to 28 and the programmes were becoming progressively more ambitious. In that year an overture represented Mozart, and the March of the Priests *(Athalie)*, and the Wedding March (from *A Midsummer night's dream)*, Mendelssohn. It was the policy of the Society to let prominent soloists appear with the orchestra so that many light classics and a few serious works could be included in programmes. Before the war the following soloists sang or played with Haarburger's orchestra: Percy Ould,* Florence Fraser,* Charles Israel, Marguerite McIntyre (a visiting Scottish soprano), the clarinet player August Gräder, Mme Trebelli,* Roger Ascham,* Sims-Reeves (tenor), Beatrice Stuart,* Albert Friedenthal (a German pianist) and Marie Albani (Marie la Jeunesse, the French-Canadian star of Covent Garden). — The annual number of concerts varied. Over the years a respectable rate of at least one concert during every two months was maintained. Ivan Haarburger had a difficult task to maintain his orchestra at a proper standard and had to wage a continual war against inadequate funds and a chronic lack of competent musicians. Elsa Leviseur* recounts an amusing anecdote of a rehearsal which took place after war had been declared. Haarburger distributed dance music to the orchestra, which they refused to play. The scene soon developed into burlesque with the conductor in a towering rage and his orchestra almost helpless with laughter. The last concert on record and the only one in that year was held on 13 July 1901. It took the form of a benefit concert for Mr Haarburger. In October, however, the orchestra was used to accompany a performance of *Messiah*. — Bloemfontein's enthusiasm for an orchestral body was shared in the rural districts by Jagersfontein, Boshof and

Kroonstad where orchestras were established for brief periods. As was the case in Bloemfontein, these were also individual attempts which lost their impetus when the dominating figures either left the towns or died.

2. Opera

Halls suitable for concerts or theatricals were naturally hardly available in the pioneering country that the Free State was until 1899. Impresarios and producers were forced to improvise and to make the best possible use of hotels, shops, magistrates's courts, class-rooms and even council chambers. Temporary stages were constructed from boards laid across crates and beer barrels. Oil lamps provided the light effects and décor had to be suggested rather than realistically depicted. The so-called "orchestra accompaniments" were generally supplied by a piano or a harmonium, possibly supplemented by some instruments which the players had with them or which were secured from members of the community. To stage anything at all under these circumstances required that the touring companies should have a spirit of adventure. The same spirit naturally activated the local groups who tried their hand at productions. Sustained by a sense of humour, courage and initiative, and by the enthusiasm of communities craving for entertainment, the ventures invariably succeeded. The discovery of diamonds and gold drew large numbers of foreigners who spent money lavishly and had an unquenchable thirst for any sort of entertainment. This fact and the gradually increasing prosperity of the farming community made the exhausting tours and performances worthwhile, even in quite small towns and villages. — Bloemfontein, being the capital city, developed comparatively rapidly and could offer at least one or two halls for stage productions and an appreciative audience. The Wesleyan congregation in Bloemfontein had a new church built in 1873 and they then sold their first little church measuring 16m x 8m to the Town Council for R2 200. Until 1883 when the first town hall was erected in Maitland Street, this little hall was used for the purpose. The availability of the hall improved the prospects for music making although other venues such as the Raadzaal were also adapted and used for concerts. — The Miranda-Harper Company which visited Bloemfontein in March 1869, presenting three grand operatic and national ballad concerts in the Raadzaal, was the first of a long series of companies to visit the town. They came again in 1870 and subsequently also visited Philippolis and Colesberg. Their programmes were compiled of the most attractive scenes and popular arias drawn from operas and operettas. No complete works were presented. In this they were typical of numerous companies who followed them. They all derived from England, America, Australia and later on Johannesburg, and had a personnel of generally lesser singers, usually four or five young people although more elderly and famous names occasionally joined these groups. — In this way artists such as James William Turner and Charlotte Helen Sainton-Dolby (1821-1885), for whom Mendelssohn wrote the contralto part in his *Elijah*, as well as the famous Sims-Reeves, came to South Africa. In a few exceptional cases the groups could boast of a really versatile musician such as James Hyde,* who later settled in the country, or Dan Godfrey who achieved great heights as a conductor in England. Sometimes entire opera companies would be brought from Italy or from England together with their own "orchestras". Usually the groups were small and consisted of enthusiasts who had theatre in their blood, who visited "remote parts of the world" to explore new and exciting things and to gain theatre experience. Their example was imitated by companies formed in Johannesburg who also undertook tours in the two Republics as well as in Natal and the Cape Province. — The majority of the artists were British and their repertoire was mainly English. In addition to the works of Gilbert and Sullivan, which were exceedingly popular in South Africa at the time, the names of such composers as Wallace *(Maritana)* and Balfé *(Bohemian girl, Grand duchess, Rose of Castille)* were always prominent. The works of several French composers of operettas, such as Offenbach *(Rose of Auvergne)*, Lecocq *(Fleurs-de-thé)*, Audran *(La mascotte, Nuremberg doll, La poupée)* and Planquette *(Les cloches de Corneville, Rip van Winkle)* were regularly staged. Among the more serious operas performed in Bloemfontein in these years were the following: *Il trovatore, Rigoletto, Daughter of the regiment, Cavalleria rusticana, Carmen, Faust* (a big favourite), *The barber of Seville, Fatinitza, Boccaccio* (von Suppé) and also *La sonnambula.* It should, however, be emphasized that these works were performed very rarely, by way of exception. The following groups performed in Bloemfontein in the years before 1899: The Miranda-Harper Company (March 1869 and April 1870). They presented ballads and arias from operas only. The Harvey-Turner Company (September 1875): two short operettas by Offenbach *(Breaking the spell* and *Rose of Auvergne), Faust, Bohemian girl.* This company also visited Smithfield. Dan Harvey's Italian Opera and Ballet Troupe (August 1876): excerpts from Italian opera only. They also visited Boshof, Reddersburg and Smithfield. The Vesalius Opera Company (December 1880 to March 1881 and again in July 1882): Sullivan's *Cox and box* and *H.M.S. Pinafore;* Offenbach's *Rose of Auvergne* and *Les deux aveugles;* Donizetti's *La fille de régiment;* Lecocq's *Fleurs-de-thé.* In 1882 they presented Planquette's *Les cloches de Cornville* and Lecocq's *La fille de Madame Angot.* The Carry Nelson Comic Operetta Company (November 1887): comic sketches only. The Sandiford Opera Company (September 1891): *H.M.S. Pinafore; La fille de Madame Angot; Cloches de Corneville; Fatinitza* and *Boccaccio* (both by von Suppé); *The gondoliers* and *The little duke* (Lecocq). The Rand Grand Operatic Company (January 1894): excerpts from *Faust, Maritana and Il trovatore.* The Lyric Company (May 1893) consisting of 40 members: *The Mikado; Iolanthe;* and Audran's *La cigale et la fourmi.* The Lyric Company (1894): Audran's *La mascotte;* Cellier's *Dorothy of Haddon Hall* and Audran's *Nuremberg doll;* Planquette's *Rip van Winkle;* and *Cavalleria rusticana.* The Royal Italian Opera Company (April 1895): *Il barbiere di Seviglia; Cavalleria rusticana; Il trovatore;* and *Carmen.* Searelle's* Opera Company (October 1897): three presentations, the titles of which are not known. — English productions were well supported, but the audiences were smaller when other languages were used. It is significant that the Presidents of the Orange Free State occasionally attended these performances - an indication that such evenings enjoyed a measure of social prestige. — The people of Bloemfontein began to feel that they, too, would like to attempt presentations of this nature and the Barratts, with their initiative and courage, were the obvious leaders. In 1880 William Barratt, together with members of the Bloemfontein Choral Society, staged *The merrie men of Sherwood Forest* by Birch. They were accompanied by an ensemble consisting of a piano, a violin and a cello. The pianist, Mrs Hopwood, was the official accompanist of the society and through all the years up to 1899 she was the mainstay of all similar ventures. — The Bloemfontein Dramatic and Operatic Company, a completely different group led by Alwin Busman, tackled Planquette's *Les cloches,* which had a run of one week. Some months later, in July 1882, the same group presented Sullivan's *The sorcerer* and after a two-year period of inactivity this choral society presented Sullivan's *Trial by jury*, directed by Sam Barratt who had returned to Bloemfontein after his sojourn in Kimberley and in East London. Inspired by the success of this production, Barratt started rehearsing *HMS Pinafore* in the same year. This was. a great favourite with Bloemfontein audiences, but Barratt's production was intended to be one with a difference; he cast children in all parts. The press reported rather unfavourably on this experiment and Barratt rested from his labours until 1887 when he put on a satire written by himself dealing with the sentimentalised philanthropy indulged in at the time. The title of the work is not known and it did not really make the grade with the audiences. In 1888 Barratt again put on *HMS Pinafore*, but this time with the best talent available and consequently with considerably more success. — There were large-scale festivities in Bloemfontein when the railway line to the city was inaugurated in December 1890. For the festival a group of amateurs from Jagersfontein and Fauresmith had rehearsed Sullivan's *The Mikado* and performed it in Bloemfontein's City Hall. The 700 seats were fully booked and the evening became something of a gala occasion. The three ladies who had produced it - mesdames H. Beddy, W. Brodie and C. Wood - were greatly commended for the success of their venture. This surprising performance reveals a little of the musical activities in the rural districts of the Free State about which there are very few reports. The next attempt at a local production only came shortly before the war, in December 1898. Probably taking the musical activities of the famous Wanderers' Club in Johannesburg as a model, the well-known sports club in Bloemfontein called Ramblers created a Ramblers' Musical and Dramatic Society under the direction of S.F. Deale and C.G. Fichardt. Fichardt had become known during recent years as a singer in local productions and Deale was well known as a mainstay of music in Bloemfontein. He had also published a few works by local composers. Deale was chosen as conductor of the new society. Their first choice was another operetta by Sullivan which they tackled in a professional way with an extensive committee system and staged very successfully. In August 1899 the society was ready with another venture - now Sullivan's *HMS Pinafore* and again they attracted full houses to the Ramblers' Hall. Fichardt sang in this production and Deale was the conductor. He had quite a reasonably sized string orchestra, a few wind instruments and a piano (still played by Mrs Hopwood) at his disposal. — This promising start was unfortunately curtailed by the outbreak of war. Everything was brought to a standstill, though a general meeting of the society was arranged for May 1901. Nevertheless the people of Bloemfontein had proved that they were willing and able to contribute to their own music culture and had made progress in that direction.

3. Choral societies

The capital city of the Republic of the Free State was incapable of maintaining a permanent choir. There was a genuine desire for choral singing, probably inspired by the large-scale choral festivals in England and by the German choral tradition with which many of the Bloemfontein residents were familiar, but all the attempts at choral work, some of them on a high level, failed time and again. — Sam Barratt on 16 July 1874 conducted the first choral performance which has been reported. Five excerpts from *Messiah* were sung to a supporting programme of instrumental and vocal items. The great success of this concert led to the establishment of the

Bloemfontein Choral Society under the chairmanship of Mr Brebner. It was launched with a constitution and much publicity. In July 1875 they were ready to sing excerpts from *Acis and Galatea*. The second half of the programme offered a variety which included a Mozart quintet adapted for pianoforte duet and violin. It was performed by the three brothers Barratt who also presented the overture to Rossini's *Tancredi* on a harmonium and two violins. After these ventures the society began to decline rapidly, and it was officially dissolved at a public meeting in August of the same year. — The OFS Choral Society sang in aid of the hospital in 1879, with the President in the audience. After this one performance they are not mentioned again, but the Bloemfontein Choral Society led by William Barratt, started off in a rather fumbling way but managed to produce Birch's *Merrie men of Sherwood Forest* in 1880. To keep the interest alive, Barratt shifted the emphasis in the direction of light operettas. A variety concert was given in 1881 and then he had Mendelssohn's *Hymn of praise* in view. This however failed to materialise. In October 1882 they managed to present Mozart's so-called *Twelfth Mass*. The performance had to be repeated and in 1883 they had J.F. Barnett's *Ancient mariner* as their next course. This was not exactly a success, so Barratt turned to operetta again, and presented Sullivan's *Trial by jury* in September 1884. Then follows a long silence which was broken in 1887 when the society gave a concert in the Town Hall. On this occasion Mr Voysey was the conductor, but it was so poorly attended that the society again lapsed into inactivity. — J. Tryal Beavan* revived the choral society in 1893, establishing a strong new committee and applying strict methods of selecting members. They sang Cowen's *Rose maiden* in 1894 and, to the accompaniment of a small orchestra, Gaul's *Holy city* in the same year. For a long time nothing was accomplished until Ivan Haarburger was invited to become leader of the choir in August 1897. This virtually amounted to an amalgamation of the orchestral and choral societies. After one year it had become evident that Haarburger could not cope successfully with the joint responsibilities and the Cathedral organist, P.V. King, was asked to lead the choir. At this time the Ramblers' opera productions were getting into their swing, and the choral society was vanquished without achieving anything of note. King made another attempt in April 1901 to revive the society, and in May it was actually officially re-established with Haarburger as the conductor. In October of that year, *Messiah* was performed and then they again became inactive. — P.J. de Villiers* was very active with his choir in Boshof. They often contributed to variety concerts, singing light choral songs of the Victorian drawing-room type. It has been established that there was another choral society in Brandfort which was conducted on at least one occasion by Beavan. There may have been others but their activities have not been recorded.

4. Visiting artists

After the discovery of diamonds and to a greater extent after the discovery of gold, there was a spate of visits to South Africa by individual artists and famous concert companies. They all aimed ultimately to get to Kimberley and subsequently to Johannesburg, but as a break in their journey or to supplement their incomes from the larger cities, they gave concerts at other towns as well. Bloemfontein as the capital city of a republic was naturally included, but quite often smaller places like Fauresmith, Smithfield, Kroonstad, Boshof and Harrismith also had the opportunity of hearing the visitors. This did have the effect of establishing a measure of contact with the music life of Europe and by setting standards had a beneficial effect on local music making. — The Poussard-Bailey Company was on a world tour which included South Africa. Among its members were the following people: Horace Poussard* (violin), Amelia Bailey (soprano), and Florence Calzado (serio-comic soprano). They visited Bloemfontein in September 1867. The Miranda-Harper Company* (see also I/2 of this article) had the following members: David Miranda (tenor), Henry Harper* (baritone and cellist), Annette Hirst (soprano), Madame Leffler (alto), wife of Harper. They visited Bloemfontein in 1869 and 1870. Towards the end of her second world tour (1873-1876) Anna Bishop* (1812-1884), then 64 years old, arrived in Bloemfontein together with her accompanist Charles Lascelles*. She gave a series of very light concerts from 3 to 8 July. — Annette Albu (soprano) and Rose Albu* (pianoforte) were in Bloemfontein in July 1882. In their case, as in many others' in those days, the visiting artists appeared with local musicians. They came for another visit in February 1891. — George Witte, a famous Dutch musician and conductor of a Musikverein in Essen, Germany, and Madame d'Arch (soprano), gave a concert in Bloemfontein in June 1889, at which Witte played the piano, the flute and the zither. — Avon Saxon (baritone) travelled through South Africa for many years. He visited Bloemfontein in April 1892 and performed with Florence Fraser* and other artists. His next visit was in November 1892 and then he sang with Virginie Cheron*, the "Natal Nightingale". — Henry Clements (tenor) performed with Florence Fraser in Bloemfontein in October 1892. — The Vienna Orchestra, conducted by Herr Kopetzky, visited Bloemfontein in December 1892 and was enthusiastically received. It was a wind orchestra consisting of 27 players. — The Bell sisters (12 and 14 years old), visited Bloemfontein in August 1893. — Edward Epstein (Johannesburg singer), paid a visit in December 1893; Percy Ould* (violin) on 23 January 1894. — Marguerite MacIntyre - a famous Scottish soprano who scored great successes in operas presented in England, Milan and St Petersburg - appeared in Bloemfontein in July 1894 together with Haarburger's orchestra. Their performance was a triumph. — Marie Stefanie (soprano), visited Bloemfontein in January 1895 as a member of the T.A. Conby Music Society which presented scenes from operas. She had visited Bloemfontein in 1893 as a member of the Rand Grand Operatic Company. — Camilla Urso (French violinist), Scherek (piano) and Saunders (tenor), brought a programme of an unusually high standard to Bloemfontein in January 1895, but played to small audiences. — Mademoiselle Trebelli* (soprano), Charles Saunders* (tenor) and Davies (singer) were also in Bloemfontein (1895). — Sir Charles (1819-1895) and Lady Hallé (1839-1911) were others to visit the town. This conductor and pianist of German descent was the founder of the oldest permanent orchestra in England. Together with his second wife, the Czechoslovak child prodigy Welma Neruda, who had been playing on a 1709 Stradivarius since 1876, Sir Charles visited Bloemfontein on 3 September 1895. A soprano and a tenor were included in their programme and they were received with what amounted to reverential enthusiasm. — Sims Reeves (tenor), who had retired in 1891 after a brilliant career, was forced by financial difficulties to give concerts again in 1893. At the age of 78, in September 1895, he sang in Bloemfontein with his second wife, Maud Rene, who had been one of his pupils. — The Fanny Moody - Charles Manners Company visited Bloemfontein in March 1897. Both husband and wife were at the height of their careers. Fanny Moody, at the age of 31, was one of the most successful British singers at the time. — Annie Stevens (alto), of the Melbourne Conservatoire, visited Bloemfontein with an Australian group in January 1898. — Albert

Friedenthal (1862-1921), also at the height of his career, visited Bloemfontein in August 1898 at a time when he was already prominent among pianists. He loved travelling and had visited the Far East and South America before he came to South Africa. — Marie Albani (Marie de la Jeunesse) (1847-1930), was given a royal reception when she visited Bloemfontein in April 1899. She toured with a company which presented scenes from the operas. — It can be assumed that the violinist Reményi* also visited Bloemfontein, although there is no certainty about the date.

5. Light music

Shortly before mid-century the Christy Minstrel Movement started in America. It spread to England and from there it was transplanted by travellers and immigrants to nearly all parts of the world. In Bloemfontein the movement was launched by the Bloemfontein Original Christy Minstrels (1867) who were rapidly followed by the Juvenile Christy Minstrels (1867), the Bethlehem Christy Minstrel Company, the Rosebud Christy Minstrels (1877), the Boshof Amateur Christy Club (1880), the Bloemfontein Christy Minstrels (1882), the Bloemfontein Amateur Christy Minstrels (1884), the Rouxville Christy Minstrels (1885), the Bloemfontein Mohawks (1885), the Ethiopian Brothers (1888), the Kroonstad Christy Minstrels (1889) the Snowballs (1890), the Cronstadt Christys' (1889). Among the visitors who supplied the necessary variety were a London group who toured in 1869, the Ohio Christy Minstrels, the Harvey-Dougherty-Leslie-Graham Minstrels of 1873-1874, Leslie's Anglo-American Minstrels of 1882 and McAdoo's Minstrels, a Negro ensemble with women, in 1897. — Large numbers of individuals and groups of the music hall and vaudeville type came to South Africa on account of its mineral wealth. With their dance steps, hit tunes, conjuring tricks, sketches and comic shows of an endless variety, they were able to make a good living in this country. — In the Free State and Transvaal there was such a dearth of entertainment that particularly foreigners eagerly attended shows in the larger towns, enticed by high-sounding extravagant advertisements that always referred to celebrities and named the main British entertainment centres as "till recently" their home. The first "immense attraction" in Bloemfontein was a concert organised by P. and C. Riegelhuth "professors of the accordion and concertina", in a class-room in 1861. Haygarth* followed with his Drawing Room Musical Entertainments in 1870, the Colville-Lemon-Sawyer-Johnson group came in 1873, followed by the companies of Sinclair-Dallas (1876), Palmer (1877), Prof. Lover and three sisters Cassandra (1879), Charles du Val* (1880 and later), the Hewett Musettes (1883), the Troubadours (1883), the London Surprise Party (1888), Thorn's Operatic, Dramatic and Musical Combination (1893), Luscombe Searelle's* Star Variety Company (1893 and later), Harvey's Royal Midgets (1893), Keenan's Variety Company (1893), Snazelle's Music, Song and Story (1893), the Ellis-Newton Company (1893), the Payne Bellringers* (1895 and 1897), Fitts Cinematographic Concert (1898), the New Vaudeville Company (1898) and D'Arch's Marionettes (1898). In addition to these visiting groups a few South African enterprises visited Bloemfontein, and there must have been local efforts that did not quite make the grade for press notices.

6. Music and the State

The people of the Free State realised that music could be an elevating aspect of State occasions and included it in the programmes of such festivities. The desire was there, but the ability was often lacking. In this way, for example, President M.W. Pretorius was welcomed during an official visit to Boshof in June 1860 by an address and a choral song specially contrived for the occasion by a teacher named P.H. Boonzaaier. The song had four stanzas, the first of which went as follows:

> Hoog Ed'le President
> Gun, dat ons zang talent
> tot U zich wend'!
> Ontvang den Hulde-groet
> Van Boshof's zangren stoet
> Dien U hier thans ontmoet
> Wees bly gegroet.

> (Highly honoured President
> Grant that our talent for singing
> May turn towards you!
> Accept the greeting of honour
> of the Boshof singing group
> That now meets you here.
> We greet you joyfully).

This was sung to the tune of God save the Queen and after the song had been sung, the text and the score, with the signatures of the 20 singers, were handed to him. After the President's meeting that evening a group of 4 voices sang psalms, hymns and religious songs. — A greater variety of possibilities opened when a brass band was established in Bloemfontein. The artillery band blew to some purpose during the celebration of President Brandt's birthday in 1881 and marched at the head of the procession when a corner stone of the new Presidential Residence was laid in 1885. On the English side Queen Victoria's jubilee was celebrated with music and in the presence of the President in 1887. During a visit to Bloemfontein by President Kruger four months later, the Boers celebrated his birthday with a large-scale concert in the Town Hall and when Reitz was inaugurated as President in 1889, music played quite an important part at the ceremony. When the procession entered the church the organist struck up Handel's *See the conquering hero comes;* two members of the Israel* family played the Largo from Haydn's *Symphony No. 16,* a choir sang and when the procession left the church again, it was to the accompaniment of *Onward, Christian soldiers.* The same evening the band of the President Brandt Rifles played in the festively-lit Government Gardens. Similarly, at the marriage of President Reitz, music formed an integral part of the celebrations, and when the railway line to Bloemfontein was inaugurated in 1890, brass bands shared in the festivities (see chapter I/1).

7. The "Winter Evening Entertainments" and debating societies

These societies were established after 1875 in Bloemfontein and in the other larger towns tò keep people in touch with Western culture by means of lectures and addresses on technological developments such as telephone and telegraph communication, or on cultural subjects such as Shakespeare or great composers. A regular feature of these meetings was that apart from the lectures, they included recitations, small-scale performances and musical items. This provided local artists with a forum for their skills, and favourable conditions were created for something like a cultural life among the people themselves. The programme announced in the press for 1875 indicates the nature of these evenings.

13 May: Lecture by Dr Brill on "De Landstaal".

20 May: Readings and music.
27 May: Lecture by Archdeacon Croghan on Shakespeare.
 2 June: Readings and music.

The series for 1876 began with a lecture on "William the Silent" by Chief Justice Reitz, and Dr B.O. Kellner,* at the next meeting, spoke on "Cremation". Gradually these "Entertainments" began to assume an organised form - there was a committee responsible for the organisation, season tickets were sold to interested people, a chairman was elected to conduct the programme and a variety of music items, to which all competent local artists probably contributed, was presented. From 1877 onwards the press began to publish reviews of these meetings. It was at one of these meetings on 11 June 1884 that the "Free State Nightingale", Florence Fraser, made her first appearance. By 1885 the musical emphasis had become so pronounced that the evenings could actually be described as music concerts. — In the rural districts, in Smithfield, Ladybrand, Heilbron, Rouxville and Boshof, similar meetings were held under various titles. Although the abovementioned centres were the only ones mentioned by the press, there were probably many more. — The St George's Club in Bloemfontein instituted social evenings with a difference. Called "Smoking Concerts", the programmes were presented impromptu by members who had prepared their items independently and had volunteered to perform at the meeting.

8.   Educational institutions and music

Education in the Free State made rapid advances after 1870. Many new schools were established, syllabi were systematically co-ordinated, qualified teachers were appointed and regular inspection tours were instituted. Inspectors' reports reveal that singing, even though it was limited to church songs and the national anthem, was a permanent feature of education, although the reports were frequently unfavourable because of the scarcity of competent singing teachers. This is probably also the reason why the syllabi do not stipulate specific requirements for the teaching of singing; each school had to make the best of the talent at its disposal. Nevertheless, they were able to give concerts fairly often, usually in the form of a closing function at the end of the year. In 1893 a rather more elegant closing function was held at Fauresmith. On this occasion "Professor" Reepmaker van Belle was responsible for instrumental and vocal items of a high standard. The teaching of singing was gradually extended and psalms and hymns were supplemented by simple choral works, duets, quartets and instrumental solos and duets. — In Bloemfontein it was mainly the girls' schools, and Eunice in particular, which paid a great deal of attention to music. Characteristic of the convictions held in those days is the fact that music was regarded as a desirable addendum to the social attributes of a young lady and that boys' schools were left far behind in this sphere - paying very little serious attention to music. When Eunice was established in 1874, with a staff of 4 teachers, one of them was a music teacher, probably Sam Barratt.* In 1878 the talented Trixie Gilfillan* taught singing at Eunice. She was to achieve success as a singer in Johannesburg in later years. By 1883 there were three music teachers at Eunice, including the Swiss Fraülein Von Stettler and the German Fraülein Hamma, who discovered Florence Fraser's voice and had it developed in Europe. By 1890 Eunice had six music teachers. Important musicians connected with the school until 1899 were: Mrs Carl Fischer,* Mrs Hopwood, the singer Ortlepp (who was very well known in music circles in the Free State), Helen Schmedes who often appeared as soloist, the highly competent Miss M. Kiescke who was to play an important part in chamber music ensembles in Johannesburg, and the well-known Ivan Haarburger and Charles Israel who taught violin. The concert programmes presented by Eunice were usually of a high standard, and it is significant that in 1891, the school was able to organise its own Mozart centenary festival to commemorate the composer's death in 1791. On this occasion excerpts from the *Requiem* were presented on harmonium and piano, the *Piano concerto in d* was performed on two pianos, the overture to *Don Giovanni* was presented as a piano duet and a variety of arias and one scene in costume was selected from *Figaro*. President Reitz and his wife attended this concert. — The Anglican Church School for Girls, St Michael's Home (also established in 1874), was a close second to Eunice. This school was known particularly for its performance of operettas such as Reinecke's *Snow White* (1879), Schumann's *Pilgrimage of the rose* and again Reinecke's *Cinderella* (1880). In the years following, this school offered either an operetta or a cantata as proof of its musical labours. Other items heard at their concerts invariably had a proper classical quality. St Michael's was probably also the first school to undertake tours in the rural districts. — Music also played a prominent part in the work done at Greenhill Convent, where pure instrumental music was preferred. Their concerts were, without exception, favourably reported in the local press. — On the initiative of Dr John Brebner, Superintendent of Education, the annual music examinations held by the University of the Cape of Good Hope were introduced to Bloemfontein in 1894. The first examiner was Dr Barrow-Dowling* of Cape Town. Forty-seven candidates had enrolled for the examination and 39 certificates were awarded. The examiner's written findings were fully recorded in the press. In 1895 the music teacher Beavan* assumed responsibility for the introduction of Trinity College music examinations in Bloemfontein. Miss W. Mader of St Michael's became the first Free State student to be awarded the Teachers' Diploma in Music (1898). Elsa Leviseur* was among the five students who qualified as teachers at the examination in the following year. These were the first steps towards providing the Free State with qualified music teachers, but the outbreak of war put a temporary stop to all musical activity.

II. THE PERIOD FROM 1900 TO 1939
1. Various orchestras
2. The music theatre
3. Choral and musical societies
4. Music education in the Free State schools
   (i) General
   (ii) The Bloemfontein schools
   (iii) Private teaching
5. Visiting artists in Bloemfontein
6. The lighter musical genres
   (i) Musical comedies
   (ii) Revues
   (iii) Vaudeville or variety
   (iv) Groups and soloists
   (v) Tearoom music
   (vi) Jazz

1. Various orchestras
Many years were to pass before Bloemfontein could again boast of an orchestra as

active in the city's musical life as that of Ivan Haarburger's Bloemfontein Orchestral Society. The capitulation of Bloemfontein on 13 March 1900 was marked by the bright scintillating sounds of British military orchestras playing indoors but especially outdoors in the open air at promenade concerts. Outside their purely military duties, they were at the disposal of the civilians in presentations of light musicals, by bringing music to important functions and by supporting groups and soloists from the local British civilian population. The first military unit which should be mentioned, belonged to the Sixth Division. On 16 April 1900 they performed on Market Square (later called Hoffman Square) and elicited sharp censure from Elsa Leviseur.* The reason was summarised in *The Friend* of the next day: "Everyone joined in honouring the name of the beloved Queen of England in the late capital of the Orange Free State." The next important band was that of the Royal Irish Rifles which often played for charity (e.g. with Florence Fraser in aid of the Orange River Colony and London Widows' and Orphans' Fund, on which occasion she sang *Auld lang syne* with new Imperial verses supplied by Rudyard Kipling), but they also assisted Haarburger who had reassembled his Bloemfontein Symphony Orchestra in 1900. From 1902 to 1904 the Second Battalion of the Gloucestershire Regiment was stationed in Bloemfontein. Its large orchestra impressed the local inhabitants by regular concerts at which music in the light genre was coupled to forays into the operatic world of Donizetti, Wagner, Rossini and the Britisher Sullivan. When Florence Fraser wanted to present a number of her pupils to the public in 1904, they added brilliance to the occasion, and when Elsa Leviseur returned from musical study in Germany during the same year, she was honoured with a concert at which the band of the Rifles again played a part. Apparently her attitude toward these orchestral manifestations of Imperial power had altered in the interim. A band which must be mentioned is that of the Fifth Dragoon Guards. During their long stay in the Free State capital (1904-1909) they gave regular concerts, co-operated with civilian groups or permitted individual players to augment civilian ensembles. Some of the organisations that benefited from their presence were the Caledonians, the Amateur Dramatic and Operatic Society, the Musical Society and the Arts and Crafts Society. Frank Hyde, who had abandoned a promising career in Kimberley on the death of his wife, to establish himself in Bloemfontein, organised an Operatic Society in 1904 and launched a musical series which he entitled Hyde's Sunday Concerts. Both undertakings were to a large measure dependent on the support of the Dragoons. This band was also prominent when it performed at the inauguration of two new theatres: the Empire in 1905, and the much larger and more significant Grand Theatre on 19 February 1906. They also placed themselves at the disposal of British charities, functions for church funds and in support of sport clubs. In short, there was practically no British institution or organisation which did not at some time or another benefit from the musical largesse of the Dragoons or their willingness to assist various organisations in improving their financial status. The musical achievements of the Caribiniers (stationed in Bloemfontein from 1909 to 1912) were of a similar nature. Other regimental bands who stayed in Bloemfontein for shorter or longer periods can be credited with the same willingness to assist where possible. As the war clouds gathered over Europe, the regiments and their bands filtered away from the South African scene at an increasingly rapid rate. — With so many British models playing in the Free State capital, it is not at all surprising that the Bloemfontein civilians started thinking in terms of an own wind ensemble which could act as a stabilising factor in local musical life and counteract the continual movement of British groups. A short-lived Bloemfontein Orchestra was heard in 1904 but it was not until 1909, after much discussion in the newspapers, and with many people acting in an advisory capacity, that the Bloemfontein Town Band was able to make its debut at the skating rink of the Ramblers' (the Royal Rink) and in Victoria Park. Until 1913 the director was a certain Garrett who conducted their playing with great verve. He was followed by Frank Huggett, C. Kent* and G.J. Nicholls* This band was also known as the Bloemfontein Brass and Reed Band, or as City Band (Brass and Reed), sometimes abbreviated to City Brass Band. In the ninth year of its existence it was replaced by the later well known Railways and Harbours Band, whose awesome full name read: Second Battalion Railways and Harbours Rifles, Bloemfontein Detachment Band. This name might be interpreted as an unmistakeable indication that the band was a product of the civilian military power of the railways and that they were accordingly subjected to discipline (1918). In effect, it existed for a much longer time than any other Free State band, a total of 22 years, for 21 of which the band leader was F.H. (Harry) Mitchell. They became an institution at sports functions at the Ramblers', at the annual Agricultural Show, at the Tempe military hospital, at festivals, at sports meetings, though it must be acknowledged that the disciplinary aspect gradually subsided. One Sunday afternoon only two players arrived to entertain the expectant public in the Zoo. Finally, the band of the Regiment President Steyn, the successor to the short-lived Field Artillery Band conducted by C. Linsell, should also be mentioned. The band leader was T.C. Hornsby. Though it was financially supported by the Town Council, it disappeared from the scene in 1938, to be succeeded in the following year by a municipal band directed by A.G. Tempest. Probably the most important concert of this group was on 16 September 1939 when it contributed a strident addition to Bloemfontein's Huguenot Festival. — In a serious and determined frame of mind, Haarburger reassembled his Orchestral Society after a meeting held in the Ramblers' Club during October 1900. By 28 November they were ready to play in public, offering a bright little programme which hardly extended the capabilities of his amateurs. The concert had the additional support of Florence Fraser, of a visiting British singer, Charles Lodge, and, a few instrumentalists borrowed from the Irish Rifles. After this date, the orchestra played at intervals, sometimes with the support of the Rifles Band, but regularly with the collaboration of prominent soloists. In July 1901, Elsa Leviseur's new song, *The throstle,* was sung at an orchestral performance by Florence Fraser. Elsa had dedicated the song to Miss Fraser. On this occasion Elsa Leviseur performed the Allegro from Mendelssohn's *Concerto in g minor* on a grand piano which had been transported to the hall especially for the purpose. To give an adequate account of the orchestral score, Haarburger had reduced his orchestra to an octet, whose members were equipped with the technique demanded by the music. The struggle for existence of the Orchestral Society is an example of musical perseverance and of a sustained love for the musical art. Battling against almost insurmountable difficulties, the orchestral players of the capital city were always prepared for another struggle with music scores. They might be considered to be genuine pioneers in Bloemfontein's musical history. With a choir of 77 members and an orchestra of only 13 performers, the society tackled Handel's *Messiah* in November 1901 and repeated the performance in October 1902 with the support of

Gloucestershire Band members, an Italian flute player, Signor Giulio di Trani, and Florence Fraser. — The next year Haarburger departed on a visit to Europe where he was married in Lübeck to a Miss Elly Rosenthal. Prior to his departure he was given a complimentary benefit concert in the Ramblers' Hall, but after his return as a married man he never again conducted in Bloemfontein. He gave priority to his civil ambitions and business interests. — After several years spent in Durban, Ferdinand Israel* returned to the city of his birth in 1911 and immediately exerted himself for the re-establishment of the Bloemfontein Orchestra, for which he demanded a municipal subsidy and other urban advantages. Nothing came of this and Ferdinand had some bitter comments to make: "If the Council were not prepared to donate such a small amount, Bloemfontein should bury itself or succumb to sleep." Probably as a result of a visit paid by the Cape Town City Orchestra under their conductor Theo Wendt,* a group of enthusiasts plucked up enough courage in 1923 to try for an orchestra again. With Ivan Haarburger as chairman, Otto Menge* was appointed conductor and officiated in this capacity until the orchestra collapsed in the next year. All that this "orchestra" assembled, was a small group of strings led by Victor Pohl*, with Wansbrough Poles* acting as pianist. They only played two or three times, but in 1926 Menge endeavoured to re-establish the group again. He tackled the problem in a thorough way by visualising an orchestral school in which future players could be trained. Since Menge departed from Bloemfontein in the same year, nothing came of this project. — The last orchestral effort in the period up to 1939 came in 1935 when the Free State Philharmonic Society was created. This group had a more-or-less symphonic character as far as its composition was concerned and the programmes reflect a more adventurous approach to the easier classical works for orchestra. Much to the fore in this new venture were Frances Hertslet*, Adriaan Blau and Petrus Lemmer*. From the first concert on 26 June 1935 in the Visser Hall of the Normal College, until he left Bloemfontein in June 1938, Lemmer was responsible for the rehearsals and concerts of the Society. With his departure the orchestra also vanished. But in 1935 it was launched with great acclamation under the protection of the Prime Minister, General J.B.M. Hertzog, and other high-ranking officials. Justice F.E.T. Krause delivered an oration at the first concert, in which he prophesied a bright future for the ensemble. The orchestral contributions to the musical part of the evening's events included Schubert's *Unfinished symphony* and his *Rosamunde* ballet music, the *Peer Gynt suite* and Lemmer's orchestral transcription of a song by Tchaikowsky. A variety of professionals presented solo items and some chamber music. After their debut, the orchestra appeared in public two or three times a year, sometimes with the support of professional musicians who played concertos (e.g. Sydney Rosenbloom*, who played Grieg's *Piano concerto* on 22 October 1936) or delivered vocal items and one who even conducted professionally (Pickerill* on 4 November 1936). Their services were also required at important civil occasions such as the inauguration of the new Town Hall. On 12 May 1938, however, they came to their last concert. Probably an indication of the conductor's appointment as Musical Director to the Defence Force in Pretoria, the programme contained two marches: Mendelssohn's *War march of the priests* and Schubert's *Military march*. As usual, the programme was supplemented by singers and instrumentalists. This was the last effort before 1939 to start an orchestra in Bloemfontein.

188

2. The music theatre

Foreign companies as well as others from the Rand seemed to be cautious about Bloemfontein·as far as the production of operas and operettas was concerned. The reason was not the availability of a suitable hall, since Bloemfontein had an eminently suitable venue in the Grand Theatre. It was large enough, the stage had an ample area and it even boasted of an orchestral pit which could accommodate a medium opera orchestra; its acoustical properties were quite adequate. The actual reason 'should rather be sought in the uncertainty of the impresarios about Bloemfontein's ability to support expensive productions financially. A few statistics are sufficient to prove this point: from 1904 to 1912 Bloemfontein was visited by 5 companies; and from 1913 until 1939, over a period of 26 years, again only 5 companies ventured a visit to the city. — If the "British, Hebrew and Oriental Opera Company," which concentrated on two works based on Jewish themes, is left out of account, the first impresarios who brought opera to the Free State capital were B. and F. Wheeler* (1905). The works had to be produced in the old Town Hall, a decrepit old building without facilities for large-scale productions and acoustically awful. In spite of these disadvantages, the Grand Opera Company's cast of 100 and an orchestra of 30 musicians achieved definite successes, according to enthusiastic press notices, with *Il trovatore. Carmen* and *Faust*. When the Grand Theatre was inaugurated in 1906, the first performances in the new theatre were presented by the D'Oyly Carte Opera Company. On 6 consecutive evenings they performed 6 different works by the Gilbert and Sullivan combination. The attendance of the Bloemfonteiners left nothing to be desired and the city's enthusiasm rose to such heights that the Company was moved to pay Bloemfontein a second visit in the same year. Signor Tressi* from Johannesburg had an equivalent success with three frothy works, but in 1912 the Quinlan Opera Company from Britain, with a cast of 160 (including an orchestra of 50 members), brought grand opera to Bloemfontein - only after the inhabitants and the press had succeeded in convincing the actor-impresario Leonard Rayne that the visit would be a success. The question of lodging a company of this size had its problems since the Agricultural Show was on at the same time. The resourcefulness and local patriotism of the Bloemfontein inhabitants solved these problems in an original way: the Railways made available 50 beds in passenger coaches shunted onto a side line in the station; the general dealers, Champions, offered beds in their general store; a few were accommodated in the dressing rooms of the Grand Theatre; and the Grand Hotel offered to take the rest if they were prepared to bivouac in the banqueting hall. With the cordial support of the press, the excitement of the musical public, and by sheer good acting and singing the Company scored great successes with their productions of *Tannhäuser, Faust, Carmen, Lohengrin, La Boheme* and *La fanciulla del West*. The favourite among these works, as far as action, music and production was concerned, was certainly Wagner's *Lohengrin*. With this visit to Bloemfontein Quinlan afforded the city a climax in its operatic life. It certainly was not equalled by the Sullivan productions of the Wheeler brothers in 1913 and 1920. Bloemfontein had to wait until 1931 when the Gonsalez Italian Opera Company of Milan, consisting of 60 vocalists, dancers and orchestral members again presented first-rate productions of Italian operas. The D'Oyly Carte Opera Company came to Bloemfontein for the third time in 1936 and the next year the Carl Rosa Opera Company presented 6 Italian operas in the Grand Theatre (September 1937). If the enthusiasm with which the public crowded into the theatre is any indication, Bloemfontein was hungry for opera. But one cannot help wondering what the reaction would have been if the city at any stage had been freed of its starvation diet and offered the possibility of seeing and hearing opera regularly. — The English-speaking sector of Bloemfontein's inhabitants was ardently devoted to enjoyable participation in light comedy operettas, a tradition which has been upheld by the English in South Africa right into our time. The rest of the population takes a paternal interest in the Englishman's patriotic enthusiasm for singing simple, sentimental little songs in the context of humorous stories. The first of these societies to start its activities in Bloemfontein, was the Amateur Dramatic and Operatic Society which produced Robertson's *Caste* shortly after its establishment in 1903, with Lord Milner and other notabilities in the audience. This was followed in 1904 by Planquette's *Les cloches de Corneville.* In the review of this production, the *Bloemfontein Post* offered some good-natured criticism which penetrates to an essential weakness of countless productions in this genre: "Dr Baumann has a sweet tenor voice, but his natural elegant appearance and dignified bearing, clothed in the latest thing in fishing costumes, and his beautifully curled jet-black moustache and a golden wig, did not serve to recall to the mind of the audience the tar-stained, sun-browned sailor-lad whom he is supposed to represent." Nevertheless, *The Friend* could testify: "It is gratifying to know that the membership of the Society has increased by leaps and bounds." For some unknown reason this group ceased to exist after another successful production in 1905. Frank Hyde had started his Opera Society in Bloemfontein in 1904, but after an exceptionally expensive but successful production of *Maritana* (Wallace), he failed with a production of *Mikado,* probably as a result of the competition offered by the Dramatic and Operatic Society who were rehearsing *Pirates of Penzance* at the same time. Evidently Bloemfontein could not accommodate two similar societies, but it is curious to note that *both* ceased to exist in 1905. More important was the Garrick Club which commenced in 1911, existed until 1915, and was reincarnated in the same year for a second lifetime which lasted until 1921. Directed by the able and enthusiastic J.G. McQuade, the Club did excellent work during its existence by offering diversion and entertainment during the difficult war years. Probably they had lost their *raison d'être* when peace was re-established in Europe. In 1916 they put on Cellier's *Dorothy* in the Grand Theatre with a promising soprano, Cecilia Wessels,* singing the role of Lydia. The press surpassed itself in eulogistic effusion about this effort. They presented a similar work annually and were also active in organising the visit of the Cape Town Civic Orchestra to Bloemfontein in 1919. Barely two years later the Orpheus Club succeeded the Garrick Club, with Alban Hamer* shouldering the responsibility for the musical aspect of their productions. When he left, Charles Hamer* took over the work. This club remained loyal to the tradition until 1930, when they dissolved after a production of Monckton's *The country girl.*

3. Choral and musical societies
Of the societies which supported cultural life in Bloemfontein, the Oranje Vroue Vereniging (OVV) should be mentioned. Primarily this was a society devoted to social work among the impoverished Boers; but eventually the OVV increased the range of its interests, even passing a resolution on the necessity for instrumental music in the school curricula. They had their own choir, not for public performance, but in the service of charity. At their meetings there was generally a sprinkling of

musical items. Just a year after the OVV, the Ons Taal society was established (1908). Practically without exception there were vocal and instrumental solos and some ensemble playing at their meetings. Occasionally they hazarded a play or organised concerts. These ventures enabled them to create a fund from which they paid for a piano and made a substantial contribution towards the building of a Koffiehuis. Their major achievement was taking the initiative in the creation of the Vrystaatse Kunsvereniging (Free State Eisteddfod). For many years this society acted under the patronage of Ons Taal. — The English interest in music was represented by the Caledonian Society where the musicians Florence Fraser, Arthur and George Deale, and Ivan Haarburger performed repeatedly at the *Burns' nicht.* Also conducted by this Scots society were the *St Andrew's nicht* which offered English-speaking Bloemfonteiners an opportunity of exercising their art. At various times the Caledonians also had choirs and even a music society, and, inevitably, a proud bagpipe band. The advancement of music was, however, essentially concentrated in two societies: the Bloemfontein Musical Society, which existed from 1907 to 1911, and the Bloemfontein Music Club which was created in 1928. The first of these was in reality a choral society which saw to it that *Messiah,* Mendelssohn's *Walpurgisnacht, St Paul* and *Elijah,* Rossini's *Stabat Mater* and Haydn's *Creation* were heard in Bloemfontein. These performances usually took place with the support of overseas soloists or with singers from Johannesburg; judging by the newspapers the standard must have been satisfactory. — Miss Gertrude Hobday was so conscious of the lack of active music-making in Bloemfontein towards the end of the twenties that she created a small circle of members who were given the opportunity of exercising their art publicly. Towards the end of 1927 the circle had grown steadily and there was a growing public demand for sharing in these musical benefits. Co-operating with the Federated Music Clubs of South Africa started by Beatrice Marx*, the circle presented bigger concerts introducing, for example, the pianist Elsie Hall* or the Scots soprano Helen Jaffary. In future, concerts by visiting artists alternated with others presented by the members. These were generally solo recitals or chamber music performances. The club was growing through the collaboration of prominent musical personalities in Bloemfontein and by the arrival of new musicians such as Wansbrough Poles and Maud Hobday. But eventually they decided to return to their original policy and after 1931 offered concerts by Bloemfontein artists only. The meetings were held in a variety of venues, private dwellings, small halls and public halls. The programmes were generally compiled around a theme, a composer, a country or a period, and maintained considerable variety, stretching from the Baroque to the twentieth century. After 1937, however, the club again decided to introduce visiting artists, since enthusiasm was waning. An investigation made in 1939 testified that, of 108 members only 40 regularly supported the club concerts. A list of the Bloemfontein artists who performed at meetings of the music club is, at the same time, practically a list of prominent musicians in the city. The club thus fulfilled the function of providing for public performances by Bloemfontein musicians. — Another group devoted to music was the Arts and Crafts Society under the leadership of Mrs Ashburnham, the magistrate's wife. She was a singer and pianist who played an exceptionally active role in Bloemfontein's musical life, as an accompanist and by her participation in chamber music performances. The actual function of this society was the advancement of the fine arts and handicrafts. Nevertheless, between 1907 and

1912 they arranged numerous concerts which testify to judicious programme compilation and knowledgeable insight into music. Their musical headquarters were at 82 St George's Street, where small audiences of apparently well-informed and appreciative listeners gathered for music. Trios and sonatas by the masters were presented and in April 1908 Elsa Leviseur gave the first public performance of her pianoforte pieces entitled *African pictures*. On another occasion Florence Fraser sang arias and Lieder by Wagner, Massenet and Schumann. In 1909 a programme was devoted to vocal music and the chamber music of Mozart and Beethoven. Clearly enough, Mrs Ashburnham's group was dedicated to great music, but unfortunately it did not exist for very long. Its last concert took place on 12 June 1912; this was a vocal recital by a one-time member of the German Dessauer Opera Company, Anna Allers (Mrs Otto Dalldorf). — All three these societies tried to do justice to the old British predilection for the choral art. The Musical Society organised so-called Festivals and with the collaboration of soloists from overseas, or other parts of the country, they embarked on the popular round of Coleridge Taylor, Handel, Haydn and Mendelssohn. Rehearsals and conducting were managed by the enthusiast George Deale, who commanded up to 100 choral and orchestral members. The word "orchestra" should be interpreted as being a group of about 13 strings, supported by a piano or harmonium, at times with a wind player or two. The Caledonian Society supported a choir, also a youth choir, but their main interest was centred in the singing of Scottish songs. The Arts and Crafts Society presented a different picture. The Rev. Schneider of the local Lutheran congregation commenced rehearsing small vocal ensembles which, by 1909, had advanced to the stage where they could perform a programme of choral works by Beethoven. By 1911 they had progressed even further and presented exerpts from the *St Matthew passion* by Bach, a cantata by the same composer and Mozart's *Ave verum*. When the Polytechnical College was created as a subsidiary of the **Normal College** in 1912, the work of the Arts and Crafts Society became redundant and it vanished from the scene. But Pastor Schneider continued with his choral activity and reached a rather uncertain climax when he had Bach's *St Matthew passion* performed in its entirety (April 1914). Bloemfontein soloists sang all the solo parts and Schneider assembled an orchestra of 18 members to cope with the instrumental parts. — The English-speaking section of Bloemfontein society was by no means replete with the work done by these three societies. In their churches there was scope for choral singing and there existed a few other societies practising the art in some form or other. The Irish singer Carrie Duffield made her home in Bloemfontein during 1901. After a promising concert debut she announced her intention of creating a ladies' choir. Very soon she commanded 40 voices and during the one year of its existence this group made quite an impression. But Carrie Duffield, for some unknown reason, retreated from the musical world, and the choir subsided. The Bloemfontein Choral Society could look back on a reasonably long history of waxing and waning, resuscitations and collapses when it was recreated for yet another period by P.V. King, Florence Fraser and Carrie Duffield. But King left Bloemfontein in 1902 and another year passed before the choir got under way under George Deale. After 1903 there were virtually annual performances of the usual oratorios by Mendelssohn, Rossini, Haydn and Handel. This lasted until 1907 when the choir ceased to exist, presumably because it had merged with the Musical Society. In 1920 the possibility of rebirth was discussed when the able musician Wansbrough Poles became domiciled in Bloemfontein. The prospects looked rosy at this stage since Victor Pohl, Alban Hamer and his brother Charles were also available. Moreover, John Connell* launched his comprehensive schemes of practising choral singing in South Africa on a national scale in the same year. His Philharmonic Society, in combination with the Pretoria Choral Society, visited Bloemfontein in 1921 to join the Bloemfonteiners in a massed performance of Mendelssohn's *Elijah*. After this event, the Bloemfontein choir, under the direction of Poles, sang works of Coleridge-Taylor, and in 1922 he endeavoured to crown this choral activity with a concertante performance of *Tannhäuser*. It was rehearsed for performance with the Cape Town Symphony Orchestra, who were due for a visit to Bloemfontein in that year, but the performance fell far short of expectations. Poles, nevertheless, tackled Elgar's *King Olaf* and *The tale of old Japan* by Coleridge-Taylor, but the writing was on the wall, and in 1925 the annual meeting was informed that interest in the Society was practically non-existent. Six years later (December 1931) the Choral Society was revived for the umpteenth time. Wansbrough Poles was the conductor when they sang Haydn's *Creation* in 1932. There were no further performances, and in 1935 Poles left Bloemfontein to become inspector of music in the Cape Education Department. — In the meantime the baritone Charles Hamer had established a male voice choir (May 1924) which enjoyed an existence of 12 years under his direction. They often sang in Bloemfontein but were also successful at eisteddfodau in Johannesburg and Kimberley, and enjoyed the firm favour of the Free State countryside. The idea of a ladies' choir was advanced when Jennie Hadlow became a teacher of singing at the Eunice Girls' High School in 1915. Until 1953 this meticulous and knowledgeable singing teacher played a major part in practically every vocal undertaking in Bloemfontein. She left Eunice in 1923 to establish herself as an independent singing teacher in the city. With their accurately rehearsed choral singing and their neat and professional stage appearance, the Hadlow Choir became a feature at eisteddfodau. Another choir which came to the fore in the thirties was the Voortrekker Dameskoor of Daisy Bosman*. Their ideals were undilutedly national: the accent fell on Afrikaans compositions and the choir itself was dressed in Voortrekker costume. Elsa Dekker, the wife of Prof. Leendert Dekker, was the conductor from 1936. It did very well in eisteddfodau competitions and was a regular feature at national festivals. — A capable and enthusiastic musician is the *sine qua non* of church music. Until 1939 church music, with the exception of congregational singing, played an unbalanced and uncertain function in the Afrikaans churches, so that there is hardly any reference to Afrikaans church music as an art. The churches of English origin had quite different traditions and no dogmatic handicaps at all. Provided a capable man officiated at the organ, the *musica sacra* flourished. Church music in Bloemfontein is consequently actually only a resumé of music in the English churches. Under the first cathedral organists in the Church of St Andrew and St Michael, Stainer's *Crucifixion,* Gounod's *Gallia* and Moore's *Darkest hour* more or less marked the extreme height of ambition. Cathedral music improved towards the end of 1920 when Alban Hamer became organist. His brother Charles was in the Wesleyan Church at the same time, so that a coalition of their choral forces became a possibility. They merged the choirs in November 1923 for a performance of Haydn's *Creation*, with Charles playing the cathedral organ. Alban left Bloemfontein in 1926 to be succeeded by his brother, who experienced problems in obtaining members for the choir. Consequently, cathedral music gently subsided. In the Presbyterian Church

193

the oft-named Wansbrough Poles was organist from 1920 to 1935. Before his advent, there had been practically no church music, but under his lead there were sporadic performances of rather uninteresting music by second-rate English composers; *Messiah,* or parts of the oratorios, formed the exception. George Deale was the organist of Trinity Wesleyan Church and trained his choir mainly in British choral music by composers like Stainer, William Jackson and Elgar, with an occasional interspersion of *Messiah.* George Deale resigned in 1921 to be succeeded by Charles Hamer who, apart from his co-operation with the cathedral choir, conducted Spohr's *Last Judgement* on Good Friday 1925. After 1926 Cecil Barnes became responsible for the church music and organised a few organ and choral recitals. At St Margaret's, church music only came to the fore when Arthur Tann took charge in 1914. In that one single year there were no less than 7 organ and choral recitals in this church, but the next year Tann had left for Kimberley. Andrew Hutton officiated at the organ until 1939 and, besides a few performances of British cantatas, his main claim to recognition is the institution of carol singing which became an annual event in this church. In the Afrikaans churches the principal organists were P.K. de Villiers (Mother Church, 1911-1923), P.J. Lemmer (Mother Church, 1928-1939), D.J. Roode* (Bloemfontein North, 1932-1957) and O.A. Karstel* (Bloemfontein West, 1938-1960). Organ recitals with solo items and choral singing were, with all four organists, the exception rather than the rule. D.J. Roode was the most active of the four. He produced *Messiah* in 1936 with selected soloists, a well-trained choir and with Charles Hamer at the organ. It was broadcast by the Afrikaans service of the SABC on the national network as an historic occasion: the work was sung in an Afrikaans translation for the first time. Choirs also sang at state occasions such as the dedication of the Vrouemonument (16 December 1913), the burial of ex-President Steyn (3 December 1916), visits of members of Royalty (1925, and again in 1934) and the official opening of the new Town Hall in Bloemfontein (1936).

4. Music education in the Free State schools (1900-1939)
  (i)   General
 (ii)   The Bloemfontein schools
(iii)   Private tuition

(i)   General
Education in the Free State revived quite rapidly from the unfortunate camp schools of the Boer War. The revival was speeded up by the import of teachers from Great Britain in accordance with the conquerors' policy of reshaping the country to the British way of life. This had far-reaching results on education as well as music. Music teaching was given an Anglo-Saxon appearance which it has retained until the present time. In the schools, the teaching of music was severely handicapped by the absence of properly trained teachers. The teaching code in 1904 takes this fact into account when it stipulates that singing would only be accepted for inspection if a school had the services of a competent musician. The regulations governing singing during the first years of this century were marked by the conspicious part which the Tonic-Solfa system played in the curriculum. This method of pitch distinction had been developed in the 19th century by John Curwen for use in British Sunday Schools. Since trained staff was practically non-existent, the method could not achieve real results in the Free State beyond acquainting the children with the basic principles of melody, rhythm and the aural distinction between pitches. Shortly after her appointment as lecturer for singing and elocution at the Normal College (1923),

Daisy Bosman exerted herself to cope with the shortage of music teachers and to remove from the curriculum a variety of abuses. She was supported in her attempts by Dr. C.F. Visser (later principal of the Normal College), Charles Hamer and after 1927 by Wansbrough Poles. By writing articles for *Die skoolblad,* by lectures and a memorandum for the Education Commission, she insisted on more singing during school hours, the early introduction of staff notation, the introduction of Afrikaans songs in the curricula, the appointment of a vocal instructor, education in singing as a necessary qualification for admittance to the Normal College, and on the revision of the school music curriculum. P.J. Lemmer also committed himself to this problem. In his report of 1929 he pointed out the weaknesses in the vocal instruction and in 1931 published an article in *Die skoolblad,* in which he advocated the methods of Emile Chevé for introduction in Free State schools. O. van Oostrum published in the same periodical some thoughtful considerations about the singing of folk songs at schools as well as about sound educational principles which testify to his insight and knowledge of the subject. All these attempts were relegated to the background when singing competitions were introduced into the schools. Probably this followed on the work which Fred Farrington had done for schools in the Eastern Province of the Cape. The competitive principle forged rapidly ahead and by 1930 the Director of Education, Henri Pellissier,* reported that the competitions had gained ground in 8 out of 10 inspectorial circuits. He describes this as "an improvement of singing". High-ranking officials were willing to act as patrons, prominent musicians acted as adjudicators and at the prize-winners' concerts audiences of up to 1 100 were the rule. During the depression the high cost of these competitions as to time and money, gave rise to doubt and criticism. For the sake of cutting costs, the competitions were divided into a northern and southern section. Nevertheless, the inspectors' circuits were beginning to react against them, the circuit of Lindley as early as 1934. It had gradually become clear that singing was not the principal aim, but the competition as such. By 1939 they had been completely eliminated and their place was taken by singing festivals which emphasised the art aspect. These are still in existence in the seventies. A further characteristic of the Free State approach to school music was the emphasis on the Afrikaans song. This had been repeatedly advised by *Die skoolblad* with reference to the songs of Johannes Joubert*. In the thirties there was even a competition for South African composers to supplement the meagre repertoire. — As far as instrumental music is concerned, there were very few opportunities for promising pupils. The Free State Education Department had 67 pianoforte teachers in 1921 and the annual cost in terms of salaries and instruments was about R27 000. Tuition fees were raised and in 1922 the Department decided to abrogate all instrumental tuition. An exception was made in the case of children who had chosen music as a school subject for Junior Certificate or Matriculation. Music teachers were mainly taught at the Normal College, an institution which had been established as a Normal School in 1898. The College was amplified in 1912 by the creation of a polytechnical section which also provided for teaching in singing and instrumental playing. Daisy Bosman became the first lecturer in singing, Victor Pohl the first lecturer in violin and P.K. de Villiers, who came to Bloemfontein in 1911, was the pianoforte teacher. The students were regularly entered for musical examinations of the University of South Africa and the results were satisfactory. One of the most promising pupils of P.K. de Villiers was P.J. Lemmer. The two divisions existed concurrently until 1918 but then

195

they were separated and the polytechnical section eventually became the Free State College for Advanced Technical Education. — An Education Committee appointed in 1922 recommended that singing form an integral part of teachers' training and to implement this resolution Daisy Bosman was appointed for singing and elocution. Instruction in instrumental playing and role singing vanished from the scene and only class singing remained. Mrs Bosman was responsible for this until 1928. P.J. Lemmer succeeded her in 1930 and he maintained the position until 1939 when he left Bloemfontein. His successor was O.A. Karstel.

(ii)   The Bloemfontein schools

Of the schools in Bloemfontein, the private and church schools paid a great deal of attention to musical education. They generally appointed trained teachers on their staff, mostly from overseas, regularly entered the pupils for the music examinations and saw to it that the results were published. Of these, the Girls' High School Eunice takes pride of place. They had no less than 11 staff members for music in 1921, all well qualified persons, who also took part in the city's musical life. Apart from individual tuition in pianoforte, violin and singing, they emphasised choral work, for which Eunice had a firm reputation. Lecture recitals by visiting artists such as Danza* and Elsie Hall* and quarterly concerts by the Eunice Music Club were among their activities. At one stage the school even had an ensemble which boasted of the name of "orchestra". At the Anglican Church school for girls, St Michael's, more or less the same pattern existed. They had their instrumental group, choirs, individual teaching and a Music Circle which was responsible for concerts and lectures by guests. At this school the Chassevant method was applied. They had 104 pupils for piano in 1916, 5 for violin, 2 for singing and 31 studying harmony and theory; the Chassevant class had 7 sections in which a total of 42 children were taught. At the girls' school Oranje there was considerable musical activity in the form of cantata performances, alternated at times with an operetta. These were generally rehearsed with the assistance of P.K. de Villiers. The school was also active at the eisteddfodau and their examination entries were rewarded with good results. Naturally, the music tuition at this school was given by South Africans: with a few exceptions, all were Afrikaans-speaking. The Greenhill Convent School concentrated on careful pianoforte tuition and could boast of excellent results at the music examinations. At odd times they also produced an operetta. Of the boys' schools, Grey College should be mentioned first of all, primarily because Baldwin-Tann trained an "orchestra" at this school which performed successfully in public. They were generally supported by the school choir, Victor Pohl's violin playing, and pianoforte solos by various artists, of whom Mr Baldwin-Tann was one. In 1913 they even performed Sullivan's *Trial by jury* in the Town Hall. There are signs of a collapse after this, but in 1923 Victor Pohl again conducted a small "orchestra" consisting mainly of his own string pupils. Other teachers who contributed to this school's reputation were Wansbrough Poles, Tom Rayne, and finally Leonard Shepstone.* At St Andrew's school the music teacher was at times also organist in the cathedral. This was the case with Alban Hamer in 1920. After him Charles occupied both positions. During their period the emphasis at this school was on choral singing. At the Central High School M. Casaleggio* maintained a fine standard of choral singing at the school competitions and eisteddfodau.

(iii)   Private tuition

All the musicians named in this survey were also music teachers in Bloemfontein and all of them used the music examination system to have their pupils tested and to advertise their teaching by publishing the results. A few of them aimed at results by organising concerts at which their pupils performed. These were usually reported in the press. Among them there were Nellie Watson and C.E.M. Wright, principal of the Orange River Colony College of Music. At times the teachers also co-operated with one another to offer joint programmes of singing, violin, cello and piano. The emphasis throughout was very strong on pianoforte playing. At a very early stage (1921) the music teachers started protecting their professional interests by creating an Orange Free State Music Teachers' Association. The dispute about the abolishing of instrumental music posts at the school was quite acute at that time and the new Society attracted some attention by the firm way in which it put the case for instrumental teachers. The SASMT established a branch in Bloemfontein in 1928 and since it had a national character, the members of the Association soon joined the SASMT.

5.   Visiting artists in Bloemfontein

Many of the visitors to South Africa mentioned in the article on Touring Theatre Groups and Concert Artists in South Africa* also appeared in Bloemfontein. There is an interesting connection between economic prosperity and public concert life. This has also been established by Dr C.G. Henning* for the musical life of Graaff Reinet. Dr Japie Human* points out that up to 1903, immediately after the South African War, there was not a single visiting artist in Bloemfontein, whereas the number increased to 22 by 1910. Then there was a decrease up to 1913 and during the First World War there was a reduction to 6. In the post-war period, until 1922, during the depression, only one. This nadir was a direct result of the economic crisis which had originated in Germany. Up to 1929 there was relative prosperity and the number increased to 21, but during the depression of 1930 to 1933 the number subsided to an average of 3 per year and remained stationary at this figure until 1939. The number of South African musicians who visited Bloemfontein is quite large. There were 14 singers, 7 pianists, 6 violinists and cello players, one symphony orchestra (from Cape Town) and a number of vocal groups and a few military bands. Of the Bloemfontein artists who repeatedly performed in the capital city, some 16 vocalists can be named (Florence Fraser, Elsa Leviseur, Alfred Baumann,* Maud Barlow,* the two brothers Smit, Marie Wood, Daisy Bosman, Anna Dalldorf, Jennie Hadlow, Cecilia Wessels, Florence and Helen Cutmore, Bé du Preez, Maxie Bosman, Charles Hamer), 9 pianists (Josephine Fischer, Jean Ashburnham, Ellen Watson, Lillian Terry, Frances Hertslet, Sydney Rosenbloom, Ruby van Renen, Mary Stuart, Gertrude Hobday), 9 organists (P.K. de Villiers, Harry Rowe, Tom Raine, Wansborough Poles, Andrew Hutton, Alban Hamer, P.J. Lemmer, D.J. Roode, S. le Roux Marais) and 8 other instrumentalists (Victor Pohl, Ferdinand Israel, Otto Menge, Maud Hobday, Jessie Sheffield, Irene Hambleton, Alma Boshoff, and Joseph Fainsinger).

6.   Light music

(i)   Musical comedies

The period 1903-1929 was the great era of scintillating musical theatre, in Bloemfontein as elsewhere in South Africa. At first, these works were performed in South Africa by British companies, but after 1912 local players acquired a share in the performances. Impresarios were B. and F. Wheeler before 1913, then Leonard Rayne and to an increasing extent in the twenties, African Theatres. The most reasonable explanation for the sudden collapse of comedy theatre after 1929 is probably the spectacular rise of the film industry. African Theatres, the most important impresario of the time, simply diverted its attention to this new entertainment and stopped the expensive and elaborate theatre presentations. Reasons for the popularity of musical comedy are practically self-evident. One explanation is the excitement of colour and costume, another is the charm of simple melodies built around sentimental words, or the transparent orchestration which never insists on sharing in the events on stage, or the syrupy tales of young ladies in love with young gentlemen far above their station. These meagre skeletons were clothed in shifting panoramas of singing and dancing which polished the entertainment's smooth and amusing fabrications. The titles reveal the content to a large extent: Sally; No, no Nanette; The belle of New York; The girl from up there; My sweetheart; The little rebel; Madcap Loo; The Casino girl; The Geisha; The broken melody; Three little maids; The shop girl; The rose of the Riviera; The orchid; The Quaker girl, The Arcadians; The maid of the mountains; The girl in the taxi; The pink lady; Oh, oh Delphine; Hit the deck; etc., etc. The companies were generally announced as "straight from their successful season" in London or New York or some other place. They called themselves by some name such as London Musical Comedy Company, Royal Australian Comic Opera Company, Gaiety Company, London Gaiety Company, The Serenaders, Juvenile Musical Comedy Company, New Gaiety Company, Royal Comic Opera Company, Musical Comedy Company, or else it employed the name of the organiser, such as Leonard Rayne's ...., Williamson's ...., African Theatres' .... Initially the performances were given in the old Town Hall, but when the Grand Theatre was completed in 1906 it became a favourite venue for these presentations.

(ii)   Revues

These fabrications were built around some unexpected element, with singing and dancing, and emphasised laughable situations. They were offered in Bloemfontein until 1937. Sometimes, one single person was responsible for the whole revue, as in the case of Mel Spurr who entertained the Bloemfontein public on 1 July 1903. The names of the groups are representative of their transient and ephemeral nature: The Smart Set; The Ginger Girls; Million Dollar Girl Revue; Look Who's Here; Bubble and Squeak Revue; Nine Scarlet Troubadours; Merry Mascots. They all have in common the comical element, rapid changes of scenery and content, quick changes of costume, bright music and well rehearsed dance items. After 1913 they were usually coupled with a film presentation, but eventually the film industry embarked on revues adapted to its own particular possibilities. Since that time living theatre revues gradually subsided in Bloemfontein.

(iii)   Vaudeville or variety

These entertainments concentrate on a light touch, music, dancing, humour and amusing stunts following one another in quick succession, with the co-operation of conjurors, acrobats and even circus athletes. The vaudeville in South Africa was, as in the case of the revue, of the American variety. A quite sensational example of the feats of which vaudeville participants were capable, is reported in *The Friend* of 11 January 1916. One reads: "(his) weight lifting was quite remarkable, but his final effort, in which, while lying down, he supported a piano and player on his chest, and while lifting a heavy weight with his left hand, held a post horn in the other and sounded the call". This powerful man was called Signor Rogotta and probably came from Italy.

(iv) Groups and soloists

The most popular group to visit Bloemfontein before 1939 was the Steele-Payne Bellringers* who gave in all ten concerts in Bloemfontein. The Kennedy family can be mentioned next, but then there is a sharp deterioration to Buster Girls and Musical Stiffs. These entertainers were mostly singers who came to the city alone or in groups to present the lighter side of music. A fine example is Margaret Cooper who accompanied herself on the piano whilst singing her speciality, humorous songs mostly of her own fabrication. Likewise popular was Harry Lauder, who was entertained as an honoured guest by the Scottish community. Gracie Fields visited Bloemfontein in 1936 and had a great reception as famous singer, comedienne and actress. Her concert took place in the Grand Theatre.

(v) Tearoom music

As elsewhere in South Africa, quite a smart fashion came to Bloemfontein in the years before, but especially after, the First World War. Professional players, generally a duet or a trio, were engaged to play in restaurants or in cafes in two or three sessions of continuous music per day. The idea was to provide entertaining sounds while the guests were having refreshments. This meant that the localities concerned were fulfilling a social function since they became popular meeting places with a lively social intercourse between the guests. The fashion required that all should be dressed neatly and fashionably and that the musicians should provide a background of light, classical and popular music. A few of these locales were the Palace Tearooms, Wright's Tearoom (where the well-known conductor Jeremy Schulman* at one time earned his keep) and the Anglo-French Tearooms where exceptionally good musicians played until 1935. This Tearoom had the distinction of presenting at one time an ensemble of 7 instrumentalists, the largest company of musicians to play in a Bloemfontein cafe. Other rendezvous were Fichardt's Coffee Lounge, the Lounge Tearooms, The Arcade Restaurant (where singers were also employed) and the Rendezvous Restaurant which had, for many years, as its main attraction the entertainer Ready-Money Rodney. His revues were generally built around the person of an unrefined Boer called Van Tonder, who stumbled from one laughable situation to another and had a section of the Bloemfontein public in roars of laughter.

(vi) Jazz

Beginning in the 'twenties, the dance music collectively known as Jazz moved into Bloemfontein. First of all there was Kahn's Jass (sic!) Band (1922); followed by the Syncopated Four, Hildred Smith's Band, Klasie Fourie's Ambassadors (later restyled The Lyricals) and a number of other evanescent groups. In this connection it should also be noted that Bloemfontein's first Boere-orkes was established in June 1938 when there was great enthusiasm for everything with an Afrikaans colour. This was the year in which the cornerstone of the Voortrekker Monument was laid. Their leader was M. Casaleggio.

BIBLIOGRAPHY

HUMAN, J.L.K.: *Musiek in die Oranje Vrystaat vanaf 1850 tot aan die begin van die Anglo-Boereoorlog.* M.Mus. dissertation. UOFS, 1963. HUMAN, J.L.K.: *Die musieklewe in Bloemfontein, 1900-1939.* Doctoral thesis, UOFS, 1976. (This study contains a full list of books and lists all the relevant sources).

SOURCE
The Bloemfontein Post: January 1901-September 1901.
—J.P.M.

BLOEMFONTEIN ORCHESTRAL SOCIETY   Victor Pohl

BLOEMHOF SCHOOL   F.W. Jannasch, Elise de Villiers

BLOMKAMP, CHRYSTAL (DE ROO), *28 February 1918 in Cape Town;   now in Johannesburg. Pianist.

The exceptional musical talent which Chrystal Blomkamp revealed at an early age was developed by Franziska Witt* in Cape Town (1927-1929), Franz Moeller* in East London (1930-1935) and Douglas Mossop* in Johannesburg (1936-1939). During her years of study she passed music examinations with distinction. At the age of 14 Chrystal Blomkamp made her debut with the East London Orchestra in a performance of Grieg's piano concerto and the following year repeated the achievement with the Cape Town Municipal Orchestra* under Dr William J. Pickerill.* From 1934 she was heard on radio as a soloist and with orchestras conducted by prominent South African musicians; in 1942 she gave the first SA performance of the Delius piano concerto in Johannesburg. In 1947, after a period of preparation under Adolph Hallis*, she left for Holland to study under Cor de Groot and Jaap Spaanderman. Her successes in South Africa were followed by radio broadcasts from Hilversum, Paris, Oslo, Brussels and London and appearances in the Concertgebouw in Amsterdam as well as in Haarlem, Rotterdam and The Hague. Before leaving Holland in 1949 she appeared with Annie Woud and Laurens Bogtman and played at the South African Legation in The Hague. — In South Africa Chrystal Blomkamp resumed her concert tours and played concertos with the SABC Symphony Orchestra. In 1951 she was married to the violinist Leo de Roo* with whom she gave joint concerts in various centres in Europe and South Africa. A feature of Chrystal Blomkamp's programmes is the inclusion of music by South African composers and the introduction to this country of works by contemporary Dutch masters. — Thus she has for example interpreted works by the South African composers Peter Dakin, Eva Noel Harvey* and Klaas van Oostveen* at the University of the Witwatersrand. In support of Leo de Roo's work with the Orchestra of Johannesburg North she has quite often played concertos with their support.

—Ed.

BODENSTEIN, HANS, *3 January 1924 in Estcourt, Natal; now in Johannesburg. Musician of the Evangelisch-Lutherische Kirche, Hermannsburg. Choir leader.

Since 1948 Hans Bodenstein has been leader of the Singewochen of the Evangelisch-Lutherische Kirche in Süd-Afrika (Hermannsburg).* After training for one semester at the Kirchenmusikhochschule in Hanover in 1956 he became the leader of the Christoferus choir in Hermannsburg. With this choir he took part in a number of radio programmes and made several records during his eleven years as choir leader. In 1956 he was a co-founder and the first leader of the choral society of Lutheran church choirs. In 1961 he was a co-founder, and secretary from that year onwards, of the Advisory Commission of the Evangelisch-Lutherische Church in South Africa (Hermannsburg). Among other duties, his responsibilities include giving advice on the installation of organs, on the choice of choir music and on the training of organists and choir leaders. In 1966 he founded the South African branch of the Internationale Heinrich Schütz Gesellschaft and since 1967 he has been closely engaged in developing the indigenous church music of the Bantu.

PUBLICATION
Lutheran Hymn Book in 8 languages. Lutheran Co-ordinating Committee, 1970.

—Ed.

BODKIN, A.A. Diocesan College

BOKWE, JOHN KNOX, *18 March 1855 in Ntselamanzi, Lovedale; °22 February 1922 in Lovedale. Xhosa minister of religion; composer and journalist.

Named after the great Scottish reformer, John Knox, Bokwe was sent to the Lovedale Missionary Institution when he was very young and in January 1867 became house and stable boy to the Rev. James Stewart, the newly appointed head of Lovedale Institution. He remained at school from 1867 to 1870, when he was taken into the Lovedale Office as messenger. In 1876 the missionary promoted him as a part-time assistant in the publication of the Lovedale periodical *Kafir Express* and eventually he became telegraphist and bookkeeper of the Institution. During his twenty years' service, Bokwe also acted as choirmaster. — While still a boy, he had managed to learn to play both piano and organ with the assistance of Mrs Stewart, and this, together with his deep and sincere interest in the vocal music of the mission, led him to attempt composition himself. His first works date from 1875; they were written in staff notation (not Tonic Solfa) in beautiful calligraphy. — In 1897, after 27 years' service, Bokwe left Lovedale to join J.T. Jabavu as joint editor of a newspaper, the *Imvo Tsabantsundu,* but journalism was not his métier, and in 1900 he set to work to become a clergyman. He spent 1900 and 1901 in Scotland for ministerial training. On his return he acted successively as Evangelist and Probationer, and in 1906 he was ordained. But failing health compelled him to resign in 1920 and he returned to Lovedale to work with Dr J. Henderson. — Since Bokwe was a self-taught composer, his choral music contains a number of blemishes that would not have occurred had he been fortunate enough to find a teacher who could give him a thorough grounding in the principles of part-writing. However, these blemishes pale into insignificance when the man's achievements in spite of his · difficulties are taken into consideration. The hymn-book, *Amaculo ase Lovedale* (Lovedale Music) is a monument to Bokwe's insight and industry. Originally published in 1875 as a small booklet containing about a dozen original songs with Xhosa words and the music in Tonic Solfa notation, it was enlarged and reprinted in 1894, and again, still further enlarged, in 1910. — In its final form it consisted of three sections: the first of these contained four-part religious music by Bantu composers including Bokwe himself; the second, chiefly English hymn-tunes to which Xhosa words had been adapted; and the third, original music composed by Bokwe. Included in the book is the only authoritative version of the very first composition by a Xhosa convert to Christianity, the well-known "Ntsikana's Hymn", *Oluthixo Omkhulu.* In his transcription of this, Bokwe endeavoured to write down the original harmonisation as he had heard it when a boy. It displays the phenomenon of "parallelism", which is so characteristic of Bantu vocal music. — What distinguished Bokwe from almost every other musician who had adapted Bantu words to Western melodies, was his insistence on preserving the correct accentuation of the Xhosa vernacular, a point frequently disregarded by

201

missionaries. Naturally, he was not able to achieve this in all cases, and, as he wrote in four-part harmony, he occasionally had to ignore the Bantu principle whereby the meaning of words depended upon the pitch of the various syllables, which, if followed strictly, would have made independent harmonic part-writing impossible. What is still more unusual is that for one of his vocal duets, *The heavenly guide,* Bokwe wrote a simple pianoforte accompaniment which, though elementary, shows that he had realised some of the essential differences between vocal and instrumental writing.

WORKS
Amaculo ase Lovedale (Lovedale Music). Lovedale Press, 1875.   The peace of God. 'Ms., Lovedale, 19.1.1890.   Plea for Africa (words by a Glasgow lady). Paterson, Sons and Co., Glasgow, 1892.   Her last words. Ms., Lovedale, 17.10.1893.   Send the Light. Paterson, Sons and Co., Glasgow, n.d.   Vuka Deborah. Ms., n.d.   Ntsikana's Hymn, Oluthixo Omkhulu (Thou great God). Ms., Lovedale, 1904.   Ntsikana, the story of an African convert. Ms., Lovedale, 1914.   Welcome home! (Poem: Samuel Mzimba). Printed. Details unknown.   Bawo Ndixolele (Father forgive). Ms., Lovedale, n.d.   God bless the Prince of Wales. Ms., Lovedale, n.d.   Guquka. Ms., Lovedale, n.d.   The heavenly guide - a duet. Ms., Lovedale, n.d.   Iminiye nkosi. Ms., Lovedale, n.d.   Kugqityiwe (It is finished). Ms., Lovedale, n.d.   Lovedale holiday song - a part song. Ms., Lovedale, n.d.   Mayenzeke inlando yako (Thy will be done). Ms., Lovedale, n.d.   O! Ye hova vuka. Ms., Lovedale, n.d.   Moya Oyingowele (Holy Ghost). Ms., Lovedale, n.d.   Nakubatina namhla Sipilile. Ms., Lovedale, n.d.   Intlaba mkosi yakwa Tixo (Proclamation of God's war cry). Ms., Lovedale, n.d.   The Saviour died - a communion hymn. Ms., Lovedale, n.d.   Sindulule sinoxolo. Ms., Lovedale, n.d.   Thou Saviour of sinners. Ms., Lovedale, n.d.   Umanyano (unity). Ms., Lovedale, n.d.   Unganxami, ungapumli (Haste not, rest not). Ms., Lovedale, n.d.   Uzuko ku Tixo (Praise to God). Ms., Lovedale, n.d.   Yesu hlala nam (Jesus abide with me). Ms., Lovedale, n.d.

BIBLIOGRAPHY
VAN DER MERWE, F.Z.: *Suid-Afrikaanse Musiekbibliografie,* 1787-1952. J.L. van Schaik, Pretoria, 1958.

SOURCE
Cory Library for Historical Research, Rhodes University Library.

—Ed.

BOLDER, BOB   Barberton IV, Johannesburg 1, Pretoria 1, Touring Theatre Groups 4

BOLLEWYN QUARTET   Johannesburg 3 (ii), E.F. Schneider

BOLUS, HARRY, *28 April 1834 in Nottingham; °25 May 1911 in Oxted, England. Business man, botanist and music lover.

Bolus arrived at Algoa Bay in March 1850, through the agency of a Grahamstown merchant, William Kensit, who had encouraged Bolus to join him. A few years later he became the bookkeeper of a business firm in Port Elizabeth, and towards the end of March 1855, he settled at Graaff Reinet, where, until December 1874, he played a part in both the business and cultural life of the town. He married a sister of Kensit in 1857. His interest in South African flora dates from 1862. — He was the first secretary of the amateur dramatic society (1858), served on the committee of the agricultural society, contributed articles to the *Graaff Reinet Herald,* and was a founder member of the Athenaeum Club (13 August 1862), at the first meeting of which he delivered an address, *The science of recreation,* setting out the cultural and educational principles of the club. Harriet Rabone recorded that shortly after his arrival he played flute trios with her brother and Alfred Essex. She described him as a good flautist and mentioned that he possessed a beautiful instrument. Bolus and Essex clubbed together to buy a harmonium, but he was apparently able to play only slow tunes on it. His musical interest lay in choral singing and his connection with the Graaff Reinet Choral Society probably dates from 1859. Although Harriet Rabone did not mention his name once, her notes for 1859 indicate that the choral society was practising Mozart's so-called *Twelfth mass,* a work which Bolus presented in its entirety in 1866. She was the society's accompanist. — In 1864 Bolus took over the direction of the choral society and worked at improving musical and vocal standards. — For three years in succession on 6 October 1864, 5 August 1865, and 12 July 1866, he gave public concerts at which choral music was sung. The following works appear on his programmes: *Te Deum and jubilate* (G.B. Allen); the *Hallelujah chorus* (Handel); several choruses from *The creation* (Haydn); *The twelfth mass* (Mozart); ensembles and choruses from operas by Mozart and Gounod, some madrigals by Elizabethan composers and a few glees by British contemporaries. — After 1866 Bolus was no longer active in Graaff Reinet's music; he began to devote more attention to South African plants and to his business interests. After a visit to England he lived in Cape Town after 1878.

BIBLIOGRAPHY

HENNING, C.G.: *The cultural history of Graaff-Reinet, 1786-1886.* D. Phil. thesis, UP, 1970. Published by T.V. Bulpin, Cape Town, 1975, as *Graaff-Reinet: a cultural history (1786-1886).* RABONE, H. and ESSEX, A.: *The records of a pioneer family.* Struik, Cape Town, 1966. *South African biographical dictionary I.* Nasionale Boekhandel Ltd., Cape Town, 1968. *Standard encyclopaedia of Southern Africa II.* Nasou Ltd., Cape Town, 1970.

SOURCES

Graaff Reinet Herald: 1855-1874. *Graaff Reinet Advertiser:* 1860-1874.

—C.G.H.

BOLUS, WALTER, *in Nottingham, England. Businessman and musician.

Walter Bolus was a brother of the famous botanist, with whom he had business and musical interests in common. He probably came to South Africa in 1855 and settled in Port Elizabeth, where he started in business as trader. Harry Bolus* operated a branch of the business at Graaff Reinet. The musical interests of the two brothers were similar - both were flautists and singers. In February 1860, Walter was one of the foundation members of the Athenaeum Musical and Choral Society, of which he was first honorary secretary, and for about 6 years, treasurer; two years later, Harry was one of the foundation members of a similar society in Graaff Reinet. Walter played in Dr Dunsterville's* little orchestra, from about 1856 to 1860. — The musical life of Walter Bolus centred at first around the Glee Club, which was in existence from 1855 to 1866. So popular was the singing of this young male group of amateurs and professionals, that they were in demand when distinguished personages, such as Sir George Grey, HRH Prince Alfred (in 1860) and Sir Philip and Lady Wodehouse (in February 1864) visited the city. The Glee Club sang at the Theatre Royal and gave performances in Uitenhage and as far afield as Grahamstown. In September 1863, Walter was one of the soloists in the PE Theatre Dramatic Club's production of Balfé's opera *The rose of Castile;* and in the following year he was leader of St Mary's Church Choir, which gave a series of sacred concerts. — Like his brother, he no longer took a leading part in musical affairs after 1866. When he left Port Elizabeth in May 1872, the older members of the Glee Club and amateurs sang him a choral farewell on the quayside. He settled in Cape Town with his brother and became a well-known businessman.

BIBLIOGRAPHY

HENNING, C.G.: *A cultural history of Graaff Reinet, 1786-1886.* D. Phil. thesis, University of Pretoria, 1971.

SOURCE

Eastern Province Herald: 1859-1872.

—C.G.H.

BON, GERRIT, *9 November 1901 in Amsterdam; now in Salisbury (1977). Organist and composer.

Gerrit Bon's musical career had at the outset the advantage of a musical father whose influence has stayed with him throughout his life. Willem de Vries (organ) and Leon C. Bouman (pianoforte and violin) contributed to his musical growth and the boy progressed so rapidly that at the age of 14 he was awarded the Netherlands Organ Diploma. On the strength of this he became organist at the Lutheran Church in Nijmegen and three years later he was a choral conductor and an assistant organist in Amsterdam. At this stage in his life however, legal studies took precedence, though he maintained his interest in music and even had instruction in certain technical aspects of this art. But when he turned 21 he abandoned his study of law and emigrated to South Africa where he settled in Pretoria as a teacher of piano and organ. Until he left the city 34 years later to settle in Salisbury (1957), Bon played a dynamic part in almost every form of serious music practised in the capital. He improved his qualifications by gaining the FRCO in 1933 and the degree of Mus.Bac. from the University of Durham in 1946, and composed a considerable amount of music. — Primarily Bon was an organist all his life. In Pretoria he at first played the organ in the DR Church in Bosman Street (1924-1928) but then he switched to the DR Church Pretoria East where he remained organist until his departure for Rhodesia. After a large new organ had been inaugurated in the City Hall (1937) he commenced weekly recitals which led to his official appointment as City Organist in 1938. This position was created for Bon and he has been the only person to occupy it. The climax of his organ career came in 1950 when he performed all Bach's organ works in a series of 26 recitals to commemorate the composer's 200th birthday. The venue for this series was the Presbyterian Church. He has since repeated the feat in Salisbury, where he has given a total of 276 organ recitals, also including the complete organ works of Max Reger. At present (1976) he is the organist of the DR Church in that city. — When Petrus van den Burg's* ASAF Choir* ceased to exist in 1926, Bon started the Gemengde Koor Zanglust* which he directed until 1943. Notable performances were *Die Johannes Passie,* sung in the Bach Year to Bon's own translation, *The damnation of Faust* (Berlioz), Haydn's *Creation,* Mendelssohn's *Elijah,* the same composer's *Hymn of praise* (to commemorate the invention of printing), and the Brahms *Requiem* to mark this composer's centenary. These performances were presented either in the Church where Bon was organist, or in the City Hall. From 1929 he was a part-time lecturer in Music at the Pretoria Normal College (now the College of Education) and after 1935 he occupied the same position in a full-time capacity. The University of Pretoria had employed him as a part-time lecturer in Music since 1933, but in 1936 the University suspended the department. At the Normal College he inaugurated extra-mural classes in Music and created an Erato Choral Society for the College students. For major performances this body was generally amalgamated with the Zanglust group. After he had left Pretoria, Bon was for a short while a lecturer in Music at the University College of Rhodesia and Nyasaland, situated in Salisbury, and also played the organ in Salisbury Cathedral. After a short interim (1960-1962) during which he acted as music master at the Boys' High School in Pretoria, he finally settled in Rhodesia. His wife died in 1963 and two years later Bon again married. His second wife is Dulcie Bell, the Rhodesian-born composer of pianoforte music, with hom he often plays chamber music in various combinations. He continued his career as organist at the Cathedral and by 1975 he had given approximately 250 performances entitled *"Four centuries of organ music"*. Nowadays he devotes much time to research on Bach and Leopold Mozart on whom he has written various articles. At different times of his career Bon has been chairman of The South African Council for the Advancement of Music*, director of the Pretoria Bach Society, chairman and member of the Afrikaans Kerkmusiekvereniging, vice chairman of the Radio Board and a member of the Editorial Board of *Res Musicae*.

WORKS

A. Vocal

Ons eie kerkkoorreeks, edited by Gerrit Bon. Transvaalse Uitgewersmaatskappy, n.d.: 1. Verlossing (G.F. Handel) 2. Prys U Naam, o Heer (?) 3. Maak my U weë bekend (Bon) 4. Gebed (Bon) 5. God is Gees (W. Sterndale Bennett) 6. Die woord van my mond (Bon) 7. Jesus gaan ons voor (Adam Drese) 8. Heilig, heilig, heilig (Fr. Schubert) 9. Loflied (Bon) 10. Seënbede (Bon) 11. Verbly julle (Bon) 12. Spreuke 20 (Bon) 13. Hoop op God (Bon) 14. Die eerste Saligsprekinge (?) 15. Verootmoediging (Bon) 16. Aandgebed (Bon) 17. Die Koning van ere (?) 18. Barmhartigheid (Bon) 19. Salig is die sagmoediges (Bon) 20. Die Heer is getrou 21. Boetelied (Bon) 22. Lukas 19:10 (?) 23. Barmhartig en genadig (Bon) 24. Goedertierenheid (Bon). Bybelkantate (Scriptures). Ms., 1st performance in Heidelberg, 1933. Bosmankantate "Ter gelegenheid van het afscheid van Dr. H.S. Bosman". Ms., 1926. Jubileumkantate. Ms., n.d. Van Riebeeck Te Deum, for choir, soloist and organ. First performed 16 March 1952 in the Pretoria City Hall. Psalm 23. Ms., first performance 12 November 1955 in the City Hall, Pretoria. Psalm 46. Ms., first performance 15 March 1942 in Pretoria. Psalm 100. Ms., first performance 21 October 1949 in Pretoria. Psalm 126. Ms., n.d. Christmas Carol, no. 25 of South African Carols. Voortrekker Pers, 1968. Die hoogste offer, passion music according to St Mark's Gospel, for soloists, choir, orchestra and organ. Ms., first performance 29 April 1945 in the City Hall, Pretoria. Voortrekker feessange, for choir and orchestra. Duplicated ms., 1 December 1938: 1. Die Voortrekker se vaarwel (Leipoldt) 2. Nimmer of nou (A.G. Visser) 3. Vegkop (Totius) 4. Oggendskof (Theo Wassenaar) 5. Ons loof U feestelik (Theo Wassenaar) 6. Oproep (J.S. Barnard) 7. Hou koers (Theo Wassenaar) 8. By die mylpaal (Theo Wassenaar). Gebed van Paul Kruger, for choir and orchestra. Ms., n.d. Voor in die wapad brand 'n lig, for choir and orchestra. Ms., n.d. Geloftelied (own text). Ms., 1933.

B. Theatre Music

Jarriago, opera in 3 acts, for soloists, choir and orchestra (C.F. Rudolph). Ms., first performance at Normal College, Pretoria, in 1952. Incidental music to plays produced by Volksteater,

Pretoria.   Marionette-opera, for voices and strings. Ms., n.d.

C. Songs

Beurtsang, duet. Ms., n.d.   Lied van Mali die slaaf (Leipoldt). Ms., n.d.   Die rose van herinnering (Visser). Ms., n.d.   Consolation. Ms., n.d.   Sannie. Ms., n.d.   Amoreuse liedeke (Mostert). Ms., n.d.   Winter (A.D. Keet). Ms., n.d.   Berusting (T. van den Heever), FAK Volksangbundel no. 230. HAUM, Cape Town, and J. de Bussy, Pretoria, 1937.   Skoppensboer (E. Marais). Ms., n.d.   Die stil avontuur, with string quartet (E. Eybers). Ms., n.d.   Verlange (A.D. Keet). Ms., n.d.   In die klooster (Visser), for soprano and string quartet. Ms., n.d.   O blye nag. Ms., n.d.   Sterrelied. Ms., n.d.   Die roos (Visser) Ms., n.d.   Was ek 'n sanger (Visser) Ms., n.d.   Kom dommel (Mostert) Ms., n.d.   Berusting (J. Celliers). Ms., n.d.   Ritrympie (T. van den Heever). Ms., n.d.   Swaansang (Visser). Ms., n.d.   Prinses van verre (Visser). FAK Volksangbundel no. 110, Nasionale Boekhandel, 1961.   Kollegelied (C.F. Rudolph). Ms., 1942.   'n Eenvoudige liedjie (Van Bruggen). FAK Volksangbundel no. 172. HAUM, Cape Town and J.H. de Bussy, Pretoria, 1937. FAK Volksangbundel no. 217. Nasionale Pers Bpk., 1961.

D. Instrumental

Rapsodie oor Oud-Nederlandse liedjies, for small orchestra. Ms., n.d.   String quartet no. 1. Ms., n.d.   Quartet for oboe, violin, viola and cello. Ms., n.d.   Trio for flute, violin and viola. Ms., n.d.   Variations on Hansie Slim, for oboe, clarinet and bassoon. Ms., n.d.   Nine snaps, for oboe and pianoforte. Ms., n.d.   Psalmus Praetorianus, for organ: 1. Fantasie en fuga   2. Pastorale, based on Ps. 23.   3. Toccato festivo, based on Ps 146. Ms., first performance 6 November 1955 in the City Hall, Pretoria (Pretoria Centenary celebrations).   Siciliano, for organ. Ms., n.d.   Rondino, for organ. Ms., n.d.   Fantasia and fugue on "For all the world" (melody of Vaughan Williams), for organ. Ms., n.d.   Festival march in honour of Totius, for organ. Ms., n.d.   Etudes and variations for pedal solo, for organ. Ms., n.d.   Eight arrangements of Bach chorales, for organ. Ms., n.d.   Sonata for pianoforte. Ms., n.d.   Sonatina for pianoforte. Ms., n.d.   L'Hiver, for pianoforte. Ms., n.d.   Pianoforte suite in 14 parts. Ms., n.d. Improvisation on a hymn tune. Ms., first performance 29 April 1957.

PUBLICATIONS

Kerkmusiek. *Die nuwe Brandwag* 1/2, May 1919.   Die modernisme in die musiek. *Nuwe Brandwag* 1/4, November 1929.   Die musiekbiblioteek. *The SA Music Teacher* 5, October 1933.   Musiek en demokrasie. *Castalia,* October 1934.   Volksang en musiek. Jaarboek, *Tydskrif vir Wetenskap en Kuns* XIII, 1938/9.   Ons volksang. *Die Huisgenoot* XX/2, 6 January 1939.   Kuns en volksmusiek in Suid-Afrika. *Jaarboek van die Skrywerskring,* Johannesburg 1941.   Eyssen se Bybelkantate. *Die Brandwag,* 29 December 1944.   Bybelkantate oor die eter. *Kultuur (Filma)* 2/2, January 1945.   Bach (1750-1950). *Lantern* XX 1/2, February 1951.   Marks and remarks. *SASMT pamphlet* series 2 conference speeches, 1955-1957.   Robert Schumann (1810-1856). *Res Musicae* III/1, September 1956.   Enkele beskouings oor Mozart. *Lantern* V/4, 4 May 1956.   The President's message, *The SA Music Teacher,* June 1957.   Die Bach-kultus. *Res Musicae* VII, June 1961.   The violin bow Bach used. *Res Musicae* VIII/5, September 1962.   Some suggestions for a different approach to the teaching of harmony. *Res Musicae* IX/1, December 1962.   Johann Sebastian Bach - the complete organ works presented and performed in 20 weekly recitals. *Unitas Press,* Salisbury, 21 May 1970.

BIBLIOGRAPHY

BENTUM, ALPHIA: *Gerrit Bon,* B. Mus. script, UP, 1965.   VAN DER MERWE, F.Z.: *Suid-Afrikaanse musiekbibliografie, 1787-1952.* Van Schaik, Pretoria, 1958.

SOURCES
Res Musicae: III/1, 2, 4; VIII/2; XI/1. Die Burger: 21 Desember 1938. Pretoria News: 23 November 1949, 21 June 1950, 28 September 1956, 4 April 1957. Transvaler: 26 September 1938, 20 December 1938, 4 August 1948, 1 October 1949, 17 January 1952, 19 February 1955. National Documentation Centre for Music, HSRC, Pretoria.

—J.P.M.

Bon, gerrit, *23 June 1938 in Pretoria; at present in Durban. Son of Gerrit Bon (sen.)*. Oboist.

After receiving his first music lessons from his mother, Gerrit Bon was a violin student of Harold Ketelbey* for five years but, while still at school, he abandoned the violin and began to concentrate on the oboe under the guidance of Jos de Groen.* In 1957 he went to Holland where he continued his studies under Jaap and Haakon Stotijn. On his return to South Africa in 1958, he accepted a position as third oboist with the SABC symphony orchestra, but by 1961 he had been promoted to acting principal oboist of the orchestra, a position he permanently filled from 1962 to 1972. Gerrit Bon frequently plays as soloist or in chamber groups, in radio broadcasts as well as in concerts. In 1972 he was appointed lecturer in woodwind instruments in the new music department of the Natal University. — He is still very keen on his career as a soloist however, and has given first South African performances of works by H.W. Henze and Penderecki. Lately he has also taken to the hobo d'amour and applies himself to the dissemination of knowledge about musical instruments at schools and over the radio.

— Ed.

Bonamici, arturo (arthur), *July 1849 in Florence; °29 January 1907 in Port Elizabeth. Theatrical manager and impresario.

Bonamici appeared on the South African scene as manager of the new Standard Theatre* which was opened in Johannesburg on 12 October 1891. The following year he joined forces with Edgar Perkins to form the Lyric Opera Company and in 1895 he brought out the complete Royal Italian Opera Company of 51 artists including the soprano Anita Protti and the baritone Michele di Padova, an orchestra with two conductors, a chorus master and a ballet company. It was probably the greatest musical venture undertaken in South Africa up to that time. This ambitious undertaking was followed by some famous singers who came to South Africa under his aegis. On 17 April 1899 Madame Albani sang at a special benefit concert for Bonamici to celebrate his "20th year as an impresario". — Little is known of his private life. He was married to Rose Sophia Toler, but they had no children. He probably retired to Port Elizabeth during the Ánglo Boer War, and died there a few years later.

BIBLIOGRAPHY
Wolpowitz, L.: James and Kate Hyde and the development of music in Johannesburg up to the First World War. J.L. van Schaik, Pretoria, 1969.

SOURCE
Register of estates Cape Colony: MOOC 6/9/564, DN 390.

—C.G.H.

Boneggio, g. Cape Town Studio Orchestra, M. Molina, Spanish Dancing in South Africa.

BONICOLI, VENCESLAO, *in Florence; probably died in Italy. Nineteenth century bandmaster, clarinet player and composer.

Before Bonicoli came to South Africa in 1865 as bandmaster of the first battalion of the Ninth Regiment, he had been a clarinet artist in Vienna, St Petersburg and Paris. According to *De Zuid-Afrikaan* he was member of the Haydn Society, the Guido Monaco (of Arezzo) Society in Rome, and the Sainte Cécile Society in Paris. He lived in Cape Town from 1865 to 1867, and then in King William's Town until 1870. During his free hours he was an exceptionally industrious musician. Following his first public appearance at an agricultural show in Cape Town (14 November 1865), he participated in concerts organised by the Cape Town Musical Society, the Apollo Union, and the German Liedertafel Germania, to which he contributed vocal and instrumental works of his own composition and arrangements for various combinations. — His programmes were usually long - extending to sixteen items in a single evening - but Bonicoli saw to it that they ended cheerfully. One evening he concluded a concert with a clarinet solo *The farmyard dance, or Burlesque for clarinet* which the *Cape Argus* described as follows: "He introduced all sorts of animals, if not in bodily presence, at least vocally, to the audience. Ducks and drakes quacked, cocks crowed, hens clucked, turkeys cluttered, donkeys brayed, cows lowed, calves bellowed and pigs grunted through his clarinet, to the very life." — In King William's Town he reinforced his programmes with local talent; after his "grand farewell concert" in June 1870 he received R58 from the mayor as a token of appreciation. After five industrious years (during which he married a South African girl, née Hiddingh) he returned to Europe, eventually to settle in Florence, his birthplace. In 1883 he was knighted with the Order of the Crown of Italy by King Umberto I, to whom he dedicated a composition.

WORKS (compiled from reviews).
The Scotch mountaineer variations, for clarinet.   Grand quartet, for piano, harp, harmonium and clarinet.   Grand fantasia, souvenir de Bellini (based on extracts from the operas La Straniera, Beatrice, Norma and I Puritani) for E flat-clarinet and piano.   Grand quintet, for clarinet, cornet, alto horn, trombone and piano.   The dead bride, song.   The foundling, song.   Receive my song with kindness, song.   Midnight galop.   The farmyard dance, or burlesque for clarinet.   The Cape Town waltz, 1867.

SOURCES
Het Volksblad: 1865-1867 and 1883.   *The Cape Argus:* 1865-1867.   ROSE, JOHN E.B.: *Diary*, ms. in the South African Public Library, Cape Town.   BOUWS, JAN: Sy boerewerfdans was treffer by Kaapse gehoor. *Die Burger*, Cape Town, 9 February 1967.
—J.B. (amplified)

BONIFACE, CHARLES-ETIENNE, *2 February 1787 in Paris; °2 December 1853 in Durban. Playwright and actor, teacher of languages and music, journalist.

The prison warder Antoine Boniface and his wife Bénigne (née Fleurot), whom he married in 1790, managed to survive the Reign of Terror with their son Charles-Etienne, who was three years old at the time. During the Directorate, Antoine, like other French citizens, was banished to Mahé on the Seychelles Islands for his revolutionary sympathies. It is said that he illegally tried to marry a widow there. His wife, who reportedly enjoyed the favour of the English admiral, Sir Sydney Smith (who had been imprisoned in Paris during the Reign of Terror), stayed in Paris with two sons. The available information seems to point to the fact that Charles-Etienne visited the Seychelles in 1805, after the death of his father, with a view to possible inheritance. A Portuguese ship possibly brought him from the Seychelles to South Africa in February 1807, so that he was 21 years old when he arrived in Cape Town equipped with a knowledge of German, Italian, Spanish and Portuguese. At times he had to exercise this ability to earn his keep. — In Cape Town, among French compatriots, he encountered a "Fransche liefhebbery toneel" which presented French works, with and without music, in their own theatre. Prior to his arrival he had probably gained some theatre experience, because in the very year of his arrival he put on his own comedy *L'Engagé*. From then on his career in Cape Town was interwoven with the theatre, frequently to his material embarrassment. His adaption of Lamartélière's *Robert chef des brigands* landed him in such financial trouble that he attempted to run from his creditors. But he was arrested, and released only on the cognisances of F.A. Heyneman (later to be his father-in-law) and J.L. Petersen* (who became a collaborator). — Musical and a good amateur player of the Spanish guitar, possessing sufficient musical knowledge to write (in beautiful calligraphy) simple melodies and guitar accompaniments, Boniface is an example of the typical French predilection for theatre in which dramatic fare is integrated with music and dancing. His French texts were at first translated by the school principal, P.C. Schonegevel, but later he himself translated them into Dutch; he even wrote in Dutch and actually employed a kind of Coloured people's Afrikaans in *De nieuwe ridderorde of De temperantisten* (1832). He also succeeded in obtaining the collaboration of local musicians and dancing masters such as F.C. Lemming*, Jacques Bertrand*, J.L. Petersen and Monsieur Cesar, but as frequently he estranged collaborators and friends with his excitable temperament. — With the exception of *Les deux chasseurs et la laitière* (an opèra comique by Duni), *De barbier van Seville* (an opera buffa adaptation with music by Paisiello as well as Rossini), *Het beleg en het nemen van Troje* (a ballet pantomine) and *Sapho* (sic) (a ballet with dialogues and dancing), all Boniface's productions were plays (his own, translated or adapted), into which he had introduced songs and dance numbers. — In order to make a living he pursued a variety of occupations, either individually or simultaneously, but without ever prospering. He advertised himself as a teacher of languages, as a dancing master and teacher of the Spanish guitar; he sold musical instruments and strings, and in 1827 he established the first SA lending library of printed music. For six months in 1830 he was the editor of the new newspaper *De Zuid-Afrikaan* and in 1839, for a somewhat longer period, the editor of *The Moderator/De Meditator* - all this without achieving any lasting success. His tempestuous relationship with Mietjie Heyneman was consummated with their marriage in 1817, but this, and the birth of a son in 1818, merely added to his responsibilities. In 1827, after repeated changes of address, he was declared bankrupt. — Eventually, in 1844, he left the Cape in the company of a former slave woman to settle in the newly proclaimed British colony of Natal. After acting for a time as editor of *De Natalier en Pietermaritzburgsche Trouwe Aantekenaar* and quarrelling with his printer-publisher, he tried to form a drama and music company and to teach the guitar, but he steadily declined. Finally in his 66th year he committed suicide.

WORKS

Requeil des chansons avec accomp.t de guitarre à Mlle H. Joubert; 24 ariettas and chansons with his own guitar accompaniment. Eight, probably original songs, attached to the manuscript of De Burger Edelman. Les adieux en romance (Buyske collection); composer problematic but the guitar accompaniments by Boniface. Slotzang van dorp aan de grenzen (J. van Lennep). Le douze Août, song with guitar accompaniment in four verses. Composed for the family Cloete in Pietermaritzburg in 1848. Six bluettes, Pietermaritzburg, 1846, borrowed tunes by Boniface. La morte du latanier, vaudeville, Pietermaritzburg, 1846; contains 18 melodies of French and Dutch origin with Boniface's own accompaniments. Dago or De Spaansche bedelaars, contains vocal items with guitar accompaniment by Boniface. Variations on a French folk song, for guitar. Clasius or Het proces om een komedielootje, Cape Town, 1834, contains arranged and original melodies.

— The cultural significance of Boniface is far greater than the importance of his music. The small number of melodies with guitar accompaniments which have been discovered and can be attributed to him with some measure of certainty, are all in the manner of light French brunettes, pastourelles and bergerettes with accompaniments consisting of simple arpeggio progressions. His numerous borrowings from folk music and the contemporary opèras comiques do testify to an active interest in music; in the history of South African music they are only of interest in an appreciation of Boniface which places him among the pioneers of theatre coupled with music and dancing.

BIBLIOGRAPHY

BOSMAN, F.C.L.: *Drama en toneel in Suid-Afrika, 1652-1855, Deel I.* Pretoria/Cape Town, 1928. BOSMAN, F.C.L. and DREYER, A.: *Hollandse joernalistiek in Suid-Afrika gedurende die negentiende eeu.* Cape Town, 1930. BOSMAN, F.C.L.: *Inleiding tot De Nieuwe Ridderorde of De Temperantisten.* Johannesburg, 1945. BOUWS, JAN: *Die musieklewe van Kaapstad, 1800-1850, en sy verhouding tot die musiekkultuur van Wes-Europa.* Cape Town/Amsterdam, 1966. NIENABER, G.S.: *Van roem tot selfmoord.* Johannesburg/Pretoria, 1939. NIENABER, G.S.: *Bluettes by Charles Et. Boniface, early Natal author and wit.* Photocopied issue with introduction, University of Natal, 1963.

SOURCES

De Kaapsche Stads Courant en Afrikaansche Berigter, 1807 and later. *De Zuid-Afrikaan,* 1830. *The Moderator/De Meditator,* 1837. FRANKEN, J.L.M.: Uit die lewe van Charles Et. Boniface. *Annals of the University of Stellenbosch,* April 1937. SCHOLTZ, J. du P.: Boniface en Afrikaans 1830-1832. *Tydskrif vir Wetenskap en Kuns,* December 1939. VAN DER MERWE, F.Z.: Die musiek van C.E. Boniface. *Tydskrif vir Wetenskap en Kuns,* April 1949. BOUWS, JAN: Charles Et. Boniface en die musiek. *Kwartaalblad van die Suid-Afrikaanse Biblioteek* XVIII, Cape Town, 1963. CORNEVIN, ROBERT: Charles Et. Boniface (1787-1853) journaliste et écrivain trilingue d'Afrique du Sud. *Annales de l'Université de Madagascar 9,* Tanarive, 1968. BOUWS, JAN: Charles Et. Boniface en sy ghitaar. *Die Burger,* Cape Town, May 1964. BOUWS, JAN: Kaap in 1824 binne grense van beskawing. *Die Burger,* Cape Town, 13 November 1968. BOUWS, JAN: 'n Nuwe lig op Boniface, die Kaapse Kruidjie-Roer-My-Nie. *Die Burger Vol. 54,* Cape Town, 12.7.1969. BOUWS, JAN: The first musical circulating libraries of Cape Town. *Libraries and people,* Cape Town, 1970.

—J.B. (amplified)

BONNAR, ELEANOR, *1887 in Durban; °28 May 1970 in Cape Town. Music teacher.

Eleanor Bonnar was educated at Durban Girls' College, where she also received her first music lessons. Later, she studied at the RCM and obtained the LRAM and ARCM diplomas. In her will she endowed this institution with scholarships. After continuing her studies in Munich under Godowsky and in Vienna under Hartricksen, she returned to Durban, where she taught privately until 1922, when she was invited by W.H. Bell* to join the staff of the South African College of Music* in Cape Town. She served the College until 1945, befriending and assisting a number of talented students financially. After her retirement, she continued teaching privately until the day of her death. — Among her pupils was Hilda Seeligsohn (née Leaman, *1900 in Durban (?); °14 February 1970 in Cape Town). After pianoforte training under Eleanor Bonnar, Hilda Seeligsohn won the Unisa Overseas' Scholarship in 1918. She was the scholarship's inaugural student.

SOURCE
S.A. Music Teacher 78, June 1970.

—Ed.

Boosey & Hawkes (South Africa) (Pty) Limited, dealers in and publishers of music. Prior to the formation of this company as a subsidiary of Boosey & Hawkes Limited of London, the South African representatives of the British company had been African Music & Book Co., in Cape Town. On 28 May 1947, when Boosey & Hawkes (SA) (Pty) Ltd was registered, the premises and business previously conducted by African Music and Book Co. were taken over and the proprietor of this firm, Mr Weiss, became a minority shareholder in the new company. The first managing director was William Goldbourn, who had come to South Africa from London. The object of the company is to offer the facilities of stocks of everything musical or related to music, including sheet music and the publication of new works. — The company made good progress, despite difficulty in obtaining import permits during the immediate post-war years. Goldbourn retired in June 1956, and was replaced by James Gibbs, during whose term of office the company moved into larger premises in Cape Town. In 1959, the firm opened a branch in Johannesburg, which occupied Time House in Eloff Street Extension, and a year later this became the Head Office. Gibbs then returned to the parent company in England and was succeeded by Stuart Pope in 1961. — There was rapid expansion during the next years, including the establishment of the Hammond Organ Company of South Africa (in which Boosey & Hawkes Manufacturing (SA) holds a substantial share), and its subsidiary, Boosey & Hawkes Manufacturing (SA) (Pty) Ltd. In August 1966, the well-known music company, Darters (Pty) Ltd, was purchased and became a wholly owned subsidiary. Recent acquisitions are a portion of the equity of Dennis van Rooyen (Pty) Ltd, and the flotation of a wholly owned subsidiary - Darters (Randburg) (Pty) Ltd, both companies engaging in retailing musical instruments and sheet music. — The present Board of Directors (1970), headed by A.R. Clapham (Chairman), consists of A.M. Richards (Managing Director), Mrs K.E. Webb, A.R. Terry and A.S. Findlay.

—A.M.R.

Booth, Leslie Webster, *in Birmingham; living in Knysna in 1968. Tenor.
Webster Booth started his singing career as a solo chorister at Lincoln Cathedral, England. When his voice broke he returned to Birmingham, studied commercial subjects and gradually started singing again. Dr Richard Wassell, organist, choir-

211

master and conductor of the City of Birmingham Orchestra eventually took charge of his musical education. After singing in the chorus of the D'Oyly Carte Opera Company for four years, there followed an engagement to sing in *Messiah* with the Royal Choral Society, engagements at Covent Garden to sing in *Rosenkavalier* and *The magic flute*, and a contract to appear in *Faust*, the first colour film to be made in England. This film led to his meeting with Anne Ziegler (Irene Frances Eastwood, 10 years his junior), who had been engaged to play the part of Marguerite, and to the forming of the Booth-Ziegler partnership. In addition to oratorio singing, they appeared in films, countless musicals, variety shows and operetta productions. After visiting South Africa briefly in 1948 during a world tour, they returned in 1955 for concert appearances in Cape Town and Rhodesia. This was followed by a third visit early in 1956, and in July of the same year they decided to settle here permanently. — Their career in South Africa includes appearances, singly or as a team, in *Angels in love* (Johannesburg), *A night in Venice* (Johannesburg and Durban), *Waltz time* (Springs and East London), *Merrie England* (East London and Johannesburg), *The vagabond king* (Durban and Springs), *Jack and the beanstalk* (East London), and *The glass slipper* (Johannesburg). Booth has sung in performances of *Messiah, Elijah, Creation* and *Dream of Gerontius* in Port Elizabeth, and sang the tenor part in Beethoven's *Choral symphony*, conducted by Sir Malcolm Sargent, during a Johannesburg Festival. He and Anne Ziegler were well-known personalities on Springbok Radio and the English Service of the SABC, and had a studio for singing and stagecraft in Johannesburg.

—Ed.

BORCHERDS, MEENT, *3 September 1762 in Jemgum, East Friesland; °28 February 1832 in Stellenbosch. Clergyman, music dilettant.

After theological studies in Groningen, Borcherds joined the East India Company in 1784, and in the same year was sent to the Cape where, on 13 May 1785, he became the third minister of the Cape Town community. He married shortly afterwards and, on his own request, was transferred to Stellenbosch where he remained in service until December 1830. — It is apparent from two extant notebooks that, in addition to historical and poetical works, Borcherds dabbled in music. The notebooks include a number of copies, with a few Dutch translations, from C.P.E. Bach's *Gellerts geistliche Oden und Lieder*. Most important is the earlier notebook in which fifteen short pieces for piano or harpsichord appear without the name of a composer. Nine of these are minuets, four have "Murky" basses, and two are gigues. The second gigue, called *Commolan*, was definitely written by a different hand. It is the work of a music amateur, possibly Borcherds himself. — It is almost self-evident that Borcherds would have taken an active interest in congregational singing and the installation of his community's first church organ. When the jubilee of his fortieth year as minister was celebrated, Wilhelm Brandt, organist of the Lutheran Church in Cape Town, arranged and conducted a performance of vocal and instrumental music in Stellenbosch, members of the orchestra having been selected from the "most respectable classes of Young South Africans".

WORKS
Six minuets from the Ms. of Rev. Meent Borcherds. Edited by Jan Bouws, Cape Town, 1964. (These minuets are attributed by the editor to Rev. Borcherds).

BIBLIOGRAPHY

BORCHERDS, CLAUDE: *A Borcherds tapestry* (stencilled 1965). BORCHERDS, P.B.: *An autobiographical memoir*. Cape Town, 1861. BOUWS, JAN: *Musiek in Suid-Afrika*. Brugge, 1946. BOUWS, JAN: *Die musieklewe van Kaapstad, 1800-1850, en sy verhouding tot die musiekkultuur van Wes- Europa*. Cape Town/Amsterdam, 1966. CONRADIE, E.J.M.: *Hollandse skrywers uit Suid-Afrika I*. Pretoria, 1934. VAN WARMELO, WILLEM: *Liederwysies van vanslewe*. Cape Town, 1949.

SOURCES

BOUWS, JAN: Ds. Meent Borcherds en die musiek. *Tydskrif vir Geesteswetenskappe* IV/2, Pretoria, 1964. BOUWS, JAN: Ons eerste komponis? *Die Huisgenoot* XLII/2378, Cape Town 27 November 1967. *Kaapsche Courant* XVI/829, 1 December 1821. *The South African Chronicle and Mercantile Advertiser* III/116, 24 October 1826. *The South African Commercial Advertiser* II/60, 1826. Two ms. notebooks of Rev. Meent Borcherds. DR Church Archives, Cape Town.

—J.B.

BOROWSKY, BOB, *23 June 1929 in Pretoria; living in Iohannesburg in 1977. Baritone and pharmacist.

Son of a cantorial tenor and the younger brother of the tenor Jules Borowsky*, Bob began singing solos in a synagogue at the age of six. He is still active in synagogical music. After matriculating in 1946, he qualified as a pharmacist. — In 1947 he sang in the choirs of John Connell's Johannesburg Municipal Opera seasons. While studying singing with Bruce Anderson* between 1952 and 1954, he sang roles in operas, operettas and oratorios for the Johannesburg Operatic and Dramatic Society* and the Johannesburg Philharmonic Society*, including *Trial by jury* (Gilbert and Sullivan), *The gypsy baron* (J. Strauss) and *Yeomen of the guard* (Gilbert and Sullivan). An interpreter at the Australian Legation in Rome from 1954 to 1955, his vocal talent was developed by Gilda Alfano. Since his return to South Africa in September 1956, he has sung baritone roles for the Rota Opera Company, the National Opera of South Africa and the South African Federation for Opera*; since 1963 he has sung for PACT in operas by Puccini, Verdi, Donizetti and Strauss. — His light music partnership with Doris Brasch* has become widely known in South Africa and Lourenço Marques as a result of commercial records and extended concert tours. For broadcasting he has sung in solo recitals and with orchestras. He has also had roles in a number of radio recordings of operas.

—Ed.

BOROWSKY, JULES, *7 May 1922 in Poland; presently (1977) in Johannesburg. Tenor and pharmacist.

The eldest son of David Borowsky, a cantorial tenor, and brother of Bob Borowsky*, Jules was brought to South Africa at the age of 4 when his family emigrated from Poland. As a child he sang solos in synagogue choirs and still sings much cantorial and sacred music. He matriculated in 1938 and qualified as a pharmacist; immediately afterwards his voice was developed by Bruce Anderson*. In 1952 he studied singing in Italy with Fernando Calcatelli and Paolo Silveri. He has broadcast frequently for the SABC as soloist in opera, oratorio and concerts, and sang the tenor roles in *The telephone* (Menotti) and *The barber of Seville* (Rossini) in 1960 and 1961 respectively. He toured for PACT as Eisenstein in *Die Fledermaus* (J. Strauss).

213

Borowsky has become known throughout South Africa as an exponent of light music in partnership with Rita Roberts* and Doreen Distiller.

—Ed.

BORRIUS Potchefstroom 1

BORWELL, EILEEN.   Johannesburg 3(ii)

BOSHOFF, ALMA B. Kok

BOSHOFF, HESTER CATHARINA CECILIA (NÉE BARNARD), *6 June 1895 in Senekal; °15 June 1969 in Potgietersrust.

After initial vocal instruction under Miss Wimble, a teacher, S.P.E. Boshoff* (afterwards professor), advised her in 1913 to go to Stellenbosch where, until the end of 1914, she had singing lessons from Ruby Spear. Subsequent to her marriage to Professor S.P.E. Boshoff in September 1915, she made frequent concert appearances in Potchefstroom when her husband was employed there. In 1920 they went to Amsterdam where she continued her studies under Hendrik van Oort at the Music Conservatoire. They returned to Potchefstroom towards the end of 1922. She frequently sang in concerts, gave singing instruction at the Potchefstroom College of Music* and adjudicated at eisteddfodau. — She and her husband settled in Pretoria in 1932, and Hester Boshoff appeared in concerts and as soloist with the Gemengd Koor Zanglust* until 1949, when poor health obliged her to end her singing career. — She collaborated with Dr Japie Schonken in collecting and recording the melodies of folk songs, which appeared in the anthologies *Afrikaanse volksliedjies Deel I: Pieknickliedjies* (J.H. de Bussy, 1918), and *Afrikaanse volksliedjies Deel II: Minneliedjies* (J.H. de Bussy, 1921). Comments on the texts of the songs were written by her husband and Professor L.J. du Plessis.

—Ed.

BOSHOFF, JANIE (MRS BURGER)   Middelburg

BOSHOFF, STEPHANUS PETRUS ERASMUS, *14 July 1891 in Senekal district; °20 April 1973 in Potgietersrust.

S.P.E. Boshoff received his schooling at Riebeek West and at Grey College in Bloemfontein. After receiving his BA (Hons.) degree in 1911, he obtained the MA degree through private study and studied in Amsterdam from 1913 to 1914. In 1915 Boshoff was appointed temporary professor and in 1917 permanent professor of Afrikaans-Nederlands at the PUC for CHE. From 1920 to 1922 he studied in Europe for the D.Litt. degree. After two years in Cape Town (1930-1932) he was Director of Education in the Transvaal until 1934. After his retirement he took over and expanded a correspondence college. — In Potchefstroom he collaborated with his wife, Hester C.C. Boshoff*, and Prof. L.J. du Plessis in collecting and publishing Afrikaans folk songs. A notable result of these endeavours was the publication of a series of articles in *Die Huisgenoot* (2 October 1931-18 December 1931) in which he deals systematically with the language, poetical worth, wisdom and general character of Afrikaans folkloristic creations.

PUBLICATIONS (only in respect of music)
Afrikaanse pieknickliedjies. Words and explanatory notes (in conjunction with L.J. du Plessis). Part I(a): Die Lied, die Volkslied, etc. J.H. de Bussy, Pretoria, 1918.   Part I(b): *Afrikaanse*

214

piekniekliedjies, words and melodies, 24 songs. J.H. de Bussy, Pretoria, 1918. Part II: *Minneliedjies*, words and melodies (noted down by Dr Japie Schonken and Mrs Boshoff): 62 items, of which 13 are based on Dutch folk songs, 11 on art songs and translations, 15 are more or less genuine Afrikaans folk songs and 22 are fragments. J.H. de Bussy, Pretoria, 1921.

—Ed.

BOSMAN, DAISY (NÉE MAARTENS), *21 June 1878 at Edenburg; °11 December 1943 at Tegernsee, Germany. Soprano and choral conductor, who interested herself in Afrikaans art songs.

After leaving Eunice School in Bloemfontein, where she had received piano and singing lessons from Miss Schmedes, Daisy Maartens qualified as a teacher, and in 1899 married the painter Jacques Bosman. Their son was born in a concentration camp in Kroonstad while her husband was a prisoner of war in Admednagar in India. Some years after peace had been negotiated, the Bosmans lived near Clanwilliam and left for Germany in 1905, and stayed there for four years. Daisy studied singing at the State Academy in Munich. The Director of the State Theatre in Munich, Felix Mottl, invited her to sing roles in Wagner operas. But, she preferred the concert stage. In 1909 they returned to South Africa. — Following a concert tour through South Africa, Daisy Bosman was appointed lecturer in music at Bloemfontein Normal College (around 1912). She held this post until 1932, and went on concert tours, sang with orchestras and in early broadcasts. According to Bosman di Ravelli* she did not possess outstanding dramatic talent, but "could make of the smallest song an unforgettable experience". She contributed significantly to the musical aspirations of the Afrikaner and became the first vocalist to publicly sing an Afrikaans song: in 1909, at a pianoforte recital given by her brother-in-law, Bosman di Ravelli, in Bloemfontein, she sang his setting of *Winternag,* a poem by Marais. After she and her husband had moved to the Free State, she was often heard in Bloemfontein, as well as in the country towns, with Afrikaans songs generally included in her programmes. This feature was noticed e.g. by the *Volksblad* which reported: "Mrs Bosman is doing missionary work by educating our public to an awareness of our own original creations". This was by no means all, since she also exerted herself in articles for the cause of the Afrikaans song and when new music syllabuses had to be drafted for the Free State schools, she included Afrikaans songs in the repertoire. At national festivals, such as the internment of Emily Hobhouse's ashes in the Vroue Monument, in 1929, she conducted her Voortrekker Choir in performances of for example the National Anthems of the Free State and the Transvaal. Her career in Bloemfontein was interrupted on two occasions, when she left on a visit to Germany and Switzerland in 1922, and again in 1932, when she visited Munich and Vienna for the purpose of making a study of vocal methods and opera. In 1930 she resigned from the staff of the Normal College and resumed her concert career, regularly emphasising the Afrikaans song as represented in those days by le Roux Marais, Doris Beyers, Lettie Joubert and D.J. Roode. The Columbia Record Company made a number of recordings of her interpretations of songs in Afrikaans. — In February 1939 Daisy and Jacques Bosman took their daughter Maxie*, who had a serious illness, to Germany for a possible cure. All three died in Germany: Maxie before the outbreak of war and her parents during the war.

PUBLICATION
Die Sangkuns. *Die Huisgenoot,* 25 July 1924.

—Ed.

BOSMAN DI RAVELLI VERE, (JAN GYSBERT HUGO BOSMAN), *24 February 1882 in Piketberg; °20 May 1967 in Somerset West. Concert pianist. Bosman adopted the pseudonym Di Ravelli in 1902 in Leipzig, when he began his career as a concert pianist. His father was a Bosman of Bottelary in Stellenbosch and his mother, whose maiden name was Boonzaaier, came from Winkelshoek, Piketberg.

His brother, ten years older than himself, took lessons with Dr Barrow-Dowling* in Cape Town and his sister (eight years his senior) had lessons with Professor Jannasch* at Bloemhof, Stellenbosch; but it never occurred to anyone that Jan Gysbert was particularly musical. In Murraysburg, about 1893, his sister "taught him his notes", but apart from accompaniments, he played nothing out of the ordinary before he was 16 years old. Then, in the year before his final BA examination, he heard the spiritualised Chopin-playing of Apolline Niay* in Cape Town and, by way of contrast, the physical virtuosity of Friedenthal. No other career but music was possible after these experiences. In spite of great consternation in the family, Bosman had his way and on 1 October 1899 he sailed for Britain on the "Briton", stayed in London for a short while and then completed his journey to Leipzig where he found himself among pro-Boer Germans. — He was interviewed by Professor Reinecke, head of the Conservatoire and became a pupil of Dufour, assistant to Winterberger (professor of piano at the Conservatoire) and when he had advanced beyond the initial stages, Winterberger took Bosman as his pupil (1901). Exceptionally charming by nature, mentally alert and of an intellectual maturity far beyond his years, Bosman had no difficulty in making friends. Especially significant for the future course of his career was his friendship with the American-born Princess Wolkonski and her two children Sergei and Varvara. Through her good offices the young man was initiated into the aristocratic circles of Italy, Paris and Berlin and made the acquaintance of persons who had the power to promote his career. In July 1902 the Wolkonskis left Leipzig and although Bosman remained in touch with them until 1914, he never saw them again. — In the meantime his receptive mind absorbed everything that Europe had to offer in the way of architecture, the fine arts and music. Even after January 1900, when the remittances from South Africa failed to materialise, he persevered in his chosen career by giving lessons in English and the classical languages. One of his language pupils was the well-to-do young German, Hesse, conductor of a choir and a chamber orchestra with whose assistance Bosman appeared for the first time in public in November 1902. Soon afterwards he joined Hesse and his orchestra on a tour through Saxony and developed an inflated opinion of himself. He was cured of this through Tauber's training in Berlin and by the privilege he had of attending Pachman's practices for concerts: an awareness of genuine artistry was awakened within him, of the spiritual moulding of sound into significant unities. On his return to Leipzig he had become a different person. — In 1903, on Winterberger's recommendation, he went to Berlin where he made his debut with Chopin's second piano concerto, supported by Hesse and his chamber orchestra. Typically, the Princess von Bülow exerted herself to make the concert a success. This was followed by an extended tour through Germany. Bosman's student years had come to an end and he was launched on a career which took him to London, Paris, various German cities and the French spas. He had become the first South African who had forged into Europe's musical life as a pianist. — In September 1905 Bosman returned to South Africa to visit his parents and to establish himself in this country. In the ensuing five years he gave a great many concerts in the Cape, the Free State and the Transvaal without showing any notable profit. Between his tours he enjoyed the friendship and freedom of the house in several homes in Pretoria, including those of General Smuts and General Beyers; Dr Klaas Hoogenhout offered him the hall of the Teachers' Training College for lectures; Mrs Bal van Lier* assisted him at his lectures with her Conservatoire choir; and Gustav Preller wrote on his behalf to some 25 towns for guarantees of R50 per year for one concert, and a lecture-recital at a school. Only four replies were received. — From his conversations with Preller came the idea of an indigenous South African music based on Bantu motives. In this matter Preller and Bosman erred, although Bosman seriously tried to study Zulu traditional music during a ten days sojourn with Dinizulu, chief of the Zulu people. His three songs to Afrikaans words are musically Western and reveal little trace of Bantu influences. Their only claim to remembrance is the fact that they were the first attempts at setting Afrikaans poetry to music. On another level Bosman propagated old church music in which he recognised great beauty, and exerted himself for a cause which must have been very close to his heart - the creation of a national academy of music. Also important are his contributions to *Die Brandwag* (1910-1912) which represent pioneering writing on music by an Afrikaner. However, he was far in advance of his time: there was too much political and national unrest for music to prosper. Disappointed, he returned to Europe on the "SS Bulawayo" on 28 November 1910 to resume his chosen career as a pianist. — Travelling with him was the talented composer of Afrikaans songs, Charles Nel* and another musical Afrikaner, Lionel Meiring. Back in Munich, he taught them the basic techniques of playing the piano and then entrusted their studies to the guidance of properly qualified teachers. The concert bureau of Wolff in Berlin remembered him from earlier years; Sgambati in Rome offered him the opportunity of playing with an orchestra and Emily Hobhouse helped him to organise a piano recital in Rome. His career got into stride again but in 1914 the War brought virtually everything to a standstill. He was in London when it started and was seriously ill with Spanish "flu" after the war came to an end. He convalesced in Locarno (1919) and used his forced idleness to study Arabic, supplementing his studies by delving into Hebrew, Chaldean, Samaritan, Syrian and later also Persian. One result of his studies was the compilation of an Arabic-English glossary for the Koran, which for a number of years was used by Sir Thomas Arnold at the Oriental School of the London University; another was his translation of an Arabic travel book of the 12th century, which could not be published because of the Second World War; and thirdly he translated various poems from the time of Mahomed and even earlier, into English. His volume of English poems, *In an Italian mirror,* was also written shortly after the War and published in 1921. — In 1921, Bosman resumed his career as a concert pianist when he played in Paris, and in quick succession in five other French cities. Sharp's of England became his sole concert agents and from then on his worries were at an end. During the approximately nine cold months each year, he gave up to 80 concerts, extending from Spain in the south to Scandinavia in the north. He used the summer months to prepare himself for the tours of the next year and to continue his oriental and classical studies. Florence became his headquarters after 1932. — The outbreak of World War II finally destroyed Bosman's world. Not until 1952 was his house in Florence restored to him. Two years later, while preparing himself for a second return to the concert world, he nearly lost his right arm in an accident. In

217

February 1956 he decided to return to South Africa and stayed with Maggie Laubscher in Somerset Strand. Rumours of his return spread rapidly after a radio broadcast about him in 1958. In 1959 the South African Academy* elected him as an honorary life member and in 1964 his fable about *St Theodore and the crocodile* was published.

PUBLICATIONS

Fantasie o'er die lewe van die komponis Chopin. Six articles published in *Die Brandwag* I, 31 May - 15 October 1910. Griekse en Gregoriaanse kerkmusiek. *Die Brandwag* 3/8, September 1912. *In an Italian mirror,* a book of poetry. London, 1921. *St. Theodore and the crocodile.* Tafelberg Press, Cape Town, 1964.

WORKS

Three songs: 1. Die howenier (Totius) 2. 'n Winternag (E.N. Marais) 3. Die veldwindjie (Jan Celliers), dedicated respectively to G. Preller, Mrs. Jan Smuts and Lady Rose-Innes. Die Volkstem, 1909. Zulu wedding chant for piano, dedicated to General and Mrs Beyers. Ms., 1910. Zulu funeral chant, for piano, dedicated to General and Mrs Beyers. Ms., 1910.

BIBLIOGRAPHY

BOUWS, JAN: *Suid-Afrikaanse komponiste.* C.F. Albertyn Bpk., Stellenbosch, 1957. BOUWS, JAN: *Komponiste van Suid-Afrika.* C.F. Albertyn Bpk., Stellenbosch, 1971. PRELLER, GUSTAV: *Literarische Interludië.* J.L. van Schaik Bpk., Pretoria, 1930. VAN DER MERWE, F.Z.: *Suid-Afrikaanse musiekbibliografie, 1787-1952.* J.L. van Schaik Bpk., Pretoria, 1958. VERMEULEN, ELIZABETH: *Die musieklewe in Pretoria tussen 1902-1926.* M.Mus. dissertation, UP, 1967.

SOURCES

Bosman di Ravelli: Music's Exile. *Vita Musica.* June, September and December 1963; August 1964. *Die Volkstem:* 8 August 1906, 19 November 1912 (advertisement of Drie Liederen), 12 June 1904. Letters from Bosman di Ravelli to Dr F.V. Engelenburg, 1910-1914 in the National Documentation Centre, HSRC, Pretoria. REENEN, RYKIE VAN: Rykie van Reenen gesels met 'n gevierde komponis. Supplement to *Die Burger,* 18 January 1958. WEGL: Bosman di Ravelli. Op die spoor van ons eerste Afrikaanse kunslied. *Die Burger,* 20 February 1959. WEGL: Bosman di Ravelli. Die Boerseun het Europa geestelik verower. *Die Burger,* 23 May 1967.

—J.P.M.

BOSMAN, FREDERIK CHRISTIAAN LUDOLPH, *17 May 1898 in Kuilsrivier; in 1977 in Pretoria. University lecturer and music organiser.

After an outstanding career as a student, Dr Bosman became a lecturer in Dutch and Afrikaans at the University of Cape Town. From 1948 to 1955 he was secretary of *Die Suid-Afrikaanse Akademie vir Wetenskap en Kuns* (The South African Academy for Science and the Arts) in Pretoria. — In addition to important research on drama and theatre in South Africa and his interest in theatrical and other cultural matters, Dr Bosman also worked actively in furthering South Africa's music life. In 1951 he was a co-founder and vice-chairman of the South African Music Council*, and became chairman in 1957. His efforts led to his obtaining state subsidies for concerts and, in 1953, he was the driving force behind the creation of the magazine, *Res Musicae* (formerly *Newsletter)* as the organ of the South African Music Council and also as a general music magazine. On the establishment of the

218

Performing Arts Council for the Transvaal in 1962, the Music Council was disbanded and Dr Bosman became chairman of the new body's Music Committee. Since 1967 he has been connected with the University of Pretoria as Honorary Professor of the History of Drama. He became a member of the editorial board of the reorganised periodical *Lantern* in 1975.

PUBLICATIONS (only those touching on music)
Drama en toneel in Suid-Afrika, Deel I, 1652-1855. HAUM, Kaapstad, 1928.   De nieuwe ridderorde of De temperatisten, 1932, door C.E. Boniface. (Edition of the text with commentary on the oldest published play in South Africa) 1954.

ARTICLES
Die Toneel in Suid-Afrika, *Helikon* 4/19 & 20, March 1955.   Prof. P.R. Kirby. *Res Musicae* VI/3, March 1960.   Prof. J.P. Malan. *Res Musicae* VII, December 1960.   Opera in Suid-Afrika. *Huisgenoot* 42 (2016), 1960.   Prof. Georg Gruber. *Res Musicae* VII, March 1961.   Prof. Gerrit Bon. *Res Musicae* VIII/2, December 1961.   Gideon Fagan. *Res Musicae* VIII/5, September 1962.   Kunsindrukke van my jongste besoek aan Europa. *Res Musicae* VIII/5, September 1962.   The Jewish Guild Young People's Orchestra. *Res Musicae* VIII/4, December 1962.

SOURCES
National Documentation Centre for Music, HSRC, Pretoria.

—Ed.

BOSMAN, MAXIE, *2 November 1903 in Clanwilliam; °30 June 1939 in Munich. Soprano.
After initial training by her mother, Daisy Bosman*, Maxie went to Vienna, to study repertoire and sang in Europe with much success. Bosman di Ravelli* remembers that the critic of the Paris journal, *Le Temps,* said of her that "one could almost not believe that this was a human voice". He himself added: "She was a 'finer' soprano than her mother, (she) felt deeply and (was) musical. Some of Brahms's things I have perhaps never heard sung better". — On her return to South Africa (1938), Maxie Bosman was for a time lecturer in music at the Normal College in Bloemfontein. During her second South African concert tour which she made with her mother, it appeared that she had cancer of the spine. In February 1939 her parents took her to Munich for treatment, but she died there.

SOURCE
Die Huisgenoot: Article by Bosman di Ravelli on M. Bosman, 23 June 1939.

—F.S.

BOTHNER, CHARLES (CARL BÖTHNER OR BOETTNER), *14 September 1879 in Vevey, Switzerland; °18 February 1943 in Cape Town. The founder of the Bothner organisation.
Charles Bothner attended school in Lausanne, and was then apprenticed to a piano maker. He came to Cape Town in 1901 and set up business as a piano maker and tuner in the Huguenot Memorial Building, where his neighbours were Percy Ould*, Mme Lillie Myers (singing), M. Reid and "professor" Henry Clements (a teacher of singing). Bothner next opened a shop on the corner of Burg and Wale Streets (1904) advertising himself as a "Piano Importer" and as "pianoforte maker and tuner" (1905). From the beginning he maintained a good relationship with the theological

seminary at Stellenbosch and advertised regularly in *De Kerkbode* and the Annual of the DR Church. By 1907 he had also become an organ builder. During the First World War, on 13 May 1915, his shop and stocks were destroyed during the *Lusitania* riots, but he rebuilt his business and expanded it to include violins, wind instruments and sheet music. In October 1915, as "Carlos" Bothner, he became vice-consul for Spain in Cape Town. — After the war he opened a branch business in Rissik Street, Johannesburg, and in 1926 he entered into partnership with a certain Starck, with whose assistance he expanded the branch and moved to a shop situated between Loveday and Rissik Streets. The partnership with Starck did not last long, and within two years he had Frank and William Lincoln as partners. The name of the firm was changed to Bothner, Lincoln and Co. In these years the gramophone sales soared and Bothner expanded his business to market, first, the Aeolian Vocalion and later, having obtained the agency for the products, Columbia and Regal. The organ section was extended to Johannesburg and he decided to open a branch in Bloemfontein (1928). At this time the radio, or "wireless" as it was then called, came on the market. Bothner saw new marketing possibilities and in 1928 he advertised that he had for sale a Brunswick Radiola Panatrope which could also transmit "wireless" concerts. — The wave of prosperity of the Roaring Twenties ended in the great depression of 1929-1932. Bothner was obliged to curtail his business enterprises. In 1931 he withdrew from Johannesburg and the company's name was changed to Lincoln Brothers Ltd. His name disappeared from his Bloemfontein branch. However, there was compensation in the form of refrigerators and electric washing machines, which started appearing in his advertisements. In 1932 South Africa abandoned the gold standard and business started improving. — In order to maintain family control of the business, Bothner brought his sons Paul Charles and Maurice E. (Bobby) Bothner into the firm in the 1930s. He reopened the Johannesburg branch, directly opposite the firm of Lincoln Bros. The business was such a success that much larger premises had to be found, but by then the Second World War had broken out. Carl Bothner died on 18 February 1943, but his sons carried on. By the end of the war they had four sales branches, a factory for the production of radio cabinets, establishments in Pretoria and Durban and a piano factory under their control. In order to manage these and other investments M.E. Bothner registered a new company on 8 March 1946, Bothner Holdings Ltd. — Before Maurice died in a motor accident in 1956, Paul had embarked on a merger with the Polliack group (1954). This merger added 22 retail branches and 4 wholesale distribution centres and new agencies. Control was jointly exercised by John Polliack and Paul Bothner. Two years later the Polliack family sold out completely and Paul Bothner found himself in sole control of a giant company. In December 1963 the Bothner Group Ltd was taken over by a consortium under the management of Wit Extensions Ltd and re-named Wit Industrials Ltd. The wholesale and retail branches of this company were eventually taken over by Phil Morkel, although Wit Industrials retained a share in the company. — **Paul Charles Bothner** was born in Cape Town and went to school at the South African College. He then attended the Ecole Nouvelle in Switzerland, returned to the University of Cape Town, and finally went to Harvard University in the United States, returning to South Africa to play his part in the business. — **Maurice (Bobby) E. Bothner** was born in Cape Town in about 1907. He died in Johannesburg on 10 October 1956 after a motor accident. He was known as a Grand Prix racing driver and he also

220

took part in the South African speed boat championships. Before joining his father, he studied in the Frigidaire section of General Motors (early 1930s) and managed the Johannesburg branch of the firm. He was closely connected with the South African Society of Music Teachers* from 1947, when, in the name of the Transvaal Piano Dealers' Association, he established a Bothner prize in composition. After his death a Maurice Bothner Memorial Bursary for music teachers was created.

—Ed.

BOTHNER, (BOBBY) MAURICE E. Charles Bothner

BOTHNER, PAUL CHARLES Charles Bothner

BOTHNER PRIZE A. Wegelin, M. Whiteman

BOUGUENON, F. Free State String Quartet, E. Lowenherz, R. Masin

BOUWS, JAN, *28 July 1902 in Purmerend, North Holland; °26 January 1978 in Cape Town. Musicologist and educationist.

Jan Bouws was trained for the teaching profession at the Rijkskweekschool in Haarlem and became a teacher at a private school in Amsterdam, of which he was the principal from 1938 to 1960. He was trained in music by Ulfert Schults (pianoforte), Leo Smit and Willem Pijper (theory of music) and Ernest W. Mulder (counterpoint). Bouws also attended the lectures on musicology given by K. Ph. Bernet Kempers and W. Smits van Waesberghe at the University of Amsterdam. — His interest in the musical history of South Africa moved Bouws to systematically gather material about this subject and by 1946 he was ready to publish a short South African musical history. He attended the FAK's Congress on Folk Music and Folk Singing at Stellenbosch in 1958 and two years later the University of Stellenbosch made him director of its institute for folk music, with the additional commitment of lecturing on musical history and paleography in its music department. He has worked in this dual capacity right up to the present time (1976). This university awarded Bouws the degree of D. Phil. in 1965 for his thesis on the musical life of Cape Town between 1800 and 1850. Two years later the South African Academy distinguished the same thesis by awarding Bouws the Stals prize for cultural history. — Numerous publications by Bouws on South African musical history, South African composers and on South African folk songs have appeared in this country and in South West Africa since 1930, but also in The Netherlands, Belgium, Switzerland, Hungary, Germany and Denmark. The Medal of Honour for Music was awarded to him by the South African Academy in 1959, and he was honoured by the Netherlands-South African Society in Amsterdam with the Jan van Riebeeck Award in 1969 and by the FAK with an illuminated address in 1972. Dr Bouws is a member of the South African Academy, the Society for Netherlands Musical History in Amsterdam, the Society for Netherlands ·Literature, the Internationale Gesellschaft für Musikwissenschaft in Basel and the International Folk Music Council seated in Illinois.

PUBLICATIONS

1. Books
Musiek in Suid-Afrika. Brugge, 1946. *Suid-Afrikaanse komponiste van vandag en gister.* Cape Town, 1957. *Die Afrikaanse volkslied.* Johannesburg, 1958. *Woord en wys van die Afrikaanse lied.* Cape Town, 1961. *Die volkslied, weerklank van 'n volk se hartklop.*

Cape Town, 1962. *Maatgespeel.* Cape Town and Pretoria, 1964. *Die musieklewe van Kaapstad, (1800-1850) en sy verhouding tot die musiekkultuur van Wes-Europa.* Cape Town and Amsterdam, 1966. *Die volkslied, deel van ons erfenis.* Cape Town and Pretoria, 1968. *Komponiste van Suid-Afrika.* Stellenbosch, 1971. *Geskiedenis van die musiekonderwys in Suid-Afrika (1652-1902).* Cape Town, 1972.

2. *Articles* (A complete list still needs to be compiled)
Numerous articles in South African and overseas' periodicals, specialised periodicals and daily newspapers.

3. *Contributions* (Details lacking)
To MGG (Barenreiter, Kassel), The *Standard Encyclopaedia of Southern Africa* (Nasionale Pers Ltd., Cape Town), and *Encyclopaedia of the World(?).*

4. *Books concerning music education*
Blokfluitboekje I, II. Broekmans en van Poppel, Amsterdam, n.d. *Liedjies vir klavier.* Broekmans en van Poppel, Amsterdam, n.d. *Pianoboek I, II, III.* Broekmans en van Poppel, Amsterdam, n.d. *Speelliedjies van overal.* Broekmans en van Poppel, Amsterdam, n.d.

WORKS
Elf Afrikaanse liedere (Leipoldt, Celliers, Eitemal, Keet, Visser, Van Bruggen, Beukes), composed 1931-1937. Studio Holland, Cape Town, 1974. Afrikaans songs in the FAK Sangbundel: Dis al (Jan F.E. Celliers); Op my ou ramkietjie (C.L. Leipoldt); Ou Magjaarse liedjie (Eitemal).

—Ed.

BOWLLY, ALBERT ALEX (AL), *7 January 1898 in Lourenço Marques; °17 April 1941 in London. Singer, banjo and guitar player.
At a very early age, Al Bowlly came to Johannesburg with his parents, where he later opened his own barber shop, learned to play the banjo and guitar and in the evenings sang with one of several dance bands. In 1923 he joined Edgar Adeler's* dance band and toured with him through South Africa and further afield as far as Mombasa, Bombay and Java. He never returned to South Africa. — After leaving Adeler's dance band in Java, he appeared in India, Germany, England and also in the United States as singer with the bands of Fred Elizalde, Ray Noble and others. According to the latest research, he made about 850 gramophone recordings of which approximately twelve were sung in Afrikaans. He died during an air raid on London.

BIBLIOGRAPHY
BARRIER, PAMELA: *The magic of Bowlly.* Vintage Jazz Mart Magazine, 1961-1964   HARVEY, C.M. and RUST, B.A.L.: *The Al Bowlly discography.* Rust's Rare Record Ltd., Middlesex, England, 1964.
—C.G.

BOWMAN, LIONEL, *11 June 1919 in Koffiefontein; living in Stellenbosch in 1970. Concert pianist and lecturer.
At the age of eight Lionel won a scholarship to the South African College of Music* in Cape Town, where the family were living at that time. During his student years he was awarded nine scholarships, played in concerts with the Cape Town Orchestra*, and toured as a recitalist. In 1937 he won the scholarship of the University of South Africa, entered the RCM and became a pupil of Vivian Langrish. He played with the student orchestra on several occasions, studied horn, cello and clarinet, and followed a conductor's course under Henry Wood. He received the Chappell Gold Medal, The

222

Matthew Phillimore Prize, and the Roller Memorial Prize as a Beethoven exponent, prior to his return to South Africa in 1940. — Bowman was a member of the staff at the South African College of Music from 1941 until 1944, and played in an ensemble that broadcast from Cape Town on Sunday afternoons in 1942. On his second visit to England in 1946, he undertook tours in Great Britain as joint soloist with Gigli, Richard Tauber, Peter Dawson and Paul Robeson. In this year he also broadcast on the BBC Home Service, and appeared in solos and concertos at the Promenade Concerts and on television. In 1948 he undertook his first tour of the Continent, and visited Holland, Belgium, France, Italy, Sweden and Greece. Tours of America (1948), Africa (1950, 1952, 1954, 1955 and 1957) and Europe (1951, 1952 and 1954) always brought him back to England, where he appeared with leading orchestras. — Bowman joined the staff of the University of Stellenbosch in 1958, though since settling in South Africa he has toured England and the Continent four times. He frequently broadcasts for the SABC, performs with different orchestras in the country, and records exclusively for EMI on the Parlophone label. — In 1964 he was elected a Fellow of the RAM.

—Ed.

BOXALL, DOROTHY RUTH, *19 July 1895 in King William's Town; °23 December 1951 in Johannesburg. Music teacher who devoted herself to orchestral activities among the youth.

Dorothy Boxall's father came from Brighton, England, and made his home first in King William's Town and then in Johannesburg. She matriculated at Jeppe High School, won a scholarship to study at the University of the Witwatersrand, and became musically qualified by obtaining the UTLM, LTCL and FTCL diplomas. After completing her diploma course at the Witwatersrand University, she sought the B.Mus degree and obtained it with distinction three years later, being the first South African to do so at that University. — In 1926 Dorothy joined the staff of R. Pritchard's* studio, as lecturer in music history. She then taught at Maud Harrison's Conservatoire, until Maud was married in 1930, when she opened her own studio with Clarice Greenstone. Her spare time was spent scoring music for children's percussion bands, and in 1932 she announced Saturday afternoon classes for children in percussion instruments and musical appreciation. By 1945 she had attained her ambition of forming a children's orchestra, thus helping young people who displayed talent and a love for music, but had not the necessary financial resources. — Recruited from her percussion bands, the little orchestra made astonishing progress. Rehearsing every Saturday morning in the Johannesburg Teachers' Training College, the Young Citizen's Orchestra gave its first concert at the College in April 1946. A choir of 1 000 children sang under Miss Boxall's direction at the music festival in October of the same year, accompanied by the children's orchestra. In 1947, a massed choir sang under her direction during the Royal visit and she was presented with a gold medal by the King for her educational work in music. Her Children's Festival became an annual event, and by 1950 included not only the massed chorus and the Young Citizens' Orchestra, but also a percussion band, a recorder band and the percussion band of St Vincent's School for the Deaf. The original orchestra of strings had increased to over 100 players (including brass and woodwind), many of whom travelled from Pretoria and the Reef towns for rehearsals. Alex Murray, who became a member of a London orchestra, and Derek Ochse*, who now directs a music school in Rustenburg, were early members of

223

Dorothy Boxall's orchestra. — She was a lecturer in music at the Johannesburg Normal College for seventeen years (1934-1951), taught at the Parktown and Jeppe Girls' High Schools, and was organiser of music to the Rosettenville Junior Government School. The Johannesburg Junior Orchestra and Theatre were launched in 1949, followed in 1950 by the first Annual Play Festival for schools and colleges. In co-operation with Mr Woodhouse, organist of St Mary's Cathedral and later of the Mayfair Anglican Church, Dorothy Boxall organised the first South African Carols by Candlelight at the Zoo Lake. In the year of her death she had established the Witwatersrand College of Music, with a new approach in music teaching, to ensure that children learnt to play instruments for which they were psychologically suited. Miss Boxall served on the executive council of the Johannesburg Musical Society*; on the music committee of the Transvaal Teachers' Association; on the Research and Education committee of the SASMT*, and she was twice chairwoman of the Witwatersrand University Musical Society. She was the founder of the Transvaal Teachers' School Music Association, and acted as chairwoman for 14 years. — In 1952 the Children's Music Festival Society, the Transvaal School Music Association and the Johannesburg Junior Orchestra and Theatre merged to become the Dorothy Boxall Young People's Music and Drama Movement. This group held a memorial concert for her in September 1952.

PUBLICATIONS

Possibilities with percussion bands for children. *SA Music Teacher*, October 1931. Investigations into children's music in London. *SA Music Teacher*, April 1932. *Percussion band book for English and Afrikaans junior schools*. Novello & Co., London, n.d.

BIBLIOGRAPHY

VAN DER MERWE, F.Z.: *Suid-Afrikaanse musiekbibliografie, 1787-1952*. J.L. van Schaik, Pretoria, 1958. W.H.K.: *The arts in South Africa*. Knox Publishing Co., Durban, 1933.

SOURCE

MARSH, ANNA: Dorothy Boxall. *SA Music Teacher*, June 1952.

—L.W.

BOYS, R.W. Potchefstroom 3

BRADLEY, F.A. Organs 2(ii), Port Elizabeth I/2

BRADLEY, LEO PAUL, *5 February 1889 in Bangalore, India; °16 February 1968 in Pretoria. Director of Music to the South African Police, composer.

Paul Bradley received his initial musical training from his father, Francis Bradley, bandmaster of the Oxfordshire Light Infantry, which was stationed in India at the time of his birth. At the age of ten he was sent to school in Yorkshire. Bradley, who also started his career in the Oxfordshire Light Infantry in January 1903, studied at the Royal Military School of Music (Kneller Hall) from 1905 until 1913, winning the Cousins Memorial Prize Medal for the most promising pupil in 1906, the Commandant's Prize for composition in 1910 and the medal of the Worshipful Company of Musicians for the most talented student in 1913. In 1910 he obtained the licentiates in orchestral conducting and military conducting, and in 1913 the licentiate of the RAM (theatrical conducting). From 1911 until his appointment as bandmaster of the Royal Irish Fusiliers in October 1913, he was "sub"-professor of violin and cornet at Kneller Hall and assistant to the director of music. — After twenty years' service as bandmaster of his regiment in Egypt and later Bombay, he became Head Constable and Bandmaster of the South African Police Band in November 1933. He was promoted to the rank of Lieutenant in December 1936, to Captain in May 1944, Major in February 1949, and Colonel in April 1963. Under his leadership the band of the South African Police developed from a band of twenty-five bandsmen into one of fifty-two, with an impressive repertoire of the best military band music and transcriptions of symphonic works. The band, which maintained an exceptionally high standard, performed at national festivals, state occasions and at open-air concerts in Burgers Park, Pretoria, as well as on radio. Colonel Bradley retired in December 1964. — He was also active in other musical spheres: in 1947 he conducted the first performance of the Pretoria City Orchestral Society, in 1959 he was appointed first director of the newly-formed Bantu Police Band and for some time he also conducted the Pretoria String Orchestra.

WORKS
Ich Dien, march for military band. Ms., 1911.   Homage, march for military band. Ms., 1938.   The Fiddler's Bow, operetta. Ms., 1942.   The Gift of Ah-Woo-Wong, Chinese fantasy. Ms., 1948.   The protea, selection of folk songs arranged for military band. Ms., 1950.   The Western Desert, symphonic suite. Ms., before 1957.   Pretoria blink uit in voortreflikheid, song (Dr Jan Pienaar). Ms., 1958.   South African folk songs, Volkspele melodies. Standard Military Band Journal No. 60. Boosey & Hawkes, 1958.   Arrangements for military band of *Die Stem van Suid-Afrika* and folk songs. Ms., n.d.   Bells of South Africa, selection of folk songs arranged for military band. Ms., n.d.   Irish slumber song, for military band. Ms., n.d.   Jack and Jill, for military band. Ms., n.d.   Men of South Africa. Ms., n.d.   Piano sonata. Ms., n.d.   Psalm 71. Ms., n.d.   Steadfast and true - Altyd getrou, song of the South African Police (Dr Jan Pienaar). Ms., n.d.   String quartet. Ms., n.d.   Trio for oboe, flute and bassoon. Ms., n.d.   Trois amour (sic), ballet. Ms., n.d.   African Rhapsody, for piano and orchestra. Ms., n.d.   Violin sonata. Ms., n.d.

BIBLIOGRAPHY
VAN STADEN, G.E.: *Kolonel L.P. Bradley en sy aandeel in die ontwikkeling van musiek in die Suid-Afrikaanse Polisie.* B.Mus. script, UP, 1967.

SOURCES
Pretoria News, 19 February 1968.   *SARP,* magazine for the South African Police, April 1968.   VISSER, SERGEANT: Die Suid-Afrikaanse Polisie-Orkes. *Newsletter of the South African Society of Music Teachers,* May 1965.
—Ed.

BRAHAM, EDITHA   J. de Wet, Higher Educational Institutions III/2, B.M. Marx.

BRAILSFORD, M.   Port Elizabeth I/5.

BRANDON, HEATHER.   Music teacher and choral conductor in Durban.

Heather Brandon was born in London of musical parents who were both singers. In Yorkshire, she was trained in pianoforte playing from her fifth year; by the age of 16 she had obtained the ATCL followed by the diplomas FTCL, GTCL and LRAM. In South Africa, Heather taught at Kingsmead School in Johannesburg, and then in Rhodesia. In 1963, when her husband was transferred to Durban, she opened a studio in Durban North, and since then has been a teacher of pianoforte, choral conducting, harmony, counterpoint and musical history. — The Oriana Chamber Choir of 24 voices was formed by Heather Brandon in 1964, and has since sung an annual programme "Music and Song" in both Durban and Pietermaritzburg. Another yearly feature is the appearance of this choir at the Christmas concerts of the Durban Music Society. The choir has also recorded commercially and has undertaken tours to Natal centres for NAPAC. The Durban Symphonic Choir of 120 voices was formed by Heather Brandon at the request of the Mayor of Durban in 1966. Together with the Durban Civic Orchestra* this choir has participated in Mahler's *Second symphony*, Kodaly's *Psalmus Hungaricus*, Poulenc's *Gloria*, Bach's *St John Passion*, Brahms's *German Requiem*, Verdi's *Requiem*, Fauré's *Requiem*, Beethoven's *Choral symphony* and Handel's *Messiah*.

—G.S.J.

BRANDT, JOHAN WILHELM CHRISTIAAN, *1804 (1803?) in Cape Town; °30 August 1873 in Cape Town. Organist and music teacher.

As the son of the verger of the Evangelical Lutheran Church in Strand Street, Brandt may have received his training in organ, piano and violin playing from the organist of this church, J.F. Osmitius*. In any case, on 4 December 1820, after a trial period, he was recommended as the successor to Osmitius and held this post until 1838. In that year he resigned after years of strife with the Church Council, especially over his small salary as organist and his assistance to L. Beil* who trained a children's choir for the church. After this he played the organ in Wynberg (1849- ?), Malmesbury (consecrated 1860), and at his freemason's lodge, De Goede Hoop. When he re-applied for the vacant organist post at the Lutheran Church in 1864, the church council gave preference to an English-speaking musician, A.J. Geden. — In the Cape's musical life and especially in connection with music for the theatre, Brandt's name turns up frequently. He was among the people associated with Boniface*, and played various roles in the productions of the company "Honi soit qui mal y pense" (1825). When Weber's *Der Freischütz* was produced in 1831, he was an important member of the orchestra. On one occasion he is even named as the composer of incidental music for the tragedy *Montoni of 't Kasteel van Udolpho* which was staged in 1836 by the company "Vlyt en Kunst". His name appears in the list of choir members who sang under the direction of Ludwig Beil at the laying of the foundation stone of the NG Kerk on Kuiperplein (1833). He was also a soloist at a concert in the building " 't Nut" (1842). — In addition to these scattered activities, he conducted the orchestra of the Amateur Musical Society at a concert in the Exchange at which Madame Chardon* assisted as solo pianist (1845). With Nicolaas Wetrens* he gave a *soirée musicale* in the Goede Hoop Lodge (1858) where works for orchestra and violin were performed. In 1862 he was director of the short-lived choral society "Harmonie en Eendragt", which was disbanded in February of the following year. — Among the lesser talents who played a part in the musical life at the Cape at this period, Brandt deserves mention as a South African musician who, with a persistence unusual for those days, was involved in a variety of musical activity.

BIBLIOGRAPHY

BOSMAN, F.C.L.: *Drama en toneel in Suid-Afrika I*. Pretoria, Cape Town, 1928.   BOUWS, JAN: *Die musieklewe van Kaapstad, 1800-1850, en sy verhouding tot die musiekkultuur van Wes-Europa*. Cape Town, Amsterdam, 1966.   OTTERMAN, R.E.: *Die kerkmusiek in die Evangeliese Lutherse Kerk in Strandstraat, Kaapstad, tussen 1780 en 1880*. M.Mus. dissertation, US, 1963.

SOURCES

The South African Chronicle and Mercantile Advertiser III, 1826. Commercial Advertiser VII, 1831. *De Verzamelaar III*, 1842. *De Zuid-Afrikaan XXXI*, 1860. *Het Volksblad III*, 1858 and *XVIII*, 1873. BOUWS JAN: 'n Musiek-immigrant se wel en wee. *Die Burger*, Cape Town, 22 July 1967. SUASSO DE LIMA, J.: *Ter herinnering aan de godsdienstige plegtigheid by het leggen van den hoeksteen der nieuwe Nederduitsche Hervormde Kerk in Kaapstad op den 18 April 1833*. Cape Town, 1833. VISAGIE, J.C.: Die Anreith-skool. *Africana Notes and News* 17/8, December 1967.

—J.B.

BRANDTS-BUYS. A Dutch family of musicians; for two centuries the name Brandts has been linked with that of Buys. Songs (or arrangements of songs) by well-known members of the family are included in Afrikaans song-books. The name was quite well-known in Transvaal musical circles.

Ludwig Felix, (*20 November 1847 in Deventer; °29 June 1917 in Velp) was an organist, choir-master and lecturer in Deventer, Zutphen, and in Rotterdam from 1874 to 1907. He became known as a composer of various songs and compositions for male-voice choir. His most popular song was *Mijne moedertaal* (words by Frans de Cort; published by G. Alsbach & Co., Amsterdam). In 1907 Dr N. Mansvelt* included this song in the *Hollands-Afrikaanse Liederbundel,* together with another song by Brandts Buys, *Transvaal en Nederland,* op. 31a (words by J.S.B.B. - Jan Sebastiaan Brandts Buys - son of the composer). His choral composition *Een stem in Rama,* was performed in Pretoria on 13 November 1917 (shortly after his death) by Petrus van den Burg*. *Transvaal en Nederland* was issued in a special edition printed by the firm of F.B. Dittmar of Rotterdam in December 1899 in aid of the Republican Red Cross and "dedicated to the nation of the Transvaal and the Orange Free State". This publication was paid for by voluntary contributions of Hollanders. The family of Brandts-Buys were most outspoken in their support of the Boer cause. — **Marius Adrianus,** (*31 October 1840 in Deventer; °13 January 1911 in Eerbeek) was known as an organ virtuoso since his teens. The song chosen for inclusion by Dr Mansvelt in the 1907 collection, *Een nieuw lied van een meisje en een schipper* (words by A.C.W. Staring), is typical of "the people's style", a type which enjoyed a great vogue at the time. — **Jan Willem Frans,** (*12 September 1868 in Zutphen; °8 December 1939 in Salzburg) son of Marius A.B-Buys and internationally the best-known of the family, studied at the Raff Conservatoire in Frankfurt and settled in Vienna in 1893. Of his operatic works, *Der Schneider von Schönau* (1916) is sometimes still produced. His contribution to Dr Mansvelt's collection is the *Lied van die Natal-Voortrekkers* from *Vijftig Uitgesogte Afrikaanse Gedigte* (1888), edited by F.W. Reitz. Taking the reference "Tune of Ps. 130" as his point of departure, the composer wrote a four-part chorale with a prelude, an interlude and a postlude. This song is also included in *Die Hollands-Afrikaanse Liederbundel.*

SOURCES

REITZ, F.W. (editor): *Vijftig uitgesogte Afrikaanse gedigte.* Amsterdam, 1888. MANSVELT, N. *Hollands-Afrikaanse Liederbundel.* Amsterdam, 1907. VAN NIEKERK, JOAN: *Die groot Afrikaanse-Hollandse Liederbundel.* Cape Town, 1907. PAAP, WOUTER: Toonkunst Arnheim 60 jaar. *Mens en Melodie XI,* Utrecht, 1956.

—J.B.
(slightly amplified)

BRASCH, DORIS (MRS NATHAN COOPERMAN), *19 September 1929 in Johannesburg; living in Johannesburg in 1977. Soprano.

Doris Brasch received vocal training since the age of 14, and when her family settled in Johannesburg in 1947, she studied with a former pupil of Lili Lehmann, Sophie Ginkewitz. Since then she has become known through Lieder recitals and by her interpretations in radio performances of works such as *Amelia goes to the ball* (Menotti) (in Afrikaans), *Eugen Onegin* (Tschaikowsky) and *The marriage of Figaro* (Mozart). — She has undertaken frequent tours with the baritone Bob Borowsky*, appeared with the Symphony Orchestras of Johannesburg, Cape Town and Durban, and made numerous commercial recordings. The roughly 30 recordings of children's songs in which she is partnered by Dawie Couzyn* (for the Afrikaans songs) and by Bob Williams, Jimmy Rayson and Ronnie Wilson (for the English songs) were in great demand. Most of these songs were written and composed by Betty Misheiker*. As soloist, and in conjunction with Dawie Couzyn, she has also recorded Afrikaans traditional and popular music. Since the Regional Councils have been launched, Doris Brasch has toured for PACT and NAPAC and also visited SWA under the auspices of the SA Association of Arts. — She was soloist at the investiture of the Republic's first State President (1961) and sang the part of the witch in *Hänsel und Gretel* (Humperdinck) at the Inaugural Festival of the Civic Theatre in Johannesburg. Since 1973 she has presented educational music programmes at schools.

—Ed.

BREBNER, DR. J. Bloemfontein I/8

BREDELL. The Bredell family came from Germany; two of its members became organ builders in the Cape Colony.

Peter Bredell was born in 1791 and married Anna Maria Stronck, born in Russia in 1796. It is assumed that he immigrated to the Cape in 1830 or a few years later. He farmed in the Stellenbosch district on the farm Moddergat, where his wife died on 3 June 1863. Peter Bredell died on 27 April the following year - also at Stellenbosch. Seven sons were born of this marriage: Adam, Paul, Peter, Anton, Johann, Carl and Jacob. Adam and Jacob became organ builders and installed instruments in the Cape Colony for a total of fifty years. Adam (born at Schweppenhausen on the Rhine in 1821, died on 18 January 1893 in Cape Town) started organ building in Cape Town around 1860. He was probably not very successful - when he died there was barely enough to defray his funeral expenses. In 1877, he erected the first organ for the congregation of Noorder-Paarl. They had ordered this instrument from a firm in England. Of his 3 daughters Pauline Bredell* (Bredelli) became a famous singer who often visited her parents in Cape Town. Jacob Bredell* settled in Port Elizabeth in 1866 and left immovable property valued at R1 940, an indication that he had been more successful.

SOURCES
Register of estates, Cape Province: MOOC 6/9/313, DN 259; 8328 of 1925; MOOC 6/9/105, DN 719; MOOC 6/9/107, DB 1051.

—C.G.H.

BREDELL, JACOB, *1838 in Cape Town; °22 June 1925 in Port Elizabeth. Organ builder.

About 1866 Jacob left Cape Town, where he had been a partner in the firm of his brother Adam (Adam Bredell and Son, Piano Warehousemen, Organ Builders and Tuners), to open a similar business in Port Elizabeth. His earliest advertisement in the

EP Herald is dated January 1867, but he had probably started during the previous year. No other organbuilders are known to have been in Port Elizabeth, though in August 1866 a new organ was completed in St Mary's and in December a new one was installed in the Wesleyan Trinity Church. Another one was inaugurated at Richmond on 9 December 1866. — This last instrument had nine stops, one coupler and three composition pedals. It had been donated by two businessmen and was purchased in London for R700. Bredell was paid R60 for the installation plus travelling expenses, but eventually, as a token of their appreciation, they paid him an additional amount of R40. On the day of its inauguration, he played an Introduction, Grundlingh of Graaff Reinet accompanied the congregational singing and, for the first time, a choir sang in the church. The *GR Herald* says that the congregation "were for the most part struck speechless at the innovation (the choir) and the beautiful effect of the organ". A description of the instrument reads: "The external case is of stained oak, and the front is Gothic work, with deep reverse mouldings, and pleated blue damask filling the spaces between the pillars. On each side is an angel, carved in composition, with outspread wings, gilt, and drapery finished with blue and gold. These hold a harp and a flute, also gilt. The front pipes are richly decorated with the fleur de lys and Maltese cross". — Three years later, on 22 December 1869, St Paul's in Port Elizabeth inaugurated a new organ which Bredell had built for R400. This little instrument had "great volume and delicacy of tone, the flute tones being especially good", 7 stops and 1 coupler (Open Diapason 16', Bourdon 8', Principal 4', Stopped Diapason 4', Salicet 4', Wald Flute, Fifteenth: in all, 342 pipes). — Bredell continued to advertise himself as an organ builder and piano tuner although he was also selling pianofortes and harmoniums in November 1873. Since 1867 he had become Juta's neighbour in Main Street. St Augustine's had an organ constructed in memory of a certain Murphy in 1875. With subsequent additions, this instrument was praised by Horace Barton*. It had been built by Walker and had cost R3 088. Bredell received R450 for erecting it and the inauguration took place in January of the next year. — In June 1881, Bredell completed the overhaul and enlargement of the instrument in St Mary's, a Walker for which the Church had paid R644 in 1866. Bredell added a Trumpet (56 pipes), a Mixture of four ranks (224 pipes) and added an Oboe of 44 pipes to the Swell. The original nine stops and 600 pipes had been increased to 12 stops and 924 pipes, 2 couplers and three composition pedals. Bredell announced that the new pipes were made of the "best spotted metal and the Trumpet stop mitred as much as possible to keep out the dust". The "accessories" included "cheeks for the sound reflectors of the Great and Swell, 5 gallons of best elastic oak varnish, 10 gallons of best boiled oil, screwplate die for trackers, wire of three different kinds (tinned, iron and brass), and a windgauge". — The church was destroyed by fire on 9 March 1895. A new organ was installed into the rebuilt church and consecrated on 13 September 1896. The cost of this instrument was R2 178; further additions in 1911 pushed the amount up to R3 200. It was once again a manufacture of Walker and Sons. Correspondence written by the precentor, the Rev. C.E. Mayo and dated August 1895 mentions that it would be wise to have the new organ "fitted for handblowing when required, as water may be cut off in dry seasons". The organs in Port Elizabeth were apparently often dependent on a water supply to keep the wind pressure constant. This system caused St Mary's difficulties but it also left St Paul's in the lurch. They had to have a new hydraulic motor in 1903 (supplied by Bredell) and St Peter's instructed Bredell to install a new hydraulic motor in 1904. Hydraulic pressure was also used in Cape Town in the Groote

Kerk (see *Organs: Groote Kerk*) and in Grahamstown, in the Cathedral (see *Organs: Cathedral, Grahamstown*). There are actually no records of this system operating satisfactorily in South Africa. On 5 November 1902, the *PE Herald* stated that Bredell had just fixed a new hydraulic engine for St Mary's organ and "that he has introduced a new system of his own invention which appears to stand every test". Pneumatic action had been desired for the new organ, but it was ultimately decided to use tracker action, "as rapid changes in atmosphere upset the pneumatics". It had three manuals with 23 stops, pedals with three stops and three couplers. — In November 1883 Bredell installed a new three-manual organ with 34 stops and 1820 pipes, built by Conacher and Sons of Huddersfield, in Trinity Church Central. A fire destroyed this church in 1897 and the next year, on 20 January, Roger Ascham* inaugurated a new three-manual instrument built by Bevington. Ascham had been the organist of this congregation since 1890 and occupied this position until his death in 1934. This instrument was never very satisfactory, but in 1904 Bredell managed to remedy some of the faults and to do renovating work for R150. — St Paul's were prepared to sell their organ for R1 000 in 1884, but it was ultimately bought by the Baptist Church in Queen Street for R200. St Paul's inaugurated their new instrument on 5 March 1885 and in 1903 Bredell supplied them with a new hydraulic engine. Another small organ probably installed by Bredell, was the one in St Peter's Church (consecrated 1880). He was paid R7,50 for "tuning and repairs" about 1897. This was another case of hydraulic troubles. The repair and maintenance of the organ in the Feathermarket Hall was entrusted to Bredell though he had nothing to do with the ordering and installation of this instrument. In July 1903 he was asked to overhaul and clean it, eliminating the feathers in the instrument and "exterminating the rats", which had caused severe damage. — Bredell was married to Catherine Woollacott (*October 1847 in Devonshire; °4 January 1918 in Port Elizabeth). They had one son, Claude Bismarck Bredell, who took over his father's business shortly after 1900.

BIBLIOGRAPHY

BIRCH, J.L.: *Pipe organs in the Anglican Churches of Port Elizabeth.* B.Mus. script, RU, 1969.   TROSKIE, A.J.J.: *The musical life of Port Elizabeth, 1875-1900.* M.Mus. dissertation, UPE, 1969.

SOURCES

GR Herald: 29 December 1866.   *EP Herald:* January 1867 - December 1874; 5 November 1902; 9 July 1903.   Register of Estates CP: No. 8328/1925.   Research and draft article by C.G. Henning.

—J.P.M.

BREDELL, J. PAULINE G. (MRS RICHARD SACKSEN), *in 1843 in Cape Town. South African soprano, operatic and concert singer; daughter of Adam Bredell, the Cape organ-builder.

After studying at the Julius Stern Conservatoire in Berlin, she made her debut there singing Susanna's aria from *Le nozze di Figaro* (Mozart). She received favourable reviews from the Berlin press for her interpretation of songs by Mendelssohn and Schubert. In 1864 she appeared in Cape Town in a concert given by the German Liedertafel Germania conducted by Gustav Boëttger. After her marriage to Richard Sacksen of Berlin, she revisited South Africa in 1879, 1882, 1883 and 1884. In 1882, illness in Cape Town resulted in her tour being delayed by about three months. She was accompanied by the American pianist Albert Thies (who had accompanied Charles du Val* in 1881) and the singer Norman Henry. When the tour eventually got underway it took her to Port Elizabeth (November 1882), Graaff Reinet (December 1882) and in March 1883 she was in Durban. Her repertoire seems to have been of a good standard and included excerpts from *Der Freischütz, Les Huguenots* and Rossini's *Stabat Mater*. In Durban her singing was extolled as "the finest ever heard in the city". — At the time of her visit in 1882, W.H. Schröder sketched her portrait for the Cape Weekly, *The Lantern*. Reports from overseas sources mention her as a prima donna of the New York and Berlin opera houses. She can be regarded as South Africa's first female singer of international repute.

BIBLIOGRAPHY

JACKSON, GEORGE S: *Music in Durban from 1850 to 1900*. D.Phil thesis, University of the Witwatersrand, 1961.

SOURCES

John Rose, Diary, 5 September 1864 (Ms. in SA Public Library, Cape Town). *Het Volksblad:* 8 September to 1 December 1864. *The Cape Argus:* 12 June 1866. *Zingari:* 28 August 1874. *De Zuid-Afrikaan* vol. 45: 29 August 1874. *The Lantern IX:* 16 September 1882. *The South African Illustrated News I:* 16 April, 10 May and 24 May 1884. BOUWS, JAN: Madame Bredelli. *Die Burger*. Cape Town, 6 December 1969.

—J.B. (amplified)

BRENNER, PETER (FELSENSTEIN) Cato Brink

BRENT-WESSELS, JUDITH Nunez Holtzhausen.

BRETAGNE, LEONIE Johannesburg 3(iv).

BREWER, J. Port Elizabeth I/4(iv).

BREYNE-DICKEN, GERTA, *6 May 1903 in Magdeburg; living in Germany in 1971. Mezzo-soprano.

Gerta Breyne-Dicken was trained at the Musikhochschule in Berlin where she was a student of Hans Beltz and Albert Fischer. She was subsequently a soloist in various oratorio performances, including Bach's *Weihnachts-Oratorium* (with the Danziger Singakademie in the St Marien Cathedral), Bach's *Johannes-Passion* (with the Berlin Philharmonic orchestra) and Kaminski's *In Memoriam* (with the Berlin radio orchestra for the Berliner Musiktage 1947). Supplementary to her concert performances in various cities, she also broadcast programmes in Berlin, Paris, Brussels, Hilversum and South Africa. — Resident in South Africa since 1950, she sang in performances of Beethoven's *Ninth Symphony* and Gerrit Bon's* *Te Deum Laudamus* (for the Van Riebeeck festival in 1952) and in various performances with the SABC Symphony Orchestra. She was a soloist in performances of the operas *Aïda* and *Verhale van Hoffmann*.

—Ed.

BREYTENBACH, PETRUS PHILIPPUS BENJAMIN, *24 January 1904 in the Wepener district; resident in Pretoria since 1952. Prominent figure in South African drama; founder and leader of NTO, and first director of PACT.

Notwithstanding teaching obligations as head of the Witwatersrand Technical College in Krugersdorp, Breytenbach has been a zealous pioneer of Afrikaans drama since the earliest years of his career. He was a foundation member of the Dramatic Club in Krugersdorp in 1928. The club meetings had the benefit of a fixed pattern:

some members produced a one-act play and others were responsible for a musical programme after the interval. The first productions were in English and included operettas, such as the second act of *Trial by jury* in 1930. In view of similar ventures, the club's name was altered to the Dramatic Society, and thereafter to the Dramatic and Operatic Society. The City Council, which was well-disposed towards this industricus group, provided facilities for the rehearsal of plays, and permitted free use of the City Hall for public performances. Society members acknowledged these favours by changing their name to The Krugersdorp Municipal Society for Drama and Opera. Breytenbach was appointed chairman in 1934, and remained in office until 1952. Through its progress the West Rand Symphony Society could be revived and *bona fide* musical concerts were presented, usually after church services on Sunday evenings. In the course of 20 years, 45 Afrikaans, 34 English plays and 14 operettas and musical comedies were staged. — Experience with this society led to the idea of a national dramatic organisation, and Breytenbach took the initiative of organising a conference in Krugersdorp, attended by representatives from 40 different dramatic societies. From this the Federation of Amateur Theatrical Societies of Southern Africa (FATSA), and eventually the National Theatre Organisation emerged, with Breytenbach as its first chairman (1947). He became the director of the Performing Arts Council of the Transvaal (PACT) in October 1962, after the NTO had been disbanded. — The Akademie vir Wetenskap en Kuns* acknowledged his contribution to the development of drama in South Africa by presenting him with a medal of honour in 1951. There is a bust of Breytenbach by Coert Steynberg in the foyer of the theatre named after him in Pretoria.

SOURCE

STEAD, R.: Portret van 'n toneelpionier; hulde aan P.P. Breytenbach. *Lantern XVII*, 2 December 1967.   —Ed.

BRIEN, EDWARD JOHN (TED), *4 March 1936 in Durban; in 1970 in Westville, Natal. Teacher and performer on the recorder.

Ted Brien was educated at Durban High School and Natal University. While he was still at school, he played the flute in the school's military band of which he later became the leader. After qualifying as an art teacher at the University of Natal in Pietermaritzburg, he began his teaching career at Highbury School in Hillcrest; here he first became interested in recorders and their music. In 1962 he left Highbury to specialise in recorder playing; in June of that year he obtained the LTCL as performer, the FTCL in 1963 and the LTCL diploma in 1967. At the end of 1967 he accepted the appointment of senior lecturer in music at the Springfield College of Education. He still holds this position. — Well-known in Natal as a recorder player, Ted Brien has given much of his time to the promotion of these instruments through the organisation of an annual Summer School for young recorder players. In 1970 he started a youth music organisation known as the Music Workshop which offers young musicians the opportunity of playing in a chamber orchestra. Although his concerts have indicated a preference for the Baroque, he has stimulated considerable interest in the more modern music written for the instrument.

SOURCES

Sunday Tribune: 13 March 1966.   *Natal Mercury:* 21 March 1966, 11 November 1966, 14

October 1966, 2 April 1970.   *Daily News:* 2 June 1971.

—G.S.J.

BRILL, SEBASTIAN   Pseudonym of J. Rodriguez Lopez.

BRIMER, MICHAEL, *8 August 1933 in Cape Town. Professor of Music and Head of the Music Department of the University of Natal and since 1974 of the University of Cape Town. Organist, pianist and conductor.

At the age of 12 Michael Brimer's music education commenced under Eleanor Bonnar* (pianoforte); during the following eight years she greatly influenced his musical development. He was a chorister at St George's Cathedral in Cape Town and had organ tuition from Dr Alban Hamer* from 1945 to 1952, while completing his schooling and studying for a BA degree at the University of Cape Town. Meanwhile he had also been assistant organist to Dr Hamer and, after the latter's death in March 1952, he became acting organist and choirmaster of St George's Cathedral*. — A music bursary awarded by UNISA enabled Brimer to continue his studies at the RCM and the RCCM (1953-1955); he also enrolled for the B.Mus. degree at the University of London. After completing the courses for the FRCO, ARCM, LRAM and the Mus. Bac., an Organ Scholarship opened the way for further study at Clare College, Cambridge (1955-1957), where he was awarded the MA degree in Music. In the meantime, he had also furthered his pianoforte studies in England and, after the Cambridge period, in Vienna, where he was taught by Josef Dichler. — In August 1958, he was appointed Director of Music at the Church of England Grammar School in Brisbane, Australia, but returned to London in August 1960 as Headquarters Choirmaster of the Royal School of Church Music. Eighteen months later the University of Western Australia appointed him lecturer in music; he served there until January 1966, when he became senior lecturer in Music at Monash University in Melbourne, Victoria - a position which he held until 1970. During his sojourn in Australia, he founded and conducted the West Australian Bach Society, appeared as pianoforte and organ soloist with the Queensland, West Australian and Melbourne Symphony Orchestras, conducted choral concerts and performed as a concert pianist. — Michael Brimer returned to South Africa in February 1971, to become Professor of Music and Head of the newly-formed Music Department of the University of Natal in Durban. In 1973 he resigned from this post to take charge of the South African College of Music* in Cape Town.

—Ed.

BRINK, CATO (MRS. MAGDALENA CATHARINA BRINK-FELSENSTEIN), *in Rustenburg; at present resident in Düsseldorf, Germany (1969). Soprano.

At the age of eight Cato Brink was awarded a trophy for a performance at the Rustenburg Eisteddfod in the section singing, girls under sixteen. This success was followed by others at various eisteddfodau during her school years. She was trained at the Heidelberg Teachers' Training College (TED) as a gymnastics teacher and taught this subject in Johannesburg, where she devoted herself to the development of her voice. In 1953 she sang the Performers' Licentiate Examination (UPLM) of UNISA and left for Vienna (1955), where she studied at the State Academy under Professor Josef Witt, Professor Hans Duhan and Dr Erich Werba, and passed the Reifeprüfung of the opera school in 1957. She was trained in singing by Maria Hittorff. This was followed by a concert tour of South Africa (1957-1958), after which she returned to Vienna in order to study oratorio and Lieder under Professor Erich Werba. — Attached to the Gelsenkirchen opera in West Germany in 1960, she sang leading roles in Düsseldorf, Heidelberg, Mainz, Krefeld and other European opera houses. On a visit to South Africa in 1967, she sang a leading role in *Die Fledermaus* (Johann Strauss), which her husband produced for PACT. Her husband is known professionally as Peter Brenner. In 1969 he was producer at the Opera House in Düsseldorf.

—Ed.

BRITTON, PHILIP JOHN, *29 January 1911 in London; °March 1971 in Adelaide. Former music organiser to the Natal Education Department.

P.J. Britton studied pianoforte under Arthur Baynon and in 1930 entered Oxford University to read simultaneously for Bachelor of Music and Bachelor of Arts (Modern Languages). His professors were Ernest Walker, Dr William Harris and Hugh Allen. In 1936 he came to South Africa as first full-time music-master to Hilton College, Natal, as well as organist and choirmaster of the chapel. He moved to Cape Town in 1939, where at first he taught class-music at Sea Point Boys' High School, then lectured in music at Battswood Training College, Wynberg, until he was appointed Inspector of Music to the Cape Education Department in 1944. Six years later he returned to Natal to become Music Organiser to the Natal Education Department. — In 1961 Britton was awarded a Carnegie Travel Grant which enabled him to study music education in the USA. Two years later he attended the World Conference of the International Society for Music Education in Tokyo. After a short period as Inspector of Indian Music to the Department of Indian Affairs, Britton sailed for Australia in May 1967 to take up an appointment as Lecturer in Music at the University of Adelaide.

SOURCE
The South African Music Teacher, June 1955 and June 1968.   —Ed.

BRITTON, WALTER GRANVILLE, *29 December 1889 in London; °12 April 1968 in Somerset West. Violoncellist.

On leaving school, Granville Britton gained a scholarship at Trinity College in London, where he obtained the performers' licentiate. He and Harold Ketelbey* participated in the first experimental recording of a string quartet (Haydn's *Kaiser*) for the Columbia Company. In 1910 he was engaged as principal cellist at the Fécamp Casino, and after a season of opera and symphony concerts, he went to Paris where he continued his studies under M. Cros St Ange at the Conservatoire National de Musique. He then returned to London where he was accepted by Henry Wood into the Queen's Hall Orchestra (1913). He performed the Dvorak cello concerto at a promenade concert in 1924, and played principal cello in the Carl Rosa Opera Company under Eugene Goosens, in the D'Oyly Carte Opera Company under Malcolm Sargent, and in the Royal Albert Hall Orchestra under Landon Ronald and others. — After visiting Canada, the USA and European countries, he came to South Africa in 1927 to join the Cape Town Municipal Orchestra* and the teaching staff of the South African College of Music*. He gave first performances in South Africa of notable works and participated in performances of new compositions as a member of various chamber music ensembles. Britton was a member of the Ellie Marx* and Elsie Hall* ensembles, the Charles Kreitzer String Quartet* and the Virginia Fortesque Piano Trio*. Many of their programmes were broadcast. On occasion

Britton was also soloist in concertos with South African orchestras.

—Ed.

BROEDRICH, ERWIN, *27 September 1903 in Libau, Latvia; a South African since 1931 and a resident of Pretoria since 1946. Violinist.

Erwin Broedrich was trained in violin playing by Siegfried Eberhardt of the Sternsche Conservatoire in Berlin and, at a later stage, by Joseph Wolfsthal of the Staatliche Musikhochschule. By the time he was 12, he played in public and after the termination of the First World War he gave concerts in various parts of Germany and in the Baltic states. He became leader of the State Theatre Orchestra in Hamburg and remained in that position until 1930. He came to South Africa on a visit during this year and in November he immigrated to this country and opened a studio in Johannesburg. Broedrich was an acquisition to music in Johannesburg. Apart from his teaching in the city and in Pretoria, he was also an active member of various chamber music groups. — He was the founder and leader of the Johannesburg String Quartette (with Hermann Becker*, Bobby Evans - violin 2 - and Else Schneider* - viola), which achieved great success through intensive preparation for every concert and the discipline of almost daily practice together. After 1935 he was also a member of chamber music groups led by Becker and Ketelbey*. Since 1941 he played in the SABC orchestra which had recently been created and performed concertos with this orchestra and with the orchestras of Cape Town and Durban. With his wife to accompany him, he also quite often played in radio programmes. — The South African pianist, Gudrun Stein, had been his accompanist since 1934. They married in 1935 and started on concert tours which eventually took them to all parts of South Africa. Through public concerts and performances accompanied by instructional talks at primary as well as high schools, they became well-known figures, even at small centres. These journeys took place quite frequently and amounted finally to some hundreds of concerts - an important contribution to musical life, especially of the country districts. — Broedrich had been lecturer in violin on the teaching panel of the Witwatersrand University since 1933 and UNISA's examiner for violin at intervals since 1945. Jack de Wet*, Bernard van der Linde*, Yvonne Lubbe and Gretchen Swanepoel are a few of his pupils. In 1960 he accepted an appointment on the staff of the Music Conservatoire in Pretoria, but he resigned in 1964 and devoted himself to private teaching in the two cities.

—Ed.

BROOKE, DIANA Higher Educational Institutions III/2, Cecilia Wessels

BROTHWOOD, CONSTANCE EDNA, *in Durban, still in Durban (1977). Pianist and music teacher.

Constance Brothwood began her piano study under Ethel Kerkin in Durban at the age of nine and two years later she performed the Mozart *Piano concerto in A* with the Durban Civic Orchestra*. After playing in the Durban Studio Orchestra under Leonard Pearce* from 1947 to 1953, she left for London to study privately under Elizabeth Grey at the RAM. Since her return to South Africa in 1954, she has been assistant to the SABC's music supervisor in the Durban studios and official accompanist and scriptwriter for musical programmes. She performs piano concertos with symphony orchestras of Johannesburg, Durban and Cape Town, and has toured the Eastern Province and Natal extensively, giving piano recitals.

Constance Brothwood broadcasts as soloist and in chamber groups, and is leader of the Studio Piano Trio*. Apart from her work as a pianist and accompanist, she has a large teaching practice.

—Ed.

BROWN, CLAUDE ENGLEFIELD, *23 April 1901 in Melton, Mowbray, England; since his retirement in 1965, he has been living in Port Elizabeth. Organist, teacher and conductor.

Claude Brown received a thorough grounding in English church music as a chorister at Worcester Cathedral from 1915 to 1924 and then as pupil-assistant to Dr Ivor Atkins. After continued music study, he was appointed an assistant music master at Wellington College, Berkshire (1928-1934), and became a Fellow of the RCO in 1932. — In April 1934, he came to South Africa as director of music to the Diocesan College* in Cape Town and distinguished himself in this position for thirty-one years until his retirement. His achievements in South Africa have been remarkable and he became recognized, not only as an outstanding conductor of choral works, but as a music master who impressed the boys of Bishops School with a love of music far beyond the ordinary. With characteristic energy, he arranged concerts in which the school orchestra was combined with the Cape Town Municipal Orchestra*, and at the end of his first year, directed the first Carol service, establishing a new tradition at the school. During the winter of 1936 he founded the school's choral society, which performed *Haiwatha's wedding feast* (Coleridge-Taylor) the next year. — Shortly after his arrival, he was invited to take over the Cape Melodic Society, which Eveline Fincken* had started as a group of madrigal singers at the College of Music*. It was re-named the Melodic Choir and under his leadership grew in membership to between 80 and 100 voices. Claude Brown very judiciously combined the adult voices of the Melodic Choir and the boys' voices of the College Choral Society for the performance of large-scale works which, until then, had not been presented in their entirety in Cape Town. At the first joint concert in 1944 a performance of Bach's *B minor mass* was given, followed at intervals by the *Sea symphony* (Vaughan-Williams), *Requiem* (Fauré), *The dream of Gerontius* (Elgar), *Belshazzar's feast* (Walton) and at their last joint concert on 2 September 1965, *Magnificat* (Bach), *Rio Grande* (Constant Lambert) and a repeat performance of *Hiawatha's wedding feast*. — Claude Brown at first acted as chorus master for Albert Coates* and William J. Pickerill*, but later conducted the works himself, although he also made use of the services of municipal conductors, such as Enrique Jordá and David Tidboald*. The French conductor, M. Berlinsky, shared the conducting honours with him when Fauré's *Requiem* was performed. For special occasions, such as the rendering of the *Sea symphony* the Melodic Choir and the Choral Society were reinforced by a special choir composed of volunteers and pupils of the Rustenburg Girls High School and the St Cyprian's School. — Even more important from Bishops' point of view, was Claude Brown's labours to promote English church music at the school. He introduced psalm singing in modern free-rhythm chanting, a great deal of plain song, modern English church music and sung Eucharists, which have all become an integral part of the school's musical life. In addition he paid attention to the extension of facilities for musical tuition in strings and wind instruments, instituted music evenings and organised special recitals by pupils and visiting artists. For his work at Bishops and for his efforts on behalf of English church music in South Africa, an honorary Doctorate of Music was conferred on Claude Brown by the Archbishop of Canterbury in 1940; whilst his services to choral music at the Cape were recognised by a special award of the Cape Tercentenary Foundation in September 1961. He was also an Honorary Member of the Royal Society of Church Musicians and their chief representative in South Africa from 1958-1967. — His encouragement of every kind of musical expression and his assistance to many pupils to develop their musical talents, have been successful. Andrew Porter*, chief music critic of the *Financial Times*, John Joubert*, composer, conductor and lecturer at the University of Birmingham, Timothy Farrell*, who had a distinguished career at the RCM, now assistant organist at St Paul's Cathedral in London, Robert Paterson, first South African concert impresario in London and Michael Brimer*, Professor of Music at the Cape Town University, are among his most prominent former pupils.

WRITINGS
Some thoughts on organs and organists. *SAMT* 22, May 1942.

—A.P.J. (amplified)

Brown, francis   Helderberg College

Brown, gus   Durban 7, Durban Operatic Society, R. Woodroffe

Brown, j. ferguson   Durban 3, 5, Organs 2 (iv), Touring Theatre Groups 4

Browne, e.r. (teddy)   Durban 8

Browne, walter   Touring Theatre Groups 4

Brüderkirche in south africa, church music of the
The story of the Brüderkirche's church music in South Africa is inseparable from the history of the Moravian mission stations. It would be difficult to describe such a thing as typical Moravian church music; the missionaries simply cultivated the music of the German Protestant church of the eighteenth and nineteenth centuries. But the liturgical wealth that characterizes their religious life is essentially Moravian, and their music maintained its character in South Africa longer even than in the Mother Church in Europe. — The Brüderkirche has from its inception placed much emphasis on singing, pioneering Protestant singing when it published its first evangelical hymn book in Prague in 1501. The tradition was passed on to Herrnhut, the first organised community of the New Brüderkirche. Count Von Zinzendorf, under whose leadership the renewal took place at a time when the pietistic movement was gaining way, said: "Those who sing and play for their God and never tire of doing so are found only among those who belong to Him, especially in the congregations". The piety of Herrnhut was joyous, and their services were festive occasions centered on the Saviour of sinners: worshippers desired to have communion with one another, and to testify of the Lamb of the world - feelings reflected in their church music. Von Zinzendorf himself composed about two thousand hymns. — Special church services were introduced in Herrnhut. During *sung services,* members of the community edify one another by singing a number of verses. In the *liturgies,* hymns or choral pieces alternate with Bible readings. In the *litanies* the pastor reads the prayers, which are interrupted by verses from a hymn sung by the congregation. On holy days, particularly during Lent and

Easter, there are *special liturgical services*. With this background, the missionaries of Herrnhut went abroad to heathen countries; the militant songs which Zinzendorf and his associates had sung accompanied them. — The first missionary to come to the Cape arrived in 1737. His name was Georg Schmidt. He had a good voice and loved singing; one of the first things he did was to teach hymns to the Hottentots in Baviaanskloof. Unfortunately, he had to leave the country after only five years. Fifty years later, in 1792, Hendrik Marsveld, Christian Kühnel and Daniel Schwinn resumed the work Georg Schmidt had begun. Marsveld and Kühnel played the flute and Schwinn the violin. After only a few months, they began to hold sung services with the Hottentots, using a Dutch hymn-book of the Brüderkirche, the second edition of 1787, with melodies. It appeared that the Hottentots loved music and had good voices; their old, heathen traditions, which were waning, were soon replaced by Christian habits. Their dances to primitive, home-made drums and stringed instruments, were replaced by evenings during which they sat together in their kraals, singing till late into the night. Funerals, which used to be conducted according to heathen practices, became Christian burials, at which the funeral liturgy of the Brüderkirche was used. The singing at Baviaanskloof elicited the admiration of visitors and colonists came from far and wide to join in celebrating the Christian festivals, since Baviaanskloof was the only centre of worship in an extensive area. — In 1806 Baviaanskloof was re-named and called Genadendal. Five or more missionaries with their wives and families, were the patriarchal rulers of the settlement, forming a community characterized by simplicity, naturalness and friendliness. Grace at meal-times took the form of a verse from some hymn that was sung before and after each meal; while on festive occasions, such as the birthdays of the missionaries, the Hottentots spontaneously came to the homestead to sing to them. More and more liturgical forms from Herrnhut were introduced at Genadendal. On New Year's Eve it was customary to play the melody of the hymn *Danke Gott, Wir alle danken Gott* on the violin, the clarinet, the flute and the horn; and on Palm Sunday the singers would render the *Hosanna*, a responsory composed by the Moravian musician, Christian Gregor, to piano accompaniment. In addition to the important religious festivals of the Christian Church, the Brüderkirche celebrated their own special days of remembrance (e.g. on 13 August and 13 November) and the days of various groups including the children's festival, and the festival of married persons. — Under the influence of Hans Peter Hallbeck (1817-1840), mission work in South Africa progressed in many ways. This missionary was a violinist, and he often used to play to the children of the nursery school he had established, and composed little songs for them. During this time a Dutch hymn book containing about 700 hymns was reprinted at the Cape for the use of missionaries; this hymn book was used at public services, as well as in homes for private edification. The following is an extract from the introduction to the hymn book: "Daartoe heeft men zich te meer aangespoord gevoeld, om dat ons is bekend geworden, dat onze lieve Hottentotsche broeders en zusters, niet alleen, zich zeer gaarn onderling stichten door gemeenschappelijk liederen te zingen, het zij in hunne huizen, of op velden en in boschen, maar dat zij daartoe ook door den Heer met aangenaam luidende stemmen begaafd zijn, waardoor zij reeds bij vele gelegenheden aan vreemde hoorders stof gegeven hebben, om god en onzen Heiland te verheerlijken, wiens lof tans weêrgalm in streken, die sedert zoo vele Eeuwen de woonplaatst geweest zijn slechts van woestheid en onkunde". (We were inspired by the discovery that our Hottentot brothers and sisters liked to edify each other by singing in their homes, on the fields or in the bush and that they have been blessed by the Lord with pleasantly sounding voices. This has often given strangers reason to bless our Saviour, whose praise is now resounding in regions which, for ages, have been in the grip of ignorance and barbarity.) — In this way German Protestant church music and hymns were introduced into South Africa, by means of translations into Dutch. The hymn book was eagerly purchased by the Colonials and very soon there were few farms in the vicinity of Genadendal and Elim without a copy of the Brothers' hymn book. — In 1839 Hallbeck had copies printed in Holland of *Litanijen en Gezangen, behoorende tot de Liturgie der Evangelische Broedergemeenten* (Litanies and hymns pertaining to the liturgy of the Evangelic Congregations of the Brother Church.) This collection contained liturgies for Christmas, Advent and Easter, as well as church prayers and a formulary. The liturgy pertaining to Easter Morning - sung at dawn in the cemetery - was a declaration of faith made by the whole community. In 1877 the very popular *Kategismuskerkgebed* (Episcopal prayer of the Catechism) was added to the collection. It had originated at another Moravian mission station in Suriname, and was a liturgical arrangement of Martin Luther's *Klein Kategismus* (Shorter Catechism) in the form of a responsory between the Minister and the congregation, interspersed with suitable verses from hymns. — In 1832 the first organ was installed at Genadendal. Hallbeck, his wife and Dr E. Lees - the mission doctor of the station - were the first to play on it, although Hallbeck immediately began to teach Ezechiel Pfeiffer, one of the youths in the community, to play the organ. — The founding of a theological seminary at Genadendal in 1838 became an important factor in promulgating its church music. Teachers and evangelical workers were trained there; the first director, Christian Friedrich Francke, was also a very talented musician. He established church choirs at Genadendal, and subsequently at Mamre (then known as Groenekloof), concentrating on well-known German choral pieces. Members of the choir were regarded as functionaries of the congregation - as were the ministers, the teachers, the church officials, and the supervisors - and every one of them partook of the annual eucharist for religious servants. They also held regular sacred concerts in which children as well as missionaries took part. By 1840 there were seven Moravian mission stations; and all were famous for their festivals and characteristic church music. — Music was also taught at the seminary, and was a popular subject among the students, many of whom were exceptionally gifted. They were taught to play the organ, the piano or the violin, and how to conduct a choir. The seminary had a brass band which, in accordance with the custom of the Brüderkirche in Europe, roused the community early in the morning on festival days, or accompanied a funeral procession to the cemetery; it also welcomed guests, or performed in front of the church before festival services. — Students of the seminary became competent musicians by the time they qualified, and the result was that other mission stations eventually had their own bands. Thus teachers came gradually to supersede missionaries, as organists and choir-leaders of the communities they served. Ezechiel Pfeiffer (mentioned above) was the first of many. From 1842 he served as the organist, choir-leader and teacher of the nursery school at Genadendal. The first Bantu to complete his studies at the seminary was Johannes Nakin. When he returned to Silo in 1853, after an absence of eight years, he was able to play the harmonium, to the astonishment of his own people. He created quite a stir in 1875, when he played the organ in the Lutheran Church in Cape Town, during a visit to the city. — In 1859 the seminary at Genadendal started its own printing press for the purpose of printing books and other publications concerning the work of the Mission. One of the first publications was *De kleine Zang-Vriend*, printed by students of the seminary under the supervision of Benno Marx. The booklet contained a collection of school hymns printed with the music. Then there was the *Lijdensgezangen over de seven Kruiswoorden* (Passion hymns on the Seven Words on the Cross), used for services held during Lent; and in 1879 this press issued the official hymn book of the church for the first time. It was re-issued in 1893. In 1895 the liturgies were published, but without the melodies; the books of the German Brüderkirche of 1784 and 1893 were used for this purpose. — In 1890 the first coloured man, Edward Weber, was appointed as a teacher at the seminary, mainly because he was better qualified to teach music than the missionary himself. He was exceptionally gifted, also composing music. One of his compositions for piano, harmonium, two violins and cello, was sent to Herrnhut to be performed there, and he became known for his performances on the organ in various Anglican Churches in the Cape. He had the knack of training students for the task of conducting choirs and wind bands. — The Moravian congregations among the Bantu in the Eastern Cape - which became a separate province in 1869 - had their own hymn books, published in Xhosa, consisting of a selection of Moravian hymns. But the bands that were started by these congregations did not survive long, and they were also unable to maintain the festival days of the Brüderkirche. Other church missions became more influential among them, and the Moravian church customs gradually died out. — But among the Coloured congregations of the Western Cape, Moravian customs have been upheld to this day, and some of them have retained liturgies and choral pieces of the nineteenth century that have disappeared among congregations of the Brüderkirche in Europe. Among these there are works by Praetorius, Händel, Bach, Haydn, Mendelssohn, as well as works by a few Moravian composers, such as Latrobe, Gregor and Hellstroem. Several hymns, together with essential church prayers and a formulary, were published in Afrikaans for the first time in 1947 and 1949. The latest hymn book, published in 1959, contains more than seven hundred hymns and several liturgies. In 1964 the Brüderkirche published its first harmonized hymn book in South Africa. These last two books contain a wealth of old hymns and tunes that are now again made available to the churches of today.

BIBLIOGRAPHY

HUTTON, J.E.: *A history of the Moravian Church*. London, 1909.

SOURCES

Collection of old hymn books, liturgical books and choral works in the archives of Genadendal.   Diaries of the mission stations in the archives of Genadendal, Elim, Clarkson and Silo.

—B.K.

BRUGHES-BRISCOE, E.B. J.F. Endler

BRYANT, H Guild of Church Musicians, Johannesburg Philharmonic Society, E.M. Slatter

BRYANT, R.M. J.S. Yates

BUCHAN, REV. AND MRS.   Potchefstroom 2

BUCKINGHAM, LESLEY   A. Parkerson

BUNTING, S.P.   Johannesburg Musical Society

BURGERS, PRESIDENT T.F. AND MRS. BURGERS (MARY BRYSON)   Graaff Reinet 3, Pretoria
1, C.F. van Rees, Volkslied - Transvaalse

BURGESS, A.M.E.   Port Elizabeth I/5

BURNE, GARY, *20 April 1936 in Bulawayo, Rhodesia; at present in Cape Town. Ballet
dancer.

A pupil of Elaine Archibald, he was advised by Dolin and Markova on their first visit
to Rhodesia in 1948, to pursue his career overseas. In England he studied with Ruth
French in 1951, and then joined the Royal Ballet School. Promoted to the Royal
Ballet Company four months later, he became soloist in 1956, and subsequently first
soloist. He toured America and the continent with the Royal Ballet, and in 1960
joined John Cranko* as guest artist in Stuttgart for eighteen months. — In 1963
Burne was appointed Ballet Master and Principal Dancer of Ballet Transvaal (later
PACT). During this time he was guest artist, twice, with NAPAC Ballet. Since 1965
he has been principal dancer of the CAPAB Ballet Company. — Gary Burne danced
in *Mamzelle Angot, The lady and the fool, Checkmate, Prince of the pagodas* and
other ballets with the Royal Ballet, and in the classic repertoire at Stuttgart.

—M.G.

BURNS, GRAHAM DOUGLAS, *21 March 1922 in Lameroo, South Australia; living in
Johannesburg in 1977. Bass-baritone.

Burns studied singing at the Elder Conservatorium in Australia from 1941 to 1950,
giving broadcast recitals during this period. Since settling in South Africa in 1951, he
has sung as soloist in *Messiah, Elijah* and *The creation* in Johannesburg and Port
Elizabeth, apart from appearances with orchestras in Johannesburg and Durban. He
has also given broadcast recitals. — Graham Burns is the founder-conductor of the
Christian Choral Society which gave performances of *Messiah* and the *St Matthew
Passion* (Bach) in Johannesburg in 1961 and 1962.

—Ed.

BURNS, R.R.   East London III

BURNS-WALKER, W.   Nunez Holtzhausen, Louis Knobel, Isobel McLaren

BURTON, DR A.W.   King William's Town 8

BUSS, FRITZ JOSEPH, *26 December 1930 in Cologne; in Johannesburg in 1977.
Guitarist.

Fritz Buss, who took up the guitar at the age of nine, is a member of a musical family.
In the early post-war period he was employed as a coach-builder and played in a
leading plucked-instrument orchestra in his spare time. He became first guitarist of
this orchestra at the age of fifteen. In March 1954, Fritz Buss immigrated to South
Africa and settled in Johannesburg. On his arrival he found that virtually no suitable
guitars, strings or sheet music were available and he was largely responsible for
rectifying this situation. In 1958 he founded the Classical and Spanish Guitar
Association of South Africa, which now has a large membership. — Throughout

241

these years his study of the guitar continued unaided; but when Narciso Yepes visited South Africa in 1960, he invited Buss to become his pupil in Madrid. Since his return to South Africa in October 1961, he has spent two more periods of study with Yepes, in 1964 and again in 1966. During the latter year he accompanied Yepes on his concert tour of Europe. — In South Africa Buss often gives recitals and broadcasts. He is at present on the staff of the Music Department of the University of the Witwatersrand*.

—Ed.

BUTTON, MRS   Barberton I, Piano Music I/2

CABINET PIANOFORTE, COTTAGE PIANO, PICCOLO FORTE PIANO, PIANINO   Piano Music, South African I/2(ii)

CALDECOTT, MADELAINE   Johannesburg 2, Johannesburg Musical Society

CALEDONIAN SOCIETIES   Bloemfontein, Johannesburg, King William's Town, Natal Mounted Rifles Pipe Band, Port Elizabeth, Queenstown, W. Tregarthen

CALUZA, REUBEN THOLAKELE,   *14 November 1895 at Edenvale near Pietermaritzburg; °5 March 1969. Zulu composer, lecturer in music at the University of Zululand.

The grandson of John Mlungumnyama Caluza, the first choral conductor at Edendale and perhaps the first Zulu to teach from staff notation, Caluza was educated at Ohlange Institute (1909-1914), where he trained a male quartet (which toured with a mixed choir). After his appointment as a teacher at this institution, Caluza devoted much of his time to the training and conducting of choirs. On two different occasions he spent a year at the Mariannhill Training College (1918 and 1921), where he also had the training of a choir. They sang his *Ixegwana* in 1921. — In 1930 His Master's Voice Gramophone Company contacted Caluza at the Ohlange Institute and arranged for a double quintet to record Zulu songs in England. In all, 150 songs were recorded, of which 45 were Caluza's own compositions, 30 his arrangements of existing tunes and the rest traditional Zulu songs. After completing this assignment, the members of the quintet returned to South Africa, but Caluza went on to Virginia in America, to study at the Hampton Institute. He was there for four years and obtained a Bachelor's Degree in Music after composing a *Rondo for orchestra* and a string quartet entitled *Reminiscences of Africa*. At Hampton Institute Caluza organised a quartet of West African students and taught them to sing traditional Zulu songs, after they had toured the Southern States of America with a programme of Negro Spirituals. From Hampton Institute he moved to Columbia University where he studied Music Education for two-and-a-half years, obtaining an MA degree for which he submitted two string quartets, based on his own *Ricksha* and *Go down Moses* respectively. — On his return to South Africa in 1937, Caluza was appointed on the staff of Adams College, as Head of Music. Here he trained a choir which toured South Africa annually, and which also broadcast on several occasions. Ten years later he retired from Adams College, to devote himself to his Sizanenjana Trading Store at Pietermaritzburg, which is now the head office for two similar stores, the Hemuhemu Trading Store at Pietermaritzburg, and the Nkumba Store at Bulwer. When the University College of Zululand was instituted in 1962, Caluza was persuaded to return to the academic field as a part-time lecturer in choral music.

— Unlike the works of most Bantu composers, Caluza's songs occasionally move chromatically, especially in the melody, and the influence of syncopated music is readily perceived. In *U Tokoloshe* he actually modulates into a related key, an extremely rare thing in Bantu music.

WORKS

A. Vocal (words by composer)

Amagama Ohlange Lakwe Zulu (Book of Zulu songs). Ama Shooting Stars ase Adams (EManzimtoti). Basundu Base Afrika (Yekan' Umona Nenzondo). Bushuka Ndabanzini (Pub. Lovedale). Elamakosi (Pub. Lovedale). Elama Zebras Asohlange. Elase Tafamasi. Emathawini. Guga Mzimba sala Ntliziyo (Pub. Lovedale). Hambani niye Emhlabeni wonke. Idiphu e Thekwini (Pub. Adams). Ihashi Elimhlophe. Inanda Seminary (Umah U Edwards ... Ugodukile Umah Edwards) (Pub. Lovedale). Influenza (Ka 1918) (Pub. Lovedale). Ingoduso (Pub. Lovedale). Intandane (Pub. Lovedale). Isangoma (Pub. Lovedale). Izimfashini. Izinsizwa Ezimbili. Izizwe Ezimnyama. Ixegwana (Ricksha song) (Pub. Lovedale, 1921). Ku nadziha ka wonhlangano (Hymn in TINSIMU) KwaMadala (Pub. Lovedale). Kwati-Belele (Pub. Lovedale). Mtaka baba (Pub. Lovedale). Mvelinqangi. Ngife Ngokuthula. Nkhensa! Moya wa nga (Hymn in TINSIMU) Nyikithi (Pub. Lovedale). Pick-up van (Pub. Adams). Sanibona (Pub. Lovedale). Sikulel' U Solomon (Pub. Lovedale). Silusapho Lwase Africa (Pub. Lovedale, 1912). Silu Sapa (Pub. Lovedale). Siyanibingelela Nina Zhlobo Zethu. Thula Mtwana (Arr. of trad.). Thuthukani. Tokoloshe. Ubhataba. U-Bungca (Ama Oxford bags) (Pub. Lovedale). Umona Neczondo. Umtaka Baba (Pub. Lovedale). Umthakathi (Pub. Lovedale). UTokoloshe. Vukani Bansundu. Vulindlela Mtaka Dube (Pub. Lovedale). Woza Mfowethu (Pub. Lovedale). Xaula Baba, Xaula Mama. Yekan' Umona (Pub. Lovedale). Yingi, sa ni nwe vamakwenthu (Hymn in TINSIMU). Ziyadhlula Izinsuku Zami (Rel.).

B. Instrumental

Rondo for orchestra. Ms., n.d. Reminiscences of Africa, string quartet. Ms., n.d. String quartet no. 2. Ms., n.d. String quartet no. 3. Ms., n.d.

BIBLIOGRAPHY

De Beer, Zelda: *Analysis of choral works by the Zulu composer, Professor R.T. Caluza.* B.Mus. script, UP, 1967. Huskisson, Yvonne: *The Bantu composers of Southern Africa,* SABC, 1969; with supplement, HSRC, 1974. Van der Merwe, F.Z.: *Suid-Afrikaanse musiekbibliografie, 1787-1952.* J.L. van Schaik, Pretoria, 1958. Supplemented for 1953-1972 by Jan van de Graaf. HSRC, Pretoria, 1974.

SOURCES

Information submitted by Prof. P.R. Kirby. National Documentation Centre for Music, HSRC, Pretoria.

—Ed.

Calvé, h.m. East London, A. Rainier

Cambrian male voice choir N.R. Ingleby

Cambridge musical society East London III

Campbell, l.h. Radio Bantu

Campbell-Rowland, a. Organs 11

CANEY, GROGAN, *16 May 1878 in London; °28 December 1966 in Hillcrest, Natal. · Baritone.

Caney was brought to South Africa when he was three years old, spent most of his early life in Pietermaritzburg, learnt to play the piano at the age of 9, and started teaching singing when he was only 18. In 1913, at the age of 35, Caney so impressed Sir Alexander Mackenzie that he arranged for him to be trained at the RAM. There he obtained the LRAM after one year and returned to South Africa in May 1915 to resume his teaching practice in Pietermaritzburg and Durban. — Caney frequently appeared as soloist in performances of oratorios, trained the choir of the Durban Musical Association (which in 1930 became the Durban Municipal Choir) and coached choruses for local productions of operettas; in some of these he sang the leading roles. Blessed with youthfulness of spirit and a great desire to help young musicians, he taught for about 70 years, his pupils including Rose Alper*, Gladys Daniel*, Peggy Whiteside and (in recent years) Thelma Whitcutt (Mrs Macdonald). In 1964 Durban awarded him civic honours, in appreciation of "a lifetime devoted to fostering the musical and cultural life of this city, and advancing worthy causes".

WRITINGS
Presidential message. *SAMT* 16, April 1939.   Kindly advice to students of singing. *SAMT* 24, June 1943.

SOURCES
Natal Daily News: 29 December 1966.   *Natal Mercury:* 29 December 1966.

—G.S.J.

CANTARE SONG SOCIETY, THE was founded in Pretoria in 1956 when, on the invitation of Helena Strauss*, a group of women met to start singing together.

Initially they only sang for their own pleasure, but since their first public performance in the Voortrekker Memorial Hall in Pretoria on 5 September 1958, they have been heard frequently, not only at concerts, but also in radio broadcasts. The membership is restricted to twenty singers, chosen in accordance with a careful disposition of high sopranos, second sopranos, and altos. However, in 1970 the membership was increased to 24 singers. — A similar choral group was formed for male voices in 1960. They were initially led by Pierre Malan*, assisted by Anton Kratz. He was succeeded by Ria Nel, then by Pieter de Villiers* and eventually in 1968 the conductorship passed on to Derik van der Merwe*. Although the two groups have amalgamated for combined performances, each retained its own identity as an independent choir. Together they have toured the country districts for PACT, and have given performances of Bach cantatas and participated in opera and oratorio performances. — The Cantare Song Society has made two long-playing records, one devoted to works by South African composers and another to the folk songs of various countries. In 1960 they were designated the best South African choir during choral competitions organised by the SABC. Pieter de Villiers has dedicated his *Op die Krovlak* to this choir.

SOURCE
National Documentation Centre for Music, HSRC, Pretoria.

—H.S.

CAPAB   (Cape Performing Arts Board), P.O. Box 4107, Cape Town.

244

CAPE COLOUREDS   Brüderkirche, Cape Malay Music, EOAN Group, J. Manca, W.L. Sammons, J.H. van Loggerenberg.

CAPE GUILD OF ORGANISTS, THE, was formed in 1923 by a group of Cape Town organists, Dr. T. Barrow-Dowling* (who became the first President), and Messrs R.N. Ingleby*, Mosdell, W.E. Ranby, A.P. Abbott and F.A. Burgess, with the objects of promoting good fellowship and mutual aid between members, and proficiency in organ and choral music, both sacred and secular. Membership of the Guild, upon which all Christian denominations are represented, is extended to persons who have filled for not less than six months the office of organist in a place of worship, and to organ builders. Bona fide students of the organ, who do not comply with the requirements for membership, are eligible as student members. Management is vested in a committee, consisting of a President, Vice President, Secretary, Treasurer-Librarian and three members. Past presidents have been i.a. Dr Barrow-Dowling, R.N. Ingleby, Dr J. Alban Hamer*, Dr Claude Brown*, Walter Swanson* and Barry Smith*. On 7 November 1925, the Guild was affiliated to the Incorporated Association of Organists, an international association based in London. — Meetings of the Guild are normally held each month. Its activities include the maintenance of a reference and circulating library of books, magazines and sheet music; the maintenance of a register of organists available for deputizing at churches; lectures; discussions; demonstrations of organ playing; inspection of organs. The Guild is responsible for the production of combined choral concerts and conducts the annual examinations for the Barrow-Dowling Organ Scholarship. The Guild has its own benevolent fund for members and periodically investigates the salaries of organists, if necessary sending recommendations and suggestions based on comparative fees and qualifications to the Church authorities concerned.

—A.S.T.

CAPE MALAYS, THE   The Cape Malays form a sub-group of about 100 000 people within a coloured community of approximately $1^1/_2$ million. Although they reveal typically Indonesian features, they are no longer regarded exclusively as members of one racial community. As early as 1652 the first of them were brought to the Cape from Batavia; in 1658 still more arrived as free servants who, however, were registered at the Cape as slaves. Slaves and political exiles from Java, Bali, Celebes, Ternate and Madagascar followed, so that gradually Islam gained a firm foothold at the Cape. Miscegenation occurred, and eventually the name Malay was no longer used exclusively for those of Malay origin, but for all who were associated with the Malays at the Cape. The term "Slamse" is now employed with the meaning of Moslems. The mixture of races took place gradually, with the result that Eastern characteristics were preserved; besides this, scrupulous observance of religious precepts has undoubtedly contributed to the Malays' quiet and dignified self-respect, in spite of one-time slavery and suppression. The designation "kings of the slaves", and later "aristocrats of the coloured people", has repeatedly been applied to them. They have a strong, intrinsic refinement, but for Western people they are also inscrutable. — For slaves who could make music, large sums were paid. When the famous bibliophile, J.N. von Dessin, died in 1761, his estate included two French horns, two violins, one oboe, two trumpets and a violoncello, the instruments on which his slaves had played. It is known that in 1756 he made a good purchase in the form of a slave from Madagascar, who could cook, make tarts and other sweet things, and "played the flute, oboe and hunting horn". Lichtenstein describes a concert by slaves in 1803 at the home of a certain Mr Van Reenen, where marches and dances were performed on clarinets, horns and bassoons. Later the same slaves played on stringed instruments and flutes. He also records that other families had similar bands and that there were a number of free men in the town who gave the slaves music lessons. Because neither the teachers nor their pupils could read, they played entirely by ear. — This was also the experience of Lady Duff Gordon, who relates how, in an hotel on New Year's Day in 1862, she sat listening to the noise of concertinas, until two Malay bricklayers came in. The one had a tambourine, while the other took over a concertina. Under his fingers the latter was transformed into an harmonious instrument, on which could be performed a great variety of dances, with a precision "only equalled by an orchestra of Strauss". He laughed heartily when she asked him if he could read music and answered that music existed in the ears and not in the eyes: he had listened to everything played by bands in the Cape. The following evening he played a new repertoire, including arias from *La traviata*. David Kennedy, a member of the company of Scottish singers who toured this country in 1879, relates that they had a large number of Malays in their audiences; what was played to them in the concert hall could be heard in the streets of the Malay quarter the next day. — The Malays are conservative and loyal, people who find it difficult to adjust themselves to altered circumstances. They do not keep pace with the tempo of modern life, which is foreign to their nature. They like to talk of bygone days, or sing of Napoleon, or imagine they are going to Batavia and Holland. Their attachment to a fairy-tale Holland exists only in the imagination and relates to a "kweningin" (queen) whom they revere, to "visters" (fishermen) on "klompertjies" (wooden clogs), to "meulens" (wind mills), and little red, white and blue flags. To these memories may be ascribed the Malays' love of old Dutch folk-songs, forgotten in the land of their origin. Street songs, which had a short-lived existence in Holland, are still sung by the Malay community, and have been absorbed into their very lives; even their speech is interspersed with sentences and expressions from Dutch songs. — To what extent the existence of these songs relies on the ear alone cannot be established with certainty. Perhaps many of the songs were temporarily neglected, and brought back into their repertoire by means of sheet music and song books. Dutch songs of the sixteenth and seventeenth centuries, such as *De twee koningskinderen, Ek ben er de groene straatjes, Zou daar een magetje vroeg opstaan,* and eighteenth and nineteenth century songs inherited from Holland, are still being sung at bridal tables, or on the street in the evening, at the turn of the year. These nightly perambulations are another old custom taken over from the Hollanders at the Cape. Songs flow in the blood of the Malays, are handed down from father to son, and are still sung spontaneously by community choirs at the annual competitions in January and February. — George French Angas (1849) and David Kennedy jun. (1879) give descriptions of Malay weddings which are of interest because from these it appears that present-day weddings do not differ greatly from those of the past, and that love songs were formerly also sung on such occasions. "The Malays are exceedingly musical", writes Kennedy. "In the beautiful starry evenings you hear their partsongs, some of the fellows singing at their open windows; and now and again a string of them extending across the broad street and shouting ballads to the accompaniment of guitar and concertina. They have quick ears". The pity is that Kennedy mentions no titles. — Charles du Val* (1882) mentions a song that throws some light on repertoire extension, after the opening of the Suez Canal (to which we shall revert). The short passage is so entertainingly written, that it is given in full: "... The men appear to be endowed with musical faculties and an immense appreciation for melodies of all kinds, and are to be met on summer nights patrolling the streets singing solos and choruses, a deep bass like a drone coming in occasionally with a most peculiar effect. I met a party one evening and listened to their song. I mentally soliloquized: 'Now I shall hear in reality some curious old oriental ballad or "Paymin" (he means, of course Paynim) chant, probably handed down from the days of the Hegira, and in which the story of Mohammed and his wondrous life will be recounted.' So I waited, and they advanced, and as the strains of their song fell upon my listening ear, I fancied I had heard the melody before, and I said: 'It is! No - it can't be. Yes, it is - My Grandfather's Clock!' - and I fled". A few pages further on Du Val describes his first Christmas at the Cape: "A motley crowd of young niggers with drums and banners marched past, singing a chorus which sounded like a blending of Rob Roy MacGregor and Marching Through Georgia". From this description we cannot say with certainty who the "niggers" were, but on Christmas, Old and New Year, and on other occasions such as Guy Fawkes Day, the Coloureds, including the Malays, still promenade to sing and make music. — According to this extract, not much has changed in the lives of the conservative Malays; but gradually English and American songs began to make their appearance. Even the Dantie brothers, who were famous for their rich repertoire of Dutch songs, began to yield to these foreign influences. Indeed, they were the people who in 1888 inaugurated the Coon tradition (the New Year carnival of the coloured people), after a visit to Cape Town by a group of Nigger Minstrels from America in the previous year. Anglicization began to gain ground after 1869 when the supply of Dutch songs dried up. After the opening of the Suez Canal, and the changing of routes to the Dutch East Indies, no more Dutch sailors came ashore in Cape Town. The Malays retained the old Dutch repertoire, especially for weddings, but new songs were taken over holus-bolus by people who just wanted to sing. — At the close of the last century, and the beginning of the present, a Dutch sailor, Frans de Jong, took the fez, joined the Malays, and with Rasdien Cornelius brought new life to the singing of Dutch songs. Mr C.J. van Rijn, a Dutch teacher in Cape Town, practised new songs with them at the piano. For this purpose song books and loose sheet music were ordered from Holland, and distributed among coloured singers. Especially prominent in this respect were Rasdien Cornelius and the Dantie brothers. The choirs that were formed sang the new songs as well as the old favourites, which, surviving dimly in memory, were soon revived and corrected. Thereafter these songs circulated once more among the people, and with the passage of time were adapted to the character of the Moslem people. Many other songs betray strong Dutch influence: for example, *Toen ek op Nederlands bergje stond/Kyk ek de see rol aan.* Dutch visitors to the Mother City are surprised to hear half forgotten songs of Holland sung in amusing distortions through which the originals can hardly be˙distinguished. That the Malayan national character differs from the Dutch is self-evident; but here we are concerned with a people in whom Eastern and Western traditions have coalesced. — Songs of the original Malays can no longer be traced, but individual Ghoema or "afklopliedjies" can be assigned to the earliest days. The "ghoema" songs were popular at picnics and lively gatherings, and were sometimes dramatized as a dance in which the men and women formed a circle round the ghoema-player (= drum player) and leading singer. Usually there followed a whole series of "ghoema" songs, one after the other. The resultant effect is disjointed, emphasised even more by the practice of adding humorous fragments arising from the excitement of the moment, or from some hidden wellspring in the heart of the singer. The words are however always subservient to the melody and the rhythm. The term *ghoema* or *ghomma* is derived from the *ghomma*, a single-headed drum made from a small cask with a skin nailed over one of the open ends. These are still in regular use among the Malays. — The so-called "moppies" may be mentioned here - genuine Cape songs with a comic intention, in which is concealed the suggestion of a story. Very well known is *Alabama, Beestepote, Jannewarie - Feberwarie - March;* not so well known are *Ou Galiema* and *Batavia*. The repertoire consists of Dutch songs and those composed by the Malays themselves, in a Dutch-Malay dialect and style, with a Cape impress inspired by the minnat songs. A popular example is *Laas toen ek een meisje bemin.* — The minnat songs (love songs, wedding songs) are sung by a precentor and a choir, in a slow drawling way, with swaying bodily movements to the sides. At a wedding reception any guest may take the lead and the whole company, all thoroughly conversant with the song which he intones, supports him in the chorus. The accompanying instruments - banjos, guitars and a cello, carried by means of a strap around the neck and called a bass - play preludes and intermezzi, usually anchored on I IV V I, which often remain unchanged for the various songs. The harmonies of the supporting choir, which comes in at the end of lines and sentences, are usually quite primitive, although at the present time, through the influence of radio and gramophone, more use is being made of occasional chromatic notes, interrupted cadences and mediant relationships. From a good choir, which may ultimately accept the role of a leader, one can hear a sort of improvized counterpoint, arising in the form of counter decorations. These decorations ("krinkeltjies" or "klossies") are Eastern arabesques, with which the leader decorates his solo. Such decoration must not, however, be compared with the ornaments of present-day Western music, where it serves mainly to adorn a melody. They neither adorn nor beautify; they are the life and soul of the song itself, and should rather be compared to the "gamakas" of Indian music. — The Andalusian singers in their "cante jondo" employ the same technique; they, too, have been influenced by the East. "Without gamakas a melody can't smile", said Stoll. A Malay once tried to sing *De twee koningskinderen* without arabesques, but gave it up after a few bars; he could not sing it in that way, and lost the thread, because so rendered, the song meant nothing to him. Not only the use of the voice is Eastern, but also the treatment of the melody that fulfils the function of a tonal pattern, which can be freely embroidered and varied in countless ways. Syllables, words and sentences are repeated, notes and musical figures are inserted, and often a new melody arises, which, however, relies heavily on the underlying structure of the original melody (Arabic: *maqām*). — To evaluate the songs of the Malays, one must not be satisfied with the commonplace observation that they originate in Indonesia, and that the technique of their performance is therefore Oriental. Originally, that is true; but just as the Malays' own songs had to make way for those of Holland, so the style of singing them had to change under the influence of unsympathetic influences, although the essential spirit remained unaltered. In the present century the Malays have proved on two occasions how easily they can switch to a new style of singing. The first was when they were practising from song books at the piano; the second occurred during competitions, when inexpert judges wanted to steer them in the direction of the Italian bel canto. Other influences worked on this remarkable mixture of old Dutch songs and Eastern singing technique. In the eighteenth century Hollanders at the Cape with private bands, disapproved of their native tunes and the Malays then abandoned them to adopt Dutch songs, rudimentary notions of European harmony and the playing of such instruments as the flute, oboe, horn, violin and cello - all of which are non-Eastern. However, they began to make Western music with an Eastern colour, in the form of rhythmic irregularities, and (in the case of vocal music) oriental arabesques. Hollanders did not feel completely strange in the presence of this Malayan style of performance, since they had known it in Europe, and had themselves actually come under its influence. As late as 1884 G. Kalff mentioned this "vreemde zingen van ons volk", and one still comes across remnants in isolated communities, such as the one in Volendam. In Scheveningen the fishermen speak of "op een zeetje zingen" when referring to embellishments added to their singing, comparing it with the little waves and ripples which disturb a calm sea. — Malay choirs and choir competitions play an important part in their musical life and should certainly be mentioned. Their choral singing is of two kinds. Firstly, there is the purely social singing, which is practised on a round of visits to friends and acquaintances. The visiting group sings a few songs, alone or together with their hosts, are served with refreshments and then move on to the next stop on their itinerary. This sociable musical habit is especially in evidence on New Year's Eve, when the singing continues right through the night until dawn the next day. The singers are usually dressed in a manner suitable to the festivity of the occasion: suits or blazers and flannels, hats replacing the usual fez whilst they are on their way. Secondly, there are the annual choral festivals during which trained groups compete in the Cape Town City Hall, with adjudicators to select the prize-winning groups. A possible origin of the itinerant singers and their off-shoot, the competing choirs, might be traced to the old Boer habit of visiting friends and relations at the turn of the year to wish them well. The Malays may have copied this practice, clothing it in music, and thus established a tradition of group singing, which developed into organised choral singing when it became a question of maintaining folksong traditions in a changing world. Group singing is referred to at times during the nineteenth century. In his *Tavern of the ocean* Laidler mentions the way Malays have of wandering about the streets after sunset, singing their songs in the moonlight, and towards the end of the century *The Cape Argus* reports that a group calling themselves *The star of independence* had thanked the mayor of the City for his permission to hold a torchlight procession on New Year's Eve (7 January 1888) (also see Du Val: mentioned above). This tradition gradually grew into the idea of having competitions, primarily for the fun of it, but indirectly serving to preserve traditions which can be traced back to the 18th century. — They have proved to be extremely popular with the Malays, as an opportunity of asserting their existence in a vocal way. The festivals have grown considerably since the first efforts at the beginning of the century and nowadays about 50 choirs take part, each with a complement of about 80 lusty voices. Women never take part in these public eruptions of a vital and energetic art. The City Hall is filled to overflowing on each occasion and the festival has increased in size to comprise five consecutive evenings. Four items are prescribed for each choir: an "old" song, a "moppie", a solo and a "Dutch" song. The competitions last until late night, when the prizes are distributed and the choral groups depart homewards, singing as they go. The "old" song, also called "Combine Chorus", is regularly sung by the whole group. For some reason this type is regarded very highly by the Malays. The other songs are generally based on a responsorial pattern with guitars, banjos, mandolines and a cello, slung over the shoulder on a strap, providing the accompaniment. The solo bits are distinguished by the antics and contortions of the singer which afford the audience much cause for merriment. — As far as folk singing is concerned, the Malays are unquestionably gifted, bringing the art to life in a totally uninhibited way. But it does not seem at this stage that they are taking to serious Western music to any appreciable extent. They simply sing for the love of it and combine tradition with novelty in a wonderfully vital way. Theirs is certainly a living art, although the roots are venerable with age.

BIBLIOGRAPHY

DU PLESSIS, I.D.: *Die hydrae van die Kaapse Maleier tot die Afrikaanse volkslied.* Nasionale Pers, Cape Town, 1935.   DU PLESSIS, I.D.: *Maleise liederskat, 'n sangbundel vir die Kaapse kore.* Nasionale Pers, Cape Town, 1939.   DU PLESSIS, I.D.: *Die Maleise samelewing aan die Kaap.* Nasionale Pers, Cape Town, 1939.   DU PLESSIS, I.D.: *Tales from the Malay Quarter.* Maskew Miller, Cape Town, 1945.   DU PLESSIS, I.D. and LÜCKHOFF, C.A.: *The Malay Quarter and its people.* Balkema, Cape Town, 1953.   DU PLESSIS, I.D.: *The Cape Malays.* A.A. Balkema, Cape Town, 1972.   DU VAL, C.: *With a show through Southern Africa.* 2 Vols. Tinsley Bros., London, 1884.

—W.v.W. (amplified)

CAPE MUSICAL MONTHLY   D. Barrable, E. Mendelssohn, King William's Town 11, Queenstown 6, 7, E.W. Welch

CAPE MUSICIANS' ASSOCIATION   W. Swanson

CAPE RECORD COLLECTOR'S SOCIETY, THE   was established in Cape Town in 1957. Its first meeting was held on 9 July 1957. Messrs S. Tockar, B. Lemonsky and C. Groenewald* were the founding members and Dr C.G.S. de Villiers* is the honorary president.

The aim of this organisation is to pay tribute to the great singers of the past and to bring together the record collectors of Cape Town and vicinity. The emphasis is on historical vocal recordings, but sometimes historical recordings by instrumentalists, conductors and chamber music societies, as well as recordings by modern musicians, are included in the programmes. — Monthly meetings are held in Garmor House, Plumstead, Cape Town.

—C.G.

CAPE TOWN AMATEUR OPERATIC AND DRAMATIC SOCIETY   N.R. Ingleby, W. Versfeld

CAPE TOWN CHAMBER MUSIC SOCIETY, THE   was formed by Charles Kreitzer* and Hannes Uys* in 1947, with I.D. du Plessis as Chairman of the committee, the aim being to foster an interest in chamber music. Subsequent Chairmen have been Sir Herbert Stanley, Sir Alfred Beit, Dr. William Pickerill* and A.H. Broeksma. The Society offers seasons of four concerts in Cape Town, and has performed in various country districts. It has on two occasions been awarded grants of R1 000 by the Cape Town Tercentenary Fund. All the programmes are provided by the Charles Kreitzer Chamber Music Ensemble*.

—C.K.

CAPE TOWN CHORAL SOCIETY   T. Barrow-Dowling, N.R. Ingleby, K. Jewell, A.E. Joubert, C.N. Thomas

CAPE TOWN LIGHT OPERA CO.   J.S. Manca

CAPE TOWN MUNICIPAL CHOIR   J.S. Manca

CAPE TOWN MUNICIPAL ORCHESTRA, THE   The orchestra gave its first performance on 28 February 1914, in the Cape Town City Hall, with Theophil Wendt* conducting and Ellie Marx* leading the orchestra. The programme included the work which was to become traditionally associated with both conductor and orchestra, the overture to *Die Meistersinger von Nürnberg* by Wagner. — The first effective claims for a municipal orchestra had been put forward in 1910 by the City Councillor Walter Marshall, who felt a need for such an institution after the creation of a College of Music in that year, and as an addition to the amenities provided on the beaches and the new pier. Three years passed and on 14 August 1913, the Improvements Committee of the recently formed City Council of Greater Cape Town recommended the formation of a municipal orchestra, to consist of eighteen performers and a conductor. The provisional estimate for the first year was R9 292. The first step towards the realisation of the project was the wise appointment of Theo Wendt as conductor. He was given a free hand in selecting musicians for the orchestra, although he was expected to appoint as many suitable South Africans as possible. Artistic considerations triumphed during the initial stages and in the event the conductor selected 22 local artists and nine British musicians, giving him an orchestra of 31 members. — It became clear during the first year that the orchestra had been realised between two opposing and incompatible points of view. The Council was not prepared to burden its budget with a cultural body that did not pay its way. Its distinctively British point of view was that the orchestra should be primarily an entertainment unit, modestly capable of catering for more sophisticated musical tastes. The conductor, on the other hand, was a man of musical integrity, who was determined to shape his orchestra into a philharmonic unit worthy of the name, without neglecting entertainment or the pioneering work necessary for education. From his point of view, the cost of the undertaking was a negligible factor in comparison with the cultural and artistic mission of his orchestra. — A glance at the prescribed duties of the orchestra provides convincing proof of the uncomfortable compromise under which it laboured from the outset. The orchestra was expected to play at two weekly City Hall concerts, one on Thursday night, which was to be mainly devoted to symphonic work, and one on Sunday night, based on a popular variety of items for the general public. In addition, it had to perform at the band-stand on the Pier, at the new Sea Point Pavilion, at the Muizenberg Pavilion and in various parks. The orchestra was clearly intended to fulfil both the functions of a beach orchestra à la Bournemouth, and of a symphony orchestra on the model of its London counterparts. These duties were conscientiously amplified by the conductor in the form of lecture-concerts for the youth, promenade concerts for the public, special programmes at schools and occasional performances at Government House. In the first year he also took his orchestra to Worcester and Beaufort West, and in July and August to the main centres in the Northern Cape and Transvaal. The magnitude of Wendt's complex task of coping with all these demands and at the same time realising his artistic ideals, becomes apparent when it is remembered that he had also to labour at the cueing of symphonic scores to adapt their demands to the size of his orchestra. — The financial position of the orchestra became serious during the war years when public support waned. Fortunately the conductor did not have to bear this responsibility alone. When the symphonic concerts had to be discontinued, a society of Thursday Concert

Subscribers was formed, with J.S. Dunn as Chairman. Established in 1919, this important group exercised pressure on the Council, raised substantial donations and gradually effected improvements in the concert situation. This civic effort was rewarded in 1921, when a deputation from the Cape Peninsula Publicity Association approached the Council with a proposal to take over the responsibility of the orchestra. This was gratefully accepted by the Council and an agreement was reached under which the latter granted a subsidy of R16 000, and relinquished all further responsibility for the orchestra to the Association. — This meant that the latter body had to raise an annual guarantee of not less than R6 000. Under the agreement, the orchestra had to reside in the Peninsula for at least eight months of the year, offer two weekly concerts for the public, in addition to two educational concerts and a Sunday performance on the Pier. By 1923 the orchestra was again in financial trouble, and it became necessary to find at least 1 000 additional subscribers to maintain its existence. This period of crisis was marked by controversies and disagreements, often of an acrimonious nature, and finally led to Wendt's resignation in May 1924. — His successor, Leslie Heward*, advanced new and startling schemes to establish the prestige of the orchestra on an international basis; this, he reasoned, would have advantages, as far as local support was concerned. The entire orchestra was taken to England where it performed at the Empire Exhibition at Wembley in June 1925, subsequently undertaking a tour of various British centres. Two weeks after the commencement of the tour the orchestra was summarily recalled, since it was heading for financial disaster. The Publicity Association despaired of saving the situation after this setback, and in February 1926 the City Council resumed full control of its orchestra. A new campaign was launched to recruit 1 000 subscribers who would be willing to contribute R10 per year. This effort proved successful and in March 1926 the press announced the glad tidings that the orchestra had been saved. — Early in 1927 Leslie Heward left for England and was succeeded as conductor by William J. Pickerill*, who had been a bassoon player in the orchestra since its inception. The choice of Pickerill proved to be the turning point in the orchestra's history. A man of great musical talents, he also had the personality to reconcile the various elements, to fuse the orchestra into an artistic unit of contented musicians, and to satisfy the great variety of public demands in an equable manner. He actually succeeded in whittling down the annual deficit, guided the orchestra through the difficult years of the World Depression, which set in in 1929, and succeeded so well in fusing the roles of conductor, educator, financier, publicity agent and liaison officer, that no serious proposal was put forward during his term to abolish the orchestra. He forged a close alliance between the orchestra and ballet, which was rapidly progressing through the efforts of Helen Webb* and Dulcie Howes*. By inviting conducting celebrities of the stature of Sir Henry Wood, Albert Coates*, and Sir Dan Godfrey, and by obtaining the services of leading soloists of South African and foreign extraction, he added distinction to the reputation of his orchestra and established it firmly as a proud possession of the City. — Pickerill resigned on account of ill-health in October 1946, after guiding the orchestra through the meagre years of the Second World War, and on 11 August 1947 Enrique Jorda* was appointed as his successor, with Geoffrey Miller* as Associate Conductor. Jorda commenced his duties in January 1948 with great verve and enthusiasm, increasing the size of the orchestra by 12 additional players, working hard at a higher standard of performance, and undertaking tours of the Eastern Cape. Unfortunately frictions of an artistic as well as political nature arose between the conductor and members of his orchestra, and Jorda submitted his resignation on 4 January 1954. As a temporary measure, Frits Schuurman* and Pierre Colombo conducted the orchestra until Edward Dunn* was appointed permanent conductor from 1 October 1954. — The system of guest conductors was however continued during the 1954-1955 season, when Basil Cameron and Sir Bernard Heinze visited Cape Town; there was an even greater variety with seven guest conductors during the following season. Dunn resigned at the end of 1955 as Director of Music and Entertainment, and the conducting of the orchestra was entrusted to the guest conductors Hugh Rignold and Anthony Collins. In 1958 Charles Groves, Leo Quayle* and Charles Mackerras took charge; in 1959 Franz Litschauer, Jeremy Schulman* and Minas Christian. — The era of guest conductors ended in 1960, when David Tidboald* arrived to become orchestral director. The policy of inviting guest conductors was not dropped; until Tidboald's resignation in June 1965, a number of visiting celebrities conducted the orchestra for shorter or longer seasons. Since 1965 there has, in fact, been no permanent appointment of lasting duration, and a variety of guest conductors have shared the responsibility of leading the orchestra. — In addition to regular appearances of international artists, practically every South African soloist of repute has been invited to perform with the orchestra, some a number of times. At one stage, beginning in 1918, the City had its Municipal Choir, which rehearsed and sang with the orchestra. This was discontinued, and the practice has since been to collaborate with choral societies and with the choirs of the Universities of Cape Town and Stellenbosch, as well as those of churches and schools for the performance of choral works. Since 1949 the orchestra has also placed its services at the disposal of the EOAN Group, in opera as well as ballet and choral productions. — Under a present agreement with the Cape Provincial Administration, the orchestra undertakes an annual tour during which it performs at schools and in smaller centres in the Province. This is a provincial extension of the policy followed by Wendt in popularizing the orchestra with the younger generation. The establishment of the Cape Performing Arts Board (CAPAB) led to a provisional agreement with the Board to provide orchestral support for its choral, ensemble and opera productions. — At the present time (1970) the orchestra is consequently established as a unit in the cultural life not only of Cape Town, but throughout vast areas of the Cape Province. Its influence extends even further and can be traced in the other provinces as well. The 1919 tour to the North under Theo Wendt had successes in every centre where the orchestra performed, and acted as a stimulus to the ambitions of Johannesburg, Durban and, in a lesser degree, Pretoria, to have civic orchestras of their own. The success and artistic standing of the Cape Town Municipal Orchestra has been frequently cited as an achievement of civic responsibility in the Mother City, to be admired and emulated by other South African cities. Durban acquired its own orchestra, based on the Cape Town model, in 1922, but with even greater emphasis on the Bournemouth type of beach entertainment; and John Connell's hand was strengthened in achieving the Johannesburg Symphony Orchestra in 1946, after a long, uphill struggle. — At the première of the Cape Town Orchestra in 1914, Gen. J.C. Smuts confessed his deficiency in musical knowledge, but spoke of his appreciation at being present on a cultural occasion of historic importance. The firm establishment of the orchestra in the cultural life of Cape Town and its indirect influence on musical life in South Africa have justified Gen. Smuts's vision.

BIBLIOGRAPHY
ROSENTHAL, ERIC: *50 Years of the Cape Town Orchestra*, 1914-1964. Galvin & Sales (Pty) Ltd, Cape Town, 1964. SHORTEN, JOHN (Ed.): *The golden jubilee of Greater Cape Town*, n.d. V.D. POST, MARGARET E.: *Theo Wendt, 1874-1974*. Tafelberg-Uitgewers Ltd, Cape Town/ Johannesburg, 1974.

SOURCES
ANON: Beginjare van stadsorkes. *Die Burger*, 25 February 1960. ANON: 50 Jaar stadsorkes: nog steeds bolwerk teen musikale vervlakking. *Die Burger*, 19 February 1964. ANON: How the orchestra was born. *Cape Argus*, 13 June 1946. ANON: Musical progress of Cape Town. Cape Argus, 25 February 1939. ANON: Stadsorkes en staatsteun. *Die Burger*, 18 September 1948. ANON: Stadsorkes gaan sy 50-jarige bestaan herdenk. *Die Burger*, 30 January 1964. CHISHOLM, FIONA: City's symphony orchestra is best in Africa. *Cape Times*, 22 August 1964. GIBBS, A.: An old stager in the municipal orchestra looks back. *Cape Argus*, 12 June 1965. MARX, B.: Orchestral reminiscences. 1950. WEICH, CHARLES: Glanspunte uit 'n halwe eeu as konsertganger. *Die Burger*, 2 February 1964. National Documentation Centre for Music, HSRC, Pretoria.

—Ed.

CAPE TOWN MUSICAL SOCIETY   T. Barrow-Dowling, J. Luyt (sen.), P.E. Ould, C.N. Thomas

CAPE TOWN ORCHESTRAL SOCIETY   J. Luyt (jun.), M. Whiteman

CAPE TOWN PHILHARMONIC SOCIETY   J. Luyt (sen.), G.B. Miller

CAPE TOWN STUDIO ORCHESTRA, THE (SABC ORCHESTRA, CAPE TOWN).   This orchestra arose in 1927 from small beginnings in the early days of South African broadcasting. Soon after the broadcast undertakings in Cape Town, Johannesburg and Durban had been acquired and welded into the African Broadcasting Company by the late I.W. Schlesinger, he reacted to prodding from the Cape Town studio-manager, René Caprara*, by engaging a trio, consisting of violin, cello and piano, to provide light music for 45 minutes during the "dinner-hour" each evening. The original members of this trio were John Spink (violin), a past leader of the Cape Town Orchestra*, Mrs Routledge (piano), and Miss Elsie Walters (cello). Their programme went on for some years, though there were changes in personnel. When John Spink rejoined the Cape Town orchestra, his place was taken by George Tobias*, then a teacher of violin at the SA College of Music*. — In March 1934, after more prodding by Caprara, who was by this time Broadcast Manager in Johannesburg, Mr Schlesinger and his fellow directors agreed to the establishment of a 12-piece orchestra, led by George Tobias, to take the place of the studio trio, and to be engaged on a full-time basis. This was timed to coincide with the opening of the new studios in Riebeeck Street in January 1934. At that time Messrs African Consolidated Theatres Ltd, one of Mr Schlesinger's associate companies, possessed a 16-piece orchestra which performed in the Plaza Kinema. This was combined with the studio ensemble, under the baton of Tobias, for broadcasting purposes. The arrangement, however, lasted only a few months, as the Plaza orchestra was transferred to Johannesburg. The studio ensemble was then increased to 15 players, plus conductor, and at the beginning of 1935 Walter Swanson* joined the studio as musical producer and co-conductor. — Till then the contributions of the orchestra had been mainly confined to the provision of 70 minutes "lunch-hour" music and 45 minutes "dinner-hour" music daily, with one or two "theme" programmes each week. Now the musical activities of the studio began to expand in all directions. Symphonic music was provided by the Cape Town Municipal Orchestra, both in studio broadcasts and in the relayed public concerts and the Studio Orchestra came to be extensively used in studio productions of revues, musical comedies and, eventually, grand operas, besides collaborating with vocal groups in choral works and providing incidental music to plays. The daily lunch- and dinner-hour programmes were at first maintained; but with extra rehearsals for more important features, the orchestra was overworked. Eventually the lunch-hour music was abolished, while the dinner-hour programme was reduced to three times a week. A valuable service was the opportunity given by the orchestra to advanced students and young professional instrumentalists and singers to perform in public with an orchestra. — By the end of the Second World War the orchestra had grown to twenty members, frequently augmented for important occasions. Practically every well-known South African artist appeared with it, as well as famous overseas artists. Until 1953 the orchestra participated in some forty operas, and hundreds of light operas and musical comedies. Early in 1964 George Tobias resigned to go into business, and Walter Swanson carried on for some time single-handed. At the end of the same year he too resigned to take up academic and theatrical work, and Dodds Miller*, a former member of the Durban Civic Orchestra*, with Gilberto Boneggio of the Johannesburg Studio Orchestra, became the new conductors. Later Mr Boneggio returned to Johannesburg and was replaced by ex-Royal Marine Bandmaster John Pattinson. These men carried on the tradition of their predecessors, but the pattern of broadcasting was changing under the South African Broadcasting Corporation, established in 1936. The SABC decided to integrate broadcast programmes, with the result that only two programmes were broadcast over the entire network, to which all the stations contributed. This became possible through improvements made to landlines between the major centres. The inevitable effect was that Johannesburg, the headquarters with the largest orchestra, received the lion's share of orchestral broadcasting time, and less use was made of the smaller combinations in Cape Town and Durban. — In 1953 the Board of Governors of the SABC decided to disband these orchestras and to build the Studio Orchestra in Johannesburg into a symphonic combination of 80 players. So ended, rather sadly, almost 20 years of useful service by the Studio Orchestra. At its disbanding (30 November 1953) no less than five of its twenty-four players had been members since the inception in March 1934. Their names were Noreen O'Sullivan, Arnold Mellor, Enid Pollack, Ferdinand Weckesser and Michael McGrath.

—W.D.S.

CAPRARA, RENÉ SILVIO, *12 February 1888 on Mauritius; now (1976) in Henley-on-Klip. First Director General of the SABC.

Caprara's first music tuition was managed by his father. He graduated at the Conservatoire in Parma and after the award of a bursary for wind playing he entered the RCM in 1911. Clarinet and pianoforte were his main practical subjects. — Caprara was chosen as clarinet player for the Cape Town Civic Orchestra* in February 1921, remained a member of the orchestra until 1927, and then devoted himself to broadcasting. He became Manager of the Cape Peninsula Broadcasting Company and, when Schlesinger achieved control, Broadcast Manager of the African Broadcasting Company. From 1934 to 1936 he was General Manager and when the SABC was created in 1936, he became its first Director General. — He retired in February 1949.

SOURCE

Cape Argus: 23 June 1948.

—Ed.

CARILLONS IN SOUTH AFRICA

1. Cape Town

After the 1918 armistice, the women of Cape Town decided to purchase a carillon as a donation to the city and as a war memorial. The bells were cast by Messrs John Taylor and Co. of Loughborough, England, with inscriptions on the individual bells which were dedicated to people, places and incidents. Thus the great B-bell was inscribed "Cecil John Rhodes - Alles zal recht komen"; the C-bell was donated by employees of the Cape Town municipality in memory of members of the municipal service who had laid down their lives in the War; no. 16, D, has the name of Jan C. Smuts ("In Thy Will is our Peace"); no. 19, F, is dedicated to Louis Botha ("Volg die weg van eer en pligt"). There were 32 bells which, together with the five original bells of the city hall chimes, made a set of 37. In 1954 two more small bells were added to bring the total to 39 - more than three chromatic octaves, which were played from a keyboard in the old Belgian tradition. The bells were inaugurated on 30 April 1925 when the Prince of Wales arrived for his visit to South Africa. The carillon was played by Anton Brees, a Belgian carillonneur, who had been specially invited for the occasion. He remained in the country for about 2 months, passing on the technique to a pupil, Jan Luyt* (jun.), later the Town Clerk of Cape Town. The post of a carillon player was created in 1928 and Jan Luyt served in this capacity until 1946, when he was succeeded by the principal bassoonist of the Cape Town Municipal Orchestra*, Walter Piper. After Piper's death in 1952, J.G. Vermaak took over in 1953 and remained on until 1954, but after him the post remained vacant for ten years. On 1 January 1964 Henk van Eck was appointed city carillonneur. He remained on until 1967, and was succeeded on 1 April 1968 by Keith Jewell*, the city organist. Jewell played the carillon for the first time on 10 April 1968 at the induction of State President J.J. Fouche. Apart from Sunday evening programmes, he gives performances on Christmas Eve, on New Year's Eve and on special occasions, such as the ceremony when the South African Navy was granted the freedom of the City.

2. Pietermaritzburg

A much smaller set of 12 bells, capable of playing 14 tunes by means of a rotating drum and pegs, is to be found in the tower of the Pietermaritzburg City Hall. There are two drums with the following tunes: Drum number 1: Rockingham; Rule Britannia; God bless the Prince of Wales; Last rose of summer; Blue bells of Scotland; Tom Bowling; Auld lang syne. Drum number 2: Adeste fidelis; Old folks at home; Annie Laurie; Believe me, if all those endearing young charms; Ye banks and braes; She wore a wreath of roses; Home sweet home. — The bells can also be played by means of a chiming apparatus: small hammers inside the bells are controlled by ropes which run over pulleys into a frame, with all the sallies of the ropes level. The bells also serve the clock and strike the quarters. The first, second, third, and seventh bells are used for this purpose. The largest bell, the tenor, strikes the hours. The mechanism was purchased to replace the old clock, which was lost in 1898 when the City Hall burnt to the ground. On 16 June 1900, exactly two years after the fire, the deputy mayor, P.E. Payne, started the mechanism. It was the task of the city organist, A.H. Day*, to play the bells every Sunday before the morning service and after the evening service. The bells were provided by Messrs Gillett and Johnston of Croyden near London.

3. Port Elizabeth

Housed in the campanile near the harbour, the Port Elizabeth carillon has 23 bells which were cast in England in 1935. They had been ordered by the municipality, although the funds had come from several organisations and from descendants of the 1820 settlers. The carillon is usually played electrically, but it is also possible to play it by hand by means of a keyboard. When the bells are operated from a keyboard, the player is R.E. Selley*, municipal Director of Music. Before the Second World War and during the years 1945 to 1946, Clifton Harris* played the carillon on Sunday afternoons from 5 to 5.30. The first broadcast of a performance on this carillon was done in 1945.

4. Potchefstroom

The N.H. or G. Church of Potchefstroom North ordered a set of five bells from Petit and Fritsen in Holland, which were installed in 1956 by SA Organ Builders. Three of the five bells can be rung by hand and there is also an electrical mechanism making mechanical ringing possible.

SOURCE
Die Orrel 1/4, September 1955.

—Ed.

CARTER, JOHN CHARLES, *31 October 1917 in Pietermaritzburg; °27 April 1957 in Pietermaritzburg. Organist, conductor.

John Carter was a chorister at St Peter's Church in Pietermaritzburg from the age of six, and had organ lessons from his father, John Withers Carter*. At school he was a member of the Maritzburg College Band, later playing French horn in the Pietermaritzburg Municipal Orchestra and the Royal Natal Carbineers' Band. — In 1940 Carter went on active service with the First South African Division, until 1943, when he was transferred to the South African Permanent Force Band in Pretoria, and played French horn for the SABC orchestra. He returned to Pietermaritzburg in 1945, and then became Director of Music to the Royal Natal Carbineers' Band, in which he had reached the rank of Captain at the time of his death. — Carter formed a choral group and conducted Gilbert and Sullivan productions. In 1949 he was appointed Musical Organiser to the Pietermaritzburg City Council. In the same year he revived the Pietermaritzburg Philharmonic Society*, and was their Director until the time of his death. — He was the holder of an LTCL diploma in conducting.

SOURCES
SAMT: 52, June 1957.   Information supplied by Mrs Marjorie Cooper of Durban North.

—C.O.

CARTER, JOHN WITHERS, *16 April 1879 in Ulverston, England; °December 1958 in Pietermaritzburg. Organist, music teacher and composer.

After studying music and becoming a youthful Fellow of the RCO in 1902, Carter worked for a time in Llangollen, Wales, before he arrived in South Africa in 1910. Three years later he was appointed Borough Organist of Pietermaritzburg, a post he held for thirty-six years, until his resignation in 1949. His wife was Constance Borain, of Pietermaritzburg, a descendant of Sir William Sterndale Bennett, composer and one-time principal of the RAM. For short periods Carter was organist and choir-master at the Metropolitan Methodist Church, Pietermaritzburg, and during the First World War, at St Saviour's Cathedral. After that he became organist of St Peter's Church, Pietermaritzburg, where he served until his retirement in 1949. During this time he established himself as a teacher of pianoforte, organ and theoretical subjects. He also conducted the Pietermaritzburg Municipal Choral Society and Orchestra. — As a composer, John Carter wrote choral music (both religious and secular), as well as music for the organ, including a *Sonata in B minor*. — He was the father of John Charles Carter*.

WORKS

Come to Durban, song (Thos. Cook). Soho Press, London, 1938.   England's answer, song (Nancy Lister). P. Davis & Sons Ltd., Natal, n.d.   King's School Song (W.F.M. Davis). Lyon & Hall, Brighton; Lowe & Brydone, London, n.d.   Information supplied by Mrs Marjorie Cooper.

—C.O.

CARTER, PETER-JOHN, *30 January 1935 in Durban; now (1977) living at Dartington Hall, Devon. Violinist and one-time Music Manager for the Natal Performing Arts Council.

The son of Roy Benoit Carter*, Peter-John studied violin under Stirling Robins* and later under Paul Martens*. In 1951 he was awarded the Kimberley Art Scholarship, and in 1952 the scholarship of the Associated Board, which enabled him to study at the RCM. During this period, he played with the Royal Philharmonic Orchestra and the Philharmonia Orchestra, and toured the United States of America. In 1955 Carter was awarded a British Council Scholarship and concluded his studies at the Brussels Conservatoire under Carlo van Neste. He obtained the Conservatoire's Diploma with distinction in 1956. He was then appointed violin teacher to the Dartington College of Arts in 1958, and became a member of the Dartington String Quartet. A year later he became leader of the London Octet, of which Alexander Kok* was the initiator and first cellist. He also broadcast as violin soloist for the BBC, appeared at concerts, and made recordings in England, as well as on the Continent. — Peter-John Carter returned to South Africa in 1969, when he accepted the post of Music Manager for NAPAC. He made several tours of Natal with the NAPAC String Quartet and Sinfonia Chamber Orchestra during 1970 and 1971. For domestic reasons he was obliged to resign from NAPAC, and in the latter year returned to England as a member of the English Chamber Orchestra. He and the three other members of the original NAPAC String Quartet are now resident in England. As the "Haydn Quartet", they have recently concluded a successful tour of Great Britain.

SOURCES

NAPAC News, 7 June 1969.   Information supplied by Mrs Valerie Carter.

—Ed.

CARTER, ROY BENOIT, *28 April 1910 in Brighton, Sussex; °16 August 1968 in Cape Town. Cellist.

Roy Carter was the son of Wilfred Burnette Carter, a viola player and one of the early members of Lyell-Tayler's* Durban Orchestra. He studied violoncello at the Metropolitan Academy of Music in London, and in 1928 joined the Durban Civic Orchestra*, becoming principal cellist in 1935. He was also sub-conductor of the orchestra (1939-1951), appeared as soloist in Durban, Cape Town, Johannesburg and Pietermaritzburg, at municipal and broadcast concerts, and he was an active organiser of chamber music in Durban. In 1946 he was appointed conductor of the Durban Philharmonic Orchestra and commenced the monthly student-artist concerts. — In 1952 Roy went to England, where he played in the London Philharmonic and in the BBC Symphony Orchestras. On his return to South Africa in 1956, he joined the SABC Studio Orchestra in Johannesburg, as principal cellist. After two years as Director of the Pietermaritzburg Philharmonic Society*, he was appointed lecturer at the South African College of Music*, Cape Town in 1962, and played as cellist in the Cape Town University Quartet. Earning the warm regard of both staff and students, he served the College until his death.

SOURCES
SAMT: 41, December 1951; 51, December 1956.   Information supplied by Mrs Valerie Carter.
—Ed.

CASALEGGIO, MICHELE, *21 February 1909 in Cape Town; at present (1970) in Bloemfontein. Teacher of commerce, singing instructor and folk-dancing leader.
Michele Casaleggio passed the Final piano examination in Bloemfontein in 1941, the UTLM (singing) in 1947, and the Final organ examination in 1957. Since 1934 he has been a teacher of singing and commerce at the Central High School in Bloemfontein, where he conducts the school choir and has staged pupil performances of operettas, musical sketches and musical comedies. — He serves on eisteddfod music committees and, since 1949, he has been an accompanist in folk-dancing performances held during national festivals, such as the inauguration of the Voortrekker monument in Pretoria (1949), the Van Riebeeck Festival in Cape Town (1952), the Union Festival (1960), and the Republic Festival in Bloemfontein (1966). During the South African folk dancers' visits to Europe (1953, 1958 and 1969), Casaleggio was the official accompanist and conducted their ensemble in programmes of folk dancing, folk singing and folk music. He was also the chief editor of the folk-song anthology, *Goue gerf,* published by the National Council of Folk Singing and Folk Dancing* in 1970.

WORKS
28 folk songs for folk dancing in *Volkspelebundel.* Nasionale Raad vir Volksang en Volkspele, 1961.   Arrangements of folk songs, like: Kinders, moenie in die water mors nie, 1955; Die blink vosperd, 1955; Hessie se witperd, 1955; Horlosie in die sak, 1955; Kimberley se trein, 1955; Hier's ek weer, 1955; Ver in die wêreld, Kittie, 1955; Ken jy die Land (C.F. Visser/J. Brent-Wessels), 1965.   Ed. *Goue gerf,* volume of folk songs. Nasionale Raad vir Volksang en Volkspele, 1970.   School song for Andrew Rabie High School, Port Elizabeth. Ms., 1957.
—Ed.

CASSEN, GERALD, *in Riga, Latvia; °13 October 1976 in Johannesburg. Bass-baritone and teacher of singing.
Cassen studied violin under Professor Issay Barmas at the Klindworth-Scharwenka Conservatoire in Berlin during 1920-21, but had to discontinue these studies owing to an injury to his right hand. In South Africa (1921) he was trained as a singer by Wilfred Burns-Walker* and Cavaliere Margottini, leaving for Milan in 1925 to continue his vocal studies. After a tour of South Africa with the English violinist,

Margaret Fairless (1928), he visited Berlin for a further period of study and gave his first Lieder recital in 1930. In 1933 he went to England, where he was a member of the Sadler's Wells Opera Company in London for three seasons, and sang in Covent Garden and in the Glyndebourne Opera Festival. He also broadcast from the BBC studios. — Gerald Cassen returned to South Africa in April 1940, after a concert tour of the Scandinavian and Baltic countries. He touted in this country and sang under the direction of the impresario Alex Cherniavsky* and in opera seasons under the direction of John Connell*, before leaving for America in 1948, where he appeared in oratorio, in concerts and radio recitals. He visited South Africa briefly in 1956 to fulfil some concert and radio engagements. In August 1959, he finally returned and settled in Johannesburg as a teacher of singing.

—Ed.

CASTALIDES was the name of a society for art and culture at the University of Pretoria during the 1930s.

The Society held an Afrikaans music evening in the Pretoria City Hall on 24 August 1934. The programme was restricted to works by the South African composers S.H. Eyssen*, Walter Spiethoff*, Johannes Joubert*, M.L. de Villiers*, Sydney Richfield*, Arthur Ellis, Lettie Joubert*, John Pescod*, S. le Roux Marais*, Gerrit Bon* and Ernest Lowenherz*, as well as the Dutch composer of Afrikaans songs, Anna Lambrechts-Vos*. The works were performed by various well-known South African artists of the time, including Nunez Holtzhausen*, Dolly de Villiers*, Anna Pohl*, Louis Knobel*, and the composers themselves. The evening was an even more unique occasion because all the composers were present; a photograph was taken to record the historic event. With small variations the same programme was performed in the Potchefstroom City Hall on 13 October 1934. — The society held a concert of Afrikaans folk songs in the new City Hall in Pretoria on 18 June 1936. Apart from folk songs and arrangements of folk songs, works by Richfield, Jan Bouws*, Emiel Hullebroeck*, Arthur Ellis, Gerrit Bon, Lettie Joubert, J.P.J. Wierts* and Johannes Joubert were performed. The programme was in three parts: an introduction consisting of two orchestral works by Richfield, performed by the Pretoria Philharmonic Orchestra conducted by the composer, and a lecture by Professor S.P.E. Boshoff* on the "Significance of the Afrikaans Folk Song" constituted the first part; the second part consisted of folk music, including folk songs, folk dances and folk-dance music; and the third part demonstrated the art of song and arrangements of folk songs in works for orchestra, choir, organ, vocal quarter and vocal solos. — In 1934 the Castalides Society issued a magazine edited by Miss C. Muller and the committee consisted of the following people: Professor Dr M.L. du Toit (President), C.J. Pelser (Chairman), Miss C.H. Muller (Vice-Chairman), L. Botha (Secretary), Miss A. Groenewald (Archivist) and Miss N. Verster, W.J. Burger and I. Reid (Additional Members).

SOURCES
Three programmes of the Castalides Society. *Lantern*, December 1962. *Trek*, 1934. *Castalides-Kunsblad*, 1934.

—E.H.S.

CASTELIJN, H.W.   Hollandsch Mannenkoor, Pretoria 1

CAVALLI, S.   Johannesburg 3(iv), L.M. Veenemans

260

CENTENARY TREK SONGS. The mounting enthusiasm evoked by the symbolic ox-wagon trek of 1938 led to a remarkable attempt in the OFS to express the emotional excitement through the medium of folk songs. A large central festival was planned to take place in Bloemfontein on 7, 8 and 9 October. The chairman of the OFS branch of the ATKV (organisers of the symbolic trek), Mr Roelf Olivier, was asked by this organisation to form a trek party in Bloemfontein with the purpose of fetching the Andries Pretorius wagon from Graaff Reinet, and the Vrou en Moeder wagon from Colesberg, and to escort them to Bloemfontein. Thereafter the party was to accompany the wagons on their trip through the Western Free State via Boshof and Kimberley, until they rejoined the main trek. Eventually the party consisted of Mr and Mrs Roelf Olivier, Dr and Mrs B.A. de Wet, Mrs Annie Jackson, Mrs Judith Pellissier, and Messrs A.P. du Toit, S.P. Grové, J.J. Eksteen and G. Joubert. Much later the party was joined by J. Otto and H. Venter. In the division of duties, S.P. Grové was to act as leader of the team of oxen with his concertina, whilst guitarist and singer A.P. du Toit acted as brakeman. — They considered the possibility of introducing a programme for festivals *en route,* which would create the right occasional atmosphere and be in keeping with the Voortrekker spirit. Although they were not lacking in musical talent, it was clear that, with the exception of patriotic songs, their repertoire was very limited. Through their own efforts they were able to collect a total of 11 songs, mostly with their own suitable words, and they rehearsed a further three traditional sacred songs, *Die môregesang,* the popular tune for *Psalm 38,* and *Die aandgesang.* The complete list is as follows: *1. Saam met die wa* (words, J.C. Eyssen, music, S.H. Eyssen): *2. My hartjie my liefie* (folk tune, 2nd and 3rd verses: B.A. de Wet); *3. Die Polla van my* (folk tune - words, B.A. de Wet); *4. Laat julle kwassies swaai* (folk tune - words, B.A. de Wet); *5. Jaloers is 'n ding wat stories maak* (folk tune - words, B.A. de Wet); *6. Anjelina* (folk tune - words, B.A. de Wet); *7. Die kappie* (folk tune - words, B.A. de Wet); *8. Baardjie* (tune: Suikerbossie - words, B.A. de Wet); *9. Aan die baardloses* (tune: Suikerbossie - words, B.A. de Wet); *10. Afscheidslied* (traditional words and melody); *11. Aan d' oever van 't snelle vliet* (traditional words and melody); *12. Môregesang* (in Dutch), traditional tune; *13. Psalm 38,* traditional tune; *14. Aandgesang* (in Dutch), traditional tune. — Mrs Pellissier was able to remember number 4 from her childhood years in the George district. The original words were: Draai my, draai my, draai my om die bos,/Draai my om die bos voor die eerste hoender kraai./*Chorus:* O! Laat julle warie swaai, swaai (2x)/Laat julle warie swaai voor die eerste hoender kraai. — (Swing me, swing me, swing me round the bush,/Swing me round the bush before the first cock crows./*Chorus:* O! Let your dresses swirl, swirl (2x)/Let your dresses swirl before the first cock crows.) — Number 3 was unearthed by Mrs Pellissier in the Little Karoo. The original words were: Daar onder in die vlei, daar staan 'n bord vol bene;/Die mannetjies en wyfies paar en paar,/Die Hotnotsmeide deurmekaar./*Chorus:* Saag, o saag die waatlemoen (2x),/O saag, die waatlemoen. — (Deep in the valley there's a plate full o' bones,/The males and the females two by two/The Hottentot girls higgledy-piggledy./*Chorus:* Cut, o cut the watermelon (2x), O cut the watermelon). — The words for number 7, a concertina piece remembered by S.P. Grové, were provided by Dr De Wet. — Numbers 10 and 11 were two traditional tunes from the old days remembered by Dr De Wet. — This scanty repertoire was received with unbounded enthusiasm in 1938, and undoubted-

261

ly evoked renewed zeal for the art of singing Afrikaans folk songs. — Their national acceptance as a result of the festivals and radio broadcasts paved the way for a folksong movement which was advanced by institutions such as the FAK*, The Council for Folk Dancing and Folk Singing* and by the Spring School Movement*. Recently the Department of Cultural Affairs* has accepted the responsibility of furthering this cause. The significant part played by the *FAK Volksangbundel* (1937) (Album of folk songs publ. by the FAK) should also be stressed. An important offshoot of this movement was the formation of an Institute for Folk Music at the University of Stellenbosch, with Dr Jan Bouws* in charge. — The far-reaching effect which the slim volume of centenary songs (published in 1938) had on the emotional awakening which precipitated the Afrikaans folksong movement, cannot be underestimated. In the published edition six further songs were added: *Lebombo* (Nico Hofmeyr*); *'n Lied van Suid-Afrika* (words: Van Bruggen; music: S. le Roux Marais); *Om die kampvuur* (words: B.A. de Wet; folk tune); *Vakansielied* (words: B.A. de Wet; folk tune); *Dapper en stapper* (words: B.A. de Wet; music: Schubert); *Pak op jou kar* (B.A. de Wet; music: D.J. Roode); *'n Weeklag* (words: B.A. de Wet; folk tune); *Gesang 157* (Voortrekker tune).

PUBLICATION
Eeufeesliedjies. Nasionale Pers Ltd., Bloemfontein, n.d. (1938).

—J.Pe. (amplified)

CHAMBERS, CYRIL, *20 November 1907 in Kidderminster, England; at present (1977) in Durban. Bellringer.

Cyril Chambers was trained as a bellringer by Edwin Gilbert and Charles Woodberry, and between 1933 and 1938 rang bells in various Worcestershire and Shropshire towers. He rang three peals of Grandsire Triples at Claverley, Chaddesley Corbett and Hagley and one peal of Grandsire Caters at Kidderminster during these years. — On his arrival in South Africa in 1939, he first lived in Johannesburg, where he was a member of Canon G.H. Ridout's handbell band (1940-1941). After moving to Durban in November 1944, he rang at St Paul's for a while and then at St Mary's, Greyville (1945-1956), after which he rejoined the St Paul's ringers. Since 1957 he has been ringer, steeple-keeper and conductor at this cathedral and tutor at the cathedral school. — Cyril Chambers is the Durban correspondent of the journal, *The ringing world*. He also published in 1955 a brochure on *Calling grandsire triples into rounds.*

—Ed.

CHAMBERS, ELSIE CLIVE (NÉE BURDETT), *15 March 1900 in Stourport-on-Severn, Worcestershire; living in Durban in 1970. Music teacher and the author of some songs.

Although Elsie Chambers showed an early aptitude for music, she became a school teacher by profession. She studied organ at a London Teachers' Training College and passed the College examination in advanced music and organ with distinction. She also learnt to play the violin, participating in the orchestra of the local Choral Society, and became·known as an accompanist and country dance pianist. Her knowledge of English folk songs resulted from her meeting with Cecil Sharp and Martin and Geoffrey Shaw, while she was still at the Training College. — In 1939 she came to South Africa with her family and taught music at Fynlands Primary

262

School in Natal from 1950 to 1956. Her production of the *Old woman in the shoe* (Thomas Dunhill), which was broadcast by the SABC in 1954, was the first broadcast of its kind by a primary school in South Africa. — Since 1942 she has become known as a composer of songs, and has been distinguished with gold medals at eisteddfodau in Johannesburg and Durban.

WORKS
Come, see this little stranger, carol (Stewart Wilson). Ms., n.d.   If I were Lord of Tartary, song (Walter de la Mare). Ms., n.d.   Fairies in winter, song (Francis Carey Slater). Ms., n.d.   Charles gave Elizabeth a dodo, song (anon). Ms., n.d.   To our Nkuhla tree, song (Claire Nelson). Ms., n.d.   Home thoughts, song (Brian Rose). Ms., n.d.   The nightingale, song (Mabel Harber). Ms., n.d.   The owl and the pussycat, song (Edward Lear). Ms., n.d.
—Ed.

CHAMBERS, PATRICK JOHN, *17 March 1900 in England; now (1965) in Durban. Teacher and composer.

Patrick Chambers's father died in 1902 and when she emigrated to South Africa in 1906, his mother placed him in the care of a convent school in London. He joined her in Natal in 1909. His first acquaintance with music was in the convent school when it was discovered that he had a promising soprano voice. He went to school in Natal and studied music privately until he matriculated in 1916, when he left for Australia, returning to South Africa in 1919. — Chambers started on a serious study of the violin under various teachers in Pretoria in 1920, and earned his living by playing in tea rooms and hotels, as well as in the cinemas and music shows of African Theatres. In 1922 he was back in Durban, where he got married in 1924 and he left for Lourenço Marques in 1926 to play in theatres and cinemas. This period terminated when the silent days of cinema ended. — Having lost his employment, Chambers returned to Durban (1931) and became a member of the Civic Orchestra under Dan Godfrey*. As was customary then, he played viola in the orchestra and clarinet in the band. He also established a wide teaching practice, especially among Coloureds and Indians and in 1941 he formed a non-white orchestra of 22 players which performed in Durban and the coastal towns. — Under the guidance of Edmond Schelpe*, Chambers also applied himself to theoretical studies leading to the licentiate of UNISA. This provided a basis for the composing he has done in recent years. He also learnt to play the organ under the guidance of William Dean*, organist at the Anglican Church of St John the Divine in Durban. Associate Membership of the South African Music Rights Organisation* was granted to Chambers in 1963.

WORKS
Missa in Honorem Sanctissimae Trinitatis a quatre voci, organo comittante. Autog. G. Delporte, Mons, Belgium, n.d.   Sacred motet. Ms., n.d.   English ballads. Ms., n.d.   Scale and arpeggio manual for the pianoforte. Ms., n.d.
—G.S.J.

CHANDLER, S.C.   Organs 5(i)

CHANGUION, A. and E.   C. Schultze

CHAPMAN, D. (MRS SHEPSTONE)   L.T. Shepstone

CHAPMAN, NEIL, *8 June 1933 in Underberg, Natal; at present (1976) in Pretoria. Assistant-conductor and chorus master.

Neil Chapman had pianoforte, theory and harmony lessons from Mrs A.M. Mansergh (January 1943 - December 1950) and whilst studying at the Natal Training College, Pietermaritzburg, for the Natal Teachers' Diploma (January 1954 - December 1955), he included pianoforte, harmony, school music teaching, history of music and form in his curriculum. Four years after obtaining the Diploma, he left for Austria and further training at the Vienna State Academy of Music in pianoforte, teaching method and other subjects under Frau H. Petyrek-Lange, J. Dichler and others (October 1959 - December 1961). He is also in possession of the LRAM (Teacher's) Diploma. — During September 1957 - December 1958, and again in 1962-1964, he was chorus master for the Theatre Group of the Pietermaritzburg Philharmonic Society, for whom he conducted performances of *Messiah* and *The mikado* in 1964. During January 1962 - December 1964, he was a lecturer in music at the Natal Training College, and from January 1965 to December 1966, Musical Director of the Pietermaritzburg Philharmonic Society. During August, September and October 1966, he acted as chorus master and assistant-conductor for PACT in Pretoria, and was appointed to these two posts in 1967. He participated in performances of the Verdi *Requiem* in December 1967, Beethoven's *Ninth symphony* in 1970 as well as in the first South African performances of *Peter Grimes* and *Don Carlos* (1969). — He was guest conductor at a concert of the Durban Municipal Orchestra in June 1966.

—Ed.

CHAPMAN, WILLIAM ISAAC, *27 July 1870 in London; °3 July 1945 in East London. Organist and choirmaster.

Chapman became an organist when he was seventeen years old. Subsequently he gave organ recitals in London and Brighton and acquired considerable experience in the art of accompanying and training choirs. He came to South Africa for health reasons in 1900 and was employed as a clerk in the firm of Baker, Baker and Co., King William's Town, and as the organist of Trinity Church. This latter position he held until August 1902 when he became organist and choirmaster of the St George's Presbyterian Church in East London. He was a bachelor and until his death he lived in East London where he was prominent as a teacher of organ, pianoforte and singing. — In 1902 he started giving popular organ recitals and sacred concerts with which he persevered until 1943, shortly before his retirement. Among the works presented by his church choir are *The crucifixion* (Stainer), *Penitence, pardon and peace* (Maunder) and *The holy city* (Gaul). He was also conductor of the East London Choral Society from 1904 to 1914. Under Chapman's direction the following works were performed: *Messiah, The creation, Judas Maccabaeus, Hiawatha* (Coleridge-Taylor), *On shore and sea* (Sullivan), *Una* (Gaul), *The May queen* (Sterndale Bennett), *The daughter of Jaïrus* (Stainer), *Faust* (Gounod) and *Elijah* - often with overseas singers as soloists. The society was self-supporting and had a membership of 100-150. The Gipsy Orchestra played under his direction in East London during and after the First World War. Chapman was a well-known pianist at concerts, playing solos and accompaniments. For three successive years he was also one of the adjudicators at the Bantu choir competitions held annually in East London since 1922.

—E.H.S.

CHARDON, MADAME, French piano virtuoso who interrupted her journey from India to France in Cape Town for a few months in 1845. Apart from concerts in which her *bravura* playing impressed the public, she once appeared as a singer too. Newspaper advertisements announced that she was willing to give piano, harp and singing lessons.

WORK
Rondeau brillante, on an original theme.

BIBLIOGRAPHY
BOUWS, JAN: *Die musieklewe van Kaapstad, 1800-1850, en sy verhouding tot die musiekkultuur van Wes-Europa.* Cape Town/Amsterdam, 1966. BRADLOW, FRANK, R.: *Baron von Ludwig and the Ludwigsburg garden.* Cape Town/Amsterdam, 1965.

SOURCES
De Zuid-Afrikaan, 1845. *De Verzamelaar,* 1845. *Sam Sly's African Journal,* 1845. The Cape of Good Hope Register, 1846.

—J.B.

CHARLES KREITZER CHAMBER MUSIC ENSEMBLE, THE, was formed in Cape Town in 1945. The members of the ensemble were Nella Wissema (first violinist), Lucy Faktor* (second violinist), Charles Kreitzer* (violist) and Granville Britton* (cellist). When Nella Wissema left for Great Britain in 1961, her place was taken by Pierre de Groote*. For works needing a larger ensemble, the quartet has combined with various members of the Cape Town Municipal Orchestra*. It has also given performances with the pianists Helga Bassel*, Lili Kraus* and Harold Rubens*. The ensemble has provided all the programmes for the Cape Town Chamber Music Society* since its inception in 1947, and has given numerous broadcasts and performances in country towns. The repertoire of the group ranges from early 18th century works to modern compositions, many performed in South Africa for the first time.

—C.K.

CHARLES, RONALD WALLACE, *27 December 1919 in Cardiff; music organiser, SABC, Durban.
Ronald Charles obtained the B.Mus. degree at the University College of Cardiff in 1947, becoming an Associate of the RCO and a Fellow of Trinity College in the same year. He had been awarded the Piano Teacher's Licentiate of Trinity College in 1940. His first appointment was as Music Master at Berkhamsted School, Herts., (1947-1953), where, six years later, he was promoted to Director of Music (1953-1958). Concurrently he lectured on music at the Newland Park Teachers' Training College, Buckinghamshire (1947-1953) and in a part-time capacity at Cambridge University (1954-1958), also acting as Director of Music to the Berkhamsted Operatic Society (1950-1958). — In 1958 he left for Tanganyika, where he was Director of Music at St Michael's and St George's School (1958-1962). Since 1963, Ronald Charles has been in South Africa, where he was successively Lecturer in Music at the Johannesburg College of Education (1963-1964), Director of Music at Michaelhouse, Natal (1964-1965) and, since 1966, Organiser of Music for the SABC in Durban. He has conducted two operas by Menotti for NAPAC (*The medium* in 1966 and *The consul* in 1968), has given solo recitals as pianist and organist for the same organisation and presents several series

of music programmes for the SABC. — In 1960 he was nominated a Fellow of the International Institute of Arts and Letters in Switzerland.

—Ed.

CHERNIAVSKY, ALEXANDER, *7 November 1896 in Odessa, Russia; living in Johannesburg in 1970. Active member of a musical family, who became a well-known concert impresario in South Africa.

Alex Cherniavsky was educated in music by his father (° 1937 in Los Angeles), the conductor of a youth orchestra, a music teacher, and a performer on 65 (!) different musical instruments. Xavier Scharwenka was another of his teachers. His five brothers and four sisters all became professional musicians and toured extensively as family groups. At the age of 12 Alex gave his first recital as a pianist in the Albert Hall in London, where the family had settled in 1906, after a stay of two years in Vienna. As a member of the second Cherniavsky Trio, sometimes called the Imperial Russian Trio, he came to South Africa for the first time in 1912, accompanied by his father. Cherniavsky senior taught music in Johannesburg while Manya (cello), cousin Boris (violin) and Alex (piano) toured the country in conveyances such as Cape-carts, ox-wagons, a train carrying dynamite and a wagon transporting ice. Inclement weather added variety to their adventures and once marooned them in a black village as heavy rains flooded the river and created a stretch of quicksand. — The Trio offered attractive programmes of classical and popular music and generally drew full houses. When halls were not available, they played in the dining rooms of hotels and, on occasion, used billiard tables as platforms. Since the audiences were easy to please and enthusiastic, although sometimes troublesome, the concerts were marked by a genial atmosphere; they sometimes ended in community singing. — After a series of 600 concerts given over a period of two and a half years, the Trio returned to London in 1914. At New York in 1915 Alex formed a new quartet with his brothers Leo, Jan and Mischel, which (until 1925) toured Canada, Australia, New Zealand, India, China, the Philippine Islands, the Malayan States, Java and South America. After his marriage to Ella Frames in 1926, Alex Cherniavsky started teaching piano in Toronto, but his brothers continued as a trio until 1933. — In 1925 he had persuaded Anna Pavlova, with her company of 42 dancers, who were en route to Australia, to include a tour of South Africa in their itinerary. Five years later, memories of this venture moved him to start a new career as a concert impresario in South Africa. He brought out artists such as Amelita Galli-Curci (1932-1934), Benno Moiseiwitsch (1931-1936 and 1947), the Gonzales Opera Company (1931), Shura Cherkassky (1929, 1931), Yascha Heifetz (1932) and Richard Crooks (1939). During the war he taught music in Johannesburg, but in 1945 he resumed his work as a concert impresario in association with African Consolidated Theatres. Since then an impressive list of some two dozen musical celebrities have visited South Africa through his agency. At the end of 1957, he left African Consolidated Theatres and independently managed artists such as Arturo Michelangeli (1958), Hanlie van Niekerk* (1959) and Benno Moiseiwitsch (1962). He also acted as impresario for Marian Friedman* and guided her early pianoforte studies.

SOURCES
CAMPBELL, D.: 50 years of musical life and work. *S.A. Panorama,* October 1958. *Sunday Times:* 24 June 1956. National Documentation Centre for Music, HSRC, Pretoria.

—Ed.

CHERNIAVSKY TRIO, THE, consisted of Leo (*20 August 1890 - violin), Jan (*22 March 1892 - pianoforte) and Mischel (*28 November 1893 - cello). They were the three elder children of Abraham Cherniavsky, a music pedagogue in Kiev, who could himself play a large variety of instruments and conducted a youth orchestra. He formed the trio in 1901, when the three boys were respectively ten, eight and seven years of age; shortly afterwards they gave a performance in the presence of the Czar and members of his family. At that time they lived in Odessa, but in 1904 they moved to Vienna and in 1906 to London. — Their first concert tour through South Africa, commencing in 1908, lasted several years. After giving about 200 concerts, often in the most remote centres, they left for a similar tour of Australia and New Zealand. A younger brother, Alexander* (*7 November 1896 in Odessa) joined them in New York in 1915 and the four brothers undertook concert tours through five continents. After a partnership of 32 years, they eventually separated in 1933, when both Jan and Mischel married. Subsequently, however, they appeared as soloists, also in South Africa. In February 1959 the three brothers visited Alexander in South Africa to celebrate the 50th anniversary of their first tour in this country. — The trio should not be confused with the second Cherniavsky trio, formed at a later date by the younger brother Alexander and his sister Manya, with their cousin Boris. This group toured in South Africa between 1912 and 1914 (see Cherniavsky, Alexander*).

—Ed.

CHERON, VIRGINIE, *1854 on Mauritius; °February 1937 in Natal. Soprano, known in South Africa as the "Natal Nightingale".

Melidor Cheron, Virginie's father, left Mauritius about 1865 to settle in South Africa, chose the North Coast of Natal for his residence, and became the first successful sugar farmer in this area. The greater part of his estate has become the residential area known as Virginia, a name chosen by Cheron in honour of the elder of his two daughters, after she had become a famous singer. — Virginie was educated at Durban and instructed in music by Alice Hart*, who discovered and developed her vocal potential. In 1882 Miss Cheron was married to a Mr Richards and three years later became prominent in the musical life of Durban as a concert singer with her sister Bertie, who played pianoforte solos and acted as her accompanist. When Virginie's first marriage ended, is not known, but during the late eighties she decided to become a professional singer. — In 1887 Melidor took his daughters on a concert tour of South Africa, with Barberton as their main destination. The town was in its boom period, and gold prospectors enjoyed their concerts with vociferous enthusiasm. After this success her reputation preceded her wherever she went and when Virginie sang in Grahamstown in January 1888, the local newspaper dubbed her the "Natal Nightingale". Their return to Durban coincided with the arrival of the celebrated violinist Reményi*, who was on a protracted tour of South Africa. He arranged benefit concerts for Virginie and persuaded her father to send her overseas for further training. She left for England in July 1888, and spent two-and-a-half years at the RAM. — In the year of her return (1891), Virginie undertook another concert tour on a grander scale, including Ladysmith, Harrismith, Bloemfontein, Johannesburg, Pretoria, Kimberley, Cape Town, Port Elizabeth, Grahamstown, Queenstown, King William's Town and East London in her itinerary. Although she was undoubtedly one of the most accomplished singers in South Africa during the last century, reviews of her singing after her return from England were noticeably cooler. Some maintained that her high notes sounded unpleasantly shrill, and the *Kimberley Independent* bluntly stated on 19 July 1891, that all Miss Cheron possessed was a physique for singing. — Undaunted, she returned to Kimberley during the great Exhibition in September 1892, this time in the company of the Canadian bass-baritone, Avon Saxon, who had been giving concerts in Bloemfontein during April/May of that year. After their Kimberley engagement, they gave a joint concert in Bloemfontein on 14 November, and then apparently continued on a tour of the Eastern Province; it has been established that a concert was given in Queenstown in May 1893. Afterwards, they returned to Durban, where they were married in July 1893. Henceforth Virginie was known as Madame Cheron-Saxon; but in Durban, where they opened a singing studio, the couple were simply known as the "Saxons". — In 1895 the Saxons again visited the Eastern Province, with the contralto Katherine Timberman and the cellist Renzo Rotondo. The party gave concerts in King William's Town on 14 and 15 November, and in Queenstown on the next day. Other centres were probably included in the itinerary, but the evidence is lacking. In common with other visiting celebrities, they co-operated with local musicians who acted as accompanists and contributed items of their own. This was an established practice; but it seems that they engaged the Durban cellist Renzo Rotondo to accompany them once or twice, for instance at concerts in Bloemfontein (11-13 January 1897). — During the Jubilee festivities in Durban in 1897, the Durban Musical Association* gave performances of Mendelssohn's *Elijah,* with Saxon singing the part of the Prophet. The performance moved the music critic of the *Natal Mercury*, Milligan, to write a most uncomplimentary notice disparaging the Saxons, and he was assaulted by the enraged Prophet in his office the next day. After the resulting scandal, the Saxons seem to have roamed through the country giving concerts; they visited England with the object of forming their own opera company, to present operatic performances in South Africa and Australia (1901). Details of this project are, however, lacking. — Their marriage broke up in 1903, and after the death of her father in 1905, Virginie was again in Durban, teaching singing there and in Pietermaritzburg. Up to the outbreak of the Great War, she often appeared as a soloist in choral performances of the Durban Musical Association. She married Mr A. McCausland in 1905, and when she finally retired from the musical scene in 1921, they lived at Umhlanga Rocks. — A grandson from her first marriage, Mr C.R.C. (Reg) Richards, inherited much of her talent. He still lives at the old estate on the North Coast in Virginia (1971).

—G.S.J.

CHERRY, RICHARD JOHN, *17 December 1897, in Ilford, Essex; at present (1976) in Johannesburg. Composer, bassoonist and lecturer.

Richard Cherry studied at the Trinity College of Music in London, where he had bassoon lessons from Fred James and instruction in harmony and counterpoint. After active service during the First World War, he became principal bassoonist of the municipal orchestra at Margate in 1921. The next year he was recruited by Lyell-Tayler* for the newly-formed Durban Municipal Orchestra*, as second bassoon player. He played with the orchestra as soloist, arranged symphonic pieces to suit its size and orchestrated compositions and vocal items for concerts and plays. He also taught at the Durban College of Music. — Cherry became principal bassoonist to the Cape Town Orchestra* in June 1928, following W. Pickerill*, and also acted as librarian to the orchestra. Again he performed as soloist, and taught at the College of Music*. He conducted his own *Suite for strings on South African tunes,* on 7

268

September 1935. In this year he left Cape Town and settled in Johannesburg, as bassoonist in the Broadcast Orchestra of Theo Wendt*, and stayed in broadcasting for 20 years. He became part of the musical life of the city, and played a prominent role in the promotion of ballet. His ability as a composer, orchestrator, arranger and conductor was invaluable during the Second World War, when he was able to provide a great deal of incidental music for broadcast and film productions, and plays. — Most of Cherry's bigger works were composed during the 40's and 50's. He associated himself with the Festival Ballet Society, from its foundation in 1940 to its dissolution in 1952. *An afternoon at the swimming bath* (1945) and *Incidents at a ball* (1946) are two of his original ballets and he also acted as musical director of the Johannesburg Festival Ballet Society (1948-1952), whom he conducted in seasons at Johannesburg, Pretoria and Durban. In addition, he conducted the Ci-bonne Ballet Company and Gwen Ashton's ballet in seasons at the Pretoria City Hall (1954-1958). He was connected with the Mercedes Molina* Spanish dance theatre for a long time. — Since he came to Johannesburg, Cherry has also been active as a private teacher of harmony, composition and bassoon. He joined the staff of the University of SA in 1959, in a part-time capacity. In a full-time capacity he lectured in composition, harmony, counterpoint and orchestration from 1965-1967. Captain E. Kealey*, K.F. Heimes* and H. Edmund Dawes* were among his most prominent pupils. He was awarded composition prizes by the SABC in 1948, 1952 and 1956.

WORKS

Cadenzas for Mozart's concerto for bassoon. Ms., 1927 (performed with Durban Municipal Orchestra).   Tell me where is fancy bred, for vocal quartette (from Shakespeare's *The merchant of Venice*). Ms., performed on 6 October 1927.   Minuet, bassoon solo. Ms., performed by composer, City Hall, Cape Town, 23 January 1932.   The Shantyman, bassoon solo. Ms., 1936.   Little suite for six wind instruments. Ms., first peformance on 11 September 1938, with the composer conducting the Cape Town City Orchestra.   Concerto for cello and orchestra. Ms., 1942.   An afternoon at the swimming bath. Ballet suite performed at Standard Theatre, Johannesburg, 1945.   Incidents at a ball. Ballet suite written for Johannesburg Festival Ballet Society, produced 1946.   Suite for strings on South African tunes. Ms., first performance 1947.   In laude regis orientalis, for baritone, choir and orchestra. Ms., 1947.   To Electra, song (R. Herrick). Ms., 1950.   Festival overture 1652, for Van Riebeeck Festival. Ms., 1952.   Pioneers, o pioneers (Walt Whitman), for chorus and orchestra. Ms., 1954.   Captain Stratton's fancy, song (J. Masefield). Ms., 1957.   Variations for string orchestra on a theme by Saint-Saëns, composed for YSAC Orchestra. First performance 14 June 1958.   How sleep the brave, song (W. Collins). Ms., 1962.   Cape cart (based on "Saai die waatlemoen"). Ms., 1958 and scherzo on "My hartjie, my liefie". Both performed by SABC Orchestra in Johannesburg City Hall, 1958.   Springboks on parade. Ms., performed 19 October 1959.   Two Christmas pieces for small orchestra. Ms., 1962.   South African pastorale, French Hoek, for piano. University of South Africa, 1964. Also in Braille by Worcester School for the Blind.   Suite, salute to Brahms, for piano. Ms., 1969.   Suite for wind quintet. Ms., n.d.   Slave dance, for harp. Ms., n.d.   Fuga doxologia, for mixed chorus (Anglican Book of Common Prayer). Ms., 1971.   Suite in three movements, for piano. Ms., 1974:   1. Passacaglietta   2. Meditation   3. Fugue.

Incidental music for

(a) radio programmes

The story of Juliet. Produced by Marie Ney; incidental music 1946.   Hamlet (in Afrikaans). Ms., 1947.   Fugue for SA voices. Produced by P. Baneshik; incidental music, 1946.   Spirit of

269

the water (Uys Krige). Ms., 1942.   This is SA, feature programme, 1947.   The Great Trek, feature programme, 1947.   Alter Ego, feature programme, n.d.

(b) plays

Servant of God. Standard Theatre, 1943.   And so to bed. 1944.   Granite. Johannesburg Repertory Players, 1944.   Periandros van Korinthe. NTO, Technical College, Johannesburg, 1956.

(c) films

Pondo story, SA documentary film, 1948.   The fox has four eyes, documentary film, 1959 (produced at Cannes Festival by Jamie Uys).   Rip van Wyk. Jamie Uys Film Productions Ltd., 1961.

Orchestral arrangements for ballet

The numerous orchestrations Richard Cherry wrote for ballet, include Peter and the Wolf (Prokofiev); La boutique fantastique; Carnival at Pesth, Constantia; Coppelia; Romeo and Juliet; Corregidor's folly; Shepherd boy (based on music by Grieg); The willow pattern plate; In old Pekin (Kameneff); Chinese suite (Hubert Bath); Pas de deux of doves, composed by Cherry; Foyer de la danse; Le lac de cygnes (Tchaikovsky); The tempest; Les sylphides (Chopin); Aurora's wedding; Giselle; Carnival; La carousel; The judgement of Paris; The sleeping beauty (Tchaikovsky).

—L.W.

CHERTKOW, BEDANA CECILY (MRS COETZEE),   *19 September 1932 in Johannesburg; at present 1977 in Johannesburg. Pianist and teacher of pianoforte.

A member of the fourth South African generation of a musical family, Bedana Chertkow had her initial music training from her mother, Mrs Betty Chertkow, a pianoforte teacher in Johannesburg. She completed six years of pianoforte study under Isador Epstein* in 1951 and studied at the University of the Witwatersrand in Johannesburg (1948-1950), where she obtained the B. Mus. degree (1950) and the Melanie Pollak Scholarship* (1951) to continue her studies at the RAM (1952-1957). There Bedana Chertkow received the Henry Eyers Prize for Aural Training, the Frederick Shinn Prize for History of Music, the Scott-Huxley Prize for pianoforte accompaniment, the Alexander Roller and Kate Steel Prizes for pianoforte, and obtained the LRSM, ARCM and LRAM diplomas. Subsequently, she was admitted to the international master classes at the Accademia Chigiana, Sienna, Italy, where she studied pianoforte under Guido Agosti and chamber music with the Quintetto Chigiano (1957-1959). — During the whole of this period she was active, first in South Africa and later in London and on the continent, as a radio pianoforte soloist and as soloist with the symphony orchestras of Cape Town, Durban, Johannesburg and the RA Orchestra in London. In addition, she taught pianoforte in London. — In 1965 she returned to Johannesburg, where she practises as a pianoforte teacher, examines for UNISA (since 1969) and is a pianoforte soloist. Evelyn Green is among her prominent pupils. Since 1976 she has been a part-time teacher of piano at the Music Academy of the University of Pretoria.

—Ed.

CHEW, GEOFFREY ALEXANDER,   *23 April 1940 in East London; at present in Johannesburg. Pianist.

After initial training with Agnes F. Scholl and Dr J.P.G. Wise*, he studied pianoforte, organ, harmony and counterpoint at the RCM, obtaining the ARCM diploma (1958-1961). From 1961 to 1964 Geoffrey Chew studied at Gonville and Cains College, Cambridge, for the Music Tripos (BA) and Mus. Bac. Since 1965 he has been engaged in doing research for a Ph. D. degree at Manchester University. — Geoffrey Chew was awarded the Ffennell Prize and received an Associated Board scholarship in 1958 and an organ scholarship at Cains College in 1961. In England he performed at the RCM chamber concerts, gave recitals in Cambridge and was conductor of an undergraduate choir in Cambridge. Currently, he is a teacher of keyboard instruments at the University of the Witwatersrand.

WORKS
Four songs (Stephen Gray). Ms., 1965.

—Ed.

CHIROPLAST   F. Logier

CHISHOLM, ERIK,   *4 January 1904 in Cathcart, Glasgow; °8 June 1965 in Cape Town. Dean and Director of the South African College of Music*, composer, conductor and all-round musician.

Chisholm received his initial training at the Athenaeum School of Music in Glasgow (now The Royal Scottish Academy of Music), with pianoforte playing (Philip Halstead) and organ (Herbert Walton) as his practical subjects. He started composing at an early age, and performed his own piano sonatina at a British Music Society concert when he was 13 years old. Three years later (1920), he made his debut as a pianist in a performance of the Liszt *Piano concerto no. 1* in Hull. Subsequently he continued his piano studies with the Russian pianist, Leff Pouishnoff. — Until 1928, Chisholm lived in Canada, where he was music master at the Pictou Academy in Nova Scotia and, concurrently, organist and choirmaster at the Westminster Presbyterian Church in New Glasgow, Nova Scotia. Besides his official duties, he toured, giving piano recitals in which he introduced the music of Bartok and Schönberg to Canadian audiences; he also played as pianist with the German violinist, Berenice Stultz. Returning to Scotland, he was organist and choirmaster at the Barony Church in Glasgow, and established a reputation as an organist, pianist, conductor and enthusiastic supporter of contemporary music. The Society for Contemporary Music was especially busy under his direction (1930-38) and gave first performances of about two hundred new compositions by living composers, who often performed in recitals of their works. In the meantime he studied at the Edinburgh University with Sir Donald Tovey, and graduated as a B.Mus. (1931) and as a D. Mus. (1934). From 1935 to 1940 he acted as musical director of the Celtic Ballet for whom he composed folk ballets. — After resigning as organist, Chisholm was active in the re-organization of the Carl Rosa Opera Company (1940-1941) and toured with them as conductor, and later as advance publicity manager. He was conductor of the Anglo-Polish Ballet Company for three years (1941-1944) and accompanied them to Italy. As pianist, he concentrated especially on new and rarely heard works, such as Bartok's *Concerto no. 1*, Medtner's *Concerto no. 2*, the Delius *Concerto*, piano works of Schönberg and Szymanowsky's *Pianoforte sonata no. 3*. At the outbreak of war Chisholm joined ENSA and organized orchestral concerts in India and in the Far East. Under war conditions scores were hardly available, and he often had to write scores by listening to gramophone records. — In 1946 he arrived in Cape Town to assume his duties as Professor of Music and Dean of the Faculty of Music at the University of Cape Town.

271

The appointment had originally been made in 1939, but the war retarded the possibility of putting it into effect. — Chisholm promptly reorganized the staff of the College of Music, creating twelve new full-time appointments; extended the curriculum from 32 to 75 courses, adding new degrees and diplomas; established an opera school (1954) with a full-time director (Gregorio Fiasconaro*); revived the weekly Hiddingh Hall concerts; and led the University Opera Company in widespread tours. At the same time he founded and organized the South African section of the ISCM (1948) and gave concerts of contemporary music, including a series of orchestral concerts with the Cape Town Municipal Orchestra*. — The repertoire of Chisholm's University Opera Company included numerous contemporary works by Bartok, Chisholm, John Joubert*, Martinu, Menotti, and other rarely heard works such as *The Portuguese inn-keeper* (Cherubini), *Iphigenia in Taurus* (Gluck), *Suor Angelica, Gianni Schicchi* and *Il Tabarro* (Puccini), and *Prodana Nevesta* (Smetana). This dynamic activity culminated in a musical festival by College students and members of the staff which Chisholm presented in London and Glasgow (December 1957 - January 1958). The six Wigmore Hall concerts each included at least one first performance, or first London performance. This was the first venture of the kind undertaken by a South African student group. — In 1957 Chisholm was invited to the Soviet Union to conduct two concerts of the USSR State Orchestra, which included performances of his *Second piano concerto*. In the same year he was nominated a member of an international jury to adjudicate 200 new compositions. In 1962 he was nominated as musical delegate from Scotland, to study music educational methods in the USSR; on two occasions he was invited to attend the Janáček Music Festival in Czechoslovakia, as a guest of honour. He was also awarded a Carnegie Travel Grant for an extended tour of the United States and Canada, where he lectured on the music of South African composers at 43 universities and music schools. — These vigorous activities, often spiced with pungent and sometimes visionary articles in the South African press, still left him time for a steady output of new works, of which several were conspicuously successful. The one-act opera *Dark sonnet* (libretto, Eugene O'Neill), which is part of a trilogy called *Murder in three keys*, was televised by the BBC in December 1953, and the whole trilogy ran for 10 weeks in New York in the summer of 1954. His operas *The inland woman* and *The pardoner's tale* were successfully performed in Cape Town, and various major instrumental works were given performances in England, America and elsewhere. A thorough study of his numerous and varied compositions is still in abeyance. Of his dynamic influence on the music and musical education in South Africa there can be not the slightest doubt.

WORKS

1. Operas

The feast of Samhein, a Celtic romantic opera in three acts (libretto by the composer after the novel of the same name by James Stephens). Ms., 1941. Black roses. Ms., n.d. Lady Lancing. Ms., n.d. Caucasian circle. Ms., n.d. The inland woman, opera in one act (libretto adapted from a short story by Mary Lavin - *The black grave and the green grave*). Ms., 1951. Murder in three keys, three one-act operas linked: 1. Sweeny Agonistes (libretto T.S. Eliot) 2. Dark sonnet (libretto Eugene O'Neill) 3. Simoon (libretto August Strindberg). Ms., 1953. The midnight court, opera in one act (libretto by the composer after a free English translation by Frank O'Connor of the Irish Gaelic poem by Bryan Merryman).

Ms., 1959. Canterbury tales, a comedy in three acts (libretto after Chaucer): 1. The wyf of Bathe's tale (a fairy romance) 2. The pardoner's tale (a tragedy of greed) 3. The nonnes preestes tale of a cok and hen (Chauntecleer and Pertelote) and a fox. Ms., 1961. The importance of being Ernest, opera in three acts (libretto based on the Oscar Wilde comedy). Curwen's, London 1963. Robert Burns - his life, his loves, his songs. A folk opera in three acts (libretto based on the narratives, letters and poems of the poet himself, and on the narratives by his brother, Gilbert, and other contemporaries). Ms., 1963.

2. Ballet

The forsaken mermaid, ballet in five scenes, composed for Celtic Ballet in 1936. Dunedin Publications have published an arrangement for two pianos in association with the Oxford University Press. The earth-shapers, symphonic ballet in a prologue and one act, composed for Celtic Ballet in 1939. Boosey & Hawkes have published the second movement as *A Celtic wonder tale*. Piobaireachd, burlesque Scottish ballet in 4 scenes, composed for Celtic Ballet in 1940/41. The Hoodie, ballet in one scene, composed for Celtic Ballet in 1947. The pied piper of Hamelin, ballet in one act. Ms., 1937. From the land under waves. Ms., n.d.

3. Orchestra (in alphabetical order)

Adventures of Babar, the baby elephant, for narrator and orchestra. Ms., 1941. Agamemnon, overture for orchestra. Ms., n.d. Cherubini's tune. Ms., n.d. Cantos gitanos, for pianoforte and orchestra. Ms., n.d. A Celtic wonder tale. Boosey & Hawkes, n.d. Ceol Mor dances. Ms., 1943. Chaconne for orchestra. Ms., n.d. Concerto no. 1, The Piobaireachd, for piano and orchestra. Ms., 1936. Concerto no. 2, The Hindustani, for piano and orchestra. Schott & Co., London, 1951. Concerto, for violin and orchestra. Ms., 1950, reorchestrated 1953. Dance suite, for piano and orchestra. Ms., 1932. Dunedin suite, for strings: 1. Sarabande 2. Caprice 3. Strathspey 4. Jig. Ms., n.d. Enchanted island. Ms., n.d. From the Western isles, suite for strings. Ms., 1939. Gipsey. Ms., n.d. Hebridia. Ms., n.d. O Son of God, it is a great grief. Ms., n.d. Overture for orchestra. Ms., n.d., arranged for pianoforte. Pageant of music, Cutty Wren and the peasants' war. Ms., May 1939. Prelude in G. Ms., n.d. Straloch, suite for orchestra. Ms., 1933; pianoforte arrangement published by Dunedin Publications. Sword dance. Ms., n.d. Symphony for strings. Ms., n.d. There was a time when I thought far sweeter. Ms., n.d. The true edge of the great world, ten orchestral preludes: 1. Ossianic lay 2. Stravaiging 3. Sea sorrow 4. Song of the Mavis 5. Sheiling lullabye 6. Spinning song 7. Port-a-Buel 8. The hour of the Sluagh 9. Rudah Ban 10. Sea tangle. Ms., 1943. The friars of Berwick, overture for small orchestra. Ms., 1933. The midnight court. Ms., n.d. Two pictures from Dante, after the engravings by Doré: 1. Inferno 2. Paradiso. Ms., 1948. Van Riebeeck concerto for orchestra. Ms., 1951, also arranged for two pianofortes.

4. Pianoforte

Cameos. Curwen, London, 1926. Ceol Mor dances, arranged for four pianofortes. Ms., n.d. Cuckoo and nightingale. Maurice Senart, Paris, 1926. Dance Bacchanal. Ms., n.d. Dance of the Princess Jachta: 1. Scheema 2. Oriental 3. Minuet 4. India. Ms., n.d. Four elegies. Ms., n.d., revised in 1951. Highland sketches, six small piano pieces. Ms., n.d., revised in 1951. Hour of the slough. Ms., n.d. Minstrelsey. Ms., n.d. Miscellaneous pieces: 1. Fashion portrait of a woman 2. Tango 3. Minuet 4. Christ in the garden 5. Wet Sythes 6. Dance 7. Minstrels 8. Prelude no. 1. Ms., n.d. Night song of the bards, nocturnes for piano after an anonymous Gaelic poem. Ms., 1944/51. Petite suite: 1. Harris dance 2. Skye dance 3. Allegretto grazioso 4. Moderato 5. Mermaid's song 6. Churning croon. Ms., n.d. Pieces for pianoforte: 1. Study 2. Caprice

3. Moto perpetuo 4. Esplanade. Ms., 1923/24.   Pipa passes, suite after Browning:
1. Morning 2. Noon. Ms., n.d.   Preludes for pianoforte: 1. Prelude 2. Chopsticks
3. Caprice 4. Intermezzo 5. Finale. Ms., n.d.   Scottish airs, arranged for the piano.
Ms., n.d.   Sonata no. 1 for piano. Ms., 1939.   Sonatina ecossaise: 1. Allegretto 2.
Lament 3. March 4. Strathspey 5. Reel. Ms., n.d.   Sonatina for piano. Ms., 1922.
Sonatinas for piano, e praeterita: 1. After Luis de Narvaez, in four movements 2.
After an Obrecht Agnus Dei and after Andriques de Valderravano, three movements
3. After ricercari by Dalzu, Ganassi and Spinaccio, in four movements 4. Movements
one and three after a lute dance by Neusiedler, movement two after a 13th century dance,
three movements 5. Two movements 6. After three dances by Claude Gervaise: Basse
dance, Aria, Burlesque. Ms., 1947.   Süss communes with Mialni. Ms., n.d.   Two
Piobaireachd laments. Ms., n.d.   Two piano pieces: 1. Viewed from a starpoint 2.
Sorrow for a queen. Senart, Paris, 1926.   Two Scottish pieces: 1. The braes o' glen
Braon, phantasia 2. Morris dance. Ms., 1920.   Two's and three's. From Pro Musica,
OUP, London, 1932.   Wisdom book, solo pieces. Ms., n.d.   With clogs on. Ms., n.d.
(Numerous arrangements for pianoforte of own and other composers' works, folk songs, etc.)

5. Chamber music

Double trio for clarinet, bassoon, trumpet and violin, cello, bass. Ms., 1930.   Sonata for viola.
Ms., n.d.

6. Vocal

Afternoon tea, song. Ms., n.d.   Biogadh, song. Ms., n.d.   The comforters; Snail, snail shoot
out your horn; Galoots, for voice and pianoforte. Ms., n.d.   Cool tombs, a Highland dirge,
arranged as part-song. Ms., n.d.   Crabbed age and youth, for chorus and mixed voices. Curwen,
London, 1926.   Cradle song for chorus of equal voices. Curwen, London, 1928.   Diarmait's
sleep, song. Ms., n.d.   Dismal is the life for me, for piano, tenor and orchestra. Ms., n.d.
Dun Liur, Gaelic bardic song. Ms., n.d.   The first daffodil, song. Ms., n.d.   Go heart, unto the
lamp of licht, song. Ms., n.d.   I arose one morning early, Scottish folksong. Ms., n.d.   The
jolly beggars, four-part songs. Ms., n.d.   A king's brother who became a hermit, for tenor,
strings and piano, with a narrator. Ms., n.d.   The last song of Oisean, son of Fionn (James
MacPherson), song. Ms., n.d.   Marbhna eoghain ruaidh ui Neill, song. Ms., n.d.   The mask of
anarchy, song. Ms., n.d.   Mungo, cantata for baritone, chorus and orchestra. Ms., n.d.   No
churchman am I, song. Ms., n.d.   The seagull, song. Ms., n.d.   Sixty cubic feet, song for
baritone. Workers' Music Association, London, 1941.   The song of the women, for SSA.
Curwen, London, 1928.   Tho' oot your shadows, part-song. Ms., n.d.   The treasure ship,
song. Ms., n.d.

7. Arrangements of Folksongs

A Celtic song book, an anthology of Celtic poetry from the 9th to the 20th century, presented as
songs. All vocal melodies were chosen from MacDonald's *Collection of airs and dances of the
Scottish Highlands and Islands* (1784). The texts and the music were arranged by Chisholm.
USSR State Music Publishers, Moscow, n.d.

8. Publications

The life and works of Leos Janáček. Pergamon Press, n.d.   South African Festival in London.
Res Musicae III/2 & 3, December 1956, March 1957.   The Mozart Year in South Africa. *Res
Musicae* III/2, December 1956.   How fast is music? *Res Musicae* VI/3, March 1960.
Chamber music in the contemporary idiom. *Res Musicae* VI/4, June 1960.   Music in British
schools. *SAMT* 31, December 1946.   Contributions to the *Cape Argus:* 15 September 1937,
11 December 1958.   Contributions to the *Cape Times:* 26 September 1955, 31 May
1958.   Contribution to the *Daily Mail:* 10 July 1961.

BIBLIOGRAPHY

BLOM, ERIC: *Grove's dictionary of music and musicians,* vol. 1. Macmillan, 1954.   SCHOLES, PERCY: *Oxford companion to music.* O.U.P., 1943.

SOURCES

ANON: New Director of the South African College of Music. *SAMT* 30, June 1945.   CHISHOLM, DINAH: Reminiscences. *Opus* I/5.   GALLOWAY, DAVE: Dr. Erik Chisholm - a retrospective profile. *Opus* I/4.   GLASSER, STANLEY: Erik Chisholm. *Res Musicae* VI/4, September 1960. *Die Burger:* 19 January 1951; October 1952; 19 February 1954; 3 January 1956; 25 April 1956; 1 June 1957; 28 August 1957; 30 December 1957; 30 June 1959; 2 July 1959; 22 February 1963; 9 June 1965.   *Cape Argus:* 1 July 1950.   *Cape Times:* ? November 1949; ? October 1950; 23 January 1952; 5 February 1954; 12 July 1954; 9 June 1965.   *Dagbreek en Sondagnuus:* 21 July 1957.   *SABC Bulletin:* 1 August 1953.   *Transvaler:* 19 January 1952; 6 March 1959; 10 June 1965.   National Documentation Centre for Music, HSRC, Pretoria.

—J.P.M.

CHOSACK FAMILY, THE   provided twelve musicians in four South African generations over the last 70 years.

Rachmiel (Robert), the head of the family, came to South Africa from Russia at the beginning of the century. He was then 30 years old and was accompanied by his wife and son, Joe. Two elder sons remained in Russia, but later followed their father. Rachmiel played the flute, violin, viola or violoncello in the permanent orchestra of Dvinsk, his birthplace, toured Russia with the orchestra and sometimes appeared as soloist. He was best known in South Africa as a flute player, and occasionally acted as choir leader. He died in Johannesburg in October 1942. — Of his three sons, **Louis** was born in Dvinsk in 1885 and died in Johannesburg. He was a clarinettist and accompanied his father, as a child, on concert tours in Russia. In 1905, at 20 years of age, he came to South Africa and originally played in Max Weinbrenn's* orchestra. Later he joined David Foote's* ensemble at the Empire Theatre in Johannesburg, became a member of John Connell's* Johannesburg Municipal Orchestra, and eventually played in the first SABC orchestra. He was a collector of sheet music. It was claimed that he had the "largest music library in the Southern hemisphere'. He became Librarian of the Music Department of the Johannesburg Municipality and, ultimately, Chief Music Librarian of the SABC. When, after his death, the Johannesburg Municipal Orchestra was discontinued, the Municipal Music Library was closed and part of it was included in the SABC music library. — **Joe** was born in 1895(?) in Dvinsk and came to South Africa with his parents when he was about five years old. He received piano instruction from Drutman and became known chiefly as a performer of light music. He formed his own dance band, Chosack and Geers, which became very popular in Johannesburg. In his later years he was a cinema manager for African Theatres and eventually became the owner of his own cinema. He died in Johannesburg. — **Israel** was the percussion player of the Cape Town City Orchestra (separate article). — The family's musical ability was inherited by Louis's children. Louis was Rachmiel Chosack's eldest son and had seven children of whom *two* sons and *two* daughters became musicians: — **Idor** was active for many years in the sphere of light music in Johannesburg, both as pianist and as composer. — **Harry** was a bass singer and took part, amongst others, in the productions of operas by John Connell* and P.R. Kirby* in

275

Johannesburg. —**Betty (Mrs Chertkow)** was trained by her grandfather and her father and was active in Johannesburg's chamber music groups and restaurant orchestras, as a cinema pianist before the advent of the "talkies", and as accompanist. After her marriage she became an outstanding piano teacher. Her daughter Bedana Chertkow* inherited her musical talent. — **Yetta (Mrs Klass)** is a competent cellist and the mother of Sylvia Jane Klass, known as Silvia Durán*. — **Hilary,** the daughter of Idor, gained a B.Sc. from the university of the Witwatersramd in 1969, with distinction in Music History. She actively participated in the University's music performances and in 1970 was editress of the scientific journal, *Probe.*

SOURCES
Cape Argus: 24 April 1965.   *Cape Times:* 24 August 1968; 18 December 1971.   *Die Burger:* 3 August 1968.

—Ed.

CHOSACK, ISRAEL, *26 June 1888 in Dvinsk, Russia; now (1976) in Cape Town. Timpanist, percussionist and concert xylophonist.

Second son of Rachmiel Chosack (head of the musical Chosack family* in South Africa), he received his musical training, including violin and piano lessons, from his father and other members of his family in Russia, but is mainly selftaught. At the age of sixteen he served as percussionist in the Don Cossack Symphony Orchestra and at the beginning of the twentieth century played in the orchestras of several Russian opera companies. In 1906 at the age of 18 he emigrated to South Africa and until 1911 he was with David Foote's* Empire Theatre Orchestra. Between 1911 and 1918 he toured South Africa as xylophone virtuoso. — He began his long association with the Cape Town City Orchestra* on 1 July 1918, when he was appointed percussionist and timpanist, a position he held with a break of 13 months (May 1927 to June 1928), until he was pensioned on his sixtieth birthday. During the last eighteen months of his service he was chief percussionist. A month later he was re-appointed as temporary chief percussionist until 18 November 1949, and since then he has at times acted as temporary part-time second percussionist. Thus he has been associated with the Cape Orchestra in various capacities for more than 52 years. — On the occasion of the visit to South Africa by Granville Bantock, Chosack was the soloist in the first South African performance of this composer's six *Tympani concerti.* In 1925 he played the xylophone in Buckingham Palace in an orchestra conducted by Leslie Heward*. He taught several student timpanists, including the timpanist of the Durban City Orchestra, E. Edwards.

—Ed.

CHRIMES, PAMELA, *28 April 1922 at Three Anchor Bay; at present (1977) in Cape Town. Ballet dancer and teacher.

Pamela Chrimes received her training from Dulcie Howes* in the UCT Ballet* in Cape Town, and created and performed many roles for the Cape Town Ballet Club*. In 1945 she went to England, where she joined the Sadler's Wells Theatre Ballet, dancing with them until 1947, when she became ballet mistress for the Sadler's Wells Opera Ballet. On her return to South Africa in 1949, she joined the Cape Town University Ballet School, as teacher, and danced in the Company. She is now principal of the school, and a full member of the Imperial Society of Teachers of Dancing (Cecchetti).

She has produced *The haunted ballroom* and *Swan lake* for the Cape Town University Ballet Company, and has done the choreography for many operas and children's ballets.

—M.G.

CHRISTELIJKE JONGELINGS VEREENIGING   Pretoria 2

CHRISTELIKE SANGVERENIGING ASAF, THE   was established on 10 June 1909 at the instigation of Dr S.O. Los, minister of the Gereformeerde Kerk in Pretoria. The choir was to be conducted by Petrus van den Burg*, organist of the Gereformeerde Kerk; it can be assumed that he actually took the initiative in founding the choral society. The Gereformeerde Kerk took the lead, but choir membership was not restricted to members of this church. In addition to choir members, the society had the support of art lovers generally, and of sponsors who each donated R2,10 per annum. The choir never gave more than two concerts a year and sang sacred music only. Initially, the programmes included shorter, four-part choral pieces by Mendelssohn and contemporary Dutch composers such as Verhulst, Bernard Zweers and Brandts-Buys*, but they were gradually extended to include more ambitious works. Choral items at these early concerts were usually supplemented and varied by instrumental ensembles in which local artists performed. The orchestra that accompanied the choir was assembled before each concert and rehearsed by Van den Burg. — The first concert was presented in the old City Hall in Pretorius Street on 22 July 1910. During the seventeen years of its existence, the choir gave performances of such works as: *Simson* (Handel), *Opstandingskantate* (Sam de Lange), *Lofgesang* (Mendelssohn), *Een stem in Rama* (Brandts-Buys), *Elia* (Mendelssohn), *Een vaste burg is onze God* (Bach), *Die skepping* (Haydn), *Josua* (Handel), and *Judas Maccabeus* (Handel). Local amateurs, rehearsed by Van den Burg, sang the solo parts. In addition to the two annual concerts, the Asaf Choir also performed at almost all the significant cultural occasions in Pretoria. — When Van den Burg retired as conductor of the Asaf Choir in April 1926, after its 25th concert, the association was dissolved. In September 1926 the Gemengd Koor Zanglust*, conducted by Gerrit Bon*, took its place. — The success achieved by the Asaf Choir was ample proof that the Dutch-speaking public of Pretoria appreciated choral singing of a high standard. The concerts were always fully supported; many of the older generation of Pretorians still speak enthusiastically of this choir (1968). Part of their success can probably be attributed to the fact that Van den Burg translated the texts of German and English works into Dutch, and subsequently also into Afrikaans. This enabled Afrikaans-speaking people to sing in a related, or in their own language.

BIBLIOGRAPHY

HENNOP, ELMA: *Petrus van den Burg*. B. Mus. dissertation, UP, 1965.   VERMEULEN, ELIZABETH: *Die musieklewe van Pretoria tussen 1902 en 1926*. M.Mus. dissertation, UP, 1967.

—Ed.

CHRISTIAN BROTHERS' COLLEGE, KIMBERLEY   C. Rybnikar

CHRISTIAN NATIONAL EDUCATION   C.G. de Jonge, Pretoria 2, H. Visscher

CHRISTINA GREIG MEMORIAL TRUST   Christina Greig

CHRISTUSKIRCHE, WINDHOEK   Hans Müller, Windhoek 1, 2, 3

CILLIÉ, GABRIEL GIDEON. *13 July 1910 in Stellenbosch; now (1976) in Bloemfontein. Astro-physicist, organist, choir conductor and composer of Afrikaans sacred music. Cillié received his training in natural sciences at the University of Stellenbosch (B.Sc., 1928; M.Sc. 1929), at the University of Oxford on a Rhodes Scholarship (D. Phil. in Astro-physics, 1930-1933), and at Harvard University, after being awarded the Commonwealth Fund Fellowship (1933-1935). He taught at the Universities of the Witwatersrand and Pretoria for three and a half years, and in July 1939 was appointed to a position as professor in Mathematics at the University of Stellenbosch. — His interest in music runs parallel to his career as a scientist; in fact, it provided a simultaneous career and is a prominent South African example of the mathematical-musical union in one person. During his school and student days in Stellenbosch he received piano lessons and tuition in harmony; but it was mainly under the influence of Professor Jannasch*, who taught him organ, that Cillié came to love the *musica sacra*. While at Oxford, he was an active member of the Oxford Bach Choir, and one of Allchin's organ pupils at the RCM in London. At Harvard he was actively engaged in G. Wallace Woodworth's male voice choir, the Harvard Glee Club. The training he had received from Jannasch, whose place he was to take as a church musician, and the experience of university choirs he gained at Oxford and at Harvard, were the determining factors in his musical life. — From the time of his appointment to a chair in Stellenbosch, until his resignation as a church musician in 1964, Cillié was prominent in Afrikaans church music circles for about a quarter of a century. As organist of the congregation of the Dutch Reformed Church in Stellenbosch from 1939-1964, he revived the tradition of having choral singing in the divine service in the Mother Church during the mornings, and in the Students' Church (now the Central Church) in the evenings. He extended, by translation, by arrangements of liturgical songs, and by his own compositions, the limited repertoire of Afrikaans religious choral works. His activities in the field of church music gradually became more comprehensive; he wrote articles, collaborated in a revision of the *Nuwe Halleluja* (1951), contributed to the compilation of the harmonized version of the Hymnbook (1956), assisted in the revision of the Afrikaans Psalm tunes, and co-operated in the envisaged extension and revision of the Afrikaans hymn book. In addition, he collected popular church melodies (liederwysies), and tried to re-establish many of these old tunes in congregational use. — The example Cillié set with the Mother Church Choir led to other things; in 1941 he was invited to assume the leadership of the Stellenbosch University Choir*, and in 1946 he was asked to conduct the newly-established Choir of the Theological Seminary*. This was the beginning of an upsurge of choral singing in Stellenbosch. In 1946 the Students' Song Festival was held, the first of what became an annual event, that steadily drew more participants and showed an improved quality of repertoire each year. Choral singing in Stellenbosch achieved a national reputation when the Seminary Choir (from 1946) and the University Choir (from 1952) went on tour. Cillié was the conductor of both, a musical consultant and a stimulating example, an arranger of Afrikaans folk songs and other music for the growing demand. He must be considered the prime mover behind the early development of Afrikaans choral singing. He became a member of the FAK's music commission and was also creatively engaged in the revision of the *Nuwe FAK-Sang-bundel* (1961). — Eventually he found it impossible to do justice to his academic work and to these musical activities; at the end of 1951 he handed the Seminary Choir, and at the end of 1955 the University Choir, to other competent people. In 1964 he also re-

278

signed from his work as an active church musician. — The South African Academy for Arts and Science acknowledged his contributions to South African music by the award of a medal of honour on 28 April 1965.

WORKS

Van goedertierenheid sal ek vir ewig sing (Ps. 89). Commissioned for the investiture of the first State President in 1961. Die aarde behoort aan die Here (Ps. 24). FAK, 1968. Maria Wiegelied, no. 1 in *South African Christmas Carols.* Voortrekkerpers, 1968. Die ontvoerde bruidjie, school operetta (Ela Spence). DALRO, 1975. Short cantata on the Totius versification of Ps. 8, for soloists, choir and organ, commissioned by the SABC in 1976. Ms. Geloftedagkantate, commissioned by the SABC. Ms., n.d. Kersfeesstuk. Ms., n.d. Two-, three- and four part arrangements of Afrikaans folk songs.

SELECTED PUBLICATIONS

Die kerklied in Suid-Afrika. *Die Huisgenoot,* 5 May 1944. Koor- en orrelmusiek in ons kerke. *Die Huisgenoot,* 12 May 1944. Die musiek van die Afrikaanse Gesangboek. *Die Huisgenoot,* 9 February 1945. Wonderskone lydensliedere in ons Gesangboek. *Die Brandwag,* 4 April 1947. Die volkslied gaan kerktoe. *Die Huisgenoot,* 2 May 1952. Die Afrikaner se gewyde volksmusiek. *Res Musicae* IV/1, September 1957. Hoe die bundel van 1562 tot stand gekom het. *Die Burger,* 11 September 1962. See also Afrikaans church music 3, bibliography.

SOURCES

HARTMAN, ANTON: Huldigingswoord aan G.G. Cillié. *SA Akademie Jaarboek,* 1965. *Die Burger:* 18 June 1952; 21 September 1957; 3 October 1957; 7 November 1964. *Die Transvaler:* 9 November 1964.

—Ed.

CLASSICAL AND SPANISH GUITAR ASSOCIATION OF SOUTH AFRICA F.J. Buss

CLAUSET, ABRAHAM F., *1 April 1849 in Rotterdam; °13 May 1935 in Hengelo, the Netherlands. Composer.

Clauset worked in Pretoria during the last decade of the nineteenth century. He translated a German operetta by Richard Leunder and Carl H.C. Reinecke, *Geluksvogel en ongeluksvogel,* into Dutch. This operetta was presented on 2 September 1893 by pupils of Henrietta Bal van Lier* in Pretoria's President Theatre, with a repeat performance two weeks later. Clauset was the first composer of the *Zuid-Afrikaanse Volkslied* (O land, gekocht door bloed) (Dutch text by Nico Hofmeyr). This song was originally published by J.A.H. Wagenaar in Utrecht, the Netherlands, and in 1907 it was included in Dr N. Mansvelt's* collection entitled *Hollands-Afrikaanse Liederbundel.* This song was also issued in a two-part version intended for use in schools.

SOURCES

Letter from A.F. Clauset to Dr N. Mansvelt, 16 June 1907 (Amsterdam), in archives of the Nederlands-Zuidafrikaanse Vereniging, Amsterdam. MANSVELT, DR. N.: *Hollands-Afrikaanse Liederbundel.* Amsterdam, Cape Town/Pretoria, 1907. VAN NIEKERK, JOAN: *Die Groot Afrikaanse-Hollandse Liederbundel.* Cape Town/Pretoria, 1927. *Cape Argus* XXXVIII/8378, 9 Sept. 1893.

—J.B.

CLAY, REGINALD C.A. Yutar

CLEBER, JOS N. Crawford

CLEMENT, DANIEL, *13 June 1902 in Izegem (West-Flanders), Belgium. Composer and organist.

Daniel Clement comes from a family of organists (four succesive generations), was trained at the Royal Conservatoire of Ghent and later settled in the place of his birth as an organist. His vocal compositions include one of J.R.L. van Bruggen's poems entitled *'n Eenvoudige liedjie.* He found further original texts in Afrikaans in the *FAK-Volksangbundel* and within a short while he had composed 42 songs. In 1944 the Flemish leader of festival singing, Willem de Meyer, requested Clement to arrange a further 24 Afrikaans folk songs in four parts. In addition, he prepared a solo edition of these songs that was to be distributed by the Vlaams Nationaal Zangverbond, but the collection was probably lost during the confusion of the last year of the war. However, his original Afrikaans songs with piano accompaniment were preserved and published in 1948 under the title *Suid-Afrika vorentoe.* This collection contains 43 items, one of which, *Gebed van Paul Kruger* (J.D. Wetsels), is in Dutch, but the rest are in Afrikaans: 1. Die Afrikaanse volkslied (C.P. Hoogenhout, A. Pannevis, D.F. du Toit, S.J. du Toit) 'n Ieder nasie het sy land 2. Gebed van Paul Kruger (J.D. Wetsels) 3. Die Afrikaanse taal (J. Lion Cachet) 4. Land, volk en taal (A.G. Visser) 5. O boereplaas (C.F. Visser) 6. Japie (C. Louis Leipoldt) 7. Siembamba (C. Louis Leipoldt) 8. Ouboeta (H.A. Fagan) 9. Wiegeliedjie (Eitemal) 10. Tuiskoms van die banneling (Eitemal) 11. Na die oorlog (Theo. W. Jandrell) 12. Vergewe en vergeet (Totius) 13. Dis al (Jan F.E. Celliers) 14. Slampamperliedjie (C. Louis Leipoldt): "Gee vir my 'n trouring" 15. Slampamperliedjie (C. Louis Leipoldt): "Ek sing van die wind" 16. Met dapper en stapper (Theo. W. Jandrell) 17. Die somertyd roep my (Eitemal, after E. Geibel) 18. Die kêrel van die onderveld (C.F. Visser) 19. Die wapad (A.G. Visser) 20. Voëllegende 21. Bethlehemsvelde (Theo. W. Jandrell) 22. Kersies (T.J. Haarhoff) 23. Winternag (Eugène N. Marais) 24. Eensaamheid (Jan F. Celliers) 25. 'n Eenvoudige liedjie (J.R.L. van Bruggen); in this publication, the title of the song has been given as: Een simpel liedjie 26. Verplante blommetjies (A.G. Visser) 27. Somer lag oor die velde (Eitemal) 28. Na rëen volg sonneskyn (D.P. Viljoen) 29. Oktobermaand (C. Louis Leipoldt) 30. Al die veld is vrolik (C. Louis Leipoldt) 31. Santjie van Soendal (Eitemal) 32. My nooientjie woon in Heidelberg (D.P. Viljoen) 33. Sannie (A.G. Visser) 34. Kalwerliefde (A.G. Visser) 35. Marietjie, Maraia, Maryne (Eitemal) 36. Soveel groete stuur ek jou (Theo. W. Jandrell) 37. Liefde in die bone (Eitemal) 38. Klaas Vakie (Theo. W. Jandrell) 39. Slaap hartediefie (Theo. W. Jandrell) 40. Drinklied (Eitemal) 41. As jy jou man kan staan (Theo. W. Jandrell) 42. Op die dood van die uil (P.H. Langenhoven) 43. Kyk die dronk gedoentes (Eitemal).

BIBLIOGRAPHY

BOUWS, JAN: *Woord en wys van die Afrikaanse lied.* HAUM, Cape Town/Pretoria 1961.

SOURCES

BOUWS, JAN: *Die Burger,* 10 August 1968.   POSSEZ, GUIDO: Daniël Clement, de stille toondichter. *De Weekbode,* Belgium, 24 November 1972.   V.D.V., E.: (EUGENE VAN DE VELDE): Dan Clement-Suid-Afrika vorentoe. *De Standaard,* Belgium, 12 August 1948.   National Documentation Centre for Music, HSRC, Pretoria.

—J.B.

CLEMENTS, R.   King William's Town 7, 8

CLIFFORD, I.   Durban 5, 10, Durban Municipal Bantu Brass Band, Durban Orchestra

CLOUGH, ROBERT ARNOLD, *11 September 1936 in Holmfirth, Huddersfield, Yorkshire; at present (1977) in Pretoria. Lecturer and composer.
Clough studied pianoforte, organ, theoretical subjects and composition under Dorothy Bradley, Dr Hubert Beever and Professor Lancelot Appleby, and singing under Edwin Sandford. In South Africa his pianoforte and composition studies were continued under Peter Rorke* and Nina Barry between 1955 and 1963. — Robert Clough was organist and choirmaster at Netherthong Parish Church before coming to South Africa in 1955. Here he held appointments from 1957 onwards as assistant to Peter Rorke (1957-1959), as teacher of pianoforte and theoretical subjects at the Rustenburg Conservatoire of Music (1960-1962) and concurrently at the Brakpan Technical College (1960-1961). He also taught privately (1959-1962). He was appointed lecturer of harmony and counterpoint at the University of Pretoria (1963-1970). — Robert Clough has often appeared as solo pianist and accompanist, was repetitor for the Pretoria Opera Group* from 1957 to 1959, secretary of the Pretoria Musical Festival in 1958, and repetitor and pianist for PACT in opera productions. He has also toured for the PACT music department as solo pianist and accompanist. — Since 1970 he has been a teacher of theoretical subjects at the Pretoria College for Advanced Technical Education*.

WORKS
Barcarolle, for pianoforte. Ms., 1957.   Parting at morning, song for baritone. Ms., 1958. Echo, song for soprano. Ms., 1958.   Polsato, for pianoforte. Ms., 1959.   Be strong and of good courage, anthem for SATB. Ms., 1960.   Piano concerto no. 1. Ms., 1960.   A family tale, children's suite for piano. Ms., 1961.   Toccatina, for pianoforte. Ms., 1962.   A South African impression, suite for piano and full orchestra. Ms., 1962.   Four pieces for pianoforte, wood-wind, strings and percussion. Ms., 1962.   Allegro for clarinet, cello and pianoforte. Ms., 1965. Concertino for piano, trumpet, woodwind and strings. Ms., 1965.   Cameos, set of 12 short pieces for pianoforte. Ms., 1968-1969.   Psalm 51, for SATB and orchestra. Ms., 1970.
—Ed.

CLÜVER, D.H.F.C. (FRIEDRICH)   Evangelical Lutheran Church Music in the Cape, Organs I(iv)

COATES, ALBERT, *23 April 1882 in St Petersburg, Russia; °11 December 1953 in Cape Town. Albert Coates was an internationally known musician, who gained the status of a leading conductor before he was 30 years of age. The scope of this article is confined to the few fruitful years he spent in South Africa at the end of his life.
In 1946, shortly after his return from a wartime sojourn in the United States of America, and his marriage to the South African-born singer, Vera de Villiers*, he accepted the invitation of John Connell*, then Musical Adviser to the City Council of Johannesburg, to become the first conductor of the newly-formed Johannesburg Municipal Orchestra. Coates at this time was in his sixty-fourth year, and an international celebrity. He nursed the infant orchestra through its teething troubles, but unfortunately the Reef altitude did not suit his health and he was compelled to relinquish the post after only three months. — He decided to settle in Cape Town, the birthplace of Vera de Villiers, and their home at Milnerton soon became a meeting place for local and visiting musicians. Almost at once he busied himself (and

281

his wife) with the formation of a South African Opera and Ballet Company, which he idealistically intended as an effort to co-ordinate isolated attempts to promote music, and especially operatic music, in South Africa. — Lacking the support of higher authorities, the Coates' accepted financial responsibility for their company, and undertook the direction and management in collaboration with Walter Swanson*. Gluck's *Orfeo* was their first major production in 1947. It was performed in Cape Town, Stellenbosch and Paarl, with the combined orchestras of the Stellenbosch University (director: Hans Endler*) and the Paarl Amateur Orchestral Society. The principals and chorus were mainly amateurs and students, but the Coates' spared no effort with this inexperienced team, and the results were remarkable. — In December of the same year, Coates put on a large-scale production of *Hänsel und Gretel* (Humperdinck), with a partly professional cast and the Cape Town Municipal Orchestra. This was followed in 1948 by a production of *Die Walküre* (Wagner), with a cast that included Vera de Villiers, Timothy Farrell*, Samuel Morris and Johanna Uys*. He was assisted in this venture by Henry Edwards-Plaut, a German-born South African musician, Swanson having accepted the conductorship of the Labia Opera Company. Wagner's work was produced under great difficulties in the Cape Town City Hall. At this stage Prof. Chisholm* proposed an amalgamation of the South African Opera and Ballet Company with the newly-formed Opera Company of the South African College of Music. His offer was accepted, and the Coates's operatic activities in Cape Town came to an end, with the exception of an Afrikaans performance of *Hänsel und Gretel* in Stellenbosch (1951), and his own last work. — During this time and in the years left to him, Coates appeared as guest conductor at symphony concerts by the Municipal Orchestra. In composition Coates was occupied with the score of an opera on the theme of Sir James Barrie's *The boy David,* but he put it aside when he was commissioned by the organizers of the Van Riebeeck Tercentenary Festival to compose an opera with a South African background. He chose the old Portuguese legend of Van Hunks and the devil, which he moulded into an operatic scenario, creating both the text and the music. Prof. L.I. Coertze and the singer Johanna Uys subsequently translated it into Afrikaans, under the title *Tafelberg se kleed.* This was a big undertaking. Coates's health was failing, and he was harassed by the fact that the work had to be ready in a limited time. By leaving sections of the opera in dialogue, he managed to complete the task, and the opera was duly performed under his personal direction during the Festival Celebrations in March, 1952. He then set to work to complete *Van Hunks and the devil* as a grand opera and had just begun the scoring for full orchestra, when he was crippled by thrombosis. The orchestration was completed after his death by Walter Swanson. — Coates became a naturalized South African citizen, and after his death his wife bequeathed his considerable collection of books, scores and original manuscripts to the library of the University of Stellenbosch.

WORKS

1. Opera
Assurbanipal (libretto, Madelon Holland). Ms., 1915.   Sardanapalus. Ms., 1916.   The myth beautiful (libretto, Madelon Holland). Ms., 1917.   Samuel Pepys (libretto, Drury and Richard Pryce). Ms., 1929.   Pickwick (libretto adapted from Charles Dickens by the composer). Universal edition, London, 1936.   Gainsborough's duchess (libretto, C. Reginald Grundy). Ms., 1939.   The boy David (libretto, De Pieteri, from the play by James M. Barrie). Ms., October 1948.   The duel (libretto by composer, from a comedy by Chekov). Ms., October

1950.   Van Hunks and the devil (libretto by composer). Ms., first performance 7 March 1952.

2. Orchestral works

Suite ancienne. Ms., 1910.   Suite for string orchestra. Ms., 1920.   The eagle, symphonic poem in memory of Nikisch, for SATB and orchestra. Ms., 1925.   Lancelot symphony. Ms., 1929.   The taming of the shrew. Ms., 1931.   Piano concerto in C major. Ms., 1933.   Cello concerto. Ms., 1934.   Little Alfie, for narrator and orchestra (Robert S. Robinson). Ms., 1939. Scherzo. Ms., 1942.   Three oriental dances. Ms., Hollywood, 1942.   A Russian suite. Ms., 1944.   Suite Slav. Ms., 1945.   Sinfonia concertante. Ms., 1950.   Symphony no. 3 in F sharp minor ("John Smith"). Ms., 1951.   Intermezzo on words by Beddoes: "How many times". Ms., 1950.   Adagio dolorosa (in memoriam). Ms., first performance in Cape Town, 1952.

3. Songs with orchestral accompaniment

The robber nightingale, for soprano. Ms., 1922.   Sunrise. Ms., 1935.   The defense of Guenevere. Ms., 1935.   Shy one (Yeats). Ms., 1935.   Three lullabies of a small child to her doll: 1. Verushka 2. Sleep volumnia 3. Vespers. Ms., 1935.   Last song. Ms., 1937. Three songs from Edward Lear's *Nonsense rhymes:* 1. The Quangle-Wangle's hat 2. The owl and the pussycat 3. The new vestments. Ms., 1941.   The 23rd Psalm. Ms., 1947.

4. Songs with pianoforte accompaniment

A song of the Don Cossacks (Madelon Holland). Ms., 1920; also orchestrated.   Elaine's song of love and death (Tennyson). Ms., 1933.   Evening (Matthew Arnold). Ms., 1934; also orchestrated.   Ave Maria. Ms., 1935; also orchestrated.   Harmony (Alexander Pringle). Ms., 1937; also orchestrated.   To an isle in the water (Beddoes). Ms., 1937; also orchestrated. The redwoods (Joseph Strauss). Ms., 1937.   The new vestments (E. Lear). Ms., 1941.   Excuse me please (E.B. Goodman). Ms., 1942.   The Lord's prayer. Ms., 1944. Browning's religion. Ms., 1947.   Three birthday songs. Ms., 1950, 1951, 1952.

5. Film music

The song of Russia.   Two girls and a sailor.

PUBLICATION
Opera for South Africa. *SAMT* 32, June 1947.

BIBLIOGRAPHY
Grove's *Dictionary of music and musicians,* 5th edition, 1954.   *The international cyclopedia of music and musicians,* 5th edition, 1949.   *Die Musik in Geschichte und Gegenwart.* Kassel, 1952.   *The Oxford companion to music.* OUP, 1942.   PAUW, N.E.: *Die lewe van Albert Coates (1882-1953) gevolg deur 'n oorsig van sy werke.* M.Mus. dissertation, US, 1968. Riemann's *Musiklexikon.* Mainz, 1959.   *The world of music* (Ed. Sandved). London, 1954.

SOURCES
Albert Coates (1882-1953). *SAMT* 46, June 1954.   *Die Brandwag,* 24 January 1947.   *Die Naweek,* 31 July 1947.   *Sondagnuus,* 28 September 1947.

—W.D.S. (amplified)

COATES, ISABELLE   Johannesburg 2, H.S. Marleyn

COATES, MABEL   Johannesburg Musical Society

COERTSE, MARIA SOPHIA (MIMI),   *12 June 1932 in Durban, the youngest of three children of a Railway inspector; now (1977) in South Africa. Dramatic coloratura soprano.

Having completed her schooling in Germiston and Johannesburg, Mimi Coertse, to the disappointment of her parents, set about preparing herself with great determination for a singing career. She undertook intensive studies in speech, singing, pianoforte and drama, from teachers such as Twinkle Hanekom, Aimèe Parkerson* and Taubie Kuschlik, while earning her living as a singing and piano teacher. From 1951, successes at eisteddfodau, in radio broadcasts and concert appearances in variety programmes, drew attention to her great possibilities. Proceeds from concerts, supplemented by the Johannesburg Skakelkomitee and the FAK, made it possible for her to study in Europe. Shortly after her first marriage (to Dawid Engela* in 1953) she left for Vienna where, in 1954, she studied under Maria Hittorff, and at the State Academy for Music and Drama, under Joseph Witt. — 1955 was the year of Mimi's discovery in Europe. In January she signed a contract with the Vienna Chamber Opera Company. Conducted by Karl Böhm, this company performed *Parsifal* and *Don Giovanni* in the Neapolitan San Carlo Theatre, with Mimi Coertse as First Flower Maiden in Wagner's work. She had further successes as a member of the Academy Theatre Group (as Constanze in *Entführung,* and Zerbinetta in *Ariadne auf Naxos*) when it performed in Schönbrunn (Vienna) and Bad Aussee, where both critics and audiences celebrated her as the vocal discovery of the year. After a successful summer visit to South Africa, she was an oustanding success in Basle in the role that made her famous, and which she was to sing over 500 times in various European opera houses: the Queen of the Night in Mozart's *Die Zauberflöte.* Having repeated the Basle success in Naples, she made her début in the same role in the Vienna State Opera (17 March 1956). This resulted in a three-year contract, which was renewed, and led to a permanent appointment. — After her first season with the State Opera, she appeared at Covent Garden and Salzburg, and has since then sung in theatres in Cologne, Glyndebourne, Athens, Aix-en-Provence, Brussels, Barcelona, Palermo, Berlin and Geneva, as well as in Austrian centres other than Vienna. Meanwhile, she was extending the repertoire within her versatile vocal range, to include practically all the important dramatic coloratura roles of opera, as well as a number of comic parts, and solo parts in various oratorios and passions. Two achievements deserve special mention: her successes in R. Strauss's operas culminated in March 1968, when she sang the title role in a Viennese première of *Die schweigsame Frau;* and she enjoyed a remarkable triumph of singing and acting by interpreting all three leading female roles in the *Verhale van Hoffmann* (Offenbach) in South Africa (1962), as well as in the Vienna State Opera (1967/1968) (in the German version). — Since 1970 she has added to her roles in Strauss operas by appearing in *Die Aegyptische Helena* and *Daphne,* both produced in the State Opera in Vienna, made her first appearances on TV and participated in the filming of a script on the life of Robert Stolz, the prominent operetta composer. The Musikverein Concert Hall saw her in a performance of Schubert's *Lazarus fragments* and Mahler's *Das klagende Lied,* but since her marriage to Mr Werner Ackerman in 1970 her European career has gradually drawn to a close. She appeared in the Vienna State Opera for the last time in 1973 and has since then finally settled in South Africa. — In previous years she had regularly visited South Africa and appeared as a celebrity in major centres, for instance at the inaugurations of the Aula of the University of Pretoria (1958), the Civic Theatre in Johannesburg (1962), and of the Amphitheatre of the University of Pretoria (1962). Since her return to this country, Mimi has continued her close association with the South African Universities by singing at the inaugural concerts of the auditoriums erected by the Rand Afrikaans University, the UOFS, and the Port Elizabeth University. She was also invited to sing with the National Symphony Orchestra conducted by Anton Hartman at the opening of the SABC's new concert studio in Auckland Park in 1976. Proud of her achievements, South Africa has repeatedly called on her to practise her art at national festivals such as the unveiling of the Afrikaans Taalmonument in Paarl or the Language Dedication Concert at the Voortrekker Monument in Pretoria (both in 1975). Previous festival occasions had been the Half-Century Festival of the Union of South Africa (1960) and the Republican Festival of 1966. Apart from these official honours, Mimi Coertse has continued her concert career in co-operation with the pianist Pieter de Villiers* in the Republic as well as in South West Africa, completed a series on her singing career for TV and launched a new tradition of Christmas concerts in the Nico Malan Theatre in Cape Town. There have also been a few appearances in opera in the Transvaal and the Cape. — She was presented with the Medal of Honour for Music by the Suid-Afrikaanse Akademie vir Wetenskap en Kuns on 17 May 1961, and on 5 October 1966 the President of the Austrian Republic bestowed on her the title of Kammersängerin. Thus, within ten years of the commencement of her career, the two countries that most benefited from her vocal art, acknowledged and rewarded her exceptional achievements. — In 1959 she donated a bursary carrying her name to the University of Pretoria to enable promising young vocalists to further their careers overseas. Funds were made available from concerts that Mimi gave for this purpose, in the University's Aula, to be supplemented by concerts given by winners of the bursary after their return to South Africa. The following singers had the advantage of this support in their studies: Gert Potgieter* and Wolfgang Anheisser (1960), Hans van Heerden* (1961), Noreen Hastings and Carla Nel (1966).

BIBLIOGRAPHY

KUTSCH, K.J. and RIEMENS, LEO: article "Mimi Coertse" in *Unvergängliche Stimmen, Kleines Sängerlexikon*, 2nd edition, 1968.

SOURCES (a few representative titles compiled by the National Documentation Centre for Music, HSRC, Pretoria).
Anonymous: Jeugdige nagtegaal. *Rooi Rose*, April 1953. Anonymous: Mimi Coertse's rise to fame. *Lantern* XI/2, December 1961. Anonymous: Mimi lei 'n liefdelose lewe. *Die Brandwag*, 19 August 1961. Anonymous: Mimi se mooi rokke. *Die Huisgenoot*, 5 October 1973. ESTERHUYSEN, L.: Mimi Coertse. *Res Musicae* VIII/5, September 1962. P.,M.: Boerenooi met die goue stem. *Die Huisgenoot*, 7 September 1962. PIENAAR,M.: Mimi kan 'n hou slaan met 'n sambok. *Die Huisgenoot*, 24 September 1962. RADEMEYER, C.: Onse Mimi. *Rooi Rose*, November 1956. RIO-NEUHOF, J.A.: Mimi Coertse. *Die Staatsamptenaar*, August 1961. STEYTLER, H.: Boernooi maak naam oorsee. *Sarie Marais*, 22 August 1956. STEYTLER, H.: Op pad na roem. *Die Huisgenoot*, 24 September 1956. WALZL-ZAAYMAN, M.: Mimi verower Maria se pronkrol. *Die Huisgenoot*, 23 January 1961. *Die Burger:* 5 October 1956; 24 October 1957; 2 December 1957; 31 August 1969. *Cape Argus:* 16 November 1957. *Dagbreek:* 27 October 1957. *Pretoria News:* 30 September 1958. *Rapport:* 6 August 1972. *Sunday Times:* 21 June 1970. *Die Transvaler:* 4 September 1957; 18 August 1962. *Die Vaderland:* 28 July 1965; 13 July 1971.

—J.P.M.

COETZEE, CONNIE   R. Müller (Pty) Ltd

COETZEE, H.P.A.   Potchefstroom University for CHE's Institute for South African Music

COETZEE, JAN CHRISTOFFEL,   *10 April 1912 in Steynsburg; at present (1977) in Pretoria. Lecturer in music and composer.

Jan Coetzee had his initial training in pianoforte under Horace Barton*, Isador Epstein* and Lorenzo Danza*, while Rosa Nepgen* instructed him in organ. When he had turned 24, he possessed the Teachers' Licentiate of Trinity College and started teaching music in Johannesburg. At a later date (1950) he also acquired UNISA's Teachers' Licentiate and the LTCL in organ playing. From 1950 until 1961 Jan Coetzee was a lecturer in Music on the staff of the Teachers' Training College in Graaff Reinet. In the latter year he was appointed a lecturer in Music in the Music Department of the UOFS. In 1954 he continued his pianoforte studies at the RAM and acquired the diplomas LRAM and ARCM. At the same time A. Nieman guided his original work. — In Bloemfontein he had the responsibility of teaching students pianoforte and organ as well as of lecturing in harmony and counterpoint. His term in Bloemfontein was interrupted twice for further study in Paris, the first time in 1969, and again in 1971. During his first visit he continued his study of the piano but also concentrated on harmony, counterpoint and composition with various teachers, including Nadia Boulanger. The purpose of his second visit was chiefly to have further guidance in his original work. During the last years of his appointment in Bloemfontein, Jan Coetzee was a Senior Lecturer in the Music Department. He retired at the end of 1976 and settled in Pretoria, where he is dedicating most of his time to composition. — After 1958 he acted as examiner for the practical music examinations of UNISA and as adjudicator at eisteddfodau in various centres.

WORKS

(Jan Coetzee is very critical regarding his own work and has withdrawn many manuscripts dating from earlier years. The following list contains all that he is willing to acknowledge in 1977).   Sonata, for pianoforte, Ms., first two movements, Paris 1969; third movement, Bloemfontein 1970. First performance in Bloemfontein, 12 November 1971.   Two songs, for soprano. Ms., London, 1969: 1. The bereaved swan   2. The rain.   Two pieces for cello and pianoforte. Ms., Bloemfontein, 1971: 1. Elegy   2. Allegretto. Kein Trost, song for soprano. Ms., Bloemfontein, 1976.   Phantasy for pianoforte and orchestra, commissioned by Oude Libertas. Ms., Bloefontein, 1976. First performance, 18 November 1976.

— Ed.

COETZEE, J.V.   Afrikaans Church and Mission Music I/4, 5

COHEN, DAVID,   *20 September 1902 in Sunderland, England; °December 1957, in Durban. Pianist, conductor and music teacher.

Educated in Durban, Cohen was awarded an overseas scholarship by the Natal Society for the Advancement of Music* in 1921 and studied at Trinity College. Here he was awarded a further scholarship, became a student of Charton Keith and obtained the FTCL diploma. He received the Chappell Gold Medal for piano playing in 1923. After returning to Durban in 1924, he appeared as soloist with the Cape Town and Durban Orchestras, and toured as soloist and accompanist to Leo

Cherniavsky* (1928). He was principal of the David Cohen Pianoforte School of Music in Durban, and a member of the Royal Society of Teachers, England. In 1952 he was elected President of the South African Society of Music Teachers*, having served as Chairman of the Durban Centre for several years. He was the founder and conductor of the Durban Jewish Club Orchestra, and choirmaster of the Durban United Hebrew Congregation.

BIBLIOGRAPHY
K.,w.h. *The arts in South Africa.* Knox Printing & Publishing Co., Durban, 1933.

SOURCE
SA Music Teacher: 39, November 1950; 42, June 1952; 44, June 1953; 54, May 1958.
—E.H.S.

COHEN, PETER LAWRENCE, *17 May 1937 in Johannesburg; at present (1977) in Germany. Attorney, lecturer in music and composer.

As a child Peter Cohen received music lessons from Ruth Rome and Brigitte Wild, and studied composition under Stewart Hylton Edwards*. He commenced composing at the age of 12, and in 1954, when he was 17, performed a pianoforte sonata of his own composition for the SABC. He matriculated in the same year, and in 1955/56 studied for six months at the Guildhall School of Music, London, when he returned to South Africa at the wish of his parents to study law. He obtained the Diploma in Law (1958) at the University of the Witwatersrand, was admitted as an attorney of the Supreme Court of SA (Transvaal Provincial Division), and of the High Court of Swaziland (1961), and practised law until 1964. During these years he made an intensive study of the life and works of C.P.E. Bach, and continued composing and studying pianoforte. UNISA appointed him ad hoc external authority on C.P.E. Bach, and commissioned him to contribute lecture notes on this subject for their students. — With the assistance of his father, Peter Cohen was enabled to abandon his legal practice in 1966, to become a full-time music student at the University of Pretoria. In 1967 he obtained the UTLM (piano) and in 1968 the UTLM (harmony and counterpoint) diplomas. In his final year he wrote a paper on "Structural synthesis in the 14 last rondos of C.P.E. Bach", and was awarded the B. Mus. (cum laude) with 5 distinctions. He thereupon became lecturer in music at the University of Port Elizabeth. The next year he became assistant editor for music to *New Nation.* In 1969 he was awarded the German Akademischer Austauschdienst Bursary of R2 200, for study in Berlin from February 1970 - April 1971, in order to complete his doctoral research on the works of C.P.E. Bach. — After the completion of his studies, Dr Cohen earned his living as a school teacher in Germany until 1975, when he accepted an appointment in the Music Department of Wits University*. At the end of 1976 however, he resigned in favour of an appointment in Germany. In his earlier years in Johannesburg and Pretoria he was a foundation member of the Rare Music Guild* and of Musica Rara. Some of his compositions have been accepted by the SABC for broadcasting and others were publicly performed in Pretoria.

WORKS

A. Instrumental

1. Pianoforte
Miscellaneous, op. 1: 1. The bird song of liberty. Ms., 1949 2. Minuet. Ms., 1949-1950

287

3. The cello. Ms., 1949-1950   4. Court dance. Ms., 1949-1950.   Suite, op. 2 :   1. Prelude
2. Sarabande   3. Minuet   4. Rondo. Ms., 1951.   Seven imperial inventions, op. 3:
1. Allegro con spirito   2. Allegro con vivacita   3. Larghetto con calma   4. Allegro con
delicatezza   5. Allegro con bravuro   6. Presto con forza   7. Presto con fermezza.
Ms., 1952-1953.   Sonata in G min., op. 5, performed by SABC in 1954. Ms., 1954.   Sonata in F,
op. 6. Ms., 1955.   Rondo in C, op. 7. Ms., 1956.   Six Sonatas, in F, A, C min., D min., B and
G, op. 9. Ms., 1957-1958.   Siciliano, op. 10. Ms., 1958.   Andante, op. 11. Ms., 1960.
Sonata in F, op. 12. Ms., 1960(?)   Phantasy sonata, op. 13. Ms., 1964.   Intermezzo,
op. 15. Ms., 1964.   Sarabande, op. 16. Ms., 1965.   Five bagatelles, op. 19. Ms., 1967.
Sonatina, op. 22. Ms., 1967.   Incidental film music for *Om te wil wees,* op. 24. Ms., 1968.
Sonatina, op. 28. Ms., 1970.

2. Various
Incidental music to *The Merchant of Venice,* op. 18:   1. Overture for harpsichord
2. Three fanfares for harpsichord   3. Three leitmotifs for harpsichord   4. Tell me where is
fancy bred (Shakespeare), song for alto and harpsichord. Ms., 1966.

3. Chamber music
Trio for clarinet, bassoon and pianoforte, op. 23, performed by SABC in 1969. Ms., 1968.
Sonatina for clarinet (or violin) and pianoforte, op. 25, performed for the State President in 1969.
Ms., 1968.   Partita for flute and violin, op. 29. Ms., 1969.

B. Vocal
Encouragement to a lover (Sir John Suckling), song for tenor and pianoforte, op. 4. Ms.,
1953.   The man from Islington (Oliver Goldsmith), song for soprano and pianoforte, op. 8.
Ms., 1957.   Drie ernstige liedere, song cycle for baritone and pianoforte, op. 14:   1. Die
begrafnis (Eitemal)   2. Vaalvalk (W.E.G. Louw)   3. Weemoed (A.D. Keet). Ms., 1964.
Loflied, Paul Kruger (Jan Celliers), for chorus and accompaniment, op. 17. Ms., 1965.   Marc
groet 's morgens de dingen (Paul van Ostayen, 1930), song for alto and pianoforte, op. 20. Ms.,
1967.   Wenn Du es wusstest *(Cäcilie,* Heinrich Hart), song for alto and pianoforte, op. 27.
Ms., 1967.   Vroegaand, Clifton (Wilhelm Knobel), song for alto and pianoforte, op. 26. Ms.,
1968.   Skoollied (Prof. T.J. Haarhoff), arrangement of original music by J.C. van Vuuren, for
children's choir: (a) accompanied   (b) unaccompanied, op. 27. Ms., 1969.

PUBLICATIONS
Carl Philipp Emanuel Bach (1714-1788). Library, UNISA, 1965.   *Die toepassing van die
affekteleer deur C.P.E. Bach.* Library, UNISA, 1967.   *Structural synthesis in the 14 last
rondos of C.P.E. Bach.* Library, UP, 1968.   *Modern audiences and modern music.* New
Nation, Pretoria, Nov. 1969.   *Theorie und Praxis der Clavieraesthetik Carl Philipp Emanuel
Bachs.* Hamburger Beiträge zur Musikwissenschaft no. 13. Karl Dieter Wagner Verlag,
Hamburg, 1974.

—Ed.

COLEMAN, UNA JAY (NÉE RICHARDS),   *16 October 1906 at Keiskamahoek, Eastern
Province; at present (1977) in Umtali, Rhodesia. Pianist and music teacher.
After taking music lessons at the Rustenburg School in Rondebosch, where she was
awarded a Trinity College bursary in 1923, Una Coleman continued her study
at the South African College of Music* (SACM) in Cape Town (1924-1926)
under Colin Taylor* (pianoforte), Ellie Marx* (violin), Eleanor Bonnar* (singing)
and obtained the UPLM and LUCT diplomas. During this time she played as piano
and violin soloist with the Cape Town Municipal Orchestra*. At the conclusion of

these three years she was appointed student teacher at the SACM for a further two years, when she obtained a teaching post at Ceres. In 1928 she entered the RAM to study theoretical subjects and pianoforte teaching and obtained the LRAM and ARCM diplomas in 1930. — Una Coleman returned to settle in Rhodesia (1931), where she taught pianoforte, violin and class singing at Government schools in Bula̋wayo, Salisbury and other centres. She has played concertos with the orchestras of Bulawayo, Salisbury and Umtali and has accompanied local and overseas artists at concerts. She has also taken part in chamber music concerts (Arte Viva Trio), organised concerts and festivals, given lecture recitals and produced musical plays at schools, conducted a madrigal group, played as organist in Anglican churches and adjudicated at eisteddfodau.

—Ed.

COLENBRANDER, VERA HOPE NANCY (MRS BARBER), *6 June 1900 in New Gelderland, Natal; at present (1976) in Durban. Violist, violinist and music teacher.

Vera Colenbrander studied at the South African College of Music* in Cape Town under Ellie Marx* (violin) and Eveline Fincken* (singing) (1917-1921) and obtained the ULM Teachers' diploma in both singing and violin. After teaching at the Queenstown Girls' High School, where she formed and conducted a school orchestra, she entered the RAM in 1925 for violin study. For a few months in 1926 she studied violin and singing privately in Rome, before returning to London for the LRAM diploma. — In 1927 she began teaching in Durban, working for African Theatres during the evenings as violinist in a trio. She became interested in the viola and in 1936 visited London for private study under Lionel Tertis. On her return to South Africa, she was appointed principal viola in the Durban Studio Orchestra, a position which she held (with an interruption of 18 months) until 1953, when the Orchestra ceased to exist. During this period she also managed to continue her viola study in London (1949), played as violist in the Gregor Bartonyi String Quartet in broadcasts and concerts in Natal, and in 1951 formed The Concordia Ensemble. This group continued until 1954 and was later revived for another period (from 1959 until 1963). Since 1953 Vera Colenbrander has been free-lancing and has played in the Durban Civic Orchestra*. She is the teacher of the viola player Lettie Vermaak*.

—Ed.

COLES, G.   St George's Cathedral

COLJEE, JAN   German Male Voice Choir, Van der Bijl Park

COLLARD, A.   Pretoria 1

COLLEGIATE SCHOOL FOR GIRLS, PORT ELIZABETH   R. Ascham, R. Cloete, F. Crane, A.G. Dixon, C.J.H. Eberlein, Port Elizabeth I/2, 5, II/5, P. Quarterman, F. Witt, C.A. Yutar

COLLINGWOOD, W.B.   Higher Educational Institutions I/3

COLOSSEUM ORCHESTRA   M. Doré, Durban 8, H.G. Ketelbey, N. Kofsky, E.F.S.L. Schneider

COLOSSEUM THEATRE   Johannesburg 3(i), H.S. Marleyn, Steele-Payne bellringers

COLONIAL CAPE MOUNTED RIFLEMEN, THE MILITARY BAND OF THE (1878-1912)   The Imperial Cape Mounted Riflemen (CMR) was established in 1795, during the first British

Occupation of the Cape. Subsequent military re-organizations changed its name and character: in 1806, Cape Regiment, 1827, Imperial CMR, 1853, Frontier Armed Mounted Police; finally, in 1870, it was disbanded. Throughout its history, however, this Regiment, which had its own military band, was a British (Imperial) Regiment under direct control from England. — Under Act 9 of 1878 of the Cape Colonial Parliament the Colonial CMR was established, and from this date until it was dissolved in 1913, it merged with the 1st Regiment, SA Riflemen in 1913, and maintained its dual character as a police and permanent frontier military force, extremely mobile, to bear the brunt of an attack on the Cape Colony. The Regiment consisted of about 750 to 800 professional soldiers, few of whom were colonial-born, who enlisted under a three-year contract. The rates of pay and conditions of service were the same as for any Imperial Regiment (15c per day), but the Colonial Government contributed little to the finances of the band, e.g. for the purchase of printed music or stands. It was typical of the time that the bandsmen were trained as artillerists and were good shots. Their number seldom exceeded fifty, and they were regarded as the brightest and smartest men in the regiment. They had the standard course of instruction in both mounted and dismounted drills, were on call for any type of active service, and after passing recruit drills and tests in musical proficiency, received extra pay at the rate of 10 cents per day. — The history of the CMR Band can conveniently be divided into two phases, the first, from 1878 to circa 1900, under Bandmaster Michael Gould and the second, from 1903 to 1912, under Bandmaster T.J. Marshall*. — According to an old photograph, there were 26 bandsmen in 1884, of which only the following can be named: Barrett, Bulcock, Barley, Deithe, Gilder, R. Hames, M. Gould (bandmaster), Fred Hardesty*, McCabe, Lancaster and B. Williams. The names indicate the mainly English character of the band. The weekly Friday evening performances, a popular institution in King William's Town, were usually presented either on Prince Alfred's Square, near the barracks, or at Barrack Square in the military reserve. In addition, the band gave regular indoor, as well as outdoor concerts at the Botanical Gardens, the Victoria Grounds, the Town Hall and other venues. It was in great demand, particularly by visiting companies, such as the Bijou Comedy Company. The Caledonian Society's Annual Sports Gathering in 1895 was in danger of cancellation when it became known that the band was unable to attend. — The band frequently strengthened the local orchestral and musical societies. Thus, on Saturday evening, 3 February 1894, it combined with the Town Band to present a promenade concert in the Botanical Gardens, for which 10c admission was charged, in aid of funds for the Town Band. The programme exhibits the traditional mixture of operatic excerpts, descriptive music and military and musical comedy items: Festival March, *Tannhäuser* (Wagner); Overture, *Semiramide* (Rossini); Selection, *Faust* (Gounod); The Turkish Patrol (descriptive) (Michaelis); Overture, French comedy (Kelar Bela); Fantasie, *Erin* (Basquit); Valse, *Dorothy* (Buccalosi); Quick March, *Colonel's parade* (Hume). God Save the Queen. — Gould's complete repertoire for the band cannot be established, but it did include the overtures to *L'Italiano in Algieri* (Rossini) and *Alphonse and Estrella* (Schubert) and selections from *Carmen* (Bizet), the *Pirates of Penzance* (Gilbert and Sullivan) and *Patience* (Gilbert and Sullivan). Marches, dances and items of a lighter nature were presented in wide variety, and the Regimental March was *Under the double eagle*. — It is not known when Michael Gould resigned as bandmaster. He was probably succeeded by Wallace (circa 1900 to

1903), whose conductorship coincided, not only with disorders in the Black territories, but also with the Anglo-Boer War (1899-1902). This resulted in the Regiment being sub-divided into small detachments distributed over the Transkei. — Although the Band now made infrequent and irregular appearances, *Qakamba*, the monthly journal of the CMR (May 1898) records that the men exerted themselves to relieve the monotony of their life in Kaffirland. The fragmentary nature of the various detachments did not permit the organization of musical and theatrical productions, but centres such as Bizana, Barkly East, Cala, Flagstaff, Libodi, Lusikisiki, Kokstad and Mount Frere enjoyed their first taste of sport and dances, as well as amateur concerts and theatricals organized by the soldiers and their families. Umtata, where many of the bandsmen appear to have been stationed for short periods, was more fortunate. Here new societies appeared, and concerts and theatrical shows were arranged. On 2 April 1898, the Umtata Dramatic Club came into existence; in December 1898, the Artillery Group formed the Pondo Minstrels; on 31 January 1899, the Umtata ladies and gentlemen formed the Magpie Minstrels; on 4 February the Libodi Dramatic Club was formed. During 1899 three concerts (including theatricals) were given at Umtata in aid of church funds, and a visit from the touring Leigh-Pierce Company proved most enjoyable. — With the arrival of T.J. Marshall in July 1903, the band entered an era of increased musical activity. Unfortunately, after the war, the Band was at its lowest state of efficiency, having been reduced to 12-members. By means of well-planned, patient work, the experienced Marshall soon augmented the numbers to 28, and from 1904 to 1907 the band toured extensively. It not only compared favourably with the Imperial bands, but was considered "second to none" in the Cape Colony. — In October 1904, the band undertook a five-month tour of the Eastern Cape, visiting Butterworth, King William's Town and East London, where it appeared at a combined military performance on 5 November, with the band of the Kaffrarian Rifles under Levy Howe, the KWT Borough Band under E.J.C. Woodrow*, and the Pipers of the Kaffrarian Rifles. At Grahamstown the band combined with the First City Volunteers and the Kingswood College Cadets. Concerts in other cities and towns followed and thus they attracted the attention of the organizers of the Cape Town Industrial Exhibition, who engaged them for three weeks during December and January, 1904-1905. — Despite a heavy programme, which included 3 daily performances at the Exhibition, the band maintained a high standard, and was considered a success. On Saturday 17 December 1904 a complimentary dinner was given in its honour. At the end of the engagement the bandmaster was presented with an ivory and silver-mounted baton and the band received a silver cup. The success of the band was due to the comradeship among the men, and to Marshall's direction, which was described in these terms: "He conducts with the greatest skill, quietly and without fuss, and with the most evident mastery of his work ... and the band answered his every direction, like a perfectly working machine". — After the Exhibition, the band remained in Cape Town for a further 6 weeks, giving weekly promenade concerts every Thursday evening from 8 to 10 at the International Hotel; and every Sunday evening at the Good Hope Gardens, as well as performances at the Lord Milner Hotel, and at nearby towns such as Stellenbosch and Paarl. — Starting in the 1905 Christmas season, the East London Municipality engaged the CMR Band for a month. Large audiences were attracted daily to a new bandstand in Marine Park, which was beautifully illuminated and presented the appearance of a "miniature Earls Court". This was the only time during Marshall's career that he was criticized in the press, but about a dozen correspondents, including a Kaffrarian Rifle bandsman, rallied to the defence of the band to reprimand the critic, who had complained that it did not play enough "noisy" music. So popular did the CMR band become, that it was unable to accept all the offers of engagements. At the beginning of 1906 it had a heavy programme, including the agricultural shows at King William's Town, Port Elizabeth (where concerts in St George's Park and the Feathermarket Hall were given in May) and Uitenhage, where the proceeds were donated to charity. The coming and going of bandsmen did not disrupt the continuity of the band. The bandmaster preferred to engage, where possible, boys rather than adults, to fill the vacancies. An old photograph of 1906 portrays 33 bandsmen. — In compiling his programmes, Marshall judiciously combined music from the classical repertoire with selections from contemporary musical comedy, and pieces of a swinging rhythmical nature. He had under his command a few members who were versatile, clever and talented musicians; most of them could play two instruments, and many three. In theory, there were three bands: a string band, which was in great demand for concerts, dances and indoor entertainments; a brass band; and a mounted band for mounted parades. He could consequently include pieces beyond the reach of the average band, such as Schubert's *Unfinished symphony,* and a concerto such as De Beriot's *7th (Military) violin concerto* (played by B. Smith). Furthermore, he could call on woodwind and brass players to render solos with orchestral accompaniment - in contrast to most 19th century bands, which sometimes included solos with piano accompaniment! Operas, symphonies and concertos were introduced to "Kaffirland", because the best brass band in the Colony was stationed at Umtata! Weekly promenade concerts were given on Friday and Saturday evenings ("weather permitting"). The band also played when the foundation stone of the new Town Hall was laid, and helped to celebrate its inauguration on 24 and 25 April, 1908. In addition, there were variety, benefit, smokers' and charity concerts, sometimes in aid of the hospital. Sport also gained by the presence of the military, and the orchestra played for football, garrison, boating and acquatic clubs. — Bandmaster Marshall started the first choir when he established the Umtata Glee Club, consisting of about 35 members of the Anglican and Wesleyan churches. This group, accompanied by the band, sang the *Hallelujah chorus* (Handel) during the Christmas season in 1907. As has been seen, the CMR Band did not only play at Umtata. At Maclear, its six-day stay was concluded with Association football and hockey matches, as well as a ball; and in April 1909, it played during the first Agricultural Show held at Kokstad. — Between 1909 and 1911, disorder and unrest in the native territories put a stop to music in Umtata. In 1912 the British Parliament passed a law which discontinued all military brass bands, with a few motivated exceptions. Simultaneously, the South African Parliament passed a similar Act. This meant that the CMR Band had to be dissolved at the end of February, that the men were to revert to their regular regimental duties, and that all instruments were to be handed in. In the Transkeian Territories, "where for nearly 30 years the Band had been the only solace of the men sent here for duty", the Act caused much indignation. A "Requiem Service to the honour and memory of the Band" was celebrated with certain obsequies, and the last post was sounded by trumpeters on their fingers.

SOURCES

The Daily Dispatch, EL: 1878-1913. *The Daily Watchman*, KWT: 1878-1899. *The Mercury*, KWT: 1878-1913. *EP Herald:* 1900-1913. *The Territorial News*, Umtata: February and March 1912. Numerous documents, including "Qakamba" (1898-9), Harry Orpwood's "Scrapbook" and miscellaneous publications on the CMR in the King William's Town Museum.

—C.G.H.

COLVERD, A.   Pietermaritzburg

COLVILLE, S.   Kimberley, Touring Theatre Groups

COMMAILLE, JOHN MCILWAIN MOOR (MICK),   *21 February 1883 in Cape Town; °28 July 1956 in Cape Town. Baritone.

Mick Commaille received singing and violin lessons, but taught himself to play the piano. He was Assistant Master and Master of the Supreme Court in several towns before he settled in Pretoria as Master of the Supreme Court. He retired there in 1943. He was an excellent sportsman and received Springbok colours for cricket and soccer, which brought him in touch with the Rev. M.L. de Villiers*, who was a minister of the church in Simonstown at the time. Commaille was the first person to sing *Die Stem van Suid-Afrika*. He undertook several concert tours in the Boland with De Villiers, and in 1924 he made three recordings of seven of De Villiers's songs.

SOURCES
STEGMANN, FRITS: Dubbele Springbok het eerste ons Volkslied gesing. *Die Burger,* 4 April 1962.

—F.S.

COMPOSERS' LIBRARY   H.E. Dawes

CONBY, T.A.   Elsa Leviseur

T.A. CONBY'S MUSIC CO.   Touring Theatre Groups 3

CONCERT ARTISTS' TOUR SCHEME, SASMT   B. Taylor, SASMT

CONCERTO SOCIETY   L. Danza, Johannesburg 2, Johannesburg Philharmonic Society, R. Kofsky, R.B. Lloyd, B.M. Marx, Touring Theatre Groups 3

CONMÉE, IVY,   *6 April 1911 in Johannesburg; living in Johannesburg in 1970. Ballet teacher, dancer and choreographer.

When she was four years old, Henry Garvin* started her on the violin at the Johannesburg Conservatoire of Music. Two years later she continued her training in England, also taking up pianoforte. After a few years, however, she terminated her musical studies to train as a dancer under Judith Espinosa and became a member of the Association of Operatic Dancing of Great Britain. On her return to South Africa, she and her sister opened the Conmée Sisters' School of Dancing in Johannesburg.
—In July 1925 she joined the company of Anita Bronzi and Oreste Faraboni, who presented a season of ballet in Johannesburg, and subsequently toured with them through England and on the Continent. On her return in 1926, she was appointed principal dancer and choreographer of African Consolidated Theatres for ballet tours of South Africa. In 1927 she was appointed Children's Examiner for the Association of Operatic Dancing and for the South African Dancing Teachers' Association. Eleven years later she became a member of the Overseas Advisory Committee of the Royal Academy of Dancing. — In 1943 Ivy Conmée joined Marjorie Sturman*, Poppy Frames* and Lesley Hodson to present the first full-

293

length locally-produced ballet programme, in conjunction with the opera season of that year. With Marjorie Sturman and Poppy Frames, she was one of the first Children's Examiners appointed in Southern Africa by the Royal Academy of Dancing (RAD).

—H.D.

CONNELL, JOHN. *18 June 1891 in Glasgow; °21 September 1955 in Johannesburg. City organist and director of music in Johannesburg from 1916 to 1950.

Little is known about Connell's parentage or his early years. "A thorough Glaswegian", he had his schooling at the Allen Glen School and was trained in music by Alice Millar (pianoforte) and at a later stage by G.T. Pattman (organist of St Mary's Cathedral), whose assistant he became in 1906. He kept this position until 1912. In January of the latter year he became an Associate of the RCO and, after further study under Hollins, a Fellow of the same College in January 1915. Connell was on very friendly terms with this blind organist of St George's United Free Church in Edinburgh and often included works by Hollins in his recital programmes. Hollins, in turn, dedicated a Scherzo to Connell. From 1912 until 1916 he acted as organist at the College and Kelvin Grove United Free Church. He was studying organ on his own during these years and gave recitals at St Mary's on the third Monday evening of each month, a further series in his own church from 1913 to 1915 and various concerts in the Protestant churches in Glasgow. The programme notes for all these recitals were written by himself. — Hollins was on one of his concert tours of South Africa, when he was approached by the Town Council of Johannesburg for advice regarding the specifications for a proposed new organ for the Town Hall, completed on 7 April 1915. The organ was inaugurated on 4 March 1916 by Hollins himself ("really the last word in organ building") and he recommended his young friend Connell as City Organist. In all, 71 organists had applied for the position at a salary of R1 200 per annum. On 30 November 1916, when the Great War had dragged on for two years, Connell arrived in Cape Town with his bride, one month after their marriage. He gave an organ recital on the Cape Town city organ ("a very efficient instrument") and then left for Johannesburg where he played on the new organ at a concert on Sunday evening, 16 December 1916. — Throughout his career Connell was first and foremost the civic organist of Johannesburg. This was his first love, the work for which he had been trained, and it remained his vocation, although his career, especially during the Second World War, became hectic and led him into other ventures. Even after his retirement in April 1950, he gave one Sunday recital and one lunch-hour recital each month by special arrangement with the City Council's Arts and Culture Committee. These represented two kinds of recital which he had introduced, although the lunch-hour recital had started on Thursdays and then moved to Wednesdays and eventually Tuesdays, often taking place on two days, but always with a singer or an instrumentalist or (after 1930) a choir participating. On 3 November 1929 he had reached recital number 1000, a publicised fact which the large audience acknowledged with acclamation. He commemorated his 25th year as City Organist on 16 December 1941 and at the time of his death had given far in excess of 2000 recitals. — He saw in this work an opportunity of educating the masses in music, of "reaching the people *at their existing level of musical appreciation,* with the intention of gradually raising the standard of the programmes and enlarging the acquaintance of the audience with the classics" (own italics). He used the organ to educate young people especially and

294

from 1917 to 1919 he presented special programmes for schools. By arrangement with the Council the pupils could use their programmes as tram tickets, and prizes were offered to those who wrote the best essays on the series. At an early stage he introduced request programmes and carried on with these for a long time. Many of the requests originated with country visitors who attended his lunch-hour recitals. It became quite usual to see children and grown-ups walking up to the organ after the recital to have a look at the instrument and to view the organist at close quarters. — Connell also undertook tours, either in the service of "vitalising propaganda" (South African tour of January-July 1918), or to "keep in touch" with overseas music and musicians (America, September-February 1931-32; England and America, August-November 1934; United Kingdom, November-January 1934-35). Furthermore, he was regularly available for inaugurations of organs or to advise on organ specifications (City Hall of Pretoria - organ inaugurated 1935). In the course of his duties he played at civic seremonies, Christmas tableaux, stage productions, charity concerts ("...the charity concert has done more to kill the love of music and of music making than did the Battle of Marathon, the Black Plague or the Treaty of Versailles, which finally upset the concert of Europe..."), concerts for war funds, etc. Apart from his duties as City Organist, he was also organist and choirmaster of St George's Church, Parktown (1918-1926), St Mary's Cathedral (1926-1931) and the Nederduitse Gereformeerde Church, Johannesburg East (1932-1944). — Fresh from the great British choral tradition, Connell had become conductor of the Johannesburg Philharmonic and Choral Society* in 1916 and remained in this position until he finally retired. After conducting the Society in smaller works, he considered the possibility of choral festivals in which a number of choirs might participate. At the end of 1918 he conducted *Messiah* in a performance of the Pretoria Choral Society and in January of the next year he had become their conductor. On 5 Feburary, Connell combined the two societies of the two cities for an open-air performance in the amphitheatre of the Union Buildings. Two days later, Germiston was affected and when the Cape Town Municipal Orchestra* visited Johannesburg in that same year, it had become possible to present large-scale performances of *Faust* (21 April) and the *German requiem* (Brahms) (18 April). The choral movement was then expanded to include Bloemfontein, Pieter-maritzburg and Kimberley. In June 1921 a unique choral tour took place. It started in Johannesburg on the 5th of June with a performance of *Elijah* supported by the Cape Town Municipal Orchestra; the choir of Johannesburg and Pretoria then left by train to sing with the choirs of Bloemfontein, Pietermaritzburg and Durban (29 June). In the same year six choirs from six cities combined to sing *Messiah* and Mendelssohn's *Hymn of praise* during a great Christmas choral festival in Johannesburg. Yet another choir was established in Potchefstroom in 1922 and when the Durban Orchestra* came for a visit, it was supported by choral groups from Pretoria and Johannesburg in a performance of *Faust*. In 1923 Connell arranged a performance of Beethoven's *Choral symphony* to take place on 17th April. For this he enlisted, in addition to the Cape Town Municipal Orchestra conducted by Wendt* and his own Philharmonic Society, three Johannesburg school choirs and the Afrikaanse Mannekoor of J.B.Z. Keet*. Three years later, in 1926, he united 5 choirs for a performance of *Messiah* in Pretoria, but then Connell relinquished the idea of organising choral festivals on this scale. He confined himself to his own Philharmonic Society which performed *Carmen, Semele, Elijah* and

Messiah. The latter work became an institution with the Society. With the possible exception of 1930, 1936 and 1946, it was conducted by Connell every year from 1939 onwards with the ASAF Choir* supporting his own forces in performances which used Afrikaans and English in turn. This enthusiasm for choral festivals on a national scale was revived in a different form at a later stage in his career when he strove to realise a national opera. — An interesting subsidiary activity of the 1920s, was Connell's association with the Transvaal University College, now the University of Pretoria. Starting in 1921, when the Council asked Connell to conduct their newly formed College Choral Society, the authorities were led step by step from the introduction of music as a B.A. subject to the point reached in June 1923, when the Music School and the Music Department with, in all, three degree courses and three academic students, rose to the dignity of a Faculty. At this stage the B. Mus. degree was instituted and the Faculty managed to limp along until 27 March 1929 when Connell, who had only one degree student, one diploma student and 11 entries for practical music, tendered his resignation. The Music Department existed until 1936, but for Connell, this single flight into the academic sphere had sufficed to convince him that he was wasting his time. That his approach to music education was, however, sincere has become evident from his work as organist and also from his willingness to act as adjudicator at Afrikaans eisteddfodau, time permitting. Thus, in the 1930s he adjudicated in Potchefstroom a few times. His sympathetic guidance, which can hardly be called criticism, exerted a lasting and beneficial influence. This same kindly interest in youth music also governed his virtually life-long interest in arranging special concerts for young people and encouraging them to start an orchestra of their own. — When he became the conductor of the Philharmonic Choir, Connell inherited a small philharmonic orchestra which, for special occasions such as the Peace celebrations in 1918 or the Kruger Centenary Festival in Pretoria in 1925, was augmented to a respectable band of 60 players. After Connell had launched his *Music Fortnights* in 1926, the orchestra became increasingly important to accompany the occasional opera or to perform during the Beethoven Centenary Year (1927). It very soon became a permanent institution, subsidised by the City Council and re-named Festival Orchestra for the winter series of 1928 and 1929. Soundtrack films and the worldwide depression which started in 1932, left many musicians without employment, and Connell gathered them into his Festival Orchestra. Beginning in 1933, he was in a position to present short symphony seasons, but he also conducted them at popular concerts on Sunday afternoons, in popular open-air programmes and in opera. With the performance of *Tannhaüser* in 1932, a new era of opera had been launched in the musical life of the city. — In 1938 Connell signed a contract with the SABC, whereby the Radio Orchestra was combined with the City Orchestra for the performance of operas and for the broadcasting of symphonic programmes. This agreement remained in force until after the War and was still effective after the establishment of the Johannesburg City Orchestra in October 1945. From this year on Connell was often in Europe to recruit musicians for his orchestra and to engage conductors: Malcolm Sargent (1946, 1948); Desire Defauw (1947, 1948); Warwick Braithwaite; Thomas Beecham; Richard Austin; Frits Schuurman* and Gideon Fagan* (August 1949, 1951). The orchestra went on tour to Bloemfontein (1947), Pretoria (1947), Benoni (1949) and played to young people (1936, 34 concerts; 1937, 38 concerts). Out of these efforts grew the Johannesburg Young People's Orchestra in 1944. After 1946, the orchestra played in City schools and in 1949 it toured the Western Transvaal (21 February - 11 March) and played in 14 centres to 30 000 people of whom 20 000 were children ("... one of the biggest cultural things that have been done in the country ..." - Connell). — The orchestral developments are intimately associated with the history of opera and ballet in the Transvaal. From September 1925, when Connell staged *Faust* for the benefit of hospital funds, he produced operas fairly regularly until 1937 when the Carl. Rosa Opera Company played in the Empire Theatre and gave convincing proof that there was a large public for opera in Johannesburg. From 1938, Connell's *Music Fortnights* became *Music Festivals*, in which the three operas of the earlier years was increased to ten operas and two ballets by 1946. With 9 or 10 operas a year, stability was established for the years up to 1950. Connell expanded this endeavour by forming a National Opera Company, which performed in Pretoria at the conclusion of the Johannesburg season, and thereafter in Cape Town, Durban (from 1943) and Pietermaritzburg (from 1946). Thus the works that had been performed in Johannesburg were shared with four other cities, and the choral efforts of the 'twenties were repeated, testifying to Connell's national bias and idealism. Meanwhile the children were not forgotten: during the war years he even managed to achieve a Children's Theatre. The remarkable development from *Music Fortnights* to *Music Festival* was epitomised by Connell himself as a development from "sandbags to shoestrings" - these festivals were realised on an amount which never exceeded R7 000. He was often sharply criticised for inferior standards, but he had made opera a paying and a self-supporting proposition and there were times when a black market for admission tickets was openly conducted. He proved that Johannesburg wanted opera and that the patrons were not too critical about the presentation. Besides his work in connection with *Music Fortnights* and *Music Festivals*, the city's Director of Music was also active in the parks where he conducted programmes of orchestral music (with operatic excerpts) and (from 1929) also organised band performances. In 1935 these had increased to 87 performances given at a cost of R4 820. His remarkable talent for organisation was also deployed to benefit large festivals and historic functions. It must be pointed out that Connell adopted a helpful and sympathetic attitude towards Afrikaner aspirations throughout his career. He was not only an organist in an Afrikaans church, but he also conducted the singing of 12 000 children at the Show Grounds during the Kruger Centenary Celebrations in Pretoria (1925). The same afternoon he conducted the singing of 500 adults when the monument was unveiled in front of the station and in the evening he presented a huge Festival Concert at the Union Buildings where a special Kruger Centenary Festival Orchestra, composed of Pretoria and Johannesburg musicians, and supported by the Police Band, played before an audience of 8000 people, including the Prime Minister and other dignitaries. On 7 August 1933 he directed the singing of a choir at a large Scottish gathering for which he had compiled a song book; in 1937 he arranged a great pageant and organised operas on the occasion of the coronation of the British King and Queen; for the Johannesburg Golden Jubilee he organised a pageant $2^1/_2$ miles long; the Johannesburg Pageant choirs and the historical displays for the Voortrekker Celebrations of 1938 were also his work. He directed community singing during the Royal visit of 1947 and was often requested to lead mass singing. — As far back as his visit to America in 1931 the *American Organist* had written about Connell: "... more American in energy than he was Scotch. That man is dynamite." With amazing energy and a determination that never flagged, this borough organist served the cause of music for 34 years and brought about musical events in Johannesburg which no one had dreamt of. On 23 February 1938 he stated in the *Daily Express* (and this might serve as a clue to his astonishing career): "My job cannot be static, it must always have some seeds of forward movement in it".

BIBLIOGRAPHY

SMUTS, TERESA G.: *John Connell.* B.Mus. script, UP, 1971.

SOURCES

Nineteen scrap books in the possession of the Johannesburg Public Library. Research by Dr L. Wolpowitz.

—J.P.M.

CONRAD, INES-MARIA (NÉE LUCANTONI), born in Bournemouth of Italian parents; now in Durban. She is the wife of James Conrad*. Lecturer in music.

Mrs Conrad won a scholarship to the RCM where she met James Conrad to whom she was married in 1959. Apart from music she also studied for the post-graduate Teachers' Training Diploma. When her husband became Head of Opera in the NAPAC organisation, she became involved in his work as opera and ballet repetitor and producer. For a while she was part-time lecturer at the Indian university, but subsequently she was appointed a full-time lecturer at the Springfield Indian Teachers' Training College. She got the idea for her *Cuckoo* series in 1969. This is designed as a young children's guide to music appreciation and as an assistance to teachers responsible for the subject. Based on the methods of Kodaly and Carl Orff, *Cuckoo* is unique in that it combines subjects such as history, geography, English and general knowledge with musical instruction. Mrs Lyndsay Maritz, NAPAC's commercial artist, drew the illustrations. The first *Cuckoo* book was adapted in 13 fifteen-minute eposides for the English Service of the SABC and was broadcast in the "Programme for young people".

PUBLICATIONS

The *Let's go, Cuckoo* series. Nasou, Parow, 1971-73: 1. Let's go! Cuckoo 2. All aboard with Cuckoo 3. Let's go abroad with Cuckoo 4. Cuckoo's world of music fantasy. The series was partially translated into Afrikaans in collaboration with M. Hawkins: 1. Kammalielie Koekoek se musiek-maak-boek 2. Stap aan boord met Koekoek 3. Op besoek met Koekoek. In collaboration with M. Hawkins: Poperettes - Sing and play Cuckoo's way.

SOURCES

SABC Bulletin: 1 March 1971. *SAMT* 83, January 1973. National Documentation Centre for Music, HSRC, Pretoria.

—Ed.

CONRAD, JAMES (JACOBUS JACOBS), *19 July 1932 in Carnarvon; now in Durban. Tenor; Head of opera and ballet for NAPAC.

After attending school in Carnarvon and Victoria West, Conrad entered the Conservatoire of Music* in Stellenbosch and obtained the diplomas ODMS, LTCL, and UTLM in singing, with violin and pianoforte as subsidiary practical subjects (1949-1953). 1955 was an important year for James Conrad. He became junior lecturer in singing at the College of Music* in Cape Town, sang in opera for the first time (two works by Mozart and *The consul* by Menotti) and then visited Britain with

the University of Cape Town's Opera Company in December. On this tour he sang in *The consul* and gave a recital of songs by Janáček in the Wigmore Hall. — He accepted a position as an Afrikaans radio announcer in the BBC and continued his singing studies, no longer as a bass-baritone, but as a dramatic tenor. He sang in the Glyndebourne production of *The magic flute* in 1960. This performance led to a recommendation by Set Svanholm for a German exchange scholarship which enabled him to enter the Detmold Music Academy where he studied voice production and repertoire from 1960 to 1963. During holidays he sang in the Bayreuth Festival Chorus and learnt Wagner roles. Kiel Opera House engaged him as junior tenor in 1964 and Sadler's Wells obtained his services as dramatic tenor in 1965. The next year he was invited to become principal tenor of PACT and at the same time he was offered the position of Head of Opera in NAPAC (1966). He accepted the latter offer and in 1968 he was also made Head of Ballet. — In Natal, James Conrad has turned to the production of operas. Altogether about nine operas by Menotti, Verdi, Bellini, Mozart, Donizetti, Puccini, Bizet, Mascagni and Leoncavallo have been presented in Durban under his direction and in some instances also in Bloemfontein up to 1972. He married Ines-Maria Lucantoni in 1959. She is a music lecturer and author of educational books and radio plays.
—G.S.J.

CONSTABLE, G (MRS QUARTERMAN)   P. Quarterman

COOPER, GILL AND TOMKINS (PTY) LTD   The firm of Cooper, Gill and Tomkins (Pty) Ltd was founded by William Charles Cooper, who emigrated to South Africa from England in 1888, as the representative for the organbuilding firm of J.J. Binns of Leeds, England. He was not only a very capable organbuilder, but also an organist of unusual merit; it was not surprising that he was often asked to inaugurate new organs which he himself had installed. — When the work became too much for one man, Cooper obtained the assistance of another employee from Messrs Binns of Leeds in Harold Gill, who emigrated from England to join him in 1900. They decided later to go into business on their own, and formed a company in 1902, which was known as Cooper & Gill. The first factory was situated at the top end of Wale Street, Cape Town; but, as circumstances demanded, it moved at times to different premises. — South Africa attracted the attention of another English firm, that of Norman & Beard of Norwich, England. In 1902 they sent out one of their best men, Alfred Maberley Fellows Tomkins, to cope with their expanding interests in this country. In 1916 he obtained for his firm the order for the large organ in the City Hall, Johannesburg. In 1906 Tomkins joined forces with Messrs Cooper & Gill, as third partner, with the task of serving the Northern provinces, thus completing the firm Cooper, Gill & Tomkins. Tomkins covered all of the Transvaal, Orange Free State and Rhodesia, from no. 10 Pope Street, Bellevue, Johannesburg, his business headquarters. When larger premises were needed, two shops at Klein Street, Hillbrow, Johannesburg were taken; but in 1937 the firm moved to the present factory at 33 Staib Street, New Doornfontein, Johannesburg. — In the meantime the firm's activities extended in the Cape and Natal areas, and another organ-builder from Leeds, Harry Williams, joined the firm in 1914. He later became a director, and retired in 1960. The present director of the firm in Cape Town - Alex Smith - returned to South Africa in 1928, after concluding his training with Rushworth & Dreaper in Liverpool; he joined the firm in May of that year. — In 1922 a further increase in staff was deemed advisable, with the

299

arrival of Albert Victor Allen, who was responsible for the rebuilding of several large organs in the Cape, amongst them the three-manual organ at Paarl Dutch Reformed Church. W.C. Cooper retired from the company in 1926, when he left for overseas to become general manager of Rushworth & Dreaper of Liverpool. Thus the trend of organ-builders leaving England for Africa was reversed. — A.V. Allen was then appointed to the staff in the Transvaal, where he was responsible for the large organ installed in the Pretoria City Hall in 1935. He later became a director, and worked for the firm to the time of his death in 1960. The present Johannesburg director, William Tozer, succeeded Allen in Johannesburg, arriving in South Africa in 1935. He had served his apprenticeship with the amalgamated firms of Messrs Wm. Hill & Son, and Norman & Beard. — A.M.F. Tomkins died in 1941, W.C. Cooper in 1952 and H. Gill in 1964, so that all the original founders have passed away. — The present directors are A.X. Smith, in charge of the Head Office at Cape Town, and W. Tozer, responsible for the Johannesburg and Durban branches; the latter is assisted by A.B. Hill in Johannesburg, and R.A. Kitchener in Natal.

—W.T.

COOPER, w.w.   Port Elizabeth I/2, Port Elizabeth Amateur Choral and Orchestral Music, Prince Alfred's Volunteer Guard Band

COPELAND, GLEN (PSEUDONYM)   N.V. Griffin

CORDER, T.   St George's Cathedral, Touring Theatre Groups 2

COULTHARD, HENRY BARLOW, *11 May 1879 in Kent; °30 August 1932 in Johannesburg. Theatre and hotel manager who was a proficient pianist and produced operettas.
Coulthard came to South Africa in 1902 as the Business Manager of Darter's* in Cape Town. Shortly after his arrival he was involved in the creation of a Cape Amateur Opera Society of which he acted in succession as secretary, chairman and business manager. As a pianist he often accompanied visiting artists. The case of Mark Hambourg is quite remarkable: this pianist performed Tchaikovsky's *First pianoforte concerto* in the Opera House* with Coulthard playing the orchestral part on a second pianoforte (1907)! — About 1909 he became the musical director and then the business manager of Bert and Frank Wheeler's* theatre enterprises in Johannesburg and delivered convincing proof of his capabilities as an organiser and a producer in His Majesty's Theatre*. To all the imported "girls", he added a South African *Girl from Springfontein*. The libretto was written by Lewis Rose MacLeod, at that time editor of the *Sunday Post*. This work was also performed in other centres in South Africa and must have enjoyed considerable popularity, since Darter's published separately a few of the tunes occurring in the work. — The Wheelers did not renew their hire of His Majesty's Theatre after 1914 and Coulthard joined I.W. Schlesinger's organisation. After a few years in Schlesinger's Natal concerns, he became manager of the Carlton Hotel in Johannesburg. With the active support of Schlesinger's African Consolidated Theatres, Coulthard personally interested himself in the affairs of the Johannesburg Amateur Opera Society* (1920-June 1932) as a result of which a number of works by Gilbert and Sullivan together with *Dorothy* (April 1920) and *The merry widow* (1924 and 1927) were performed in the twelve years before he died. — Since 1926 he had been a member of Johannesburg's publicity society and since 1930 its chairman.

WORKS

Four short songs (Lynn Lyster). Darter & Sons, Cape Town, n.d.: 1. Amaranth 2. Asphodels 3. The night has a thousand eyes 4. When we are old. The girl from Springfontein (Lewis Rose MacLeod). Darter & Sons, Cape Town, 1913. Only four songs from this musical were published by Darter's: 1. I'm lonely 2. Love is in season all the year 3. My lady of dreams 4. To. our land. The outspan, barn dance. Printed by C.G. Röder, Leipzig; publ. Darter & Sons, Cape Town, n.d. Reveries of the Cape. Printed by C.G. Röder, Leipzig; publ. Darter & Sons, Cape Town, n.d. The VCTA (Voluntary Civilian Training Association), song (F.E. Walrond). Mackay Bros., Johannesburg, 1914.

BIBLIOGRAPHY

VAN DER MERWE, F.Z.: *Suid-Afrikaanse musiekbibliografie, 1787-1952.* J.L. van Schaik, Pretoria, 1958.

—L.W.

COUTTS, DIANE BURDETT, *5 January 1942 in Durban; now (1977) in Durban. Pianist, organist, flautist and official accompanist to the SABC since 1970.

After early study under Elizabeth Sivertson* (pianoforte), Joseph Slater* (flute and recorder), and Errol Slatter* (organ), she obtained a Fellowship of Trinity College and licentiates of the RAM for organ and pianoforte as well as South African licentiates. Her study in London was made possible through an annual bursary awarded by the Natal Society for the Advancement of Music* (1955-61). She also won the Gustav Hallé bursary twice for the most outstanding competitor at the Durban Eisteddfod, and on two occasions won the Gertrude Buchanan Bursary awarded to runners-up for the Overseas Bursary of UNISA. Miss Coutts has given two piano recitals and organ-and-oboe concerts with her sister Janet; she has also broadcast as pianist and organist for the SABC, and has been organist at Emmanuel Cathedral and St Joseph's Roman Catholic Church in Durban since 1971. She teaches pianoforte, flute and recorder, and has formed the Purcell Recorder Ensemble for her talented pupils. She composed and performed the flute music for an Afrikaans production of Sophocles's *Antigone,* by the Natal Teachers' Training College. Well-known as an organ recitalist in Natal and the Transvaal, Diane Coutts has formed a pianoforte duo with Ronald Charles* and often teams up with chamber music groups. — Diane is the eldest of three sisters who are all musical. The youngest of the trio is Janet who has distinguished herself as an oboist in solo recitals and concertos with orchestras in South Africa and England. As a member of various chamber music groups she has performed widely in Natal, for NAPAC and the SASMT. After a successful study at the RAM, she returned to South Africa to become oboist in the Durban Symphony Orchestra. At present she is an oboist and cor anglais player in the PACT Orchestra, Pretoria.

—Ed.

COUZYN, MAURITZ DAVID WILHELMUS (DAWIE), *27 June 1925 in Pretoria; now (1977) in Pretoria. Baritone.

Dawie Couzyn was a boy-soprano during his early schooldays in Pietersburg. After he had matriculated, he continued his singing lessons in Pretoria, first under Stella Blakemore* and later in Johannesburg from 1945 onwards, under Margaret Roux, Bruce Anderson* and especially under Olga Ryss*. In 1948 he took part in opera performances for the first time. In 1955 he went to the Staatsakademie für Musik und Darstellende Kunst in Vienna where he studied under Josef Witt, Viktor Graef

301

and Erich Werba and passed the Staatliche Reifeprüfung after two years. Some time later he continued his studies under Maria Schultz-Dornburg in Salzburg and Adelaida Saraceni in Milan. Meanwhile he had appeared on programmes of the BBC in London and on Radio Wien and as soloist with the Viennese Kammeroper. — In June 1957 Dawie Couzyn made his debut as a professional concert singer in the Albert Hall in London. This was the first of a series of recitals and broadcasts that he gave in England. After that, he was invited to appear as guest singer in various German and English opera seasons and in 1959 he became the leading bass-buffo of the Landestheater in Salzburg. From 1964 onwards, he sang roles for the Salzburger Mozartoper on their extensive annual tours through Italy, France, Switzerland, Luxemburg and Germany. During the Salzburg Festival he took part in the Baroque programmes at the Palais Mirabel; at the same time he continued his studies at the Mozarteum and under Bernhard Paumgartner Dawie Couzyn became a specialist in the operas of Mozart. — He has sung the part of Figaro 78 times; the part of Guglielmo (in *Cosí fan tutte*) 65 times and the title role in *Don Giovanni* 26 times (up to 1972). As Tarquinius in Britten's *Rape of Lucretia,* as Antinous in Franz Schmidt's *Ulysses,* as Consul in Menotti's *The consul* and in *Die Kluge* (Orff) (all in continental productions). Dawie Couzyn has proved his ability to interpret contemporary music. During 1969 and 1971 he went to the United States to sing seven baritone leading roles in opera seasons presented by the National Opera Company of America. From August 1971 he was attached for one year to the Linz opera in Austria as baritone. Among the parts he sang there was the title-role of Verdi's *Rigoletto.* — Since 1960 he visited South Africa regularly every year, and took part in productions presented by the Regional Councils for the Performing Arts. He appeared in operas such as *Cosí fan tutte, Carmen, The consul* and *Norma,* and in recitals throughout the country, has made commercial recordings and become well-known for his interpretation of songs for children. — Dawie Couzyn has taken part in oratorios under leading conductors in London, Huddersfield, Salzburg and elsewhere, and has earned himself an excellent reputation as a singer of Lieder on radio programmes in England, South Africa, Germany and Austria. In 1963 and 1964 he was invited to sing the baritone solo part in the Santa Cecilia presentation of Britten's *War requiem* in Rome. His overseas career was terminated in 1974 when he succeeded Xander Haagen* on the staff of the Music Department of Pretoria's College for Advanced Technical Education as Head of the Opera School under Josias van der Merwe*. He remained in this position for three years and gave the opera department a firm basis by presenting an annual opera production in the Aula of the University of Pretoria. In June 1977 however, he resigned.

ARTICLE
Hoogtepunt van die musiekfees in Salzburg. *Vita Musica* I/4, December 1963.

SOURCES
SACK, JOE: Couzyn's century of Figaro roles. *Opus* V/1, October 1973. *Rooi Rose:* January 1955. *Die Burger:* 19 March 1960; 15 June 1967. National Documentation Centre for Music, HSRC, Pretoria.

—Ed.

COWEY, VIOLETTE   L. Strauss Smith

CRAIB, DORIS (NÉE VEVERS), *1906 in Bristol, England; now (1977) in the district of Somerset East. Cellist and composer.

After receiving an Associated Board Scholarship at the age of seventeen, Doris Craib studied under Herbert Walenn (cello) and Dorothy Howell (composition) at the RAM. There she won awards and prizes for cello and gained the Performer's Licentiate. She was also made a Sub-Professor and in 1931 became an Associate of the Royal Academy of Music. Her professional career has included recitals for the BBC and concert engagements in many parts of England. Since she settled in South Africa, Doris Craib has played in different parts of the country and has broadcast for the SABC. She plays on a cello of approximately 1735, made by Giorgio Tanigard, who lived and worked in Rome.

WORKS

A Lullaby, for cello and piano. Ms., 1925.   Intermezzo, for piano. Ms., 1927.   Chanson sans paroles, for cello and piano. Ms., 1929.   Elegy, for cello and piano. Ms., 1929.

—Ed.

CRANCH, W.   Pretoria 2, 3, Theatres and Concert Halls VI/1

CRANE, FRANCIS.   British singing teacher, organist and choral conductor who was active in South Africa during the last decade of the 19th century.

Little is known of his early career, except that he had been a "broker and commission agent"; and that he had received his musical training at the Milan Conservatoire where he studied singing under Signor C. Emeric. — The date of Crane's arrival in South Africa is not known, but early in 1881 he accepted an appointment as singing teacher at the Collegiate School, Port Elizabeth at a salary of R146 a year. From September 1881 to about July 1882 he was organist at St Mary's Collegiate Church, and for a period of about 18 months he directed the activities of the Uitenhage Musical Society. In October 1881 he revived the Port Elizabeth Choral Union and in December of that year he became founder, organiser and conductor of the Port Elizabeth Amateur Operatic Company which opened its first "season" of seven nights on 7 January 1882 with Gilbert and Sullivan's *The sorcerer*. He was given a farewell concert in Uitenhage, and, probably in 1882, he left for Fauresmith where he became accountant to the Board of Executors. — Francis Crane's wanderings then took him to Kimberley where he became organist at the Anglican Church of St Cyprian's. He made his first appearance in Durban in 1884, advertising himself as "prepared to receive pupils in Production and Cultivation of the Voice and Singing". He soon became associated with Duncan MacColl*, conductor of the Durban Philharmonic Society*, and during the latter part of this year, was appointed conductor of the Pietermaritzburg Philharmonic Society*, a position he held for about a year. After one of the concerts given by this Society in April 1885, a press report in the *Natal Witness* commended him as a "promising tenor". In 1887 he appeared in Johannesburg as a singing teacher and the first organist at St Mary's Hall, Eloff Street - the forerunner of the Anglican Cathedral of St Mary's. On 2 February 1888 he was conductor at a concert in aid of St Mary's Hospital, given under the patronage of Captain and Mrs Von Brandis. — His re-appearance in Durban about the middle of 1890 was opportune. MacColl's failure to keep his choir intact led to the disintegration of the Durban Philharmonic Society and the formation of the Berea Choral Society under Francis Crane. The newly-formed choir made its first public appearance in the old Town Hall on 30 August, giving evidence

of "excellent training" in their rendition of some unaccompanied part-songs.
— By September 1890 Crane had considerable musical resources at his command. The
Berea and Durban Choral Societies had amalgamated and simultaneously members of
the Durban Orchestral Society* (still trained by Herr Eberlein*) joined forces under
his baton. This amalgamation of musical forces proved very successful and on 19 December 1890 a choir of 160 voices, supported by a small orchestra, gave a performance
of Mendelssohn's *Elijah*. During the next three years the new society, which called
itself the Durban Choral Union, presented a series of subscription concerts
including such large-scale works as *Messiah, Hymn of praise* (Mendelssohn) and
The revenge (Stanford). By March 1894 the Durban Choral Union had become the
Durban Choral and Orchestral Union and in December, with 200 voices, it
presented two performances of Handel's *Messiah* in a special week of festivity to
celebrate the inauguration of the new Town Hall organ. — The appointment of the
first borough organist brought to a close Francis Crane's career as a civic choral
conductor in Durban. The choirs he had formed and trained were later re-established
as the Durban Musical Association* under R. Houston Macdonald*. Meanwhile
Crane had formed Durban's first Male Voice Choir (April 1893) and had trained
smaller vocal groups. One of his last public appearances in Durban was at a Christmas
Concert in the old Town Hall on 21 December 1895 when he conducted a combined
choir, a Glee club and a Ladies' choir, 27 singers in all. — By August 1897
reports in the *Diggers News* and *Natal Advertiser* stated that he had resumed his
music teaching practice in Johannesburg. Unfortunately these are the last available
references to him.

BIBLIOGRAPHY

JACKSON, G.S.: *Music in Durban.* D. Phil. thesis, UWits, 1961.   TROSKIE, A.J.J.: *The musical life of
Port Elizabeth, 1875-1900.* M. Mus. dissertation, UPE, 1969.   WOLPOWITZ, L.: *James and Kate
Hyde and the development of music in Johannesburg up to the First World War.* J.L. van
Schaik, Pretoria, 1969.

—G.S.J.

CRANKO, JOHN, *1927 in Rustenburg; °26 June 1973 during a flight over Europe.
Choreographer and director of the Stuttgart Opera Ballet.

Before his career as a dancer and choreographer started in Cape Town, Cranko had
received ballet tuition from Marjorie Sturman* in Johannesburg. In Cape Town he
did his first ballet for the Cape Town Ballet Club* in 1944, *A soldier's tale* (music by
Stravinsky), and he joined the University of Cape Town Ballet* in the next year,
doing the choreography for two ballets before leaving for England in 1946. Shortly
after his arrival, he joined the Sadler's Wells Theatre Ballet, becoming Resident
Choreographer for the company after Ninette de Valois had seen his ballet, *Tritch
tratch* (music by Strauss). *Bonne bouche* was written for the Sadler's Wells Covent
Garden Company in 1952, and his first full-length ballet *Prince of the pagodas,* with
specially commissioned music by Benjamin Britten, for the Royal Ballet at Covent
Garden. Since 1960 Cranko was Artistic Director of Ballet at the Stuttgart State
Opera in Germany, where he had a company of high standing, which had recently
formed its own school. — John Cranko choreographed ballets for the Cape Town
Ballet Club, the UCT Ballet, the Sadler's Wells Theatre Ballet (among them *Sea
change, Beauty and the beast, Pineapple Poll, Harlequin in April),* the Covent
Garden Ballet *(The prince of the pagodas, Antigone* etc.), and the State Opera of

Stuttgart (*Daphnis and Chloe, Eugene Onegin, Jeux des cartes, L'Estro armonico, Romeo and Juliet,* etc.). — To the memory of John Cranko, a bursary was started in 1976.

BIBLIOGRAPHY

WINKLER-BELZENDAHL, M.: *The Sadler's Wells theatre ballet.* A & C Black & Co., London, 1956. WINKLER-BELZENDAHL, M.: *Ballet in Stuttgart.* Chr. Belzer, Stuttgart, 1964.   WILSON, G.B.L.: *A dictionary of ballet.* Penguin, 1957.   WILSON, G.B.L.: *A dictionary of modern ballet.* Methuen & Co., London, 1959.   WORRAL, JOHN (ED.): *Ballet in South Africa.* Howard Timmins, Cape Town/Bodley Head, London, 1950.   HASKELL, ARNOLD; CARTER, MARK; WOOD, MICHAEL (editors): *Gala performance.* Collins, London 1955.   DE VALOIS, NINETTE: *Come and dance with me - a memoir.* Hamish Hamilton, London, 1957.

SOURCES

WILLIAMS, P.: What makes a company? *Dance and dancers,* July 1976.   DU PREEZ, A.: Half a century in the forefront of ballet. South Africa's place in the world of dance. *Lantern,* September 1976.   *E.P. Herald:* 1 June 1976.   *Die Burger:* 23 July 1957.   National Documentation Centre for Music, HSRC, Pretoria.

—M.G.

CRAWFORD, NIGEL, *4 January 1924 in Johannesburg, where he lives at present (1977). Jazz pianist, composer and teacher of light music.

Nigel Crawford commenced taking music lessons at the age of six, with a Mr Jolly and later with Clarice Smith. Although he was trained in serious music, he soon developed an individual style as a jazz musician, and formed an orchestra while still at school. On returning to South Africa after service in the Second World War, he began a school of pianoforte playing in Johannesburg, and established a light orchestra which he led for five years, playing at the Skyline Hotel. In 1948 he married Nadene Logan, a pianist and a music teacher. He has been in Johannesburg ever since, except for a period in 1955-1956 when he led a dance orchestra at the Windsor Bowl, East London. — On several occasions Nigel has been invited to play the piano, or to assemble and conduct a light band, on chartered sea-voyages to England offered by the Overseas Visitors' Club. In Johannesburg he has been active broadcasting as a pianist, and as the leader of light ensembles. He accompanied Roy Martin's singing group, The Melodians, during their concert tour of the Reef in the early 1960s. He has also played the piano with the SABC Light Orchestra under Jos Cleber, in a series of fourteen recorded broadcasts. Crawford has to his credit many commercial recordings, some of which include light music composed since his early youth. Songs that have become known in England and America through records are: *Zulu lullaby; Hamba lala* (Little Zulu boy); *Tell me again; I know the reason why; You are the one I love; Loving you; Alice in Kwelaland; Better take care.*

—Ed.

CREE, EDGAR   Johannesburg 3(iii), Opera Societies 1, 4

CREMERS, HARRY, *1903 in Holland; living in Cape Town (1970). Cellist.

Harry Cremers studied at the Musik-Hochschule in Cologne (Germany), and at the Royal Conservatoire in Liége (Belgium). He was awarded the Premier Prix for cello-playing and chamber music and subsequently continued studies under the cellist, Emmanuel Feuermann. After touring several European countries as a soloist, and as a member of the Franz Schätzer Quartet, he was appointed principal cellist of the Hilversum Radio Symphony Orchestra in 1933, a position he held for fourteen years. Cremers came to South Africa in 1947 to take up an appointment as principal cellist of the Johannesburg Symphony Orchestra*, but two years later he moved to Cape Town, where he was principal cellist of the Cape Town Municipal Orchestra*. Here he was a foundation member of the Arte Viva Trio, and with this combination he toured the main centres of the Republic and the Rhodesian Federation. In 1960 he joined the OFS String Quartet* in Bloemfontein, and became Head of Chamber Music in ·the music department of the University of the OFS. Among the works specially written for, and dedicated to Harry Cremers, is a fugue for cello and piano by Professor Georg Gruber*. He left Bloemfontein at the end of 1968 for Cape Town where he was appointed to the staff of the South African College of Music.

—Ed.

CRITERION THEATRE, DURBAN   Durban 5, Durban Amateur Operatic Society

CRONJÉ, J.P.   E.M. Tamassy

CROSSLEY, F.   Pietermaritzburg, Pietermaritzburg Philharmonic Society

CRUSE, PETER   L.B. de Kock, H. Greenwood, J. Pierre Malan, S. Smuts, SASMT II/3

CUBITT, MRS. J.   Durban 2, Durban Philharmonic Society, Organs 2(v)

CUERTON, RICHARD, *1767 (1766?) in England; °26 August 1815 in Cape Town. Tailor who entertained Cape Town audiences between 1813 and 1815 with pantomimes and harlequinades.

In the July 1813 issue of the *Kaapsche Courant* there is a notice to the effect that Richard Cuerton would be presenting a military concert and a harlequinade with a garrison company in the Afrikaans Theatre. This venture was obviously successful because during the following two years he also presented *Robinson Crusoe or Harlequin Friday* (Sheridan and Linley?); *Don Juan or The libertine destroyed* (a ballet supplemented by harlequin items); *The old grown young*, or *Harlequin's gambols; The padlock* (Charles Dibdin?); and *The shipwreck*, a "ballet of action" which could have been a translation of Villet; and Lemming's* *De schipbreuk, of De Korsaren op het eiland Ivica* of 1810. — Cuerton produced these shows and took part in them, either singing or whistling or playing the part of Harlequin himself. By introducing pantomimes and harlequinades, Cuerton brought light entertainment and British-style wit to Cape Town.

BIBLIOGRAPHY

BOSMAN, F.C.L.: *Drama en toneel in Suid-Afrika I.* Pretoria/Cape Town, 1928.   BOUWS, JAN: *Die musieklewe van Kaapstad, 1800-1850, en sy verhouding tot die musiekkultuur van Wes-Europa.* Cape Town/Amsterdam, 1966.   REBLING, E.: *Een eeu danskunst in Nederland.* Amsterdam, 1950.

SOURCES

Kaapsche Courant en Afrikaansche Berigter: 1813-1815.

—J.B.

DA COSTA, RAIE, *19 April 1905 in Cape Town; °26 August 1934 in London. Pianist and composer.

While studying at the South African College of Music* in Cape Town during the early 'twenties, Raie da Costa played with the Cape Town Municipal Orchestra*. In

1924 she went to London where her solo piano recitals were received with great acclaim but her performances became less frequent. In 1926 she composed a jazz song entitled *When I say good-bye to you*. This was an immediate success and led to her first contract with a recording company. After 1926 she concentrated on recordings until her death, following an operation. With few exceptions, the records contain jazz only, although the tunes and their arrangement almost invariably have classical overtones. On a few recordings she sang to her own accompaniment. — Her piano recordings are on Parlophone and HMV records, and on Imperial records under the name of Roy Dennis (see Discography of S.A. Recordings).

ARTICLE
Personalities I have met. *The Outspan*, 17 November 1933.

A FEW MELODIES
When I say good-bye to you, song (Joe Pessach). Keith Prowse, London, 1926.   You're in the way, song. Music Publishing Co., London, 1930.   At the court of Old King Cole, song (Paul Boyle). Keith Prowse & Co. Ltd., London, 1934.

BIBLIOGRAPHY
WINBUSCH, ROGER: *The gramophone*, October 1934.   VAN DER MERWE, F.Z.: *Suid-Afrikaanse musiekbibliografie, 1787-1952*. J.L. van Schaik Bpk., Pretoria, 1958.
—C.G.

DAINES, THOMAS   *1829(?) in London; °1880 in King William's Town. A dentist who propagated the tonic solfa system in South Africa.
During the period of his professional training in London, Daines attended singing classes arranged by a certain G.W. Martin, and was a member of a special choir which sang in St Paul's Cathedral. He became acquainted with the tonic solfa system, still new at the time, and when he was appointed to the permanent staff of Grey's Hospital in King William's Town (c.1860), he advertised a series of 30 classes in sight-singing and part-singing. During 1862 he applied the solfa method to Bantu choirs and on 22 December, 16 pupils of St Matthew's Mission School sang sacred and secular works. Five years later he conducted a Bantu choir of between 200 and 300 voices in partsongs, hymns and in a work by Purcell. The students also exhibited their prowess at singing from a modulator. — This culturally active man was responsible for the establishment of the library at King William's Town; a plaque perpetuates his memory.

SOURCES
The Daily Watchman: 1867.   Dr Burton's notes.   Interview with Daines's daughter, April 1970.
—C.G.H.

DALBERG, EVELYN,   *23 May 1939, in Leipzig; at present in Cape Town. Mezzo-soprano.
A daughter of Frederick Dalberg* and the German soprano Ellen Winter, Evelyn was trained at the Guildhall School of Music in London (1956-1957) where she obtained a Performer's Diploma. Her professional career began in the extra chorus at Covent Garden in 1953. After moving to Germany in 1957, she sang in *Tannhäuser* (Wagner), *The marriage of Figaro* (Mozart) and other works at the Coblenz Opera, but she also had further tuition in singing in the centres Munich, Mannheim and Coblenz. — Some months after her marriage to the German

bassoonist Werner Eichler (now a member of the Cape Town City Orchestra*), she came to South Africa (1964). Until her appointment at the South African College of Music as a lecturer in singing (1967), she sang mezzo-soprano roles for PACT. In addition to her work at the College, she continued to sing for CAPAB, in 1971 at the opening of the new Opera House in Cape Town, and in an opera production of NAPAC in 1970. She has also sung in *Messiah* and in *St John's passion,* and taken part in Bach cantatas performed by Barry Smith's* St George's Singers. The operas in which she has appeared in South Africa include *Un ballo in maschera, Falstaff, Martha, Madame Butterfly, Macbeth* and *Aïda.*

—Ed.

DALBERG (DALRYMPLE), FREDERICK, *7 January 1908 in Newcastle-on-Tyne; now in Stellenbosch. Bass.

Frederick Dalberg came to South Africa as a child of 12 and grew up in Pretoria, where he was a choirboy in St Alban's Cathedral for many years. He was the only boy soprano in the Pretoria Musical Association, of which Sydney Rees* was the conductor, and sang as soloist in concerts. At the age of nineteen he started taking lessons from Ernesto Ferri in Johannesburg, winning the bursary for the most promising singer at the Johannesburg Eisteddfod and recording songs in Afrikaans for the Columbia Gramophone Company. — With the financial assistance of Stanley Lezard he left South Africa in 1930 to study in Dresden. In 1931 he joined the Leipzig Opera, becoming first bass three years later. Whilst in Leipzig he sang in the Gewandhaus and in performances of Bach's works at the St Thomas Kirche, where for a number of years he sang the part of Christ in the annual Good Friday performances of either the *St Matthew* or the *St John passion.* After a period as first bass at the Berlin State Opera, he joined the Munich State Opera as principal bass (1946-1949). He returned to South Africa at this time to sing in the Johannesburg opera seasons and in concerts in various parts of the country. In 1951 he became first bass in Covent Garden, and participated in first performances of works by Benjamin Britten and William Walton, but in 1957 he resigned to accept the position of first bass in the Mannheim Opera. He stayed there until January 1970. During the latter part of this period, he was also a senior lecturer at the Musikhochschule in Mannheim. Some of his pupils are employed in the opera houses of Mannheim, Mainz and Würzburg. — During his career, Frederick Dalberg performed in many other opera centres, in Rome, Paris, Vienna, Lisbon, Brussels, Hamburg, Cologne, Stuttgart, Frankfurt and Düsseldorf, and was engaged for the Bayreuth Festivals to sing in *Götterdämmerung* (Hagen), *Meistersinger* (Pogner), *Ring der Nibelungen* (Fafner) and other Wagner works. He also sang in the Berlin, Glyndebourne and Schwetzingen Festivals and was well-known as a Lieder singer in German cities. For his achievements as operatic, oratorio and Lieder singer, the title of *Kammersänger* was conferred on him in Germany and he has the distinction of being listed in the second edition of the lexicon, *Unvergängliche Stimmen.* — In all these years Dalberg rarely sang in South Africa. In 1956 he appeared at a symphony concert of the Cape Town Municipal Orchestra; in 1960 he sang Sarastro in the *Magic flute* during the Union Festival in Bloemfontein; in 1963 he had the part of the school teacher in Lortzing's *Wilddief* produced by the Pretoria Opera Society* and in 1964 he sang the part of Mephisto in PACT'S production of Gounod's *Faust.* In his earlier years he recorded a few Afrikaans songs. He is married to the German soprano Ellen Winter; their daughter, Evelyn*, has been a lecturer in singing at the South

African College of Music*, Cape Town, since 1967. In January 1970, Frederick Dalberg returned to South Africa and assumed a part-time appointment as lecturer in singing at the Stellenbosch Conservatoire of Music*.

BIBLIOGRAPHY

KUTSCH, K.J. & RIEMENS, LEO: *Unvergängliche Stimmen: kleines Sängerlexikon,* 2nd edition, n.d.

SOURCES

STEGMANN, FRITS: Dis Dalberg se droom. *Die Huisgenoot,* 28 September 1962.   STEGMANN, FRITS: Frederick Dalberg vir die Eikestad. *Die Burger,* 8 January 1970.   Anonymous: Beroemde bas kom terug na Suid-Afrika. *Die Transvaler,* 15 January 1970.   VAN RENSBURG, MARY-ANN: Frederick Dalberg, ons eerste bekende sanger in Europa. *SAMT* 86, July 1974. National Documentation Centre for Music, HSRC, Pretoria.

—Ed.

DALE COLLEGE   King William's Town 10

DALRO   Dramatic Artistic and Literary Rights Organisation (Pty) Ltd, P.O. Box 9292, Johannesburg. Music publishers. See SAMRO.

DANIEL, GLADYS CONSTANCE,   *23 March 1890 in Kimberley; °7 August 1930 in Cape Town. Coloratura soprano, generally known as the "Natal (or even South African) Nightingale". Her real surname was Daniels, but she chose Gladys Daniel as her stage name.

Gladys Daniel received singing lessons from Frank Proudman*, Mme. Hooper-Rees* and Mme. Marie Louise Mazery in Kimberley, and then continued her studies in Durban under Grogan Caney* and Margaret Jewel. With the aid of funds raised by music-lovers, she went to London in 1919 (or 1920) and became Frederic King's student at the RAM for three years, receiving several medal awards. Her concert tour in South Africa in 1923 created such a stir that mounted police had to control the crowds outside the Cape Town City Hall on the night of her first concert. — At the beginning of 1924 Gladys Daniel went to Milan, where her voice was irrevocably spoilt by faulty teaching. From December 1926 until August 1927, and from March 1928 until June 1928 she was on concert tours in South Africa. During her last visit to England she got married and while there, she made several records. On 21 July 1929 she returned to South Africa to settle in Durban for a short while before going on a last tour which ended in Cape Town.

SOURCES

STEGMANN, FRITS: Gladys Daniel se sopraanstem het duisende bekoor. *Die Burger,* 24 August 1961.   STEGMANN, FRITS: Die Natalse nagtegaal wat haar stem laat verwoes het. *Die Burger,* 16 November 1961.   STEGMANN, FRITS: Gladys Daniel. *Dagbreek en Sondagnuus,* 21 April 1963.

—F.S.

DANTIE BROTHERS   Cape Malays

DANZA, LORENZO,   *10 October 1887 in Forli, near Naples; in 1966 back in Naples, after a distinguished career as pianist and teacher in South Africa.

Danza only started on a serious study of pianoforte playing when he was 13 years old. E. Marciano of Naples was his teacher and he completed the requirements for the Neapolitan Conservatoire Diploma before 1911, when he decided to settle in Johannesburg. The fortunes of musicians were at a low ebb at the time and in common with many other prominent performers, Danza had to play in restaurants and gardens. In May, he was employed by the Anglo-Austrian Café, together with his compatriot, Sign. Pizzo, to give popular Sunday afternoon concerts with their "orchestra". In the next year Danza was playing at the piano saloon of White & Sons during the mornings. He was known as a pianist by this time and gave a recital with the violinist, Selma Sacke (Whitehouse)*, for the Johannesburg Musical Society* early in 1913, and again in November, in the Caledonian Hall. They became a team that, until 1923, played frequently in Johannesburg, Pretoria and other South African centres. Their association continued after Selma Sacke's marriage to James Whitehouse* in 1914. — In this year they gave a successful recital for the Concerto Society, and in 1915 inaugurated the historic series of educational chamber music concerts in the Grand National Hotel. Assisted by Robert Kofsky*, they gave a series of four during the winter season; this became an annual event during the war years, and a feature of the City's musical life. Artists such as Mrs H. Durell, Frank Ferramosca, Mrs Hollins, Hermann Becker* and Otto Elias were enlisted for the performance of quartets and quintets. The programmes were of a uniformly high standard and covered the range of great composers, such as Mozart, Beethoven, Schumann, Arensky, Tchaikovsky, Dvořak, Franck and Elgar. C.A.O. Duggan*, music critic of *The Rand Daily Mail*, acknowledged their worth, and after a particularly successful chamber recital on 15 August 1918 singled out Danza for his artistry: "It is the delicacy of his delivery and the peculiarly appropriate grasp of a composer's requirements that makes his playing so distinctive and so essentially musical". — In the Selborne Hall on 17 August 1922, Danza's ensemble gave Elgar's *Quintet* its first South African performance; the work had to be repeated on demand at a special educational concert in the University Hall on 16 September. Early in 1923 Danza decided to return to Italy and an enthusiastic audience assembled in the City Hall for a farewell concert given by a number of artists who had been closely associated with him (26 March 1923). Lissant Collins* of *The Star* acknowledged "his excellent work for the elevation of artistic taste", and described the concert as "an altogether unmistakable sign of public recognition of the immense debt we owe him". — It is known that he taught at the Forli Conservatoire in Italy and that he gave many recitals on the Continent, but in November 1928, Mrs Whitehouse (Selma Sacke) announced in the *Natal Advertiser* that he intended leaving Europe for London to teach and give recitals with her. The London *Daily Telegraph* reported a successful joint recital given in the Aeolian Hall; but in September 1929 Danza was back in Johannesburg, co-operating with Isobel McLaren* in the City Hall. He was on the staff of Maud Harrison's Conservatoire, and when this changed hands in 1930, he established a private studio in Fatti's Building. For the next 27 years he again took the lead in chamber music and served the art with little financial advantage to himself. He formed a new group in 1931, with Ferramosca and Goldberg, which often performed in Johannesburg and Pretoria. Together with Bram Verhoef he formed the Johannesburg Piano Quartette in 1932, and performed with this violinist in recitals of violin sonatas by Beethoven, Schumann and Strauss. The next year he also co-operated with Hermann Becker's City String Quartette. — With the advent of national broadcasting (1936), he became a member of the Johannesburg Trio (Michael Doré*, Becker and Danza), which broadcast fortnightly. In addition, he performed concertos and gave numerous recitals for the Johannesburg Musical Society, alone and in conjunction with local and visiting artists, such as Bobby Evans (Debussy Festival, 1937), Margaret Fairless (1940),

Betsy de la Porte* (1940, 1944), Nella Wissema and Betty Pack* (1945) and Mischel Cherniavsky* (1953). Reasonably often, he played as soloist in Pretoria, Potchefstroom and other centres. During his last year in Johannesburg, before again leaving for Italy (1957), he gave a recital with Esther Mentz*, and at the 55th Anniversary Concert of the Johannesburg Musical Society in July, he was honoured by Prof. P.R. Kirby* for his selfless service to music, and for his long association with the Society. — At the instance of Count Labia, Italian Minister Pleni-potentiary in South Africa, Danza was nominated Cavallero d'Italia by King Victor Emmanuel of Italy for outstanding services to music in South Africa (January 1933). In 1933, he was Chairman of the Johannesburg centre, and vice president of the Transvaal section of the South African Society of Music Teachers*. For many years he acted as examiner in music for the University of South Africa and the Witwatersrand University, and he was at one time President of the Dante Alleghieri Society in Johannesburg.

ARTICLE
Music examinations in South Africa. *SAMT* 3, December 1932.

BIBLIOGRAPHY
K., W.H.: *The arts in South Africa.* Knox Printing & Publishing Co., Durban, 1943.

SOURCES
BENDER, ANNA: Uit toeka se dae. *Opus* 3/4, July 1972.   *The Star:* Johannesburg, 1923-1956. Who's who? *SAMT* 39, November 1950.   Details submitted by the Secretary of the Dante Alleghieri Society in Johannesburg.

—L.W.

D'ARCH FAMILY   Bloemfontein, Port Elizabeth I/5, Touring Theatre Groups 3

D'ARCY, PAUL   Johannesburg 1

D'ARCY READ OPERETTA COMPANY, THE.   This was a group of London entertainers who toured in South Africa between 1868 and 1874. D'Arcy Read initially specialized in farces such as *The ring and the keeper, The cousins* and *Belgravia,* works usually described as "charming and clever". They appeared in Graaff Reinet during 1868, stayed for 18 days and gave nine performances. In August 1869 they turned up in Durban, where they introduced a dramatic element into their variety programmes: on 20 August in Houghting's Hall they performed Dibden's ballad opera *The waterman,* with the support of H.A. Greene and a group of amateurs. — Although the public of Durban tired of Mr and Mrs D'Arcy Read within a few months, he continued to present variety programmes in Houghting's Music Hall until April 1871. During February and March his "spectroscope" attracted bigger and noisier audiences to a store situated at the lower end of West Street; it consisted of a large piece of plated glass, which he cleverly manipulated to create the illusion of moving ghosts in a play of light and shadow. Mr Read's "Ghostology" became the talk of the town, and attracted many Indians, for whom special shows were arranged. In more serious mood, there was a musical background of extracts from *Faust,* to accompany the performance of his so-called "impersonators". By the middle of April, Durban had nothing more to offer him, and he left for Port Elizabeth, where between 1 May and 5 July 1871 he gave 13 performances of Bouller's operetta *The ring and the keeper,* crammed in together with dramas, solos, duets and Negro spirituals. He must have offered his Ghostology there too, because it was on the programme when he began to play in Albany Hall, Grahamstown, during July. In Port Elizabeth, between May and June 1872, he enlarged on the supernatural element, to create entertainments entitled *Faust or the Virginian mummy* and *A haunted mill.* — In July the group were again in Grahamstown, where they gave six performances of an operetta entitled *Ghost.* The press found it "charming". From Grahamstown the D'Arcy Reads went to Kimberley, and in 1874 they returned to Graaff Reinet with two enormous wagons having some likeness to the mausoleum of an Indian Prince; they were also described as castles-on-wheels. The town hall in Graaff Reinet was too small for Mr Read's ghostly performances; so he hired the steam mills, where he let heads float about, devils and angels appear and vanish, while voices in the background sang arias from Gounod's *Faust.* After Graaff Reinet he announced further visits to Uitenhage and Port Elizabeth, which did not materialise.

BIBLIOGRAPHY
HENNING, C.G.: *A cultural history of Graaff Reinet, 1786-1886.* D. Phil. thesis, UP, 1971, published as *Graaff-Reinet, a cultural history.* Bulpin, Cape Town, 1975.   JACKSON, G.S.: *Music in Durban, 1850-1900.* Witwatersrand University Press Publication Series No. 6, Johannesburg, 1970.

SOURCES
Graaff Reinet Herald: September 1868 and January 1874.   *Eastern Province Herald:* May-July 1871, May-June 1872, 6 February 1874.

—G.S.J. amplified by C.G.H.

DARTER: A family engaged in the South African music trade after the middle of the 19th century. In February 1945 (nearly a hundred years later) their headquarters in Adderley Street were completely destroyed by fire, leading also to the loss of their archives. The following is a skeletal reconstruction of the history of the family to which the firm owes its name.

George Blackford Silver Darter (born in Reading, Berkshire about 1803) came to South Africa in about 1849-1950 with three children born from his first marriage with Anne Giles. He was married for the second time to a certain Mary Elizabeth Underwood by whom he had a daughter, Harriet Silver. Of the first three children, two were boys: **George Silver** (born September 1833 in Reading) and **William Silver** (born June 1838 in Reading). George (senior) was a qualified piano tuner, and quite well-to-do. In his estate his profession was described as "gentleman". When he established the firm (1850), his eldest boy was about 17 years old and the second boy 12. — The firm specialised in selling sheet music and in importing pianos, although they probably sold other musical instruments as well. It prospered, and when G.B.S. Darter died on 27 July 1879, he not only owned the firm in Cape Town, but he also had a fully furnished house, including a silver service, in London. He had a contract drawn up on 30 March 1874 in which he left the Cape business to his sons George and William. His testament of 18 April confirms the legacy. It was firmly established at the time and so successful that GBS regarded it as sufficient provision for his two sons. The rest of his estate, the house and the bank account in London and other movable property, he left to his second wife and their daughter Harriet. — Of the two sons who inherited the business in Cape town, George Silver was a pianist and an active young man. William died in the fashionable St John's Wood Park in London on 28 February 1911. His profession was given as "retired dealer". George died on 20 March 1894, in Rondebosch and his wife, a South African, Elizabeth Johanna Jurgens, who had borne him five children, died in June 1898.

William Silver must have retired from the business between 1898 and 1910. — Very little is known of George Silver Darter's career. Before Neumann Thomas* was appointed to play the organ in St George's Cathedral*, George had been the organist, though he was actually a pianist and the composer of a few salon pieces. For the visit of Prince Alfred (later the Duke of Edinburgh), he composed a *Bicycle galop* and a song, *Prince Alfred's welcome,* which was sung by Mr Ashley of Cape Town; a copy printed on satin was handed to the young prince. These, and his other works were printed by the firm of Darter and Sons. Darter describes himself as being "pianist to HRH the Duke of Edinburgh". From this date (1860) onwards, and until 1943, the firm continued to publish the compositions of South Africans. As far as can be established, they were mostly songs of a lighter or of a patriotic genre. — In November 1864, George became responsible for the opening of a branch of Darter's in Main Street, Port Elizabeth, which still existed in 1916, and before 1912 the firm had further branches in Grahamstown, Stellenbosch and Uitenhage. During his stay in Port Elizabeth, George played piano at the Grey Institute (9 May 1865), and again in June of that year when he co-operated with Mosenthal and Walter Bolus*, but by 1868 he had returned to Cape Town and was then official accompanist to James Harper's* touring company.

WORKS BY G.S. DARTER

Bicycle galop. Published by Darter & Sons and printed by Chappel & Co., London n.d. The Cape Volunteer Artillery march. Darter's Pianoforte and Music Warehouse, 1860. Platte klip, for pianoforte. Published by Darter & Sons, printed by De Villiers & Co., Cape Town, probably in 1860.   Prince Alfred's welcome song (Major Longmore). Published by Darter's Pianoforte and Music Warehouse; printed by De Villiers & Co., Cape Town, 1860. Two polkas: 1. The grotto 2. Le jour de naissance. Darter & Sons, Cape Town, and B. Williams of London, n.d.   The Volunteer Rifle Corps waltzes. Darter & Sons, Cape Town, 1860.   Marche funébre. Darter & Sons, Cape Town, 1882.   Reverie by the waterfall. No details

BIBLIOGRAPHY
VAN DER MERWE, F.Z.: *Suid-Afrikaanse musiekbibliografie, 1787-1952.* J.L. van Schaik, Pretoria, 1958.

SOURCES

EP Herald: November 1864 - October 1865.   Information on Harper supplied by Dr Jan Bouws.   Correspondence with A.H.W. Penver of Cape Town, 1962.   Registrar of Estates, CP: MOOC 6/9/71, DN 7513   MOOC 6/9/327, DN 77 MOOC 6/9/678, DN 2816   Testament of G.B.S. Darter.   Research by Dr C.G. Henning.   Research by J.M. Smalberger, Cape Town.

—Ed.

DAVIES, A.W   Wellington

DAVIES, DUDLEY, *7 February 1928 in Springs; at present in Bloemfontein. Ballet dancer, teacher and director of PACOFS Ballet.

Davies received his early training from the Gardener sisters in Springs. Later he was taught by Arnold Dover, Cecily Robinson* and Dulcie Howes*. He was a member of the Johannesburg Theatre Ballet, then of the Cape Town University Ballet*, and in London in March 1952, he was accepted by the Sadler's Wells Theatre Ballet for a tour on the Continent, in Rhodesia and England. During the 1954 South African tour he married the ballerina, Patricia Miller*. — He returned to South Africa with his wife in 1956, to join the staff of the University of Cape Town Ballet, opening his own studio two years later. In 1962 Davies moved to Johannesburg, where he was invited to produce *Coppélia*, the first ballet staged in the Civic Theatre* for the Johannesburg City Ballet. He became principal of the City Ballet's Academy, and worked for the newly-formed Ballet Transvaal. In 1964 he was appointed Director of Ballet to the Performing Arts Council of the Orange Free State (PACOFS).

—M.G.

DAVIS, P. AND SONS   Piano Music II/2, Port Elizabeth

DAWES, HERBERT EDMUND, *30 April 1897 in Lydenburg, Transvaal; at present in Durban. Composer.

In Durban, he studied with Florence Cheesbrough (piano), William Deane* (organ), Amon Bilmark* (cello) and Richard Cherry* (composition), obtaining the Teacher's Diploma of Trinity College in 1922. At the Natal Eisteddfodau of 1920 and 1921 he received gold and silver medals for composition, and for the next three years served as Secretary on the Eisteddfod Committee. With the introduction of a broadcasting system in Natal towards the end of 1924, he was invited to become music controller. In 1927 he was appointed Studio Manager. Transferred to the Head Offices of the SABC in Johannesburg in 1947 he was Director of English Programmes and later became Supervisor of Music and Drama. Edmund Dawes retired in 1959. — In a broadcast talk in November 1939, he launched the South African "Composer's Library", the primary objects of which were to encourage composers in South Africa, and to collect their works in a representative library. The idea was partially realized, and a valuable collection is now housed in the Music Library of the SABC in Johannesburg. During 1948 Edmund Dawes organised the SABC National Competition for South African composers, and in the following year the SABC Festival of South African Music.

WORKS

A. Vocal

1. Songs
To the sea, for contralto (Lola Fearnley). Ms., 1920.   Give me a song, for baritone (J.R. McCarthy). Ms., 1925.   If I were king, for baritone (J.H. McCarthy). Ms., 1925.   A song of the sea, for baritone (Allen Cunningham). Ms., 1926.   Venetian night, for soprano (Hugo von Hofmannsthal). Ms., 1935.   Appeal, for soprano (Ruth Pryor). Ms., 1935.   April, for soprano (John Hanlon). Ms., 1936.   Under the eucalyptus trees, for soprano (Dawes). Ms., 1943.   Late leaves, for mezzo-soprano (Walter Savage Landor). Ms., 1952.   So, we'll go no more a'roving, for mezzo-soprano (Byron). Ms., 1954.

2. Church choir and organ
Thou wilt keep him, anthem (words Biblical). Ms., 1937.

B. Instrumental

1. Orchestra
Allegretto for strings. Ms., 1923.   Gavotte (in the old style). Ms., 1924.   Two pieces for orchestra. Ms., 1927:   1. Summer evening   2. Autumn leaves.

2. Pianoforte
Barcarolle. Ms., 1923.   Sea idyll. Ms., 1924.   Impromptu in C minor. Ms., 1924.   The sea.
Ms., 1930.   Legend. Ms., 1940.

—Ed.

DAWS, GEORGE, Violinist in the Cape Colony between 1875 and 1893.

In 1875 Daws arranged *God save the Queen* for the laying of the foundation stone of the new Houses of Parliament, Cape Town; it had a concluding stanza by the Very Reverend the Dean of Cape Town. He toured South Africa in 1880 with his wife (a pianist from the Crystal Palace School of Arts), who acted as accompanist; they were assisted by Miss Emily Seaton, a contralto and female tenor, famous for her vocal impersonations. The repertoire of the violinist included a Beethoven sonata, duets for piano and violin, and various arrangements calculated to appeal to unsophisticated audiences. Daws is known to have given three performances in Graaff Reinet, on 10, 11 and 15 May, at which George Hind* assisted as player on the piccolo and clarionet. After that, Daws was in Cape Town, where he conducted the Cape Town Choral Society. — In January 1887 he appeared in Queenstown, where he composed a *Jubilee March* for the Jubilee Concert organised by the *Queenstown Free Press.* Until 1893 he performed at about 16 concerts, mostly fund-raising efforts for the Anglican and Methodist churches; also at smokers' concerts for the local cricket club, variety concerts, and one for Mr Welch*. Daws must have been organist of the Dutch Reformed Church, for he is mentioned on several occasions in this connection: in September 1888, he inaugurated the new organ for the Molteno DR Church; in January 1889, he played a new harmonium presented to the Queenstown church and in September 1890, Daws officiated at a service to mark the Rev. S.P. Naudé's* 30th year as minister. He also revived the Choral Society, now called the Philharmonic Society; after rehearsing for 6 months, the group performed selections from *Messiah* in December 1891. In August 1892 Daws made his last appearance in Queenstown, leading the Wesleyan Church choir. Later he took part in a fundraising concert for the Anglican Church at Dordrecht (August 1893).

WORKS
The National anthem, arranged for the laying of the foundation stone of the new Houses of Parliament, published by Van de Sandt de Villiers & Co., Cape Town, 1875.   Jubilee march, for the *Queenstown Free Press.* Ms., 1887.

BIBLIOGRAPHY
HENNING C.G.: *A cultural history of Graaff Reinet, 1786-1886.* D. Phil. thesis, UP, 1971, published as *Graaff Reinet, a cultural history (1786-1886).* Bulpin, Cape Town, 1975.   VAN DER MERWE, F.Z.: *Suid-Afrikaanse musiekbibliografie, 1787-1952.* J.L. van Schaik, Pretoria, 1958.

SOURCES
Graaff Reinet Herald: 8-15 May, 1880.   *The Queenstown Free Press:* June 1887 - August 1893.

—C.G.H.

DAY, CHARLES WILLIAM. Builder and bandmaster in King William's Town between 1876 and at least 1902.

Day was associated with amateur brass bands in King William's Town for about thirty years. In all, he established three: The Town Volunteer Artillery Band, which lasted from 1876 to 1889 (although one source states that Day's "First Town Band" was established in 1881); the Band of the KWT Athletic and Gymnastic Club in 1891, and the Town Guard Band which, unlike the previous two, continued to exist, because it was merged with the KWT Borough Band (1902-1970). Apart from the creation and conductorship of these bands, little is known of Day's activities, except that he published a few compositions.

WORKS

The KWT volunteer artillery schottische. *Cape Colonist,* 10 March 1883.   Charter march. C.A. Jay (late J. Hyde), King William's Town, 1897.   Rhodesia bold, march. Darter & Sons, Cape Town, n.d.   Heroes of Mafeking, march for the pianoforte. M. Heller & Co., London. Composed for the Mafeking celebrations in KWT, and played by the Town Guard Band, under the direction of the composer, n.d.   Zambezi Falls, waltz. Robert Whiteaker, Aylesburg, England, n.d.

BIBLIOGRAPHY

Van der Merwe, F.Z.: *Suid-Afrikaanse musiekbibliografie, 1787-1952.* J.L. van Schaik, Pretoria, 1958.

SOURCES

Dr Burton's notebooks.   KWT Museum: miscellaneous material, programmes etc.

—C.G.H.

Day, james   Port Elizabeth I/4(i)

Deale, george henry,   *1864 in Dublin; °24 January 1923 in Bloemfontein. Conductor and organist.

Deale was educated at Wesley College in Dublin, and subsequently at St Patrick's Cathedral School, where he was a member of the Cathedral choir; later he was a chorister in the choir of the Chapel Royal. Whilst an organ student at the Royal Irish Academy of Music, he was employed as organist by churches in Dublin, including St Ardoen's Parish Church and the Molyneux Church. — Deale came to South Africa in June 1902 on account of ill-health, entered the Department of Public Works in the OFS and settled in Bloemfontein, where he opened a bookshop and became organist of the Trinity Wesleyan Church, a position he held until shortly before his death. Sacred concerts and choral performances under his direction, such as *The crucifixion* (Stainer), *Messiah, Ruth* (Gaul) and *The daughter of Jaïrus* (Stainer), enlivened church music in the town. Shortly after his arrival he revived the defunct Bloemfontein Musical Society. He gave performances of *Hiawatha* (Coleridge-Taylor), *The creation* (Haydn), *St Paul* (Mendelssohn), *Stabat mater* (Rossini) and *The revenge* (Stanford), before the society collapsed in 1911. — During the four years of the revived Society's existence, it held an annual Festival, generally in August, at which the choir sang with visiting British soloists. After the first successful effort in 1907, they proudly announced that they had obtained the patronage of distinguished personages including Lord and Lady Methuen and the Earl and Countess of Selborne. As a result of representations to the Railways, a special concession was introduced for country enthusiasts who wished to attend the Festival. The performance of *St Paul* by more than 100 choir and orchestral members marked a climax. The stage of the Grand Theatre had to be enlarged to accommodate these large forces, unfortunately to the detriment of co-operation between singers and instrumentalists. For the performance of *Elijah* in 1911, the military band of the Cameronians strengthened the Bloemfontein orchestra, but the press criticism became more outspoken on this occasion and the *Bloemfontein Post* described the instrumental contribution as being "a little ragged". Deale had had considerable difficulty in assembling musicians for this performance and after 1911 the Society again subsided into obscurity. — Deale was also keenly interested in amateur operatic work, and became responsible for the musical direction of the Bloemfontein Amateur Dramatic and Operatic Society's productions in 1904-1905 of *Les cloches de Corneville* (Planquette) and *The pirates of Penzance* (Gilbert and Sullivan). In 1916 and 1918 he directed *Dorothy* (Cellier) and *Iolanthe* (Gilbert and Sullivan), which were produced for the Garrick Club. The role of Dorothy was sung by Cecilia Wessels*, appearing in her first production at the age of 21. — One of Deale's last appearances as conductor was at the Peace Sunday concert in August, 1919, when the massed choirs of Bloemfontein sang in the Grand Theatre, under his direction. Indifferent health during the last years of his life compelled him to relinquish most of his musical duties.

BIBLIOGRAPHY
HUMAN, J.L.K.: *Die musieklewe in Bloemfontein 1900-1939.* D. Phil. thesis, UOFS, 1977.

SOURCES
The Friend: 1904-1922 and 25 January 1923. *The Bloemfontein Pelican:* 17 December 1904, 3 June 1905.

—E.H.S.

DEALE, S.F Bloemfontein I/2

DEANE, WILLIAM, *in 1869 in Eastbourne; °7 September 1954 in Durban. Organist and music teacher.

Deane received his training as an organist at Christchurch, Oxford under Dr C.H. Lloyd, and in Paris under Louis Viérne - both celebrated in their day as organists and composers. To the former Deane owed his deep affection for the Anglican Church service and to the latter his life-long enthusiasm for French organ music. — He first appeared on the South African musical scene in 1894 when he was appointed organist of the Cathedral of St Michael and St George in Grahamstown in succession to his brother-in-law A.H. Day*, who had relinquished the post after three years, to become the borough organist of Pietermaritzburg. Deane's musical activities in the Eastern Province sometimes took him to Port Elizabeth; it is known that on Friday 18 September 1896 he was guest organist at the Church of St Augustine in a performance of the *Messe solennelle* by Gounod. — In 1910 he moved to Johannesburg to become organist of the Anglican Church of St Mary's. This new and more active environment offered him and his musical wife more scope for their talents and with the co-operation of other artists they presented a series of pianoforte and organ recitals sufficiently varied to include works by J.S. Bach, a symphonic poem by Sibelius and César Franck's *Variations symphoniques.* One of their concerts was devoted entirely to Russian music. But the centre of his musical activities was St Mary's where he directed performances of *The last judgement* (Spohr), *Messiah* (Handel) and *Te Deum* (Sullivan). — Deane left Johannesburg in 1920 to go to Durban, where he spent the remaining 34 years of his life. Frank Proudman*, who had held the dual positions of borough organist and organist at St Paul's since the year 1908, resigned both to take up the post of borough organist in Kimberley. Deane arrived in August to take up his new appointment at St Paul's.

317

It was however his wife, Grace Batchelder, who first played in public in the Art Gallery (August 1920). She had been trained at the RCM and was regarded as a highly gifted pianist. She was also an organist and a singer and appeared in the Town Hall as one of the finalists in the vocal section of the 1922 Natal Eisteddfod. Unfortunately her career as a peformer was considerably marred by the increasing deafness of her later years. — For 17 years Deane was organist and choirmaster at St Paul's, being assisted in the later stages by Mr W. Everett, a local bank manager who trained the choir. When in 1937 the latter gentleman agreed to assume the duties of organist and choirmaster - which by virtue of his professional occupation he was obliged to do in an honorary capacity - Deane sought an appointment elsewhere. This he succeeded in obtaining at the Anglican Church of St John the Divine in Clarke Road. — By vocation and temperament Deane was essentially a church organist, and although he was meticulous in training a church choir he very rarely appeared in the role of choral conductor. His recital programmes revealed the traditional preference for the works of J.S. Bach and Mendelssohn, but most of all he loved to play the works of Guilmant and Marcel Dupré. On the few occasions when he returned to Europe on vacation he made a pilgrimage to the church of Saint-Sulpice in Paris to pay homage at the shrine of Marcel Dupré. After that he would go to London where he attended one service after another - sometimes as many as four on a Sunday - just to compare different styles of organ-playing. — A number of church organists in South Africa owe their early training to William Deane. From all of his pupils he demanded meticulous execution. He offered two main precepts: learn by listening to others; and (as he would so often say) "Never be dull. Let the words of the service go across." If this remarkably eventempered and self-effacing musician betrayed any kind of pique in criticising his pupils, it was usually for the reason that they had neglected to infuse the words of the service with meaning by an appropriate organ registration. — He is still remembered as somewhat prone to eccentricity. As a short, fair and rather stockily built young man, he had rescued some small boys from a blazing school room and his face was heavily scarred as a result of burns. This disfigurement, combined with a very prominent lower lip, gave him an aspect of severity which belied his true feelings. In later life he was highly strung and nervy. — At the funeral service of William Deane his instrument maintained an eerie silence. A power failure in the early afternoon necessitated the use of a piano.

WORKS

Cinderella, petite valse pour pianoforte. Grocott & Sherry, Grahamstown, printed by C.G Röder, Leipzig, before 1909.   Danse gracieuse, for pianoforte. Stanley Lucas, Weber & Co., London, n.d.   Prayer of the African people (John McCormack). Mackay Brothers and Argus Co., Cape Town, n.d.   The Southern Cross grand waltz. Grocott & Sherry, Grahamstown, printed by Vincent Music Co., n.d.   Victoria waltz. Grocott & Sherry, printed by C.G. Röder, Leipzig, n.d.   Violetta, valse de salon. Stanley Lucas, Weber & Co., London; printed by C.G. Röder, Leipzig, 1897.

BIBLIOGRAPHY

VAN DER MERWE, F.Z.: *Suid-Afrikaanse musiekbibliografie, 1787-1952.* J.L. van Schaik, Pretoria, 1958.   WOLPOWITZ, LILY: *James and Kate Hyde and the development of music in Johannesburg up to the First World War.* J.L. van Schaik, Pretoria, 1969.

SOURCES
Natal Mercury Pictorial: September 1920 to November 1922. Additional information from: Mr Patrick Chambers, Durban; Mr W.A. Gardner, Natal; Mr Errol Slatter, Durban; Mr E.C. Vincer, Durban.

—G.S.J.

DEAS, PROF. S. W.H. Bell, Higher Educational Institutions I/2, M. Whiteman

DE BEER, ANGELIQUE Pierre de Beer, Discography, C.W. Israel, Johannesburg 2, Johannesburg Musical Society, Theatres and Concert Halls VI/1

DE BEER, DAWID Higher Educational Institutions II/3

DE BEER, DOREEN MARIE (MRS RUMBELOW) Pierre de Beer

DE BEER, MRS PIERRE Pierre de Beer, Discography

DE BEER, PIERRE JOHANNES MARCELLUS, *30 November 1877 in Breda, Northern Brabant; °20 August 1932 at Camps Bay, Cape. Concert pianist.

Since early childhood the brother and sister, Pierre and Angelique de Beer, children of Marcelis and Elizabeth (née De Haan), were known in Holland as concert artists and, it is said, appeared together before the Queen. It is presumed that Pierre received his training at the Amsterdam Conservatoire and won a silver medal for exceptional achievement in a music examination. His fellow student, who won the gold medal, was Mark Hambourg. — About 1899 the brother and sister emigrated to South Africa where Pierre intended accepting employment in the Mount Nelson Trio in Cape Town. Here his sister was soon married to a Portuguese doctor, Dr Lomalino of Lourenço Marques, where she settled after her marriage, giving music lessons and playing in concerts. Beatrice Marx* describes her as follows: "She was a highly-talented, temperamental creature, with Pierre's blonde colouring and a beautiful white skin. Had she been less brilliant as a pianist, she might have made her name as an opera singer. At one of these concerts she sang the big Santuzza duet from *Cavalleria rusticana* with a visiting Belgian tenor, tossing off the accompaniment at the same time". These concerts took place in about 1906; both Beatrice Marx and Pierre de Beer took part in them. — Pierre's marriage to the 18 year-old soprano, Lilian Elizabeth de Marillac (stage name, Lilian Holbrook), originally from England, was solemnised in 1900. In 1917 he became a South African citizen and of the three sons and two daughters born of his marriage, Doreen Marie (now Mrs Rumbelow) was talented as a pianist. After De Beer's death she took over her father's teaching practice and continued it for a number of years. — Fellow-members of Pierre de Beer in the Mount Nelson Trio (1900) were Jan Luyt* and S.M. van Erkel; apparently they played together until 1906, when Pierre moved to Johannesburg. He and Beatrice Marx gave a great many recitals in the city and also in other centres (including Lourenço Marques). From 1909 to 1911 he was conductor of the Pretoria Hollandsch Mannenkoor* for whom he ordered sheet music from Holland from the Maatschappij tot Bevordering der Toonkunst, Afdeling Amsterdam. — During the years 1911 to 1912 Pierre had the post of musical director of the Grand Theatre Company, Empire Theatres, Johannesburg. Early in 1912, however, he gave a piano recital in Hawthorndene, Wynberg, Cape; it is quite possible that he had resigned his position at the theatre to take up a post at the South African College of Music* in Cape Town. Before starting on his new duties, he and his wife undertook a tour during the closing months of 1912 and the early part of 1913 with a concert party under the direction of Gregor Cherniavsky, which was described as "The World Renowned Russian Violinist and His Famous Concert Party". — One of the first of the many prominent South African musicians trained by Pierre de Beer, was the *diseuse*, Pattie Price*, who was his pupil at the SACM from 1914 to 1919. He also gave piano lessons to the soprano, Cecilia Wessels* (1917-1920). Between 1913 and 1930 he played at Denholm Walker's* organ recitals (1913), **with Theo Wendt's* Orchestra (1915-1930), made records for the Edison Bell Company (see Discography) with his wife, appeared with Elsie Hall*** (1925), and accompanied Anna Pavlova and her 42 dancers who came to South Africa in 1926. — His health was failing and after the tour with Pavlova he had to relinquish all his musical duties. He was in Europe for medical treatment during 1928-1929 and on 27 January 1930, he was welcomed back by an announcement in the *Cape Times* that he was to play Liszt's *Piano concerto in E flat* with the Municipal Orchestra on the 30th. However, his health remained precarious and he died eighteen months later. — Pierre de Beer had an engaging personality. His colleagues and pupils spoke of him with affection and from newspaper cuttings dealing with his activities as an artist, it appears that he had endeared himself to the critics and the public. After his death the Cape Town Municipal Orchestra, under the direction of William Pickerill*, gave a concert in which the first item was dedicated to his memory. On the programme (25.8.1932) it was framed in black and read: "In Memory of Pierre de Beer who devoted the major portion of his life to the cause of music in South Africa. Andantino ... Haydn".

SONG

SA Union, national anthem (words and music). Ms., n.d.

BIBLIOGRAPHY

MARX, BEATRICE: *She shall have music. The memoirs of Beatrice Marx*. W.J. Flesch & Partners, Cape Town, 1961.

SOURCES

Cape Times: January - March 1930. Cutting from a Pietermaritzburg newspaper, dated 3 November (?). Programmes 19.12-1932, loaned by Mrs L.T. Hopkins (his daughter). Correspondence with members of the family and original correspondence addressed to Pierre de Beer.

—E.C.

DEDEKIND, O. AND W. Evangelical Lutheran Church (Hermannsburg 2)

DEFRIES (DE VRIES) DANIEL N., °27 October 1920 in Johannesburg. Conductor.

Diamonds attracted Defries to Kimberley, where he was remembered later as "a good-natured diamond-broker, who played an enormous trombone". He was probably the conductor of the Kimberley Orchestral Society, which performed at his farewell concert on 11 August 1884. On this occasion he also directed a choir consisting chiefly of members of the Kimberley Choral Society*. During the first gold rush he turned up in Barberton where he was one of the founders and the first conductor of the Barberton Orchestral Society (March 1887). He was also chairman of the Smoking Club, which arranged weekly entertainments for men, and a member of the committee which founded the Philharmonic Society in July 1887. His farewell concert took place in January 1889. — Although he informed the newspapers that he was returning to England, Defries remained in Johannesburg. There he succeeded Francis Crane* as temporary conductor of the Wanderers Orchestra, which from

320

November 1889 gave performances in the Wanderers Hall every Sunday afternoon, until James Hyde* was appointed permanent conductor of the Wanderers in 1892. Since that date he must have devoted himself to his business interests. He is not mentioned in the press again.

BIBLIOGRAPHY
MARÉ, BLYDA: *Die musieklewe van Barberton tussen die jare 1885 en 1914.* B.Mus. script, UP, 1967.

SOURCES
The Diamond Fields Advertiser: 1884 and 19 February 1930.   Information supplied by Dr L. Wolpowitz.

—E.H.S.

DE GROEN, JOSEPH SAMSON (JOS), *24 April 1914 in The Hague; °28 July 1978 in Johannesburg. Bassoonist and teacher of woodwind instruments.

Jos de Groen studied at the Royal Conservatoire in The Hague from 1927 to 1930 and, at the age of seventeen, became a member of the orchestra at Groningen. Four years later he was invited to join the Israel Philharmonic Orchestra (initially conducted by Toscanini) as chief bassoonist. In 1939 he joined the Orchestre National de Belgique as chief bassoonist. At the same time he was lecturer in bassoon at the Royal Conservatoire of Music in Brussels. — In 1946 he came to South Africa where he joined the Johannesburg City Orchestra as chief bassoonist and remained with this orchestra until it was disbanded. He was then recruited into the National Symphony Orchestra of the SABC. From 1966 until 1977 he was senior lecturer for four woodwind instruments in the Department of Music of the University of Pretoria. His pupils include Gerrit Bon*, Eva Tamassy*, Jos de Groen Jnr (at one time chief bassoonist of the Mexico Symphony Orchestra), Jimmy Reinders (second clarinettist of the National Symphony Orchestra of the SABC) and L. Hurwitz (chief bassoonist of the London Symphony Orchestra). — Jos de Groen was also the founder of chamber music societies - including the Riet Trio* - and the coach and conductor of the Pretoria Youth Orchestra, the Potchefstroom Symphony Orchestra, the Johannesburg Baroque Orchestra and the Wonderboom Band. As a soloist he was well-known in South Africa.

SOURCES
SABC Bulletin: 27 March 1954; 7 September 1967

—Ed.

DE GROOFF, HILDA   Middelburg

DE GROOT, M.   Pretoria 1

DE GROOTE FAMILY ENSEMBLE, THE, consisted of Pierre de Groote and members of his family: Hermina (his wife) and his sons Oliver, Philip and Steven. Chamber music group.

Pierre de Groote comes from a well-known musical family in Brussels, Belgium. During childhood he practised the art with his mother, sister and brothers (one of whom, Lucien, lived in Johannesburg for a while) and perpetuated this tradition of music in the family circle in later years. He married Joyce Harriette Mace in Europe, and they had four sons. In 1947 they emigrated to South Africa with the two eldest children, André and Oliver, Pierre having accepted a music post in Johannesburg. The youngest sons, Philip and Steven, were born here. Even before André returned to Belgium in 1956 for music specialization, the De Groote parents had played chamber music with him and Lucien, and had formed the Pierre de Groote quartette. — After the death of Joyce in 1960, Pierre moved to Stellenbosch with the three youngest boys, and became lecturer in violin at the Stellenbosch Conservatoire*. In 1961 he was married again, to Hermina Verster (violinist). The family settled in the suburb Voëltjiesdorp (now known as Onder-Papagaaiberg), and there the three children were introduced to serious music. The piano was always open, sheet music on the stand, and a number of recorders and other instruments at hand. Consequently, games were frequently interrupted as the boys took up instruments and played through music that happened to be on the piano. Then followed attempts to sight-read chamber-music scores, often on instruments other than those specified by the composer; until one day, just "for fun", Pierre played through Mozart's *Piano trio in G* with the two elder boys. Subsequently the family played chamber music together, until Oliver suddenly declared that they needed a viola and that he would play it. And so the De Groote family ensemble came into being. — In due course the group was requested to participate in concerts. Initially, they performed single items, then they presented a recital during a refresher course at the Stellenbosch Conservatoire, an evening concert at the Stellenbosch Arts Festival, concerts by invitation of the Cape Town University, and at schools, music societies and churches in the Peninsula. Since 1965 the group has played for the Cape Town Concert Club, undertaken a tour for PACOFS (1966), given a series of concerts for CAPAB (1968) and broadcast several times for the SABC. — In January 1969, within the framework of the cultural treaties between the Republic and The Netherlands and Germany, the De Groote Family Ensemble was invited to tour for four weeks in these countries. On their own initiative, they organised further concerts in Belgium and in Switzerland, so that there were altogether 14 performances, including three in Brussels (in which the eldest son, André, professor in Brussels, participated), two in The Hague (one presented in the historical Mauritshuis), and six in Germany (Bonn, Kassel and Hamburg), as well as one television performance in Geneva. — Since this tour and in the normal course of events, the group has dispersed.

SOURCES

Suid-Afrikaanse musiekaand. *Res Musicae* III/2, December 1956. Jong Musikante. (André de Groot). *Res Musicae* III/3, March 1957. STEGMANN, FRITS: Die tweede Stellenbosse Kunsfees. *Res Musicae* VIII/2, December 1961. National Documentation Centre for Music, HSRC, Pretoria.

—E.C.

DE GROOTE. **Pierre,** *7 December 1913 in Brussels, Belgium; now in Cape Town. Violinist, senior lecturer, former head of the string section of the South African College of Music*, at present part time teacher of violin, SACM.

Pierre's father was André de Groote, private tutor of the future Leopold III of Belgium. Together with his mother, Berthe Busine-de Groote (twice winner of the Belgian Prix-de-Rome for composition), Pierre, his brothers and a sister already played chamber music during their childhood. At the Conservatoire Royal de Musique, Brussels, he studied violin under Albert Zimmer (1929-1934) and chamber music under Maurice Dambois (1930-1933) and obtained the Institute's diploma for virtuosity in chamber music (1933) and another for violin playing (1934). Two years

322

later he became the leader of the Belgian National Orchestra, as well as a member of the Gertler quartette; in 1942 he established a De Groote string quartette. Highlights of his career in Europe were a performance of Alban Berg's *Lyrical suite* by the André Gertler string quartette at the International Festival of Contemporary Music in Venice (1937), and six broadcasts for the BBC by the De Groote string quartette (1946-1947). — In Johannesburg De Groote was lecturer in music at the University of the Witwatersrand (1947-1960), and in 1953 leader of the Johannesburg City Orchestra*. From 1954 he was also leader of the SABC Studio Orchestra. He formed the second Pierre de Groote quartette, together with his first wife, his brother Lucien and his son André. At Stellenbosch in 1961, after his marriage to Hermina Verster, they and the three boys formed the De Groote Family Ensemble, which he led until 1969. As senior lecturer and head of the string section he also became leader of the string quartette of the SACM at the University of Cape Town in 1965. Vincent Frittelli*, Roy Malan, Derek Rabin and Pierre Maroleau are among his prominent pupils. From 1974-78 he was coach and conductor of the Orange Free State Youth Orchestra. — De Groote is known in South Africa and in Europe as a violin soloist, and as a leader of orchestras and chamber orchestras. During the Van Riebeeck Festival in Cape Town (1952) he and Szymon Goldberg gave a performance of Bach's *Concerto for two violins*. The next year, the University String Quartette performed all the Beethoven string quartettes for the SABC with himself as leader. This series was repeated at the University of Cape Town. — **Joyce Harriette (née Mace)** (first wife of Pierre de Groote and mother of his sons), *8 January 1914 in Brighouse, Yorkshire, England; °1960 in Johannesburg. Violinist. Joyce de Groote was trained at the Conservatoire Royal de Musique in Brussels where, after two years' violin study under Albert Zimmer, she won the conservatoire's first prize for violin playing. She continued her violin study from 1931 to 1934 in Frankfurt, Germany, under Hans Benda, and in London under Max Rostal (1942-1944). During her two years in London, she was also a member of the Dartington chamber music group. During the Second World War she toured Britain with ENSA's classical music group. When the family moved to South Africa in 1947, Joyce performed as soloist with the SABC symphony orchestra. — **Hermina (née Verster)** (second wife of Pierre), *17 January 1934 in Dundee, Natal; now in Cape Town. Violinist and music teacher. — Hermina de Groote had her earliest musical instruction from her mother and Miss Munroe in Ladysmith and during her high school days in Bloemfontein was taught the violin by Victor Pohl*. At the University of the Witwatersrand Pierre de Groote was her lecturer in violin and after the award of the B.Mus. degree, she was appointed a member of the SABC orchestra. In 1955 she obtained the UPLM and UTLM diplomas of UNISA, and the Barclays' Bank bursary for overseas study. She continued her study of violin at the Akademie für Musik und Darstellende Kunst in Vienna, Austria under Franz Samohyl, and took further tuition in piano, viola and conducting. On her return, she taught music at the Jan van Riebeeck primary school in Cape Town, and at the Rhenish Primary School, Stellenbosch, as well as privately (1956-1957) in Cape Town. — **André**, *28 March 1940 in Brussels, Belgium; now again in Brussels. Pianist, chamber musician, professor of music. — André's parents brought him to South Africa when he was seven years old; in Johannesburg he received musical tuition from **Brigitte Wild** (1947-1955). In 1956 he returned to Brussels to study at the Conservatoire Royal de Musique under Eduardo dal Pueyo (pianoforte) and Louis

Poulet (chamber music) obtaining the diploma for virtuosity in pianoforte (1958). A further three years of study commenced in 1959 at the Chapelle de la Reine Elizabeth in Waterloo, Brussels, under Dal Pueyo and Franz André; this culminated in the awards of the Agregé de la Chapelle Musicale of the Institute, the Diploma Superieure of the Belgian Government, the Arthur de Greef prize for pianoforte playing, and the Harriet Cohen medal. In 1966 he won the international Tchaikovsky competition (Moscow), and in 1968 the Queen Elizabeth competition in Brussels. In Teneriffe he was also the winner of the Spanish international competition. After a recital in the Wigmore Hall, London, he undertook concert tours in West and East Europe, and in South Africa, and was appointed additional professor at the Conservatoire Royal de Bruxelles in 1967. During the European tour of the De Groote Family group in 1969, he participated in their chamber music concerts in Brussels. — **Oliver,** *13 December 1947 in Brussels, Belgium; now in Johannesburg. Clarinettist. — Soon after his birth, his parents brought Oliver to Johannesburg, where he had clarinet tuition from Mario Trinchero from his twelfth year. While he was a high school pupil at the Paul Roos Gymnasium, Stellenbosch, he was a member of the 1st Bugler Cadets and, until matriculation, continued his clarinet study at the Stellenbosch Conservatoire under George Elson. Subsequently (1965-1969) he studied clarinet at the South African College of Music* in Cape Town, under Wolfgang Simon, David Woodman and Harald Strebel, obtained the LRSM diploma and won the Gertrude Buchanan Memorial Prize. He was a member of the De Groote Family Ensemble from early childhood, playing violin and viola. His family regard him as the most versatile member: he has also become known as a recorder virtuoso. In Cape Town he was a presentation assistant at the SABC, until his appointment as clarinettist in the SABC Symphony Orchestra in April 1969. — **Philip,** *on Christmas Day 1950 in Stellenbosch; now in London. Cellist. — Philip received his primary school education at the Paul Roos Gymnasium and had lessons in violoncello from Granville Britton*, from his twelfth year. Whilst attending the Westerford High School (Cape Town), he received further tuition in violoncello from Roy Carter* at the South African College of Music; when he was 17 years old, he passed the final examination of the Royal Schools, and won the Ellie Marx* bursary, as well as the RSM Overseas Scholarship. Since the beginning of 1969 he has been a student of Eileen Croxford at the RCM in London. He has appeared as soloist with the orchestras of the SACM and the SABC in Cape Town, and participated in recitals of the string quartette of the University of Cape Town. From 1967 until his departure for London, he was sub-leader of the violoncello section of the Cape Town Municipal Orchestra*. — **Steven,** *12 January 1953 in Johannesburg; now (1971) in Europe. Pianist. — Steven is the youngest son of the family and became a member of the ensemble as a nine-year old boy, after receiving pianoforte tuition for four years from Lola Porter. Rosalind Allderman was his pianoforte teacher at the Paul Roos Gymnasium, Stellenbosch and while at the Westerford High School, he continued study in pianoforte at the SACM under Lamar Crowson and Michael Isadore. At sixteen he passed the final examinations of the RSM and UNISA, both institutions awarding him bursaries. As a pianoforte soloist, he has given recitals in the schools of the Peninsula, and in the Young South Africa programmes of the SABC. He has also appeared with orchestras of Cape Town, Durban and the SABC. In 1970 he won the Overseas Scholarship of UNISA, and is now (1971) studying in Europe.

BIBLIOGRAPHY
International who's who in music, 8th edition, Melrose Press, Cambridge, 1977.

SOURCES
Die Burger: 26 March 1962; 20 September 1965; 25 June 1966; 3 August 1969.   *Die Huisgenoot:* Die De Grootes is geen bloukouse nie. 12 September 1969.   *SABC Bulletin:* 30 January 1954; 12 May 1969.   National Documentation Centre for Music, HSRC, Pretoria.

—E.C.

DE JONGE, CARS GEERT,   *10 October 1865 aboard his father's ship in the Brazilian harbour Bahia; °on 21 October 1899 in the battle of Elandslaagte. Teacher, inspector of schools, composer of school songs. — De Jonge was educated in Wildervank in the province of Groningen where in 1885 he successfully completed an examination to qualify as a teacher. He continued his studies and in 1887 qualified in Amsterdam as a principal of schools for Christian education. While studying he taught at Wildervanksterdallen and in the city of Utrecht until deteriorating health forced him to emigrate to the Transvaal in 1887. — He was associated with Wessel Louis's school until 1889; then he became principal of a school at Rustenburg and eventually an inspector of schools in the ZAR. In 1897 he became Secretary of Education. De Jonge was a staunch Calvinist and an at times stormy protagonist of Christian Education through medium of the Dutch language. During the 1899 educational crisis, he maintained his point of view and opposed the introduction of English as a medium of instruction. He was also an active co-founder of the Dutch Corps in which he served as a lieutenant until the end of his career. — De Jonge's significance is mainly due to his singlemindedness as an educationist and to his share in the volume *Liederen voor de Scholen der Zuid Afrikaansche Republiek* which he published in collaboration with H. Visscher*. The words of song 3 (Zij zullen het niet hebben) and song 5 (De Moedertaal) were written by De Jonge himself; both reflect his deeply religious and patriotic nature.

BIBLIOGRAPHY
VISSCHER, H. and DE JONGE, C.G.: *Liederen voor de scholen der Zuid Afrikaansche Republiek.* J.C. Juta & Co., Johannesburg, Cape Town, Port Elizabeth, 1896.

SOURCES
PLOEGER, J.: Die geboortebewys van Cars Geert de Jonge. *Historiese studies,* Pretoria, June 1943.
PLOEGER, J.: Onderwys en Onderwysbeleid in die Suid-Afrikaanse Republiek onder ds. S.J. du Toit en dr. N. Mansvelt (1881-1900). *Argiefjaarboek vir S.A. Geskiedenis,* vol. I, 1952.
PLOEGER, J.: Van een Groninger buitengaats. *Dorp en Stad,* Groningen, July 1950.   PLOKHOOY, c.: Gedenkt den slag van Elandslaagte. *Hollands Weekblad voor Zuid-Afrika,* Pretoria, October 1946.   VAN DALSEN, J.: Die Hollanders in die Zuid-Afrikaansche Republiek. *Historiese studies,* Pretoria, June 1943.

—J.P.

DE KOCK, DENIS   Heidelberg 3, B. van Biljon-Couzyn

DE KOCK, JOHANNES JACOBUS,   *26 February 1816 in Cape Town; °12 April 1863 in Cape Town. Attorney and official translator, compiler of folksong verse.

Although De Kock's share in the Cape's music life was largely that of an active and intelligent amateur, he was an important key figure whose humorous contributions to folk lore shed light on several facets of the music conditions at the time, as well as on principals of the cultural life in Cape Town and their relationships. — De Kock was partial to theatre, dancing and music. This brought him into the sphere of Boniface* when he was nine years old and danced the Turk in a Boniface production of *De burger edelman* (Molière). From then onwards he was a supporter of the Frenchman and had a share in his attempts to ridicule J. Suasso de Lima. Two years after he had played the part of Leonora in *Clasius of Het proces om een komedilootjie*, written by Boniface as a satire on De Lima, his *Verzameling van Hollandsche liederen* was published. De Kock was then 21 years old. — Some time later this seemingly innocent little collection of songs led to a harsh polemic in the *Commercial Advertiser* and in *De Zuid-Afrikaan* on account of its hidden barbs, and eventually to a law suit against De Kock in which he was found guilty. However, the amateur group *Vlyt en kunst*, of which De Kock had been the secretary for several years, organised an evening of theatrical entertainment and paid his legal costs out of the proceeds. — The publication contains a collection of songs together with indications of the melodies to which they were to be sung. From this it is immediately obvious that the influence of British melodies was still negligible, while it proves that any number of French melodies were still known at the Cape in 1836. *Der Freischütz* (Weber), which had been presented in 1831, must have made an impression, because two melodies from this work are prescribed in De Kock's booklet. — The choice of texts was clearly influenced by a tendency towards active involvement: some are reminiscent of the Belgian uprising of 1830/1831, while others are related to South African conditions at the time. Examples of these are the songs in praise of the "Kaapsche burghers" and of the "brave old Field commandant Nicolaas Joh. Linde", as well as texts from Boniface's *De burger edelman,* which had been performed in 1834, or from his production of Jacob van Lennep's *Het dorp aan de grenzen*. It is obvious, particularly from the last group of texts, that the youthful compiler supported Boniface in the latter's merciless ridiculing of De Lima. To Capetonians at the time, phrases such as "Leen is as grimy as a pig" and "Leentjie is a dogthief" must have been obvious references to Miss Magdalena Theron, with whom De Lima stayed after the failure of his marriage; and the references to Klaas, after the performance of Boniface's *Clasius,* were clearly aimed at De Lima. Boniface is however sharply profiled by the fact that he wrote a farce, shortly before leaving the Cape, entitled *Kockincoz* in which he in turn ridiculed his staunch supporter, De Kock. — De Kock's second publication was his merry *Almanak* (1840), which also contains a few texts of songs. The rhymed descriptions entitled *Ontmoetingen,* seem to indicate that the lively descriptions of law suits published in *Het Volksblad,* some twenty years later, must also have been written by De Kock. — In 1852 both De Kock and De Lima published new collections of texts for songs; an indication that their competitive poetizing was still responsible for a great deal of tension between them. De Kock's collection, *Nieuwe Hollandsche gezelschapsliederen,* was more than a second edition of the 1836 collection. Especially significant is the fact that seventeen new texts had been added, all written to English melodies, and that there were fewer French melodies than in the first collection; but most of the 71 texts were still written with Dutch melodies in mind. — As was the case in the first collection, there was a general predisposition to active involvement and a number of the texts refer to incidents that occurred during the period 1848-1852, such as the anti-convict movement, which features prominently. — The humorous series entitled *Toneelen uit het Politiehof* (Scenes from the police court) which appeared during 1860 and continued till 1863, contain references to several folk songs and songs of the Boniface period. This seems to indicate that De Kock probably wrote the scenes himself. — This interesting Afrikaner with his French predilection for mockery was a provocative feature of Cape cultural life as editor of the first South African song album and as humorist. His example was not equalled for a long time.

PUBLICATIONS

DE KOCK, J.J.: *Verzameling van Hollandsche liederen.* Cape Town, 1836.   DE KOCK, J.J.: *De Zuid-Afrikaansche blygeestige almanak en naamlyst voor 't jaar onzes Heeren 1840.* Cape Town, 1840.   DE KOCK, J.J.: *Nieuwe Hollandsche gezelschapsliederen.* Cape Town, 1852.

BIBLIOGRAFIE

BOSMAN, F.C.L.: *Drama en toneel in Suid-Afrika I.* Pretoria/Cape Town, 1928.   BOUWS, JAN: *Die musieklewe van Kaapstad, 1800-1850, en sy verhouding tot die musiekkultuur van Wes-Europa.* Cape Town/Amsterdam, 1966.   CONRADIE, E.J.M.: *Hollandse skrywers uit Suid-Afrika I.* Pretoria, 1934.   NIENABER, P.J.: *'n Beknopte geskiedenis van die Hollands-Afrikaanse drukpers in Suid-Afrika.* Bloemfontein, 1943.   SCHOLTZ, J. DU P.: *Uit die Afrikaanse volkskultuur. Afrikaans uit die vroeë tyd.* Cape Town, n.d. (1965).

SOURCES

BOUWS, JAN: *Die eerste liederboeke van Suid-Afrika.* Dietsland-Europa (Gantois-nummer), 1964.   BOUWS, JAN: 'n "Liederlyke" liedboek. *Die Burger,* Cape Town, 21 October 1965. BOUWS, JAN: Hofverslae, 'n bron van kennis van die Afrikaanse volkslied. *Die Burger,* 30 December 1965.   *Baptismal register 1816,* NG Church Archives, Cape Town.   *Commercial Advertiser,* Cape Town, 1836.   *De Zuid-Afrikaan,* Cape Town, 1836.

—J.B.

DE KOCK, LOURENS BOSMAN,   *31 January 1922 in Potchefstroom; °14 August 1967 in Pretoria. Organiser of Music at the SABC and subsequently Deputy-Director and Director of PACT.

De Kock received his early training in music from M.M. van der Bent* in Potchefstroom. As a BA student at the University of Pretoria, he continued his study of music under P. Cruse (pianoforte) and Hilda Harries (singing), and while teaching in Potchefstroom during 1944 and 1945, he obtained the University of South Africa's licentiates in singing and in pianoforte. He resigned from the teaching profession in 1945 and joined the staff of the SABC as compiler of music programmes, organiser of programmes and organiser of music. He remained in broadcasting until 1962. When PACT was established, he became its Deputy-Director in January 1963 and Director on 1 February 1967. — Bosman de Kock had a flair for music as well as for languages. He began writing at an early age and eventually started translating operas as well as operettas by Preud'homme* into Afrikaans. While working for the SABC he did much for Afrikaans folk music: he was the leader of two groups, the Boeresangers and the Minnesangers, for whom he arranged several folk tunes *(Al lê die berge nog so blou; Slaap, kindjie, slaap; Doedoe kinnie van ma;* and several others). He displayed the same enthusiasm in his active support for the annual nativity plays presented by Volksteater in Pretoria (1942-1944). In his capacity as Deputy-Director, Bosman de Kock played an important part in establishing PACT's orchestra in 1964.

WORKS

A. Operettas

327

Willemien (words and music), operetta written for SABC in 1951; often performed at high schools.   Potjierol, children's operetta (Sita). Afr. Pers, Johannesburg, 1950.   Soetkoek, children's operetta (Sita). Afr. Pers, Johannesburg, 1950.

B. *Opera translations*
Martha (v. Flotow) for SABC broadcast.   La Bohéme (Puccini) for PACT production.   Die Fledermaus (Strauss) for PACT production.   Il Seraglio (Mozart) for PACT production. 'n Soen val uit die hemel (Preud'homme).   Uit die purper heide (Preud'homme).   Van Dyck en Isabella (Preud'homme).

SOURCES
Dagbreek en Sondagnuus: 13 August 1967. *Die Perdeby:* 18 August 1967. *Die Transvaler:* 16 August 1967. *SABC Bulletin:* 29 August 1960; 24 April 1961. National Documentation Centre for Music, HSRC, Pretoria.

—Ed.

DE LA FONTAINE, GOVERNOR   Organs I(v)

DE LANGE, JOHANNES   H. Greenwood

DELAPORTE, A .   Johannesburg 1, Theatres and Concert Halls IV/3, Touring Theatre Groups 4

DE LA PORTE, ELIZABETH JACOBA (BETSY),   *16 June 1901 in Wolmaransstad; °18 August 1977 in Johannesburg. Mezzo-soprano.
A pupil of Madame Hodgson Palmer, Betsy de la Porte won the University of South Africa's overseas scholarship in 1924, entitling her to three years' study at the RCM. She entered the College in 1925, obtained the ARCM and LRAM in the following year, and later became the recipient of an operatic bursary for a further two years. While still a student, she started singing in public in London and the counties, making her first appearance in the Royal Covent Garden international opera season in 1928. — On the completion of her studies in London, Betsy de la Porte went to the Munich Academy, where for two years she studied operatic roles under Anna Bahr-Mildenburg, and was awarded the Munich State Opera Diploma for operatic roles and stagecraft. After her return to England in 1930, she sang for six years in opera seasons at Covent Garden and for two seasons in the Glyndebourne Festival. She also distinguished herself in operatic roles at the Old Vic and Sadler's Wells, in addition to singing at concerts, in oratorios and for broadcasting. — After her marriage to Mr W.J.C. Tomlinson in 1935, Betsy de la Porte returned to South Africa, where she became known as a concert and radio recitalist and as an opera singer. Her invaluable service to South African music since 1936 needs to be mentioned with due appreciation: with unusual generosity she placed her musical and vocal talents at the disposal of South African composers (of whom W.H. Bell* should be named), by regularly including a number of their songs in her recital and broadcast programmes, locally as well as overseas. The beneficient effects of this selfless policy on South African composers and their works as well as on the reaction of the public, have ensured Betsy de la Porte of the high esteem of all who foster South African music. — Revisiting England in 1947, she accepted an invitation from Benjamin Britten to join his newly-formed English Opera Group. At the Glyndebourne Festival she created the role of Mrs Herring in his new comic opera *Albert Herring,* later appearing in the same role at the Scheveningen and Amsterdam Festivals, and at the International Musical Festival in Lucerne. In 1954

328

she and Arnold van Wyk* represented South Africa at the festival of the International Society for Contemporary Music, held in Israel. On this occasion, she sang Van Wyk's song cycle, *Van liefde en verlatenheid.* After the festival she broadcast it on the Third Programme of the BBC, and also in Belgium, Holland and Norway. — In the fourteen years between 1956 and 1970, Betsy de la Porte was highly regarded as a singing teacher and as a connoisseur of the vocal art. Among those who were trained by her have been Dr Jan Schutte,* Sarie Lamprecht*, Rita Roberts*, Doris Brasch*, Elizabeth Heyns*, Peggy Haddon*, Anne Hamblin, Isolde Traut and Margaret Rodseth. Apart from her sympathetic and knowledgeable treatment of voices, she commanded an exceptionally broad repertoire which continually drew prominent singers to her studio for assistance in compiling programmes and in polishing their repertoires. She also owned a large library of solo vocal music, to which she continually added representative items. It contains a variety of mss. of South African vocal music. — In recognition of her services to music in South Africa, she was awarded the Medal of Honour of the Suid-Afrikaanse Akademie vir Wetenskap en Kuns in 1958, the first singer to be honoured in this way. Her daughter, Elizabeth de la Porte, won the overseas bursary of UNISA for pianoforte playing in 1960 and used it for harpsicord study at the RCM and the Tonkunstakademie in Vienna. Since then two long-playing records of her playing have been made.

BIBLIOGRAPHY
DU PLESSIS, HUBERT: *Letters from William Henry Bell.* Tafelberg-Uitgewers Bpk., Cape Town, 1973.

SOURCES
Betsy de la Porte, pro and con. *SAMT* 51, December 1956.   Elizabeth de la Porte. *Opus* 3/3, March 1972. The SA Council for the Advancement of Music. *Newsletter* I/2, January 1954; I/4 June 1954; II/1, March 1955.   National Documentation Centre for Music, HSRC, Pretoria.

—Ed.

DE LIMA, J. SUASSO   C.E. Boniface, J.J. de Kock, W.L. Sammons, Songbooks with Dutch words

DE NETTRE, A.   Ballet VII, IX, XI, XII

DENHOLM, CHARLES GRAHAM *9 October 1911 in Edinburg; now (1974) in Durban. Violinist and conductor.
Educated at the Royal High School, Edinburgh, he won the Sibbald Bursary and first prize for violin playing in 1925. In 1928 he commenced his studies at the RAM, where he was a medallist in aural training in the following year. He became a violinist in the Scottish Orchestra in 1934, under the baton of John Barbirolli. A course of study at Edinburgh University on which he had entered in 1939, was interrupted by war service, but eventually completed in 1947, when he graduated as Bachelor of Music, also winning the Niecks Essay Prize awarded for History of Music. — Charles Denholm joined the Durban Civic Orchestra* in September 1947 and became Chorusmaster to the Durban Civic Choir (1948-1965). He was appointed Deputy Conductor of the Durban Orchestra in 1954. Since that time he has conducted hundreds of popular lunch-hour concerts. In the absence of a permanent conductor for the Durban Orchestra he virtually became their full-time

conductor for symphony concerts, ballet performances and light orchestral concerts. Until recently he was also responsible for training the Junior Civic Orchestra and the Durban Philharmonic Orchestra*.

—Ed.

DENNIS, ERNEST JOHN, *20 January 1911 in Redruth, Cornwall, of South African parents; at present (1976) in Cape Town. Tenor and senior lecturer in singing. After settling in South Africa with his parents in 1924, Dennis was educated in Johannesburg and Durban, where he was vocally trained by Perla Siedle Gibson* and Xenia Belmas*, from his eighteenth year. On the strength of a four-year scholarship, he entered the RAM in 1936, winning awards such as the Parapa Rosa Gold Medal. In September 1940, he enlisted in the British Army. He was made an Associate of the RAM in 1945. — Dennis had established himself in England as a concert artist, taking part in oratorio and operatic work at Covent Garden and Glyndebourne, but returned to South Africa in December 1947, to become lecturer in singing at the South African College of Music* in Cape Town, and eventually senior lecturer. In August 1967, he was promoted to the new post of Organiser for Music and Drama at the University of Cape Town. An active member of the University of Cape Town Opera Company, he is also their business manager, and has achieved a reputation as a concert artist and opera singer in the Republic. — He is married to Thelma Finch, concert pianist and former accompanist to the SABC in Durban. She is an opera repetitor of the UCT Opera Company.

—Ed.

DENNIS, R.   Raie da Costa

DEPARTMENT OF EDUCATION, ARTS AND SCIENCE (NOW DEPARTMENT OF NATIONAL EDUCATION)   Higher Educational Institutions IV/1

DE ROO, LEONARDUS CORNELIS (LEO DE ROO), *17 July 1922 in Pretoria; presently (1977) in Johannesburg. Violinist and conductor of the Johannesburg North Orchestra.

Leo de Roo had a predilection for violin since an early age and when he was eight years old, his Christmas present was the first violin he ever owned. This was followed by a period of rather haphazard tuition which only got into its stride, when first Erwin Broedrich* and then Bram Verhoef took charge. While studying at the University of the Witwatersrand for the degrees of B.A. and B.Mus., he gathered experience of orchestral playing in the orchestras of the Collosseum and the City of Johannesburg. He left for the Netherlands in 1947 to continue his study under the guidance of Oskar Back; there, for a while, he was the leader of the Amsterdam Concertgebouw Youth Orchestra. One of the artists he met there, and with whom he co-operated, was the South African pianist Chrystal Blomkamp*, whom he married in 1951. — After his return to South Africa he was a member of the SABC Orchestra (now the National Symphony Orchestra), but he eventually resigned to enter the service of the Transvaal Education Department. Since 1976 he has been violin teacher in the music centre of the Blairgowrie Primary School, where he also has the responsibility of training the pupils' orchestra. In 1966 De Roo created the Johannesburg North Orchestra, one of the few suburban orchestras in South Africa. Under his direction they often perform in aid of charity, or of schoolfunds, churches or societies. At times they also visit country towns where orchestras are rarely if ever heard. A highlight of the orchestra's history was their performance during the centenary festival of education in the Transvaal, at which they played under the patronage of the Educational Trust (1976). On this occasion they had the co-operation of Chrystal Blomkamp and a combined choir in a performance of Beethoven's *Choral fantasia.* — As violinist Leo de Roo has performed and conducted Mozart's *Concerto in D,* and has often played with his wife in a duet team, on occasions with the addition of his son Wilbert (cello), to form a trio, which has given concerts for the Linden Music Circle and at the University of the Witwatersrand. Their three children are all very musical: Leonora is a pianist and a music teacher at the Randburg High School, Wilbert is a capable cellist and pianist who is now studying cello in Vienna and Christopher is a performer on the clarinet.

—Ed.

DEUTSCHE ST MARTINI KIRCHE, CAPE TOWN   German Evangelical Lutheran Church Music in the Cape, W. König, G.W. Kühn, W. Kühn, H.H. Maske, C.L.R. Müller, Organs I(iii)

DEUTSCHE ST MARTINI SCHULE   See above

DE VILLE, P.B.   J.S. de Villiers, Graaff Reinet 2, 5, 6, 7, 8

DE VILLIERS.   A South African family which descended from the three Huguenot brothers Pierre, Abraham and Jacques. All the members of this family were remarkably musical - undoubtedly a hereditary tendency. Because there are two musical and relatively distantly related branches of the family - descendants of the eldest and of the youngest ancestors - one should take the family's musical potential into account, although it is possible that musical talent was introduced into the family by marriage and that it remained latent. An example of the latter possibility is what became known as the Catorzia de Villiers branch (the Katorse), in which musical talent is traditionally ascribed to the Neapolitan, Quatorcia. This branch of the De Villiers family is the largest of the De Villiers descendants. — The following family tree, compiled according to a method developed by Christoffel de Villiers, illustrates how the musical De Villiers family is constituted:

a1 Pierre (1657-1720) x (Marie) Elisabeth Taillefer (1674-1735)
  b1 Pierre 1695 x Hester Roux
    c1 Pieter 1725 x (1) Helena Basson;
      x (2) Johanna de Villiers
      d6 Matthys Johannes 1764 x Elisabeth Dojema
        e6 Jan Jeremias 1801 x S.M.M. du Toit
          f5 Andries Stephanus 1842 x C.G. Swart
            g6 C.G.S. de Villiers*.

      d5 Johannes Albertus 1766 x Susanna Dojema
        e2 Pieter Jan Albert 1797 x D.D. Gräbe
          f3 Coenraad Gräbe 1822 x B.W. Taute
            g5 Christoffel Coetzee x S.S. Cilliers
            h
              i Dr Louis Scholtz de Villiers

d14 Susanna Martha (mother, Johanna de Villiers) x Jan Stephanus de Villiers

  e Abraham Matthys de Villiers (18.5.1814 - 8.9.1888) x Gertruida Catharina Catorzia* (31.8.1819 - 24.6.1902)

    f. Rocco Catorzia de Villiers* (27.2.1838 - 21.5.1902) x M.M. Louw d. 27.2.96.

C3 Jan 1729 x Anna Hugo

  d3 Hester Maria 1759 x Izaak de Villiers
    (a3 - b8 - c9)

    e1 Abraham Josua x M.J. de Vos

      f3 Elizabeth Maria de Villiers 1809 x Jan Stephanus de Villiers

      g Jan Stephanus de Villiers (Jan Orrelis*)

B2 Jan 1699 x Hester Mylius ("Melius")

  c5 Jacob 1741 x Debora du Toit

    d11 Jan Stephanus 1778 x Susanna Martha de Villiers
      (a1 - b1 - c1 - d14)

      e6 Abraham Matthys Johannes (1814 - 1888) x Gertruida Catharina Catorzia (1819 - 1902)

        f1 Rocco (1838 - 1902) x Maria Magdalena Louw (died 1896)

          g1 Abraham Matthys 1862 x E.H. Marais 1864

            h1 Rocco (1888 - 1918)

              H5 Abraham Marais 1894 x T. Gericke

              i Elise*

          g8 Pieter Kuyper* ("P.K.")

        f8 Dirk Izak* x Tina Smith

        g Marthinus Lourens*

        h Dirkie*

        g Len

          h Pieter J.*

        g Septimus C.*

      f9 Pieter Jakob* x Ellen van Heerden

A2 Abraham x Susanne Gardiol

  b4 Susanna 1697 x Pierre Joubert

    c Elisabeth Joubert 1721 x Jan de Villiers 1717

      d Susanna de Villiers 1743 x (1) Izaak de Villiers (2) Jan Hilbrandus (son Dojema)

      e Elisabeth x M.J. de Villiers

      Susanna x J.A. de Villiers

a3 Jacques (o. 1735) x Marguerite Gardiol

  b8 Abraham 1707 x Johanna Lombard

c9 Izaak 1750 x Hester Maria de Villiers 1759
(a1 - b1 - c3 - d3)
d1 Abraham Josua 1794 x M.J. de Vos
e3 Elisabeth Maria 1809 x Jan Stephanus de Villiers d. Aug. 1864
f Jan Stephanus de Villiers ("Jan Orrelis") 15.3.1827

b10 Jan 1717 x Elisabeth Joubert (a2 - b4 - c)
c1 Jacob 1739 x M.E. Marais
d1 Jan Stephanus x C.S. van Niekerk
e Jan Stephanus x Elisabeth Maria de Villiers
(a3 - b8 - c9 - d1 - c3)
f Jan Stephanus ("Jan Orrelis") x Maria v.d. Lingen
g Elizabeth Johanna Hendrika von Wiellich*
h Maria van der Lingen (Fismer*)
g Nancy Wilhelmina de Villiers (Mrs Lategan*)

c3 Susanna 1743 x J.W. Dojema
d Elisabeth Dojema x M.J. de Villiers
e6 Jan Jeremias 1801 x S.M.N. du Toit
f5 Andries Stephanus 1842 x C.G.S. Swart
g6 C.G.S. (Con) de Villiers
d Susanna Dojema x J.A. de Villiers
e Pieter Jan Albert 1797 x D.D. Gräbe (grandparents of Christoffel
de Villiers)

Both the eldest brother, Pierre, and the youngest, Jacques, had descendants who were
musical. Jan Stephanus ("Jan Orrelis") is related to the second brother, Abraham, by
way of the Joubert family. (Abraham, the progenitor, had no other descendants who
showed much musical talent). But Jan Stephanus is also a descendant of the eldest
brother, Pierre, through his mother and her grandmother, Hester Maria de Villiers
a1 - b1 - c3 - d3 - so that he, in fact, represents all three branches. — On his
mother's side of the family he is also related to his well-known contemporary, Rocco
de Villiers*. Rocco's musical talents are probably not entirely due to his link with
Rocco Quatorcia but could be traced partly, or to a large extent, to the De Villiers
heritage.

SOURCES
DE VILLIERS, C.G.S.: Die musikale Viljees. *Die Burger,* 17 November 1956.   RENIER: Musikale
familie. *Die Burger,* 28 November 1957.
—C.G.S. de V.

DE VILLIERS, CORNELIUS GERHARDUS STEPHANUS (CON), *16 December 1894 at
Dunghay Park ("Donkiespad"), Caledon; °25 November 1978 in Ceres. Writer,
connoisseur of music and singing, collector of records.
Con de Villiers was educated in the farm school "Solitaire", at the village school in Caledon and later at the Victoria College in Stellenbosch. After a period as lecturer at the
Transvaal University College in Pretoria, he received a Ph. D. degree in Zürich in
1919/20. In 1923 he was appointed professor of Zoology at the University of

Stellenbosch. In addition to his many outstanding academic achievements, he has published articles on music and on music affairs since the 'twenties; and his talks on and enthusiasm for music and for the annual Stellenbosch Song Festival did much to stimulate student interest in music. His lively interest in folklore is evidenced by his adaptations of foreign folk music and in his collection of Afrikaans folk tunes, some of which have been included in the *Nuwe FAK-sangbundel*. — In 1967 the University of Stellenbosch conferred an honorary. D. Phil. on Dr De Villiers in recognition of his valuable contributions to culture and science in South Africa. During the 60th annual meeting of the SA Akademie vir Wetenskap en Kuns* in Pretoria in 1969, Dr De Villiers was accorded Honorary Membership for his sustained, comprehensive and significant contributions in respect of science, culture and literature in South Africa.

PUBLICATIONS ON MUSICAL SUBJECTS

Giacomo Puccini. *Die Huisgenoot*, 12.12.1924. Die oorsprong van ons gesange en psalms. *Die Huisgenoot* 11.9.36; 18.9.36; 2.10.36; 16.10.36; 30.10.36. Die Geneefse Psalmboek 400 jaar oud. *Die Huisgenoot* 25.6.1943. Onwelluidende Psalmwysies. *Die Huisgenoot*, 19.11.43. Die Strydpsalm van die Hugenote. *Die Huisgenoot*, 26.11.43. Die Korale gebaseer op Psalm 46. *Die Huisgenoot*, 10.12.43. Kersliedjies en Kersvierings. *Die Huisgenoot*, 17.12.43. Die Afrikaanse kunslied. *Die Huisgenoot*, 9.6.44. Die voordrag van die kunslied. *Die Huisgenoot*, 21.7.44. Die meesters van die kunslied: 1. Franz Schubert. *Die Huisgenoot*, 11.8.44. 2. Robert Schumann. *Die Huisgenoot*, 18.8.44. 3. Johannes Brahms. *Die Huisgenoot*, 8.9.44. 4. Hugo Wolf. *Die Huisgenoot*, 15.9.44. 5. Richard Strauss. *Die Huisgenoot*, 1.12.44. Hedendaagse groot sangkunstenaars: 1. Soprane. *Die Huisgenoot*, 1.2.46. 2. Mezzo-soprane en liedersangeresse. *Die Huisgenoot*, 8.2.46. 3. Tenore. *Die Huisgenoot*, 15.2.46. 4. Baritons en basse. *Die Huisgenoot*, 22.2.46. Hans Endler. *Die Stellenbosse oudstudent*, December 1947. Die belangstelling in die Westerse volkslied is 'n eeu oud. *Res Musicae* IV/1 & 2, September and December 1957. *Musici en mense*. Nasionale Boekhandel Bpk., Cape Town, 1958. Tristan en Isolde. *Res Musicae* VI/1, September 1959. *Die Burger:* 27.3.37; 31.7.37; 17.11.56; 1.10.57. Several collections of sketches, as well as translations.

BIBLIOGRAPHY

NIENABER, P.J.: *Hier is ons skrywers*. Afrikaanse Pers Boekhandel, Johannesburg, 1949.

SOURCES

Verteenwoordiger van Die Huisgenoot: Con de Villiers. *Die Huisgenoot*, 19.3.48. Prof. dr. C.G.S. de Villiers. *Die Burger*, 8.6.68. WESSELS, MARIE: Fluit, fluit, prof. Con se storie is uit, so sê hy. Supplement to *Die Burger*, 16.11.48. STEGMANN, FRITS: Dr. Con word 70. *Die Burger*, 16.12.64. STEGMANN, FRITS: Dr. Con en die musiek. *Eikestadnuus*, 15.12.67. *Die Volksblad*, 3.7.69. *Die Transvaler*, 4.7.69. National Documentation Centre for Music, HSRC, Pretoria.

—F.S.

DE VILLIERS, DIRK IZAK, *12 June 1859 in Paarl; °27 August 1937 in the Strand. Organist and music teacher in Wellington. Second youngest son of Abraham and Gertruida de Villiers.

Dirk de Villiers grew up in the same atmosphere as his gifted brothers and revealed so much talent for music that when Dr Andrew Murray appealed to his eldest brother Rocco de Villiers* for an organist for the Wellington congregation, Dirk was equipped for the position within a few months through a rapid course at Caledon (c. 1898). For forty years, starting in 1898, he remained the organist and music teacher in Wellington. — He married the musically talented Tina (Catharina Susanna) Smith (°2 March 1936; a pupil of J.S. de Villiers* of Paarl) and with her assistance started a Music Institute which offered training in pianoforte, organ, wind instruments and theoretical subjects. They had up to 200 pupils a year at R3 a term and gave an annual recital of the work done by the pupils, in which the De Villiers children gradually played an increasingly important part. De Villiers also started his own band which practised in the attic of the wagon factory of A.J: Malan, who blew on the cornet in this group. At least one notable occasion at which the band officiated has been noted: when the Lady Loch bridge over the Berg River was opened in 1891, the band was installed on an open wagon near the bridge to provide suitable music and accompaniments. At times this band combined with the string orchestra which De Villiers had formed out of his pupils. — Like Rocco, he seized his opportunities, bought the old organ of the Wellington congregation very cheaply in 1893 and had it rebuilt in his home. Today this organ is used in the Adendorf church in Graaff Reinet. Apart from his musical interests, De Villiers also traded in bicycles in a shop next to his home. In later years he bought the first motor car seen on the streets of Wellington, and switched from bicycles to motor cars. — The couple had six sons and a daughter, all active in music-making. It was more especially the eldest son Marthinus Lourens* ("M.L."), and Septimus* who excelled in later years.

WORK
Band march for the Blouvlei and Wellington brass band. Ms., n.d.

BIBLIOGRAPHY
DREYER, A.: *Ons Kerk.* Samuel Griffiths, Cape Town, 1927.   DE VILLIERS, D.P.: *A history of the De Villiers family.* Nasionale Boekhandel Bpk., 1960.   DE VILLIERS, M.L.: *Die Catorse. Meer 'n memorandum - in toto - as 'n dokument.* Ms., 1962.

SOURCE
DE VILLIERS, CON G.S.: Die musikale Viljees. Supplement, *Die Burger,* 17 November 1956.
                                                                —E.V. (with additions)

DE VILLIERS, DIRK IZAK CATTOGIO (DIRKIE), *1 November 1921 in Simonstown; in 1977 Head of Music in the Free State Education Department. Organist and composer. Son of M.L. de Villiers*.

Dirkie de Villiers had his first instruction in pianoforte and organ under Adrienne Joubert* in Wellington. In later years Professor Eric Grant, Dean of the new College of Music* at the Cape University, guided his efforts in composition. Jan Coetzee* assisted him in his study for the UTLM of UNISA, which he acquired in 1955. — At the former Huguenot University College in Wellington he completed the requirements for the degree of BA, and afterwards taught at schools in Vredenburg, Parow, Bellville and Grabouw (1941-1954). For the next two years he was a senior lecturer in School Music at the Teachers' Training College in Graaff Reinet and then he became Inspector of School Music in the Education Department of the OFS. He was promoted to Head of Music in the same Department in 1974. Since 1956 he has been organist in the NG church Bloemheuwel. — During the Union Festival in Bloemfontein (1960) De Villiers was responsible for the music section. The Free

335

State Youth Choir* which he personally trained and conducted until 1974, was started in 1964. This choir has, on an average, given 20 concerts per year. The OFS is at the present time the only province in the Republic which can boast of a children's choir. Since 1974 he has been very active in organising an educational programme for orchestral instruments, which again is an idea which only the OFS has advanced. In 1977 there were 24 full-time teachers instructing about 700 pupils in Free State schools in the playing of all symphonic orchestral instruments, excepting the harp. — As a church musician De Villiers has been a member of the Revision Committee which is responsible for reshaping the Psalms and Hymns of the church (1961-1976). Together with C.G. Cillié* and J.D. Malan he had the task of harmonising all the melodies in use in the NG church. He became a member of the Music Committee of the FAK in 1952 and acted as chief editor of the new *FAK-sangbundel* in 1960. For the past 21 years he has also been a member of the Joint Advisory Committee for Music Examinations of the University of South Africa. —Apart from his contributions as conductor of the Youth Choir, accompanist and organist, he has become well-known through his contributions to radio and TV. Two of the children born of his marriage to the clinical psychologist Hendrina C. Grobbelaar, are gifted musically: in 1977 Johan succeeded Philip McLachlan as conductor of the Stellenbosch University Choir*; Johan's sister, Suzanne, is a violinist, who distinguished herself as the best violinist to play at the International Festival of Youth Orchestras at St Moritz in 1970. Since then she has studied under Max Rostal in Switzerland and under Galamian in America.

WORKS

Songs

Net maar gesien (A.D. Keet). Ms., 1937.   Winternag (Eugène Marais). Ms., 1938. Daeraad (H.H. Joubert). Ms., 1939.   Lied van 'n koningsdogter (I.D. du Plessis). Ms., 1941.   Voorwaarts (S. Ign. Mocke). Ms., 1941.   Grense (N.P. van Wyk Louw). Ms., 1941.   Ons is die geeste wat dwaal (N.P. van Wyk Louw). Ms., 1942.   Skoppensboer Eugène Marais). Ms., 1942.   Winterbome (N.P. van Wyk Louw). Ms., 1942.   Waar die nag in ademlose stilte (Doll de Villiers). Composed 1973. *Suid-Afrikaanse Kersliedere deel II*. NG-Kerkboekhandel, 1976.

Choral

Wiegelied (C.J. Langenhoven), commissioned by the SABC for Langenhoven year, 1973.   Repos ailleurs (Totius), commissioned by the SABC for Totius festival, 1977.   Dit is maar ligte liedjies (Totius), commissioned by the SABC for Totius festival, 1977.

Official songs

The green heritage year (J.F. Spies), commissioned by the Government. Studio Holland, Cape Town, 1973.   University song of the UPE (J.F. Spies), commissioned by the UPE. Ms., 1975.

School songs

More than 100 school songs for schools throughout the 4 provinces and SWA.

Nuwe FAK-sangbundel (Nasionale Boekhandel Bpk. Cape Town, 1961-1969): Komaan (Jan F.E. Celliers); Kom, Afrikaners (A.D. Keet); numerous arrangements of songs.

BIBLIOGRAPHY

International who's who in music, 8th edition. Melrose Press, Cambridge, 1977.

—Ed.

DE VILLIERS, DOROTHEA COMBRINCK (DOLLY) (MRS DU BUISSON), *26 September 1903 in Heidelberg, Transvaal; living in Pretoria in 1966. Soprano.

Dolly de Villiers studied singing under Professor Margottini and Signor Alberto Terassi in Johannesburg and made her debut in the Pretoria City Hall in 1918. After teaching music at Amersfoort and at Volksrust, she joined the staff of M.M. van der Bent's* Music College in Potchefstroom. In 1924 she went to Paris, France, to continue her studies and one year later she joined the staff of the Stellenbosch Conservatoire*. There she played an active part in Hans Endler's* annual productions of operettas and often performed as soloist in the concerts of the Cape Town City Orchestra*, until her marriage in 1928. — After her husband's death in 1932 she again settled in Pretoria where she taught singing and pianoforte, and was active in the musical life of the city. In 1934 she was actively involved in the first comprehensive Afrikaans musical evening presented by the Castalides* Society of the University of Pretoria in the local city hall.

—F.S. (amplified)

DE VILLIERS, D.S.　Organs 10

DE VILLIERS, FAITH.　Artistic Director of the PACT Ballet Company, ballet dancer and teacher.

Faith de Villiers began her dancing career at the age of eleven as a pupil of Audrey Grose, continuing under Dolphine Thompson and Madge Mann. In 1938 she left for London, joined the Carl Rosa Ballet Company, and accompanied them on extensive tours. At the outbreak of the Second World War she returned to South Africa and joined the Johannesburg Ballet Club, for whom she danced the *Sugar plum fairy* during the 1940 season. Soon afterwards, she was appointed ballet mistress for productions of African Consolidated Theatres. In 1947 she was elected to the committee of Ballet Theatre, a company formed to promote professional ballet in the Transvaal. For them she choreographed ballets such as *Rhapsody in blue.* — In 1950 Faith joined the National Ballet in Cape Town and choreographed some of the classics for them. On her return to Johannesburg in 1957 she joined Yvonne Mounsey and Denise Schultze in the launching of a company known as Johannesburg Ballet. She produced many ballets for this company, which performed not only in Johannesburg, but in various centres in the Transvaal and in Lourenço Marques. The company was renamed the Johannesburg City Ballet in 1959, and given financial assistance and temporary premises by the City Council. At the end of 1960 Faith de Villiers left Johannesburg for Durban, where she taught at the Technical College Ballet School. She returned to Johannesburg at the end of 1961 and was appointed Artistic Director of the PACT Ballet Company at the beginning of 1964. — One of the leading teachers of the Cecchetti method in Southern Africa, she is a prominent member and senior examiner of the Imperial Society of Teachers of Dancing, for whom she has organised many summer schools. She has also acted as adjudicator at ballet festivals and competitions.

—H.D.

DE VILLIERS, GERTRUIDA CATHARINA (CATORZIA), *31 August 1819 in Paarl; °22 June 1902, in Paarl. Ancestor of the musical Catorzia de Villiers.

Gertruida Catharina de Villiers, the only child of Rocco Quatorcia and Charlotta Theron, married Abraham Matthys de Villiers in 1837. They had eleven children who inherited their mother's musical talent and perpetuated this talent into the present time. Some of the direct descendants of this family who took up music as a profession are the following: Rocco Catorzia (1839-1902), Abraham Matthys (1862 -   ), Elise (1921-1959), Pieter Kuyper (1874-1949), Dirk Izak (1859-1937), Marthinus Lourens (1885-1977), Dirk Izak Catoggio (1921-   ), Pieter Johannes (1924-   ), Septimus C. (1895-1929), Pieter Jakob (1861-1937).

—E.V.

DE VILLIERS, GERTRUIDA ELIZABETH (ELISE), *24 April 1921 in Villiersdorp; °27 September 1959 at the Strand. Violinist.

Elise de Villiers commenced violin lessons at the age of six in Villiersdorp, where her father was the school principal. Her tutor was E.J. Sangster, who had formerly been on the staff of the College of Music in Cape Town. His thorough teaching over a period of ten years enabled her to continue her studies under Ivy Angove* at the Stellenbosch Conservatoire*, where she acquired the performer's and teacher's licentiates in violin and pianoforte. — She taught violin and pianoforte in Worcester and at Bloemhof Girls' High in Stellenbosch for a few years and in 1948 she was appointed lecturer in violin at the Stellenbosch Conservatoire. She visited London in 1952, where she obtained the LRAM diploma. — She was a well-known concert and radio artist and played as soloist with the Cape Town City Orchestra*, conducted by Enrique Jordá, in Cape Town as well as in Stellenbosch. Enrique Jordá advised her to continue her studies in Brussels, under Arthur Grumiaux, and in 1954 she eventually left on a grant from the Drie-Eeue Stigting in Cape Town, for a period of two years. — Elise de Villiers was an exceptionally gifted artist, whose playing was distinguished by warmth and sensitive musicality.

SOURCES

STEGMANN, FRITS: Obituary in *Eikestadnuus,* September 1959.   Obituaries in *Cape Times* and *Die Burger,* 28 September 1959.   Obituary in *SAMT* 57, December 1959.   National Documentation Centre for Music, HSRC, Pretoria.

—F.S.

DE VILLIERS, ISAAC MICHAEL, *13 March 1916 in Johannesburg; still in Johannesburg. Music teacher, dance band leader, pianist and composer of light music.

De Villiers studied serious music and obtained the ATCL teacher's diploma at the age of eighteen, but had in the meantime become interested in light music. In 1932 he began his career as pianist in a light orchestra playing at the Anglo-French Café in Bloemfontein. As a member of Hendrik Susan's orchestra, which he joined a few months later, he played in various cafés and clubs in Johannesburg and Pretoria, until Susan formed the first Afrikaans broadcast band, of which de Villiers became the pianist. — In 1936 De Villiers began teaching piano and piano-accordion in Johannesburg, and eventually opened a school of music in Eloff Street, where he was assisted by six teachers. The Boere-orkes leaders Duffy Ravenscroft*, H. van Loggerenberg* and Arnout Malherbe are among those who received their musical training from him. An accordion band, which he formed from his pupils in 1937, undertook a tour of South Africa for African Theatres, and broadcast regularly each week for about five years. Michael de Villiers was often heard over the radio as a solo pianist and as leader of his Afrikaans broadcast band. In addition, he formed a dance band, which played in night-clubs and hotels in and around Johannesburg. —

338

His melodies include i.a. *Ou Vaalrivier, Kom ons skiet 'n leeu, Nie te laat* and *Lente*.
—Ed.

DE VILLIERS, JAN STEPHANUS, *15 March 1827 in Paarl; °2 May 1902 in Paarl. Church musician and composer.

Jan Stephanus was the eldest son of the Paarl blacksmith and wainwright, Jan Stephanus de Villiers (°1864), and Elizabeth Maria de Villiers (1809-1884). He was a direct descendant of the Huguenot, Jacques de Villiers but, on his mother's side, he was also a descendant of the two other Huguenot De Villiers's, so that all three branches of the family were represented in him. — From 1837 to 1847 his mother had music lessons from the Paarl organist Pieter Hugo; the boy often attended his mother's lessons and attracted Hugo's attention with his musicality. He was consequently included in the tuition, and very soon surpassed his mother. After hearing Jan play the pianoforte, the Cape governor, Sir George Napier, offered to send the boy to Europe at his expense for musical study (after January 1838). Due to his extreme youth, his father could not agree to this and Jan's tuition was entrusted to Frederick Logier* (1840-1847), with organ as his principal subject, although he was also instructed in pianoforte, violin, harp and in theoretical subjects. When he was 18, Jan Stephanus gave two concerts in Cape Town, in which he performed some of his own compositions and a set of brilliant variations by Herz. *Sam Sly's journal* reported succinctly: "(He) gave universal satisfaction by the power of his execution" (1845). — On 1 November 1947, De Villiers became organist of the "Thatched-roof Church" in Paarl, at an initial salary of R60 per year, with a subsidy of R24 for tuning and keeping the organ in working condition. He remained in this position until 1875 when a commission of the Ring, after drawn-out negotiations, eventually decided to create a new congregation for the Northern Paarl. The Northeners were quite enthusiastic about the policies of the Genootskap van Regte Afrikaners, and several church members insisted that Rev. S.J. du Toit be called as minister of the new congregation. Jan Stephanus was a supporter of the Society (see below) and became a member of the Northern Paarl congregation and naturally their "organist", although he only had a harmonium at his disposal, on which he played without compensation until 1877. When the congregation had financial difficulties in 1883, he was again requested by the Church Council to waive his salary, which had been fixed at R100 per year. This situation lasted until 1889. The new organ was inaugurated in September 1877. It had been built in London at a cost of R1 600 and was erected in the Paarl by A. Bredell* of Cape Town. At the services during the day there was much choral singing and organ solos given by the organist and Rocco de Villiers*; after the evening service they played the Hallelujah chorus from Handel's *Messiah* as a duet on the new instrument! After serving the congregation for 50 years, the organ was sold to Observatory in 1927. Jan Orrelis played on it until three days before his death in 1902. He was succeeded by his daughter, Nancy de Villiers*, who led the congregational singing on the same instrument until 1905. — To teach his pupils, Jan Stephanus used to ride his dapple grey horse to their homes. One of them was the daughter of Rev. Van der Lingen, Johanna Maria Wilhelmina (1834-1897), who was taught by him for seven years and then became his wife (c. 1855). Thirteen children were born of the marriage, of whom nine were still living when Jan Stephanus died in 1902. There were two talented daughters among them - Elizabeth Maria* (Mrs Von Wielligh*, the mother of Maria van der Lingen - Maria Fismer*) and Justina Wilhelmina Nancy* (Mrs Lategan) who was prominent when the Stellenbosch Conservatoire* was founded. This marriage into a minister's family greatly influenced the career of Jan Stephanus. His father-in-law was sincerely interested in Jan's music, and proved it by supporting sacred song festivals, by co-operating in the writing of a text for an oratorio, and by arranging for a performance of De Villiers's Philharmonic Society before the Synod. The influence of the church is also attested by the 13 new tunes which Jan wrote in 1883 for the proof edition of a new hymn book, called *Halleluja, psalmen en gezangen der Ned. Geref. Kerk van Zuid Afrika.* Four of these tunes were eventually used in the Afrikaans Psalter of 1936 (Psalms 26, 31, 48 and 71). — De Villiers's accompaniments to congregational singing must have been extraordinary - even his death notice mentions how well he managed the art of attuning his organ playing to the character of the message delivered by the Minister: "one felt that it was not a machine that one was listening to - it was the heart of a Christian making itself heard in complementary tones." —

From his close connection with the Church came his appointment as a curator of the Gymnasium, which had been established by his father-in-law in 1857 and was placed under the supervision of Northern Paarl in 1876. In 1872 he had acquired a little private school, in Paarl, from Mrs Hugo and transformed it, with the assistance of his wife, into a Ladies' Seminary. The seminary also was placed under supervision of Northern Paarl by De Villiers, in 1876. He and his wife shared the management of the school and its hostel until 1890 when it was bought from him by Rev. Andrew Murray as the Paarl branch of the Wellington Huguenot Seminary. In 1912 the school's name was changed to La Rochelle on the recommendation of the principal, Miss M.H. Cillié. — Apart from his duties to the church, De Villiers exerted himself for the advancement of music in Paarl and created the Paarl Philharmonic Society in 1864. This began in a small way, but grew steadily and eventually had 120 members. It was mainly a choral society, whose singing was supported by organ or pianoforte, and a variable instrumental ensemble which possibly sometimes justified the title of "orchestra". The members rehearsed each week and sang mainly sacred music, inter alia the first performances of De Villiers's four oratorios: *De Epiphanie* (1856), *Zion en Babylon* (to words of Rev. Van der Lingen and Arnoldus Pannevis, 1866), *De Sulamith* and *Maranatha.* The work of this society attracted attention even in Cape Town. In 1867 the German musician, Carl Junghenn*, reported on *Zion en Babylon* for *Het Volksblad,* saying that it was an "imitation" and a "mixture of recitatives, songs and choral pieces with pianoforte accompaniment". His criticism caused a sharp reaction in Paarl, echoed in distant places, such as Graaff Reinet and Bloemfontein. Junghenn later pursued his criticism by counselling De Villiers "to perform the great masters ... then he will no longer be regarded as the wonder of Paarl, but each sincere musician will extend to him the hand of brotherhood." De Villiers conducted the society until 1884, when he was succeeded by his pupil Rocco de Villiers. The story of the society still has to be investigated. — The Genootskap van Regte Afrikaners, with Rev. S.J. du Toit as its undisputed leader, and with C.P. Hoogenhout, D.F. du Toit and later Pannevis and Von Wielligh as active members, was causing a stir in Paarl after August 1875. Completely ignored in the extant histories of the Genootskap, the contributions of J.S. de Villiers were nevertheless important. He wrote music for the patriotic *Di Afrikaanse Volksliid* of Pannevis and Du Toit. This attracted some attention, encouraged the society and caused the over-enthusiastic Du Toit to describe De Villiers as "The Afrikaans Beethoven". This song never became popular, but De Villiers had more success with his composition of Du Toit's *Di Fiirkleur*. In general, De Villiers's endeavour to advance the cause of Afrikaans music in an Afrikaans town was motivated by the same ideals as those announced by the Afrikaans Genootskap. His labour on behalf of Afrikaans music, whatever its quality, deserves more attention, much as the paltry rhymes of the Patriots are quoted as initial attempts at poetry in Afrikaans. *Die Kerkbode* was conscious of this point when it wrote, after his death (5 May 1902): "(he) played such an active part in the history of his time that he must be regarded as a vital link between the present and the past." This vision of De Villiers's importance has been lost, and will have to be recaptured. Other works with a specific Afrikaans tendency were the piano piece, *De Transvaalsche jager*, a festival song to words of Celliers, *Sestien Desember* and *Slaap rustig* to words of Theo Jandrell (see list of works). — De Villiers was also a citizen of a colony under British control and so he honoured Prince Alfred, Duke of Edinburgh, with four occasional works on his visit to South Africa: *Africa's welcome to HRH The Duke of Edinburgh* (publ. 1860), *Prince Alfred's grand march* (publ. 1860) (written for the Prince's visit to the Paarl), *Prince Alfred's quick march* (1860) and *Prince Alfred's galop* (1867). For the Jubilee Festival of Queen Victoria in 1887 De Villiers wrote a *Jubilee fantasia*. Several of his works had English titles, such as the five songs which were published as *Echoes from the Cape of Good Hope*. The *Grand march* was performed by a band directed by J.S. de Villiers, which accompanied the young Prince from Klapmuts to Paarl. Other occasional works of De Villiers were concerned with the Zulu war against the British in 1879: *Op den dood van Prins Napoleon* (words C.P. Hoogenhout), *Rorke's drift* and *Isandula*. — The services of Jan Stephanus were in great demand when a new organ had to be inaugurated. On such occasions his own compositions usually featured on the programme (Wellington, 1861 - *Hij komt!;* Graaff Reinet, 1887 - *Wij zullen ingaan in zijne woningen).* De Villiers had a prominent pupil playing the organ at Graaff Reinet - P.B. de Ville, who dedicated his own *Recollections of the Paarl waltz* to "Professor" J.S. de Villiers in 1887. Nancy de Villiers says that he received a Royal letter after the visit of Prince Alfred, in which he was addressed as Professor; after that it was customary to acknowledge the honorary title. The origin of the name *Jan Orrelis* is unknown. It probably originated in the old Boer habit of distinguishing between people of the same family by nicknaming them. Reményi* was another acquaintance of De Villiers: "I have a friend in one of the De Villiers's ... a long-haired De Villiers ... and I need not tell you that his name is John de Villiers". Reményi was after a violin possessed by Jan Stephanus, but the organist refused to part with it.

WORKS

A. Sacred music

1. Oratorios

De Epiphanie. Oratorio for soprano, tenor, bass, vocal ensembles, choir and orchestra in two parts and 26 items. Ms., probably 1856. From this oratorio De Villiers later published a few items as Christmas Songs (cf. next section).   Maranatha. Oratorio for soprano, tenor, bass, vocal ensembles and choir in three parts, on a text from the Bible. Ms., between 1856 and 1866. De Villiers published items from this oratorio in the collections entitled (a) Hemelvaart (b) Gewijde Feestliederen (cf. next section).   Zion en Babylon. Oratorio for soprano, tenor, bass, vocal ensembles and choir, a single composition of 32 items; text by Rev. G.W.A. van der Lingen and A. Pannevis. Ms., about 1866. Two items from this oratorio were published by De Villiers in his Pinksterfeesliederen (cf. next section).   De Sulamith. Ms., between 1856 and

1866, mentioned by Jan Bouws in his *Musiek in Suid-Afrika* (1946) and by Nancy de Villiers in her unpublished biography of Jan Orrelis, National Afrikaans Literary Museum, Bloemfontein.

2. Choral Collections

Zes gewijde feestliederen vir koor: 1. Hoe lievelijk zijn op de bergen (Isaiah 52: 7, 8, 9), for solo and choir 2. Wij zullen ingaan in Zijne woningen (Psalm 132: 7, 8, 9) 3. Komt, en laat ons opgaan (Micah 4:2), with soprano solo 4. Want alle volken (Micah 4:5) 5. Wij zullen juichen, recitative, duet and chorus on Psalm 20:3, 5, 6. (cf. Slaap rustig, section B 1) 6. Juicht den Heer, for soprano, duet and chorus, five items (Psalm 98: 4-9). Printed by D.F. du Toit & Co., De Paarlsche Drukkerij and published by Byrne & Co., Cape Town, 1883. Pinksterfeestliederen: 1. Zend Heer Uw licht, for contralto and chorus (Psalm 43: 3, 4) 2. En te dienzelvden daage, recitative and chorus (Isaiah 12: 1, 2) 3. En gijlieden, for soprano recitative and aria and chorus. (Isaiah 12: 3, 4, 5) 4. Juicht en zingt vroolijk, chorus only (Isaiah 12:6) 5. Om Zion's wil, soprano solo (Isaiah 62:1 and 12) 6. De Heer heeft Zion verkooren, for female voices (Psalm 132: 13 and 14). Printed by C.G. Röder, Leipzig and published by Höveker & Wormser, Amsterdam/Pretoria, probably 1880. Hemelvaart: 1. God zal opstaan, bass recitative and soprano solo (Psalm 68: 2, 3, 4) 2. Zingt gode, for chorus (Psalm 68:5) 3. Wie zal klimmen, for tenor (Psalm 24: 3, 4, 5) 4. Heft uw hoofden, for chorus, solo and chorale (Psalm 24: 7, 8 and 10) 5. Dat de rivieren met de handen, for soprano and choir (Psalm 98: 8 and 9). Printed by C.G. Röder, Leipzig and published by Höveker & Wormser, Amsterdam/Pretoria, probably 1880. Het Lam voor den Troon: 1. En ik zag en ziet, recitative and chorus (Rev. 5: 6-10) 2. En ik zag en ik hoorde, recitative and chorus (Rev. 5: 11, 12) 3. En alle schepsel, recitative and chorus (Rev. 5:13). This collection was published together with the previous Hemelvaart. Kerstfeestliederen: 1. Hij komt! for choir 2. Wat heerlijkheid straal, for soprano 3. Hallelujah, looft den Heer, for female voices and mixed choir 4. Herders lofzang, for male voice choir 5. O Herders, for soprano 6. Laat ons met de herders gaan, for choir 7. Aan den nacht des heils, for quartet and mixed choir. Printed by C.G. Röder, Leipzig and published by Höveker & Wormser, Amsterdam/Pretoria, probably 1880.

3. Unpublished sacred music

Feestliederen bij de toewijding van nu (sic!) kerkgebouwen: 1. De hart naar boven (C.P. Hoogenhout), for choir. Ms., 17 November 1885 2. Wij prijzen en danken, for choir 3. Hij mag in zijn genade, for duo, soprano and tenor 4. Meld den roem van onzen God, for choir. Wat buigt g'neder, for soprano (Psalm 42: 6, 7). Hoop op God, for choir (Psalm 42:12). Gelijk een, for soprano. Tot hoe lang, for bass duet (Daniel 12: 6, 9, 10). Hoe lieflijk, for quartet (Psalm 84: 2, 3). Ziet donkere van den nacht, for soprano. Heer onze God, for contralto and choir (I Kings 8: 56, 57). Als mij eens van traanen moede, for solo and choir. Accompaniments to Psalms 47 and 150.

B. Secular works

1. Vocal

Op den dood van Prins Napoleon, cantata for soprano, tenor, three-part male voice choir and four-part choir (C.P. Hoogenhout). Ms., 1879. Rorke's drift, cantata for soprano and mixed choir (Miss C. de Villiers). Ms., 1879. Isandula, cantata for soprano, tenor and four-part choir. Ms., 1879. Noodkreet uit de Kalahari woestijn, for choir. Ms., perf. 28 March 1879. Transvaal is vrij, for four-part choir. Ms., probably 1881. Kom nu, een feestzang aangeheven ('n loflied vir Transvaal), for soprano. Ms., composed about 1890 for Nancy de Villiers. Di Afrikaanse Volkslied (Pannevis and Du Toit). *Ons Klyntji* I, 1896. Twee Transvaalse Volksliederen: (i) Di Fiirkleur (ii) Di Vierkleur van Transvaal. D.F. du Toit

& Co., Paarl, c. 1881. Slaap rustig, dapper helde (music of Wij zullen juichen, joined to words by Theo. Jandrell and published in *Die Boerevrou,* 1926). *Nuwe FAK-Sangbundel,* no. 220, 1961. 16 Desember (J.F.E. Celliers), festival song. No details. Feestlied (C.P. Hoogenhout). Paarlsche Drukkerij, 1885. Africa's welcome to HRH, The Duke of Edinburgh (Miss A.L.S.) Darter & Sons, Cape Town, 1867. Albert and Alexandra, for the wedding of the future King Edward VII to Princess Alexandra of Denmark. Cocks & Co., England, c. 1864. Echoes from the Cape of Good Hope, a song collection. Robert Cocks & Co., London, n.d. Recollections of home, song. Ashdown & Parry, London, n.d. O call it not death, song in memory of Miss Anna Knoblauch. Ms., n.d. Woman's prayer, for voice, violin, two horns and piano. Ms., n.d. There's a little mischiefmaking elfin, for violin and three female voices. Ms., in the handwriting of J.S. de Villiers, n.d.

2. Instrumental

Fantasia offertoire, quartet for piano, organ and two violins. Ms., n.d. Jubilee fantasia. Ms., probably 1887. Grand fantasia, trio for piano, organ and violin. Ms., n.d. Grand fantasia, theme and five variations for piano. Ms., n.d. Trio for piano, harmonium and violin. Ms., n.d. De Transvaalsche jager, for piano. Holland, 1875; *Vita Musica* I/2, June 1962. Prince Alfred's grand march and Prince Alfred's quick march. Darnell & Murray, Cape Town, 1860. Prince Alfred's galop. Published 1867. The steam printing press movement, for pianoforte. A.S. Robertson, Cape Town, 1855. Recollections of home, pianoforte arrangement of the song. Ashdown & Parry, London, n.d.

3. Arrangements for orchestra and four-part choir of:

The brook; Now tramp o'er moss and veld; items from Offenbach's *Orfée;* items from Balfe's *Bohemian girl; The Queen;* for orchestra only: *Spring song* (Pinsuti); *The pearl diver* (Hatton).

J.S. de Villiers composed an estimated 80 works of which 48 were printed. Of the composition total, 46 are sacred pieces. His major contribution to Afrikaans church music is contained in the collections *Gewijde feestliederen, Kerstfeesliederen, Pinksterfeestliederen* and *Hemelvaart.* Although the composer acted as organist for more than 50 years, it appears that he left no proper organ music whatever. Liturgically he is represented by 13 melodies, which were printed in the proof edition of *Halleluja* in 1883. The major part of his sacred music was written to compensate for the lack of suitable Dutch-Afrikaans vocal works, experienced by the Paarl Philharmonic Society. — In 1973 Mr Jan van de Graaf discovered manuscripts of J.S. de Villiers in the garage of Mrs Hitchings of Stutterheim, a granddaughter of the composer. The manuscripts are certainly not in a condition to be printed; they have rather the appearance of rough drafts. The numbering of the items often varies, and extraneous music is sometimes written in the part books of the choral works. Most of the works are incomplete, probably as a result of single copies only written for vocalists, which were lost while in the singers' possession. As a result of Dr C.G. Henning's work on these manuscripts it has since 1974 become possible to assess the importance of this Afrikaans musical pioneer (see Sources). — The works are those of a talented but untrained composer, who compensated for his lack of technical facility by drawing on laborious practical experience. Thus the register of voices in the manuscripts exceeds the capabilities of choral singers and had to be transposed to a lower pitch; similarly, echo effects and crescendos reaching from pp to ff show signs of musical passion, expressed in an elementary and clumsy way. De Villiers's melodies are generally musical and attractive, but the harmonies are of the simplest, with numerous parallel thirds and sixths, and the phrasing is restricted to monotonous successions of two- and four-bar constructions. There are bare traces of counterpoint - the instrumental accompaniments generally double the vocal parts. Solo melodies are often characterized by a tendency to a flowery, ornamental style (the availability of facile singers?). On the other hand, the extracts from the oratorios, which De Villiers prepared for publication during the 1880s, are written in a convincingly simple, four-part choral style, suited to the average Afrikaans church choir. — An interesting aspect of his vocal music is the musical illustration of words: "Hell and Satan have fled" is set to a series of rising, rapid quaver figures. "You will be pushed down to Hell" is clothed in the musical form of a drawn-out descending octave; and when rejoicing or praise of the Creator is mentioned, the melodic lines revel in triadic themes. — De Villiers cannot be considered an important composer, and Junghenn was probably right when he referred the composer to the great masters. His significance is rather of a cultural and historical nature; he is important as the first Afrikaner to compose significant music. A revaluation of his work against the background of the Western Province cultural situation in the nineteenth century, is probably due.

BIBLIOGRAPHY

BOUWS, JAN: *Komponiste van Suid-Afrika*. Stellenbosch, 1971. BOUWS, JAN: *Die musieklewe van Kaapstad, 1800-1850 en sy verhouding tot die musiekkultuur van Wes-Europa*. Cape Town, 1966. BOUWS, JAN: *Musiek in Suid-Afrika*. Brugge, 1946. BOUWS, JAN: *Suid-Afrikaanse komponiste van vandag en gister*. Balkema, Cape Town, 1957. KITSHOF, M.C.: *G.W.A. van der Lingen*. D.Phil thesis, Groningen, 1972. OBERHOLSTER, J.A.S.: *'n Driekwart-eeu van God's liefde. Noorder-Paarl 1875-1950*. Paarl, 1950. Kwartmellennium-gedenkboek van die NG Gemeente Paarl, 1691-1941. Paarl Drukpersmaatskappy, 1941: Chapter 3 - Die orrelgeskiedenis van die gemeente, by J.C. Pauw, p. 197; and chapter 6 - Onderwys in Drakenstein, by P.S. du Toit, p. 283. VAN DER MERWE, F.Z.: *Suid-Afrikaanse musiekbibliografie, 1787-1952*. J.L. van Schaik, Pretoria, 1958. VAN DER WALT, J.J.A.: *Die Afrikaanse psalmmelodieë*. Pro Rege Press, Potchefstroom, 1962.

SOURCES

ACTA, handelingen van de Synode der NG Kerk van Zuid Afrika: 1852, p. 7; 1880, p. 44; 1890, p. 61. BOUWS, JAN: Jan Orrelis, Suid-Afrikaanse geleentheidskomponis. *Cabo* II, Cape Town, 1973. BOUWS, JAN: Langs die wapad van die Afrikaanse musiek. *Res Musicae* VII, September 1960. BOUWS, JAN: Suid-Afrikaanse vlagliedere. *Lantern* XV/4, Pretoria, 1966. *The Cape Monitor:* 1 August 1855. *De Getuigde* XXIV/8, August 1902: advertisement on page 160. *Halleluja. Psalmen en gezangen der NG Kerk van Zuid Afrika*, Cape Town, 1883. HENNING, C.G.: Jan Orrelis van die Paarl. *Tydskrif vir Geesteswetenskappe* XIV/3, September 1974. HENNING, C.G.: The music and manuscripts of J.S. de Villiers. *Africana Society of Pretoria, Yearbook I*, 1975. HENNING, C.G.: Die eerste Afrikaanse oratoria. *Musicus* 3/1, 1975. HENNING, C.G.: *South African biographical dictionary* III. HSRC, Pretoria, 1977. HENNING, C.G.: Research, draft article and compilation of sources. *In Memoriam: Johanna M.W. de Villiers*. Paarl, December 1897. In Memoriam: Johanna M.W. de Villiers. *De Kerkbode*, XIV/52, 30 December 1897. In Memoriam: J.S. de Villiers. *De Kerkbode* XIX/19, 15 May 1902. Estates: J.S. de Villiers (jun.): MOOC 6/9/450, DN 1560; Elizabeth M. de Villiers: MOOC 6/9/209, DN 8636; J.S. de Villiers (sen.): MOOC 6/9/148, DN 865. Manuscripts and published works, De Villiers collection no. 367, National Documentation Centre for Music, HSRC, Pretoria. Manuscripts and published works, De Villiers collection, National Afrikaans Literary Museum, Bloemfontein. Manuscripts discovered at Stutterheim by J. van de Graaf. *Sam Sly's journal,* Cape Town, 26 September 1845, 18 November 1845. VAN DER MERWE, F.Z.: Op soek na gister, iets omtrent die musiek van J.S. de Villiers, *SAMT* 49, December 1955. VAN DER MERWE, F.Z.: Transvaalsche Jager, *Vita Musica* I/2, June 1963. *De Zuid Afrikaan,* 14 December 1857 (advertisement). Information supplied by Miss M.C. Bodley.

—J.P.M.

DE VILLIERS, JUSTINA WILHELMINA NANCY (MRS LATEGAN), *21 January 1871 in Paarl; °19 September 1957 in Parys, OFS. Soprano, pianist, music teacher.

Nancy de Villiers was the twelfth child of J.S. de Villiers*, who was also her first teacher. From 1899 till 1902 she studied at the Berlin Conservatoire, where she was trained in piano, organ, composition, singing and elocution. She returned to South Africa after the Anglo-Boer War and concentrated on music teaching. In 1903 she and her sister, Mrs Von Wielligh*, founded the "Villieria School of Music" at Stellenbosch, and two years later they established the Stellenbosch Conservatoire of Music* together with F.W. Jannasch* and Hans Endler*. Nancy de Villiers taught there until 1910, the year in which she married A.H. Lategan, who had been one of her pupils. She and her husband then went abroad for a while, after which they settled at Cradock where they lived for 17 years. In 1946 they moved to Parys in the Orange Free State. Although Mrs Lategan composed several works for pianoforte, violin and for singing, only one of her compositions was published.

WORKS
Lied van Vroue-Landbouvereniging Kaapprovinsie (E.H. Nellmapius). Published, n.d.   Lied ohne Worte, for violin and pianoforte, op. 1. Ms., n.d.   Der stille Thal, op. 2 no. 1. Ms., n.d.   Seitdem die Mutter heimgegangen ist, op. 2 no. 2. Ms., n.d.   Moment musical in E major. Ms., n.d.   Rondo in B major. Ms., n.d.   Rondo in F major. Ms., n.d.   Mazurka no. 1 in A major. Ms., n.d.   Op die moment (improvisation). Ms., n.d.   Romanza for violin and pianoforte in G major. Ms., n.d.

BIBLIOGRAPHY
VAN DER MERWE, F.Z.: *Suid-Afrikaanse musiekbibliografie, 1787-1952.* J.L. van Schaik, Pretoria 1958.

SOURCES
HENNING, C.G.: Nancy de Villiers (Miss Nancy). *Musicus* 3/3, 1975.   STEGMANN, FRITS: Nancy de Villiers se bydrae tot ons musieklewe. *Die Burger,* 13 July 1961.   VAN ZYL, MARIE: Sy was een van ons geniaalste musici. *Dagbreek en Sondagnuus,* 22 August 1948.   National Documentation Centre for Music, HSRC, Pretoria.

—F.S.

DE VILLIERS, MARTHINUS LOURENS ("M.L."), *31 July 1885 in Paarl; °17 May 1977 in Wellington. Composer of *Die Stem van Suid-Afrika.*

M.L. de Villiers is the son of Dirk de Villiers* and Tina Smith, who founded an Institute of Music at Wellington three years after the birth of their son. His mother taught him to play the piano and his father gave him organ and violin lessons as well as instruction in harmony. He also learned to play the clarinet and was able to join his father's Wellington Brass Band. After 1920, while he was a minister of the DR Church in Simonstown, he resumed his musical studies under Professor Henry Bell*, head of the South African College of Music* of the University of Cape Town, who guided him in harmony and counterpoint for three years. — Although his

345

exceptional talent for music was evident at an early age (he started composing in 1899) he studied at the Huguenot University College from 1901-1904 and took a conventional BA degree, after which he accepted a teaching post at Wepener in the OFS (1905-1907). He practised music in Wepener and continued to write music, became a student of Theology at the Victoria College (the present University of Stellenbosch) in 1908, after which he served as minister of the Dutch Reformed Church in Beaufort West (1912), in Bedford (1912-1918) and in Simonstown (1918-1930). While in Bedford the vicarage became a centre of unprecedented musical activity: he organised thanksgiving concerts, held evenings of chamber music at the vicarage, gave organ recitals in the church and even established a chamber orchestra consisting of five violins, a 'cello, a clarinet and a piano. In Bedford, and later in Simonstown, he remained musically creative. — In 1931 the pattern of his life changed. He resigned as minister of the Dutch Reformed Church and settled in Wellington, where he died in 1977. During his first fourteen years as a free-lance musician he undertook 17 tours of the country, gave organ recitals and hundreds of concerts, as well as talks on music at different schools. Important extras were the composition of about 250 school songs (often written to his own texts), and the promotion of his own compositions. This turbulent existence was curtailed by the Second World War and came to an end in 1945. — As a musician, M.L. de Villiers was an energetic supporter of the Afrikaners' cultural life. He identified himself with their drive towards cultural progress and was emotionally involved in their hopes and aspirations, composing Afrikaans school songs, songs for festivals and special occasions and music to Afrikaans poems. His greatest truimph came when his melody for Langenhoven's *Die Stem van Suid-Afrika* was accepted as the national anthem. Thereafter he became a well-known musical personality, who was often honoured by the Afrikaners. Because he was committed to many things outside music - his religious vocation, his studies - he was never really able to fully develop his musical talents. Nevertheless, the fresh spontaneity of his melodic gifts left an indelible impression on the Afrikaans cultural life. The most convincing demonstration of this fact is the way in which his melody for the *Stem van Suid-Afrika* awakened a resonance in the bosom of his people. — Public recognition of his services were not lacking: in 1940 the Suid-Afrikaanse Akademie vir Wetenskap en Kuns* awarded him a medal for music and, after his melody for the national anthem had been accepted by Parliament, the state provided him with a life-long pension. In 1957, during the Folk Music Congress of the FAK at Stellenbosch, official tribute was paid to him and in 1961 a special M.L. de Villiers-evening was held in Simonstown, where he had been a minister for twelve years. His melody for the national anthem was written there. — In June 1911 he married Jemina Susanna du Plessis; they had two daughters and two sons, one of whom - Dirkie de Villiers* - chose music as a profession.

WORKS

A. Vocal

1. Choral

Zijt Gij de Koning der Joden? (M.L. de V.). Dedicated to the choir of the DR Church in Wepener. R. Müller, Cape Town, 1905-1907 (?).

2. Solo songs

Adieu song. Vaarwel (Vera Nicholls - Eng.; M.L. de V. - Afr.). Dogilbert, Brussels, n.d.   Empire Exhibition love song on the Milner Park waltz (M. Catoggio, M.L. de V.; also in Afrikaans). Cape Times Ltd., 1937. Fyn soos 'n vlinder (M.L. de V.). No. 96 in *Nuwe FAK -sangbundel.* Nas. Boekhandel, Cape Town, 1961.   Gebed van die polisiedienaar (M.L. de V.). Cape times, Cape Town, 1937.   Hoe die liefde kom (after Totius). Nas. Pers, Bloemfontein, 1920.   I dreamt. Ik droomde. (M.L. de V.). Joseph Williams Ltd., London, 1915.   Melkbosch-by-the-seas. Melkbosch-aan-die-see. Cape Times, Cape Town, n.d.   Roses. Rose (Vera Nicholls - Eng.; M.L. de V. - Afr.). Dogilbert, Brussels, 1924.   Ses Afrikaanse kunsliedere: 1. Komaan (J.F.E. Celliers) 2. Terugblik (Celliers) 3. 'n Doornkroon (Celliers) 4. Die branders (Celliers) 5. Rus en stilte (I.D. du Plessis) 6. Lig en donker (Celliers). Dogilbert, Brussels, 1921.   Salut d'amour (A.G. Visser). No. 111, *Nuwe FAK-sangbundel.* Nas. Pers Boekhandel, Cape Town, 1961.   Sewe Afrikaanse stapliedere (E.M. Nellmapius). Nas. Pers, Cape Town, after 1940.   Six Stoneman songs (Bertha Stoneman, principal of the former Huguenot University College in Wellington). Darter & Sons, Cape Town, 1943.   Starlight. Sterrelig (Vera Nicholls - Eng.; M.L. de V. - Afr.). Dogilbert, Brussels, n.d. Afr. edition 1924.   Twee lewensliedere. Ms., n.d.   Vier Afrikaanse liedjies. Almal se liedere no. 6. R. Müller, Cape Town, 1918-1930.   Waai, windjie waai (M.L. de V.). No. 138 in *Nuwe FAK-sangbundel.* Nas. Boekhandel, Cape Town, 1961.

3. Patriotic songs
Afscheid naar kommando, 1899-1902. Cape Times, Cape Town, n.d.   Die stem van Suid-Afrika (Langenhoven), comp. 1919. *Almal se liedere* no.1. Nas. Pers, Cape Town, n.d. Many reprints for solo and/or choir, also by other publishers and in collections.   Dingaansdag, 'n feeslied vir 16 Desember. Darter & Sons, Cape Town, n.d.   Reprints in various collections.   Dit daag al oweral (J.F.E. Celliers). Dogilbert, Brussels, n.d.   Drie eie nasieliedere. *Almal se liedere*-reeks. Nas. Pers, Cape Town, after 1940. Drie liedjies vir die volk. *Almal se liedere* no. 4. Nas.Pers, Cape Town, n.d.   Ek ken 'n liefste volksman (on Pres. M.T. Steyn) (M.L. de V.). Het Volksblad-drukkerij, Bloemfontein, 1915.   Geen vaderland (after Totius). Nas. Pers, Bloemfontein, 1939.   Helpmekaar: aan alle Afrikaners die hulle volk werklik lief het. Performed at Slachtersnek, 9 March 1916. Het Volksblad-drukkerij, Bloemfontein, n.d. (also in four-part edition).   Hugenotelied, vir gedenkfees 1939 (Ps. 42). E.M. Needham Co., Cape Town, 1939.   Ons volksgebed. Aan my volk (M.L. de V.). Nas. Pers, Bloemfontein, 1920.   Oproep tot stryd vir die moedertaal (N.J. Brümmer). Printed by C.G. Röder, Leipzig, and published by Darter & Sons, Cape Town, 1911.   Soet is die stryd (I.D. du Plessis). Nas. Pers, Cape Town, n.d.   Strydlied (J.F.E. Celliers). No. 9 of Volksliedere byeenversamel deur die Werda-studentebond. Pro Ecclesia, Stellenbosch, 1922.   Trou (J.F.E. Celliers). *Almal se liedere* no. 3. Nas. Pers, and Cape Times as "national edition", n.d.   Twee gedenkliedere: 1. Slachtersnek (also in four parts); 2. Ons voorgeslacht (M.L. de V.). 'Het Volksblad-drukkerij, Bloemfontein, n.d., and R. Müller, Cape Town, n.d.   Voortrekkerlied (J.F.E. Celliers). No. 12 of Volksliedere byeenversameld deur die Werda-studentebond. Pro Ecclesia, Stellenbosch, 1922.   Vertel mij. Dedicated to Young South Africa (M.L. de V.). De Nationale Pers, Bloemfontein, 1920.   Vyf vaderlandsliedjies. *Almal se liedere* no. 5. R. Müller, Cape Town, 1915-1930.   Werda-lied (Langenhoven). No. 1 of Volksliederen byeenversameld deur die Werda studentebond. Pro Ecclesia, Stellenbosch, 1922. Also printed as no. 20 in *Nuwe FAK-sangbundel,* 1961.

4. Songs for societies, schools and incidental songs
Alma mater (M.L. de V.). *Die Huisgenoot,* jubilee edition, 1896-1946. Wellington, 1946.   Die lied van die ATKV (M.L. de V.), publ. in 4-part arrangement in *Die Taalgenoot,* 2935.   Lijksang (in commemoration of Prof. C.F.J. Muller), for solo or choir (M.L. de V.). *De Goede Hoop,* 15 September 1915.   Music Institute song. Vive l'institute! Dedicated to his

347

parents and fellow students at the Institute. Darter & Sons, Cape Town, n.d. Nuwe volkspele: 30 liedjies (M.L. de V.). Pro Ecclesia, Stellenbosch, 1942. Ons eie volkspele. Uniale Raad vir Volkspele en Volksang, April 1955 (nos. 9, 10, 14, 16, 20, 26, 27, 35, 42, 46). Ons verdedigingslied. Dedicated to genl. J.C. Smuts. Darter & Sons, Cape Town, n.d. SA Military College song (M.L. de V.). Dogilbert, Brussels, n.d. SA Field Artillery song (M.L. de V.). Dogilbert, Brussels, n.d. Twintig skoolliedjies (in collaboration with P.K. de Villiers). Composed by M.L. de V.: nos. 2, 4, 6, 8, 10, 12, 14, 16, 18, 20. Approximately 158 school songs, composed mainly between 1931 - 1945.

B. Instrumental

1. Pianoforte

Caprice to a butterfly. Aan 'n vlindertjie. Perry & Co., Cape Town, 1923. Empire Exhibition March. Cape Times, 1936/37. March for the students at the Huguenot University College, Wellington; also distributed as *National March for South Africa* during the Empire Exhibition, 1936/37; also in Afrikaans as *Volksmars vir Suid-Afrika*. Cape Times, 1936. On the pier, intermezzo. Perry & Co., Cape Town, 1916. Seven wonders waltzes. Milner Park waltzes. Sewe wonders-walse. R. Müller, Cape Town, 1936. Three piano sketches. Darter & Sons, Cape Town, n.d.

C. Melodies to Psalms and Hymns

April 1919: Psalm 15 and Psalm 35. July 1921: Psalms 5, 20, 57, 78, 86, 112, 128, 131. 1926: Psalms 22, 41, 50, 104. Hymns 26, 102. 1937: Ps. 131.

D. Unpublished works

Admissiebondlied (M.L. de V.), 1954. Allegro vivace, dedicated to his mother, Tina de Villiers, 1905. Andante religioso, for organ. Afrikaner Boere-orkesmars, for pianoforte. Algemene Bybellied (M.L. de V.). Calm, for organ. Die Afrikaner vrou (M.L. de V.), 1925. Die goue kalf, a cantata. Die simboliese ossewatrek-lied (M.L. de V.), 1938. Die sonnige Suide, for pianoforte. Dink aan my (J.F.E. Celliers). Three songs on words by Cassie le Grange: 1. Lentelied 2. Dit was 'n maanligaand 3. Wiegeliedjie. Edel, edel held! For four-part chorus. Eie klaslied (own class song), for students at the theological seminary at Stellenbosch. Fiat lux (M.L. de Villiers). Here, Here, God! For choir. Glen Lyndon, inaugural march and aria, for organ. Goudlied (M.L. de V.). He blew his pipes (B. Lane), for choir. Herfs (M.L. de V.) Hou koers! (M.L. de V.). Jukskeilied (M.L. de V.). Laat Israel vertrou! For choir. Landboulied (Rev. Martins), for fourpart-chorus. Looft Hem, volk'ren geeft Hem eer! For organ and chorus. March, published by D.I. de Villiers in 1903. Details lost. Mid streams and glen, for pianoforte. Môre op die Groot-Karoo, 1912. Najaarswind, for chorus. 'n Vas- en biddag, for chorus (M.L. de V.). Ons eie lied (G.B.A. Gerdener). Ons openingslied (P.J. van der Merwe). Raindrops, for organ. Reddingsdaadlied (after Langenhoven). Salonstück for violin, pianoforte and organ, 1902. String quartet in C, dedicated to Dr W.H. Bell. South African Air Force song (M.L. de Villiers). Spaarsaamheidslied (M.L. de V.). Special Service Battalion song (M.L. de V.), 1934. Storm scene, for organ. Piece for violin and piano, SA Eisteddfod prize, 1923. Sunset at the Cape, for pianoforte. The busy Rand, for pianoforte. The roar of the elements, for organ. The song of the veld, for pianoforte. 't Is morgen vakantie (Nico Hofmeyer). Though storms may rage, for organ. Wedding march in C, between 1908 and 1911. Voorslag (A.G. Visser). Waar seemeeu sit, for pianoforte. Won't you come aroaming, for chorus, 1922. 1910, for organ.

WRITINGS

Oproep tot stryd vir die moedertaal: Wij zullen handhaven. Stellenbosch, 1911. Mijn eigen taal. *The Stellenbosch Student's Quarterly* XII/2, July 1911.   Die Afrikaanse lied. *Populair Wetenskaplike Leesboek* IV, Cape Town, 1920.   *Die Huisgenoot:* articles on composers, performers and musical matters on 30 November 1923, 7 March 1924, 24 October 1924, 19 December 1924, 27 June 1924, 9 May 1924, 8 and 15 August and 5 September 1924, 15 November 1924, 16 January 1925, 30 January 1925, 13 February 1925, 6 March 1925.   *Die Burger:* Septimus de Villiers. 1 October 1929.   *Die Catorse - a memorandum.* Ms., 1962.

BIBLIOGRAPHY

BOUWS, JAN: *Musiek in Suid-Afrika.* Uitgeverij Voorland, Brugge, 1946.   BOUWS, JAN: *Suid-Afrikaanse komponiste van vandag en gister.* A. Balkema, Cape Town, 1957.   BOUWS, JAN: *Komponiste van Suid-Afrika.* C.F. Albertyn Bpk., Stellenbosch, 1971.   GROBBELAAR, E.P.: *Die kulturele betekenis van ds. M.L. de Villiers.* D. Phil. thesis, US, 197--   FENEYSEY, S.F.: *Die NG gemeente Glen Lyndon gedurende 'n honderd jare, 1829-1929.* Commemorative publication Nas. Pers, Cape Town, 1930.   Golden Jubilee edition of *De Hugenoot,* 1896-1946. Wellington, 1946.   NIENABER, P.J.: *Manne van betekenis.* Afrikaanse Pers Boekhandel, Johannesburg, 1950.   OBERHOLSTER, J.J.: *Wepener, 1869 - 1969.* Nas. Pers, Bloemfontein, 1969.   POTGIETER, J.H.: *'n Analistiese oorsig van die Afrikaanse kunslied.* D.Mus. thesis, UP, 1967.   VAN DER MERWE, F.Z.: *Suid-Afrikaanse musiekbibliografie, 1787-1952.* J.L. van Schaik, Pretoria, 1958.

SOURCES

ANON: M.L. de Villiers - uit sy hart 'n volkslied. *Die Kerkbode,* 3 September 1969.   ANON.: Gaan ons nooit dankie sê? *Die Brandwag,* 17 May 1957.   ANON.: Simonstad, die vlootdorp, geboorteplek van ons volkslied. *Commando,* June, 1962.   BOUWS, JAN: Sy naam sal voortleef. *Die Taalgenoot,* January 1962.   COETZEE, P.: Agt note in drie jaar. *Die Brandwag,* 24 September 1963.   GOLDBLATT, S.: Die Stem van Suid-Afrika. *Die Huisgenoot,* 11 August 1933.   GOLDBLATT, S.: Die Stem is vyftig jaar oud. *Die Huisgenoot,* 31 May 1968.   GOLDBLATT, S.: Preface to *Collected works of C.J. Langenhoven XVI.* Cape Town, 25 September 1957.   HOOGENHOUT, I.: Komponis van Die Stem vier goue bruilof. *Die Huisgenoot,* 25 August 1961.   LAKE, A.S.: Volkslied 'n skandaal. *Mense,* September 1956.   THERON, R.: Langenhoven, Die Stem en M.L. de Villiers. *SAMT* 84, July 1973.   VAN DER MERWE, J.: Die Stem van Suid-Afrika. *Afrikaans-Nederlandse Maandblad,* November 1957.   *De Koerier* (Beaufort West): 1 February 1912.   *Bedford Enterprise:* Criticisms between 1912 and 1918.   *Die Burger:* 5 September 1922, 14 November 1924, 1 January 1935, 3 January 1936, 12 November 1940, 24 March 1956, 3 March 1957, 4 May 1957, 24 April 1964, 8 May 1965; four articles by Sarah Goldblatt published 12-15 August 1957.   *Parliamentary records:* 26 July 1938, 29 July 1938, 25 August 1938, 7 February 1939, 23 February 1954, 23 March 1956, 2 May 1957.   *Die Volksblad:* 28 June 1971.   *Hoofstad:* 29 June 1971.   National Documentation Centre for Music, HSRC, Pretoria.

—Ed.

DE VILLIERS, O.T   Piano music II/1

DE VILLIERS, PIETER JAKOB, *10 December 1861 in Paarl; °11 March 1937 at Porterville. Organist and music teacher.

Pieter Jakob received his musical training from his eldest brother Rocco C. de Villiers* and in 1884 he emigrated to take up the positions of organist, music teacher and town clerk in Boshof. Four years later he married Ellen van Heerden, sister of the Rev. P.S. van Heerden and in 1891 he brought out his *Muzikale gids,* a manual written in Dutch for music teaching. He was employed in Ladybrand from 1896 to 1903, in Noorder-Paarl from 1906 to 1916, in Queenstown, where he was attached to Queen's College, from 1916 to 1929, and in Porterville from 1929 to 1937 and gave lessons in piano, violin, cello, organ and wind instruments. A characteristic of his career was that he regularly trained men and boys to play wind instruments, and thus created bands in the centres where he lived. — He had three children. One of the daughters, Gerty, was a singer; the son, Abraham M. de Villiers, became a competent clarinettist. — Like other members of his family, P.J. de Villiers distinguished himself as an enthusiast who took the initiative in several musical fields. By sheer love of music he was able to do important pioneering work. Compositions of his which have survived, betray only an elementary knowledge of creative art; but the significance of his work lies in what he did for music in a predominantly rural country with the recitals he gave, by his teaching of a variety of instruments, in training choirs, and finally in forming military bands, of which he was particularly fond.

WORKS

Fantasia. Pianoforte solo dedicated to the Boshof Amateur Orchestral Society. Ms., n.d.   Au revoir. Something for the piano from your brother. Ms., n.d.   Review march, for brass band. Ms., n.d.   The night is calm. Music by your brother. Ms., 1887.   Wij zullen juichen (Ps. 20), a choral composition. Ms., n.d.   Zendingslied. Ms., 25 September 1887.

PUBLICATIONS

De muzikale gids. W.A. Richards & Zonen, Cape Town, 1891.

BIBLIOGRAPHY

DE VILLIERS, D.P.: *A history of the De Villiers family.* Nasionale Boekhandel, 1960.   DE VILLIERS, M.L.: *Die Catorse - 'n memorandum.* 1962.   DREYER, A.: *Ons Kerk.* Samuel Griffiths, Cape Town, 1927.   OBERHOLSTER, J.A.S.: *Een gedenkboek van die Ned. Ger. Gemeente - Noorder-Paarl, Driekwart Eeu.* Paarl Printers, 1950.

SOURCE

MALAN, J.P.: Arbeiders in die musikale wyngaard. No. 1, P.J. de Villiers. *Vita Musica* I/4, February 1964.

—E.V. (amplified)

DE VILLIERS, PIETER JOHANNES, *19 June 1924 in Klerksdorp; now (1978) in Potchefstroom. Professor of Music, composer.

After obtaining his BA degree at the University of Pretoria, Pieter de Villiers went to Stellenbosch where he studied at the Conservatoire of Music* under Maria Fismer* (piano, organ, history of music, teaching methods, harmony and counterpoint), Miss E. Lubbe and Walter Swanson* (orchestration and composition). After two years he qualified as a school and music teacher (1948), obtained the UPLM, UTLM and UALM diplomas of the University of South Africa and continued his studies under Pollard in London for the diplomas LRAM and ARCM. — Since then Pieter de Villiers has often appeared in South Africa as a soloist (on the piano and the harpsichord), also with the Cape Town City Orchestra* and the SABC Orchestra. He often broadcasts, is an enthusiastic participant in chamber music and has become known throughout the country as an accompanist to prominent South African singers such as Cecilia Wessels*, Betsy de la Porte*, Mimi Coertse*, Hanlie van Niekerk*, Joyce Barker* and Emma Renzi (Emmarentia Scheepers*). — As choral conductor Pieter de Villiers has also contributed to South African music. Between 1948 and 1953 he accompanied the Stellenbosch Seminary Choir* on five concert tours as pianist and as conductor, and since 1962 he was largely responsible for the recording of all the

Afrikaans psalms and hymns for the radio by the Sangluskoor*. This task was completed in May 1969 after seven years. — He taught mainly pianoforte at the Stellenbosch Conservatoire of Music (1948-1953), and then became a lecturer in the Department of Music of the Potchefstroom University for Christian Higher Education*. After seven years Pieter de Villiers moved to Johannesburg, as transcription-organiser for the SABC, and in 1963 he was appointed lecturer at the Music Academy of the University of Pretoria*, mainly for organ tuition. In January 1968 he resigned to become a professor of Music at the Potchefstroom University for CHE.

WORKS

A. Choral works

Die Slamaaierwinkel (C.L. Leipoldt), for unacc. mixed choir. MS., 1967.   In die Hoëveld (Toon van den Heever), for four-part male voice choir. Ms., 1967.   Psalm cantata, Lof en smeking. Ms., 1967.   Dis al (Jan F.E. Celliers), for unacc. four-part choir. Ms., 1968.   Cantata for the centenary festival of the PU for CHE. Ms., 1969.   Op die Krovlak (Boerneef), for ladies choir with pianoforte acc. Ms., 1969/70:   1. Ek het 'n vreemde voël hoor fluit   2. Wyn rym met pyn   3. Dit spook hier woes met nuwemaan   4. Ek is dankbaar op die Nuwejaar   5. Die eikeblare loop en loop   6. (a) Losringtrens en rolletjiestang (b) Deuntjie draai al deur my kop   7. Waar skuil ek teen die son se steek?   Danklied van die feesvierende menigte (Ps. 118: 1-6, 27, 28). Ms., 1971.   Die woorde sonder prys (C.J. Langenhoven), for unacc. mixed choir. Ms., 1972.   Raaisel (C.J. Langenhoven), for two-part choir and pianoforte. Ms., 1972.   Ses liedjies vir latenstyd (Boerneef), for mixed choir and pianoforte. Ms., 1972:   1. Die jonggroen van 'n eikeboom   2. Die reën sak uit by Koorsteenberg   3. Horie patryse ennie fisane   4. My hart blom wit   5. Niks hang so rooi soos wingerdblaar by Hexrivier   6. Jy's man alleen.   Met rym en klank (Boerneef), for ladies choir with pianoforte, dedicated to Helena Strauss and the Cantare Ladies Choir. Ms., 1972/73:   1. Kattekruie en roosmaryn 2. Jy's hond alleen   3. Kaliefos en doepablare 4. Ou Soelsman speel met rym en klank   5. (a) Laat bokspring die kram   (b) Bantom hom so en flennie die snare   (c) Laas was dit droog.   6. Die duikerooi was dragtig   7. Smaak die ghaap vir jou te bitter? Drie Leipoldt-liedjies, for unacc. mixed choir. Ms., 1973:   1. Soos 'n borrelende vink 2. 'n Treurlied 3. Klim op, klim op met die slingerpad. Ses gedigte uit Leitourgos (I.L. de Villiers), for unacc. mixed choir. Ms., 1973:   1. Trisagion   2. Nagmaal   3. Doop   4. Stuurwielgebed Du Toitskloof   5. Maria 6. Wonder. Sing tot eer van die Here 'n nuwe lied (Ps. 98), for unacc. mixed choir. Ms., 1974.   Die Here is my Herder (Ps. 23), for soprano, choir and chamber orchestra, commissioned by the Transvaal Choral Council for the Year of the Language Festival, 1975. Ms.   Die herders van Bethlehem (Lucas 2: 8-14), for solo voice, mixed choir and organ or pianoforte. South African Christmas Carols Part II. N.G. Kerk Boekhandel, 1975.   Die Heer regeer, a psalm cantata for unacc. chorus, commissioned by the SABC for the Totius Year. Ms., 1976:   1. Die Heer regeer (Ps.93) 2. My hart is nie hoogmoedig, Heer! (Ps. 131)   3. Loof God, loof Sy naam alom! (Ps. 150). Vergewe en vergeet (Totius), two-part chorus with pianoforte acc. Ms., 1976/77.   Ps. 8 for soprano and baritone, mixed choir and pianoforte or organ, composed for the unveiling of the Totius monument, Potchefstroom, on 19 February 1977.   Vreemde prooi, for ladies choir and pianoforte. Ms., 1977:   1. Manna oor die duine (I.L. de Villiers)   2. Lied vannie gamiente vannie Here (Adam Small) 3. Hoe Christus sy kerk op aarde (en in ons stad) gestig het (N.P. Van Wyk Louw).   My tong sal U Woord besing, for four-part chorus. Duplicated, n.d.   Sproeireën (D.J. Opperman), for unacc. chorus. Ms., n.d.

B. Songs

Die geskenke (E. Eybers), a song. Ms., 1961.   Sewe Boerneefliedjies, dedicated to Betsy de la Porte. FAK, Johannesburg, 1961: 1. Blaas op die pampoenstingel 2. Klein Piedeplooi 3. Die berggans het 'n veer laat val   4. Waarom is die duiwel vir die slypsteen bang? 5. Aandblom is 'n wit blom   6. My koekiesveerhen jou verkereveer   7. Daar bo teen die rant.   Ek hou van blou (A.D. Keet), a song. MS., 1967.   Kleuterland, for voice and pianoforte. FAK, Johannesburg, 1967. Seesonnet (T. Wassenaar), a song. Ms., 1968.   Heilige nag, *South African Christmas Carols* no. 7. Voortrekkerpers, Johannesburg, 1968.   Kliprivier Primary School Song. Ms., 1970.   Four Psalms, for baritone and piano, commissioned by CAPAB. Ms., 1970/71.   Waar ou Heidelberg hang aan die Suikerbosrand (A.G. Visser), for solo voice and pianoforte. Ms., 1974.   Middagslapie (A.G. Visser), for solo voice and pianoforte. Ms., 1974.   As dit fluit-fluit gaan (A.G. Visser), for solo voice and pianoforte. Ms., 1974.   Kersaand ('n gebed) (I.L. de Villiers), for solo voice and pianoforte, *South African Christmas Carols* Part II. N.G. Kerk Boekhandel, 1975.   Lied sonder woorde, for soprano and pianoforte. Ms., 1975.

C. Pianoforte

Klein Pretoria-suite, for pianoforte. Ms., 1977:   1. Somernamiddag: Magnolia-dal 2. Oom Paul 3. Rugby op Loftus.

SOURCES

Career of Prof. De Villiers. *Opus* I/1, December 1969.

—Ed.

DE VILLIERS, PIETER KUYPER DE VOS.   *16 September 1874 at Caledon; °17 December 1949 in Cape Town. Organist, son of Rocco Catorzia de Villiers*.

"P.K." was musically trained by his father and at the beginning of 1894 he became organist and music teacher in Richmond, where he was also leader of a band. He filled his father's post as a music teacher in Paarl in May 1896 and a few months later he entered the RAM where he studied for four and a half years. He received medals for organ playing in 1899 and in 1900, gave a few organ recitals, and became one of the earliest South Africans to receive the ARAM diploma. In January 1900 he also obtained the ARCO diploma. — After his return to South Africa he taught music at Stellenbosch, but when Hans Endler* became his assistant in 1903, he revisited England for a few months at the end of the same year. Returning to South Africa, he settled at Worcester and became well known in the Western Province as the founder and conductor of an amateur band (1904-1910), as the organist of the DRC, as the founder and conductor of a Philharmonic Society, and as a music teacher. In addition to his organ recitals at Worcester (1904-1910), he gave some eighteen recitals in far-flung places such as Montagu, Graaff Reinet, Molteno, Philippolis and Bloemfontein-seven of which were at organ dedication ceremonies. He was responsible for the specifications of eight new organs during this period. — After a third visit to England, De Villiers settled in Bloemfontein in January 1911 as organist of the DRC and, initially, as a private music teacher. From July 1912, however, he also taught music at the Normal and Polytechnic Colleges, the Grey University College, and at various schools. Apart from organ recitals in other centres in the Free State, he gave lectures in Bloemfontein and organised pupil concerts. In October 1922 he paid his fourth visit to England and this time he also went to Germany. Several months after his return, in January 1923, he left Bloemfontein to become the first Inspector of

Music (Western Province) in the Cape Education Department in October 1923. He lived in Cape Town until his retirement in 1935, but frequently travelled on official duties. After his retirement he was the organist of the DRC in Caledon, but in 1939 he again made his home at Worcester. During the last years of his life De Villiers occasionally substituted as organist in other towns, gave organ recitals and inaugurated new or reconstructed organs. In October 1943 he became the conductor of the Worcester Choral Society, a position which he apparently held until 1946. He died in 1949 in Groote Schuur Hospital, Cape Town, after a road accident. — Among De Villiers's prominent pupils were P.J. Lemmer*, Douglas Mossop*, M.M. van der Bent*, O.A. Karstel*, Septimus de Villiers*, and S. le Roux Marais*. He was awarded the medal of honour of the Suid-Afrikaanse Akademie vir Wetenskap en Kuns* in 1944 in recognition of his pioneering work in the field of music, not only as a school inspector, but also as a composer. The citation of the award made special mention of his new melodies for several psalms and hymns.

WORKS

A. Instrumental
Andantino in D flat, for pianoforte. Joseph Williams, London, 1929.   In memoriam, for pianoforte. C.J. de Jong, Worcester, composed 1918.   Melody, for pianoforte. Laudy & Co., London, n.d.   Memories, for piano. Augener Ltd, London, 1936.   Romance pour piano. Darter & Sons, Cape Town, n.d.   Toccata for pianoforte. Laudy & Co., London, 1912.   Valse caprice pour piano. Darter & Sons, Cape Town, n.d.   Cantiléne Aurelia, for organ. Published in *Ecclesiae Organum* Vol. XII, The Vincent Music Company, 1912. This work was composed during his studies and called Cantiléne Nuptiale.   Chorale with variations, for organ. Augener Ltd, London, 1936.   Canzona pour violon, with piano accompaniment, Schott & Co., London, n.d.   Fugato, for pianoforte. Joseph Williams, London, n.d.   Fantasie op "Dat's Heeren zegen op u daal", for pianoforte. Ms., n.d.   The Worcester valsette, for pianoforte. Ms., n.d.   Prelude and fughetta, for pianoforte. Ms., n.d. (lost).

B. Vocal
Across the sea, song (anon.). Weekes & Co., London, 1898.   The bowlers' song (poem by composer). *The Cape Times*, 18 March 1948.   Koorstukke vir kerk, kollege, skool, en gewyde stukke vir die orrel. Joseph Williams Ltd, London, 1929:   1. Uren, dagen, maanden, jaren   2. Geloof, hoop en liefde   3. Och! Heer geef nu heil en voorspoed   4. Zalig zijn de doden   5. Dat's Heeren zegen op u daal.   Kruis tot kroon, cantata. Printed by Cape Times, n.d.   Dat uw Geest den leeraar sterk, also in English, arrangement of hymn no. 87, verse 3. R. Müller, Cape Town, n.d.   Twintig skoolliedjies (collaborating with M.L. de Villiers*). Pro Ecclesia-drukkery, Stellenbosch 1926. The ten tunes composed by P.K. de Villiers are: 1. 'n Les (Maria Vorster)   3. As Pa saans huistoe kom (Maria Vorster)   5. 'n Sportliedjie (M.L. de Villiers)   7. Vakansie (Maria Vorster)   9. Alles loof die Here (Maria Vorster)   11. Klaas Vakie (M.L. de Villiers)   13. Die Tok-tokkie (Hilda Postma)   15. Grootpraat ("Huge-noot")   17. Krismisliedjie (Maria Vorster)   19. Na die griep (Hilda Postma).   Vader-landse liefde, for solo voice and pianoforte (C.P. Hoogenhout). Darter & Zonen, Cape Town, 1909.   Studentelied van het Normaal- en Polytechnies Kollege, Bloemfontein (R. Hoekstra). Bloemfontein Litho Co., n.d.   Hul boodskap: 1838-1938, four-part chorus (Dr Gerdener). Ms., 1938.   Huwelikslied (L.A. Schoonees). Ms., n.d.   Heilig, heilig is die Here, chorus. Ms., n.d.   Og, dat ek nader by U kom, chorus. Ms., n.d.   Settings of the following Psalms: 2, 4, 5, 6, 7, 12, 14, 18, 51, 57, 64, 69, 100, 102, 109, 110, 112, 114, 119, 120, 125, 130, 142, 144 and 147. These melodies were included in the Psalter of the Afrikaans churches (1937). Settings of the following

Hymns: 30, 71, 73, 83, 90, 104, 115, 123, 134, 159, 174, 175 and 188. These melodies were included in the Psalter and Hymn book of the Afrikaans churches (1943). Heilige nag (E. Eybers), a Christmas carol. Ms., n.d.

ARTICLE
Ons psalm- en gesangwysies. *Die Huisgenoot*, 19 October 1945.

BIBLIOGRAPHY
STANFORD, H.J.: *Die lewe en werke van P.K. de Villiers*. M.Mus. dissertation, US, 1965.   VAN DER MERWE, F.Z.: *Suid-Afrikaanse musiekbibliografie, 1787-1952*. J.L. van Schaik, Pretoria, 1958.

SOURCES
Anonymous: Prof. P.K. de Villiers. *Die Brandwag*, 3 February 1950.   SCHOONEES, L.A.: 'n Musikus gehuldig. Lewe en werk van prof. P.K. de Villiers. *Die Huisgenoot*, 28 July 1944. BOUWS, JAN: Langs die wapad van die Afrikaanse musiek. *Res Musicae* VIII, September 1960.   *Die Burger:* 30 July 1935; 16 November 1943; 19 December 1949.   National Documentation Centre for Music, HSRC, Pretoria.

—Ed.

DE VILLIERS, ROCCO CATORZIA,   *27 February 1838 in Paarl; °21 May 1902 in Paarl. Organist, music teacher and composer.

This eldest son of the marriage between Abraham de Villiers and Gertruida Catorzia* was educated privately under P.J.S. du Toit and was trained in music by J.S. de Villiers*. In the course of his career as church musician he was organist at Caledon for 22 years (1865-1887) and organist of the Mother Church at Paarl for 15 years (1887-1902). Rocco was married twice: to Maria Magdalena Louw (°1896) by whom he had fourteen children and to Johanna Albertyn, eldest daughter of the Rev. P.K. Albertyn of Caledon. Three of his offspring followed a musical career: Abraham Matthys whose granddaughter, Elise*, was a violinist at Stellenbosch; Pieter Kuyper de Villiers* ("P.K."), and Rocco (13 December 1888 - 14 October 1918), who was in the music trade in Paarl. — Rocco de Villiers occupied the post of organist with an elegant distinction which has become almost legendary. On Sundays, attired in frock coat and top hat, he arrived at the church in a blackhooded carriage drawn by a smart pair of horses. His fiery energy at the organ was renowned. More than once he gave recitals for charity. Fittingly, Prof. A. Moorrees, in his funeral oration on Rocco de Villiers, mentioned the way he could penetrate the spirit of the psalms and hymns and interpret them in accordance with the words. Usually he did this from the tune itself, although he published his own chorale book with short preludes and interludes, giving the secular tunes for Psalms 130 and 146, as well as a new tune for Hymn no. 30, devised by himself. The chorale book was distributed by Rocco jnr. from his music shop in Paarl. — The income he received as an organist, he supplemented by selling pianos that he had imported from Germany, a business which was carried on by Rocco jnr. In one of the out-buildings on his property he re-built the old organ of the Kruiskerk (cruciform church) in Paarl and used it for practice and for giving lessons.

WORKS
Koraalboek. Harmonisations of the Psalms and Hymn Tunes. Includes his portrait. Published by himself in the Paarl, n.d.   Mijn Land, mijn volk, mijn taal. *Ons Tijdschrift* I, 1896.   True love's desire. London Musical Bureau, n.d.   Welkomstlied. *Ons Tijdschrift* V, 1897.   Zalig zijn de dooden. Stanley Lucas, Weber & Co., London, n.d.   Een Zuid-Afrikaansch volkslied. Jacques Dusseau & Co., Amsterdam-Cape Town; also in *Ons Tijdschrift* I, 1896.   Klaaglied van

die os (S.J. du Toit). No details, 1896. Hear my prayer (Ps. 55). Stanley Lucas, Weber & Co., London, n.d. Gezang 36 (new melody). *De Kerkbode*, 30.5.1917. Heft uwe hoofden. Ms., n.d. The Alfred quick march. Published, no details. When mother's in Salem, vocal duet. Ms., n.d. Voluntary in F, piano solo (The Jubilee). Ms., n.d. Voluntary in C, piano solo. Ms., n.d. Grand wedding march, piano solo. Ms., n.d. Halleluja! Looft God in zijn heiligdom. Ms., n.d. De Heere regeert, chorus. Ms., n.d. Aria devotionale (in D and A flat). Ms., n.d. Juich en verblijd u, gij dochter van Zion. Ms., n.d. Geloof zij de Heere. Ms., n.d. Dedication. Ms., n.d. Zegt onder de heidenen. Ms., n.d. Fantasia (originally for piano). Ms., n.d. De Heere zegene u. Ms., n.d. Troumars, in G. Ms., 1883. Troumars, in B flat. Ms., n.d. Fantasia pour l'orgue, composed for the inauguration of the organ in the NG Church, Paarl-North. Ms., n.d. 6 Preludes in E flat, B flat, F, G, E min., G min.

BIBLIOGRAPHY

BOUWS, JAN: *Komponiste van Suid-Afrika*. E.C.F. Albertyn, Stellenbosch, 1971. DE VILLIERS, D.P.: *A history of the De Villiers family*. Nasionale Boekhandel, 1960. DREYER, ANDRIES: *Ons Kerk*. Samuel Griffiths, Cape Town, 1927.

SOURCES

DE VILLIERS, C.G.S.: Die musikale Viljees. Supplement, *Die Burger*, 17 November 1956. DE VILLIERS, M.L.: Die Catorse - 'n memorandum. 1962. MOORREES, A.: In memoriam. Funeral tribute to Prof. R.C. de Villiers - 1902. Preface to *Koraalboek* by R.C. de Villiers. OOM FRANSIE: Neef Rocco Viljee en zijn klavier. *De Goede Hoop,* March 1909. National Documentation Centre for Music, HSRC, Pretoria.

—Ed.

DE VILLIERS, SEPTIMUS CATORZIA, *29 June 1895 in Wellington; °25 September 1929 in Ermelo. Son of D.I. de Villiers*, younger brother of M.L. de Villiers*. Composer and music teacher.

At the early age of eight Septimus de Villiers played the organ during divine service at the DR Church, Paarl. After completing his musical training and obtaining the ARCM diploma at the RCM, he established himself in Oudtshoorn as a music teacher and organist of the DR Church (1914-1925). As a violinist he played in the Western Province and became known, not only as a performing artist, but also as a composer. During the 1920s he was one of the first Afrikaners to be approached by the Cape Town Broadcasting Station for recitals of his own compositions. Unfortunately most of his works disappeared after his death. In 1929 he entered a new sphere of activity in Ermelo where he was organist and in charge of a school of music, but he died in the same year. By that time he had already assembled a string orchestra.

WORKS

Liedjies vir die kleintjies. Burger-Boekhandel, Cape Town, n.d: 1. Môrelied 2. Die skilpad 3. Pieriewiet 4. Die by 5. Winkel-toe 6. Die trapsoetjies 7. Oggend 8. Dis tyd vir ou kleintjies 9. Lentetyd 10. Slaapdeuntjie. Liedjies vir die kleintjies, Boek II. W.G. Schaap, Uniondale Road, 1929: 1. Môrestond 2. 'n Wieglied 3. Sneeu 4. Landbou 5. Die meerkat 6. Awendstond 7. 'n Rondte vir drie stemme 8. Die haas 9. Die sterretjie. Verdere liedjies vir die kleintjies, 1929: 1. Die klokke 2. Die rosie 3. In sy wiegie 4. Die engeltjie 5. Slaapliedjie 6. Vroeg opstaan 7. Die wind 8. Breiliedjie 9. Alleen 10. Krismisliedjie 11. Kaal voetjies 12. Die slak 13. Die koue boompie 14. Die diertjies in die veld 15. Herfs 16. Vaarwel, moeder lente. Remembrance, for piano. Ms., before 1915. A lullaby (E.H.W.). Joseph Williams Ltd, London, 1916. Slaapdeuntjie. Ms., 1922.   Wedded. Ms., 1922.   In a chrysanthemum garden. Ms., 1922.   Love's toast. Ms., n.d.,   Sea lavender. Ms., n.d.   My garden. Ms., n.d.   In exile. Ms., n.d.   Uit die vreemde, song (Johan G. Smit). Published, Oudtshoorn, n.d.   Riverside rhapsody, for piano. Ms., n.d.   Firefly, for piano. Ms., n.d.   Three minuets. Ms., n.d.   Die osse stap aan deur die stowwe, song for mezzo-soprano (Jan Celliers). Ms., n.d.   Herinnering, song (anon.). Ms., n.d.   Vonkel, sterretjie, vonkel, song. Ms., n.d.   Die verlore seun, cantata. Ms., 1923.   Requiem. Ms., n.d.   I will lift up mine eyes (anthem), for choir. Ms., n.d. Oudtshoorn Training College song. M.s., n.d.   Children of nature and children of Thee. Ms., n.d.   Verhef uw loflied. Ms., n.d.   Slaapt nu voort. Ms., n.d.   Gezang 83. Ms., n.d.   Zingt den Heer 'n nieuw lied. Ms., n.d.   Leer ons. Ms., n.d.   Laat ons juichen. Ms., n.d.   Gij doorgrondt en' kent mij. Ms., n.d.   Het heilig avondmaal. Ms., n.d.   Heer, neig uw oor. Ms., n.d.   Uren, dagen, maanden, jaren. Ms., n.d.   Gezang 84. Ms., n.d.   Ik ben de Alfa en de Omega. Ms., n.d.   De zeven kruiswoorden. Ms., n.d.   Gezang 124. Ms., n.d.   Zijt ons genadig. Ms., n.d.   Hervormingslied. Ms., n.d.   Stille nacht. Ms., n.d.   Gezang 22. Ms., n.d.   Zendinglied. Ms., n.d.   Pinksterlied. Ms., n.d.   There is evidence of other music, violin and chamber music, but the manuscripts have been lost.

BIBLIOGRAPHY
VAN DER MERWE, F.Z.: *Suid-Afrikaanse musiekbibliografie, 1787-1952.* J.L. van Schaik, Pretoria, 1958.

SOURCES
Diamond Fields Advertiser: 27 September 1929.   *Die Burger:* 1 October 1929.   Correspondence with Mrs D.I. Hartman, Alexandria, CP.   Correspondence with his daughter-in-law, Mrs M. de Villiers, Grahamstown. .   National Documentation Centre for Music, HSRC, Pretoria.

—Ed.

DE VILLIERS, T.C.   Higher Educational Institutions II/3, Potchefstroom University for CHE's Institute for South African Music

DE VILLIERS, VERA (JOHANNA VÉRONIQUE WATERSTON GRAAFF, MRS ALBERT COATES),   *26 September 1891 in Sea Point, Cape Town; living at Hermanus in 1969 where she devoted herself to painting. Dramatic mezzo-soprano.

Vera de Villiers is the only daughter of Sir Jacobus and Lady De Villiers Graaff. She attended school in Brussels, in Bedford and in Dresden and was only launched on her career as a singer eight years after her marriage to Dr P. Daneel, when she was awarded a gold medal at the South African Eisteddfod in Cape Town (1922). At that stage she had only been trained as a singer for a few months. After this success she studied in England under Raimund von Zur-Muehlen for nine years, giving her first Lieder recital in the Wigmore Hall on 18 October 1928. After singing with the London Symphony Orchestra in the Albert Hall in 1932, the conductor, Hans Weisbach, invited her to join a concert party which was scheduled to give concerts in Paris, Berlin, Amsterdam, The Hague, Rome, Prague, Zürich, Düsseldorf, Stockholm, Oslo and Vienna. — She created a sensation in Vienna when she was invited on various occasions to sing with the Vienna Philharmonic Orchestra conducted by Weingartner, Bruno Walter and Albert Coates. In the same year, she was honoured by being nominated as an Honorary Member of this orchestra - until then, the only singers to be honoured in this way had been Richard Mayr, Lotte Lehmann and Elizabeth Schumann. In November 1933 she made her debut in America, appearing in three concerts in New York, Boston and Chicago respectively, after which she returned to Vienna in 1934 to sing with the Philharmonic Orchestra conducted by Bruno Walter. A further honour was the award of the "Ritterkreuz" by the chancellor, Dr Schusschnigg. She was also invited to open the Music Festival at Salzburg with a recital of Lieder (1934). — In 1936 she was the soloist at a symphony concert in London conducted by Albert Coates. Her next appearance was in Russia where, with Albert Coates as her accompanist, she gave a series of eight concerts. She had, until that time, concentrated on Lieder but, after meeting the Russian producer Stanislavsky, her career changed direction and she began to concentrate on the production techniques of opera. On her return to England she, in association with Albert Coates and Vladimir Rosing, established the British Music, Drama and Opera Association. During the Second World War they were in America where they established a similar organisation - the Southern Californian Opera Association. These associations were intended to train singers in stage craft, and also in the technique of opera production and presentation. Stanislavsky's principles and methods were adopted throughout. — In 1945 she was married to Albert Coates in London and, when he was appointed conductor of the newly-established Johannesburg City Orchestra in 1946, the couple came to South Africa. Three months after their arrival, they had to leave Johannesburg for Cape Town on account of Albert Coates's health. There they established their third opera company - The South African Opera and Ballet Group - without any financial aid. Vera de Villiers acted as producer of their presentations, and also sang the main roles. — After the death of her husband, she retired from musical life. Her last appearance was with the London Symphony Orchestra on 1 July 1959, in a concert to the memory of Albert Coates. The programme was devoted entirely to his works; Vera de Villiers sang the three songs, *To an isle in the water,* and two arias from his opera, *Gainsborough's duchess.* — During her period of study in England she was married to F.J. Nettlefold, who had done much to encourage her in her career as a singer.

BIBLIOGRAPHY
McCOY, GUY: *Portraits of the world's best-known musicians.* Theodore Presser Co., Philadelphia. USA, 1946.

SOURCE
STEGMANN, FRITS: Vera de Villiers in lied en opera uitgemunt. *Die Burger,* 20 July 1961.
—Ed.

DE VISSER, J.J.   Hollandsch Mannenkoor, Pretoria 2

DE VLETTER, ANTONY, *1 January 1841, in Poortugaal (near Rotterdam); °13 September 1896 in Dullstroom. Author of a collection of patriotic songs.

Antony de Vletter was related to the editor-publisher, Johannes Servaas de Vletter of Bloemfontein. He arrived in Durban in 1882, having qualified as a teacher of physical training, became a private teacher on the farm Waaikom near Newcastle, and then transferred to the farm Middelpoort in the district of Vrede. In 1884 he joined the Boer Commando that crowned Dinizulu and subsequently took part in an armed offensive against Usibepu, after which he helped to survey farms and determine the boundaries of the "New Republic" of Vryheid. From 9 June 1885, he was the Post Master, Public Prosecutor, Scrivener and stamp distributor of the New Republic; but

357

he resigned on 14 September 1886, to become a gold-digger in Barberton. In 1887 he went to live on the farm Groot Suikerboschkop - which later became Dullstroom - where he stayed for the rest of his life, as a teacher and as Post Master. — His collection entitled *Een achttal vaderlandsche liedjes bij-eenverzameld door A. de Vletter te Groot Suikerboschkop, Zuid-Afrikaansche Republiek* was published by W. Jonker's Snelpers-drukkerij in Pretoria in 1888 or 1889. This was the press of *De Volksstem.* — De Vletter was a restless, energetic, cultured man. By nature given to wanderlust, a competent writer and an almost legendary figure among his contemporaries, he was also an excellent teacher. In 1890 his little school, called Vletterhof, was regarded as the best school in the district of Lydenburg. His publication of *Vaderlandsche liedjes* was probably an attempt on his part to encourage the teaching of language through singing. There are no signs of music in this collection, but the verse forms seem to be devised for several well-known tunes. His poetic inclination is evident in his farewell song entitled *Weemoed, berusting en vertrouwen;* it can safely be assumed that he wrote several texts himself. The collection includes the following: 1. Transvaalsch Volkslied (C.F. van Rees) 2. Vrijheid 3. Eendracht maakt macht 4. Amajuba, Spitskop 5. Het Hollandsch hart vergeet zijn broeders niet (C.S. van Adama van Scheltema). 6. Transvaalsch Volkslied *(Algemeen dagblad van Neërlandsch Indië)* 7. Transvaalsch vlag 8. Het Vaderland. — In some instances detailed sources are given of songs that refer to the period before, during and shortly after the First War of Liberation (1880-1881), but in other instances no sources are given at all. It should be mentioned that Carel Steven Adama van Scheltema (here incorrectly called C.S. van Adama van Scheltema) was a poet and minister of the church in Amsterdam, who became famous for his poems and writings on religious and social themes (1815-1897). The *Algemeen Dagblad voor Nederlandsch - Indië* (incorrectly referred to as the *Algemeen Dagblad van Neërlandsch-Indië*) was established in the early seventies by the well-known Dutch literary figure Conrad Busken Huet (1826-1886) in Batavia. The origins of the other texts are unknown, unless it is assumed that De Vletter wrote them himself. — The Transvaalsch Volkslied, no. 6, had its origin in 1879, following on national gatherings at Kleinfontein and Wonderfontein, which, in turn, were preparations for the mass-gathering at Paardekraal in December 1880. It is an early, stirring patriotic song in Afrikaans.

SOURCES

DE VLETTER, A.: *Een achttal vaderlandsche liedjes. Bijeenverzameld door A. de Vletter, te Groot Suikerboschkop, Zuid Afrikaansche Republiek.* W. Jonker's Snelpersdrukkerij, Pretoria, n.d.
PLOEGER, JAN: Uit die briewe van Antony de Vletter, huis-onderwyser, staatmaker in diens van die "Nieuwe Republiek", wildjagter, gouddelwer, eerste onderwyser en posmeester van Dullstroom (1882-1888). *Historia* 7/2, Pretoria, June, 1962.

—J.P.

DE WET, JACK. *25 August 1927 in Aliwal North; now (1978) in Port Elizabeth. Professor of violin playing ·and chamber music at the UPE, violinist and former conductor of the Free State Youth Orchestra*.

Jack de Wet showed early signs of musical talent and was instructed in violin playing by various teachers including Erwin Broedrich*. In 1945 Editha Braham taught him in Cape Town and from 1946 to 1949 he was a student at the Cape Town University. A bursary of the City of Amsterdam was awarded to De Wet in 1950, and with this he studied under the First Professor at the Amsterdam Conservatoire, Herman Leydendorff (a pupil of Carl Flesch) for one year. His study continued the next year at the Muzieklyceum under Oskar Back (a Hungarian violinist and First Professor at the Lyceum), with whom he studied until 1955. He visited England in 1951 and obtained the LTCL and FTCL diplomas. — De Wet returned to South Africa in 1956 and until 1959 he was a first violinist in the SABC orchestra. He departed for Bloemfontein in 1960 to become lecturer in violin at the UOFS (senior lecturer in 1968) and eventually leader of the Free State String Quartet*. This quartet was a joint effort of the City of Bloemfontein and of the University and succeeded in achieving a national reputation. The Free State Youth Orchestra* was started by De Wet in 1962 and with these youthful players, he toured the country districts of the Free State and some of the major South African centres including contemporary works in their repertoire. In 1970 he led his orchestra to St Moritz where he achieved great success at the International Youth Musical Festival. — In 1973 De Wet accepted a chair in violin and chamber music playing at the University of Port Elizabeth. In the achievement of his aims, he strives at an early and correct development of young musicians and at giving them the experience of joyful participation in ensemble playing. Students and music teachers are similarly encouraged to participate in orchestral playing. In connection with this work he has undertaken tours to the USA and to Dr Suzuki at Matsumoto in Japan. As fruits of his specialisation he has now created in Port Elizabeth a chamber orchestra and a junior orchestra for young string players. On occasion he has been invited to act as adjudicator at the International Festival of Youth Orchestras held at St Moritz and in Lausanne. In 1977 he was the South African representative at the Strathclyde International Festival of the Violin held in Glasgow.

PUBLICATION
Teaching the violin. *Lantern* XXII/1, September 1972.

SOURCES
Anonymous: Jack de Wet. *Res Musicae* VIII/5, September 1962. Anonymous: Violinist appointed professor and member of senate at UPE. *Opus* IV/2, December 1972. GALLOWAY, D.: The musical future of South Africa. *Opus* I/4, 1966. SACK, J.: Port Elizabeth has plans to make city a vital music centre. *Opus* IV/3, March 1973. *Die Burger:* 24 December 1970. *The Friend:* 23 December 1970; 30 January 1971; 13 March 1971. *The Star:* 29 January 1971. *Die Transvaler:* 4 February 1950. National Documentation Centre for Music, HSRC, Pretoria.

—Ed.

DE WET, LILIAN   Charles Nel

DIAMOND FIELDS MUSIC ASSOCIATION   Kimberley, C. Rybnikar

DICKINSON, LOUIE   Potchefstroom 2

DIETMANN, P.   R. Müller (Pty) Ltd, Piano Manufacturers of South Africa

DIGGENHOF, A.   Discography, G. Fagan

DILLON, FREDERICK JOHN LAMB,   *1880 in Grahamstown; °4 June 1937 in Pretoria. Violinist and singer.
Rémenyi* heard Frederick Dillon play the violin at the age of five and urged his father,

Dr Thomas Dillon, to let him pursue a musical career. During the late '90s, Frederick entered the RAM for study under Hans Wessely, continued at the RCM, gained an exhibition for violin playing and was awarded an ARCM. During these years Walter Ford took charge of his vocal training. His studies were interrupted by the South African War and an injury to his left hand eliminated the possibility of a career as a violinist. After this injury Dillon concentrated on singing and made a living by giving solo recitals in Queen's Hall, Bechstein Hall, the Crystal Palace and in the British counties. He also taught singing and acted as choirmaster for the Marie Brema opera productions at the Savoy Theatre. Shortly before Christmas 1909, he took part in a concert sponsored by wealthy South African patrons, to raise funds for the Rand Regiment's Memorial. Other South African artists featured on the programme were Elsa Leviseur*, Selma Sacke (Whitehouse)*, Annie Visser*, Ada Forrest*, Vera Wise, Grace Hazelhurst and Dillon's wife, Geraldine. — In 1924 ill health forced him to leave London and come back to South Africa where he opened a singing studio in Pretoria. He was approached by P.R. Kirby* to serve on the panel of the Witwatersrand University's Department of Music* as a singing teacher, and John Connell* obtained his services in a similar capacity for the music department of the Transvaal University College. Together with Harold Ketelbey*, Dillon was responsible for the training of the cast and chorus of *Der Freischütz* and *Shamus O'Brien* produced for the Pretoria University at the Opera House* in 1930 and 1931 respectively. He was also an examiner in singing for UNISA.

OBITUARIES
Pretoria News, 5 June 1937.   *SAMT* 13, December 1937.

—Ed.

DIOCESAN COLLEGE, MUSIC IN THE   Established in 1849 at Protea (now Bishopscourt) by Robert Gray, first Bishop of Cape Town, the Diocesan College School ("Collegiate School", "The Bishop's College", "Bishops") moved to its present site in Woodlands, Rondebosch in 1850. Although a Church School, Bishops had no music master and hardly any practical music-making until the advent of George Ogilvie (headmaster 1861-1886), a trained musician with a fine tenor voice. Before long he had borrowed a harmonium for the Chapel and when the "new" Chapel (now the Brooke Library) was completed in 1880, this historic instrument was moved to its organ chamber. 1880 is also the year in which Prof. A.A. Bodkin joined the staff of Bishops and brought additional life to its music. He arranged concerts, organised and trained an orchestra, pressed the harmonium into service for performances of "toy symphonies", formed the first choir (1887), and led the way so energetically that Bishops's first Chapel Organ could be dedicated in September 1891. This organ (of unknown ancestry) did duty for 35 years and was eventually replaced by an instrument by Rushworth & Dreaper of Liverpool in 1933. The second organ was installed in the new War Memorial Chapel, which had been completed in 1926. — Although the scope of musical activities at Bishops had broadened considerably through the efforts of Ogilvie, Bodkin and others, the only official recognition of music was the weekly singing class for juniors, over which Dr T. Barrow-Dowling* presided with infectious enthusiasm for many years. He did not have the opportunity of making musicians, but he understood the art of instilling a love of music in the boys. When the Rev. Harold Birt became principal in 1919, Dr Barrow-Dowling's weekly visit was the only item of music in the school curriculum. Among the many sweeping reforms that Birt inaugurated, his new emphasis on music, leading to the appointment of the first music master, paved the way for future developments. The pioneers who blazed the trail as music makers, were successively Dr J.H. Alden, B. Hilliard and K.T. Scovell, who were encouraged and assisted by Dr Elsie Hall* and Ellie Marx*. Shortly after the dedication of the new organ in 1933, Claude Brown* arrived, to take over the duties of music master. With him, Bishops was launched on a new era of music-making on a high level. He arranged concerts in which the school orchestra played with the Municipal Orchestra, directed the first Carol service at the end of 1934, founded the Choral Society during the winter of 1936, started sung Eucharists and Music Evenings, and continued the tradition of special recitals by visiting artists. His Choral Society became especially prominent in Cape Town, with its participation in large-scale performances of choral works. — Even more important for the School's musical life, is the increasing attention given to music in the Chapel. The Psalms are now sung to modern, free-rhythm chanting; a great deal of plain-song has been introduced, and much of the best Anglican Church music is sung. Significantly, there has also been an increase in the opportunities for making music on strings and wind instruments. Music students from Bishops, such as John Joubert* and Michael Brimer*, have won high honours. Dr Brown's qualities of sound musicianship and leadership have, in one generation, raised music at Bishops to one of the most potent influences in the life of the school.

—J.P.M.

DISCOGRAPHY OF SOUTH AFRICAN RECORDINGS
  I. Historical introduction.
 II. The record industry in South Africa.
III. Discography.

I. HISTORICAL INTRODUCTION.
In his *Encyclopedia of Southern Africa* Eric Rosenthal mentions the photographer Arthur Elliott who recorded the voice of Paul Kruger, presumably on a wax cylinder. Hitherto there has been no trace of this important recording. It is known that during the Anglo-Boer War, European sympathy with the Boers found expression in the publication of various compositions, copies of which have been preserved in the Kruger Museum in Pretoria, the Africana Section of the City Library in Johannesburg and the collection of F.Z. van der Merwe in the library of the University of Pretoria. Not ·so well known is the fact that Thomas Denijs in Amsterdam and Betsy Schot in Berlin made recordings of the *Transvaalse Volkslied*. Furthermore, in 1904, the Dutch baritone, Arnold Spoel*, recorded and distributed his own song *Vereenigd Afrika,* also in Amsterdam. These three records, each pressed on one side only, are the only Africana recordings mentioned by Robert Bauer in his *New catalogue of historical records, 1898-1908/9.* — As far as can be ascertained, Annie Visser* was the first South African singer to make a recording of the *Transvaalse Volkslied.* This was done in London in 1908 and the record was distributed by GCR. The same piece was recorded in 1909-1910 for Zonophone by the British Black Diamond Brass Band. A copy of this historical recording was presented to the author by Hendrik Neethling of Lydenburg. On the reverse side the same band plays a *Trauermarsch (sic!) ter herinnering aan het overlijden van Staats-president Paul Kruger* (Funeral march in memory of the death of State President Paul Kruger), a composition by Willem Anthonie van Oosten*, in which the composer uses the tune of the national anthem of the Zuid-Afrikaansche Republiek. The first South African to have the Volkslied of the

361

Transvaal recorded in South Africa was Kate Opperman*, who sang it for the Zonophone Company when they visited Johannesburg (see below). During this visit the Zonophone Company also recorded her rendering of the national anthem of the OFS. — The Springbok rugby touring side of 1906 made four single-sided records in England. Mainly speech and in the novelty of "the Taal", these were manufactured for The Gramophone and Typewriter Limited and Sister Companies, forerunners of His Master's Voice. This "sporting" introduction of the Afrikaans language to England was followed by a number of single-sided recordings by the singers Joey Marais (2 records), Ada Forrest* (3 records) and Annie Visser (22 records, including psalms and hymns). (Here and elsewhere, the number of recordings given in brackets after the names of various artists is based on our present knowledge. Further research will undoubtedly modify many of these figures which must therefore be regarded as an approximate indication only, and not as final.) Items of elocution were rendered on other recordings by C.V. Becker (2 records) and Johannes J. Smith (7 records). — These earlier efforts must have proved very successful, because in 1912 the Zonophone Company sent a recording company to South Africa. The accuracy of this date is beyond dispute, because the manuscripts of Willem Versveld's* sketches were all dated 1912; there is further confirmation by Miemie Eberlein* and from various advertisements which appeared in periodicals and newspapers. During their visit the Zonophone Company made a number of recordings (by then done on double-sided records): renditions by the Choir of the Mother Church under the direction of Denholm Walker* (14 records), and by several soloists of whom Mrs David de Villiers (5 records), Joey Stramrood* (7 records), Connie Thomas (5 records), Mrs Danie de Villiers (3 records), E.G. von Bonde (2 records) and J.J. Smith (1 record) may be mentioned. The voices of Melt Brink (4 records) and the humorist Willem Versfeld* (13 records) have been preserved on records as "artistic orators". In Johannesburg the soprano Maud Baury (1 record), Kate Opperman* (6 records), Sofie Deys-Draaier (3 records) and the Double Quartette of Ten Brink* (1 record) appeared before the recording unit's microphone. Mr Hendrik Neethling of Lydenburg presented the author with a copy of the recording by the Ten Brink quartet of two excerpts from Henri ten Brink's *Unie kantate* sung to words by Jan Celliers: *Heerlik land van son en blyheid* and *Afscheid van de Voortrekkers*. The latter item is, of course, the traditional parting song "Ziet ons skei nou van elkander Hier op deze aardse dal..." ("Behold, we part from one another, here upon this earthly vale ...") which at the time was described by Gustav Preller as "an insipid little curiosity of folklore". According to an article in *Die Volkstem* (22 September 1909) Dr E.D. Kan heard this song sung by the Boers in the 1850s. He traced the words to Somerset Strand and afterwards he sang the tune (from memory) to Ten Brink. — At the time of their South African visit Zonophone made available the London recordings already mentioned (with the exception of those by Ada Forrest) in new editions as double-sided discs. The list of South African recordings was later supplemented with those of the sopranos Irene van Dyck (1 record) and Aletta Meiring (2 records). According to correspondence between Aletta Meiring writing from London and her family in South Africa, these were made in 1913. As far as can be ascertained, Aletta Meiring also sang for other recording companies, including Pathé, but the details have been lost. Besides Zonophone, a number of Jumbo records "in Taal" appeared on the market, which had presumably been manufactured in England between 1911 and

1912. Perhaps a few of them were recorded in South Africa, but they were all pressed in England by the Fonotipia Company. The artists were sopranos Klara de Villiers (4 records) and Katie Hofmeyer (2 records), the contralto Florill Florein (3 records), the baritone J. van Mylius (2 records) and the elocutionists Jan Haantjie (3 records) and Jan Smuts (1 record). — During the First World War there was a break in the sequence of South African recordings and it was not until 1924 that activities were resumed with the arrival of the Edison Bell Company in Cape Town. The date of this visit has been confirmed by newspaper advertisements and independent evidence supplied by Joan van Niekerk* and Mrs De Kock. Following on this visit the company recorded and marketed 50 double-sided discs, made in accordance with the prevailing method of "acoustic" recording. They were mostly recordings by the Cape Town City Orchestra* conducted by Theo Wendt* (20 records). Jan Luyt* (violin) and Pierre de Beer* (piano) made five recordings, Ellie Marx* (two), the Waldorf Trio (six), soprano Mrs Pierre de Beer (two), mezzo-soprano C.M. de Jongh (one), contraltos Joan van Niekerk (two) and Violet Turnbull* (one), baritones Con Morris (two), Nick Commaille* accompanied by M.L. de Villiers* (three), Walter Spiethoff* (two) and Norman Hart* (one). — In 1925 the electric recording technique superseded the old acoustic method and from then on the record industry expanded rapidly, increasing the number of South African artists who recorded, mainly for English companies. A few prominent personalities with the number (in brackets) of their recordings that have been traced so far, were: John van Zyl* (7), Gladys Daniel* (6), Betsy de la Porte* (7), Deborah Joubert (3), Adelaide Turnbull* (3), Gideon Fagan* (as accompanist to Betsy de la Porte and as composer of light music under the pseudonym "Diggenhof"). The majority of these recordings were made for the HMV Company, soon followed by Columbia who launched their first recording enterprise in South Africa in 1930. Some discs were released under the Regal label: these included the voices of General Hertzog and General Smuts and music recorded by Cecilia Wessels* (2), Nunez Holtzhausen* (1), Ester Mentz* (1), Dolly de Villiers* (1), Flippie Theunissen (2), Cornie Olivier, tenor (6), Stephen Eyssen* (7), Fred Dalrymple (Frederick Dalberg*) (1), Mrs Jan Luyt's* choir (1), Charles Weich's* DRC Choir, Kuils River (2 records), J.B.Z. Keet's* Asaf Choir* (4), Isador Epstein* (piano) (1), the Cape Town City Orchestra conducted by W.J. Pickerill* (2). A large number of light music items was recorded, much of it by Chris Blignaut*. — During the early 1930s the FAK, in conjunction with the HMV Company, made seven records of Afrikaans songs in Johannesburg, for which the co-operation of the following musicians was enlisted: Nunez Holtzhausen, Anna Steyn (contralto), Annette Opperman (contralto), Cornie Olivier, Barend Mellet (tenor), Stephen Eyssen and the ABC Orchestra conducted by Arthur Ellis. HMV used this opportunity for preparing another varied selection of recordings ranging from Boeremusiek (represented by groups such as Die Vier Transvalers and Die Vyf Dagbrekers) to recordings of psalms and hymns played on the organ by John Connell*. — The early 1930s was also the period when Gallo (Africa) Limited started their own South African factory for the manufacture of records. Under the labels of Singer and Gallotone a long series of recordings by Hendrik Susan* with Chris Lessing as vocal soloist, and also with David de Lange and Dan Bothma appeared on the market. On a more serious level, Dr Silbernagel's Johannesburg Male Quartet, the sextet of Louwtjie and Albie Louw and the Bloemfontein Centenary Choir of P.J. Lemmer all made recordings under this label. — With the exception of the recordings by Ada Forrest, whose first record was cut in 1907, all of the Afrikaans records were released in South Africa only. Between 1907 and 1912, however, the Ada Forrest records, both in "the Taal" and in English, were distributed overseas. Then followed Jenny Sonnenberg* who sang for Polydor in Germany. Several others appear in overseas record catalogues: Xenia Belmas* (Polydor), Adelheid Armhold*, Garda Hall*, Lilli Kraus* (as Lilli Dreifuss), Rose Alper*, Dorothy Clarke, Webster Booth*, Francis Russell*, Lord Lurgan, Lloyd Strauss-Smith*, Elsie Hall*, Adolph Hallis*, Isador Goodman, Hubert Greenslade, Victor Hely-Hutchinson*, Leo Cherniavsky*, Joseph Slater*, Paul Kerby, Gideon Fagan, Georg Gruber*, Albert Coates* and Frits Schuurman*. Some of these artists were South African-born and others were already established as recording artists before they arrived in this country as immigrants. Well-known for their recordings of light music were Al Bowlly* (with nearly 1 000 titles to his credit), Josef Marais (actually Pessach), Raie da Costa* and the guitarist Len Fillis*. Since World War II most of the prominent South African artists have made records, many of which have been sold in Europe. In this connection it should be mentioned that musicians from other countries have also made recordings in Afrikaans: Heinrich Schlusnus, Jan Peerce and the Vienna Boys' Choir.

II. THE RECORD INDUSTRY IN SOUTH AFRICA

Before World War II virtually all South African recordings were pressed in England. In 1936 John Hecht, trained in the record industry in Berlin since 1898, started the first gramophone record press for Gallo. It was first used to press specimens of South African recordings, but with the great record shortage during the War, it was also used to press a number of commercial records for distribution in this country. To combat the great shortage, the well-known radio personality Cecil Wightman, started the Radio Van Riebeeck Record Company and pressed some best-seller records fabricated overseas in Cape Town. With the co-operation of Walter Swanson*, he also made recordings by Lionel Bowman* (piano), Paula Richfield* ("Paula du Toit"), "Jan van Ryneveld" (actually Jack Gibson) and Dirk Lourens*. However, shellac was in short supply and the discs were not of a high quality. — After World War II this pioneer work by Hecht and Wightman developed into South Africa's own record industry. From about 1948, matrices from other countries were used to make local pressings and this procedure was continued after the introduction of long-playing records. In 1969 the turnover of 7 inch microgroove, as well as the larger long-playing records reached a yearly total of five million records. Besides this, a large market for Bantu music recordings has been exploited. This reached a turnover of $1^1/_2$ million records a year in 1969. By far the majority of the records sold in South Africa are still pressed from overseas matrices, but many recordings by local artists e.g. Gé Korsten*, Nellie du Toit*, Dawie Couzyn* and Lionel Bowman* have become available. Light music is well represented with recordings by Virginia Lee, Albie Louw, Nico Carstens* and Min Shaw. Children's records have a wide circulation in South Africa, e.g. presentations by Dawie Couzyn and Doris Brasch* of children's songs and musical dramatisations written by Betty Misheiker*. Quite a number of writers, composers and performing artists cultivate this kind of entertainment through the medium of both official languages of the country. — A record industry with such a wide scope induced local manufacturers to institute their own awards. Thus, for instance, after 25 000 copies of a particular record have been sold, a Golden Record is awarded to the artist. About

50 artists in South Africa have already had this distinction. Moreover, in 1964, this industry, in conjunction with Springbok Radio, instituted an annual SARI award. In spite of such tremendous progress, there is a noticeable lack of recordings of works by South African composers which should be made available commercially. Hitherto HMV has released only *Klassieke fees* (Festival of classics) which includes piano works by Arnold van Wyk*, Hubert du Plessis*, Stefans Grové* and John Joubert*; while HAUM has issued *Nagmusiek* (Serenade) by Arnold van Wyk and the *Trio for piano, violin and cello* by Hubert du Plessis. HAUM was also responsible for the series of records entitled *Skrywers aan die woord* (Authors at the microphone), but without government aid it is unlikely that the present situation will alter greatly.

—F.S.

III. Discography

So far a discography of South African records has not yet been published or compiled; what follows here must be regarded as a first attempt. This is a neglected field in the collection of Africana, in which only a few individuals have shown any interest. Apart from the small collection in the Africana section of the City Library in Johannesburg, no organisation has been very concerned about it. Of course, it may be assumed that the SABC has at its disposal the great majority of those important recordings which might qualify as Africana, but no details are available. Certainly the importance of printed documents, buildings, works of art, even household utensils, has not been overlooked, and ample provision has been made in every kind of library and museum for displaying the cultural achievements of South Africans, but hitherto no provision has been made for the systematic collection (and study) of recordings by South African artists. The two collectors already mentioned have collected much material from the early days of recording, but it probably represents only a small percentage of the sum total of records that have been issued over the years. Thus, the first great problem in connection with compiling a discography is the availability of the recordings. The meagre data available, had to be supplemented by a laborious process of collecting information from advertisements in newspapers and periodicals and from the catalogues of different gramophone companies. In the case of advertisements, the numbers of the records are not usually given and this leaves a gap in the compilation. Information on South African gramophone record manufacturers before World War II is no longer available and cannot be consulted. — The discography given below covers the period until 1939, i.e. the outbreak of the Second World War. The year 1939 was chosen as a temporary line of demarcation, because the War gave rise to a very rapid growth of the South African record industry which has become a multi-million Rand industry. The period following the War can thus be regarded as a second great era. Unless the task of making a systematic collection of South African records is undertaken fairly soon, many problems are likely to arise in connection with the complete documentation of South African music in the near future. — Naturally the years prior to 1939 fall into two periods. During the first, which ends in 1925, records were made acoustically. In the second (until 1939) the technique of electrical recording made rapid strides, quite as sensational as the development in microgroove technique after World War II. The growth of the industry as a whole was as much dependent on improved recording techniques as on improved methods of pressing. However, it should be remembered that the introduction of this type of "canned music" at the beginning of the century, created a sensation in South Africa. People thronged to hear the voices of great artists on the crude record-playing machines of those days and in all centres in South Africa concerts of recorded music were held. The demand for this new kind of entertainment was so great, that it contributed significantly to the diversion from community music to the music of professionals. — With the compilation of this discography a number of important editorial decisions had to be made, which are accounted for in the following numbered list:

1. Pre-electrical recordings are indicated thus ★, and where available, the approximate date of manufacture is given.

2. Often the spelling on the earlier records is extremely odd. For the sake of interest, the original spellings, as they appear on the label, have been retained. These are indicated by an (!). Even unlikely cases are in accordance with an original spelling. The irregular use of capital letters has similarly been maintained.

3. On the earlier recordings the composer is rarely mentioned and it would be an impossible task even to attempt to establish his identity. The first recordings "in Taal" are often translations from English ballads, the composers of which have long since been forgotten.

4. Where essential information is lacking in this classification a question mark (?) appears.

5. This discography must in no way be regarded as complete. The great majority of recordings were of light music. In many instances the artist was perhaps South African, but lived and worked in England, so that the direct connection with South Africa is only slender. Thus there had to be a selection of recordings in accordance with the following criteria .

   (i) that there must be some connection with South Africa as regards title, language, origin, historical significance or subject matter;

   (ii) that it would be superfluous, for example, to give details of the large number of "boeremusiek" recordings.

An example of 5(i) is the appearance in England of an Al Bowlly discography containing about 1 000 titles. Only the Afrikaans titles have been taken from this catalogue and the reader is referred to the complete discography of his recordings. As far as we know, Raie da Costa made only two records with Afrikaans titles; and, as a matter of interest, only a selection from her earliest recordings abroad is available. There are no Afrikaans titles among the recordings of Len Fillis and only a few of the earliest overseas recordings have been included here. Chris Blignaut and David de Lange were very popular in their day and consequently 40 of their records (80 titles) have been included in the list. The number of small ensembles that have made recordings of "boeremusiek" has been narrowed down to those which, being better known, enjoyed the greatest turn-over in sales. In the case of the very popular Hendrik Susan the choice has been limited to the oldest recordings, these being of the greatest historical interest. Where necessary notes have been added to direct the reader's attention to these matters.

6. Artists of international reputation who became South African citizens, have also been included in the discography.

7. The entries have been made in accordance with the following system:

   (i) name of the artist, followed by the type of voice (if this is known), or the instrument(s) played;

   (ii) make of record;

   (iii) catalogue number of the record;

(iv) title(s) of composition(s) followed by the name(s) of the composer(s); the type of accompaniment; the name of the accompanist (if known); and the type of music. In isolated instances, the name of the town where the recording was made is also available.

(v) A diagonal stroke "/" indicates the reverse side of a record.

8. The following abbreviations have been used for the commercial names of the records:

B	Broadcast
BR	Berliner Record
BT	Broadcast Twelve
COL	Columbia
DEC	Decca
EBVFR	Edison Bell Velvet Face Record
ELEC	Electrola
G & T	Gramophone and Typewriter Ltd.
GCR	Gramophone Concert Record
GMR	Gramophone Monarch Record
GRAM	Grammavox Record
GS	Gallotone-Singer
HMV	His Master's Voice
HOM	Homochord
J	Jumbo
O	Odeon
P	Pathé
PAR	Parlophone
POL	Polydor
RE	Regal
RE-ZON	Regal-Zonophone
SING	Singer
UPHON	Ultraphon
WIN	Winner
ZON	Zonophone

Afrikaner Quartet
COL AE 540 : (a) Die Afrikanervrou   (b) Dingaansdag ('n Feeslied) (De Villiers)/Ons voorgeslag.

Rose Alper*, soprano
RE-ZON (under the pseudonym Violetta) : MR 2991: Sadko (Rimsky-Korsakov): Song of India/Merry Widow (Léhar): Vilia Waltz, acc. Joe Loss's dance band.
COL FB 2193 : The Dancing Years: Waltz of my heart/I can give you the starlight. (Intro.: Leap year waltz), acc. London Theatre Orch.

Adelheid Armhold*, mezzo-soprano
ELEC EG 3592 : An die Nachtigall (Brahms)/In der Fremde (Schumann).
ELEC EH 963 : Freischütz (Von Weber): selection, with Anni Frind, Walter Ludwig, Wilhelm Strienz, and choir.

Asaf choir*, cond. J.B.Z. Keet*
RE GR 30 : Psalm 146/Gesang 12. Organ, John Connell*.

COL LE 16 : (a) Ere zij God in die hoge (b) Alles loof die Heer/Wie is Hy? (Halleluja 340, verses 1, 2, 7, 8), with piano.

COL LE 21 : Psalm 134, verses 1, 2, 3/Psalm 118, arr. of verses 7, 10, 14.

COL LE 22 : Gedenk/Mijn herder is God (Psalm 23, part 1).

Die Baanbrekers: D.F. Scholtz, J. Hooneberg, R. Meyer

COL AE 509 : Vat jou goed, polka/Sannie gee my brood, settees.

COL AE 510 : Ek het jou lief, polka/Vaalrivier, waltz.

COL AE 511 : Reisiesbaan, settees/Portugese wals.

COL AE 512 : Jamkoek, polka/Soetlief, waltz.

Maude Baury, soprano

ZON 4067 : Op het kerkhof (Arnold Spoel)/Liefste het is dag (Aylward) (Afrikaan soprano accpt. by Mde Bal* of the Conservatorium, Pretoria) (Johannesburg 1912).

C.V. Becker, singer and diseur

★ GCR GC 1429 : The Gun Licence, "Afrikaans talking" (London c. 1910).

★ GCR GC 1430 : In Self Defence, "Afrikaans talking" (London c. 1910).

★ ZON 4011 : The Gun Licence/See Johannes J. Smith (c. 1910).

★ ZON 4012 : In Self Defence/See Johannes J. Smith (c. 1910).

★ ZON 4162 : A Coloured Conversazione, humorous monologue (parts 1-2) (1912).

★ ZON 4165 : Springbok Rympies, humorous monologue by W. Versfeld (parts 1-2) (1912).

★ ZON 4166 : A Cape Girl's Lament, humorous monologue by C.V. Becker (1912)/See C.W. Leönard.

HMV FJ 25 : Die voetball match (Versfeld) (Springboks v. All Blacks), (parts 1-2), descriptive.

HMV FJ 31 : A Cape Girl's Lament (Becker)/Sarie Maré (trad.), acc. Ian Stewart.

HMV FJ 40 : Ma, kijk vir Japie (Ma, look at Charlie) (Hedges)/Vryer moet ek kry (Gonna find a girl) (Lewis, Simon and Ash), acc. Gerald Steyn.

RE GR 47 : 'n Heel flukse kêrel (A gay Caballero) (C.V. Becker)/Lui die klok, slaan die trom! (Jingle Bells) (C.V. Becker).

COL LE 54 : Die hemelike trap te klim (C.V. Becker)/Swart botteltjie (C.V. Becker).

Xenia Belmas*, soprano. She most probably made other recordings.

POL 522296 : The lark (Glinka)/Doubt (Glinka).

POL 66631 : Bohème (Puccini) : Si, mi chiamano Mimi/Sono andati.

POL 66635 : Trovatore (Verdi) : Tacea la notte placida (parts 1-2).

POL 66636 : Madame Butterfly (Puccini) : Un bel di vedremo/Manon (Massenet) : Gavotte (also on POL 66749).

POL 66715 : Huguenots (Meyerbeer) : Cavatine du page/Cavalleria Rusticana (Mascagni) : Voi lo sapete.

POL 66716 : Christmas Eve (Rimsky-Korsakov) : Aria/Elégie (Massenet).

POL 66746 : Mignon (Thomas) : Connais-tu le pays/Styrienne.

POL 66747 : Tosca (Puccini) : Non la sospiri la nostra casetta/Vissi d'arte.

POL 66748 : The Fair at Sorochinsk (Moussorgsky) : Parissia's song/The Rose and the Nightingale (Rimsky-Korsakov).

POL 66847 : Pagliacci (Leoncavallo) : No, più non m'ami (parts 1-2), duet with W. Domgraf-Fassbänder, baritone.

POL 66849 : Aïda (Verdi) : Su dunque (parts 1-2), duet with W. Domgraf-Fassbänder, baritone.

POL 66857 : Aïda (Verdi) : Ritórna vincitor (parts 1-2), with orchestra.

POL 66883 : Ernani (Verdi) : Surta è la notte/La Dame de Pique (Tchaikovsky) : Scène et air de Lise, with orchestra.

POL 66999 : If I had known (Tchaikovsky)/The Bride's Complaint (Tchaikovsky).

POL 67001 : Pagliacci (Leoncavallo) : Ballatella/The Snow Maiden (Rimsky-Korsakov) : To go berrying.

UPHON FP 110 : Coq D'or (Rimsky-Korsakov): Hymn to the Sun/Sadko Rimsky-Korsakov): Song of India.

The Black Diamonds Band

★ ZON 4019 : Transvaal Volkslied (Van Rees)/Trauermarch(!) (ter herinnering aan het overlyden van Staatspresident Paul Kruger) (W. van Oosten*) (1909-1910).

Chris A. Blignaut, bass-baritone

COL LE 8 to 62, acc. by Jansen quartet.

COL LE 8 : Die prisonier se gesang/Onder ses voet grond.

COL LE 9 : Een, twee, drie, vier (trans. Blignaut)/Potpourri van Afrikaanse wysies (trad., arr. Blignaut).

COL LE 10 : 'n Kêrel van die Pêrel (Crumit, trans. Blignaut)/Mooirivier se maan (Davis and Burke, trans. Rousseau).

COL LE 11 : Lenie Louw (trans. Versfeld)/Daar oorkant die spruit (trad.).

COL LE 12 : Op die trein na Pretoria (trans. Versfeld)/O boereplaas (Van Niekerk).

COL LE 13 : Ou tante Koba (trad.)/Sarie Marais (trad.).

COL LE 60 : Kom ons gaan blomme pluk (Owen)/Ek gaan terug na Stellenbosch (trans. Versfeld).

COL LE 61 : Daar onder op ons plaas/Ver oor die see (Steyn).

COL LE 62 : Rooi wang/Om die ou plaas weer te sien.

COL LE 74 : Die brug op ons plaas/Ou Transvaal.

COL LE 75 : Smokkelaar se dogter/Sal jy met haar wil trou?

COL LE 76 : Sing maar almal Halleluja (trans. Versfeld)/O Susanna (trans. Versfeld), with Jansen quartet.

COL LE 87 : Nat en Sap/Nuwejaar.

COL LE 88 : My man kom laat (trad.)/Die ou ruwe Kruis (trans. Willie du Toit), with Blignaut's Wolbekke; piano, Dan Bothma.

COL LE 89 : Sy's 'n baie mooi ding (Blignaut)/Skeeloog Annie (tant Koba se dogter) (Blignaut and W.S. Cooper), with Blignaut's Wolbekke; piano, Dan Bothma.

COL LE 90 : Kom terug my liefling (Blignaut and W.S. Cooper)/My Annetjie (Blignaut and W.S. Cooper), with Blignaut's Wolbekke; piano, Dan Bothma.

COL LE 94 : Kleine maat/Rympies.

COL LE 95 : 'n Seun se beste vriend is Moeder (trans. I.D. du Plessis)/Die ou wiegelied (trans. I.D. du Plessis), piano, Dan Bothma; banjo, P. Fysh.

COL LE 96 : Die wit broek sit nie mooi nie (Blignaut)/Vrystaat se nooiens

(Blignaut), with Blignaut's Wolbekke; piano, Dan Bothma.

COL LE 98 : Bruilof (W.S. Cooper and Cissie Budke)/Oom Kool (tant Koba se man) (Blignaut and Cooper), with Blignaut's Wolbekke; piano, Dan Bothma.

COL LE 99 : Agter die ou kraalmuur (F. Crumit)/Gee pad ou man, gee pad (F. Crumit), with Blignaut's Wolbekke; piano, Dan Bothma.

COL LE 100 : Sannie/Maanskyn en rose (with Dolly Neiman), piano, Dan Bothma.

COL LE 101 : As Oktobermaand weer hier is (Woolsey and Sauer, trans. F.P. Rousseau)/Maanlig op die Vaalrivier (Moll and King, trans. F.P. Rousseau), with Blignaut's Wolbekke; piano, Dan Bothma.

COL LE 102 : In die hemel/Ek wag nog vir jou. -

COL LE 103 : Los my/My mooi nooi.

COL LE 104 : Lê my by die roosboom neer/Mooiriviervallei.

COL LE 105 : Die liewe ou kerk in die vlakte (Kahn, Arnold, Van Alstyne), piano, Dan Bothma, guitar, P. Fysh/As die maan so skyn oor die berge (H. Woods), with Blignaut's Wolbekke; piano, Dan Bothma.

COL LE 106 : Ek wens ek was weer ongetroud/Rooi vlooi, mooi vlooi.

COL LE 107 : Die swart-omlynde brief (trans. I.D. du Plessis), piano, Dan Bothma/Sal die huiskring onverdeel wees?, with organ and violin.

COL LE 108 : Moenie aan my vat nie/Suid-Afrika.

COL LE 109 : Glimlag weer/Smart en pyn.

COL LE 110 : Daar by die boomtree (Blignaut)/Tannie met die rooi rokkie (Blignaut), with band.

COL LE 111 : By die ou meulstroom (Tell Taylor)/Daar's 'n huisie in die Vrystaat (Blignaut), with band.

COL AE 593 : Ou Pieta was 'n wewenaar (Blignaut)/Die ounooi sal koek en tert gee (Blignaut), with band.

COL AE 594 : Daar onder waar die pampoene groei/Die nooiens van die Vrystaat.

COL AE 595 : Die Vader van die wese (Blignaut)/Gee my 'n huis (Blignaut and Goodwin), with band.

COL AE 596 : Hannetjie verjaar (Blignaut and Cooper)/Ry maar aan ossewa (Blignaut and Kennedy), with band.

COL AE 600 : Daar onder by die ou kantien (Blignaut)/Kom luister na my (Blignaut), with band.

COL 601 : Daar onder in die olei (vlei)/Liewe Moeder (Blignaut), with band.

COL AE 611 : Lekker wedevrou (Blignaut)/Tot rooi dagbreek (C.J. Frean), with band.

COL AE 613 : Wiegenlied (Brahms)/Liewe Sannie (Blignaut), with band.

COL DE 100 : Oom Boggem (W.S. Cooper and Cissie Budke)/Suikerbossie, (trad., arr. Blignaut).

COL DE 101 : Die piekniekaand (W.S. Cooper and Cissie Budke)/Lentjie (W.S. Cooper and Cissie Budke).

COL DE 120 : Voortrekkers dans (Cissie and W.S. Cooper)/Opsitaand (Cissie and W.S. Cooper), piano, Charmion Kantor; guitar, C. Macrow.

COL DE 159 : Langs die strand (C. and W.S. Cooper)/Antjie, my liewe Antjie (C. and W.S. Cooper).

COL DE 160 : Die donkie (C. and W.S. Cooper)/Moederhuisie (C. and W.S. Cooper).

COL DE 178 : My Oupa het 'n perd (Blignaut)/Ek het jou waarlik lief (C. Jacobs-Bond), with band.

Webster Booth*, tenor. This singer made many recordings. He can be heard in a shortened version of *Gondoliers* (Gilbert and Sullivan), in works by i.a. Bach, Bizet, Handel, Mendelssohn, Mozart, Purcell and Wagner, and also with the following singers: Joan Cross, Joan Hammond, Edith Coates, Nancy Evans, Denis Noble, Norman Walker, Arnold Matters, Noel Eadie, etc. The following list contains most of the earliest recordings in his career. See Webster Booth and Anne Ziegler, Dorothy Clarke, Garda Hall.

HMV B 3283 : Dance away the night/Let me dream in your arms (Nicholls).

HMV B 3319 : I love the moon (Rubens)/A brown bird singing (Haydn Wood).

HMV B 3448 : Princess Elizabeth (Crean)/London Palladium Orchestra.

HMV B 3758 : Moonlight and you (De Crescenzo)/Always as I close my eyes (Coates).

HMV B 3778 : Heavenly night/Along the road of dreams.

HMV B 8360 : Love passes by/As I sit here (Sanderson).

HMV B 8385 : Heart's Desire - Vocal gems (parts 1-2).

HMV B 8393 : Pale moon (Logan)/The world is mine tonight (Posford).

Webster Booth and Anne Ziegler*, vocal duets

HMV B 8982 : If you were the only girl in the world (Ayer)/A paradise for two (Fraser-Simson and Tate).

HMV B 8996 : I'll see you again (Coward)/Wanting you (Romberg).

HMV B 9051 : Ah, sweet mystery of life (Herbert)/Lover, come back to me (Romberg).

Miemie Botha, soprano

RE GR 26 : Mamma, ek wil 'n man hê/My bruin oë.

COL LE 25 : Fragmente (trad.)/My hartjie, my liefie (trad.), with piano-accordeon, Alec Benjamin; guitar, Billie Wright.

Dan Bothma (piano) and his orchestra,(alsoChris Blignaut, Hendrik Susan and Dan Bothma)

SING GE 247 : Hy sal huis toe kom/Boet Muller se plaas.

SING GE 248 : 'n Dansparty/Vuurwarm, barn dance.

SING GE 249 : Die siel van Suid-Afrika/Die lekkerpolka.

SING GE 250 : Sarie Marais/Transvaalse Volkslied.

SING GE 260 : Die braaivleisaand/Die Bolandjol.

Al Bowlly*, baritone. Only his South African records are given here. For a full list of records see: Harvey, Clifford M. and Rust, Brian A.L.: *The Al Bowlly Discography* (2nd edition) Rust's Rare Records, Hatch End, Middlesex, England, 1967. According to the above authors, Bowlly also made Afrikaans records under the *nom-de-plume,* Jannie Viljoen.

HMV FJ 97 : Kleine maat/The lonesome Road, in Afrikaans.

HMV FJ 100 : Alleenig (Diggenhof), piano, Albert Diggenhof/Ou Kaapstad is my hemelland (Croom and Johnson), with orchestra and piano.

HMV FJ 103 : Sal die eng'le hulle harpe speel vir my? (Hirsch and Wilhite)/Voetslaan op oom Jacob se leer (Heiser), with concertina, guitar, cello and mouth organ.

371

HMV FJ 120 : Daar is geen rou in die hemel/Die ou lelievallei.
HMV FJ 133 : Bandietlied/Jy's in die pad.

Melt Brink, diseur
★ ZON 4083 : Mijn land, mijn volk, en taal (Melt Brink)/Japie zyn nieuwe stevels en Tante Tryntjie (Melt Brink) (Cape Town 1912).
★ ZON 4097 : Een schutter zoo als jij mier vindt (Melt Brink)/Jan wat naar kinders gewens het (Melt Brink) (Cape Town 1912).
★ ZON 4114 : Die vrome meid, part 1 (Melt Brink)/Die vrome meid, part 2 (Melt Brink), "Afrikaan talking" (Cape Town 1912).
★ ZON 4131 : Die pakkie met spelde (Melt Brink)/Ou Klaas Lap (Melt Brink) (Cape Town 1912).

The Hon. W. Brownlow, baritone
★ COL DB 79 : I pitch my lonely caravan at night (Horey and Coates)/I look into your garden (Wilmot and Haydn Wood).
COL DB 179 : Now sleeps the crimson petal (Tennyson and Quilter)/Weep you no more (Quilter).
COL DB 772 : Two eyes of grey (McGeoch)/I did not know (Bingham and Trotere).
COL DB 1072 : Sylvia (Scollard and Speaks)/Blue moon (Westrup and Fisher).
COL DB 1126 : This lovely rose (Sievier and Ramsay)/When I think of you (Lockton and Tate).
COL DB 1240 : I still love Mary/One kind word.
COL DB 1650 : Ballads of yesterday, no. 1 (parts 1-2) (Guy d'Hardelot).
COL DB 1694 : Ballads of yesterday, no. 2 (parts 1-2) (Teresa del Riego).

Leonard Burchell, tenor
COL LE 51 : (a) Jou het ek lief   (b) Daar's 'n Boernooi (M.L. de Villiers*)/Die ossewa (S.C. de Villiers), with piano.

Marjorie Burger, diseuse
COL LE 36 : Kaatjie ontvang 'n foonboodskap (Versfeld)/Kaatjie bel die loodgieter op (Versfeld).
COL LE 37 : Kombuisgeklets, part 1 (M. Burger)/Kombuisgeklets, part 2 (M. Burger).
COL LE 38 : Die nuuskierige ou man (M. Burger)/Die nuuskierige ou vrou (M. Burger).
COL LE 39 : Kaatjie saai uit (Versfeld)/Luidrugtige Kafferbediendes (M. Burger).
COL LE 112 : The Jubilee (M. Burger)/The Duke of Kent's visit to South Africa (M. Burger).
COL LE 113 : Kaatjie Kekkelbek phones the Butcher (M. Burger)/The Census Forms (M. Burger).
COL LE 114 : The Coronation/Unknown.

Cape Town Orchestra*, cond. Theo Wendt*. All these records were cut in Cape Town during 1924
★ EBVFR J 32 : L'enfant Prodigue, selection 1 (Wormser)/L'enfant Prodigue, selection 2 (Wormser).
★ EBVFR J 33 : Sylvan Scenes, suite no. 1 : Sylvia Dances (Fletcher)/Sylvan Scenes, suite no. 3 : At the Pool of Narcissus (Fletcher).

★ EBVFR J 34 : On the Steppes of Middle Asia, selection 1 (Borodin)/On the Steppes of Middle Asia, selection 2 (Borodin).

★ EBVFR J 35 : Praeludium (Järnefeldt)/La Fée Tarapatapoum, Suite Française no. 2 (J.H. Foulds).

★ EBVFR J 36 : Chanson ("In Love") (Rudolf Friml)/The Bull Frog Patrol (Jerome Kern).

★ EBVFR J 37 : Botha's Boys, march (Theo Wendt)/La Paloma, valse (Yradier).

★ EBVFR J 38 : Wood Nymphs, valsette (Eric Coates)/Serenade no. 2, from suite "Joyous Youth" (Eric Coates).

★ EBVFR J 39 : Naila, intermezzo (Delibes)/Cortége du Sardar (M. Ippolitow).

★ EBVFR J 40 : Minuet (Boccherini)/Loin du Bal, valse (E. Gillet).

★ EBVFR J 41 : Varen (Grieg)/Les Vendredis, polka for strings (N.S. Kolow).

★ EBVFR J 42 : Andante for Strings (Mozart)/Romance (Mozart).

★ EBVFR J 43 : Irish Tune from County Derry (P.A. Grainger)/Pizzicato (R. Drigo).

★ EBVFR J 44 : En Badinant (A. d'Ambrosio)/Reve, valse lente (A. d'Ambrosio).

★ EBVFR J 45 : Berceuse (Järnefeldt)/(a) Doux Propos (H. Fevrier) (b) Dame Galante Suite (A. Spink).

★ EBVFR J 46 : Valse lente (R. Drigo)/Valse bluette (R. Drigo).

★ EBVFR J 47 : Serenade ("Les Millions d'Arlequin") (R. Drigo)/Reconciliation (R. Drigo).

★ EBVFR J 48 : My Lady Dragon:, no. 1, Dance of the Silver Pool; no. 2, Golden Days (Finck)/Träume (Study from "Tristan and Isolde") (Wagner).

★ EBVFR J 49 : Rustic Revels Suite: no. 1, Dancing on the Green (Fletcher)/Rustic Revels Suite: no. 2, At Quality Court (Fletcher).

★ EBVFR J 50 : Rustic Revels Suite: no. 3, All the Fun of the Fair (Fletcher)/Summer Days Suite: no. 3, At the Dance (E. Coates).

★ EBVFR J 51 : Summer Days Suite: no. 1, In a Country Lane (E. Coates)/Summer Days Suite: no. 2, On the Edge of the Lake (E. Coates).

Cape Town Orchestra, cond. Wm. J. Pickerill
COL LE 80 : Evening on the Veldt (Pickerill)/Veldblommetjies (Kirby*).
COL DE 301 : Die Stem van Suid-Afrika (M.L. de Villiers)/Botha Boys, march (Theo Wendt).

Arthur Carnaby, pianist. See Dorothy Wienand.

Tom Carrick and Jan Kool, dialogue
HMV FJ 110 : Mnr. Rooinek word afslaer (Carrick and Diggenhof)/Mnr. Rooinek se motor breek (Carrick and Diggenhof).

Dorothy Clarke, contralto, with Webster Booth, tenor, and Foster Richardson, bass-baritone
HMV C 2961 : Songs that have sold a Million : Somewhere a voice is calling, Little grey home in the west, Until, Love's old sweet song, Lost chord, Roses of Picardy, Because, Goodbye.
HMV C 3050 : Songs that have sold a Million, second set : Rosary, Silver threads, Ah, sweet mystery of life, God sent you back to me, For you alone, Homing, Parted, Trees.

Albert Coates*, cond. The pre-electric records were cut in c. 1918-1925. This conductor made a large number of records. The following list represents some of his earliest recordings (see Vera de Villiers). On the following records he conducts a symphony orchestra:

★ HMV D 590 : Die Meistersinger overture (Wagner).
★ HMV D 607 : Rienzi overture (Wagner).
★ HMV D 620 : Children's Corner, no. 6 (Debussy)/Kikimora (Liadov).
★ HMV D 624 : Der Freischütz overture (Von Weber).
★ HMV D 732-4 : Coq D'or (Rimsky-Korsakov).
★ HMV D 649-650 : Siegfried idyll (Wagner).
★ HMV D 658 : Ruslan and Ludmilla overture (Glinka)/Snow Maiden : Dance of the Tumblers (Rimsky-Korsakov).
★ D 670-1 : Don Juan (R. Strauss).
★ D 708-9 : Mother Goose Suite (Ravel).
★ D 759-764 : Symphony no. 5 (Tchaikovsky).
★ D 795 : Prince Igor overture (Borodin).
★ D 842-849 : Symphony no. 9 (Beethoven).

On the following records he conducts excerpts from operas, with different singers:
★ HMV D 677 : Rheingold (Wagner), with Radford.
★ HMV D 700-2 : Siegfried (Wagner), with Austral, Davies, e.a.
★ HMV D 703-6 : Götterdämmerung (Wagner), with Austral, Radford, Davies, e.a.
★ HMV D 745-757 : Meistersinger (Wagner), with Austral, Radford, Davies, Walker, e.a.
★ HMV D 899 : Faust (Gounod), with Chaliapin.
HMV D 1025-1030 : Parsifal (Wagner), with Radford, Widdop, Baker, e.a.
HMV D 1101 : Lohengrin (Wagner), with Widdop.

On the following records he conducts the London Symphony Orchestra:
HMV D 1359-62 : Symphony no. 41 in C major (Mozart).
HMV D 1429-30 : The Fountains of Rome (Respighi).
HMV D 1521-24 : Petroushka (Stravinsky).
HMV D 1525-26 : Tod und Verklärung (R. Strauss).
HMV D 1528 : Prins Igor, ballet music (Borodin).
HMV D 1560 : Phantasia and fugue (Bach).
HMV D 1616-7 : Les Préludes (Liszt).
HMV D 1746-50 : Concerto in B flat major, for piano and orchestra, opus 83 (Brahms). Soloist Arthur Rubinstein.
HMV D 2010 : Night on a bare mountain (Moussorgsky).
HMV DB 1554-6 : Symphony no. 2 in B minor (Borodin).

Ian Colquhoun, tenor
★ ZON X 348 : Marching on Pretoria, Patriotic Song, with orchestra (c. 1900).

M.J. Commaille*, baritone. Piano, the Rev. M.L. de Villiers
★ WIN J 3 : Die Stem van Suid-Afrika (C.J. Langenhoven)/(a) 'n Doornekroon (b) Terugblik
★ WIN J 4 : Trou (Ek hou van 'n man) (J.F.E. Celliers)/Die lig-blou meer (N.(!) de Villiers).
★ WIN ? : Komaan (M.L. de Villiers)/Vaarwel (N.(!) de Villiers) (Cape Town 1924).

374

John Connell*, organist. See Asaf choir. Played on the organ of the D.R. Church, Irene, Plein St., Johannesburg:

HMV JA 1 : Psalm 25 ('K hef mijn ziel o God der Goden)/Gezang 7 (Op bergen en in dalen).

HMV JA 2 : Gezang 9 (Waar zijn de wijzen die mij zeggen)/Psalm 65 (De lofzang klimt uit Zions zalen).

HMV JA 3 : Gezang 11 of Psalm 42 (Heilig God! voor ween steeds waarheid)/Gezang 156 (Houdt Christus Zijne Kerk in stand).

Raie da Costa*, pianist and singer. This artist made a large number of records, only two of which are South African, as far as is known. The list that follows contains some of her earliest records.

(All the labels of this firm are entitled "The Parlophone Girl").

PAR R 121 : Can't help lovin' dat man (Show Boat)/Ol' man river (Show Boat).

PAR R 122 : Why do I love you? (Show Boat)/Cotton Blossom and Hey Feller (Show Boat).

PAR R 123 : Teach me to dance like Grandma (This Year of Grace)/An' furthermore (Clowns in Clover).

PAR R 130 : That's a Good Girl - selection (parts 1-2).

PAR R 150 : The one I'm looking for (That's a Good Girl)/Fancy our meeting (That's a Good Girl).

PAR R 176 : The Varsity drag (Good News)/Good News (Good News).

PAR R 177 : The best things in life are free (Good News)/Lucky in love (Good News).

PAR R 189 : Hollyhock/Razor blades.

PAR R 225 : Paradise Square (Virginia)/Roll away clouds (Virginia).

PAR R 228 : Funny Face (Funny Face)/My one and only (Funny Face).

PAR R 229 : S'Wonderful (Funny Face)/He loves and she loves (Funny Face).

PAR R 274 : Every little moment (Mister Cinders)/Spread a little happiness (Mister Cinders).

HMV FJ 150 : Die Afrikaanse pop/Mamma, 'k wil 'n man hê.

HMV B 3418 : C.B. Cochran's 1930 Revue, medley (parts 1-2).

HMV B 3441 : No, no, Nanette, medley/Rio Rita, medley.

HMV B 3450 : High Society Blues, medley/Cryin' for the Carolines.

HMV B 3500 : Fledermaus selection (parts 1-2).

HMV B 3755 : The King's horses/Medley of Marches.

HMV B 3777 : Whoopee, medley/Monte Carlo, medley.

HMV B 3814 : I'm yours/You're driving me crazy.

HMV B 3877 : Blue again/Parade of the minutes.

HMV B 3878 : White Horse Inn, medley/Millionare Kid, medley.

Raie da Costa and Hugh Morton, song duets, with Raie da Costa, piano

HMV B 4487 : I've got the world on a string/When my little Pomeranian.

HMV B 4490 : A bedtime story, medley/Isn't it heavenly.

Friedrich Dalberg*. See Frederick Dalrymple.

Frederick Dalrymple, bass

COL LE 50 : Daar is geen dood (Geoffrey O'Hara)/Die blinde aan die ploeg (R. Coningsby-Clarke), with piano.

O 3654 : Don Carlos (Verdi) : Monolog des Philipp - Sie hat mich nie geliebt.
O 3655-6 : Don Carlos (Verdi) : Duet, Act 1 - Philipp und Posa (with Theodor Horand, baritone). (Acc. on Odeon records : Stadt- und Gewandhaus-orchester, Leipzig, cond. Paul Schmitz).

Gladys Daniel*, soprano. Piano, Mme. C.A. Lucas, except where otherwise stated
HMV FJ 41 : Oktobermaand (Pescod)/Die roseknoppie (Pescod).
HMV FJ 42 : Wiegeliedjie (Langenhoven)/Ek sing van die wind (Daniel and Amyot). Piano, Etienne Amyot.
HMV FJ 43 : The Night Wind (Farley)/The Russian Nightingale (Alabief, arr. Liebling).
HMV FJ 55 : The Songs my Mother sang (Grimshaw)/At the Well (Hageman).
HMV FJ 68 : Slampamperliedjie (Lucas)/Die skoenlapper (Lucas).

Mrs Pierre de Beer, soprano; piano, Pierre de Beer*; violin obligato, Rolf Wehner
★ WIN J 8 : Wiegenliedjie (E. de Roubaix)/Uit pure pret (E. Hullebroeck*) (Cape Town 1924).
★ Moederke alleen (E. Hullebroeck)/Aan den oever van de Minnetonka (Cape Town 1924).

Miss C.M. de Jongh, mezzo-soprano
★ WIN J 11 : Afrikaanse wiegeliedjie (C.J. Langenhoven)/O Boereplaas (M.L. de Villiers) (Cape Town 1924).

David de Lange. A large number of records by this artist were cut. The following list contains some of his earliest recordings
SING GE 216 to 219 are accompanied by Die Naglopers.
SING GE 216 : Die kalfie-wals/Daisy-polka.
SING GE 217 : Susanna/Liewe Goudstad.
SING GE 218 : Jakkalsdraai-polka/Die verneuk-seties.
SING GE 219 : Die lekker dop/Die mosbeskuit.
SING GE 220 : Ma sê, Pa sê/Die Elanders-wals, acc. Van Niewenhuizen's Elanders.
SING GE 221 : Saartjie/Skaapvel-seties, acc. Van Niewenhuizen's Elanders.
SING GE 232 : Waar is Moeder?/My soetlief, vocal duets with his sister.
SING GE 235 : Die bedelaar/Kalfie-wals no. 2, acc. Vastrappers.
SING GE 251 : Wattels-wals/Hessie se wit perd, acc. Kruger and Marais's band.
SING GE 252 : Liewe Annie/Op die slagveld, with his sister and Baby Kruger.
SING GE 264 : Roosterkoek-seties/Suikerbossie, acc. Welgens's band.
SING GE 265 : Grietjie/Hendrik se wals, acc. Gert Hattingh's band.
SING GE 266 : Pieta, acc. Die Lekker Kêrels/As die maan opkom oor die berge, acc. Welgens's band.
SING GE 267 : In die vallei/Vaarwel, with his sister and Baby Kruger.
SING GE 269 : Die wapad-vastrap/By die turksvye, acc. Kruger and Marais's band.
SING GE 273 : Bosveldliefde-vastrap/Rooidag-seties, acc. Welgens's band.
SING GE 277 : Soet gedagtes/Die lekker kêrels, acc. Hansie van Loggeren-berg and Die Lekker Kêrels.
SING GE 278 : Huis toe gaan/Oom Willie se vastrap, acc. Hansie van Log-gerenberg and Die Lekker Kêrels.

SING GE 279 : Bosveldhuisie/Die ou armstoel, acc. Welgens's band.
SING GE 280 : Lettie Brand, acc. Singer dance band/Singer dance band.
SING GE 281 : Dorpsmusiek/Hoogmoedige Jan, acc. Welgens's Suikerbossie band.
SING GE 282 : Vra, Lammie, vra, acc. Welgens's dance band/Welgens's dance band.
SING GE 283 : Koos van Buffeldorings/Loekie, Loekie, Loekie, acc. Hansie van Loggerenberg and Die Lekker Kêrels.
SING GE 284 : Ver in Christiana/Minnie se verjaardag, acc. Hansie van Loggerenberg and Die Lekker Kêrels.
SING GE 286 : Sarie Marais, acc. Welgens's dance band/Arme vroutjie, acc. Kruger and Marais's band.
SING GE 289 : Ek hou van piesangs/Marie, acc. Welgens's Suikerbossie band.
SING GE 290 : Die bont rok, acc. Singer dance band/Tannie moet nou ja sê, acc. Kruger and Marais's band.
SING GE 293 : Ti-pi-tin/Rusbankie, acc. Welgens's Suikerbossie band.
SING GE 295 : Jan Pierewiet/Vrolike musiek, acc. Hansie van Loggerenberg and Die Lekker Kêrels.
SING GE 296 : Bekkie-seties/Die karringvat, acc. Dan Lourens's Outydse Orkes.
SING GE 297 : Die kierie-wals/Ek wil terug na die plaas, acc. Dan Lourens's Outydse Orkes.
SING GE 299 : Valse liefde, barn dance, acc. Welgens's Suikerbossie band/ Daar kom die wa, with Burger and Van Dyl.
SING GE 304 : Die Hoëveld-dans/Tien mooi nooiens, acc. Welgens's Suikerbossie band.
SING GE 306 : Die jaloerse minnaar/Die ou leuningstoel, with Hendrina Schrimper and band.
SING GE 309 : Willie, die fluitspeler se vastrap, acc. Welgens's Suikerbossie band/Ou Dan se seties, acc. Dan Lourens's band..
SING GE 310 : Waar is Bettie?/Treur, Baba, treur, acc. Welgens's Suikerbossie band.
SING GE 311 to 334 are accompanied by his own band.
SING GE 311 : Die sambreelmaker/Die vlei-vastrap.
SING GE 314 : Sonop/Meisie van my drome.
SING GE 315 : Ekskuus (Cissie and Willie Cooper)/Voortrekkerdans (Cissie and Willie Cooper).
SING GE 316 : Hier wag vir 'n trein/Ek fluit 'n deuntjie.
SING GE 317 : Belet my nie om te droom/Fluister-vastrap.
SING GE 323 : Hardloop, hasie/Petronella.
SING GE 333 : Sy's 'n mooi nooi (Cissie and Willie Cooper)/Ons land (Cissie and Willie Cooper).
SING GE 334 : Die biervat-polka/Eggo.

Betsy de la Porte*, mezzo-soprano
BT 5177 : O dry those tears (Del Riego)/Good-bye (Tosti), with orchestra.
BT 5219 : My little Irish cottage (Summers)/By the waters of Minnetonka (Lieurance), with orchestra.
HMV FJ 83 : Die Stem van Suid-Afrika (Langenhoven and Gideon Fagan), parts 1-2, piano, Gideon Fagan.

HMV FJ 98 : Byna bewogen (Hymn 179)/Nog is er plaats (Hymn 181), organ, Mirian Duncan.
HMV FJ 105 : (a) Soos die windjie wat suis (J.J. Fagan) (b) Die soekende moeder (J.J. Fagan)/Die duifie (Gideon Fagan), piano, Gideon Fagan.

Betsy de la Porte, mezzo-soprano and Guy Marshall, tenor
    BT 5150 : O lovely night (Ronald)/Homing (Del Riego).

Thomas Denijs, baritone
★ BR 92048 : Transvaalsche Volkslied (Amsterdam 1901).

Mrs Danie de Villiers, contralto
★ ZON 4071 : Rozige kop (Forder)/Bid voor ons (Piccolomini) (Cape Town 1912).
★ ZON A 4703 : Wees mij nabij (Liddle)/Houdt gij mijn hand (Cape Town 1912).
★ ZON A 4704 : Die zwoegers (Piccolomini)/See Joey Stramrood* (Cape Town 1912).

Mrs David de Villiers, soprano
★ ZON 4070 : De zwaluwen (Bingham-Cowen)/Tot alle eeuwigheid (Mascheroni), "Afrikaan songs" (Cape Town 1912).
★ ZON 4089 : Liefder gezang (Molloy)/Des levens belofte (Cowen) (Cape Town 1912).
★ ZON 4102 : Min my en maak my bly (E. Ball)/Regen en sonnenschyn (Blumenthal), "Afrikaan vocal" (Cape Town 1912).
★ ZON 4120 : Geliefste het is dag (F. Aylward)/Oprechtheid (Emile Clarke) (Cape Town 1912).
★ ZON 4144 : De rozekrans (Nevin)/O droog elke traan (T. del Riego) (Cape Town 1912).

Dolly de Villiers*, soprano
    COL LE 53 : O Heer myn God/Nader my God.

Klara de Villiers, soprano
★ J 754 : Grietjie/Antwoord van Grietjie (c. 1911).
★ J 755 : Die meisies van di Kaap (C. v.d. Linden)/Uitnodiging an Annie (Wierts), "Sung in Taal", with piano acc. (c. 1911).
★ J 756 : Tant Kati haar dogtertjie/Ons eige lied (Wierts), "Sung in Taal", with piano acc. (c. 1911).
★ J 757 Afrikaansch Volkslied/Het lied der Afrikaanders (c. 1911).

Rev. M.L. de Villiers*, composer and pianist. See M.J. Commaille.

Vera de Villiers*, soprano
    HMV Special Records
    HMV GR 4 : The Pilgrim's Song (Tchaikovsky)/Pique-Dame (Tchaikovsky) : Romance of Pauline, piano, Gerald Moore.
    HMV GS 12 : (a) Du bist wie eine Blume (Schumann) (b) Liebesbotschaft (Schubert)/Georgian Love Song (Rachmaninov), piano, Gerald Moore.
    HMV GS 13 : (a) Da unten im Tale (Brahms) (b) Who is Sylvia? (Schubert)/Der Tod und das Mädchen (Schubert), piano, Gerald Moore.
    HMV GS 14 : A Life for the Czar (Glinka) : Vanya's Aria (parts 1-2) acc. London Symphony Orchestra, cond. Albert Coates*.

HMV ? : Prince Igor (Borodin) : Konchakovna's Cavatina/A Life for the Czar (Glinka) : Vanya's Aria, acc. London Symphony Orchestra, cond. Albert Coates*. HMV ? : Evening/A Child's Lullaby to her Doll, acc. London Symphony Orchestra, cond. Albert Coates.

Sofie Deys Draayer, contralto
★ ZON 4069 : Vereenigd Zuid-Afrika (Spoel)/Sannie Beyers (Wierts) (Johannesburg 1912).
★ ZON 4119 : Antjie Schut (Wierts)/Uitnodiging an Annie (Wierts) (Johannesburg 1912).
★ ZON 4154 : Ons eige lied (Wierts)/Antwoord van Grietjie (Wierts) (Johannesburg 1912).

Diggenhof and his Music Makers (Diggenhof en sy musiekmakers)
HMV GX 33 : Ek soek na my Dina/Ou tante Koos, polka.
HMV GX 40 : (a) Hier's ons weer (b) Ma sê, Pa sê/(a) Japie, my skapie (b) Staan, Pollie, staan.
HMV FJ 135 : Vat jou goed en trek, Ferreira (arr. Gideon Fagan)/Vanaand gaan die volkies koring sny (arr. Gideon Fagan).

Lilli Dreifuss, contralto, and Ria Ginster, soprano
★ HOM 48971 : Requiem (Verdi): Recordare, Jesu piè (early nineteen-twenties)/See M. Gitowsky, bass.

The Dutch Trio: Pierre de Beer, piano; Jan Luyt*, violin and Jean Amorison, cello
★ WIN J 12 : Ouwe Zuid Afrikaanse melodies/O sole mio (Di Capua) (Cape Town 1912).
★ WIN J 14 : Serenade (C.M. Widor)/Serenata (Toselli) (Cape Town 1912).
★ WIN ? : High Jinks, selection 1/High Jinks, selection 2 (Cape Town 1912).

P.J. du Toit, diseur
★ ZON 4096 : N'dronkliedge van' n' Mozambique en N'Jolly Hotnot/Die ou' man (Johannesburg 1912).

Isador Epstein*, pianist
COL 5563 : Waltz in C sharp minor op. 64 no. 2 (Chopin)/Waltz in E minor (Chopin).

Stephen H. Eyssen*, baritone. See Cornie H. Olivier and Stephen H. Eyssen; Nunez Holtzhausen* and Stephen H. Eyssen; N. Holtzhausen; A. Steyn; S. Eyssen and B. Mellet
COL LE 47 : Segelied (Stephen H. Eyssen)/Prinses van verre (Gerrit Bon*); with piano.
COL LE 64 : Pikanienie-wiegelied (W. Spiethoff*)/(a) Kinderlied (b) Sneeu (W. Spiethoff).
HMV issued at request of the FAK
HMV FJ 142 : Duisend-en-een (A.G. Visser - A. Ellis), with ABC Radio Orchestra, cond. A. Ellis/See FAK choir.
HMV FJ 145 : Was ek 'n sanger (A.G. Visser - G. Bon), with piano/See Nunez Holtzhausen.

Gideon Fagan*, composer and pianist. This artist also appeared on records under the nom-de-plume Albert Diggenhof. For records on which he appears, also those on which his compositions are performed, see under the following artists:

Al Bowlly
Tom Carrick and Jan Kool
Betsy de la Porte
Diggenhof and his Music Makers
Josef Marais
Josef Marais and the Diggenhof-Marais-Bosvelders
Josef Marais and Johanna Lol
Al Witkin

FAK Choir
HMV issued at request of the FAK
HMV FP 6 : Dingaansdag, ballad (A. Ellis) (parts 1-2), with the ABC Radio Orchestra, cond. A. Ellis.
HMV FJ 142 : Die Stem van Suid-Afrika (C.J. Langenhoven - S. Eyssen), with the ABC Radio Orchestra, cond. A. Ellis/See Stephen H. Eyssen.

Len Fillis*, guitar, Hawaiian guitar, banjo, ukelele. A large number of records by this artist were pressed. The following list contains some of his earliest recordings
COL 4161 : (a) No, Sir that's not my Girl   (b) Chinese moon/Tamin' the tenor, banjo.
COL 4372 : Because I love You, guitar/Meadow Lark, guitar.
COL 4383 : Sort of uncertain, banjo/My Rose, guitar.
COL 4643 : Banjoviality, banjo/Uncanny banjo, with piano by Sid Bright.
COL 4678 : Souvenirs, guitar/When You played the Organ, guitar, with piano by Sid Bright.
COL 4920 : Butterfingers, banjo/Blues Serenade, banjo, with piano by Sid Bright.
COL 5010 : My Pet, banjo/Just a matter of Chords, Spanish guitar, with piano by Sid Bright.
COL 5282 : A matter of Notes, Spanish guitar/Bluebird, sing me a song, banjo, with piano by Sid Bright.
COL 5698 : Progressions, banjo, with piano by Sid Bright/Anita Waltz, with guitar by Al Bowlly, piano by Sid Bright.
COL DB 91 : Now I'm in love, banjo and guitar, with piano/In the Moonlight, banjo, with piano.
COL DB 256 : High Society Blues, banjo, with piano by Arthur Young/Moon is low, Hawaiian guitar.
COL DB 276 : Swanee River Medley, banjo en Hawaiian guitar, with piano (parts 1-2).
COL DB 304 : Evergreen - Dancing on the Ceiling, Hawaiian guitar/No Place but Home, Hawaiian guitar, with piano by Arthur Young.
COL DB 354 : Banjokes, banjo/Dizzy Digits, banjo, with piano by Arthur Young.
COL DB 498 : Three little Words, banjo, with piano/World is waiting for the Sunrise, Hawaiian guitar, with piano..
COL DB 686 : I believe in You, Hawaiian guitar, with piano/For You, Hawaiian guitar, with piano.
COL DB 705 : Sweet and Lovely, Hawaiian guitar, with piano/At Your Command, Hawaiian guitar, with piano.

COL DB 723 : No. 13 Blues, Hawaiian guitar, with piano/In "A", Spanish guitar, with piano.
COL DB 788 : Home, Hawaiian guitar/Just Friends, Hawaiian guitar.

Sir Percy Fitzpatrick KCMG. See Gen. J.B.M. Hertzog
COL 9151-2 : South African National Memorial, Delville Wood, Unveiling Ceremony, October 10, 1926. Speech at the Unveiling Ceremony (parts 1, 2, 3, 4).

Floriel Florean, contralto
J 426 : Hul sal dit tog nie kry nie/Overtuiging (c. 1911).
★ J 427 : Ou tante Koos/Grietjie (c. 1911).
★ J 428 : Mamma, 'k wil 'n man hê/Toe zê de magistraat, with orchestra (c. 1911).

Ada Forrest*, soprano
★ GCR GC 3712 : "Hondt" het Fort (c. 1907).
★ GMR 03104 : Di ster van Bethlehem (Adams) (1908).
★ HMV 3911 : Nymphs and Shepherds (Purcell) (1912).
★ P 5245 : There's a land (Allitsen)/When love is kind (Moore), with orchestral acc. (c. 1911).
★ P 5246 : Rose softly blooming (Spohr)/A Savannah Lullaby (Batten), with orchestral acc. (c. 1911).
★ P 8644 : Slaap zacht (S. de Lange)/Ik ken een lied (Willem de Mol). "Sung in Taal", with organ and piano (c. 1911).

The Goeie Hoop Quartet
COL LE 17 : Stille Nag (Halleluja 49)/Kersfeeslied (Halleluja 50), with organ.

The Grammavox Military Band
★ GRAM 138-9 : Commemorative Record of the Union of South Africa. Selection A-B (c. 1910). (Each side of the record has a different catalogue number: 138 and 139).

J.B. Grossouw, soprano
★ GCR GC 3773 : Grietjie (The Hague 1908).
★ GCR GC 3798 : Z.A. Volks Zang. "Sung in Taal", with organ (London c. 1909).

Jan Haantje, singer and diseur
★ J 738 : Oom "Hendrith" en di gouverneur/Di verjaardag van tant Bet.
★ J 739 : Di boer en di smous/Simson en di vosse, "Sung in Taal" (London August 1911).
★ J 740 : Allie Brand/Glo jy dat di wereld draai, "Sung in Taal" (London August 1911).

Elsie Hall*, pianist
HMV FJ 116 : Prelude and Fugue, in F minor, no. 36 (Bach)/Sonatine (Ravel). From Syllabus of Trinity College Music Examinations (Diploma), Associate List.
HMV FJ 117 : Gavotte and Musette in D minor and D major (Bach)/Arabesque (Schumann). From Syllabus of Trinity College Music Examinations;

Senior Group 4.

Elsie Hall and Leslie Heward*, pianoforte duet
DEC F 1613 : Military March, Op. 51 (Schubert)/Waltz no. 3 in F major (Chabrier).

Garda Hall, soprano
COL DE 1 : Oktobermaand (C.J. Pescod)/My klein rooi rosie (C. Jacobs-Bond).
COL DE 2 : Die sterretjie (Leipoldt and Hullebroeck)/Afrikaanse Wiegeliedjie (Langenhoven and Hullebroeck).
COL DE 3 : Verlange (Keet and Wierts)/'n Goue dag (C. Jacobs-Bond).
HMV B 2335 : Soft-footed snow (S. Lee)/The Second Minuet (M. Besly), with piano.
HMV B 2523 : Down in the Forest (Ronald)/Cherry Ripe (arr. Lehmann), with piano.

Garda Hall and Walter Glynne
HMV B 4271 : Who tied the Knot? (Gypsy Baron by J. Strauss)/Solo by Walter Glynne.

Garda Hall and George Baker
HMV C 2412 : Musical Comedy, selection (parts 1-2).

Garda Hall, with various other singers
HMV C 2903 : Theatre Land at Coronation Time (part 1): Song of the Vagabonds - Stuart Robertson and Choir, Music in May - Garda Hall, At the Balalaika - Webster Booth, Sing something in the Morning - Garda Hall and choir/Theatre Land at Coronation Time (part 2): The Night is young and you're so beautiful - Garda Hall and Webster Booth, I've got a thing about You - Sam Costa, If all the world were mine - Webster Booth, Swing along - Stuart Robertson and choir.

Garda Hall and John McKenna, with Columbia Light Opera Company and orchestra
COL DX 735 : A Fantasie of Sleep (part 1). Solos by Garda Hall: Träumerei, Lullaby, Sweet and Low, Cradle Song, Rocked in the Cradle of the Deep, All through the Night/A Fantasie of Sleep (part 2). Garda Hall and John McKenna: Träume, Go to sleep my little Piccaninny, Cradle song, Lullaby, A Dream, Awake.

Adolph Hallis*, pianist
DEC K 891-6 : 12 Etudes (parts 1-2) (Debussy).

Harmony Quartette
★ WIN ? : Banks of Allan Water/The Land o' the Leal (Cape Town 1924).

Norman Hart, singer
★ WIN ? : 'Tis the Day (Leoncavallo), The Rose and the Lily (Schumann), What care I now? (Schumann). Piano acc. Walter Hely-Hutchinson (Cape Town 1924).

Walter Hely-Hutchinson*, pianist. See Norman Hart.

Gen. J.B.M. Hertzog (MLA). See Sir Percy Fitzpatrick
COL 9153 : South African National Memorial, Delville Wood, Unveiling

Ceremony, October 10, 1926. Speech at the Unveiling Ceremony (parts 1-2).
COL LE 500 : 'n Boodskap aan Afrikaners/A Message to South Africans.

Katie Hofmeyer, soprano
★ J 879 : Houdt het fort, with organ/Bijna, with piano acc. "Gezangen, gezongen in de Taal" (c. 1911).

Nunez Holtzhausen*, soprano. See Stephen H. Eyssen and Nunez Holtzhausen.
COL LE 49 : Eggo (C. Eckert)/Die nagtegaal (Alabief), with piano.
HMV issued at request of the FAK
HMV FJ 145 : Lentesang (I.S. Mocke and L. Joubert), with piano/See Stephen Eyssen.
HMV FJ 146 : Die Pêrel se klokkies (A.G. Visser and A. Ellis)/Wiegeliedjie (E. de Roubaix and H. Endler), with piano.

Nunez Holtzhausen and Stephen H. Eyssen, issued at request of the FAK
HMV FJ 143 : Die aandklokkie lui in die verte (mus. Cath. van Rennes), with piano acc./See following entry.

N. Holtzhausen, A. Steyn, S. Eyssen and B. Mellet
HMV FJ 143 : O Boereplaas (C.F. Visser and Johannes Joubert), with ABC Radio Orchestra, cond. A. Ellis/See previous entry.

Deborah Joubert, soprano
HMV with piano acc. by Walter Fennell
HMV FJ 47 : (a) Aandblik (Beyers) (b) Sneeu op die berge (Beyers)/ (a) Moedersskat (Wierts) (b) Waghondjies (Wierts).
HMV FJ 69 : Net een (Lambrechts-Vos)/(a) Styging (Beyers) (b) Lied van die wonderboom (Beyers).
HMV FP 2 : (a) Serenade (Beyers) (b) Aan blomme (Beyers)/Rose van herinnering (Beyers).

Dorus Keesing, Dutch operatic baritone, acc. by Hal Wallace and his orchestra, leader Ted Staves
BT CTC 1001 : Afrikaanse deuntjies (part 1): Daar lê die ding, Waar kry jy daardie hoed?, Die Kaapse nooiens, Gertjie, Vat jou goed en trek, Ou Japie jou jakkals, Die Afrikaanse Pop/Afrikaanse deuntjies (part 2): Óu tante Koba, Die Stellenbosch-boys, Die steweltjies van Sannie, O brandewyn laat my staan, Mama 'k wil 'n man hê, Daar kom die wa, Die vaal hoed, Ek sal jou kry.
BT CTC 1002 : Maar ek wil nie/Orchestra and solo.
BT CTC 1003 : Ou tante Koos/Afrikaanse melodietjies: Vrystaatse minne-lied, Wiegelied, Slaap kindjie slaap, 'k Het my wagen vol geladen, Pollie ons gaan Pêrel toe, Rokkies wou sy dra, Staan Poppie staan, Siembamba, Vanaand gaan die volkies koring sny, Ver in die wêreld Kittie, Wat maak oom Kalie daar? Malaboch, Vra vir jou ma.
BT CTC 1005 : O Boereplaas/Gertjie.
BT CTC 1006 : Sarie Marais/Die Stem van Suid-Afrika.
BT CTC 1007 : Slaat hom/Afrikaners landgenote.

Paul Kerby, conductor of the Vienna Symphony Orchestra
COL DB 1064 : Skaters Waltz (Waldteufel)/Schoenbrunner Waltz (Lanner).
COL DB 1268 : Peer Gynt (Grieg), with choir. Act 2: In the Hall of the Mountain Kings. Act 3: Prelude/Death of Ase. Act 4: Solveig's Song.

COL DB 1269 : Peer Gynt (Grieg). Act 4: Prelude, Morning/Anitra's .Dance.

COL DB 1363 : Spanish Dances (Moszkowski): no. 1 and 2/no. 3 and 5.

COL 69065 D : Le Calife de Bagdad overture (Boieldieu)/Mireille overture (Gounod).

COL DFX 86 : Le Calife de Bagdad overture (Boieldieu)/Eine Nacht in Venedig overture (Strauss).

COL DF 426 : Morgenblätter Waltz (Strauss).

Paul Kerby, conductor of the Vienna State Opera Choir
COL DFX 178 : Lohengrin: Bridal chorus (Wagner)/Tannhäuser: Pilgrims' chorus (Wagner).

Tom Kinniburgh, bass
★ GCR GC 42048 : The Dawn of Union (c. 1910).

Lilli Kraus, contralto. See Lilli Dreifuss and Ria Ginster.

Charles W. Leönard, humorist
˙★ ZON 3052 : Oosthuisen at the Circus (Leönard)/Oosthuisen's Lion Hunt (Leönard) (1912)
★ ZON 4157 : De opening van de spoorweg (Leönard)/Oosthuizen en de muilen (Leönard) (1912).
★ ZON 4166 : (a) From whom all Blessings flow (b) Oosthuizen at the Revenue Office, humorous monologues written by Chas. W. Leönard (1912)/See C.V. Becker.

Chris Lessing, bass, with Hendrik Susan and his orchestra
SING TJ 3000 or GE 436 : Perdeby/Bobbejaan klim die berg.
SING TJ 3001 or GE 437 : Hier's ek weer/Ver oor die see.
SING TJ 3002 or GE 438 : Wanneer kom ons troudag, Gertjie?/Suikerbossie.
SING TJ 3003 or GE 439 : Jan Pierewiet/Tant Mina kook stroop.
SING TJ 3008 or GE 442 : (a) Waar kry jy daardie hoed? (b) Daar kom die wa/(a) Ver in die wêreld Kittie. (b) Wat maak oom Kalie daar?
SING TJ 3009 or GE 443 : Kom laat ons dans/Hier moet ons nou skei.
SING TJ 3010 or GE 425 : Hoe ry die boere/Daar's 'n hoender.
SING TJ 3012 or GE 426 : O kom na my (Di Capua)/My droombeminde (Herbert).
SING GE 339 : Die ossewa (Jan Swart)/Huisie in die berge.
SING GE 350 : In die Vaalrivier se water/Die windmeul draai.
SING GE 366 : Daar onder in die Kaap/Gertjie is die bruid.
SING GE 418 : Kaapse draai (Danie Bosman)/My skat (Danie Bosman).
SING GE 458 : Ons lag, sing en dans/Band alone.

Johanna Lol. See Josef Marais and Johanna Lol.

Tina Louw
★ WIN ? : Mamma, 'k wil 'n man hê/Ons twee (J.F.E. Celliers), with piano acc. (Cape Town 1924).

Lord Lurgan, baritone. See The Hon. W. Brownlow.

Jan Luyt (jr.)*, bass. See Mrs Jan Luyt's Choir.

Jan Luyt (sr.)*, violinist, with piano acc. by Pierre de Beer

★ WIN J 18 : Hej! Haj! (F. Drdla)/Liebeslied (Kreisler) (Cape Town 1924).
★ WIN ? : Le cygne (Saint-Saens)/Liebesfreud (Kreisler) (Cape Town 1924).

Mrs Jan Luyt's Choir
COL LE 73 : Silwerdrade, soloist Jan Luyt (jr.), bass/Die ruwe kruis.

Joey Marais, soprano
★ ZON 4010 : Danie en Lenie (Hofmeyr)/Nader mijn God bij U, with piano and organ acc. (London 1910).

Josef Marais, baritone
DEC acc. by his Bushveld Band:
DEC 18046 : (a) Stellenbosch Boys (b) Tante Koba (Diggenhof and Marais)/Stay, Polly, stay (Diggenhof and Marais).
DEC 18047 : Vat jou goed en trek (Diggenhof and Marais)/Here am I (Diggenhof and Marais).
DEC 18048 : Sarie Marais (Diggenhof and Marais)/Henrietta's Wedding (Diggenhof and Marais).
DEC 18230 : Marching to Pretoria (Marais)/My heart is so sad (Marais).
DEC 18231 : There's the Cape cart (Marais)/Meisiesfontein (Marais).
DEC 18232 : (a) Siembamba (b) "Ai, ai" the pied crow cry (Marais)/As the sun goes down (Marais).
DEC 18233 : (a) There comes Alibama (b) Train to Kimberley (Marais)/Jan Pierewiet (Marais).
HMV acc. by the Diggenhof-Marais-Ensemble:
HMV GX 527 : Ek dans die polka/My liefling.
HMV GX 528 : Sy's die nooi vir my/Trane.
HMV GX 534 : Ek droom/Almal se deuntjies, no. 3.
Acc. by the Diggenhof-Marais-Bosvelders:
HMV GX 546 : Boo-hoo die klein bobbejaan/Die klank van die Bosveldlied.
HMV GX 547 : As die jakkals deur die hele nag huil/Karoo, Karoo.

Josef Marais and Johanna Lol
HMV FJ 131 : Koos en Johanna vier witbroodsdae (Diggenhof and Marais), dialogue and song (parts 1-2) with "Pasop vir die diener". With chord harp, guitar and cello.

Ellie Marx*, violinist
★ EBVFR J 31 : Thaïs (Massenet)/Allegretto (Boccherini - Kreisler) (Cape Town 1924).
★ EBVFR ? : Canyonella (A. d'Ambrosio)/Melodie (Gluck - Kreisler) (Cape Town 1924).

Aletta Meiring, soprano
★ ZON 4121 : Lentelied (Sir Meiring Beck)/Ons land (Sir Meiring Beck).
★ ZON 4122 : Een vaste burg is onze God (Luther)/Zie den Mensch (Hässler - Bach) (1913).

Harold Melck, tenor
COL LE 28 : Walsliedjies, with ukulele and banjo/Voetballiedjies, with ukelele and guitar.

B. Mellet, tenor. See N. Holtzhausen, A. Steyn, S. Eyssen and B. Mellet.

385

The Melodiants, male quartette: Percy Daniel, Walter Rees*, William Matthews* and
Wilfred Hutchings*, with Rupert Stoutt*, piano
  COL LE 52 : Lonel (Whiting and Burke)/Indrukke van Naturelle-liedjies
  (arr. Wm. Matthews).
  COL LE 67 : Die droomvissertjie (Gaynor)/Ons Karooplaas (P. de V. Pienaar).

Esther Mentz*, soprano
  COL AE 508 : Maar een Suid-Afrika (Keet and M.L. de Villiers), with piano/
  In Stellenbosch bloei weer die bome (R. Stolz and Kurt Robitscheck), with cello
  and piano.

Joan Michie, mezzo-soprano, acc. by the McKay trio
  HMV GX 518 : 'n Wiegeliedjie (S. Richfield*)/Die stem van Suid-Afrika
  (M.L. de Villiers).
  HMV GX 558 : Heimwee (S. le R. Marais*)/O Boereplaas (Joubert).

Het Moeder Kerk Koor (The choir of the Groote Kerk, Cape Town). All the labels
bear the inscription: "Onder leiding van den Heer G. Denholm Walker"* and
"Afrikaan vocal". These records were all cut during 1912 in Cape Town.
  ★ ZON 4074 : O God van Bethel/Roem in het Kruis.
  ★ ZON 4075 : Gezang 1/Gezang 20, verzen 1 en 2.
  ★ ZON 4076 : Psalm 68, verzen 7 en 10/Psalm 134.
  ★ ZON 4090 : Gezang 22/Psalm 146, verzen 1, 3 en 8.
  ★ ZON 4091 : Zyt gij moede/De beste Vriend.
  ★ ZON 4104 : Heft aan met geweld/Looft den Heer, O my ziel.
  ★ ZON 4105 : Heilig, Heilig, Heilig/Rots der eeuwen.
  ★ ZON 4106 : God is ons Hoop en Kracht/Leer mij, O Heer.
  ★ ZON 4123 : Och, had ik de vleugelen/O kom laat ons bidden.
  ★ ZON 4124 : Rots der eeuwen/De dag breekt aan.
  ★ ZON 4125 : Gezang 39/Gezang 49.
  ★ ZON 4155 : De rust dag/De trouwe Herder.
  ★ ZON 4156 : Voorwaarts Christen stryders (Sullivan)/Redt die verloren gaan.
  ★ ZON A 4702 : Rust mijn ziel/Nu zijn dag taak is gedaan.

Con Morris, baritone
  ★ EBVFR J 29 : My Sweet Sweeting (F. Keel)/Maire (!), my Girl (G. Aitken),
  with piano acc. (Cape Town 1924).
  ★ EBVFR ? : Love, could I only tell thee (J.M. Capel)/Son of Mine (Wm.
  Wallace) (Cape Town 1924).

Nellie Nagel. See NG Church Choir, Kuils River.

Dolly Neiman. See Chris Blignaut.

NG Church choir, Kuils River. Cond., Chas. H. Weich
  COL LE 20 : Zingt onze God lof, unacc./Nader my God by U (Halleluja
  209), unacc. in Dutch. Solist: Miss Nellie Nagel.
  COL AE 538 : De Allerverachtste/Jesus, Woord van God.

R.C.E. Nissen, humorist. These records were cut during 1912 in Johannesburg
  ★ · ZON 4080 : Klaas, hou op met kille (Lauder)/To Pa will leg de tapijt op de
  trap.
  ★ ZON 4081 : Ringen op mij vingers/Alice, waar zijt gij?

386

★ ZON 4094 : Suartje Belle/Iks bang om T'huis te kom en de nacht.
★ ZON 4107 : Daar's soepe in die bottle ver de morre/Mrs. Dennepietje.
★ ZON 4129 : Ek wille weggaan van mij ou pondok ver jou/Waar krij je daar die hoed.
★ ZON 4159 : Kom wordt mijn regenboog (Wenrich)/De onbestorven weduwnaar.

J.D. Noonan, humorist
★ ZON 4095 : Jeremiah's love making/Coloured conversazione (Johannesburg 1912).

Cornie H. Olivier, tenor
COL LE 48 : Lied van Malie die slaaf (Gerrit Bon), with piano acc./Berusting (Gerrit Bon), with string ensemble, leader J. Schulman*.
HMV FJ 144 : Die aandblom (P. de V. Pienaar and A. Ellis), with ABC Radio Orchestra, cond. A. Ellis. Issued at request of the FAK/See Annette Opperman.

Cornie H. Olivier and Stephen H. Eyssen, song duets
RE GR 25 : Omruil huishou (arr. J.A.A. Ellis)/Die apie se bruilof (arr. J.A.A. Ellis).
COL LE 26 : Oom Jan en sy nooi/As die blare verkleur.
COL LE 40 : Bobbejaan klim die berg (arr. J.A.A. Ellis)/Die kat kom terug (arr. J.A.A. Ellis), with "peculiar" accompaniment.
COL LE 41 : Die arme Boer (arr. J.A.A. Ellis)/Die arme Engelsman (arr. J.A.A. Ellis).
COL LE 65 : Neef Jannie se ma (arr. J.A.A. Ellis)/Die windmaker- Engelsman (arr. J.A.A. Ellis).

Annette Opperman, contralto
HMV FJ 144 : Die wapad is my woning (A.G. Visser and A. Ellis), with piano acc. Issued at request of the FAK/See Cornie H. Olivier.

Kate Opperman*, contralto. These records were all cut in London, 1912-1913.
★ ZON 4065 : Seuns van die Suid (James Hyde*)/Ons land (James Hyde), "Afrikaan vocal".
★ ZON 4066 : Het volkslied van de Zuid Afrikaans Republiek/Dingaansdag, N'Feeslied "16 Dec." (M.L. de Villiers), "Afrikaan songs".
★ ZON 4086 : Afscheid (Henri T. Brink*)/Alleen (L.M. Giesen).
★ ZON 4115 : Goei morre Ma! (Brandts-Buys*)/Het lied der Afrikaners. "Holland Afrikaane Lieder Bundel."
★ ZON 4116 : Eenzaam (Nicolai)/Volkslied van de Oranje-Vrystaat. "Holland Afrikaane Lieder Bundel."

Kate Opperman and Wilfreyda Jamieson
★ ZON 4160 : Het vaderland (Visscher)/(a) Het angelus klept in de vert (b) Gedank, op. 5 no. 1 (C. van Rennes) (c. 1912).

Orchestra with effects and quartette
HMV FJ 104 : 'n Dag op 'n Boereplaas (part 1) (Richfield): Sonop, Die ossewa vertrek na die mark, Op die lande tussen die golwende koring/'n Dag op 'n Boereplaas (part 2) (Richfield): Ná die werk, By die Kafferkraal, Sononder, Aandgesang, 'n Sterrelug, Goeienag.

Peerless Orchestra

★ ZON 4018 : Vat jou goed en trek Ferreira (Hyde)/Tikkiedraai - selections of popular Afrikander songs and airs (**Stephanus Mare**) (1909-1910).

Francis Russel*, tenor. Apart from his performances on the undermentioned records, this singer can also be heard together with the following artists: Harold Williams, Isobel Baillie, the Columbia Light Opera Company; and in *Crucifixion* (Stainer), *Faust* (Gounod) and *Bohemian girl* (Balfé).

COL 1537 : Kathleen Mavourneen/Killarney (Balfé).

COL 2889 : Maritana - There is a flower (Wallace)/Solo by H. Nash.

COL 2898 : Maritana - Yes, let me like a soldier fall (Wallace)/Solo by P. Jones.

COL 4158 : I heard you singing (Barrie and Coates)/Blind ploughman (Clarke).

COL 4501 : Give (Clarke and Lohr)/Mother o' mine (Kipling and Tours).

COL 9508 : Queen of Sheba (Gounod): Lend me your aid (parts 1-2).

COL 9746 : Flying Dutchman (Wagner): Erik's song/Steerman's song.

COL 9924 : Meistersinger (Wagner): Prize song/Judas Maccabaeus (Handel): Sound an alarm.

COL DX 128 : Lost chord (Sullivan)/Holy city (Adams).

COL DX 261 : My dreams (Weatherly and Tosti)/I'll sing thee songs of Araby (Wills and Clary).

Betsy Schot, soprano

★ ZON 86 : Transvaalisch volkslied.

J. Schulman*. See Cornie H. Olivier.

Die Ses Hartbrekers, leaders: S. Viljoen and Gerry Snyman

HMV GX 11 : Askoek, settees/Uit die Boland, waltz.

HMV GX 20 : Môrester, waltz/Eina, jy maak my seer, polka.

HMV GX 25 : Boesmansdraf, polka/Sarie Marais, march.

HMV GX 31 : My oupa se perd, polka/Deurmekaar trap, settees.

HMV GX 38 : Lettie se wals/Maanskyn, waltz.

Jan J. Smith, bass

★ ZON 4099 : Gesust in d'boezem van de zee (Knight)/Voorvaders van Zuid Afrika (Cape Town 1912).

Johannes J. Smith, recitation. These records were al cut c. 1910 in London

★ HMV GC 1436 : Die prokureur sijn hond (anon.), "Afrikaans talking".

★ HMV GC 1438 : Ondervindings op tog (Engela), "Afrikaans talking".

★ HMV GC 1439 : Klaas Geswind en sijn perd (Reitz), "Afrikaans talking".

★ ZON 4011 : Die prokureur sijn hond (anon.), "Afrikaans talking"/See C.V. Becker.

★ ZON 4012 : Verliefd Jan (Melt Brink), "Afrikaans talking"/See C.V. Becker.

★ ZON 4013 : Ondervindings op tog (Engela), "Afrikaans talking"/See Die Springbokke.

★ ZON 4014 : Klaas Geswind en sijn perd (Reitz), "Afrikaans talking"/See Die Springbokke.

★ .ZON 4015 : Die afslaer en die togrijer (Engela), "Afrikaans recitation"/See Die Springbokke.

★ ZON 4016 : Windvool vertel hoe hij die Kangogrotte ontdek het (Conradie)'

"Afrikaans recitation"/See Die Springbokke.
★ ZON 4017 : Aan mijn moeder (Heine - trans.), "Afrikaans recitation"/'n Eresarsie, "Afrikaans recitation".

W.S. Smook, humorist
★ ZON 4082 : Morre tante, morre oom/Mijn naam is Melingo Hooi, "met lachen" (Johannesburg 1912).

Gen. J.C. Smuts
HMV C 12-13 : The Scientific World Picture of Today. Conclusion of the Presidential Centenary Meeting, London, 1931. (Parts 1, 2, 3, 4).
COL LE 91 : Boodskap aan Suid-Afrika/Message to South Africa.

Joe Snyman, vocalist
COL LE 4 : Die aap se bruilof (Melt J. Brink)/Hou jou roksak toe, comic songs with guitar acc.
COL LE 33 : Die kelkie sonder voet/Die steweltjies van Sannie.
COL LE 34 : Japie Olin/Afrikaanse raad.
COL LE 84 : Die Afrikaanse pop/Meisies van die Kaap.
COL AE 586 : Die mieliepit (G. Bakker and Reitz)/Tipperary (Judge and Williams).

Jenny Sonnenberg*, contralto. She probably made further recordings
★ POL 66080 : Samson und Delila (Saint-Saëns): Sieh' mein Herz/Gioconda (Ponchielli): O welcher Engel (Berlin early 1920s).
★ POL 66082 : Don Carlos (Verdi): O don fatale/Samson und Delila (Saint-Saëns): Sieh' mein Herz (Berlin early 1920s).
★ POL 66083 : Dido and Aeneas (Purcell): Recitativ et aria/Orfeo ed Euridice (Haydn): Del mio core (Berlin early 1920s).
★ POL 66084 : Orfeo ed Euridice (Haydn): Del mio core/Nebbie (Respighi) (Berlin early 1920s).
POL 66657 to 66663 : Ninth Symphony (Beethoven), with Lotte Leonard, soprano; Eugen Transky, tenor; Wilhelm Guttmann, bass, and the Bruno Kittel Choir, with the Berlin State Opera Orchestra, cond. Oskar Fried.
UPHON A 941 : Golden Light (Bizet and Mary Chater)/Rezitativ und Arie (Largo) (Handel), with piano.
UPHON A 942 : Wohin? (Schubert)/Lied eines Schiffers an die Dioskuren (Schubert), with piano.
UPHON A 943 : Pilgrim's Song (Tchaikovsky and Paul England)/At Sunset (Coates and Charles Hutchins), with piano.
HMV 62604 : (a) Das Mädchen Spricht (b) Wiegenlied (Brahms)/Der Tod und das Mädchen (Schubert), with piano by Joh. Heidenreich.

The South African Quartet, vocal quartet with organ
HMV FJ 80 : Heer, Uw schepping, aard en hemel (Hymn 32)/U alleen, U loven wij (Psalm 75).
HMV FJ 90 : Lieve Jesus, zie ons zaam (Hymn 93)/Looft, looft nu aller Heeren Heer (Psalm 134).

Bernard Sowman, baritone
★ WIN J 24 : Die Stem van Suid-Afrika (C.J. Langenhoven)/Slaap sag (Karel Castells), with piano acc. (Cape Town 1924).

Walter Spiethoff, baritone
★. WIN J 5 : (a) Ek sing van die wind (L. Leipold) (b) Skat van my drome (A. du Biel)/(a) Afrikanerlied (H.A. Fagan) (b) Die stryd (J.F.E. Celliers), with piano acc. (Cape Town 1924).

Arnold Spoel*, baritone
GTR 92364 : Vereenigd Afrika (Spoel).

Die Springbokke. (The Springbok rugby team of the late Paul Roos, 1906.) These records were all cut in London, 1906
★ GCR GC 1320 : Boer recitation "Transvaal talking; In the Taal" (London).
★ GCR GC 1330 : Springboks conversing in the Taal, "Afrikander talking" (London).
★ GCR GC 4608 : Springbok Chorus and War Cry, "Afrikander descriptive" (London).
★ GCR GC 4608 : Springbok Chorus and War Cry, "Afrikander descriptive" (London).
★ ZON 4013 : Springboks conversing in the Taal/See Johannes J. Smith.
★ ZON 4014 : Springbok Chorus and War Cry/See Johannes J. Smith.
★ ZON 4015 : Boer recitation/See Johannes J. Smith.
★ ZON 4016 : Boer dialogue/See Johannes J. Smith.

St Andrew's Presbyterian Church Choir, cond. R.J. Lonsdale
★ WIN J 23 : Fierce raged the tempest (J.B. Dykes)/Saviour again (E.J. Hopkins) (Cape Town 1924).

A. Steyn, contralto. See N. Holtzhausen, A. Steyn, S.H. Eyssen and B. Mellet
HMV FJ 147 : Dis al (J.F.E. Celliers and Johannes Joubert*)/My liefste raaiseldom (C.F. Visser and Johannes Joubert), with piano acc. Issued at request of the FAK.

Betty Steyn, soprano
ZON T 4172 : Die Stem van Suid-Afrika (De Villiers)/Afrikaans wiegeliedjie (Hullebroeck) with piano acc.
ZON T 4173 : Die lig-blou meer (De Villiers)/Ik ken 'n liefste volksman (De Villiers), with piano acc.
ZON T 4174 : Klaas Vakie (Wierts)/(a) Wiegeliedjie (Endler) (b) Waghondjies (Wierts), with piano acc.

Gerald Steyn, baritone, with Ian Stewart, piano
HMV FJ 21 : In die willeboom (Steyn)/Maarie (Steyn).
HMV FJ 81 : Snags, dags en saans (G. Steyn)/Luister na my (G. Steyn).
HMV B 4784 : Kaptijn Pretorius (Steyn)/Jan Piedewiet (!) (arr. Steyn).
HMV B 4785 : Slaat hom (Steyn)/Ver oor die see (Steyn).
HMV B 4786 : Waar was Jan (Steyn)/Vat jou goed en trek Ferreira (arr. Steyn).
HMV B 4787 : Ek sal hom krij (Steyn)/Sing 'n liedjie (Steyn).
HMV B 4789 : Brandewyn laat mij staan (arr. Steyn)/Pretoria (arr. Steyn).
HMV FJ 24 : Potpourri of Afrikaans Melodies (arr. Steyn)/When the Ivories go mad (Steyn), piano solos.

Gerald Steyn and Ian Stewart, vocal duets
BT 2 : The Face in the Moon (Steyn)/Please forget (Steyn), piano acc. Billy

Thorburn.
HMV B 4790 : Someone, Somewhere, fox-trot (Steyn)/Believe me, I don't know why, fox-trot (Steyn).

Rupert Stoutt*, pianist. See The Melodiants.

Joey Stramrood*, mezzo-soprano, piano acc. G. Denholm Walker*. These records were cut during 1912 in Cape Town
★ ZON 4068 : Drie groen hoedjes/De dageraad (Somerset).
★ ZON 4087 : Zuid Afrika/Toen Jan en ik.
★ ZON 4100 : Slaap en vergeet (White)/Alle zielen dag - als eens in Mei.
★ ZON 4117 : Kruip 'n beetje nader toe/Als uw blauw oogen.
★ ZON A 4701 : De Heer is mijn licht/De engelen zang (Braga), violin obligato Jan Luyt.
★ ZON A 4704 : O mijn hart is moede! (Goring Thomas)/See Mrs Danie de Villiers.
★ ZON A 4705 : Blijft bij mij Heer (Liddle)/Leid gunstig licht.

Students of the University of Stellenbosch
COL LE 30 : Studenteliedjies (part 1)/Students' Songs (part 2).
COL LE 31 : Studenteliedjies (part 3)/Students' Songs (part 4).

Students of the University of Cape Town
COL LE 32 : Students' Songs (part 1)/Studenteliedjies (part 2).

Hendrik Susan, violin, and Dan Bothma, piano
COL AE 554 : Minnie my liefling, barn dance (Dan Bothma)/In die helder maanlig, waltz (Dan Bothma).
COL AE 568 : Liefdeslied/Soetste en liefste.
GS GE 495 : Stille diep rivier, waltz (Dan Bothma)/Pragtig, mooi en lieflik, settees (Dan Bothma).

Hendrik Susan and his band. See Chris Lessing. A considerable number of records have been made by this orchestra, the following being the earliest recordings traced:
SING GE 367 : Oom Bossie van die Bosveld (Danie Bosman)/Op 'n braaivleisaand (Danie Bosman).
SING GE 381 : Susan se wisseldans, no. 1/Susan se wisseldans, no. 2.
SING GE 382 : Susan se wisseldans, no. 3/Susan se wisseldans, no. 4.
SING TJ 3004 or GE 440 : Ons is almal vrinde, with refrain/Vanaand gaan die volkies koring sny, with refrain.
SING GE 458 : Kliprivier-polka/See Chris Lessing.
SING GE 469 : Die Koloniewals/Die suikerriet.
SING GE 479 : Oslo-wals/Piet en Hendrik se wals.

Ten Brink's* Double Quartette
★ ZON 4077 : Gedeelte uit de "Unie Kantate"/Afscheid lied van de Voortrekkers (Ten Brink) (Johannesburg 1912).

Philip Theunissen, boy soprano
COL LE 23 : Afrikaners, landgenote/O Boereplaas (Van Niekerk), with piano acc.
COL LE 24 : Die brug op ons plaas/By die ou meulstroom.

Connie Thomas*, soprano. These records were all cut during 1912 in Cape Town
★ ' ZON 4072 : Er is een heuvel (Gounod)/O mijn Heer en verlosser.
★ ZON 4088 : Een aand in Mei (Goring Thomas)/Vaarwel (Tosti).
★ ZON 4101 : De dageraad (D'Hardelot)/Slaaplied (Somerset).
★ ZON 4118 : Blyf bij mij (Barnby)/De krans.
★ ZON 4153 : Gebied my niet u te verlaten/Ik hoor uw stemme weer (Marshall).

Adelaide Turnbull, contralto
HMV FJ 48 : Moederke alleen (Hullebroeck and De Clerq)/Die Stem van Suid-Afrika (Spiethoff).
HMV FJ 49 : Ons twee (Spiethoff)/Skat van my drome (Spiethoff).
HMV FJ 70 : Vaarwel (De Villiers)/Die strijd (Spiethoff), piano Margery Renaut.

Violet Turnbull*, contralto
★ WIN J 10 : Moederke alleen (Emiel Hullebroeck)/Die lig-blou meer (M.L. de Villiers), with piano acc. (Cape Town 1924).

Die Twee Springbokke: Cleverley and Rich, vocal duets
COL DE 4 : Kry jou koers, ou man/Afrikaanse liedjies: Ou tante Koba, Daar lê die ding, Sarie Marais, Moet nie huil nie, Vat jou goed en trek Ferreira, with guitar and harmonica.
COL DE 5 : Sarie Marais, with guitar and harmonica/As die maan se strale op die berg val, with guitar and saxophone.
COL DE 6 : In die kou grond, with guitar/Sing, ou boetie, sing, with guitar and harmonica.
COL DE 7 : Minnelied van 'n Kaapse jong, with guitar and harmonica/'n Treursang, with guitar and saxophone.

Ans Uithof, soprano
COL AE 505 : Rosekrans (The Rosary) (Nevin)/(a) Amors konfetti (Doris Beyers) (b) Serenade (Doris Beyers).

J. van Dyck, soprano
★ ZON 4145 : Het Bondslied (Wierts)/Ons Verdedigingslied (c. 1913).

J. van Mylius, baritone
★ J 973 : Kloppend, wie is daar (Ira D. Sankey)/Daniels Bende, "gezongen in de Taal", with piano acc.. (c. 1911).

Joan van Niekerk*, contralto, with piano acc. by Pierre de Beer
★ WIN J 20 : Studentelied (Emiel Hullebroeck)/Sarie Marais (Cape Town 1924).
★ WIN ? : Verskoning (J.R.L. van Bruggen)/Kom ons gaan blomme pluk (Van der Sandt de Villiers) (Cape Town 1924).

John van Zyl*, bass, with piano acc. by John Pescod
HMV FJ 1 : Ek hou van 'n man (Hullebroeck)/Die oorwinning van Dingaan (arr. Somerville).
HMV FJ 2 : Afscheid van de Voortrekkers (Brink)/Die wildeby (Pescod).
HMV FJ 3 : Die ossewa (Pescod)/Die roseknoppie (Pescod).
HMV FJ 6 : Song of the Flea (Moussorgsky)/Vulcan's Song (Gounod).
HMV FJ 19 : Sarie Marais (arr. Van Niekerk)/Ek sing van die wind

(Spiethoff).
HMV FJ 56 : Hoe sal ek maak (Warff)/'n Gebed (Morks).
HMV FP 1 : Die wandelaar (Schubert)/Die elwekoning (Schubert).

W. Versfeld*, tenor and diseur. These records were all cut in Cape Town, 1912
★ ZON 4078 : Blikbout Jan die Hotnot man/Sy kost my twinting shillings.
★ ZON 4079 : Yeup! taralle trala trala (Abb-Flynn)/Die voetbal match (W. Versfeld).
★ ZON 4092 : Die Kaapse jubelsang/Carolus van Dyke.
★ ZON 4108 : Die motor bicycle/Die kanarie man.
★ ZON 4109 : Yach! yach! ya!/Bier, bier, bier.
★ ZON 4110 : Japie sing in die gramophone/Sakabona sonki.
★ ZON 4111 : Toe zê die magistraat/See W. Versfeld and Minnie Laubser
★ ZON 4126 : Ik gaan met hom/Die spook in die kerkhof.
★ ZON 4127 : Oom Jan sij eetpartij/Een vlukse meid.
★ ZON 4128 : Meneer Van der Westhuizen/Jou stem is naby als ik slaap.
★ ZON 4150 : Niks/Die kat kom weer.
★ ZON 4158 : Een shilling in mijn sak/Wag een beetjie.

W. Versfeld and Minnie Laubser, voçal duet
★ ZON 4111 : Wil Minie vryers kry/See W. Versfeld (Cape Town 1912).

Die Vier Springbokke, leaders P. Prinsloo and H. Rex
HMV GX 1 : Lekkerdraai, polka/Môrester, polka.
HMV GX 2 : Seleksies van polkas/Hoekom het jy my verlaat?, waltz.
HMV GX 3 : Die droomwals/Moenie aan my vat nie, settees.
HMV GX 4 : Kruiwa stoot, settees/Die springbokpolka.
HMV GX 21 : Grieta, jou liewe ding, polka/Seleksies van ou walse.

Die Vier Transvalers, leader Faan Harris
HMV GX 5 : Soutpansberg se seties/Soutpansberg se polka.
HMV GX 6 : Rooidag toe, polka/Wals van tant Sannie.
HMV GX 10 : Plat toon, polka/Hartseer, wals.
HMV GX 16 : Eileen Alannah, waltz/Moenie, oom Kool, settees.
HMV GX 23 : Kromdraai, masurka/Anna Pop, settees.
HMV GX 28 : Ek is Mama se kind, waltz/Hier jy!, polka.
HMV GX 42 : Lief Fransie, waltz/Warm pampoen, settees.
HMV GX 54 : Neef Frans se polka/Hartlamwals.

Dr. W.J. Viljoen, M.A. Ph.D., D.C.L. (Oxon.), Superintendent-General of Education, Cape of Good Hope
★ WIN J 1 : A Message for Union Day (parts 1-2) (Cape Town 1924).

Annie Visser*, soprano. These records were all cut during 1908-1910 in London
★ GCR GC 3771 : Das Volkslied von Transvaal. "Sung in the Taal". Piano acc., Leo Weinthal.(N.B.: The title was later changed to "Transvaalsche Volkslied").
★ GCR GC 3772 : Vereeniga Africka (!). "Sung in the Taal". Piano acc. Leo Weinthal.
★ GCR GC 3854 : Overtuiging, with orchestral acc.
★ GCR GC 3869 : Gezang 58, verzen 7 en 9 (Ruwe stormen mogen woeden), with organ acc..

★ ZON 4000 : Di veldpartijtji/Mamma, 'k wil 'n man hê, with piano acc.
★ ZON 4001 : Grietje/Ou tante Koos.
★ ZON 4002 : Afrikaans volkslied/Gertji.
★ ZON 4003 : Afrikaans bruiloftslied/Di Afrikaanse pop.
★ ZON 4004 : Zuid Afrikaans volkslied/Transvaalsche volkslied.
★ ZON 4005 : Gezang 58, verzen 7 en 9 (Ruwe stormen mogen woeden)/ Gezang 180, verzen 1 en 3 ('K wil U o God mijn dank betalen).
★ ZON 4006 : Psalm 25, verzen 1 en 2 ('K hef mijn ziel, o God der Goden)/ Psalm 89, verzen 7 en 8 (Hoe zalig is het volk dat naar Uw klankens (!) hoort).
★ ZON 4007 : Gezang 21 (Diepe wijsheid zijn Uw paden)/Gezang 68 (Zalig, zalig niets te wezen).
★ ZON 4008 : Gezang 83 (Heer waar dan heen)/Gezang 96 (Halleluja, eeuwig dank en eere).
★ ZON 4009 : Gezang 62 (Heilige Jesus, mij ten leven)/Psalm 68 (De Heer zal opstaan tot den strijd).

Etto von Bonde*, bass, with piano acc. by G. Denholm Walker
★ ZON 4073 : Rust in de diepte (Petre)/Oprechtheid (E. Clarke) (Cape Town 1912).
★ ZON 4103 : De Heilige Stad (S. Adams)/Kalvarie (Rodney) (Cape Town 1912).

Voortrekker quartet, leader S.B. Solomon
COL LE 1 : Daar kom die Alibama/Voortrekkerwals.
COL LE 2 : Lekker dans, oom Jan/Vanaand gaan die volkies koring sny.
COL LE 3 : Dagbreek/Outydse baandans.
COL LE 69 : Generaal Jackson/Vuiltrein.
COL LE 70 : Die blomkool, polka/Die uitskop, polka.
COL LE 71 : Skoppelmaai/Kettings.

Die Vrolike Trio: Zabow, De Cola, King
COL music composed by Stephanus Mare.
COL LE 5 : Tikiedraai lansers (fig. 1)/Tikiedraai lansers (fig. 2).
COL LE 6 : Tikiedraai lansers (fig. 3)/Tikiedraai lansers (fig. 4).
COL LE 7 : Tikiedraai lansers (fig. 5)/O brandewyn laat my staan.

Die Vyf Dagbrekers, leader Silver de Lange
HMV GX 7 : Verloof, waltz/Witwortel, polka.
HMV GX 19 : Dik Anna, polka/Kom, laat ons dans, fox-trot.
HMV GX 36 : Een druk en een soen, fox-trot/Spaanse wals.
HMV GX 44 : Mielieblare, settees/Warm patat, polka.
HMV GX 56 : Hoekom het jy my laat staan?, waltz/Dierbaar is jy, fox-trot.

Die Vyf Vastrappers, leaders J.P. Bodenstein and H. Zeller
RE GR 27 : Polka/Waltz.
RE GR 28 : Polka/Settees.
GE GR 53 : Eenpas-dans/Waltz.
GE GR 54 : Polka/Settees.
COL AE 513 : Ek en my soetlief, polka/Die fluisterwals.
COL AE 515 : Wals, with two concertinas/Connie met die rooi rokkie, polka.

Waldorf Trio: R. Koorland, violin; Percy Rees*, cello; Irene Leach, piano. These

records were all cut during 1924 in Cape Town
- ★ WIN J 27 : Rosalba (B. Miles Pizzi)/Ma chere coeur (Percy Elliott).
  The catalogue numbers of the following titles are unknown::
- ★ Love come to me in a song (R. Bradley)
- ★ Andalusian serenade (G. Lind)
- ★ Danse Bosinaque (L. Balieron)
- ★ Vale (Farewell) (Kennedy Russell)
- ★ Ave Maria (Gounod)
- ★ Serenata (Schubert)
- ★ Novellettes (part 1) (Serenade miniature) (Chas. Aucliffe)
- ★ Novellettes (part 2) (Love lilt) (Chas. Aucliffe)
- ★ Marcheta (V.L. Schertzinger)
- ★ Liebestraum (F. Liszt).

Chas. H. Weich*. See NG Church choir, Kuils River.

Cecilia Wessels*, dramatic soprano
COL LE 57 : Vrystaatse volkslied, with Wurlitzer-organ acc. by Frank Lean/ Transvaal volkslied, with piano.
COL LE 78 : Die Stem van Suid-Afrika (C.J. Langenhoven and M.L. de Villiers). Recorded in the Alhambra theatre, Cape Town, with Wurlitzer-organ acc./Afrikaners landgenote, with piano.
N.B.: At the same time as the above, test recordings were made of the following titles, but to our knowledge, the records did not appear commercially
O Divine Redeemer
The Lost Chord
Largo (Handel)
Ave Maria
Vissi d'arte (Tosca)
During the 1940s one more record by her appeared (Columbia DE 304).

Dorothy Wienand, soprano, with piano acc. by Arthur Carnaby
HMV GX 525 : Rooi dagbreek, waltz (Kate Kruger*)/The Cape is calling (D. Wienand).

Engel Wilson, diseur. These records were all cut during 1912 in Johannesburg
- ★ ZON 4084 : Die vergetende Voortrekker, 1 (J. Lub)/Die vergetende Voor-trekker, 2 (J. Lub).
- ★ ZON 4085 : Die omslagtige tant Lenie (C.J. Langenhoven)/Paardegang (E. Laurillard).
- ★ ZON 4098 : Die ingewikkelde boodskap, 1 (C.J. Langenhoven)/Die ingewik-kelde boodskap hiernaast, 2 (E. Laurillard).
- ★ ZON 4112 : Lachebekje, 1 (J.W. van Hall)/Lachebekje, 2 (J.W. van Hall).
- ★ ZON 4113 : Die president gaat voorbij, 1 (J. Lub)/Die president gaat voorbij, 2 (J. Lub).
- ★ ZON 4130 : Te wees of niet te wees nie (from "Hamlet", trans. G.S. Preller)/ Antonius lykrede (from "Julius Caesar", trans. G.S. Preller).

Al Witkin, baritone
HMV FJ 134 : My oupa se klok/Twee dogtertjies in blou, with Diggenhof players.

Anne Ziegler*, soprano. See Webster Booth and Anne Ziegler.

BIBLIOGRAPHY AND SOURCES
BAUER, ROBERT: *The new catalogue of historical records, 1898-1908/9.* Sidgwick & Jackson Ltd., London, 1947.   BENNETT, JOHN R.: *Voices of the past,* vol. 1. The Oakwood Press, Lingfield, Surrey, n.d.   *Cape Argus:* Cape Town, 13 March 1924 (advert.).   CLOUGH, FRANCIS F. and CUMING, G.J.: *The world's encyclopedia of recorded music.* Sidgwick & Jackson Ltd., London, 1952.   DARRELL, R.D.: *The gramophone shop encyclopaedia of recorded music.* The Gramophone Shop Inc., New York City, 1936.   HARVEY, CLIFFORD M. and RUST, BRIAN A.L.: *The Al Bowlly discography,* 2nd edition. Rust's Rare Records, Hatch End, Middlesex, 1967. *   LESLIE, GEORGE CLARK, (advisory editor): *The gramophone shop encyclopaedia of recorded music.* Simon & Schuster, New York, 1942.   Record catalogues and lists of most of the recording companies whose records were included in the discography.   REID, ROBERT H., (advisory editor): *The gramophone shop encyclopedia of recorded music,* Crown Publishers, New York, 1948.   SEARLE, AMY M., Groot-Brakrivier: private correspondence.   SMITH, MICHAEL: *Voices of the past,* vol. 5. The Oakwood Press, Lingfield, Surrey, n.d.   STEGMANN, G.F. (FRITS): articles in *Die Burger* during 1961-65, radio programmes during 1962-63 and correspondence.   South African Broadcasting Corporation: private correspondence.

—C.G. assisted by F.S.

DIXON, ARTHUR GEORGE   The son of the English organist, Dr George Dixon, Arthur was assistant organist at Westminster Abbey for three years before sailing for South Africa in the late 1870s to become the organist of St Cyprian's in Kimberley. He exchanged Kimberley for Port Elizabeth in October 1882, where he acted as organist of St Mary's and as music master at the Girls' Collegiate School. Within a few weeks of his arrival he conducted Lecoq's operetta *La fille de Madame Angot* in a production of the PE Amateur Operatic Society. — At his organ recitals, Dixon sometimes included major works such as the *St Anne's fugue* of Bach and Mendelssohn's *Second sonata.* Vocal items were contributed by the Orpheus Glee Club, his own church choir and prominent city soloists. The respect in which he was held as an organist is indicated by the fact that he was chosen to inaugurate new organs in Queen Street and the DR Church in Humansdorp. On his initiative, two choral festivals were organised in Port Elizabeth, with choirs from Grahamstown and Uitenhage participating. On the first occasion, in August 1884, 150 singers shared in the singing and at the second meeting Dixon conducted 80 voices and an "orchestra" in a programme consisting of extracts from oratorios and an anthem composed by his father. In June 1886 he revived the old PE Philharmonic Society and conducted them in five concerts between September 1886 and September 1887. During the same year he also managed an amateur minstrel group facetiously called The Canaries, and led the PAVG Band in a Grand Jubilee Concert for Queen Victoria. — In 1888 he was involved in a scandal concerning questionable conduct, and although he was found judicially innocent, his career in Port Elizabeth had come to an end. He simply vanished from the South African musical scene.

BIBLIOGRAPHY
TROSKIE, A.J.J.: *The musical life of Port Elizabeth, 1875-1900.* M.Mus. dissertation, UPE, 1969.

—A.J.J.T. and C.G.H.

DOLIN; A.   Ballet I/10, II/1, 2, A. Godfrey, G. Lewis, M. Sturman, W. Swanson

DOMMISSE, HERMIEN (MRS C.J. McCAUL),   *27 October 1915 in Ermelo; at present (1977) *

in Johannesburg. Producer of plays and operas.

From her early years, until the time she settled in Johannesburg in 1956, Hermien Dommisse had been closely associated with the theatre. She toured as a professional actress with the theatrical companies of Huguenet, Hanekom, Marda Vanne and Gwen Ffrancon-Davies and after 1942 established a reputation as a producer in Krugersdorp, Johannesburg and Cape Town. In 1946/47, and again in 1955, she visited America and the European continent for study and to obtain experience. After joining the Opera Society of South Africa* (OPSA) in 1957, she began to produce opera in Johannesburg and Pretoria. In 1959 she revisited Europe for further study, paying particular attention to operatic production, and in 1960 she enjoyed the distinction of producing *Die towerfluit* for the Union Festival. Since 1960 she had also devoted attention to ballet. She became a member of the Johannesburg City Ballet, and organised this art form on a professional basis for the entire Transvaal. With the establishment of the Performing Arts Council for the Transvaal (PACT), she was nominated chairwoman of the Ballet Committee and held this position with zeal and enthusiasm up to 1966.

WRITINGS
Afrikaanse teaterterminologie en verklarende teaterterminologie. Unpublished.   Articles on the theatre and acting in *Die Huisgenoot, Standpunte, Die Transvaler, Die Burger, Die Vaderland, Het Toneel* (Belgium), *Streven* (Belgium), *Jaarboek van die Afrikaanse Skrywerskring, Helikon, Ons eie Boek* and *Dagbreek.   Die dramaturg en sy gemeenskap.* Perskor-uitgewery, Johannesburg, 1976.

—Ed.

DOPPER, CORNELIS, *7 February 1870 in Stadskanaal, The Netherlands; °18 September 1939 in Amsterdam. Dutch composer and conductor.

Dopper studied music, mainly under Carl Reinecke, at the Conservatoire of Leipzig. From 1908 to 1931 he was the second conductor of the Concertgebouw Orchestra of Amsterdam. Of his orchestral works, seven symphonies and the *Ciaconna Gotica* became well-known. Dopper had a particular predilection for children's choirs. One of his most successful works was *De wilgen,* based on a text of C.S. Adama van Scheltema. Later he was attracted to Afrikaans texts: Waghondjies (Jan F.E. Celliers) for two voices and piano;   Four choral pieces, based on texts by Dr A.D. Keet (1930): 1. Winter, rondeau for three equal voices, with an accompaniment of four violins (ad libitum) 2. Klaas Vakie, canon for two voices, with an accompaniment of four violins 3. Sneeu, for four voices, with an accompaniment of four violins 4. Kinderlied, for three voices, with an accompaniment of four violins. These four choral pieces were conducted by H.J. den Hertog in the Concertgebouw in Amsterdam in 1931. They were sung by a large children's choir to the accompaniment of a string orchestra.

SOURCES
BOUWS, JAN: Nederlandse musiek. *Die Huisgenoot,* Cape Town, 4 July 1939.   BOUWS, JAN: Afrikaanse kinderkoorwerke op tekste van A.D. Keet. *Die Burger,* Cape Town, 8 September 1965.

—J.B.

DORÉ, MICHAEL, *12 September 1883 in Moscow; °26 October 1968 in Cape Town. Violinist.

397

Michael Doré entered the Moscow Conservatoire of Music in 1891 to study violin under the direction of Jule Conus, and harmony and counterpoint under Hrimaly and Taneieff. He won a scholarship in 1893 and a silver medal in 1902; when he was 19 he left the Conservatoire after the award of its highest diploma (1902). A tour of Russia followed, from Siberia to the Caucasus, during which he performed in some of the principal cities. On his return he became sub-leader at the Bolshoi Imperial Theatre, a position he held for five years (1903-1908), playing under conductors such as Nikisch and Albert Coates*. Subsequently he became conductor of the Pavlosk Symphony Orchestra for three years and in 1911 conducted a performance of the Mendelssohn *Violin concerto,* with Jascha Heifetz as the young soloist.. He became well acquainted with Rimsky-Korsakov, Cesar Cui, and Glazounov, whose violin concerto he himself performed in 1911, with the composer conducting the orchestra. — In 1912 Doré left Russia and played in the principal German centres, making a timely move from Berlin to England in 1914. He worked there for 20 years, playing, conducting and acting as musical adviser and conductor to Paramount Theatres. In 1934 Doré left England to settle in Johannesburg, where he became conductor of the Colosseum Orchestra. When the SABC came into being in 1936, he joined their orchestra as a violinist and sub-conductor, positions which he held for nine years. He also taught violin, viola and conducting and was active as an ensemble player in the Johannesburg Pianoforte Trio (Doré, Hermannnn Becker* and Lorenzo Danza*) and the Johannesburg String Quartette (Doré, Bobbie Evans, Else Schneider* and Herman Becker). After 1940 he had his own string quartette (Doré, Noreen O'Sullivan, Else Schneider and Betty Pack*), which frequently became a quintette, in association with Danza. The group played in a series of chamber concerts for the radio, and for the Johannesburg Musical Society*. Doré married Else Schneider in 1941. — In 1946 he became leader of John Connell's Johannesburg City Orchestra, and performed in concertos under various conductors during the next seven years. Upon the dissolution of this orchestra in 1953, he left Johannesburg to settle in Cape Town, where he became senior lecturer in violin at the SA College of Music* (1956-1958). He retained his interest in playing and ensemble work during the last ten years of his life. His hobby was violin making, and at least nine instruments exist to testify to his skill in this art.

SOURCES ·
Obituaries: *Cape Argus,* 28 October 1968; *Die Burger,* 5 November 1968; *SAMT* 75, December 1968. Obituary Else Doré: *SAMT* 80, June 1971.

—L.W.

DORKAY HOUSE   Bantu Music Corporations of Johannesburg

DOVE, NEVILLE   A. Hallis

D'OYLY CARTE OPERA COMPANY   Bloemfontein, Durban 5, 8, Johannesburg 1, Kimberley, Pretoria 1, 2, Theatres and Concert Halls, Touring Theatre Groups 4

DRAKENSBERG CHOIR SCHOOL   Durban 10

DRAMATIC, ARTISTIC AND LITERARY RIGHTS ORGANISATION (DALRO)   G. Roos, South African Music Rights Organisation (SAMRO)

DRAMATIC HALL   Pietermaritzburg

DRAYCOTT, EDWIN GEORGE,   *13 April 1886 in Little Bolton, England; °26 July 1945

in Port Elizabeth. A school master who was active in Port Elizabeth's musical life. Draycott came to South Africa in 1913 to join the staff of the Grey High School in Port Elizabeth. In England he had obtained a BA degree at the University of Manchester in 1908 and then became a school master in Brighton. No details of his musical training are available, but he was a capable organist and very fond of choral work. He had a special liking for his great English contemporary, Sir Edward Elgar, whose choral and organ works he introduced to Port Elizabeth. He became acting rector of Grey High School in 1928 and when the Grey Junior School was opened in 1930, he was appointed its first headmaster, a position he occupied until his death. — From 1916 to 1941 he was organist and choir master of the Hill Presbyterian Church and from 1941 until his death, organist of Holy Trinity Church. He directed his Presbyterian choir in performances of Mendelssohn's *Hymn of praise* (24 July 1918) and *Athalie* (1921). He was also closely associated with the Eisteddfod in Port Elizabeth and acted as their accompanist in 1913; in 1927 he suggested that the Eisteddfod which had relapsed during the War, be revived (1927). At the competition in 1933, George Draycott was awarded a gold medal for the singing of his junior school choir, his ladies' choir and the Hill Concert Choir, which he had established in 1923. He was also associated with the Port Elizabeth Male Voice Choir, the Port Elizabeth Scottish Association Choir and with various school choirs, especially those of the Boys' High and the Grey Junior Schools. — Draycott was keen on the works of Gilbert and Sullivan and directed the Port Elizabeth Amateur Operatic and Dramatic Society in their performances of *Mikado* and *Gondoliers* (1930 and 1931). In 1932 he became a founder of the Port Elizabeth Gilbert and Sullivan Society, of which he remained the musical director and president until his death. The new society gave three concert versions of works by Gilbert and Sullivan and produced at least one stage version annually. — Edward Elgar died on 23 February 1934 and Roger Ascham* on 31 March 1934. Between these two occasions, Draycott, as acting municipal organist, gave a special concert on Sunday 4 March, which took the form of a tribute to Elgar. At the beginning of the concert he played the funeral march from *Saul,* during which the audience stood. A choir sang two numbers *(As torrents in summer* and *Aspiration)* and the organist played Elgar's *Chanson de nuit.* The rest of the programme consisted of works by Sullivan, Macpherson, Mendelssohn, Franck and Von Weber. The soloists were Merle Loveless, Solveig Hart and Eyolf Haslem. After this concert, Draycott shared the organist's duties with G. Clifton Harris* and C. Pellow-White*. — Edwin Draycott had been associated with the orchestra of Mr Sangster* in 1915 and after 1942 he succeeded Lionel Field as conductor of the Port Elizabeth Orchestral Society. When he died three years later, Robert Selley* became their conductor.

SOURCES
Eastern Province Herald: 1913-1920; 6 March 1934.   Correspondence with Mrs Elaine Dexter (née Draycott).

—C.G.H.

DREYER, W.   Organs I(iii)

DUFF, JOCK   Durban 10, Durban Orchestra

DUFFIL, C.C. & SONS AND DUFFIL, S.E.   Organs 2(iii), (v)

DUGGAN, CORNELIUS ANDRIES (ANDREW) OTTO (CON),   *12 July 1885 in Hopetown;

°August 1943 in Johannesburg. Music teacher and a highly regarded music critic and eisteddfod adjudicator.

Duggan received his piano tuition from Ernshaw, an English pianist, and after 1907, while teaching music in Kimberley, he had occasional tuition from Roger Ascham* in Port Elizabeth and from Pierre de Beer* in Johannesburg. With youthful enthusiasm Duggan founded a "symphony orchestra" in Kimberley which he conducted until the outbreak of World War I. After his discharge, following two years of active service in South West Africa, he settled in Johannesburg where, on 23 February 1916, he gave a public concert with Sign. Alberto Terassi. Thereafter he devoted most of his time to teaching and music criticism. He was a piano teacher at the Yeoville College of Music from the day it was opened by Mrs A. Landau on 15 January 1917. From that time he began to write on concert and music matters in *The Rand Daily Mail, The Sunday Times, The South African Pictorial,* and later in *The Star.* He had a wide knowledge of piano literature, and his reviews and critiques are characterised by sound technical knowledge and journalistic talent. — In 1925, assisted by his wife Mabel Duggan*, he founded the Mayfair Academy of Music. The Academy was established in a building especially adapted for the purpose, as it had a hall and a platform designed for group tuition. In his article entitled *Getting away from the old pianoforte drudgery,* he formulated his ideas on a scientific approach to piano tuition, especially in the intitial stages, and advocated group tuition and the application of classroom principles and discipline in the practical field of music. He gave a demonstration of his methods on 6 August 1932 when a class of ten pupils - all of whom had received music tuition for a period of from three to six weeks only - gave a performance on ten pianos in the City Hall, supported by John Connell* at the organ. Duggan also advocated the value of educational performances and lectures for his pupils and both he and his wife took an active part in giving them. Through such performances and lectures he aimed at giving his pupils a wider knowledge of the piano, and of its literature. Duggan was also a member of P.R. Kirby's* panel of practical piano teachers since the formation of the Music Department of the University of the Witwatersrand. — His aptitude for critically evaluating the performing art found its fullest expression in music adjudication at eisteddfodau and Afrikaans competitions. He adjudicated in every important centre in South Africa. His principle was that a critic should be appreciative before he was critical, and generous before he pronounced his verdict. This gained him the respect and admiration of literally thousands of competitors in all age groups throughout South Africa. When he adjudicated the Afrikaans Eisteddfod for the tenth consecutive year in 1931, he was awarded a special gold medal. In April 1941, he adjudicated the National Eisteddfod* in Johannesburg for the 25th consecutive year. Forming a part of the educational work which Duggan achieved in his lifetime as a writer, teacher and adjudicator, were the special radio programmes which he produced under the title *Achievements of youth.* Assisted by his wife, he was probably the first person to broadcast short discussions and performances of examination pieces prescribed by Trinity College.

—L.W.

DUGGAN, MABEL (NÉE JAMES).   Pianist, teacher of music and poetess, in Johannesburg in 1966.

Her parents took Mabel Duggan to England when she was an infant and she had her education in Cornwall; music lessons were given by a Miss Thomas. After her return to Johannesburg in 1912, she had lessons with Barclay Donn, Horace Barton* and eventually with C.A.O. Duggan*, to whom she was married in 1920. A gifted pianist with a natural flair for transposition and accompaniment, she became the first candidate in South Africa to obtain the FTCL diploma by examination (1922). A performance of Grieg's *Pianoforte concerto* with the Johannesburg Symphony Orchestra in July 1926 and two joint pianoforte recitals with her husband at their Mayfair Academy of Music in 1927, impressed the critic R.A. Nelson, who described her as a magnificent performer. — She was greatly attracted to teaching, and had an outstanding career in music education. In 1943 she was invited by Prof. Kirby* to take the place of her late husband on the panel of teachers and examiners of the Music Department of the Witwatersrand University*. She also lectured at this University in 1965-1966, and carried on her husband's work as adjudicator in all the main centres of South Africa, along the Reef and also at Bantu festivals. She has written articles for papers and periodicals on musicianship, and the technical aspects and poetics of music. Since 1947 she has also written a large number of poems, several of which were published in the magazine *Milady*. Poems about musicians have been broadcast on several occasions, and a book of children's stories was prescribed for use in standard three.

PUBLICATION

The giraffe who wanted to wear a white collar. Book of children's stories, also translated into Afrikaans. Afrikaanse Pers, Johannesburg, n.d.

—Ed.

DUGMORE, HENRY HARE, *27 April 1810 in Birmingham; °14 June 1897 in Queenstown. Dugmore was an extraordinarily versatile man, who made his mark as a theologian in the Eastern Province, and as a missionary among the Xhosa; but he also exerted a cultural influence on the 1820 Settlers and their descendants in the 19th century. This article is concerned with his cultural work, in which music was a prominent factor.

Dugmore was 10 years old when his parents came to South Africa with the 1820 Settlers. He was apprenticed to a saddler, Mr Wright, of Grahamstown, finding much benefit from the night school inaugurated by the Reverends William Shaw and Boyes. Gifted with a sharp intelligence and an excellent memory, he was largely self-taught, but managed to pick up a working knowledge of music which enabled him to write simple melodies, and to share in and even lead the amateur music-making of the Settlers. — After his apprenticeship, Dugmore was authorised to act as an "exhorter" of his church in the rural areas around Grahamstown and as a missionary at Mount Coke. After his ordination in Grahamstown, he was married on 13 November 1838 to Miss Elizabeth Simpson, and became resident minister in and around Grahamstown. At this time he co-operated with several others in the translation of the Bible into Xhosa. When the 25th anniversary of the Settlers came, there were church festivities in Grahamstown, Bathurst and Salem, at which music played its part. Dugmore contributed a *Commemoration anthem* which was heard again when the foundation stone of the Commemoration Chapel was laid on 10 April 1845. In 1854 he preached the first service in the new Methodist Church, Queenstown, and became resident minister of this congregation in February 1864. With one long interruption of about 10 years, his career was interwoven with

Queenstown's history up to the time of his death. — The Mechanics Institute, which had been formed in 1859, became a cultural organisation in Dugmore's hands. There were learned and topical lectures, and musical items of such an elevating nature that a reader complained in the *Free Press* about all the music of Haydn and Mozart, and demanded something less "scientific" (31 May 1865). Dugmore joined in the amateur singing and playing, and in 1867 established an ensemble which consisted of the Rev. Naudé* (violin) and members of the Dugmore family: Herbert (cornet), George (violoncello), Arthur (harmonium), a daughter (piano) and the Rev. Dugmore himself (flute). The Institute had now become the Young Men's Mutual Improvement Society, and their meetings were in the main actual concerts, at which glees, ensembles and instrumental and vocal items were presented. At first the meetings were held in the Institute's Reading Room, sometimes in the Town Hall or in the Library; but the Wesleyan school-room served fairly regularly as a venue. Extending this cultural work, Dugmore established a Volunteer Brass Band, for which he composed a march *Tramp, tramp, tramp*. In 1869 he gave the first sacred concert in Queenstown, and it was then proposed to establish a choral and philharmonic society, with Dugmore as president; but nothing came of this. — In 1870 there were Settlers' Jubilee celebrations in Grahamstown, at which the music performed was arranged for and performed by an "orchestra" and a chorus of 100 performers. One of the pieces was a choral march. According to a letter written by Dugmore to the secretary of the Methodist Missionary Society in London, the "orchestral" arrangements were done by himself. The other items were *Prospect and retrospect, The dear old land* and *The sunny land*. This music was heard at a lecture lasting four hours, given by the Rev. Dugmore, in which he reviewed the history of the Settlers. Musical items introduced the lecture, were heard at intervals, and at the end. The lecture was later published as *Reminiscences of an Albany settler*. — From 1873 to about 1883, Dugmore's movements included a stay at the Lesseyton Mission Station, for which he composed a *Quick march;* there was also a second visit to England, but there is some confusion as to dates and places. Without his leadership the YMMIS waned. In the twelve years before 1876 there had been approximately 400 concerts in Queenstown, of which the Minister was responsible for some 180. — In 1883 Dugmore returned to Queenstown to live there for the rest of his life. Music was an integral part of the educational work at the Wesleyan Ladies' School, and choral music was encouraged, as were school concerts in which the Minister often participated. For the opening of a new Wesleyan Church Dugmore composed a *Jubilate*, and when the organ was inaugurated on 18 January 1883 the 73 year-old Minister sang two solos and had a part in a vocal trio from Haydn's *Creation*. This concert was a major effort, which led to the re-establishment of the Queenstown Choral Society, with Dugmore as president (1883-1890). He was also active in the district and organised a musical concert at Molteno, which took place in July 1883 to mark the laying of the foundation stone for a new chapel. His last known appearance was at the Wesleyan conference in April 1893, when he conducted a choir in four items of a programme of eleven, which included two of his creations - a choral march based on *God save the Queen* and a *Jubilee march of the British settlers*. — At the age of 70 Dugmore started teaching himself Greek, and then German, but his eyesight was failing. In his 83rd year he dictated *Life's review,* a retrospective poem of 150 lines. When the Settlers' celebrations took place in Grahamstown in 1970, the four pieces that Dugmore had written for the celebrations of 25 May 1870 were revived in an orchestral arrangement by Albert Honey* of Rhodes University.

WORKS

For the Queen, anthem (Rev. Thornley-Smith). Ms., 1844. Sound ye the trumpet, anthem for choir (Rev. Thornley-Smith). For the laying of the foundation stone of the Commemoration Chapel in Grahamstown, 10 April 1845. In the Children's Home Music series of publications for choral societies, singing classes, schools and the family circle: 1. Prospect and retrospect, Part 40 2. The dear old land, Part 43 3. The sunny land, Part 123. Performed by the Wesleyan Young Men's Society, Grahamstown, on 22 November 1867. God save the Queen! Let all the people sing. Jubilee choral march of the British Settlers, performed 22 November 1867. Quick march, dedicated to the Queenstown Volunteers. Published by E. Mendelssohn & Co., c. 1883, in the *Cape Musical Monthly;* Quick march, Tramp, tramp, tramp! for the Queenstown Volunteer Band, possibly the same (1870); Quick March, for Lesseyton Collegiate College, possibly the same (1872). Jubilate for choir, composed for the new Wesley Chapel, Queenstown, May 1882. Gently sighs the breeze, duet with chorus, performed October 1885. Eight tunes contributed to *Incwadi Yamaculo Kunye Nengoma Sekuvunywa,* a Xhosa hymnbook published by the Methodist Press, 1889. Ten tunes contributed to the *Wesleyan Kaffir hymn and tune book.* Published by the Methodist Press, 1898 (no copies available).

WRITINGS

An Albany settler's reminiscences; or a glance at the early history of the settlement. 22 November 1867, and 1870 Jubilee Celebrations, Grahamstown. Six poems in *A treasury of South African poetry and verse.* Edited by E.H. Crouch, pub. by The Walter Scott Publishing Co., New York, London etc, and Juta & Co., Cape Town, 1907. Reissue, edited by E.H. Crouch, printed by Birbeck & Sons Ltd., Birmingham, 1920. Translations into Xhosa of: the Psalms, St Matthew, St Mark, St Luke, Acts of the Apostles, Romans, Phillippians, 1st and 2nd Thessalonians, Titus and Philemon; the prayer book and a number of hymns. He assisted in Rev. H. Haddy's translations of Corinthians and Galatians, and also in Appleyard's Standard Translation of the Bible. Unpublished poems, writings and lectures.

BIBLIOGRAPHY

CROUCH, E.H.: *Life of Rev. H.H. Dugmore.* Hazell, Watson & Viney, London, 1920. RADLOFF, T.E.K.: *Music in Grahamstown, 1863-1879.* B.Mus. script, Rhodes University, Grahamstown, 1969.

SOURCES

Graham's Town Journal: 17 April 1845. *Queenstown Free Press:* 1863 to June 1897. Correspondence with Prof. L.A. Hewson, Department of Divinity, Rhodes University; M. Berning, Cory Research Library, Grahamstown; and Jennifer M. Henderson (née Dugmore).

—C.G.H. (amplified)

DUNBARON, MAMIE (MRS BELL) Drummond Bell

DUNN, WILLIAM EDWARD, *11 August 1902 in Manchester; °10 April 1973 in Johannesburg. Conductor.

Between the years 1913 and 1919 Edward Dunn studied at the Royal Manchester College of Music and at the Manchester University, becoming an Associate of the College in 1916. He was also elected a member of the Royal Society of Teachers and of the Incorporated Society of Musicians. Initially a clarinet player in the Hallé

Orchestra, he soon advanced to become the musical director of the London Colosseum, Ballet, the O'Mara Opera Company, then of the boroughs Buxton and Bath and was invited to tour Australia and New Zealand as a guest conductor. From 1925 to 1927 he directed his own Academy of Music in Manchester and acted as a musical editor to the publishing house of Mons Yvette in Paris. — Shortly after his appointment to the position of artistic and administrative director of the Durban Municipal Orchestra* in 1935, Dunn made a public statement in which he emphasised that the highest function of an orchestra was the playing of symphonic music, but that recognition should also be accorded to the demands of orchestral entertainments. The large audiences in the years of care-free optimism before and especially during the Second World War certainly served to emphasise the correctness of his statement. A spirit of abandon prevailed among the thousands of transit troops who attended his concerts and the "Happy Nights", presented in the Durban Pavilion on Saturday evenings on themes designed for relaxation - "Popular British Composers", "Night", "Foreign Travel" and the like. — In the immediate post-war period, Dunn founded the International Arts League of Youth, a pioneer venture intended to explore the resources of youthful musical talent in Durban and the country as a whole. For 15 years the IALY festivals attracted about 300 young delegates annually. The size of the Durban orchestra was steadily increased to 45 players; in 1948 it actually had a membership of 60 players, and the concerts featured soloists such as Betsy de la Porte*, Cecilia Wessels*, Adolph Hallis* and Harold Ketelbey*. — In 1954 Dunn resigned the musical directorship in Durban to take up a similar appointment under the Cape Town Municipality. This lasted until 1957, when he moved to Johannesburg and founded an Institute of Musical Art for the training of conductors and music teachers. He also lectured on music appreciation, and conducted courses in musicology for the Institute of Adult Studies under the aegis of the Adult Education Association. Pietermaritzburg called for his services in July 1962, and appointed him co-ordinating director of orchestral, choral and theatre groups. On Sunday night, 14 July 1968, after an absence of 14 years, he was the guest conductor before a large audience in the Durban City Hall. — As the third person to occupy the post of conductor of the Durban Orchestra, Dunn followed closely in the steps of his predecessors, Lyell-Taylor* and Dan Godfrey*, both well-versed in the art of introducing all types of music to seaside audiences.

ARTICLES, SPEECHES, ETC.
Your music pupils as missionaries of culture and peace. *SAMT* 42, June 1952.   Growing appreciation in music appreciation. *Res Musicae* III/3, March 1957.   The modern approach to pianoforte teaching. *Opus* I/5, 1967.

SOURCES
Anonymous: Festival of youth, Durban. *SAMT* 36, June 1949.   Anonymous: Fourth annual Durban Festival of the International Cultural Arts League of Youth. *SAMT* 42, June 1952.   Anonymous: SASMT students' concert tour scheme. *Res Musicae* IV/1 & 2, September & December 1957.   Anonymous: The Durban Civic Orchestra. *Res Musicae* VII/2, March 1961.   Obituary: *Opus* IV/4, June 1973.   *Cape Times:* 26 June 1954; 13 November 1954.   *Evening Post:* 5 September 1955.   *Natal Mercury:* 1935-1955, 19 April 1962.   *Natal Daily News:* 1935-1955, 15 July 1968.   *Sunday Times:* 26 January 1957.   National Documentation Centre for Music, HSRC, Pretoria.

—G.S.J.   .

DUNSTER, J.C.   Pietermaritzburg, Pietermaritzburg Philharmonic Society

DUNSTERVILLE, MISS   G. Dunsterville, Port Elizabeth

DUNSTERVILLE, GEORGE EDWARD, *1811 in England; °23 October 1877 in Port Elizabeth. Medical doctor and musical amateur.

The first amateur concert in Port Elizabeth of which independent testimony exists is dated Wednesday, 15 November 1848. The same concert was repeated two days later in aid of the funds of the Public Library. Dunsterville was responsible for these concerts and arranged a programme which contained items by a small ensemble of nine members (4 violins, viola, cello, double bass and 2 flutes). The doctor was able to play both the viola and the double bass and he participated on either of these two instruments. This little group still existed in the early sixties and must be regarded as Port Elizabeth's first "orchestral" effort. — In 1860 Dunsterville was again prominent as one of the men who established the Athenaeum Musical and Choral Society. This society organised, among other things, two classes - one for choral singing and one for instrumental playing. Dunsterville led the instrumental class. That his work was properly appreciated, appears from a farewell concert which was arranged for him on 3 April 1863. All the members of the "old" music society, the band, the string ensemble and the glee club combined to honour the doctor with a variety of contributions. — Seven years later (December 1870), Dunsterville had returned to Port Elizabeth and, although he was no longer active as a music maker, he was again chosen to be president of the choral society. A Miss Dunsterville had taken part in the first concert of November 1848 and also shared in the first historic concert given at Graaff Reinet in April 1856. She was probably a daughter or a sister of the doctor.

BIBLIOGRAPHY
HENNING, C.G.: *The cultural history of Graaff-Reinet, 1786-1886.* D. Phil. thesis, UP, 1971.

SOURCES
EP Herald: 1848-1870.   Registrar of estates, Cape Colony: MOOC 6/9/161. DN 4633.
                                                                        —C.G.H.

DU PLESSIS, HUBERT, *7 June 1922 on the farm Groen Rivier in the Malmesbury district; at present (1978) senior lecturer in Music at the Stellenbosch Conservatoire*. Composer and pianist.

Du Plessis began to play the piano at the age of 7 and, while still at school in Porterville, tried his hand at writing his own music. In 1940 he entered the University of Stellenbosch for a B.A. degree, with English and Music (since 1941) as major subjects - consequently he was also a student at the Conservatoire where two of his instructors were Prof. M. Fismer* and Alan Graham*. 1942 saw the beginning of his lessons in composition with Prof. W.H. Bell*, former Dean of the Music Faculty at the University of Cape Town*. Interesting details arising from his journeys to Gordon's Bay (often cycling the distance), have been published in the correspondence between Du Plessis and Bell (edited by Du Plessis; see list of publications). These years also saw the beginning of his broadcasting turns as pianist and his first appearances in public. — For a short while Du Plessis was employed in the Record Library of the SABC in Cape Town (1943), but soon Bell's influence had paved the way for his appointment in the Music Department of Rhodes University

College* (1944). Initially he acted as Senior Demonstrator, but after he had successfully completed the requirements for the degree of B.Mus. in 1946, he was promoted to lecturer. Prof. Friedrich Hartmann*, the head of the department, had the responsibility of supervising his work in composition and also guided his studies in 16th century Counterpoint, Harmony and Orchestration. His original work, especially for pianoforte and solo voice with piano accompaniment, attracted attention after 1945. — The award of an overseas bursary awarded by the Performing Right Society (1951), enabled him to specialize in composition at the RAM with Alan Bush and Howard Ferguson as his mentors. His original work gained a prize in 1952 and the next year the bursary was renewed for a further two years, so that he could devote himself to creative work in England until September 1954. After substituting for Arnold van Wyk* at the Cape Town College of Music in 1955, he lectured in Music in both Cape Town and Stellenbosch from 1956 to 1957. Since 1958 he has been on the Stellenbosch staff only, first as lecturer and later as senior lecturer. — Du Plessis is an excellent player of pianoforte, harpsichord and clavichord. His programmes usually arise from the music which he is studying at a particular time. Thus, at the end of 1956, he devoted a series of six lecture recitals to the music of Bach and Couperin and played Part 1 of Bach's *Welltempered clavichord* at the Cape Town College of Music on six consecutive evenings. In September 1964 his love for Bach (on whom he published his book in 1962) led to a harpsichord performance of the *Goldberg variations;* the 150th anniversary of Franz Liszt's birth was marked by special programmes in 1961; 1962 was devoted to Debussy; other evenings centred around the music of Chopin and Schumann. This concern for music in performance, also colours Du Plessis's musicological work. The most valuable part of his book on Bach is that which reflects his personal view of the work he has played or studied. Similarly his article on Couperin was dictated by his practical study of this composer's keyboard works. Since approximately 1946 there has been a kind of rhythm between his creative work and his playing: composition received preference during the long holidays, but during the terms and short vacations he devoted more attention to keyboard technique and repertoire. — As a person, Du Plessis distinguishes himself as an eminently civilised man whose complete devotion to aesthetic matters is reflected in his concern for his immediate surroundings, his friendships and his conversation. Meticulous and accurate in everything pertaining to his art, he also commands an admirable critical faculty, which is often exercised in genial conjunction with a sense of humour.

WORKS

A. Instrumental

1. Pianoforte

Four pianoforte pieces, op. 1, 1944-1945. Studio Holland, Cape Town, 1963: 1. Prelude 2. Study 3. Elegy 4. Dance. Six miniatures, op. 3, 1945-1949. Studio Holland, Cape Town, 1975. Sonata no. 1, op. 8. Ms., 1952. Sonata for pianoforte duet, op. 10. Novello, London, 1954. "Composed for H. Ferguson and D. Matthews." Cunctipotens genitor Deus, phantasy on an 11th century organum, for two pianos. Ms., 1956. Prelude fugue and postludium, op. 17. Novello, London, 1958. Seven preludes, op. 19. HAUM, Cape Town, 1964. Inspiré par mes chats, suite, op. 27. Ms., 1963-1964: 1. Déploration sur la mort de Dodo 2. L'allégresse et la sagesse de Josquin 3. Les petits pas amoureux de Tristan 4. La tendresse d'Isolde 5. Gaspard et sa souris, pas de deux 6. Tombeau 'de

Joséphine. Four pianoforte pieces, commissioned by UNISA. Ms., 1965: 1. Hommage à Fauré 2. Hommage à Ravel 3. Hommage à Chopin 4. Hommage à François Couperin (nos 1 and 3 have been published by UNISA as examination pieces). When I was a child/Toe ek 'n kind was, suite, op. 33. DALRO, Johannesburg, 1972: 1. Musical box 2. The cellist 3. Vlei folk 4. Calf love 5. River dream 6. End of term 7. Kaleidoscope 8. Night sounds. Sonata no. 2, op. 40, commissioned by SAMRO. Ms., 1974-1975. Ten pianoforte pieces for children and young people, op. 41, composed as a study project for the US. Ms., 1975. Part I (for children): 1. Heimwee van 'n Amerikaanse teddiebeer 2. Angus en oom Koos maak maats 3. Wispelturige Wilhelmina 4. Ouboet en Kleinboet voel olik 5. In die pretpark. Part II (for young people): 6. Hartseerwals 7. Kwêla 8. Mars 9. Studie 10. Scherzo.

2. Other solo instruments
Variations on a folk tune, for solo harp, op. 31, commissioned by the South African Harp Society. Ms., 1967-1968.

3. Chamber music
String quartet, op. 13, "In memory of Henry Bell", comp. 1950-1953. Novello, London, 1957. Trio for piano, violin and cello, op. 20, commissioned by the SABC. Ms., 1957-1960. Three pieces for flute and piano, op. 25. Ms., 1962-1963: 1. Sarabande 2. Waltz 3. Lullaby. Four antique dances for flute and harpsichord, op. 35: 1. Siciliano (from incidental music for *Periandros van Korinte* (D.J. Opperman)). Ms., 1972 2. Tambourin 3. Sarabande 4. Gigue (nos 2, 3, 4 are drawn from incidental music written for an Afrikaans production of *A winter's tale* (Shakespeare)). Ms., 1974.

4. Orchestra
Symphony, op. 14. Ms., 1953-1954. Musiek by drie skilderye van Henri Rousseau, op. 24, commissioned by the SABC. Ms., 1962: 1. Un soir de carnaval 2. Pour fêter le bébé 3. Le rêve.

5. Orchestrations
Die Stem van Suid-Afrika, commissioned by the SABC. Ms., 1960. Vallée d'Obermann (Liszt). Ms., 1961. Drie outas het in die haai Karoo, arrangement for chamber orchestra of an own a capella choral work, commissioned by the SABC. Ms., 1973.

6. Incidental music
Huberta the hippo (radio feature by Cecil Jubber), for chamber ensemble. Ms., 1960. *Periandros van Korinte* (Opperman), for chamber ensemble. Ms., 1972.

B. Vocal

1. Songs with pianoforte accompaniment
Vijf liedekens, for baritone or mezzo-soprano, op. 2 (P. van Ostaijen). Ms., 1946 (revised 1964): 1. Berceuse 2. Berceuse presque nègre 3. Berceuse voor volwassenen 4. Zeer kleine speeldoos 5. Mélopée. Herbst, for baritone or mezzo-soprano, op. 4 (Rilke). Ms., 1946 (revised). In den ronde, song cycle for baritone, op. 5 (H. Marsman). Ms., 1945-1948 (revised 1964): 1. Wacht 2. Vrouw 3. Invocatio 4. De blanke tuin 5. Vlam 6. Afscheid 7. De gescheidenen. Twee Middelnederlandse liedere, for baritone, op. 6 (anonymous). Ms., 1949-1952: 1. Ghequetst ben ic van binnen 2. Egidius waer bestu bleven? Vreemde liefde, song cycle for baritone, op. 7 (I.D. du Plessis), commissioned for the Van Riebeeck Festival. Ms., 1951: 1. As ek my vreemde liefde bloot moes lê 2. Ek het my aan jou oorgegee 3. Die hart van die daeraad 4. Swakkeling met vrou en kind 5. Ek

407

weet dat in die kalme samesyn 6. Nee, liewer die dood 7. Met skemering toe die vinke, 8. O vreemde liefde. Sechs Galgenlieder, for baritone, op. 9 (Christian Morgenstern). Ms., 1952: 1. Das Knie 2. Monden-dinge 3. Der Walfafisch oder das Überwasser 4. Der Hecht 5. Der Schaukelstuhl auf der verlassenen Terrasse 6. Der Nachtschelm und das Siebenschwein. Five invocations, for tenor, op. 12. Novello, London, 1954: 1. Hark, now everything is still (John Webster) 2. The river-god's song (John Fletcher) 3. God Lyaeus (John Fletcher) 4. Care-charming sleep (John Fletcher) 5. Dirge (John Webster). Three sonnets from the Portuguese, for mezzo-soprano, op. 15 (Elizabeth Barrett-Browning). Ms., 1954: 1. Go from me (Sonnet VI) 2. Unlike are we (Sonnet III) 3. Let the world's sharpness (Sonnet XXIV). Vier slampamperliedjies, for soprano, op. 23 (Leipoldt). Ms., 1961: 1. Krulkopklonkie 2. Sekretarisvoël 3. Op my ou ramkietjie 4. Boggom en Voertsek. Three diatonic settings for *Twelfth night,* for lyric baritone or tenor with harpsichord, op. 26 (Shakespeare). Ms., 1948 (revised 1963): 1. Come away death 2. O, mistress mine 3. When that I was.. Die vrou, song cycle for soprano and pianoforte, op. 30, commissioned by US and dedicated to Hanlie van Niekerk. DALRO, Johannesburg, 1969: 1. Die meisie (E. Eybers) 2. Chant d'amour (Cantique des cantiques) 3. De bruid (H. Marsman) 4. Wiegenlied (Morgenstern) 5. Die moeder (E. Eybers). Three nocturnes, for dramatic soprano, op. 36, commissioned by Oude Libertas. Ms., 1974: 1. Die rus is elders (Totius) 2. Suidoos (E. van Heerden) 3. Winternag (E. Marais), a pianoforte arrangement of *Suid-Afrika, nag en daeraad,* comp. in 1966. Three love songs, for baritone, op. 37, dedicated to Bernhard de Clerk. Ms., 1974: 1. Amoureus-lied (Bredero) 2. Klaaglied van Dawid oor Saul en Jônatan (extracts from Sam. I & II) 3. Wiegeliedjie voor de geliefde (Paul van Ostaijen). Ten Boerneef songs, for tenor, op. 38, dedicated to Helmut Holzapfel. Ms., 1974: 1. Doer bo teen die rant 2. Lappiedy lappida 3. Die berggans 4. Die koperkapel 5. By Pramberg 6. Vannie eenkant 7. Die vuur brand laag 8. Veer op my hoed 9. Duisendpoot en hotnosgot 10. Varkleerbaadjie en klinknaelbroek.

Without opus numbers
Herfsliedere (H. du Plessis). Ms., 1943-1944. Two Elizabethan lyrics, for baritone. Ms., 1948: 1. Lady, when I behold the roses sprouting 2. My love in her attire.

For use in schools
Wysies en deuntjies vir meisies en seuntjies (Mariechen Naudé), melodies by Dolly Heiberg, song cycle for schools: 1. Oggendgeluide 2. Skooltyd 3. Volksdansies 4. Etenstyd 5. Tweetalig 6. Babbelbekkie 7. Kabouterdiefies 8. Stoutigheid 9. Hoekom 10. Slaap-liedjie.

2. Choir a capella
Two Christmas carols, for SATB, op. 11: 1. A carol of the fleur de lys (anonymous). Novello, London, 1953 2. A shepherd's carol (Crashaw). Ms., 1953. Two madrigals, for SATB, op. 16: 1. Description of Spring (H. Howard). Novello, London, 1954. 2. How lovely is the heaven of this night (T.L. Beddoes). Ms., 1958-1959. Bold Robin Hood, for TBB (no opus number) (trad.). Novello, London, 1955. En Boplaas sing koortaal, for SATB, op. 32 (Boerneef), commissioned by the Free State Youth Choir. Ms., 1970: 1. Hoe stil kan dit word as sedoos gaan lê 2. Jankemalanke Langklaasfranke.

3. Choir with pianoforte, ensemble or orchestra
Slamse beelde, for SATB, clarinet, harp and strings, op. 21 (I.D. du Plessis). Ms., 1959: 1. In die Slamse buurt 2. Albassi en Fatima 3. Ramadan. Die dans van die reën, for soprano and

orchestra, op. 22 (E. Marais), commissioned for the Union Festival. Ms., 19591960. Suid-
Afrika - nag en daeraad, for soprano, chₒir and orchestra, op. 29, commissioned for the Republic
Festival 1966. Ms., 1965-1966: 1. Nag (including E. Marais's *Winternag* 2. Daeraad
(including *'n Ider nasie het sy land* with adapted words).   Drie outas het in die haai Karoo,
Christmas carol for S, M-s, A with piano (no opus number) (Dirk Opperman). Ms., 1968.   Ag
wat, dis maar 'n hond, for choir and pianoforte, op. 34 (Langenhoven), dedicated to Sarah
Goldblatt. Ms., 1972. . Requiem aeternam, for choir and orchestra, op. 39. Ms., 1974.

PUBLICATIONS
An introduction to the keyboard music of François Couperin. *SAMT* 52, June; 53, December
1957.   *Johann Sebastian Bach*. Tafelberg-Uitgewers, Cape Town, 1960.   Atmosfeer van
plesierige Maleise optog (I discovered an ideal Malay melody).   *SABC Bulletin* VI/37,
1961.   *Dagboek van Die dans van die reën*. Tafelberg-Uitgewers, Cape Town,
1970.   Dagboek van Die dans van die reën. *Die Huisvrou* 50/6, October 1971.   *Letters from
William Henry Bell*. Tafelberg-Uitgewers, Cape Town, 1973.   'n Besoek aan Bayreuth. *SAMT*
83, January 1973.   Scriabin. *Standpunte* 105, February 1973.   Hubert du Plessis' Elegie, op. 1
no. 3. The composer replies. *Musicus* IV/1 & 2, 1976.   *Die Burger:* 21 October 1961; 11
January 1963; 19 May 1966; 28 September 1966.   *Rapport:* 5 May 1974.   Hubert du Plessis.
Piano suite, op. 33. *Musicus* III/2, 1975.

Hubert du Plessis is a versatile and interesting composer who has an excellent
command of the technique of composition in all its facets. Though he has applied the
discipline of tone rows in some works (pianoforte trio, preludes, Slampamper songs)
and although generally his music has a modern sound, they all suggest a link, rather
than a break, with tradition - as Du Plessis himself has observed. Judged according to
content, his work is characterized by personal emotion; the sound effect is marked by a
distinctly vocal approach; the form exhibits self-control and a free application of
contrapuntal techniques; the meticulous finish of detail is the work of a loving
craftsman. — Vocal works (songs with pianoforte, a cappella choirs, choruses with
instrumental ensembles) dominate to such an extent that Du Plessis can be described
chiefly as a vocal composer. In his choice of texts he exhibits a cultivated literary taste
and an intimate knowledge of Afrikaans and English as well as of Dutch, German and
French poetry. As far as the musical treatment of words is concerned, the songs and
choral works reveal respect for metre and verse rhythms and sentences are rarely
interrupted in an irritating way. The general impression is one of an overall, well
thought-out congruence between music and poetic structure, quite often with musical
illustrations of words. Melismatic figures sometimes have the function of accentuating
a word or illustrating a detail, but generally they are musically organised into the
melody as a whole; melodic leaps, changes of tempo and time, rhythm, sonorities and
dissonances, phrasing, in short, all the musical elements are integrated in the same
way (the reader is referred to Dr J.H. Potgieter's* enlightening harmonic analyses in
the thesis quoted below). It amounts to a very fine aesthetic balance between tonal and
verbal expression. Supple and significant manipulation of telling motives is important
in the accompaniments. Representative examples are "Ek weet" (No. 5 of *Vreemde
liefde)* and "Krulkopklonkie" (No. 1 of *Vier Slampamperliedjies).* The overall impression is one of disciplined formal organisation, which may possibly have a retarding
effect on the immediate reactions of a listener, but is an important factor in determining
the lasting qualities of this composer's vocal work. — A tendency towards pure, absolute music dominates the pianoforte works written in London. Later works such as the

Suite, Opus 27 tend to be more playful and programmatical (see Pianoforte Music in South Africa). Du Plessis's relationship with Afrikaans folk music has an interesting history - in the beginning he regarded it as unsuitable for use in serious composition, but in later years it began to play a part in his work. For Du Plessis, folk tunes communicate certain sentiments which renders them symbolic of a nation's weal and woe. He weaves this symbolic complement into the texture of his compositions by means of melodic quotation. Thus quotations from the lay folk music are prominent in his *Slamse beelde,* although mainly employed for local colour; but in his pianoforte trio and in *Suid-Afrika, nag en daeraad* melodies from the Afrikaans folk music repertoire are used in an intentionally symbolic way. — *When I was a child* has an autobiographical character and is marked by its use of a variety of South African associations. The composer has himself written: "The programmatic nature of the pieces varies from musical phantasy and mood depiction to the realistic employment of sounds that I remember from my childhood". The epilogue of the work was written after hearing "the primary simplicity and relative timelessness" of a Coloured musician who passed his house on New Year's Eve.

BIBLIOGRAPHY

BOUWS, JAN: *Suid-Afrikaanse komponiste van vandag en gister.* Balkema, Cape Town, 1957. BOUWS, JAN: *Woord en wys van die Afrikaanse lied.* Cape Town, 1961.   *International who's who in music,* 8th edition. Melrose Press, Cambridge, 1977.   POTGIETER, J.H.: *'n Analitiese oorsig van die Afrikaanse kunslied.* D.Mus. thesis, UP, 1967.   VAN DER MERWE, F.Z.: *Suid-Afrikaanse musiekbibliografie, 1787-1972.* Amplified for the HSRC by J. van de Graaf. Tafelberg-Uitgewers, Cape Town, 1974.   *Four South African composers.* HSRC, Pretoria, 1975.

SOURCES

BENDER, ANNA: Nuwe klavier-siklus in Afrikaanse musiek-literatuur. *Opus* III/1.   BOUWS, JAN: Die Afrikaanse kunslied in die afgelope 60 jaar. *Tydskrif vir Geesteswetenskappe* IX, Pretoria, 1969.   BOUWS, JAN: Die hedendaagse musiek in Suid-Afrika. *Ons Erfdeel* VII/4, Rekkem, Belgium, 1964.   BOUWS, JAN: 'n Eie styl in die Afrikaanse musiek? *Standpunte* XX/3, Cape Town, 1967.   GROVÉ, STEFANS: Hubert du Plessis. *Bladmusik News,* November 1976.   GROVÉ, STEFANS: Ten pianoforte pieces for children and young people, Opus 41. *Bladmusik News,* June 1977.   HARTMAN, ANTON: 'n Kwarteeu van Suid-Afrikaanse toonkuns. *Standpunte* IX/3, Cape Town, 1954.   MALAN, J.P.: Akademie-onderskeiding vir Hubert du Plessis. *Vita Musica* I/2, June 1963.   PAXINOS, S.: Hubert du Plessis: Elegie, op. 1 no. 3. *Musicus* III/2, 1975.   POTGIETER, JOHANN: Hubert du Plessis. *SABC Bulletin,* 29 July 1968.   POTGIETER, J.H.: Sommige van die Afrikaanse liedere van Hubert du Plessis. *Musicus* III/1, 1975.   ROOS, J.: Hubert du Plessis, 'n biografie volgens sy outobiografiese aantekeninge. *Musicus* III/1, 1975 (The author also used *Four South African Composers,* HSRC, Pretoria, 1975). 1975).   THERON, R.: Reviews of published works by Hubert du Plessis. *SAMT* 64, 65, 66, 75, 80, 82.   WEGELIN, ARTHUR: Dagboek van *Die dans van die reën.* Review in *Tydskrif vir Geesteswetenskappe* 13/3, September 1973.   *Res Musicae:* III/2 December 1956; III/3 March 1957; VI/4 September 1960; VII/1 December 1960; VIII/1 September 1961; VIII/2 December 1961; VIII/4 September 1962.   National Documentation Centre for Music, HSRC, Pretoria.

—Ed.

DU PLESSIS, PAUL JOHANNES (BOETIE), *3 June 1932 in Bloemfontein; still in Bloemfontein. Leader of a once popular "boere-orkes" in the Free State.

Boetie du Plessis learned to play the accordion from his twelfth year at Paddy's School of music. Later he was trained by Klasie Fourie, joined his dance band and eventually became its leader. In 1950 and 1952 he was the winner of the Free State section of talent contests organised by African Theatres. After 1952 he was accordion player in Hendrik Susan's band for a long time until, for business reasons, he was obliged to return to Bloemfontein. With Tinie Coetzer, Sakkie du Toit and others, he played for charities in the Free State and from 1949 to 1959 he broadcast -initially in the well-known coffee-house concerts ("koffiehuiskonserte") of Pieter de Waal.

—Ed.

DU PREEZ, MRS M.   S. Le Roux Marais, Middelburg

DURÁN, SILVIA (SYLVIA JANE KLASS),   *14 May 1947 in Johannesburg; now (1970) in Spain. Spanish dancer.

The daughter of Morris and Yetta Klass (née Chosack), Silvia Durán belongs to the fourth South African generation of the musical Chosack family*. From 1951 she received piano lessons from her aunt Betty Chertkow, and as an eight-year-old took part in radio broadcasts. After a performance by Antonio and his Spanish Ballet in Johannesburg in 1960, she decided to leave music and to take up dancing. Shortly afterwards she became a student of Mercedes Molina*, and a few years later a member of her company. She took part in the South African tour of Luisillo in 1966, originally as temporary, but afterwards as permanent member of the troupe, under the professional name of Silvia Durán. During a European tour, and shortly before the performance at the Champs Elysées Theatre, she was promoted to dance solo parts. A tour of Australia and New Zealand followed. — After eighteen months with Luisillo, Silvia returned to Spain as soloist in the new company of Paco Ruiz (a nephew of Antonio), to perform in Estoril (Portugal), Madrid and other centres, followed by a tour of North and South America. Strengthened by an amalgamation with Carmen Rojas's group, the company gave a series of performances before Europe's royal families and the Pope. — In the meantime, Silvia Durán continued her studies in Spain, under teachers who wrote choreographies for her solo dances. At the end of 1969 she refused an offer from the Spanish dancer Miguel Sandoval to dance as his partner, in order to return to Johannesburg as partner in Mercedes Molina's dance studio. She was guest artist of the company, for whom she also choreographed several Flamenco dances. In October 1970, she was guest artist with Paco Ruiz and Carmen Rojas on their short South African tour and returned with them to Spain.

—H.D.

DURBAN AMATEUR OPERATIC SOCIETY   The first of many amateur operatic societies in Durban made its appearance in the Theatre Royal in September 1886, when *The mikado* was performed by "ladies and gentlemen who had placed themselves under the tuition of Mr J. Ferguson Brown". The "orchestra" of two violins, a cornet and a double-bass, was supported by a piano at which Mr Brown himself was seated in the capacity of conductor. In all, there were seven performances to packed houses; inevitably, patrons in the gallery ("gods") joined in some of the choruses. *The mikado* remained the best of their productions; but they also had the distinction of giving the first South African performance of *Ruddigore,* on the night of 7 June 1887. — The success of these early Gilbert and Sullivan operettas persuaded Ferguson Brown to extend the activities of his Society to Pietermaritzburg. This he did in another production of *The mikado* in 1888. By 1894 the Society had increased to 50 members,

411

and the repertoire included other nineteenth century favourites, such as *Olivette, Les cloches de Corneville* and *Dorothy*. In 1897 they called themselves the Diamond Jubilee Opera Company, and by this time Ferguson Brown had the valuable assistance of Charles Hoby* as conductor. For over 80 years operettas and musical comedies have enjoyed tremendous popularity; and Durban continues to be the South African home of this kind of theatrical entertainment. The career of every amateur operatic society or club has followed a similar pattern: once a good reputation has been established, box-office successes are assured. Professional actors and instrumentalists are readily absorbed into the company, and it is not long before many of the amateurs become professionals. — In the latter part of the nineteenth, and the early years of the present century, amateur operatic societies had to compete with visiting professional companies from overseas. Comedy and Gaiety companies fitted comfortably into the early prosperity of Johannesburg, before visiting Durban for a season of light opera. Elton's, Searelle's*, Perkins's, Frank Wheeler's, the Standard Opera - these were a few of the companies that toured South Africa in the closing years of the last century. Under such conditions Ferguson Brown was soon attracted away from amateur opera and, like several of his original members, accepted employment with visiting professional companies. The climax of the movement towards professionalism was reached in the first decade of the present century, when the Wheeler-Edwardes Gaiety Companies produced an abundance of musical comedy, and the D'Oyly Carte Opera Company presented the full range of Gilbert and Sullivan. — Ferguson Brown became the respected amateur producer again in many local performances of musical comedy before the First World War. In 1919 the Durban Opera Society was revived by Gus Brown, his son, who was more of an actor and producer, than a musician like his father. He was supported by two good singers (Harry Evans and Gladys Daniel*), and in 1922 obtained the assistance of Reg Woodroffe's* amateur orchestra of 30 players. This brought about a revival of Gilbert and Sullivan and other nineteenth century operettas at the Criterion. But in 1923 Gus Brown diverted his interests to the Bachelor Girls, a society active during the 1920s and 1930s in productions of musical comedy *(Floradora, The belle of New York, The Quaker girl.* These annual performances displayed to advantage the vocal talents of the leading lady, Thelma Whitcutt. — In 1928 Dan Godfrey* tried to stimulate interest in "grand opera". The Durban Amateur Grand Opera Society then performed concert versions of *Faust* and *Il trovatore,* but never dispelled the limitation of being a municipal choral society, enjoying the exceptional vocal talents of Rose Alper*, Rosa Kerdachi, Keppoch Macdonald, Grogan Caney* and Muriel Clark. The spirit of light opera was not recaptured until 1937, when Teddy Browne, with his natural wit and excellent diction, became a master of the patter song, in the style of Allan Hawes of the first Durban Amateur Operatic Company in 1886. Towards the end of World War II a Municipal Choral and Light Opera Society was formed, and the Criterion became the venue for a few Gilbert and Sullivan operas in 1946. Continuity was, however, broken by another burst of grand opera at the City Hall. — Operatic productions were often marred by the lack of a well-equipped theatre. After the Alhambra was opened in 1952, new operatic societies were formed. The Durban Opera and Drama Society made its first public appearance in February 1954, in an attempt to revive musical comedy. Its activities continued for eight years, a crowning achievement being the 1960 production of *Desert song* in the Alhambra, with a chorus of 80. In August 1954 Teddy Browne revived the activities of the Durban Municipal Light Operatic and Choral

412

Society in a performance of *The gondoliers* also at the Alhambra, followed in November by *The mikado*. The two independent societies continued to produce opera annually until the early 1960s. — With the coming of NAPAC, grand opera became an exclusively professional undertaking. The idea had been anticipated by Dr Heinz Haape* in 1958, when he formed the Durban Opera Company. But light opera and musical comedies are still produced annually by amateurs; the latest society to come into being is the Durban Opera Group, founded in 1968 by Miss Olive Peel.

—G.S.J.

DURBAN, CHAMBER MUSIC GROUPS IN

1. Aeolian Players
2. The Ad Artem Quartet
3. The Baroque Players
4. The Montpelier Players
5. The Studio Piano Trio

1.   **Aeolian Players** is the name of a chamber music group formed in London in 1925 by Gordon Bryan, which first broadcast chamber music for the BBC. Joseph Slater* was a member of the group, and when he came to South Africa in 1951, he formed a new ensemble with the same name, which became well-known through SABC broadcasts. The South African players were Joseph Slater (flute), Nancy Greig (cello) and Constance Brothwood* (pianoforte). A number of works have been composed for this group, both by local and overseas composers.

2.   **The Ad Artem Quartet** was formed in Durban in 1948 by Paul Martens*. Trained in Brussels, he came to South Africa in 1947 to join the Durban Civic Orchestra. He inaugurated and led chamber music groups, until his departure for Stellenbosch in 1969. The original members of the quartet were Paul Martens (violin), K. van der Velde (violin), Connie Watt (viola), J. Barbier (cello). The Quartet gave many broadcast performances, but since 1961 has concentrated on public recitals. A series given in private homes in Natal in 1962, and another at schools throughout Natal in 1963, proved extremely successful. The Quartet has worked in conjunction with the Education Department, the International Arts League of Youth, and NAPAC, doing excellent work in spreading the appreciation of chamber music throughout Natal. It also sought to encourage local composers by performing their works. When Paul Martens left Durban, the members of the Quartet were: Paul Martens and George Walker* (violins), Barbara Groom (viola) and Nancy Greig (cello).

3.   **The Baroque Players** was a group of ten enthusiastic string players, formed and led by Paul Martens*, specialising in music of the pre-classical and modern periods. They have given numerous broadcasts of music, from the accompaniment to *La serva padrona* (Pergolesi) to Bartok's *Music for strings, percussion and celeste,* and performed works by local composers, such as the *African shepherd's rhapsody,* specially written for this group by Philip Britton*.

4.   **The Montpelier Players** was formed in Durban in 1958 to stimulate interest among young people in playing sixteenth, seventeenth and eighteenth century music. They gave a number of radio and public recitals, and provided a portion of the incidental music to the SABC production of *Troilus and Cressida,* during the Shakespeare quater-centenary celebrations. The members of the group are all members of the Dolmetsch Foundation: Richard Oxtoby* (virginal and recorder), Juil

Selwyn-Smith (virginal and recorder), Monica Scott (recorder) and Ted Brien*
(recorder).

5. **The Studio Piano Trio** was formed in Durban shortly after the disbandment of
the Durban Studio Orchestra in 1953; the moving spirits were Constance Brothwood*
(pianoforte), George Walker* (violin) and Nancy Greıg (cello), previous members of
the orchestra. Soon after the formation of the Trio, they played before Prince
Bernhardt of the Netherlands during his South African visit. Subsequently the trio
toured Natal country districts, giving concerts in centres where chamber music had
hardly been heard before. They broadcast frequently, and specialize mainly. in
Romantic music.

—Ed.

DURBAN CHORAL UNION   F. Crane, C. Hoby

DURBAN CIVIC CHOIR   G. Denholm, C. Hamer

DURBAN LIGHT ORCHESTRA, THE   Originally known as the New Concert Orchestra, this
group of players made its first public appearance in 1956, as a theatre band conducted
by Captain Hugh Hind. It happened at a Durban amateur production of the musical
comedy *Floradora,* in which Dorothy Hind, his wife, sang the leading role. The group
soon acquired independent status as a concert orchestra for performances of light
orchestral classics, giving amateurs an opportunity of practising and performing
together in public. It also provided young soloists (singers and instrumentalists) with
a sonorous background at concerts, where they were to make their debut. A popular
venue was the Y Club (YMCA in Durban), where in June 1958, two clever young
harmonica players, John and Jill Walton, were the stars of the evening. In December
1959, the orchestra played at the Pinetown Civic Centre for an evening of ballet
presented by Eileen Keegan*. — For some years Captain Hind had been bandmaster
of the Natal Mounted Rifles. In 1960 he formed what he believed to be the first Boys'
Brass Band in Durban, and this group of players, like other youthful ensembles he had
encouraged in the past, was absorbed into the New Concert Orchestra for special
occasions. Many of the concerts were for the benefit of the aged, who attended free of
charge. But to ensure that the orchestra would always be in a financial position to meet
incidental expenses, members were required to pay a small monthly subscription. At a
concert in 1965 the founder and conductor collapsed and died. — Dorothy Hind tried
conducting the orchestra herself, and then approved of amalgamation with a Dutch
Orchestra (called De Noten Krakers). A substantially strong and well-balanced
orchestra of 30 players, called the Durban Concert Orchestra, came into being under a
new conductor, Theo Wiercx*. A committee was elected from the members of the
orchestra to administer the funds, derived from monthly subscriptions and the sale of
concert tickets. The conductor was to be remunerated on the basis of the number of
rehearsals and concerts at which he conducted. After a number of successful concerts
during 1967 and 1968, it became evident that the new orchestra had severed all its
associations with the original one by becoming the Durban Light Orchestra. — As a
teacher endowed with great musical and dramatic talents, Hugh Hind's widow
(Dorothy Language after her second marriage) envisaged a 40-member Pinetown
Civic Orchestra, to be used at galas, pantomimes and on civic occasions. On the other
hand, Theo Wiercx, foremost Durban teacher of the accordion, had re-shaped the
orchestra in his own special way, by including a number of accordion players to supply

the missing wind parts. During 1970 several members of the Durban Light Orchestra either resigned or failed to appear at rehearsals. Obviously the orchestra had concluded another phase in its history, and Theo Wiercx resigned. Among the few who have remained loyal to the orchestra are some members of the Dutch orchestra (De Noten Krakers), one being at present (1971) the temporary conductor. — As Pinetown is one of the rapidly growing towns of the Republic, Dorothy Language still believes in the possibility of a Pinetown Civic Orchestra in the very near future.

SOURCES

Highway Mail: 1 November 1968.   *Natal Mercury:* 29 May 1958; 2 December 1959; 16 December 1960; 13 March 1961; 4 January 1968.

—G.S.J.

DURBAN MALE VOICE PARTY   Durban, H. Evans

DURBAN MUNICIPAL BANTU BRASS BAND, THE   During the 1950s and the early 1960s non-European musicians in Durban were given opportunities to express themselves on the concert platform, through choirs and instrumental ensembles of various kinds. In 1951 James Barber, a member of the Durban Orchestra, started a brass band for African employees of the Durban Corporation's Bantu Administration. This was intended to serve as a form of recreation, entertainment and musical instruction. Others succeeded Mr Barber in his part-time occupation of training the band. In 1954 it was taken over by Ivor Clifford, who had been trumpeter in the Durban Orchestra since 1937. He had received his early training at the RCM, making a special study of band music, and of conducting under the guidance of Dr Charles Hoby*. Brass bands had a peculiar fascination for Ivor Clifford; over a period of 12 years he held three rehearsals a week for the training of this band - it became his chief recreation. By 1966 the band had reached a strength of 26 players. — Concerts were given at the King Edward VIII and McCord hospitals. The band also played at Sunday-night concerts in the City Hall, and at the annual African Arts Festival, when it usually contributed a march and selections from a well-known musical comedy. It also provided the background and publicity for a number of soloists, including the tenor Joseph Dhlamini, the mezzo-soprano Esther Makhoba and the trumpeter Ernest Zwane. Vocal quartets and groups of guitar players helped to give even more variety to these occasions. — Ivor Clifford retired from the Durban Orchestra some years ago, and with no regular conductor the band is now reduced to 16 players only. It is hoped that the training of players will soon be regarded as a full-time occupation; but at the time of writing (1971) the authority for this still has to be granted.

SOURCES

Natal Mercury: 19 March 1958; 27 January 1960; 11 November 1961; 24 May 1962; 28 January 1966.   Information supplied by Mr. Tom Roach of the Bantu Administration Department, Durban Corporation.

—G.S.J.

DURBAN MUNICIPAL LIGHT OPERATIC AND CHORAL SOCIETY   Durban Amateur Operatic Society, Durban Orchestral Society

DURBAN MUNICIPAL MILITARY BAND   Durban 7

DURBAN MUSICAL ASSOCIATION, THE   When R. Houston Macdonald*, aged 23, was

415

appointed borough organist of Durban in 1896, he accepted implicitly the responsibility of becoming the town's musical director. Besides his regular organ recitals - at least two a week - he was expected to revive and train a choral society. For this he was to receive an honorarium of R90 a year. In January 1896, soon after his arrival in Durban, Macdonald became known to the public through his organ recitals, by advertising himself as a music teacher and by publishing the following announcement in the local newspapers: "I am wishful to institute (with the assistance of Mr Crane) the following activities: (a) A Choral Society of about 100 voices (b) A small choir of about 20 voices to perform at the Sunday evening organ recitals once a month (c) An Orchestral Society. It is also proposed to hold a Grand Musical Festival in July with full Chorus and Orchestra". — The first successful attempt to form a large choir had been the Durban Philharmonic Society* which Duncan MacColl* - Durban's pioneer choral conductor - trained and conducted from 1881. When, after some seven or eight years, this society lapsed into a state of slow decline and ultimate dissolution, all that remained of its members formed themselves into the Durban and Berea Choral Union, a body of singers trained by Francis Crane*, who was a good singer and a skilful choir-trainer. Under his direction this second large choir - which on some occasions numbered almost 200 voices - continued to practise and give concerts between 1890 and 1894. Many of the singers who had belonged to either or both of these societies were only too willing to give their support to a third choral society under the direction of the newly-appointed borough organist. In fact, Francis Crane, who was to open a music studio in Johannesburg, handed over his choir to Macdonald. — In response to Macdonald's appeal through the press a meeting was called for 17 February 1896, to be held in the council chamber of the Town Hall. At the suggestion of Otto Siedle* the new society was christened the Durban Musical Association and properly constituted a fortnight later. The DMA, as it was always called, began its activities under the distinguished patronage of the Governor of Natal and Lady Walter Hely-Hutchinson. The mayor of Durban was elected President and Sir John Robinson, Vice-President. Other distinguished personalities on the committee were: H. Escombe, B.W. Greenacre, J.W. Leuchars, R. Ramsay Collins and F.C. Hollander (chairman). — The new Association had the blessing and support of the Durban Corporation, expressed in the tangible form of an annual subsidy amounting to R600 and free transport for members of choir and orchestra to and from rehearsals and concerts. Rehearsals began on 30 March 1896, with 130 singers and 19 orchestral players, and after exactly two months, on 30 May, the DMA made its debut before a capacity audience in the Town Hall in a performance of Mendelssohn's *Athalie*. In preparation for the July Festival which Macdonald envisaged, the choir was increased to 140 and the orchestra to 30. The main work chosen for this occasion was Mendelssohn's setting of the 42nd Psalm with a supporting programme of organ solos, songs, cello solos and a few items by the orchestra, including a performance of Beethoven's *First symphony*. All this took place on the nights of 16, 17 and 18 July. To add to the splendours of this three-day festival, morning organ recitals and a "sacred" concert on Sunday night were presented. — In spite of its elaborate musical fare the festival was not a success; attendance at the concerts was poor and the financial loss was considerable. Also, members of the choir and orchestra were leaving and a third performance of *Athalie* in October, to an audience of no more than 100 people, did nothing to improve the plight of the Association. The year closed with a somewhat anaemic rendition of Handel's *Messiah,* with a small choir supported by organ and

416

piano as a substitute for the 30-piece orchestra that had vanished. — Houston Macdonald was a highly sensitive man whose musical susceptibilities were easily offended. His withering sarcasm at rehearsals was more than some of the female members of his choir could endure. Orchestral players also came under the lash of his tongue - especially those regimental wind-players who filled out the orchestral tone in a robust, public-spirited way. Macdonald's approach to musical performance was essentially professional, but his lack of tact remained unforgiven and members of his choir sought retribution through the press: "I would kindly hint to the conductor", wrote a popular columnist, "that the ladies who are so essential to the success of the society are considerably annoyed over certain remarks, sarcastic and personal, and as inane as they are unwise, made during rehearsals; and unless they cease a great many ladies will resign". And a great many did resign. — Added to these personal difficulties of the conductor was the financial predicament of the association, which was expected (with the aid of the subsidy) to pay its way. In December 1896 Macdonald tendered his resignation from the post of honorary conductor to the DMA; but this, very politely, was not accepted and he was asked to continue. — The year 1897 and Queen Victoria's Diamond Jubilee made the DMA and the whole population of Durban sufficiently festival-minded to forget past animosities between conductor and choir. With choir and orchestra back to their former strength (200 in all) the July musical scene was dominated by Mendelssohn's Elijah, but the performance of this work on 10 July in the Town Hall burdened the Association with publicity of a rather disreputable kind. Avon Saxon and Virginie Cheron* (husband and wife) were two of the soloists - Saxon in the role of the Prophet. Alexander Milligan, one of the ablest yet harshest critics Durban has ever known, found the interpretation generally displeasing and wrote his criticism for the Natal Mercury, mainly to the utter disparagement of both these Durban singers. On the following morning the enraged Prophet sought out the critic and assaulted him in his office. The resulting court action became headline news. But the overall musical success of this year of jubilation restored a little of the conductor's lost prestige. — There was no disguising the truth: Macdonald was not the most suitable conductor for the DMA. At least two other musicians in Durban in the last years of the century - Charles Hoby* and Frank Proudman* - were more acceptable to both choir and orchestra. In the early part of this century Charles Hoby became foremost choral and orchestral conductor, mainly through having to deputise for Macdonald who, never robust, seemed to be declining rapidly towards his early death in February 1908 at the age of 35. — Frank Proudman's appointment to the post of borough organist after Macdonald, automatically made him the new conductor of the DMA, then growing in numbers as the population of the town increased. In 1910 the new Town Hall, with an enlarged organ, created the City Hall scene that concert-goers know so well today. At festival-choir strength the DMA had at least 200 voices, and while peace reigned before the storm of 1914-1918, it was supported by a large Philharmonic Orchestra. During the First World War and until he returned to Kimberley in 1920, Frank Proudman continued as conductor. One of his last great concerts was a performance of Elgar's King Olaf in July 1919. — As musical director and conductor of the new Durban Orchestra, Lyell-Tayler* became honorary conductor of the DMA choir which had reached a strength of 300 members. With the support of the Durban Orchestra they performed concert versions of Coleridge-Taylor's A tale of old Japan, Gounod's Faust, and various operettas. In 1922 and 1923

417

the number of choral festivals mushroomed, largely as a result of John Connell's* efforts to establish choral singing on a national scale. One of the larger efforts of the DMA was Elgar's *Dream of Gerontius.* — With Lyell-Tayler's departure in 1927 the DMA continued under Edmond Schelpe*, choirmaster of Emmanuel Cathedral. A performance of Haydn's *The creation* with a massed choir of over 500 (May 1928), was the swan song of the Association and a period of apathy to choral concerts followed. In October 1928 an advisory committee discussed ways and means of reorganising the Association. They attributed the decline in choral singing to the presence of too many veterans and "old stagers" in the choir. Only "new blood", it was said, could revitalise choral singing, but there was little encouragement from Dan Godfrey*, the new conductor of the Durban Orchestra. — In January 1929 it was decided to discontinue the activities of the DMA. Four months later the Durban Corporation agreed to liquidate the debt of R290, and in November 1929 Dan Godfrey formed a new Choral Society of 60 singers, which soon increased to 100. In November 1930 this choir was known as the Municipal Choral Society under the auspices of the Durban Corporation. But choral societies had outlived their popularity. So many people were attracted to the cinema and "talkies", and jazz was so popular that it was generally believed in the early 1930s that the choral concert had gone for ever. — In fact the great era of choral concerts ended then, and strangely enough this coincided with the death of Emily MacColl in December 1933 when she was 75 years old. Her husband, Duncan MacColl, had founded the parent choral society in 1881. As accompanist she had been associated with this and all subsequent choral societies for about 50 years. The last gesture of the DMA was in August 1929 when members presented to her (in her seventieth year) a cheque for R200 in recognition of her 48 years as accompanist. If Duncan MacColl inaugurated the 50 years of choral singing, it was Emily who saw it through to the end.

BIBLIOGRAPHY

JACKSON, GEORGE S.: *Music in Durban from 1850 to 1900.* D.Phil. thesis, University of the Witwatersrand, Johannesburg, 1961.

SOURCES

Natal Mercury: 1896-1933. *Natal Mercury Pictorial:* 1904-1921.

—G.S.J.

DURBAN, MUSIC IN

I. INTRODUCTION

The cultural life of early Durban originated in the middle-class homes of mid-nineteenth century England. The focal point of music in the home was the piano *in the drawingroom, around which members of the family gathered in the evening to play or sing. The more gifted could do both. Some played stringed or wind instruments and added the tonal colour that might transform simple, unaffected music-making into an impromptu concert. — The characteristic charm of the mid-Victorian musical evening was its informality. A formal occasion was the suburban concert, or *soirée,* where local musicians, who had gained assurance through the encouragement of family and friends at home, were elevated to the platform. Programmes at *soirées* were interminably long, and often the standard of performance regrettably low; but the promise of refreshments sustained the patience of the audience in its loyal support of "a good cause" and of the local talent that had to be endured. — England was a land of song. Singing was nearly everyone's musical diversion. An essential feature of all *soirées* was the singing of glees and part-songs - a pleasant pastime for those with good voices and musical skill. Small vocal ensembles grew into church choirs and choral societies, and these in turn helped to swell the numbers in those English festival choirs that sang choruses from the great oratorios with a powerful zest tempered with reverence.

II. EARLY CONCERTS

In the middle of the nineteenth century Durban was the gateway to a promised land. Within three years of the annexation of Natal by the British Government in December 1845, the first immigrants began to arrive. Between 1848 and 1851 over 4 000 settlers passed through Port Natal on their way to the interior where they hoped to start a new life as farmers in the "green and pleasant land" of their adoption. Disappointment compelled many of them to return to the towns where they could acquire new skills in order to earn a living. By the year 1851 Durban had a fairly settled population of about 1 200. They were the pioneers of the large commercial centre and popular sea-side resort we know today. — Three months of hardship at sea taught the early settlers to abandon their provincial and suburban ways by mixing more sociably with their compatriots from other parts of Britain. Differences in background and speech were resolved through the artistic adventure of making music together. The hazards and discomforts of a long voyage in a sailing ship were soon forgotten when shipboard concerts called for a spontaneous display of musical and dramatic talent. — The sandy desolation of Durban in the mid-nineteenth century demanded a similar musical resourcefulness if only to alleviate the boredom after sunset. Single and temporarily unattached young men frequented the public houses called "inns" or "taverns" - the kind of refuge which catered for soldiers, sailors and lonely civilian bachelors. Here a variety of diversions was offered to attract customers, including music and dances, evenings of sword exercises and short plays. One such evening haunt popular in the early 1850s, was the London Tavern in Union Street, where informal entertainment was arranged for each evening of the week, except Sunday. Tuesday was set aside for a "concert" presided over by the landlord who - in the role of mine host of the English tavern - invited talented customers to contribute the items. — The early Durban taverns certainly had their music, but it was not long before they acquired an unsavoury reputation for drunkenness - a favourite topic for denunciation at temperance meetings and from pulpits. Nevertheless, the taverns continued to increase in number and to prosper all along the main highways of Durban. Meanwhile various religious bodies, mutual improvement societies and the Mechanics Institution, offered the public more wholesome entertainment in the form of *soirées*. For this purpose some of the larger warehouses were made available by generous business proprietors. These roughly assembled wood and iron sheds, gracefully transformed within, were the first concert halls. But the *soirées* were more social than musical. Without any fear of being morally uplifted or improved, anyone could attend and enjoy a full programme of songs, vocal duets, part-songs and glees, recitations, piano solos and duets for the sum of ten cents with an additional charge of five cents for the lavish refreshments served during the interval. Thus amateurs were afforded opportunities of displaying their musical talent, or their ability to read or recite in public. — The *soirées* of the 1850s brought before the public the first Durban Philharmonic Society*, originally a group of a dozen young bachelors sworn to celibacy. Their activities started as a glee club, soon to be transformed into an "orchestra" of string and wind instruments, supported by a bass drum and harmonium, both home-made. Little is known of the repertoire of this early society. Bishop Colenso recorded that at one *soirée* he attended, they performed works by Handel, Beethoven and Rossini before "a very full, fair, attentive and delighted audience". During the year 1854 the group of players reached a maximum strength of twenty oddly assorted musicians who performed regularly under the direction of Mr Daniel Hull, seated at the harmonium. They also assumed the role of town band when, as itinerant musicians, they paraded along the streets reviving the old English custom of the "waits" by serenading prominent citizens on Christmas Eve. As there is no mention of this Society after 1855, it may be assumed that by that time marriage had claimed most of its members. — The *soirées* drew the attention of the public to resident professional musicians. From time to time they were invited to arrange suitable programmes and to contribute most of the items themselves. One of the earliest was Mrs J. Cubitt. She arrived in Durban in 1850 and soon became known as a teacher of pianoforte and singing. Though a staunch non-conformist, she was the first "organist" at the Anglican Church of St Paul's. Another popular concert personality of the 1850s was a schoolmaster, Mr J.W. Haygarth*. He was bandmaster of the first volunteer regimental band (the Durban Rifle Band) and a performer on several musical instruments. In the 1870s he was better known in South Africa as a singer of humorous Irish songs.

III.   MUSIC HALLS AND THEATRES IN THE NINETEENTH CENTURY
In the 1850s there was no hall that could be used regularly for concerts. In the 1860s *soirées* gave place to more formal concerts in churches, private homes or even in warehouses suitably transformed to look like concert halls. In 1861 the New Masonic Hall (later known as the County Hall) was erected in Gardiner Street between West and Pine Streets - the first hall that could be used for regular public entertainment. It was a tall, ungainly-looking structure, badly ventilated and unpleasantly hot in summer; in fact little better than a shed. Audiences were longsuffering. They fanned themselves continuously through some of the performances given by early touring musicians and theatrical troupes who travelled widely over South Africa, advertising themselves as "celebrated". Most of these early professional entertainments were arranged by J.W. Haygarth* who was obliged to muster the best of local talent in a supporting programme of standard pattern with solos for piano and violin, arias from well-known operas and a few popular English glees. — In 1865 the County Hall became the warehouse it had always strongly resembled. It was superseded by a larger, more substantial double-storied building in Field Street. Like earlier counterparts in England, the new hall had grown out of the "music room" of a tavern. "Houghtings

Hall" - as it was called - was an ambitious venture. With a fairly large stage and a seating capacity of 400 it was the popular venue for all the concerts and variety shows between 1866 and 1871. The "variety" concert - with songs, glees, piano solos and humorous monologues - was presented either formally, or against the more frivolous background of Christy Minstrels. Houghtings Hall attracted lively crowds to all kinds of stunt performances given by visiting illusionists, ventriloquists and magicians who would often describe themselves as "Professors" of their peculiar art. But it was also a venue for the presentation of serious music. The first Durban performance of *Messiah* took place here on 31 May 1866. By 1869 the hall had become a theatre. Two early variety artists, Mr and Mrs D'Arcy Read*, used it for a performance of Dibdin's ballad opera *The waterman*. — Almost adjacent to Houghtings Hall was the Trafalgar Hall, with its entrance in Pine Street. Opened in 1869, it had a seating capacity of 500. Early attempts to stage opera were made here. The Miranda-Harper Company toured Natal in 1870 and presented *Il trovatore* in July. This was commendable only as a pioneering effort. As a production - with gin cases used as stage props - nothing could have been worse. Six years later Anna Bishop*, third wife of the late English composer, Sir Henry Bishop, produced the same opera rather more convincingly in the same hall. At the age of 66 the *prima donna* was long past her best but could at least draw a few tears by singing *Home, sweet home*. In the line of grand opera Bellini's *La sonnambula* was part of her repertoire; but, limited by the necessity of having to use mainly local talent, she achieved considerably more success with Offenbach's *The Grand Duchess of Gerolstein,* presented in a concert version, a happy compromise adopted by choral societies in South Africa for over 100 years. — The visit of Anna Bishop aroused interest in the theatre. A few months after her visit the Trafalgar Hall was almost entirely rebuilt and converted into a theatre for the regular presentation of plays and operas. Most of the musical stage productions were French and English operettas. This new phase in the development of Durban's musical history was interrupted by the outbreak of the Zulu War in January 1879, followed by months of uncertainty and insecurity. — Durban's population started growing rapidly in 1880 as a result of new immigration schemes. The arrival of several dynamic personalities helped to revive interest in music, especially of the theatrical variety. For about 90 years Durban has loved its Gilbert and Sullivan. The founder of a well-known firm of music dealers, J.H. Mackay*, must be given the credit for rousing this enthusiasm with his production of *H.M.S. Pinafore* at the Trafalgar Theatre in August 1880. Charles Lascelles* formed an operatic company in Pietermaritzburg during the 1880s, and when he brought his company to Durban, the initial enthusiasm developed into a cult which earned him the title of "father of opera" in Natal. He was assisted by a very gifted and versatile actress, Julia Sydney. Between them they established the standard operatic repertory with performances of *The Bohemian girl* (Balfé), *The daughter of the regiment* (Donizetti), *The rose of Auvergne* (Offenbach), *Les cloches de Corneville* (Planquette) and each of the Gilbert and Sullivan operettas as soon as it became available after its première at the Savoy Theatre in London. — In 1882 Durban's first large theatre - the Theatre Royal - was completed. It stood in West Street at the end of Berea Road and was for nearly half a century both the home and shrine of theatrical entertainment. Visiting companies, called "Stock companies", alternately staged plays and operas and travelled the length and breadth of South Africa. They moved themselves and their stage properties by ox-wagon between the main population centres of the coast and interior, giving innumerable performances of the French

421

operettas by Lecocq, Planquette, Audran and Offenbach and the satirical works of Gilbert and Sullivan. However, by the year 1886 J. Ferguson Brown, a church organist at St. Cyprian's, had realized that talented amateurs could give adequate performances of these same operettas: hence the formation of the first Durban Amateur Operatic Society* in 1886 and a performance of *The mikado* in September of that year in the Theatre Royal. For the next approximately 30 years Ferguson Brown devoted himself zealously to this lighter side of theatre music. — Some months before Ferguson Brown formed the first amateur operatic society, two members of Julia Sydney's theatrical company, W.F. Clitherow and his wife Rosina Brandram of Savoy Theatre fame, took over the old Trafalgar Theatre and had it reconditioned as a children's theatre for the performance of *H.M.S. Pinafore* by a company of 40 children between six and twelve years of age. The immediate success of this production set a fashion for organizing juvenile opera companies. At different times there were two such companies of children, one in Durban and another in Pietermaritzburg. Wherever the idea may have originated, it was most profitably developed in Australia by a certain Mr Pollard, whose "Lilliputian" opera companies toured South Africa in the 1890s with an extensive repertoire of operettas. They visited Durban on three separate occasions between 1898 and 1903 and played to wildly enthusiastic audiences in the Theatre Royal. — Amateur theatrical companies had some astonishing box-office successes; but this did not deter professional companies from devoting a whole season to opera. Companies seemed to come in quick succession, presenting favourite operettas in addition to numerous - almost too many - productions of *Martha* (Flotow), *Maritana* (Wallace), *Cavalleria rusticana* (Mascagni), *Il trovatore* (Verdi), *Faust* (Gounod), *The daughter of the regiment* (Donizetti) and *The Bohemian girl* (Balfé).

IV.   EARLY CHORAL AND ORCHESTRAL SOCIETIES

Opera was in tremendous vogue in the late nineteenth century, but the standard form of musical entertainment was still the concert - a slightly sophisticated development of the *soirée* which retained the stereotyped bill of fare, i.e. songs, duets, piano solos and instrumental solos, occasionally enriched by the novelty of a military band or small chamber ensemble, or a few scenes from a well-known opera presented in a concert version. Especially characteristic of the mid-Victorian era in Durban was the singing of glees - a typically English tradition cultivated by church choirs who adopted the practice of singing glees as part-songs with several voices (male and female) to a single part. This may have helped to destroy the true art of glee singing, as practised in England during the late eighteenth and early nineteenth centuries, when a glee party usually consisted of three or four male voices; on the other hand in Durban it certainly helped to establish the first choirs and choral societies. — As early as the 1850s attempts were made to start a choral society, but it was not until 1865 that the first of the small choral groups made its appearance in public. Early choral groups were known variously as: the Sacred Harmonic Society, the Madrigal Society, the Choral Union - each endeavouring to gain public recognition through the performance of well-known excerpts from *Messiah*. At a time when mammoth choirs were singing at the Handel Festivals at the Palace Theatre in London, lovers of choral music looked forward to the day when Durban would have its own large festival choir. Until the year 1880 most of the choral work was done by church choirs, generally for sacred concerts held in the church itself. In 1880 the Rev. Page Wood, vicar of the Anglican Church of St. Paul's, foresaw the possibility of training his own church choir to sing Mendelssohn's *Elijah*. After the choir had rendered several excerpts from this work in public, its members became the nucleus of a new civic choral society properly constituted with the Rev. Page Wood as official conductor. — A difference of ecclesiastical opinion between Bishop Colenso and the Vicar, removed the latter gentlemen from the scene almost overnight, leaving St Paul's without an incumbent and the new choral society without a conductor. Fortunately a 35 year old Scotsman, Duncan MacColl* had been transferred from Port Elizabeth to Durban as representative of a shipping firm. In 1881 he took over, with missionary zeal, the duty of training the choir and small orchestra of this second Durban Philharmonic Society. The new conductor, endowed with more Scottish determination than musical knowledge, depended for his initial success on sustained patience and the generous support of the public. A number of festive occasions stimulated the rapid early growth of this society. The first was the opening of the new Theatre Royal in October 1882, with a performance of *Elijah*. The choir of 120 and orchestra of 19 provided Durban with its first musical festival. The programme was elaborately prepared and the oratorio minutely analysed in one of the local newspapers. Other festivals on a much larger scale were held at the opening of Durban's first Town Hall (now the Post Office) in 1885, and on the occasion of Queen Victoria's Jubilee in 1887. — The choral tradition of Durban began with MacColl's Philharmonic Society Singers who devoted their efforts mainly to the performance of standard oratorios. The great favourites were *The creation, Messiah, Judas Maccabeus, Elijah, St. Paul* and a number of other choral works now less frequently heard: Mozart's so-called "Twelfth Mass" (no longer attributed to Mozart), Beethoven's *Ruins of Athens,* Gounod's *Gallia* and Sterndale Bennett's *May queen.* — After the initial success of *Elijah* in the Theatre Royal - due more to the novelty of the circumstances than to musical quality - the Philharmonic Society showed signs of rapid decline. With reduced numbers in the choir it was still possible to hold at least four choral concerts a year. The first Town Hall was declared open after a rendering of Handel's Coronation Anthem, *Zadok the priest,* by a choir of 120 - a modest number compared with the great English choirs of 500. This was an exciting moment for music lovers as they envisaged a new era of choral singing. — Few people seemed to be aware of the acute financial difficulties of the Philharmonic Society. The counter attraction during this period was a new Amateur Operatic Society that drew more and more singers into its light-hearted choruses. MacColl, somewhat embittered, resorted to denouncing this rival faction through the press and appeared to lose some of his former prestige. But as a hard-working, infinitely patient conductor he was still highly regarded by the public. For a few years at least he was the leading musical personality of the town, and, by virtue of a small municipal subsidy, the Philharmonic Society had civic status. In 1887, the Queen Victoria Jubilee Celebration helped to rehabilitate the society. — The arrival of the world-famous Eduard Reményi* in 1888, not only brought the orchestra before the public as a background for the gymnastic violin playing of this eccentric artist, it also earned the great man's special commendation for the conductor's wife, Emily MacColl, who sometimes accompanied him on the piano, and for Mrs Richards (better known as Virginie Cheron*), the first Natal soprano of outstanding merit. — Reményi's visit must have fired a number of young people with enthusiasm for learning the violin. The success of the orchestral ventures in the 1890s can be attributed to the number of schoolgirls who took up violin as their principal musical study. The original 19 players of the 1881 Philharmonic Society were never quite proficient enough for anything more than uncertain renderings of a few standard overtures and operatic selections, as an occasional relief for the choir. The first purely orchestral society was started in May 1888 by a German music teacher, Herr C.J. Eberlein*, within a few months of MacColl's decision to discontinue rehearsals owing to lack of support from the choir and the public and the consequent shortage of funds. Eberlein had been Reményi's accompanist, but had quarrelled with him during their tour of the country. He planned his arrival in Durban to coincide with Reményi's departure. — During his three-year stay Eberlein was a great inspiration to young musicians. One of the first in Durban to regard orchestral concerts as something more than light entertainment provided between choral and vocal items, he felt that the public needed educating in the matter of attentive listening. With this in mind he offered explanatory comments on the more serious works his orchestra were to perform. The Orchestral Society had more than 80 subscribers and at least 30 regular players, some of whom had belonged to the now defunct Philharmonic Society orchestra. The first Durban subscription concerts were held in the Town Hall over a period of three years. The society discontinued its activities just prior to Eberlein's departure for the Kimberley Exhibition of 1892. Most of the members formed themselves into another group called the "Durban and Berea Choral Society" with Francis Crane* as choirmaster and Charles Hoby* in charge of the orchestra. The new society was formed in 1891 and paved the way for the formation of the Durban Musical Association* in 1896 - mainly a choral society conducted by Houston Macdonald*, the borough organist - that proved to be the most permanent of all Durban's musical societies. It is still regarded as the parent organisation of all subsequent musical societies sponsored by the Durban Corporation. — The Durban Musical Association was the brain child of Otto Siedle*, who was connected with it for over 40 years. Like other earlier choral societies, it started with a great flourish of public enthusiasm, the guaranteed financial backing of the Durban corporation and the patronage of leading citizens. As an amateur organisation, strengthened on occasion by professionals, the society set out to uphold the choral traditions of England by performing well-known oratorios by Handel, Haydn and Mendelssohn and works by a few aspiring British choral composers of the last century. Compared with MacColl, the first choral conductor of Durban, Macdonald was the superior musician but the inferior diplomat. Early in his career the new society showed signs of weakening. The lack of co-operation between conductor and choir soon became evident. Moreover, it was not long before Macdonald had to contend with the rival claims to public recognition of Frank Proudman*, a church organist who had recently arrived in Durban, and whose success with the revived Orchestral Society did much to prejudice Macdonald's status as the leading musician of the town. In fact, the enthusiasm for orchestral music became a noticeable feature of Durban's musical life in the closing years of the century. Refugees from Johannesburg and the Reef poured into Durban in the early part of 1899, and music societies that had been disbanded in the Transvaal started up again in Durban. Ernest Lezard*, well-known in later years as an auctioneer and art collector, had great musical talent. He was responsible for the formation of the Bijou Orchestra, of which most members had played under James Hyde at the Wanderers' Hall in Johannesburg. As conductor of this orchestra, he entertained Durban people with light music in the Town Hall each Saturday night.

V. *THE EARLY YEARS OF THE TWENTIETH CENTURY*

The early years of the present century were some of the most prosperous in Durban's musical history. The legacy of war was certainly not depression, but flourishing musical societies, symphony orchestras, mandoline bands, chamber orchestras, military bands and the theatre. At the Theatre Royal musical comedies mainly about girls, were in vogue: *The gaiety girl, A country girl, The runaway girl, The telephone girl, The gay Parisienne, The belle of New York, The girls of Gottenburg* - all presented by the "gaiety" companies of B. and F. Wheeler under the guiding genius of George Edwardes, "the guv" and master producer on the London Stage. In 1903 the D'Oyly Carte Company came to Durban with a repertoire of Gilbert and Sullivan operettas. But it was the musical comedy that held the stage, together with the Chrismas pantomime and disseminated hit tunes such as "The honeysuckle and the bee" and "Happy days in Dixey". These tunes in turn impregnated the repertoire of every light orchestra and military band. Yet there were still enough serious-minded Edwardians who preferred the uplifting strains of "The holy city", "The better land" and "The lost chord" (played on the cornet). — Through a strange set of circumstances Charles Hoby became the leading musical personality of the day. The Durban Musical Association (DMA), the only musical society blessed with civic recognition, looked thinner at each rehearsal. Houston Macdonald, its official conductor (never popular with either his choir, or the wind players who lent their exuberant orchestral support at practices), was either frequently ill or on leave overseas. Frank Proudman had built up his Orchestral Society to 42 players, but seeing no musical future for himself in Durban, he returned to Kimberley and founded the Kimberley Musical Association. Ernest Lezard had created the Saturday night "pops" and Sunday "sacred" concerts with his Bijou Orchestra, but he returned to Johannesburg to re-open his business in Commissioner Street (1903). As a result of all these departures, Charles Hoby became conductor of the DMA, the Durban Orchestral Society and the Bijou Orchestra and in addition, deputy borough organist. Nothing seemed to defy his musical ingenuity and resources. He trained adult choirs and school choirs, military bands and orchestras; he could play several musical instruments and compose to order: songs, overtures, orchestral suites and symphonies. He started what was perhaps the most successful of all music academies, the Natal School of Music, with over 100 students. A staff of 14 offered tuition in every branch of musical study. This was in 1904, when nearly every home had its own piano and those who did not play, could at least sing. These were the days of mammoth orchestras and choirs performing to audiences of 25 000 at the Crystal Palace in London; the days of Henry Wood and the "Proms" at Queen's Hall. — The desire among Durban residents to learn orchestral instruments, especially string instruments, may have sustained the efforts of the violinist Lorenzo Mancini. He started Durban's first regular string quartet in 1902. A professional instrumentmaker and repairer, Thomas Morrill, started a business in 1903 and the music selling business prospered in the firm of Jackson Brothers* in West Street. In those days there were exceptionally talented local musicians: the pianists Violet Wiltshire, Bertha Feinhols and Mrs A. Buchanan; the violinists Violet Campbell-Rowland, Mary Howard, Eugene Benzon and Beatrice Stuart*; and the cellists Ethel Beningfield and Clifford Foster; Mrs Siedle and her daughter Perla were both good pianists; Perla (Siedle) Gibson* has enjoyed the dual artistic career of painter and singer; well-known singers, among whom were Virginie Cheron, Ada Forrest* and Grogan Caney*, performed regularly in this first decade of the century. Theo Wendt*, distinguished South African conductor, was also in Durban at this time. As organist, pianist, viola player and composer he had a share in every musical activity and was one of the best accompanists Durban has known. — Charles Hoby left Durban with the Standard Opera Company in 1906 - about 13 years after his

425

arrival in 1892. He never returned, but continued his musical career in England where he became conductor of the Band of the Royal Marines. By this time Houston Macdonald had returned from overseas and appeared to be more settled. He formed his own choir called the Berea Choral Society (after absorbing a number of singers from the declining DMA). The new society had to be sustained mainly on a diet of Coleridge-Taylor's *Hiawatha*. They did, however, venture a performance of Parry's *Judith* in July 1906 in "a hall well-filled by a critical but sympathetic audience". As a social club the DMA was still very much alive and the annual "conversazione" attracted as many as 400 people, including choir members who had missed most of the rehearsals, but were happy enough waltzing round the hall to the strains of the *Eton boating song,* played by Mr Stranack's band. — These were the colourful days of theatrical gaiety and social elegance. In front of the old Town Hall, between West Street and Smith Street, were the Town Gardens. On warm summer evenings music from the bandstand filtered through the indigenous trees, while couples sat or wandered in a carefree way in an atmosphere of sub-tropical romance. Ever since the 1840s and 1850s, when the 45th Regiment used to come down from Pietermaritzburg, there had been band performances. In the early years of this century any one of three resident bands could be heard in the Town Gardens or the Town Hall: the Natal Mounted Rifles, Durban Light Infantry and the Town Band. Programmes followed a standard pattern ranging from all that was brisk and brassy to extreme sentimentality. There were overtures, selections from musical comedies and marches, with the instrumental items supplemented by solos of various kinds, especially songs, including such doubtful speculations as "Shall I be an angel, Daddy?". — These were the "good old days" that could not last. In 1903 the prize for the best design for a new Town Hall was awarded to a Johannesburg firm of architects. Excavations were soon in progress for the great edifice that stands on the site of the old Town Gardens, thus destroying one of the most treasured beauty spots of old Durban. The bandstand was removed to the beach front. All musical and theatrical entertainment began moving towards the sea. Even in 1901 there were plans for a new "Bayside Theatre" to relieve the Theatre Royal of variety entertainment and of the noisy crowds that frequented the saloon bars attached to the theatre. What was to become the Criterion Theatre on the Victoria Embankment was not opened until 1912, being preceded by two variety theatres that stood approximately on the same site in West Street between Aliwal and Stanger Streets. The first was the Holborn Theatre of Varieties which offered the kind of show that was staged in the Field Street Music Hall in the 1860s: a ventriloquist, dancer, coon impersonator and comedian, together with the overworked stunt of a one-string violinist. The same hall renovated as the Empire Music Hall in 1904 was a music hall, concert hall and theatre, and could offer the public *East Lynne* (the greatest tear-jerker of the day) in addition to such varied amusements as "boxing, wrestling, singing, etc." — Beach entertainment started in 1905. The open air *(al fresco)* concert was a continental idea that had been successfully tried out in Johannesburg and Pretoria before it was adapted to the ideal conditions of a beach front. These were free concerts except that chairs had to be rented. A certain Mr Tamplin Child provided such concerts every evening of the week on the terrace of the Beach Hotel, offering entertainment which included novelties such as "a pedestal dance on skates" and "the cake walk". In the Winter Gardens of the Bencorrum Hotel, Lago Clifford, pioneer radio announcer in Johannesburg in 1924, presented variety entertainments called "The Follies", which attracted as many as 2 000 people each night of the week. Apart from the show itself prizes were a big draw: "a double-cased gold watch" or "a beautiful ostrich fan". The characteristic beach entertainment or free concert was extended to Sunday "sacred concerts" at the Clairmont Hotel Gardens, with a concert party of at least six artists, one of whom was the singer Harry Evans* from Johannesburg. The popularity of beach entertainment was attributed to the greater comfort of being in the open air instead of in a hot, stuffy concert hall; and also to the fact that the beach and Bencorrum concerts were a local version of the English music hall and the style of entertainment associated with seaside resorts in Britain. Another form of diversion that proved a great attraction at this time, was the bioscope (a refined version of the "biograph" of the previous century) with the Bijou Orchestra or Hoby's Select Orchestra providing background for the silent pictures, and interpolated descriptive musical effects. — Variety shows were not a monopoly of beach entertainers. In 1907 the Empire Music Hall in West Street was re-opened as His Majesty's Theatre or Palace of Varieties and directed by J. Ferguson Brown, founder of the Durban Amateur Operatic Society in the previous century. This was the main variety theatre until the Criterion at the corner of Field Street and the Esplanade was opened in May 1912. — Meanwhile, serious music was not being neglected. Houston Macdonald had amalgamated two music societies, the DMA and the Berea Choral Society, to form the Durban and Berea Musical Association. After his early death in February 1908 at the age of 35, he was succeeded by Frank Proudman, who assumed control of the new choral society in his capacity as borough organist. A number of celebrities visited Durban about this time. Charles Santley, the famous English baritone, arrived in 1907. In the same year Alfred Hollins, the blind organist and composer, gave his first series of recitals on the great three-manual organ in the Town Hall. Perhaps he is best remembered in South Africa as the one who prepared the specification of the Johannesburg Town Hall organ*. Mark Hambourg, the famous pianist, made his first visit in 1908 - the year in which the Cherniavsky Trio* first arrived in Durban. — About the year 1910 choirs were much in evidence. At the opening of the new Town Hall in April 1910 the DMA choir under Frank Proudman numbered over 200. The Elsie Purvis Ladies' Choir*, in all 30 singers from Pietermaritzburg and Durban, made a first public appearance in July 1908. They were much inspired by the fine performances of the Welsh Ladies' Choir under Clara Novello Davies who visited South Africa in July 1910. Beresford Smyly, Irish baritone, was choirmaster at Emmanuel Cathedral. His choir sang at the first festival ever held by the Natal Society for the Advancement of Music* in 1910. Sydney Payne, who had a long association with the choirs, orchestra and theatre of Durban, was conductor of the choir and orchestra of a newly-formed Philharmonic Society. J. Ferguson Brown left the variety stage for the sake of reviving nineteenth century operettas. He could muster a chorus of at least 50 singers. Closely associated with all his efforts was the outstanding actress and soprano, Florence Perry (Mrs Frank Greig). Harry Evans formed his male voice choir known as the Durban Male Voice Party in 1911 - a revival of Charles Hoby's Gleemen of Durban. The largest choir heard in Durban during this period sang at the Coronation Empire Concert in the Town Hall in August 1911. On this occasion the DMA, augmented by the touring Sheffield Choir, reached a strength of 380 voices. — The opening of the new Town Hall in 1910, and the coronation of King George V in 1911, created an atmosphere of festivity and a desire to rejoice through the medium of great choral concerts. But only the tactful welding of many smaller choirs could produce one large choir of festival magnitude. One* of the foremost choir-trainers, Beresford Smyly, created a lively interest in choral music at Emmanuel Cathedral, his enterprise being greatly assisted and stimulated by the opening of a new three-manual organ in April 1912. With the emphasis on greater musical forces, two societies, the DMA under Proudman and the Durban Philharmonic under Sydney Payne, affiliated; while the instrumentalists of the Philharmonic hived off to form another Bijou Orchestra under Sydney Payne, which played nightly at the Criterion in support of silent films. The Durban Male Voice Party and the Elsie Purvis Ladies' Choir were often absorbed into larger choirs, and any combination with church choirs could yield at least another 100 singers. Yet it is surprising how little was done to stage those great choral works that had become part of Durban's musical heritage.

VI. WORLD WAR I

Frank Proudman went overseas in 1913. Just prior to his departure he conducted the DMA with orchestra in a Wagner programme - perhaps the first of its kind in Durban. On his return early in 1914 he started a series of Sunday concerts on the beach. For this purpose he had an orchestra of 40 players (leader Lorenzo Mancini). The playing of some well-known light classics anticipated by a few years what a full-time professional orchestra might one day have to do. In these days immediately preceding World War I, the main venue for beach entertainment was the "Hall by the Sea" - formerly a skating rink and large enough to accommodate holiday crowds for all kinds of shows: bioscope, variety theatre or revues "with 20 beautiful bathing belles" and bands churning out tangos and ragtime, the latest musical craze. Military bandsmen were always in evidence, either in band performances on the beach-front or as wind-players in Proudman's new orchestra. — There were ominous signs of war. One Sunday evening in the Town Hall the band of the South Staffordshire Regiment opened a concert with the *Trauermarsch* from Wagner's *Götterdämmerung*. Within a few months they were all wiped out on the battlefields in Flanders. Inopportunely, the new Cape Town Orchestra of 32 players under Theo Wendt* chose the month of August 1914 to make their first tour of South Africa. They gave only two concerts in Durban, which made people wonder why nothing had been done about forming a local professional orchestra. It was too late to do anything. War raged in Europe and people flocked to patriotic concerts to sing *It's a long way to Tipperary, Soldiers of the King, Land of hope and glory.* — Most musicians were apprehensive about the effect of war on the arts. The advice given in Durban in 1914 was: "Go to the theatre" - which they did. Every hall and theatre seemed to be bursting with all manner of entertainment, if only on the pretext of raising war funds. The Theatre Royal started off with *Charley's aunt,* before degenerating into a series of revues. The Criterion let loose the *Girls of the Ragtime Six.* The slogan, "Those who cannot fight must entertain", captured the imagination of a great many who had never thought of doing anything in the musical or theatrical line. Both the DMA and Beresford Smyly's choir increased their membership. Proudman's orchestra of 30 players with Eugene Benzon as leader continued their series of fortnightly concerts in the Town Hall and on the beach. The annual eisteddfod was held as usual. There were regular organ recitals in the Town Hall, and concerts by the Male Voice Party and the Purvis Choir. Regular chamber concerts took place in the art gallery. Musical comedy was thriving under Ferguson Brown who had by this time initiated his son, Gus Brown, into this kind of show business. — In July 1916 it was even suggested that a college of music be established in

Durban, to be affiliated to the Technical College. Mr Gustave Hallé, founder and president of the Natal Society for the Advancement of Music, suggested that his own Society should be transformed into a Natal College of Music, which he believed to be quite feasible with the financial assistance of the municipalities and the Provincial Council. Nothing ever came of this, but such was the prevailing optimism about the future of music at this period of world crisis. — During the war the people sang. There were many songs; recruiting songs (by local musicians), soon to be forgotten, marching songs and songs from revues. Among them were: *I love the girls* sung by the elderly Mr Ferguson Brown at the Criterion one night, and - topically, or for old time's sake - *Let me like a soldier fall,* by Harry Evans, the golden-voiced Welsh tenor whose great talents will be remembered with those of his war-time contemporaries Hilda Cookson Armitage*, Gladys Daniel* and Isobel McLaren*. — New orchestras were started. A certain Mrs Vincent formed a Patriotic Orchestra of 15 players to entertain soldiers in hospitals and rest camps. However, it was the military band that so many enjoyed listening to. In 1914 the Newcastle-on-Tyne Brass Band was in Durban on a three-month contract, and although the Cape Town Orchestra had made its debut in Durban a few weeks before, the glamour of musicians in uniform stirred the hearts of everyone. In 1916 Proudman conducted the first Municipal Band and inaugurated a series of band concerts on the Ocean Beach. It was an immediate success, attracting the local population and holiday-makers in great numbers. Another subsidy was therefore forthcoming for a second series of concerts in 1917, and until the end of the War, Proudman and his 34 bandsmen provided the appropriate war-time image of musicians as men in uniform. The idea of a military band as the purveyor of popular music at a sea-side resort lingered for many years.

VII.   THE NEW ERA OF THE 1920s
The War left Durban musically unimpaired, except for the death of Beresford Smyly in 1917. Large choral concerts were less frequent than in pre-war days and there were no symphony concerts, nor was there a regular symphony orchestra. In February 1919, however, the Cape Town Municipal Orchestra of 44 players celebrated its fifth anniversary with a performance of Beethoven's *Choral symphony.* In addition, a chair of music was established at Cape Town University (1920). These two achievements provided much food for wistful thinking in Durban. — The unexpected appearance of "bio-cafes" in West Street in 1918 testified to the plight of musicians. Small groups of players found employment there or in the theatre. Trade unionism among musicians expressed itself with a vengeance at the Theatre Royal one night, when the orchestra walked out before the curtain went up, as a protest against being under-paid. In the early twenties the unemployment situation assumed serious proportions. An attempt to establish the professional status of musicians was made during the War with the creation of a Natal Musicians' Union; the Music Teachers' Association was formed in 1925. — Amateur musical activities were kept alive through the Durban Amateur Operatic Society which Gus Brown had inherited from his father and from which the Durban Bachelor Girls seceded in 1928. The Bachelor Girls led to the discovery of the exceptional talents of Thelma Whitcutt and Keppoch Macdonald. Arthur Tann started the first boys' choir in 1923 and Harry Evans had a Male Voice Choir of 60. Hilda Cookson Armitage and Harold Dyer, two well-known teachers of singing, each had their own choir. The only regular amateur orchestras were a Philharmonic Orchestra conducted by Reg Woodroffe* who, for over 15 years, gave

concerts for charity, and a theatre orchestra at the Criterion to which Sydney Payne returned as conductor in 1920 after an absence of some years. — In 1920 it became evident that music as a civic matter was in a rapid state of transition. In August Frank Proudman relinquished the post of borough organist to take up a similar appointment in Kimberley. As no-one was appointed to succeed him, the post became redundant. Regular organ recitals were discontinued and the Town Hall organ again fell into disuse and a state of disrepair. The appointment of Lyell-Tayler* as Music Director in September 1921, was combined with the new venture of starting an all-professional civic orchestra. He arrived on 22 October 1921, after relinquishing the post of Director of Music Entertainment in Brighton, which he had held for 10 years. A first impression of this man with his shock of golden-yellow hair was of "a personality that is charming in spite of a somewhat obtrusive egotism". — The reason for this revolutionary change in the musical life of Durban can be explained in terms of civic status. The Cape Town Orchestra under Theo Wendt made a second visit to Durban in July 1921. It became a matter of pride that Durban should have its own orchestra, and that the successful experiment of Bournemouth and Brighton should be repeated under the direction of a personality trained in the environment of sea-side musical entertainment. The Durban Orchestra of 30 musicians, nearly all of whom were recruited from England, made a first public appearance in the Town Hall on 27 May 1922 in a programme of "melodious memories". This was soon followed by programmes of London "Prom" favourites such as Tchaikovsky's *Symphony no. 6,* and the same composer's *Andante cantabile* and *Casse-noisette suite.* The first concert at the Beach took place on 4 August 1922. — The first great choral revival since the War was held in October 1922. The DMA combined with choral societies from Johannesburg and Pretoria and, supported by the new orchestra, gave the first Durban performance of Elgar's *Dream of Gerontius.* In all, 500 performers took part in the four-day festival which included Mendelssohn's *Elijah* and concert versions of Gounod's *Faust* and *Cavalleria rusticana* by Mascagni. Subsequent concerts by the DMA and Durban Orchestra were on a large scale with at least 350 performers. All this was achieved in a town of about 45 000 white citizens. — The establishment of a professional symphony orchestra did much to improve musical taste. This was surely a period of musical enlightenment, when Durban audiences listened to live performances of the Brahms symphonies, works by Richard Strauss, the symphonies of Tchaikovsky, works by De Falla and Stravinsky. The main venues for these concerts were the Town Hall and the Beach Pavilion. The latter was first used on 12 August 1924, with Cecilia Wessels* as guest artist. By this time Lyell-Tayler was both Music Director and Beach Manager. In December 1924, when the first broadcasting studio was opened, members of the Durban Orchestra were also employed in the Studio Orchestra. Lyell-Tayler was appointed Director of Broadcasting. Music became an important part of education. The Workers' Educational Association (WEA) concerned itself with adult education. Under the auspices of this organisation, Archdeacon Hodson of St Cyprian's in Durban gave talks on "how to listen to music", with the new symphony orchestra at hand for musical illustration. He was also responsible for promoting the chamber concerts in the Art Gallery. A string quartet was formed from members of the symphony orchestra with Stirling Robins* as leader. Edgar Heap*, official accompanist in the orchestra, occasionally joined them. — The musical education of the young took new shape. Archdeacon Hodson was the first to present the new orchestra to schoolchildren of all ages in the town Hall. These lecture

430

concerts had been very successful in Cape Town and in Johannesburg, where Professor P.R. Kirby*, backed by the visiting Cape Town Orchestra, brought revelation and excitement to thousands of children when he demonstrated the wonders of the composer's "colourbox". Lyell-Tayler himself had great musical optimism when in November 1922 he predicted that Durban would become the leading musical city in South Africa. This, of course, depended on the training of young musicians in a school of music, perhaps, as someone else had suggested, through the Technical College. It also depended on the formation of a junior orchestra, and on the orchestral training of competent amateurs. This latter thought helped to revive the Durban Orchestral Society, a task undertaken by Otto Siedle*, successful businessman and music-lover. It was he who had arranged and sponsored the visit of the Cape Town Orchestra in 1921, thus preparing the way for Durban's own orchestra the following year. The Orchestral Society had two important functions: it made a number of subscription concerts financially possible and it provided a large group of amateur orchestral players to augment the professional orchestra of only 30. — In spite of the orchestra, Durban could not do without its military band. By the middle of 1924 Lyell-Tayler was in military uniform conducting the Municipal Military Band of 35 musicians, drawn from the orchestra and from various local bands. Band concerts at the beach drew crowds who could have their music free of charge. This was important in view of the approaching years of depression. More and more musicians had to earn a living by playing in tearooms and café-bios. Orchestral players and everyone else looked with apprehension to the years ahead. The order of the day was to keep smiling. In 1927 a wave of community singing swept the world. The people of Durban flocked to lunchhour gatherings of community singing in the Town Hall under the jovial baton of Lyell-Tayler. "Daddy wouldn't buy me a bow-wow" they roared. — The Durban Orchestra was certainly not paying its way. How long it would survive became a matter for anxious conjecture. In September 1927 Lyell-Tayler was attracted to Johannesburg where he became Director of Music for African Consolidated Theatres Ltd. Under the Acting Music Director, T.H. Huddle, principal trombonist, the orchestra and military band continued giving concerts at the Pavilion, the Summer Palace and the Town Hall. — Durban was not entirely dependent on a professional orchestra or a music director for its musical entertainment. There were several amateur societies including orchestras and choirs. Reg. Woodroffe directed the Durban Operatic Society using his own orchestra. Stirling Robins, the violinist, led another orchestral group and both of these groups were invited on occasion to augment the Durban Orchestra. There were a number of small choirs - the Durban Male Voice Party under Harry Evans, a ladies choir under José Smith*, and a boys' choir under Arthur Tann. The DMA, much reduced in strength, met occasionally for the singing of glees and part-songs. Sydney Payne and Gus Brown directed the shows put on by the Bachelor Girls - usually light musical comedies. — Choirs are more easily rehabilitated than orchestras. In May 1928 Edmond Schelpe*, organist and choirmaster of Emmanuel Cathedral, lifted the DMA out of its slow decline with a colossal performance of Haydn's *The creation,* involving 700 singers, most of them members of various school choirs. But the future of the Durban Orchestra remained a vexed question. From Kimberley came the almost forgotten voice of Frank Proudman: he suggested a municipal band instead of an orchestra, thus reviving what he himself had started in 1916. The suggestion was not entirely unwelcome. For many the orchestra had become an "extravagant luxury". — In May 1928, Dan Godfrey*, son of

431

the famous Sir Dan Godfrey of Bournemouth, accepted the post of Music Director. On 24 June he made his debut in Durban, a large, military-looking gentleman of 35. Both his appearance and close association with the Durban Light Infantry throughout his short career made him the ideal bandmaster. But Dan Godfrey was more than just a bandmaster. Under his baton Durban audiences heard for the first time live performances of Respighi's *Fountains of Rome,* of several Russian symphonies (including those of Glazounov) and of symphonies by Sibelius. Chamber concerts in the Art Gallery were revived and grand opera again came to the fore with a concert version of *Il trovatore,* which included singers of high reputation: Harry Evans, Grogan Caney, Muriel Clark, Keppoch Macdonald and Rose Alper*. Yet the characteristic image of Dan Godfrey remained that of the bandmaster: first as conductor of the Durban Light Infantry Band, after the retirement of T.J. Grant who had held this position for over 36 years, and then as conductor of the Durban Military Band. — Between the years 1928 and the early 1930s technical advances brought about better broadcasting, better gramophone recordings and sound reproduction, and the "talkies" - all of which constituted a real threat to live music. Singers in particular were less interested in attending rehearsals. The large choral concerts formerly associated with the DMA seemed to have lost their appeal. However, a revival of *Hiawatha,* much inspired by a sensational costume performance in the Albert Hall in London, and the choir-training of Grogan Caney brought 200 singers into action again. But another long-established style of entertainment, the "vaudeville" (or variety show) at the Criterion, had to give way to films. — Any amount of recorded music was available in shops, record libraries and over the air. In spite of this the Durban Orchestral Society, or "Symphony Concert Society" as it was often called, gave the necessary financial backing to symphony seasons. These Thursday night concerts were fashionable occasions, both at the Pavilion and in the Town Hall. Press photographers were there at the interval on the look-out for attractive patrons, while the scramble for refreshments went on relentlessly. The orchestral repertoire appeared to be as up-to-date as anything in London, with symphonies by Bruckner, symphonies and tone poems by Elgar; more and more Brahms and Dvorak, and all this with rather limited orchestral resources.

VIII. THE 1930s

A high standard of general musical education developed in the early 1930s. Memorable recordings by world celebrities could be heard in any home. The radio became a vehicle for musical education when Cyril Wright*, Natal Music Inspector, gave a series of fortnightly broadcasts for use in schools - a favourite topic being *Instruments of the orchestra.* Yet only four Durban schools were equipped with radio sets and the idea never grew much beyond the experimental stage. — While cinema organs, loudspeakers and gramophone records were replacing cinema orchestras overseas, the large cinema orchestra of the Johannesburg Colosseum absorbed a few players from the Durban Orchestra, then faced with a very uncertain future. Also at this time, the 12 year-old controversy of a national orchestra was revived. In 1935, at the peak of the Durban orchestral crisis, conductor Dan Godfrey died. He was given a military funeral. A further tribute was paid him in the performance, a fortnight later, of the great *C major symphony* by his favourite composer, Schubert. The work was conducted by T.H. Huddle, who stepped into the breach again as Acting Music Director. — From January 1935 there were to be no more concerts relayed from

Johannesburg through the Durban studio. This may have been an incentive for more Durban musicians to do something about performing over the air. The mid-1930s were years of comparative prosperity and optimism when television was expected within a year. Some people were again mooting the question of a music department at the University. According to Cyril Wright, who revived the subject, this new faculty could be a school of music with teaching personnel drawn from the Durban Orchestra. — Among the local pianists of outstanding merit who came before the Durban public at this period were: Glyn Townley*, Moira Birks*, Janet Swan and Jack Aronowitz*. Glyn Townley, an eisteddfod winner, went overseas for further study and though his home is in Durban, he has hardly rested from travel; indeed, he is perhaps the foremost of the globe-trotting South African musicians. Moira Birks, another eisteddfod winner, has for the most part devoted her musical activities to Durban as a teacher of the piano, choral conductor and concert pianist. Janet Swan, winner of the overseas scholarship of the University of South Africa in 1933, was one of the most remarkable teenage concert pianists in Durban during the 1930s and still makes her appearance from time to time on the platform of the City Hall (1970). Jack Aronowitz, acknowledged by all his contemporaries as a brilliant pianist, moved between this country and Britain, being much drawn to the latter. — The successor to Dan Godfrey was Edward Dunn*. He made his first appearance with the orchestra on 25 November 1935. Shortly after his arrival in this country he made a public statement which must have endeared him to the public for many years to come: "Much as I may think that the highest function of a good orchestra is the playing of symphonic music; and although I appreciate and encourage the work of the Symphonic Concert Society, there is no disputing the fact that the bulk of the ratepayers of any city like this regard music from the point of view of the entertainment it can afford them; and it is only fair to consider the majority". — He therefore arranged programmes with a "theme", e.g. "Popular British composers", "Night", "Foreign travel", "Happy nights", at the Pavilion every Saturday night. The dynamic, infectious enthusiasm of the new conductor, combined with the musical boom of the middle and late 1930s, brought on the widespread fashion of talent searching. One of the first talent competitions ever held in Durban took place at the Prince's Theatre (now the Colosseum) in Smith Street. The appeal was mainly to the young and led to the first Natal Schools Music Festival held in the Town Hall on Sunday, 21 June 1936. It included folk dancing, eurythmics, percussion bands, a children's orchestra and a choir of 500 supported by the Durban Orchestra. The first Municipal Dance Band (15 piece) made its debut in the same month. A Choral and Light Opera Society, also designated as "municipal", revived *Merrie England* and *The pirates of Penzance*. — When the broadcasting studio was taken over by the Durban Corporation in 1936, a new concert orchestra for radio concerts was formed under Edward Dunn - 40 players in all, with Stirling Robins as leader. Most of the players belonged to the Durban Orchestra. Edward Dunn's musical responsibility was therefore considerably increased. He was in charge of broadcast concerts, Thursday symphony concerts, lunch hour concerts, "Happy nights" every Saturday, cabaret dances and musical comedy shows. In addition to this, he was responsible for most of the publicity associated with the musical life of the city. — The main centre of musical activity in the middle 1930s was the Broadcasting Studio in Aliwal Street. George Walker*, present leader of the Durban Civic Orchestra (1970), Zoe Stacey Frost* (pianist), Roy Carter* (cellist), Dodds Miller (pianist), Theo Wiercx* (violinist) and Moira Birks (pianist) were frequently heard over the air.

433

A great many concerts, instrumental and choral, were also relayed. The large choral societies of former years were replaced by small choirs: the student choirs from the Natal Training College and Natal University under Cyril Wright, the Durban Glee Club under Rosa Kerdachi (contralto), a mixed choir conducted by Harold Dyer, and a ladies' choir under Hilda Cookson-Armitage. — In 1937 orchestras became an attraction. Besides the Municipal Orchestra under Edward Dunn, there was an unusually large amateur orchestra of 50 players under Sydney Payne. The glamour of the baton gave rise to a conductors' competition in October. The winner was a 16 year old pianist and musical prodigy, Geoffrey Frank. The great future predicted for him was cut short a few years later, when he was killed in World War II. His great talent is remembered in a memorial bursary awarded annually for outstanding performance at the eisteddfod. In November 1937 the first of the ladies' conducting competitions was won by Moira Birks. Today she conducts the choir of Emmanuel Cathedral in the four-yearly presentation of the Passion Play and an annual performance of *Messiah*. — The same year brought to light the talent of E.R. Browne ("Teddy") who devoted himself to Gilbert and Sullivan as actor and producer. This later Mayor of Westville is one of the few living links with the D'Oyly Carte Opera Company in which his father played the oboe under the baton of Sir Arthur Sullivan. Teddy Browne was responsible for many productions with the Durban Light Opera Company and other amateur groups before and after World War II. Among the accomplished singers who assisted him was the soprano Christina Greig*, daughter of Mrs Frank Greig (Florence Perry), the soprano who produced and took part in these operettas in the early part of the century. The orchestral conductor for these pre-war shows was Sydney Payne, who had been associated with Durban theatrical shows for over 30 years. In September 1938, disappointed that he did not get the directorship of the new broadcasting orchestra, he left for England never to return. The end of this era came in October when the Theatre Royal brought down the curtain on the last of their live theatre shows. — When Edward Dunn returned from his trip to England, he was more than ever convinced that Durban would become another Blackpool. For 15 years the Pavilion was the heart of all entertainment at the beach. Symphony concerts, accordion and harmonica bands, and the latest craze - talent contests - all took place here. At the height of this activity, the Pavilion was gutted by fire one Saturday night in August 1939 - almost exactly a year after its creator, Lyell-Tayler, had died in Johannesburg.

IX. WORLD WAR II

No concert hall was built to replace the Pavilion with its seating capacity of 1 000 and serious music has never found its way back to the beach. For over 30 years the site has remained vacant and the City Hall with its poor acoustics is the venue for every type of musical entertainment. The pre-war craze for talent competitions led to the conducting competition at the Twentieth Century Cinema. As war inevitably approached, there were outbursts of "Grand community singing" at the Playhouse, with hit songs from the forces - mainly on the subject of Hitler. In December 1939, with apparently little concern about the war in Europe, over 400 voices gave a confident rendering of *Messiah* in the City Hall. — As the war developed into a more serious matter a great many people sat glued to the radio for the news, and incidentally got most of their music that way. A series of talks about music was started by O.J. Horrax and this prepared the way for Charles Oxtoby*. With so many musicians in the forces the Municipal Orchestra was depleted and attendance at concerts poor. Thus

434

chamber music came into its own. The Salon Art Concert series in the Art Gallery provided chamber concerts in the late afternoon, usually with the assistance of the broadcasting studio trio (Stirling Robins, Roy Carter and Edgar Heap) and the Municipal String Orchestra. In fact, 1940 was the year of chamber music festivals in Durban as well as in Johannesburg, Pretoria and Cape Town. — A new kind of Philharmonic Orchestra came into being. Dodds Miller, the conductor, tried to recruit young musicians in the hope that they might be given the opportunity of performing in public. A similar venture involving the youth was started by Theo Wiercx in 1941. He opened his Accordion School in Hooper Lane and gradually elevated the "squash-box" to the status of a concert-hall instrument. It took him 14 years to build up an Accordion Orchestra of 40 players. — At the end of the war the Municipal Orchestra began to recover its strength as the players returned. The orchestra became powerful enough for the performance of standard orchestral works in the Thursday afternoon Master Series. Some of these were conducted by Leonard Pearce*, who had succeeded Gregor Bartonyi as conductor of the Studio Orchestra. In May 1946 the new symphony season opened with 50 players under Edward Dunn and several well-known South African musicians as soloists. Among them were the singers Betsy de la Porte*, Cecilia Wessels*, Harold Lake and Rose Alper*, the pianists Adolph Hallis* and Moira Birks and the violinist Harold Ketelbey*. Sunday evening popular concerts were given regularly. At one of them, in April 1946, Charles Oxtoby, the popular broadcaster on music, appeared on the platform to conduct some of his own compositions. — The home of the theatre - with plays, variety, operas and operettas - was the Criterion. After the War, Italian opera became almost a cult. Many of the returned soldiers had been in Italy and for the first time enjoyed live perfomances of opera. One who showed great enterprise in presenting opera, was John Connell*, the City Organist of Johannesburg. It was he who conducted the series ofoperas at the Criterion in April 1946.

X.   POST-WAR DEVELOPMENTS
In the immediate post-war years nearly every kind os musical entertainment was available to the public. Edward Dunn, during a short visit overseas, recruited new members for the orchestra to bring it up to a strength of 45 players, while the Philharmonic Orchestra under Stirling Robins had 50. The Durban Ballet Club, assisted by the Durban String Players under Roy Carter, and also inspired by the visit of the Cape Town University Ballet under Dulcie Howes*, helped to make ballet the most popular form of theatrical entertainment. The Durban Light Opera Society became the main choral society and could best prove its vocal and theatrical talents in a full-costumed presentation of *Hiawatha*. Seasons of ballet, symphony concerts, more conducting competitions, *al fresco* concerts at the Beach Amphitheatre, recorded music concerts - all these made music a somewhat serious pastime for young people who were not much inclined to let themselves go, unless it was to sing "Open the door Richard", a revival of a negro tune from the 1920s. — Several of the well-known musical personalities of today made their debut in Durban during the post-war period. Charles Denholm*, a violinist, joined the orchestra and also proved himself an able choir trainer. In recent years he has become the deputy-conductor. Errol Slatter*, the present organist at St Paul's is another able choir-master associated with the activities of the Select Choir. He was a pupil of Harold Dyer* who formed his own choral society. Slatter's predecessor at St Paul's for about 20 years, Charles Hamer*, had his

435

own ladies' choir. Among the new members of the orchestra was Paul Martens*, the violinist, whose wife Jacqueline played the harpsichord. Between them they created a new public interest in Baroque music. Over 20 years later they restored something of the lost art of creating music in the home with their family of four musical children - all string players. — The establishment of a large civic orchestra meant the belated realisation of a dream for at least one great music-lover: Otto Siedle. It had been his ideal for over 50 years. The 60-piece orchestra was founded early in 1948. He died later that same year - aged 91. He and his musical wife passed on their talents to two of their children - Perla Siedle Gibson*, pianist and dramatic soprano who was widely known as the "Lady in White". This name was given to her by the troops for whom she sang as they left Durban harbour during the war. The other child was Jack Siedle, Springbok cricketer, and cellist in the Durban orchestra of the late 1920s. Sir Thomas Beecham, the famous British conductor, visited South Africa in 1948 and in August conducted the new Durban orchestra, augmented for the occasion to 95 players. Three months later Theo Wendt, veteran conductor of the Cape Town Orchestra, appeared as guest conductor. — Nearly all post-war musical enterprise placed emphasis on youth. In 1948 the talented violinist Peter John Carter* captured public attention at the Y-Club concerts given by a youth orchestra conducted by his father, Roy Carter. Twenty years later he returned from Europe as music manager for NAPAC. Edward Dunn was responsible for the first so-called "Festival of Youth" in April 1949. Orchestras, much enlarged by immigrant musicians, came to Durban from different parts of the country. Three Durban musicians, Edward Dunn, Arthur Tempest* and Lynette James*, who worked tirelessly to promote music among the youth, gave concerts with a children's festival orchestra of 70 players. There were lectures on music, ballet and drama. An event which was later to become the International Arts League of Youth Festival (IALY), was held in Durban annually, usually in July, attended by children of all ages from all parts of the country. — A greater interest in non-European musical activity developed during the war years. The eisteddfod was extended to Indians, Coloureds and Africans. There had been Zulu choirs since the late nineteenth century and some had been on overseas tours, but very little individual talent emerged. During the 1950s there were several interesting manifestations of Zulu talent. The Municipal Bantu Brass Band* started in 1951 with a small group of musicians. The band provided a platform and a background for either solo singers or vocal quartets. In the same year while the IALY entered its ninth annual festival, and the Durban "Skakelkomitee" were launching their second Afrikaans eisteddfod with over 2 000 entries, the African Jazz and Variety Show was accepted as an annual event - soon to be followed by the Natal Festival of African Arts. Among the Africans who made a substantial contribution to musical life in Durban, were: K. Masinga, SABC announcer who made over 300 recordings of old Zulu songs; K. Mngoma*, the singer who studied in Johannesburg with Anny Lambrechts* and subsequently trained the Bantu teachers' choir in Durban; John Ngcobo, a lyric baritone, trained at the Guildhall School of Music, London; and Joseph Dhlamini, a tenor and the first African to take a three-year course in Music at the University of Cape Town. — In this same era of festivals and the search for talent, some notable South African musicians were discovered: Mimi Coertse*, the famous operatic soprano was auditioned by the Durban Studio of the SABC in the early 1950s; Joyce Barker*, soprano, was the first winner of the Kathleen Ferrier Memorial Scholarship; and Wendy Fine* made her first appearance with the Pinetown Civic Choral society under John van Zyl*. Edward Dunn* discovered the talent of John Manduell*, conductor and composer, who is now Director of Music at Lancaster University in England. In 1954 Manduell was music director for the Durban centenary celebrations - one of many in a series of festivals throughout the city's history which marked civic progress, and, like the others, it revived memories of the previous century: Christy minstrels, glees, madrigals, part-songs and children's choirs singing Victorian - favourites. The centenary celebrations gave impetus to comparatively new musical ventures. Among them were the Centenary Ballet Company which engaged the visiting South African ballerina, Nadia Nerina*, for the occasion; the Intimate Ballet Company trained by John Pygram; and a company which presented lunch-hour jive sessions. Jazz, accompanied by much talk about "rhythm", was given musical status through a civic variety orchestra. Nolan Ranger's thirteen-piece orchestra, performing this type of music, was a special attraction on the *al fresco* terrace of the Esplanade Hotel. — In 1952 the Alhambra Theatre was opened and soon became the new home of Gilbert and Sullivan productions - with Teddy Browne and William Pickerill* conducting. The latter was soon to succeed Edward Dunn as Music Director in Durban. Edward Dunn made his farewell bow on 27 August 1954 before going to Cape Town. In the same year the Durban Catholic Players Guild under Father Noel Coughlan produced the Passion Play. The massed Catholic choirs used in these early productions were trained by Moira Birks under whose baton they performed large choral works, thus bringing back the best of Durban's choral tradition. There were three other choirs of high repute: a Durban Municipal choir under Charles Denholm, the Light Opera Choral Society under Constance Munro and the Dutch Reformed Choir of 200 voices under Dr John Pauw*. — The great era of singing had returned. The first of the "Music and Song" festivals took place in May 1958. This was presented by the Durbanse Skakelkomitee in place of the usual Afrikaans eisteddfod, and brought before the public the singers Mary-Anne Adler, Eric Voysey, Michael Gritten and Mavis Hawkins. This was all part of the campaign to discover youthful talent among the "artists of tomorrow", who appeared in a series of concerts in the City Hall. Among the new discoveries were two young pianists Annette Kearney, daughter of Moira Birks, and Robert Mills, who became senior lecturer in English at the University of Natal. — A quick succession of appointments to the post of Director of Entertainments in Durban followed on Edward Dunn's resignation in 1954. His successor, William Pickerill, died on 6 May 1955. Then came Frits Schuurman*. As a Hollander with considerable overseas conducting experience, and a former music lecturer at Cape Town University, he had an aura of continental seriousness about him - a welcome contrast to the seaside heartiness of his predecessors. His wife, the violinist, Maria Neuss* (a descendant of the composer Dvořák), added even more dignity to the post of Director of Entertainments. But this did not in any way dampen the prevailing youthful exuberance of the musical community. The amateur orchestra, known as the "Philharmonic", became a youth orchestra under the direction of George Walker*, who concentrated on the art of good string playing. The youth orchestra at the Y-Club became a junior orchestra directed by the clarinet player Arthur Tempest*. There were several accordion bands, of which the largest was the "orchestra" of 48, trained and directed by Theo Wiercx, who created a fashion for this instrument through the Natal Accordion Society and the Harmonica Society. The latter helped to establish the reputation of a prominent South African exponent on this instrument - John Walton*. — The great Festival of Song in 1955 involved over 400 schoolchildren, but this was only a faint echo of the late nineteenth century when 1 200 children sang in the old Town Hall. The nineteen-year old Pierino Gamba arrived from Italy in 1956 and became the dynamic spirit behind the mid-year International Festival of Youth. In spite of jive on the dance floor and hi-fi on long-playing records, as well as the advent of the electric guitar, which displaced the accordion, young people in their hundreds were still learning to play the piano as their forebears had done in the previous century and achieving great things at the annual eisteddfod. However, the word "teenager" was already in current use and "groups" were becoming evident, especially small dance bands of electric guitar players backed by a versatile drummer in "skiffle" music. — Added to all these youthful exploits, the African Arts Festival, the Coon Carnival and the Indian Eisteddfod gave music of the late 1950s a multi-racial flavour. Music was also becoming cosmopolitan as Durban's deeply ingrained Victorianism was forced to accept the contamination of new "foreign" influences. Dutch residents of Durban contributed to the cosmopolitan flavour of the city's musical activities. So for instance, De Zang en Vriendschap Society of Natal provided both good singers and good orchestral players. — The German community has also made its contribution. In 1959 Heinrich Haape*, medical doctor, psychologist and opera director, started the Durban Opera Company. He himself was producer of several operas in the City Hall and Lyric Theatre in Imbilo Road (opened in December 1959). Among the productions were *The tales of Hoffmann, The marriage of Figaro, The bartered bride* and *Madame Butterfly.* His wife, Martha Arazym-Haape*, and Dorothy Avrich*, Hans Menck* and Bradley Harris* sang the leading roles in the earliest of these productions between 1959 and 1961. Some of the inspiration for this new operatic venture may have come from Cape Town. The season of opera presented by the University of Cape Town Opera Company under Dr Eric Chisholm* took place in the Alhambra during July 1959 and the Eoan Group* under Dr Joseph Manca* brought a season of Italian opera to the Alhambra in July 1960. — Another feature of cosmopolitan entertainment was the ever-increasing interest in Latin-American ballroom dancing, and - especially for connoisseurs and the initiated - Spanish ballet directed by Joy Shearer*. Music for the evenings of Spanish ballet, held at the Pinetown Civic Centre in December 1959, was provided by Captain Hugh Hind's New Concert Orchestra - consisting of the foundation members of the Durban Light Orchestral Society*. These musicians, together with the Durban Philharmonic Orchestra (now mainly an adult group), absorbed more and more amateurs into the musical scene of the 1960s. — In the two decades after 1950 young people of all ages devoted much of their time to acquiring proficiency on fashionable instruments: accordions, guitars, electronic organs and the wide range of percussion instruments forming the lively centre of a dance band. The electronic organ with its built-in effects and mechanisms has appealed to a great many would-be performers who have only limited musicianship. They too, lived in the hope that one day they would achieve just a little of the superb skill exhibited by such gifted players as Dennis van Rooyen*, an acknowledged master of this instrument in Durban. — In view of this characteristically youthful desire to be musically up-to-date, it is all the more surprising that so many young people should have chosen to take up the recorder. There have been recorder groups throughout the country since the 1930s but nothing quite as remarkable as the cult for obsolete instruments which began in Durban in the late 1950s. In April 1958, at the Y-Club, Jacqueline Martens gave a public recital on the harpsichord. At the same concert Richard Oxtoby* performed on recorders of different sizes. This revival of the

Baroque in music found regular expression in concerts by the Montpellier Players*, a group of recorder players led by Ted Brien* (leading exponent of the instrument in Durban) and supported by a harpsichord player. The harpsichord was made locally by Richard Oxtoby who used indigenous wood for the purpose. Ted Brien, assisted by several music teachers in Natal, was largely responsible for sustaining this interest in recorders through the concerts of the Recorder Guild* and annual summer schools. The actual making of recorders out of bamboo has been tried with some success in a few of the junior schools. — At a more mature level, music of the Baroque became the special interest of Paul Martens and his family; and also the group of string players known as the Baroque Players*. Visiting string ensembles from Europe prepared the way for the NAPAC Sinfonia of 1969 and the series of concerts in different parts of Natal under the direction of Peter John Carter. — The Durban Music Society was formed in 1950. The chairman, John Baylis, dedicates his spare time to this Society, which specialises in arranging celebrity concerts. As a result of the steadily increasing membership over the past 12 years, it can present frequent concerts by world-famous artists, of whom a few have appeared as soloists with the Durban Orchestra. This Society also gives encouragement to local performers and, like the Johannesburg Music Society*, of much longer standing, arranges chamber concerts in the Art Gallery or Jubilee Room of the City Hall. — With the accent still on youth in the 1960s, music camps attract young musicians from all parts of the country. Orchestral camps offer lectures and ensemble playing with the added attraction of fishing, swimming, riding, hiking - in fact, the whole range of holiday diversions that can be provided in the Natal Midlands in summer or on the South Coast at any time of the year. There were even ballet camps. The summer schools in post-war Britain established the fashion in other parts of the world. "Music without tears" drew many potential orchestral players to these vacation camps, or refresher courses with a difference. In Durban it started in 1949 when Edward Dunn organised the first "Festival of Youth". The object in view was a National Youth Orchestra. The man envisaged as the conductor was Pierino Gamba who has made several visits to this country as a guest conductor. By July 1963 he had 50 players and they made their first public appearance on 12 July 1964, with Annette Kearney as soloist in the Grieg *Piano concerto*. The scheme for maintaining this body of players depended on certain financial guarantees. Some of these were not forthcoming and the whole project was virtually abandoned by 1965. — In 1965 the fate of the Durban Orchestra hung in the balance. Even before Frits Schuurman's contract expired in March 1966, it was suggested that the conductor should be relieved of administrative duties. In September 1966 a larger orchestra of 70 players came into being under Alfred Walther, a German conductor. With greater orchestral resources available, some large works found their way into the Durban orchestral repertory. These included Mahler's second and third symphonies, and at least two symphonies by Shostakovitch. The concert hall atmosphere became decidedly more serious and Central European. — Alfred Walther entered the musical life of Durban through the opera house. In 1963 the Durban Opera Company, with Heinrich Haape as producer and Hans Menck* as conductor and chorus master, had a successful season in the Transvaal. In the following year the control of this company came under the wing of NAPAC with James Conrad* as opera manager. A year later, in 1965, Alfred Walther was invited to conduct the NAPAC production of Verdi's *Aïda* at the Alhambra. He was appointed Resident Conductor of the Durban Orchestra in 1966 and made his first appearance with the new orchestra on 12 September. He was more fortunate than his predecessors: all administration was placed in the hands of an Entertainments Officer, Hugh Cairnduff ("Jock Duff"), who was soon succeeded by A.A. Pletnick in 1966. — What NAPAC did for opera, it did for ballet, by absorbing the talents of Ballet Natal. In April 1970 the Alhambra was taken over by NAPAC for productions which require the combined talents of operatic singers and/or ballet dancers and the Civic Orchestra. — With a European population of less than half-a-million Durban is not a large city by world standards, yet it offers every kind of musical entertainment. At least four times yearly the population is swelled by thousands of holiday-makers, many of whom give their support to concerts of serious music. Much of the light music entertainment is associated with fashionable hotels, where groups or bands help to create the exotic atmosphere that goes so well with expensive dining. But the old world heritage from the last century is still there. — Durban is still very British. A love of singing expresses itself through a great variety of small choirs - a Symphonic Choir led by Heather Brandon*, a Male Voice Choir led by Dr John Pauw, an assortment of Cantabile Choirs led by Constance Munro, a Boys' Choir led by Gillian Randall, and there are singers in operatic groups. One of the greatest attractions is the Festival of Song arranged by Virginia Lee. Every year it attracts thousands of entries from aspiring song writers who hope to write the hit tune that will set the whole world singing and, incidentally, make a fortune for the composer. Folk-singing enjoys a long run of popularity, and is unique in combining the talents of singer and guitar player in one performer. Jack Dowle's* variety show called "World of music" has the blessing of NAPAC; as does the Intimate Concerts which in 1968 started inviting serious musicians to perform in chamber concerts. Among the pianists who have contributed to the programmes in the Little Theatre in Acutt Street, are two popular broadcasters from the Durban Studio, Ronald Charles* and Constance Brothwood*. — Light opera (or operetta) still has its hold on Durban. The Gilbert and Sullivan operettas have never lost their popularity. The Durban Opera Group, formed in 1968 under the management of Olive Peel, has almost a monopoly in being able to offer two good productions a year in Durban, Pietermaritzburg, Pinetown, Westville and as far afield as Greytown and Scottburgh. — There seems to be no limit to the number of festivals. Besides the English and Afrikaans Eisteddfodau and the Festival of Song, there is an annual Piano Festival and a "Beat Festival". Some of them assume colossal proportions. The Skakel Song and Youth Festival of June 1968 mustered 5 000 voices; the Jazz, Folk and Pop "Beat" Festival of 1970 at King's Park drew a crowd almost as large as for an international sports encounter. — Nowadays, choirs, like sports teams, go on tour - for the sake of goodwill rather than competition. Two choirs, the Natal Schools Choir and the Drakensberg Choir School are committed to this itinerant occupation. In the past University choirs have toured the country extensively - the Rhodes University Choir* under Georg Gruber* being the first and most distinguished of its kind. In spite of the efforts by Constance Munro in 1960, the University of Natal still has no well-established choir, either in Durban or Pietermaritzburg. However, both of the Students' Union Halls have become important venues for concerts. Early in 1971 the new Department of Music of the University of Natal was established on the Durban campus. Michael Brimer* was appointed the first Head of the Department, occupying the L.G. Joel Chair of Music*, created in 1969. After his departure for Cape Town in 1974, C.J. Ballantine was appointed to the chair and became Head of the Department.

440

BIBLIOGRAPHY
BARRETT, W.A.: *English glees and part-songs: an inquiry into their historical development.* Longmans Green & Co., 1886.   CAMPBELL, E.: *The 1845 - 1850 Natal Settlers, including the Byrne Settlers and their allotments of land in Natal.* Manuscript in the Don Library, Durban, n.d.   COLENSO, J.W.: *Ten weeks in Natal: A journal of a first tour of visitation among the colonists and the Zulu Kafirs of Natal.* Macmillan & Co., Cambridge, 1855.   DAWES, E.: *Landmarks of Old Durban: a series of documentary programmes broadcast from the Durban studio of the South African Broadcasting Corporation.* E.P. & Commercial Printing Co. Ltd., Durban, 1948.   DISHER, M.W.: *Victorian song.* Phoenix House, London, 1955.   GODFREY, SIR DAN: *Memories and music.* Hutchinson & Co., London, 1924.   HATTERSLEY, A.F.: *The Natalians: further annals of Natal.* Shuter & Shooter, 1940.   HATTERSLEY, A.F.: *Portrait of a colony: the story of Natal.* Cambridge Univ. Press, 1940.   HATTERSLEY, A.F.: *British settlement of Natal: a study of imperial migration.* Cambridge Univ. Press, 1950.   JACKSON, G.S.: *Music in Durban: an account of musical activities in Durban from 1850 to the early years of the present century.* Human Sciences Research Council Publication Series no. 6. Witwatersrand University Press, Johannesburg, 1970.   RUSSELL, G.: *History of Old Durban and reminiscences of an emigrant of 1850.* P. Davis & Sons, Durban, 1899.   SIEDLE, O.: *Siedle saga: reminiscences and reflections.* Knox Publishing Co., Durban, 1940.

SOURCES

Durban Advocate and General Advertiser: 1852 - 1954.   *Durban Observer and Natal General Advertiser:* 1851 and 1852.   *Durban Star:* 1897.   *Natal Advertiser:* 1878 - 1937: *Natal Advertiser and Mercantile Gazette:* 1854 and 1855.   *Natal Almanac and Yearly Register:* 1861 - 1897.   *Natal Colonist:* 1871 - 1878.   *Natal Commercial Advertiser:* 1854.   *Natal Daily News:* from 1937.   *Natal Guardian:* 1856.   *Natal Herald:* 1866 - 1870.   *Natal Mercury:* from 1852.   *Natal Mercury Pictorial:* 1904 1921.   *Natal Star:* 1855 - 1963.   *Natal Times and D'Urban Mercantile and Agricultural Gazette:* 1851 and 1852.   *Natal Witness:* from 1846.   *The Port Natal Almanac.* Printed and Published by J. Cullingworth, Durban, 1851.

—G.S.J.

DURBAN MUSIC SOCIETY, THE   This Society was started when a number of Durban music-lovers discussed the possibility of encouraging an interest in music through a non-profit organisation. The Durban Music Society was established on 8 June 1950 at the inaugural meeting held in the Mayor's Parlour in the City Hall. The objects of the Society were stated thus: to promote and advance interest in music; to provide social and cultural activities for members; to investigate matters of musical interest; to provide a concert platform for aspiring local artists; to give assistance to young artists for overseas study. — During the early years the Society's concerts were entirely dependent on members to provide musical items. The second phase in the Society's existence began in 1959 with the first international celebrity concert in the Art Gallery, featuring the Quintetto Boccherini of Rome. From then on attendance at concerts increased considerably and interest extended well beyond the members of the Society. Subsequent visits by international artists became progressively easier through collaboration with similar societies in other parts of the country. It was through the success of these concerts that membership increased substantially and after the formation of NAPAC, the Society concentrated solely on concerts by overseas artists. — One problem which was envisaged by the Society at least 10 years ago was the lack of venues for concerts; but this became less acute when the choice of venue was

441

extended beyond the City Hall and the University Students' Union to the Alhambra Theatre.

—G.S.J.

DURBAN OPERA COMPANY   D. Avrich, Durban 10, Durban Amateur Operatic Society, H. Haape, W. Heinen

DURBAN OPERA AND DRAMA SOCIETY   Durban Amateur Operatic Society

DURBAN OPERA GROUP   Durban 10, Durban Amateur Operatic Society, H. Menck

DURBAN OPERA SOCIETY   Durban Amateur Operatic Society

DURBAN ORCHESTRA, THE   For 55 years (1922-1977) the greatest single influence on the musical life of Durban has been its orchestra - a group of highly proficient instrumentalists entrusted (sometimes overburdened) with the dual task of educating and entertaining a heterogeneous community of residents and holidaymakers. — The designation Durban Orchestra was given to the first permanent professional body of musicians formed under Lyell-Tayler. This served to distinguish it from the Cape Town Municipal Orchestra*, the only other professional civic orchestra in the country at the time. At various times it has also been called the Durban Civic Orchestra - to give it status; the Durban Symphony Orchestra - to reaffirm its competence in undertaking the performance of major orchestral works; and the Durban Municipal Orchestra - to remind the public that it has to be paid for. — The Durban Orchestra was accepted in principle in February 1922, about seven months after the appointment of H. Lyell-Tayler* to the new post of Musical Director. The orchestra became a reality in May 1922. This achievement may have been regarded as a musical dream come true, or just as a realisation of a civic ambition, but the idea of a permanent orchestra had been growing in the minds of the people over a period of 40 years. — Since 1881, when the Durban Philharmonic Society* was started, there had been at least one amateur orchestra composed of hard-working string players, overpowered by exuberant regimental bandsmen who had a monotonous way of "filling in" the missing parts. The vogue for orchestral concerts which developed in the 1890s was sustained by the activities of a number of orchestral societies. No doubt the contemporary musical life of England inspired them: the experiment of Dan Godfrey's Bournemouth Municipal Orchestra in 1893 and the London Promenade Concerts under Henry Wood at the Queen's Hall from 1895 were both successful. In Durban, Lorenzo Mancini was the first to publicly raise the question of a permanent professional orchestra. In 1901, as leader of the Durban Orchestral Society*, he envisaged the nucleus of a permanent orchestra within the Society itself. The idea was prompted by the forthcoming royal visit of the Duke and Duchess of Cornwall and York (later George V and Queen Mary) and the musical requirements for a festive occasion. Mancini was thinking in terms of an orchestra of 22, an equal number of string and wind players, to be maintained at an estimated cost of R2 000 per annum. Such hopes and speculations were expressed in letters to the daily newspapers but they came to nothing. Five years later Mancini raised the subject again, this time at a specially convened meeting in August 1906 when he had the support of Houston Macdonald*, the borough organist, and Eustace Jackson, amateur cellist and head of the firm Jackson Brothers*. Nothing came of this either, for, as was pointed out at the meeting, there were too many musical cliques divided by petty jealousies to allow one permanent orchestra to remain unchallenged for very long. — Amateur orchestras

442

grew and flourished throughout the years prior to the First World War. The visit in August 1914 of the new Cape Town Orchestra under Theo Wendt*, revived the idea of a Durban Orchestra, and it is reasonable to assume that only the outbreak of war delayed steps towards its establishment. Frank Proudman*, the borough organist at the time, had a small orchestra but he, like so many others, believed the military band was the appropriate body to perform what became known as the "municipal music" of the war period. — In 1921 the Cape Town Orchestra paid another visit to Durban and re-affirmed the need for a local orchestra. But this sort of propaganda was by no means the intention of Theo Wendt and his orchestra. They were touring the country in order to remain solvent; in fact the very suggestion that Durban should have its own orchestra was interpreted as a threat to their prestige and livelihood, especially as it also implied that the touring prospects should be equitably shared between the two orchestras. — Lyell-Tayler arrived on 22 October 1921 and began his search for talent. At a time when employment was becoming difficult, musicians of professional standing hoped to gain a place in the new orchestra. However, they were disappointed and offended when, in February 1922, it became known that Lyell-Tayler, after rejecting the local musical talent, was on his way to Johannesburg to recruit players. The Musicians' Union made one last abortive attempt to vindicate their cause by cabling the International Confederation of Musicians, asking them to discourage all overseas members from accepting engagements. Finding "no suitable" players in Johannesburg either, Lyell-Tayler left for England in March 1922 and returned with an orchestra in May. All the members of the orchestra were then British, except for one Dutchman and F.J. Beswick, the bandsman who had deputised for Lyell-Tayler during his absence overseas. Harold Ketelbey* (leader), Stirling Robins* (deputy leader), Edgar Heap* (accompanist), Henry Oney (principal clarinettist) and Richard Cherry* (bassoonist) were five of the newcomers destined to play prominent parts in the musical life of the country of their adoption. — After the initial uproarious reception in the Town Hall on Saturday 27 May 1922, the conductor settled down to prepare the routine for daily concerts. His ensemble was frequently described as "Lyell-Tayler's famous Military Band and Municipal Orchestra - the finest combination in South Africa". They had to accustom themselves to play under all kinds of uncomfortable conditions and circumstances: in the Town Hall with its appalling acoustics (shortly afterwards improved at a cost of R20 000); at the windswept open-air Summer Palace on the Beach; and in the Pavilion where "you can enjoy Refreshments of Tea, Coffee, Minerals or Eskimo Pies, either in your seat or at the tables placed in the aisles. Just call the waiter and your order will be promptly executed". — In the first eleven weeks of its career the Durban Orchestra's concerts were run at a loss of R1 200. Evidently the orchestra needed to be popularised through free bandstand concerts at the Beach, operatic nights, lectures before the Thursday evening symphony concerts, and orchestral tour of the Rand. The tour took place in October 1922, but it did not help to alleviate financial difficulties, mainly as a result of insufficient publicity and a similar tour by the Cape Town Orchestra six months earlier. — In January 1925 the Durban Orchestra commenced broadcasting regularly. This was certainly financially beneficial at a time when the orchestra was facing the first of its financial and artistic crises: better prospects in Johannesburg attracted the leader and the principal cellist, and the unhappy revelation that the orchestra was still being run at a loss, forced Lyell-Tayler to accept what he had always detested - an orchestra convertible to a military band.

The high proportion of wind instruments to strings in the original orchestra did make it, sound more like a military band than a symphony orchestra (tonally acceptable in the earliest programmes which so often included Wagner's Overture to *Tannhäuser*, the Introduction to Act III of *Lohengrin*, and an orchestral arrangement of Rachmaninov's *Prelude in C sharp minor* - all very brassy and stirring). The fact was however that the parallel existence of a separate military band had always constituted a threat to an orchestra of symphonic stature. Durban had been musically educated on military bands by Frank Proudman and in a town which was rapidly becoming "the playground of South Africa where the season is always in full swing", a military band was sure to be popular. Evidently a great many people in Durban were convinced that a military band should replace the orchestra. World-wide unemployment of musicians in the 1920s and the financial struggles of two small municipal orchestras in South Africa also raised the controversial topic of a national orchestra - a scheme which Durban rejected as a matter of civic pride. — In November 1922 Lyell-Tayler drew public attention to the necessity for training young amateur orchestral players - especially string players - to augment the professional orchestra on special occasions, and in September 1925 the Durban Orchestral Society* made its debut, thereby increasing the strength of the Durban Orchestra from 30 to 65. This venture proved so successful that is was decided to dispense with the military band and continue with the orchestra only. During the third visit of the Cape Town Orchestra under its new conductor Leslie Heward*, the combined strength of the two professional orchestras was 62. — The musical history of Durban reveals that bands, military or brass, could not easily be suppressed. The municipal military band which had been eliminated towards the end of 1925, was suddenly revived in July 1926 when the New Durban Brass Band made its debut under a certain Horace Farr. Added to this musical setback was the unhappy disclosure in January 1927 that the Durban Orchestra was costing six times as much as it was earning. Lyell-Tayler was disillusioned and in September he accepted the post of Director of Music to African Theatres in Johannesburg. He left the orchestra in the care of the principal trombonist, Thomas Huddle, whose military presence on the rostrum was sustained by 21 years' service in the Coldstream Guards. In January 1928 the Durban Orchestra was described as "a mistake"; Lyell-Tayler, it was said, had been allowed to introduce "an expensive art luxury as an additional expense or more or less permanent charge on our small town". It was decided that the orchestra should not cost more than R16 000 per annum. This included a salary of R2 000 for the Musical Director and R800 for each of 28 players. The revenue, apart from an additional levy on ratepayers, came from the Broadcasting Company and the Orchestral Society. — The future of the orchestra looked uncertain. Frank Proudman, former Durban borough organist and bandmaster, recommended a municipal band in place of an orchestra, but in May 1928 Dan Godfrey* (Junior) arrived to become Musical Director, bringing an air of gaiety to Durban. He declared: "There must be a military band in a place like Durban"; in addition, a dance band, a new choral society, more light operettas; but above all, more popular entertainments at the Pavilion. By 1930 the orchestra had been reduced to 26 players but is was decided to retain it for another three years. The new military band was scheduled to make its first appearance in July 1931. — At this stage the responsibility for maintaining the artistic standard of the municipal orchestra became the special interest of the Durban Orchestral Society* under its devoted president, Otto Siedle*. They organised the annual series of symphony concerts and through their list of subscribers they helped to subsidize the subscription concerts of the "Symphony Season" and so they raised the level of musical taste. Some of the programmes were very ambitious (Elgar's *Falstaff* and *Symphony No. 2 in E flat;* Stravinsky's *Fire bird suite);* others were enhanced by the inclusion of a piano concerto rendered by such accomplished artists as Mrs Alexander Buchanan and Edgar Heap. — Every third year the Municipal Council reviewed the position of the orchestra and in April 1934 it was again in jeopardy. The country was in the grip of a depression and the orchestra was costing the Durban Municipality more than the stipulated R16 000. Compared with other amenities (Public Library, Art Gallery, Museum, Parks and Gardens) this was considered high, especially in view of a poor income of R2 000 from concerts. Furthermore, temporary musical prosperity on the Rand enticed at least six players from the Durban Orchestra to accept employment with African Theatres; E.J. Beswick, trombonist and bandmaster, died in July 1934; and in April 1935, while the orchestra was still "in the melting pot", Dan Godfrey died, leaving Thomas Huddle, the remaining trombonist, once again temporarily in command. — In response to the advertisement for a new Musical Director at a salary of R2 000 there were no less than 154 applicants. A short list of ten was submitted to Anderson Tyrer, noted British pianist, who at the time was one of the adjudicators at the Durban Eisteddfod. When, in August 1935, the appointment of Edward Dunn* was announced, the choice was highly commended. He was, according to press opinion, "a particularly successful musician from a business point of view"; besides which Durban, it was said, was growing tired of "inanimate" music through the media of gramophone, radio and film. — The new civic music policy under Edward Dunn was dictated largely by what had been tried successfully in Bournemouth. There were to be more symphony and "celebrity" concerts - if only to enhance the artistic reputation of the newly proclaimed City, more light entertainment, closer co-operation with educational authorities in Natal, and lectures on music to societies and clubs. Also, there was to be a military band which would combine, on occasion, in massed performances with visiting army bands. More publicity was essential. There would certainly have to be a choir; a students' week; and, of course, a dance band. All this, it was implied, would come within the scope of the new Music Director's duties. — Edward Dunn made his debut in the City Hall on 25 November 1935 - a gay-looking, light-hearted, pleasant-voiced Manchester man, destined to win great favour among the people of Durban. With an orchestra back to its original strength of 30, he was determined to pay attention to "what the people like". At the risk of putting showmanship before musicianship he started "to deliver the goods" in the form of "Happy Nights" at the Pavilion on Saturdays with the municipal dance band in attendance, musical comedy shows, lunch-hour concerts, music for the ballet and symphony concerts. An extra boost for the Durban Orchestra was the invitation to perform at Johannesburg's Empire Exhibition in the middle of November. — All went well with Edward Dunn and the orchestra until 1938. The South African Government assumed control of broadcasting and formed the SABC in 1936. Studio orchestras were created in Johannesburg, Cape Town and Durban and from September 1936 Dunn had the added responsibility of conducting a 40-piece Studio Orchestra. This meant that the broadcasts of the Durban Civic Orchestra were discontinued, resulting in a significant loss of revenue and a consequent reduction in the number of symphony concerts in the City Hall. Edward Dunn, dissatisfied with his heavy administrative duties and the "woeful ignorance" on musical matters of his employers, made it known that he was seeking an appointment elsewhere. In 1938 he went overseas, leaving Stirling Robins to deputise as conductor and Nat Kofsky*, newly appointed from London, as deputy-leader. A few months in England restored Edward Dunn's faith in Durban's potential for all kinds of musical and theatrical entertainment. He suggested an arts centre, a "little theatre", an open-air dance floor and a Viennese "Biergarten". Very soon the municipal band was performing regularly in the Town Gardens; accordion and harmonica bands filled the air with reedy sounds; and various sorts of young people appeared on the rostrum to prove their skill with the baton. — The orchestra of 1922 had changed considerably over the years and by September 1939, when war broke out in Europe, only four of the original members were left: Stirling Robins (leader since 1923), Edgar Heap (violinist and accompanist), Thomas H. Huddle (trombonist and deputy band conductor) and Harry Oney (principal clarinettist). Some who had joined in the late 1920s and 1930s were destined to remain a long time. Among them were Dodds Miller (flute), Robert ("Rusty") Beaton (trombone) and Edward Jacombs (oboe). Two veteran trumpeters, Charles Inglis and Ivor Clifford, retired recently. John Flanagan (flute), who joined the orchestra in 1925, died in 1940. Wartime conditions reduced the orchestral strength so drastically that full-scale concerts were possible only in combination with the Studio Orchestra. — At the end of the war, South Africa, with its sunny climate and world-wide reputation for war-time hospitality, attracted a number of musicians from different parts of Europe. In 1947 Edward Dunn was overseas for five weeks and engaged 24 musicians. Among them were Paul Martens* (violin), Ilona de Vos* (harp), Stefan Deak (violin) (who became joint leader with Ernest Hartley after the resignation of Stirling Robins in 1952 and subsequently leader of the orchestra) and G.C. Denholm*, a violinist, later to become chorus-master and deputy conductor. The new Durban Civic Orchestra of 45 players made its debut on 4 April 1948 in a Mayoral Command Performance in the City Hall. This was followed by an extensive orchestral tour of Natal, the OFS and the Eastern Cape arranged by Hugh Cairnduff (popularly known as "Jock Duff") who was manager of the Municipal Entertainments Department, and had been responsible for organising entertainments for thousands of troops passing through Durban during the war years. — During the post-war period the Durban Orchestra was involved in a great variety of musical activities: Thursday evening symphony concerts, late afternoon mid-week concerts, promenade concerts at the beach-front amphitheatre, Sunday popular concerts, ballet, opera, variety concerts, military band concerts and talent contests. Throughout the country there was much talk about youth in relation to music, and people began to think nationally. In 1949 the National Theatre Organisation made its third tour of the country and in November of that year the National Council of Music of South Africa was formed with Edward Dunn as its first chairman. The various National Arts Festivals of Youth grew out of this period against the background of the Durban Orchestra and the new Civic Junior Orchestra under Arthur Tempest*. There were happy episodes in the orchestral life of the community during the early 1950s when young and old, professional and amateur, combined to further the interests of young musicians (many of them young children) entering upon the experience of orchestral playing. The success of this "new approach" should be attributed to Edward Dunn, whose achievements on behalf of youth and music made a nation-wide impact. — During the Festival of Music to commemorate the Durban Centenary Celebrations of 1954 a Civic Orchestra of 60 players and John Manduell, a protégé of

446

Edward Dunn, achieved prominence. Manduell, a highly-gifted 26-year-old conductor and composer, chose to pursue his musical career in Britain and did not succeed Edward Dunn, who resigned from the post of Musical Director in July 1954, after 19 years' service. He made his last appearance on 26 August 1954 with three other local celebrities: Rose Alper* (soprano), Christina Greig* (mezzo-soprano) and Edgar Heap (piano). — The departure of Edward Dunn marked the end of a musical era. For 32 years the Musical Director had been compelled to fulfil the role of chief civic entertainer - on the pattern of the popular seaside conductor who has to master the art of dispensing music with a smile. After the short term of office of Dr William Pickerill*, who died in May 1955, Frits Schuurman* was appointed Music Director. Under Schuurman the orchestra assumed the dignity of a symphony orchestra with the City Hall as the most appropriate venue for its performances. He sustained the Durban Civic Orchestra, as it was usually called, over a period of recurrent crises lasting ten years. Unfortunately his term of office coincided with a period of orchestral depression. When Edward Dunn resigned, it was suggested that the orchestra be disbanded. This had been the fate of the Studio Orchestra at the end of 1953, leaving a number of musicians facing an uncertain future. The creation of a large SABC orchestra in Johannesburg was, in fact, the beginning of the "national" orchestra which was first mooted in 1922 and had remained a vague possibility since then. Orchestral players were therefore on the move: George Walker* and Else Menge joined the Durban Civic Orchestra at the end of 1953: the former to become leader in April 1958 (after the departure overseas of Stefan Deak in July 1957) and the latter sub-leader. In 1964 a salary crisis developed and musicians began to leave the orchestra - among them "Rusty" Beaton, who retired after 34 years as trombonist. Very soon the orchestra was again reduced to 40 players. — In 1963 the Municipal Council gave considerable financial backing to the Youth Music Festival of the International Arts League of Youth held in July 1964 and the Beethoven Festival of the same year, both directed by the celebrated young Pierino Gamba. The success of both festivals intensified the disillusionment of Frits Schuurman, who seemed to have lost the confidence of his public. A plan for increasing the orchestra from 45 to 60 players was discussed in August 1964 and improved salary scales were announced in March 1965. — Frits Schuurman's contract expired on 31 March 1966 and there was a strong rumour that Alfred Walther, a visiting Austrian-born operatic conductor, might be the new conductor. In October 1965 the new post of business manager to the Municipal Department of Music was established, to relieve the conductor of administrative work. The new conductor, now called the "resident conductor", was to be appointed for limited periods so that he might return to Europe each year. — Throughout its history there has always been considerable opposition to the Durban orchestra as an amenity with limited appeal and one that loses money. It has survived mainly on the assertion that an orchestra is just as essential to the life of a city, as, for example, an art gallery. The old argument was revived more fiercely than ever before in December 1965, when the maintenance of the orchestra was costing about R190 000 a year. — In the early part of 1966 a wave of sympathy for Frits Schuurman resulted in public recognition of his services and his great interpretative skill as a conductor. When his contract expired on 31 March he left the musical scene of Durban without any desire to return. A month later Alfred Walther was appointed resident conductor. With 15 new players from overseas, the orchestra was increased from 45 to 60 players and made its debut under the new conductor on 12 September. The concert

447

routine remained as before: Thursday symphony concerts each week; free Sunday afternoon concerts conducted by Charles Denholm*, the deputy conductor, and Sunday night popular concerts. Walther, like his predecessors, urged very strongly that a School of Music be started to train future players. Preliminary talks at symphony concerts revived what had been started 45 years ago by Lyell-Tayler. In 1967 two large works were added to the orchestral repertoire: Mahler's *Second symphony* and Shostakovich's *Fifth symphony*. Encouraged by a few spectacular successes, Walther left for Europe at the end of the summer concert season with the intention of recruiting more players for the new season starting in September 1967, but was quite unsuccessful. Meanwhile a winter concert season continued under the Spanish conductor Alberto Bolet who conducted a performance of Fauré's *Requiem* with the assistance of Heather Brandon* and the Symphonic Choir. When the resident conductor returned, he introduced works by Kodaly, Viktor Kalabis, Bruckner, Bartok, Karl Haidmayr and Menahem Avidom, giving his programmes a new spirit of internationalism and exoticism. — About the middle of 1968 the orchestra faced another crisis on the question of finance. A new set of statistics revealed that the orchestra was costing R250 000 and drawing only 10 000 people a year. A spirit of discontent prevailed among the players and by November the City Council was still divided on the question whether Walther was suitable as conductor; and while they agreed that the salary for the post be raised, the question of Walther's reappointment remained undecided. In the midst of this state of unrest an unexpected advertising gimmick was thrown out to the public in the form of "A Classical Beat Concert". This attracted over 2 000 people of all ages, some of whom were turned away at the door. Apart from a few rhythmic guitar and percussion effects added to a Bach Brandenburg Concerto, the programme was conventionally serious. Some members of the orchestra looked uncomfortable in their informal dress and·Alfred Walther, the conductor, was conspicuous in a red shirt. This belated publicity did remind a great many young people that Durban had its own orchestra, but there was more trouble brewing between the conductor and manager of the Municipal Department of Music and in August 1969 Alfred Walther cabled his final decision: he was not returning for the season starting in September. — Recently (1970) a committee of inquiry on the future of the orchestra recommended that the whole orchestra be handed over to NAPAC, but NAPAC found the proposal unacceptable and a compromise has been worked out to provide a temporary solution: since 1969 the services of the orchestra have been hired out to the Performing Arts Councils of Natal and the OFS. — When not occupied in this fashion the orchestra was expected to sustain the traditional sequence of symphony concerts etc. under the baton of visiting guest conductors. Its maintenance rose steadily however and in the year of its jubilee (1972) the cost of the orchestra had reached R300 000. In the end the City Council was forced to the conclusion that this institution was beyond its means and by a majority of votes the history of the Durban Orchestra was brought to a close.

BIBLIOGRAPHY

JACKSON, G.S.: *Music in Durban: an account of musical activities in Durban from 1850 to the early years of the present century.* HSRC publication series no. 6. Witwatersrand University Press, Johannesburg, 1970.   SIEDLE, O.: *Siedle saga: reminiscences and reflections.* Knox Publishing Co., Durban, 1940.

SOURCES

The Durban civic orchestra. *Res Musicae* III/1, September 1956; V/3, March 1959; VII/2, March 1961. *Natal Advertiser:* from 1878; *Natal Daily News:* from 1937. *Natal Mercury Pictorial:* 1904 - 1921. Early programmes placed at the author's disposal by Mr. George Walker and Miss Hilda Dawson.

—G.S.J.

DURBAN ORCHESTRAL SOCIETY, THE   In one of the local newspapers of July 1888, someone made the comment that musical societies in Durban seldom lasted more than three years. This was written when the Durban Philharmonic Society*, struggling into the seventh year of its uncertain existence, informed the public that it intended "going into retreat" - a way of intimating that in future the Society would not be giving more concerts. Neither choir nor orchestra actually appeared in public again. — A month later, in August, a new orchestral society was formed. The members arranged to meet for practice once a week under their conductor Herr C.J.H. Eberlein*, a newcomer to Durban, whose knowledge of music in all its branches made him an acquisition to the community. This was to be "a private society for the study and practice of music". The Durban Orchestral Society started in February 1888, when 13 instrumentalists provided the musical background for a flower show. The Society's rapid growth into an orchestra of symphonic proportions was remarkable. Invitations to join the new society soon increased the membership to 82 subscribers; and at the first concert on 18 September 1888, no less than 40 players took part in a programme which included the overture to *Rosamunde*(Schubert) and the march from *La reine de Saba* (Gounod). Young Beatrice Stuart* (later Marx*) made one of her first concert appearances as solo violinist, and Herr Eberlein, her teacher, played a number of violin solos himself. Among the singers who appeared as soloists was Otto Siedle*. He was associated with the Durban Orchestral Society for 50 years. Most of the 40 members of the new orchestra - who presumptuously called themselves the "Durban Orchestra" had belonged to the orchestra of the Durban Philharmonic Society; and when Herr Eberlein was highly praised for training a body of musicians who "stirred the musical depths of Durban", it was pointed out in the press that at least some of the credit should have gone to Duncan MacColl*, the founder of the pioneer orchestra in 1881. — In spite of the spectacular growth of the new orchestral society its lifetime was about two years, during which the expenses were about R240 per annum. With only limited funds at their disposal, the members could not afford to hire a room large enough to accommodate the orchestra for rehearsals. The Society concluded its second series of concerts on 13 December 1889, and at the same time its existence. The collapse of the Durban Orchestral Society was partly due also to lack of players, a misfortune aggravated by the quick succession of theatrical companies that arrived in Durban at this time. Competent amateurs were enticed into theatre orchestras and became, for a short period, professionals. As the vogue for operettas continued into the early 1890s, it was difficult to sustain the activities of any amateur orchestra outside of private schools. — It was unfortunate that the second Durban Orchestral Society, started by Frank Proudman* in 1899, should have created a spirit of bitter rivalry. The orchestra of the Durban Musical Association*, established with the aid of a municipal subsidy in 1896, was sacrificed to the demands of the new society, whose inauguration in September 1899 owed much to the arrival of refugee musicians from Johannesburg on the outbreak of war; the membership of the association increased rapidly to over 120. The new orchestra of 34 included a generous sprinkling of

449

professionals, and was beyond doubt the finest orchestra heard in Durban up to that time: *1st Violins:* Mrs Proudman (leader), Miss Alice Irving, Mr H. Ferranti, Mr W. Abeleven, Miss Mary Howard, Mr F. Hirst, Mr Gundelfinger, Mr P. McMahon. *2nd Violins:* Mr H.W. Slade, Mr E. Lezard*, Mr Hoyette, Miss G. Field, Miss Edith Oakes, Miss Andrews. *Violas:* Mr B. Ormand, Mr W.M. Ridgway. *Cellos:* Mr E.L. Jackson, Mr C. Hoby*. *Double basses:* Mr Taylor, Mr J.M. Hammond. *Flute:* Mr F.C. Hollander. *Oboes:* Mr C. Bell, Mr L. Jackson. *Clarinets:* Mr H. Field, Mr S.C. Baylis. *Horns:* Mr J.C. Baker, Mr Thompson. *Cornets:* Mr N.S. Thorpe, Mr Scott. *Trombones:* Mr H. Dring, Mr Ogilvie. *Tuba:* Mr E. Rasmussen. *Timpani:* Mr A.W. Cullingworth. *Conductor:* Mr Frank Proudman*. — When Proudman accepted the appointment of organist to the Presbyterian Church in Kimberley towards the end of 1899, Charles Hoby trained and conducted the orchestra for a period of about 6 years. He was fortunate in securing the services of the violinist Lorenzo Mancini as leader of the orchestra. It was Mancini who, in 1901, envisaged the ensemble of 42 players as a possible municipal orchestra. Under Charles Hoby the repertoire of the orchestra blossomed into something that was both varied and attractive; it owed much to the prevailing musical taste of London, as expressed in the earlier programmes of the Promenade Concerts under Henry Wood at Queen's Hall. The works consisted of a number of exciting, exotic pieces by Tchaikovsky and the contemporary composer Edvard Grieg; Schubert's *Marche militaire* and *Unfinished symphony;* as much Wagner as was manageable within the limitations of a small orchestra; and new successes by Elgar, including *Chanson de matin.* Beethoven was represented by the overtures *Prometheus* and *Egmont* and the first local performance of his *Fifth symphony* (August 1903). On the lighter side there was the music of Edward German; in true "Prom" style Haydn's *"Farewell" symphony* closed that season. — There had been signs in 1903 that the orchestra was declining in strength and popularity. Nevertheless the DOS boasted in 1904 that they were the only society of their kind in South Africa; and in 1906 they reasserted their claims to recognition as a Durban municipal orchestra - again without success. In the meantime the Berea Choral Society was revived and created another musical diversion for the public as well as a further attraction for orchestral members of the DOS. Moreover, in March 1904 a new Town Band was beginning to attract attention with smart uniforms and gay music offered in public parks and gardens. After Hoby's departure in 1906, no effort was made to continue the activities of the DOS. A new era of choral singing started in 1905 and lasted for some eight or nine years. The visit of the Cape Town Orchestra* created a passing interest in orchestral concerts in 1914. During the Great War orchestral playing was kept alive by Frank Proudman, whose municipal orchestra of 30 players, with Eugene Benzon as leader, performed in the Town Hall on Sunday evenings. — Towards the end of the World War amateur orchestral playing was revived by Reg Woodroffe*. In 1918 he formed the group of players (usually about 30 in number) called Reg Woodroffe's Orchestra, and continued for 15 years as trainer, and as conductor of many concerts given in support of charity. When the first all-professional Durban Orchestra was formed in 1922, amateur orchestral players suffered a temporary setback. But Otto Siedle, who was the President of Reg Woodroffe's Orchestra, re-established the Durban Orchestral Society (the third since 1888) in March 1925. The objects of the new society were twofold: (1) to interest a sufficiently large number of members, whose subscriptions would relieve the heavy financial burden on the Durban Orchestra, and who, by their support, could guarantee an annual symphony season; and (2) to encourage amateurs to cultivate the art of orchestral playing as guest members of the professional orchestra when, on special occasions, they were invited to augment it (to about 60 players). Reg Woodroffe's Orchestra was disbanded in 1934. The DOS continued to sponsor subscription concerts. The only other group that maintained a more or less permanent amateur orchestra was the Municipal Choral and Light Opera Society. — In 1937 Sydney Payne took over the conductorship of amateur players in the DOS, and at the time of his departure for England in 1938 his orchestra numbered about 50 players. They became a separate entity called the Philharmonia Orchestra, and like Proudman's orchestras of 1899 and of the War years, it was an orchestra of amateurs supported by professionals. Ultimately this orchestra gained official recognition and some financial assistance from the Durban Corporation; it thus became the responsibility of Edward Dunn*, the City's Music Director. — The DOS continued as a society of music lovers devoted to listening. The increase in membership of the Durban Orchestral Society from 98 in March 1937 to 243 in November 1939 was attributed to the success of classes in musical appreciation conducted by Edward Dunn, under the auspices of the Workers' Educational Association. Since the Second World War there has been no attempt to revive the DOS. — The twofold aims formulated in 1925 have been accepted as responsibilities by two separate societies: the Philharmonic Society Orchestra (with its off-shoot, the Junior Civic Orchestra) provides training that might one day lead to professional status; and the Durban Musical Society* sponsors celebrity concerts, which help to maintain a high standard of orchestral and chamber music. Since 1888 when the DOS was started, the aim of all societies has remained the same: to bring together as many music-lovers as possible for the enjoyment of music, either as performers or as listeners.

BIBLIOGRAPHY

JACKSON, GEORGE S.: *Music in Durban from 1850 to 1900*. D. Phil. thesis, University of the Witwatersrand, Johannesburg, 1961.

SOURCES

Natal Advertiser: 1878 - 1937.   *Natal Mercury:* from 1888.

—G.S.J.

DURBAN PHILHARMONIC SOCIETY, THE   The first society of this name was established circa November 1851 in circumstances which were suitably informal for those early days. Somewhere in Union Street - which still exists as a short narrow lane between West and Pine Streets - a few young men rented a house. Because there was no regular entertainment in the town, they provided their own during the evenings by climbing onto the iron roof for singing practices. These were conducted by one of the group who beat out the time (with much energy and noisy emphasis) for the hymn tunes and secular songs they chose to render. If only for their attempts to sing in parts, they were entitled to call themselves a "glee club"; but the disturbance they created in the process made them nothing more than a public nuisance, and the local residents requested they practise their art elsewhere. A benefactor in the person of George Cato - who became the first mayor of Durban - offered them a room on his own estate near Durban where they could sing, play or smoke in what became a young men's club. — With this change to a more favourable environment the original glee club became the

Durban Philharmonic Society, consisting of about a dozen young bachelors who were exclusive enough to make celibacy a condition of membership. Their talents were soon transferred to playing instruments, which resulted in the formation of the first "orchestra" in Durban. In 1853 it had at least 16 members: Thomas Cato, John P. Cato, D. Hull, J.J. Chapman, W. Swift, W. Palmer, W. Grant, W. Fraser, J. Cubitt, J.F. Baumann, J.L. Cullingworth, Thring, C.J. Cato, W.H. Cullingworth, W. Throssell and W. Hart. At one concert in 1855 there were as many as 20 players. It is not known with certainty which instruments they played, but early concert notices name several flautists and at least one fairly accomplished violinist (W. Fraser). William Swift, organist at the Central Methodist Church for over 60 years, was a violinist in this early ensemble. Daniel Hull, who played the harmonium and doubled as conductor, described himself as a "professional". — After 1855 there is no further mention of the activities of this society whose orchestra, or band as it really was, provided so much of the music in the early soirées and concerts. Musicians in Durban became more interested in the formation of choral societies consisting of small groups of singers who came together through the concert activities of various churches - notably the Congregational and Methodist - in the early 1860s. The first of the larger choral societies grew out of the secular glee-singing of St Paul's Anglican Church choir and became the nucleus of the choral society of 1881. — The second Durban Philharmonic Society under Duncan MacColl was thought to be at least 12 years overdue. Ever since 1868 when the Pietermaritzburg Philharmonic Society* was formed, musicians in Durban were more than a little ashamed of their own failure to establish a similar organisation of comparable strength. Unlike the Pietermaritzburg Philharmonic Society, the Durban Philharmonic Society was trained and conducted by a man who made no claim to be an expert musician: MacColl was the local representative of Dunn and Company, shipping agents. He started regular practices in June 1881 with the assistance of Gustav Monhaupt, a German horn-player whose superior knowledge of orchestral technique was a useful supplement to MacColl's limited musical experience, almost entirely restricted to choir training. The first concert took place on 15 September 1881 with a choir of 40 and an orchestra of 13. Called the "Philharmonic Orchestra" and led by J.N. Hoffman, it consisted of nine string players and four wind players. By September 1882 the choir had reached a strength of 120 and were ready to attempt the presentation of standard large-scale works. An early success, mainly from the point of view of publicity rather than technical achievement, was the performance of *Elijah* at the opening of the Theatre Royal in November 1882. — Most of the Society's concerts were given in the Oddfellow's Hall, which formerly stood in West Street in the heart of present-day Motor Town, and quite close to the scene of those early musical escapades in Union Street. The Society secured a lease on the hall at a cost of R36 a year, and provided 600 chairs and 20 lamps: thereafter the hall was known as the "Philharmonic Hall". — The Philharmonic Society had a hard struggle for survival. In 1883 it was costing R500 a year to keep it going. About half of this sum was being used to transport the members to and from rehearsals on municipal horse trams. Festive occasions, such as the opening of the Town Hall in 1885 and Queen Victoria's Jubilee in 1887, helped to keep the Society alive, but the final dissolution was inevitable. By 1888 the Durban Philharmonic Society was reduced in size and prestige to the 40 singers who were described as "MacColl's Choir". MacColl himself attributed the decline of the Society to the difficulties and high cost of transport and not in any way to lack of interest in music? — Subsequent philharmonic societies in Durban have all been orchestral. In January 1909 Sydney Payne gave his first choral and orchestral concert in the Town Hall (the present Post Office) and was assisted by two excellent tenors: Harold Payne (his brother) and Harry Evans*. Sydney Payne's musical interest was predominantly theatrical and in his presentations of such works as *Cavalleria rusticana* and *Faust,* in concert version, he was obliged to invite the assistance of the Durban Musical Association* choir. The amateur orchestra he conducted was that of the Philharmonic Society which he had revived; but soon after the death of Harold Payne in April 1912, the orchestra became affiliated to the Durban Musical Association under Frank Proudman*, the borough organist, and the Philharmonic Society lost its identity. Sydney Payne resumed his work as an orchestral conductor with the revival of the Bijou Orchestra at the Criterion, the newly-opened variety theatre, in 1912. — In April 1937 Edward Dunn devised a scheme for enlarging the Durban Orchestra for special occasions by using amateurs, who were invited to join the professional orchestra in what was then described as the "Durban Philharmonic Orchestra". They were members of the Amateur Orchestral Society under Sydney Payne. This was the origin of the present Durban Philharmonic Society of orchestral players; which is also a training school for young players who might one day aspire to professional status in the Civic Orchestra. Sydney Payne left Durban for England in September 1938 after 29 years as teacher, church organist, choir-trainer, musical director of many theatrical shows and foremost conductor of Durban's amateur orchestras, some of which attained a strength of 50 players. — One of the schemes for providing young musicians with concert experience as soloists, was the Federated Music Clubs, initiated somewhat unsuccessfully in the middle 1920s by Ellie Marx* and Beatrice Stuart*. These were revived with considerable success ten years later in various towns and cities of South Africa. Under the auspices of the South African Society of Music Teachers* Dodds Miller, flautist in the Durban Orchestra, sponsored one of the first Music Club evenings in June 1940. A year later he established what became the Durban Philharmonic Orchestra as a separate orchestra for young players. In 1948 the Philharmonic Society under the direction of Roy Carter*, principal cellist of the Durban Orchestra, came under the aegis of the Municipal Entertainments Department. The venue for rehearsals was the Elizabeth Crookes Hall, now called the "Y Club". This prepared the way for the series of post-war youth festivals and the valuable training of student orchestras by other Natal musicians: Lynette James*, Zoe Frost and Arthur Tempest. — In 1955 George Walker*, the last leader of the Durban Orchestra, was appointed conductor of the amateur orchestra of the Philharmonic Society. This afforded a number of young performers their first opportunity to appear as soloists in the City Hall. The Philharmonic Orchestra has long since ceased to be a youth orchestra. The two recognised subsidiary orchestral groups to the Durban Orchestra were the predominantly adult Philharmonic Orchestra and the Junior Civic Orchestra. Until recently the Philharmonic Orchestra was trained and conducted by Paul Martens*; the juniors are still being trained by Charles Denholm*. — The spirit of the Philharmonic Society orchestra remains the same as it was in the 1850s: amateurs, whether highly skilled or just beginners, meet regularly solely for the love of making music together. The Philharmonic Orchestra's free concerts - all too few - draw an audience of between 800 and 1 000 on a Sunday afternoon. The players have the satisfaction of appearing in public and young soloists have an opportunity to make their debut before an audience which is appreciative without being too critical.

BIBLIOGRAPHY

JACKSON, GEORGE S.: *Music in Durban: an account of musical activities in Durban from 1850 to the early years of the present century.* HSRC publication series no. 6. Witwatersrand University Press, Johannesburg 1970. MARX, BEATRICE: *She shall have music: the memoirs of Beatrice Marx.* W.J. Flesch & Partners, Cape Town, 1961. RUSSELL, G.: *History of old Durban and reminiscences of an emigrant of 1850.* P. Davis & Sons, Durban, 1899. SIEDLE, O.: *Reminiscences and reflections.* Knox Publishing Co., Durban, 1940.

SOURCES

Natal Advertiser: 1878-1937. *Natal Daily News:* 1937 onwards. *Natal Mercury:* 1852 onwards.

—G.S.J.

DURBAN SELECT CHOIR   H. Dyer, E. Slatter, T. Wiercx

DURBAN STUDIO ORCHESTRA   Durban, Durban Orchestra, T. Wiercx

DURBAN SYMPHONIC CHOIR   H. Brandon

DURELL, MRS. H.   Selma Whitehouse

DUTCH MALE VOICE CHOIR, VAN DER BIJL PARK, THE   Like the German Male Voice Choir, the Dutch Male Voice Choir - also known as the Crescendo Male Voice Choir - was formed by immigrants concerned chiefly with the steel industry in Van der Bijl Park. The choir grew out of a nucleus of twenty Dutchmen who held a gathering in Van der Bijl Park in April 1952, to commemorate the third centenary of the Dutch settlement in South Africa. In the course of time a committee was formed from choir members who were responsible for the choir's management. — Under the guidance of Mr Hough, choir-master for the first one and a half years of the choir's existence, membership continued to grow until it numbered 40, and performances were given at church functions and gatherings of cultural societies. Hough was succeeded by Te Vaarwerk in 1953. Following this take-over, more attention was given to German, Dutch, French and Russian songs, instead of the Afrikaans and English songs which, until then, had dominated the choir's repertoire. Apart from concert performances in Van der Bijl Park, the choir also sang in Vereeniging, Pretoria, Johannesburg and Welkom, as well as on radio. — Towards the end of 1960, eleven of the choir members had already left Van der Bijl Park and no replacements could be found. The choir's tenth anniversary was celebrated by only 24 members, and shortly afterwards it was temporarily dissolved. Notwithstanding a revival in 1965 (after a period of inactivity lasting three years), the choir finally ceased to exist in 1966.

—B.M.O.

DUTHIE, T.H.   R. Müller (Pty) Ltd

DU TOIT, BETTIE (MRS VAN DER WALT)   Middelburg

DU TOIT, DANIE   C.L. Venter

DU TOIT, LILIAN (NÉE ZIERVOGEL)   Graaff Reinet 8

DU TOIT, PAULA (PSEUDONYM))   Paula Richfield

DU TOIT, PETRONELLA M. (NELLIE) (MRS P. CROUSE),   *17 December 1929 in Pietersburg; now (1977) in Pretoria. Lyric soprano with dramatic qualities, teacher of singing. Nellie du Toit comes from a musical family and exhibited her natural bent for singing

454

at an early age. When she was sixteen years of age, she sang in an operetta for the first time. After completing her school education in 1946, she entered for the newly-created Diploma in Opera Singing at the SA College of Music in Cape Town and became a pupil of Adelheid Armhold*. Whilst a student she sang parts in university operas produced by Gregorio Fiasconaro*, such as *Gianni Schicchi, Sister Angelica* and *Beatrice and Benedict*. In 1952 she obtained the Diploma with distinction and left for England. Before her departure she sang in a Festival Performance of Mahler's *Fourth symphony* during the Van Riebeeck Tricentenary celebrations. — In England she studied singing under Tatiana Makushina and interpreted a number of roles for the National English Opera Company on their tours in Great Britain, including parts in *La nozze di Figaro* and *La cenerentola*. On her return to South Africa she toured through the country with Marcel Wittrisch. She continued her study of singing and impressed the examiners for the Licentiate examination to the extent of being invited to participate in the competition for the Overseas Bursary of the University of South Africa. She was successful and left for Vienna in 1956 to obtain experience and to study under Maria Hittorff for a few months. — In the period from 1957 until 1962 Nellie du Toit was actively engaged in various opera productions of Alessandro Rota's National Opera Society of South Africa*, the Opera Vereniging van Suid-Afrika (OPSA)*, the Pretoria Opera Group*, and the South African Federation of Opera*. In 1957 she sang Madame Butterfly for the first time in Rota's production. Since then she has interpreted this role more than 100 times and in 1973 was awarded the Nederburg Opera Prize for her Cape performance of the part. In all, she has been the recipient of this prize three times. Apart from her opera achievements she also sang in oratorios, notably in Pretoria, where she was engaged by the Afrikaanse Musiekklub* for their choral ventures. In 1958 she shared the honours with Gert Potgieter* in the world première of Henk Badings's radiophonic opera *Asterion* (N.P. van Wyk Louw). At a later stage she again sang in the première of a work by Badings, *Die ballade van die bloeddorstige jagter* (G.A. Watermeyer). This work was awarded an international prize in Italy in 1971. — She sang in Prof. Erik Chisholm's production of John Joubert's *Droogte* in 1958 and again under Chisholm's direction in 1961, when she had a leading role in the world première of the same composer's *Silas Marner*. After 1963 she was increasingly engaged in the opera productions of the four provincial Regional Councils for the Performing Arts and her repertoire increased to 25 different operas, including *Jenufa* by Janacek (1976). The art of singing Lieder was also cultivated, generally to the pianoforte accompaniment of Hennie Joubert*. — From 1959 to 1961 Nellie du Toit was lecturer for singing at the Pretoria Conservatoire for Music*, but since then she has taught privately only. Among those who have benefited from her teaching are Gé Korsten*, George Kok and Rikie Venter.

—J.P.M.

Du VAL, CHARLES, *1850 in Manchester; °23 February 1889 in the Red Sea. Entertainer.

Born of English and French parentage, young Charles, while in his teens, abandoned his law studies in favour of a stage career. He joined a repertory theatre at Oldham in Lancashire, and a few months later went to Dublin, where he discovered his true metier, as an entertainer rather than as an actor. It was there that he first devised his two-hour one-man entertainment, "Odds and ends", which had an immediate and lasting success. — In the early 1870s he toured England and Ireland with a ventriloquist named Arthur Fry. As a result of ill-health, Du Val was advised to take a trip to South Africa. On 29 November 1879 Charles and his wife Lily, together with Fry and his puppets, sailed for Cape Town, arriving on 18 December. He hired the Athenaeum Theatre, and over a period of 3 weeks during the Christmas season, gave 22 performances. In spite of competition and a measure of hostility from Captain Disney Roebuck and his Company playing at the Cape Town Theatre, he drew good houses and had excellent notices. At the conclusion of his Cape Town stay, Du Val arranged "a grand farewell concert and a benefit night" at the open air theatre in the Good Hope Gardens. The band of the 91st Highlanders played, and Roebuck joined him on the stage in a fine display of magnanimity. According to the *Cape Times,* the occasion was an enormous personal success for Du Val. On 10 January 1880, Fry took his ventriloquist dolls to the Castle, and demonstrated them to the Zulu King Cetewayo. — On Saturday 17 January, the Du Val Company left by train for the Diamond Fields, travelling in open cattle trucks between Montagu Road and Beaufort West, and from there by coach in 5 days to Kimberley. There he collected a Russian-Polish character called Grab, and purchased a mule wagon and four horses from him for R360. Another pair was eventually added to the team and the words "Du Val Tonight" were painted on the cover of the wagon. From February to November their itinerary took them through the Free State, down into the Eastern Cape (Graaff Reinet from 26 to 31 May), through Natal and then to the Transvaal, arriving in Pretoria on 8 November. Travelling conditions and hotels were appalling, but he describes his adventures in a good-humoured way in his book *With a show through Southern Africa* (1884). The "theatres" were often primitive: at Senekal they had a galvanized-iron wool-shed festooned with biltong; the audience sat on barrows, a couple of ploughs and a great stack of wool bales. From November 1880 to April 1881 he experienced the First War of Independence and the 100-day siege of Pretoria. In addition to putting on a show for the British troops, he took a leading part in arranging concerts and theatricals to relieve the tedium of the siege. Du Val joined the Pretoria Carabineers (or D'Arcy's Horse), took part in two engagements outside the town (in one of which he had his horse shot under him), managed to get himself attached to Colonel Gildea's staff as Information Officer and, with the help of Charles Deecker, edited and largely wrote a siege paper named *The News of the Camp,* published thrice weekly. — The siege over, Du Val left for Kimberley and Port Elizabeth (where he and Fry parted company), and finally proceeded to Cape Town, where he arrived on 17 July 1881. En route he teamed up with a young American pianist, Albert Thies, who accompanied Pauline Bredelli* on her 1883 tour. Thies appeared with him at the Mutual Hall, Cape Town, then at Mossel Bay and Oudtshoorn, and finally in a week of one-night stands in the Boland area. Before their departure for England on 13 September 1881, Du Val gave a series of "magic-lantern" lectures on the Transvaal War, in Cape Town. — From 1881-1888 he lived, chiefly in London, in very comfortable circumstances; but about the middle of March 1888, Charles and Lily were back in Cape Town. He appeared at Durban on 10 and 12 April, at Pietermaritzburg on the 13th, then again at Durban. In May he reached Johannesburg, where he played to full houses at the Theatre Royal, introducing celebrated turns, such as "Signor Howlerini", the "Agony column", "Chawley of ours", "Professore Dullbore" and the "Town crier". In July he was reported to be doing good business at Barberton. The *Gold Fields News* wrote, "who can say there is no money in the place when the Exchange was crammed on Tuesday and Thursday evenings with people, who paid 50c for standing room to see Du Val". August found him in Estcourt, Newcastle and Ladysmith; September in Kimberley; October in Bloemfontein, and by early December he was back in Cape Town. After Christmas, the Du Vals sailed for Ceylon, stopping for a few days in Durban. Soon after they arrived at Colombo, Du Val was taken seriously ill. The cause was variously given as sunstroke or "an Eastern fever". The tour had to be cancelled and a passage was immediately booked to England via the Suez Canal. As they passed through the Red Sea, he vanished overboard. — Du Val had been one of the most popular entertainers of his age, and the English and South African newspapers carried long obituaries of a famous stage personality. The bewildering speed with which he changed both costume and character was frequently remarked on. He was extremely good-looking, with an attractive singing voice and a wonderful gift of mimicry. His most famous impersonation, performed in various countries for about 15 years, was "Miss Bella Dashaway, the ballroom belle".

BIBLIOGRAPHY
DU VAL, C.: *With a show through Southern Africa*, 2 vols. Tinsley Bros., London, 1884.

SOURCE
ALLEN, VIVIENNE: Charles du Val. *Pretoria News*, 13 May 1971.

—C.G.H.

DUVE, GABRIELE, (NÉE GEIER),   *30 March 1925 in Cologne; at present (1976) in Freiburg. Harpsichordist.

Gabriele Duve's mother taught her to play the piano and after the Second World War she continued her studies at the new Staatliche Hochschule für Musik in Freiburg, Western Germany, under the guidance of Prof. K.A. Schirmer (piano) (1946-1950). She subsequently became a private music teacher and repetitor at the Conservatorium for Eurhythmics in Stuttgart-Köngen. — In 1951 she had the opportunity of leaving post-war Germany to train as a nurse in South Africa. After she had completed her training in 1954, she again turned to music with the harpsichord as her speciality. In 1956-1957 and again in 1962, she visited Freiburg, to study under Prof. Fritz Neumeyer. Since making her debut in Johannesburg in 1958 with her Musica Antiqua ensemble, of which the other members were Eva Tamassy* (flute) and Gerard van de Geest* (viola da gamba), Gabriele Duve has been heard in orchestral concerts, in ensembles, and as soloist at concerts and over the radio. She also visits Europe on occasion, and gives recitals there. A couple of records were made of her playing and distributed commercially. — Gabriele Duve is a founder member of the Johannesburg Rare Music Guild*, and was a part-time lecturer in harpsichord and clavichord playing at the Music Academy of the Pretoria University*. In 1974 she left South Africa and is at present living in Freiburg.

—Ed.

DYER, JOHN HAROLD,   *26 August 1883 in Durban; °11 July 1951 in Durban. Choral conductor, music teacher, organist and composer.

Dyer was first taught in Durban by Charles Hoby* and R. Houston Macdonald* and then in Johannesburg by Prof. Margottini (singing) and Pierre de Beer* (piano). In Durban he studied also under J. Frank Proudman* (harmony, counterpoint and composition). From 1912 to 1914 he was at the Royal Conservatoire of Music, Würzburg (Germany), and in 1931 he had lessons in London under John Morel (singing) and James Ching (piano). — He commenced his teaching career in Durban in 1915 and eventually established a Durban Conservatoire of Music. He was also organist at' the Manning Road Methodist Church for 25 years (1921-1946), and at various other Methodist Churches in Durban and Johannesburg, but it was as a choral conductor that he made his mark in Durban. A choral conductor from an early age, he led church, ladies', male, mixed and boys' choirs in Durban prior to the Second World War, in performances at public concerts and for broadcasting. In 1946 this work culminated in the formation of the Harold Dyer Choral Society. — He was responsible for the formation of the Durban Centre of the South African Society of Music Teachers* in 1923, and served as Chairman for the first two years and again in 1936-1938. He married the musical Gladys Thomas in 1919.

WRITINGS

A plea for loyalty. *SAMT* 18, May 1940 (the year in which he acted as president of the SASMT).

WORKS

Abide with me, sacred song (Henry Francis Lyte). Edwin Ashdown Ltd., London, 1922. Life's twilight, song (William Manson). Edwin Ashdown Ltd., London, 1922. My land, song (William Manson). Edwin Ashdown Ltd., London, 1922. But God, sacred song (E.P. and C.P.), 1941. Several songs and choral works. Ms., n.d.

BIBLIOGRAPHY

K., W.H.: *The arts in South Africa.* Knox Printing & Publishing Co., Durban, 1933. VAN DER MERWE, F.Z.: *Suid-Afrikaanse musiekbibliografie, 1787-1952.* J.L. van Schaik, Pretoria, 1958.

SOURCES

SAMT: 16, April 1939; November 1949; 41, December 1951 (obituary notice).

—E.H.S.

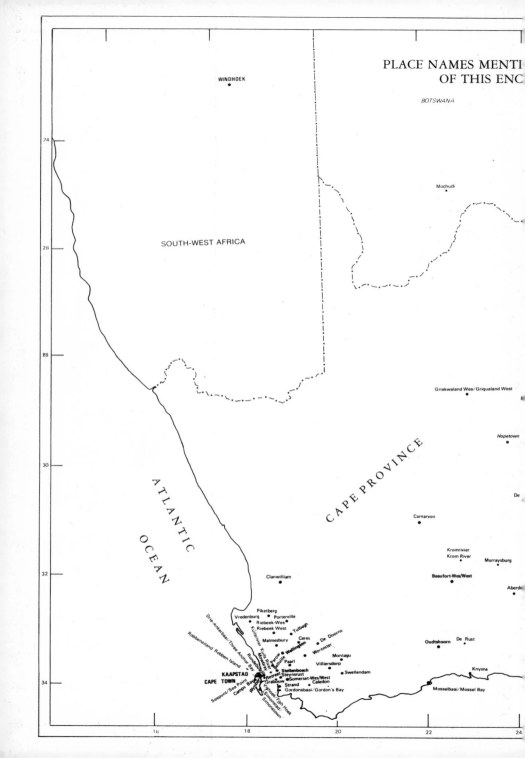